T0211734

Lecture Notes in Artificial Intelligence   11835

Subseries of Lecture Notes in Computer Science

More information about this series at http://www.springer.com/series/1244

Lourdes Martínez-Villaseñor ·
Ildar Batyrshin · Antonio Marín-Hernández (Eds.)

Advances in Soft Computing

18th Mexican International Conference
on Artificial Intelligence, MICAI 2019
Xalapa, Mexico, October 27 – November 2, 2019
Proceedings

 Springer

Editors
Lourdes Martínez-Villaseñor
Universidad Panamericana
Mexico City, Mexico

Ildar Batyrshin
Instituto Politecnico Nacional
Mexico, Mexico

Antonio Marín-Hernández
Universidad Veracruzana
Xalapa, Mexico

ISSN 0302-9743   ISSN 1611-3349 (electronic)
Lecture Notes in Artificial Intelligence
ISBN 978-3-030-33748-3   ISBN 978-3-030-33749-0 (eBook)
https://doi.org/10.1007/978-3-030-33749-0

LNCS Sublibrary: SL7 – Artificial Intelligence

This Springer imprint is published by the registered company Springer Nature Switzerland AG
The registered company address is: Gewerbestrasse 11, 6330 Cham, Switzerland

Preface

The Mexican International Conference on Artificial Intelligence (MICAI) is a yearly international conference series that has been organized by the Mexican Society of Artificial Intelligence (SMIA) since 2000. MICAI is a major international artificial intelligence (AI) forum and the main event in the academic life of the country's growing AI community.

MICAI conferences publish high-quality papers in all areas of AI and its applications. The proceedings of the previous MICAI events have been published by Springer in its Lecture Notes in Artificial Intelligence (LNAI) series, vol. 1793, 2313, 2972, 3789, 4293, 4827, 5317, 5845, 6437, 6438, 7094, 7095, 7629,7630, 8265, 8266, 8856, 8857, 9413, 9414, 10061, 10062, 10632, 10633, 11288, and 11289. Since its foundation in 2000, the conference has been growing in popularity and improving in quality.

The proceedings of MICAI 2019 contains 59 papers structured into four sections:

- Machine Learning
- Fuzzy Systems, Reasoning, and Intelligent Applications
- Computer Vision and Robotics
- Optimization and Planning

This book should be of interest to researchers in all fields of AI, students specializing in related topics, and for the public in general interested in recent developments in AI.

The conference received for evaluation 148 submissions from 16 countries: Argentina, Australia, Brazil, Cuba, Czech Republic, France, Germany, Mexico, Pakistan, Peru, Portugal, Russia, Spain, the United Kingdom, the USA, and Venezuela. Of these submissions, 59 papers were selected for publication in this volume after a peer-reviewing process carried out by the international Program Committee. The acceptance rate was 40%.

The international Program Committee consisted of 99 experts from 15 countries: Argentina, Brazil, Canada, Cuba, France, Greece, Ireland, Israel, Italy, Japan, Mexico, Portugal, Spain, the United Kingdom, and the USA.

MICAI 2019 was honored by the presence of renowned experts who gave excellent keynote lectures:

- Seth Hutchinson, Institute for Robotics and Intelligent Machines, Georgia Institute of Technology, USA
- Pablo Noriega, Artificial Intelligence Research Institute of the Spanish Scientific Research Council (III-CSIC), Spain
- Manuel Montes y Gómez, Instituto Nacional de Astrofísica, Óptica y Electrónica, Mexico
- Julian Togelius, New York University, USA

- Marley Vellasco, Computational Intelligence and Robotics Laboratory (LIRA) at PUC-Rio, Brazil

The technical program of the conference also featured seven tutorials:

- "Introduction to BDI Agent Programing with JaCa," by Héctor Xavier Limón Riaño
- "Path Planning and Control for Robots," by Rafael Eric Murrieta Cid
- "Trading Algorithms with Python: Learn to Buy and to Sell Shares on the Stock Market using Python and Artificial Intelligence Methods," by Israel Hernández and Oscar Herrera
- "Computational Intelligence for Processing and Classification of Bio-Signals," by Carlos Alberto Reyes García
- "New Models and Algorithms of Artificial Neural Networks," by Juan Humberto Sossa Azuela
- "A Walk-Though of Deep-Learning-Based Object Detectors," by Gilberto Ochoa-Ruiz
- "The RoboCup Logistics League: A Teaching and Research Testbed for Novel Concepts in Flexible Production," by Gerald Steinbauer

Six workshops were held jointly with the conference:

- HIS 2019: 12th Workshop of Hybrid Intelligent Systems
- WILE 2019: 12th Workshop on Intelligent Learning Environments
- WIDSSI 2019: 5th International Workshop on Intelligent Decision Support Systems for Industry Application
- CIAPP 2019: the First Workshop on New Trends in Computational Intelligence and Applications
- The first Workshop on Causal Reasoning
- Machine Learning for Healthcare

The authors of the following papers received the Best Paper Awards based on the paper's overall quality, significance, and originality of the reported results:

- First place: "RGB-D Camera and 2D Laser Integration for Robot Navigation in Dynamic Environments," by Orlando Lara-Guzmán, Sergio A. Serrano, David Carrillo-López, and L. Enrique Sucar (Mexico)
- Second place: "Towards Constant Calculation in Disjunctive Inequalities using Wound Treatment Optimization," by Hiram Ponce, José A. Marmolejo-Saucedo and Lourdes Martínez-Villaseñor (Mexico)
- Third place: "A Corpus-based Study of the Rate of Changes in Frequency of Syntactic Bigrams in English and Russian," by Vladimir Bochkarev, Valery Solovyev, and Anna Shevlyakova (Russia)

The cultural program of the conference included a tour to Xalapa Anthropology Museum and two of the most recognized Mesoamerican Archaeological sites in Veracruz: Cempoala and Quiahuiztlán.

We want to thank all the people involved in the organization of this conference. In the first place, there are the authors of the papers published in this book – it is their research work that gives value to the book and to the work of the organizers. We thank

Organization

MICAI 2019 was organized by the Mexican Society of Artificial Intelligence (SMIA – Sociedad Mexicana de Inteligencia Artificial) in collaboration with the Universidad Veracruzana, the Universidad Autónoma del Estado de Hidalgo, the Centro de Investigación en Computación of the Instituto Politécnico Nacional, and the Facultad de Ingeniería of the Universidad Panamericana.

The MICAI series website is www.MICAI.org. The website of the Mexican Society of Artificial Intelligence (SMIA) is www.SMIA.mx. Contact options and additional information can be found on these websites.

Conference Committee

General Chair

Félix A. Castro Espinoza	Universidad Autónoma del Estado de Hidalgo, Mexico

Program Chairs

Lourdes Martínez-Villaseñor	Universidad Panamericana, Mexico
Ildar Batyrshin	Instituto Politécnico Nacional, Mexico
Antonio Marín-Hernández	Universidad Veracruzana, Mexico

Workshop Chair

Noé Alejandro Castro Sánchez	Centro Nacional de Investigación y Desarrollo Tecnológico, Mexico

Tutorials Chairs

Roberto A. Vázquez	Universidad La Salle, Mexico
Félix A. Castro Espinoza	Universidad Autónoma del Estado de Hidalgo, Mexico

Doctoral Consortium Chairs

Miguel Gonzalez Mendoza	Tecnológico de Monterrey CEM, Mexico
Juan Martínez Miranda	CICESE Research Center, Mexico

Keynote Talks Chair

Sabino Miranda Jiménez	INFOTEC, Mexico

Publication Chair

Hiram Ponce	Universidad Panamericana, Mexico

Financial Chair

Oscar Herrera Alcántara | Universidad Autónoma Metropolitana Azcapotzalco, Mexico

Grant Chair

Félix A. Castro Espinoza | Universidad Autónoma del Estado de Hidalgo, Mexico

Local Organizing Committee

Local Chairs

Antonio Marín-Hernández | Universidad Veracruzana, Mexico
Efren Mezura Montes | Universidad Veracruzana, Mexico
Fernando M. Montes González | Universidad Veracruzana, Mexico

Local Logistics Chairs

Angel Juan Sanchez García | Universidad Veracruzana, Mexico
Fernando Aldana Franco | Universidad Veracruzana, Mexico
Andrés Lopez Velazquez | Universidad Veracruzana, Mexico
Maria Karen Cortés Verdín | Universidad Veracruzana, Mexico
Jorge Octavio Ocharán Hernández | Universidad Veracruzana, Mexico
Portillo Velez Rogelio de Jesus | Universidad Veracruzana, Mexico

Finance Chairs

Homero V. Rios Figueroa | Universidad Veracruzana, Mexico
Luis Felipe Marín Urias | Universidad Veracruzana, Mexico
Alejandro Vazquez Santacruz | Universidad Veracruzana, Mexico

Publicity Chairs

Nicandro Cruz Ramírez | Universidad Veracruzana, Mexico
Ervin Jésus Alvarez Sánchez | Universidad Veracruzana, Mexico
Héctor Gabriel Acosta Mesa | Universidad Veracruzana, Mexico

Area Chairs

Machine Learning

Eduardo Morales | Instituto Nacional de Astrofísica Óptica y Electrónica, Mexico
Raúl Monroy | Tecnológico de Monterrey, Mexico

Natural Language Processing

Esaú Villatoro	Universidad Autóonoma Metropolitana, Mexico
Noé Alejandro Castro-Sánchez	Centro Nacional de Investigación y Desarrollo Tecnológico, Mexico

Evolutionary and Metaheuristic Algorithms

Alicia Morales-Reyes	Instituto Nacional de Astrofísica Óptica y Electrónica, Mexico
Efren Mezura	Universidad Veracruzana, Mexico

Fuzzy and Hybrid Systems

Carlos Alberto Reyes	Instituto Nacional de Astrofísica Óptica y Electrónica, Mexico
Juan Jose Flores	Universidad Michoacana de San Nicolás de Hidalgo, Mexico

Neural Networks

Hiram Ponce	Universidad Panamericana, Mexico
Angel Kuri-Morales	ITAM, Mexico

Intelligent Applications

Gustavo Arroyo-Figueroa	Instituto Nacional de Electricidad y Energías Limpias, Mexico
Humberto Sossa	CIC IPN, Mexico
Antonio Marin	Universidad Veracruzana, Mexico

Computer Vision and Robotics

José Martínez	Instituto Nacional de Astrofísica, Óptica y Electrónica, Mexico
Hayde Peregrina	Instituto Nacional de Astrofísica, Óptica y Electrónica, Mexico

Program Committee

Rocío Abascal-Mena	Universidad Autonoma Metropolitana, Mexico
Giner Alor Hernandez	Instituto Tecnológico de Orizaba, Mexico
Joanna Alvarado-Uribe	Instituto Tecnológico y de Estudios Superiores de Monterrey, Mexico
Miguel Ángel Álvarez Carmona	Instituto Nacional de Astrofísica, Óptica y Electrónica, Mexico
Gustavo Arroyo-Figueroa	Instituto Nacional de Electricidad y Energías Limpias, Mexico
Jose Roberto Ayala Solares	The George Institute for Global Health, UK
Maria Lucia Barrón-Estrada	Instituto Tecnológico de Culiacan, Mexico

Ildar Batyrshin	Instituto Politecnico Nacional, Mexico
Monica Borunda	Instituto Nacional de Electricidad y Energías Limpias, Mexico
Davide Buscaldi	LIPN, Université Paris 13, Sorbonne Paris Cité, France
Nicoletta Calzolari	Istituto di Linguistica Computazionale - CNR, Italy
Jesus Ariel Carrasco-Ochoa	Instituto Nacional de Astrofísica, Óptica y Electrónica, Mexico
Felix Castro Espinoza	CITIS-UAEH, Mexico
Noé Alejandro Castro-Sánchez	Centro Nacional de Investigación y Desarrollo Tecnológico, Mexico
Ulises Cortés	BSC, Spain
Paulo Cortez	University of Minho, Portugal
Nicandro Cruz-Ramirez	Universidad Veracruzana, Mexico
Andre de Carvalho	University of São Paulo, Brazil
Omar Arturo Dominguez Ramírez	CITIS-UAEH, Mexico
Saul Dominguez-Isidro	National Laboratory on Advanced Informatics, Mexico
Marcelo Errecalde	Universidad Nacional de San Luis, Argentina
Hugo Jair Escalante	Instituto Nacional de Astrofísica, Óptica y Electrónica, Mexico
Ponciano Jorge Escamilla-Ambrosio	CIC-IPN, Mexico
Juan Jose Flores	Universidad Michoacana de San Nicolás de Hidalgo, Mexico
Gibran Fuentes-Pineda	Universidad Nacional Autónoma de México, Mexico
Sofia N. Galicia-Haro	Facultad de Ciencias, UNAM, Mexico
Milton García-Borroto	Cuban Society of Pattern Recognition, Cuba
Alexander Gelbukh	Instituto Politécnico Nacional, Mexico
Luis-Carlos González-Gurrola	Universidad Autonoma de Chihuahua, Mexico
Samuel González-López	Technological Institute of Nogales, Mexico
Miguel González-Mendoza	Tecnológico de Monterrey, Mexico
Mario Graff	INFOTEC Centro de Investigación e Innovación en Tecnologías de la Información y Comunicación, Mexico
Fernando Gudino	FES CUAUTITLAN-UNAM, Mexico
Andres Gutiérrez-Rodríguez	Centro de Bioplantas, Cuba
Yasunari Harada	Waseda University, Japan
Jorge Hermosillo	UAEM, Mexico
Yasmin Hernández	Instituto Nacional de Electricidad y Energías Limpias, Mexico
Delia Irazu Hernández Farias	Instituto Nacional de Astrofísica, Óptica y Electrónica, Mexico
Oscar Herrera	UAM Azcapotzalco, Mexico
Efren Juárez-Castillo	Universidad Veracruzana, Mexico

Angel Kuri-Morales	Instituto Tecnológico Autonomo de Mexico, ITAM, Mexico
Chris Lang	MIT, USA
Carlos Lara Álvarez	Centro de Investigación en Matemáticas (CIMAT), Mexico
Eugene Levner	Ashkelon Academic College, Israel
Fernando Lezama	Instituto Nacional de Astrofísica, Óptica y Electrónica, Mexico
Rodrigo López Farias	CONACYT-Consorcio CENTROMET, Mexico
Omar López-Ortega	UAEH, Mexico
Octavio Loyola-González	School of Science and Engineering, Tecnológico de Monterrey, Mexico
Wulfrano-Arturo Luna-Ramírez	University of Essex, UK and Universidad Autónoma Metropolitana, Mexico
Antonio Marin	Universidad Veracruzana, Mexico
Aldo Márquez Grajales	Universidad Veracruzana, Mexico
José Martínez	Instituto Nacional de Astrofísica, Óptica y Electrónica, Mexico
Lourdes Martínez-Villaseñor	Universidad Panamericana, Mexico
Maria-Gpe. Martínez-Peñaloza	Instituto Nacional de Astrofísica, Óptica y Electrónica, Mexico
José Fco. Martínez-Trinidad	Instituto Nacional de Astrofísica, Óptica y Electrónica, Mexico
Miguel Angel Medina Pérez	Instituto Nacional de Astrofísica, Óptica y Electrónica, Mexico
Iris Méndez	Universidad Autónoma de Ciudad Juárez, Mexico
Efren Mezura	Universidad Veracruzana, Mexico
Sabino Miranda-Jiménez	INFOTEC, Mexico
Daniela Moctezuma	CONACYT - CentroGEO, Mexico
Raúl Monroy	Tecnológico de Monterrey, Mexico
Omar Montaño	Universidad Politécnica de San Luis Potosí, Mexico
Manuel Montes-Y-Gómez	Instituto Nacional de Astrofísica, Óptica y Electrónica, Mexico
Eduardo Morales	Instituto Nacional de Astrofísica, Óptica y Electrónica, Mexico
Annette Morales-González	CENATAV, Cuba
Alicia Morales-Reyes	Instituto Nacional de Astrofísica, Óptica y Electrónica, Mexico
Ernesto Moya-Albor	Universidad Panamericana, Mexico
C. Alberto Ochoa Zezatti	Universidad Autónoma de Ciudad Juárez, Mexico
José Luis Oliveira	University of Aveiro, Portugal
José Carlos Ortiz-Bayliss	Tecnológico de Monterrey, Mexico
Leon Palafox	Universidad Panamericana, Mexico
Ivandre Paraboni	University of São Paulo, Brazil

Hayde Peregrina	Instituto Nacional de Astrofísica, Óptica y Electrónica, Mexico
Karina Ruby Pérez Daniel	Universidad Panamericana, Mexico
Carlos Pérez Leguizamo	Banco de Mexico, Mexico
Fernando Pérez-Tellez	Technical University Dublin, Ireland
Obdulia Pichardo-Lagunas	Unidad Profesional Interdisciplinaria en Ingeniería y Tecnologías Avanzadas-IPN, Mexico
Garibaldi Pineda García	UMSNH, University of Manchester, UK
Hiram Ponce	Universidad Panamericana, Mexico
Pedro Ponce	Tec de Monterrey, Mexico
Carlos Alberto Reyes	Instituto Nacional de Astrofísica, Óptica y Electrónica, Mexico
Orion Reyes	University of Alberta Edmonton AB, Canada
Antonio Rico-Sulayes	Universidad de las Americas Puebla, Mexico
Jorge Rodríguez-Ruiz	Tecnológico de Monterrey, Campus Estado de México, Mexico
Francisco Roman-Rangel	Instituto Tecnológico Autonomo de Mexico, ITAM, Mexico
Alejandro Rosales	Tecnológico de Monterrey, Mexico
Guillermo Santamaria	CONACYT-INEEL, Mexico
Grigori Sidorov	CIC-IPN, Mexico
Humberto Sossa	CIC-IPN, Mexico
Efstathios Stamatatos	University of the Aegean, Greece
Eric S. Tellez	CONACYT - INFOTEC, Mexico
Alejandro Torres Garcia	Instituto Nacional de Astrofísica, Óptica y Electrónica, Mexico
Juan-Manuel Torres-Moreno	Laboratoire Informatique d'Avignon-UA, France
Gregorio Toscano-Pulido	CINVESTAV-IPN, Mexico
Roberto Vázquez	Universidad La Salle, Mexico
Nestor Velasco-Bermeo	Tecnológico de Monterrey, Mexico
Esaú Villatoro	Universidad Autónoma Metropolitana, Mexico
Francisco Viveros Jiménez	CIC-IPN, Mexico
Alisa Zhila	Ntent, USA

Additional Reviewers

Ignacio Algredo
Dora Luz Almanza Ojeda
Gustavo Arechavaleta
Gabriel Aviña Cervantes
Víctor Ayala Ramírez
Eduardo Cabal-Yepez
Mario Castelán
José Arturo Cocoma-Ortega
Fernándo Correa-Tome
Israel Cruz Vega
Germán Cuaya-Simbro
Jorge De la Calleja
Sheila González
Luis González-Guzmán
Zobeida Jezabel Guzmán Zavaleta
Uriel Hernández-Belmonte
Mario Alberto Ibarra-Manzano
Jorge Jaimes
Hugo Jimenez

Rocío Lizárraga-Morales
Alfonso Martínez Cruz
Anabel Martin-González
Antonio Matus-Vargas
Manuel Mejía-Lavalle
Mariana Edith Miranda-Varela
Marco Morales
América Morales Díaz
Luis Morales Velázquez
Kelsey Alejandra Ramírez Gutiérrez
Juan M. Ramírez-Cortés
Juan Pablo Ramírez-Paredes
Reyes Ríos Cabrera
Ubaldo Ruíz
Raúl Sánchez Yañez
Omar Sandre Hernández
Luis Torres Treviño
Luz Abril Torres-Méndez
Miguel Zuñiga

Contents

Machine Learning

Optimization and Planning

Best Paper Award, Second Place

Fuzzy Systems, Reasoning and Intelligent Applications

Best Paper Award, Third Place

Vision and Robotics

Best Paper Award, First Place

Machine Learning

Road Damage Detection Acquisition System Based on Deep Neural Networks for Physical Asset Management

Andres Angulo[1], Juan Antonio Vega-Fernández[1],
Lina Maria Aguilar-Lobo[1], Shailendra Natraj[2],
and Gilberto Ochoa-Ruiz[3]([✉]) [iD]

[1] Universidad Autónoma de Guadalajara, Zapopan, Mexico
{andres.angulo, antonio.vega, lina.aguilar}@edu.uag.mx
[2] Vidrona LTD, Edinburgh, UK
shailendra@vidrona.com
[3] ITESM Campus Guadalajara, Zapopan, Mexico
gilberto.ochoa@tec.mx

Abstract. Research on damage detection of road surfaces has been an active area of research, but most studies have focused so far on the detection of the presence of damages. However, in real-world scenarios, road managers need to clearly understand the type of damage and its extent in order to take effective action in advance or to allocate the necessary resources. Moreover, currently there are few uniform and openly available road damage datasets, leading to a lack of a common benchmark for road damage detection. Such dataset could be used in a great variety of applications; herein, it is intended to serve as the acquisition component of a physical asset management tool which can aid governments agencies for planning purposes, or by infrastructure maintenance companies. In this paper, we make two contributions to address these issues. First, we present a large-scale road damage dataset, which includes a more balanced and representative set of damages. This dataset is composed of 18,034 road damage images captured with a smartphone, with 45,435 instances road surface damages. Second, we trained different types of object detection methods, both traditional (an LBP-cascaded classifier) and deep learning-based, specifically, MobileNet and RetinaNet, which are amenable for embedded and mobile and We compare the accuracy and inference time of all these models with others in the state of the art.

Keywords: Road damage · Deep learning · DNNs · Generic Object Detection

1 Introduction

Research on damage detection of road surfaces using image processing and machine learning techniques has been an active area of research in both developed and in-development countries [1–4]. This is an important issue, as roads are one of the most important civil infrastructures in every country and contribute directly and indirectly to the countries' economies and more importantly, to the well-being and safeness of their

© Springer Nature Switzerland AG 2019
L. Martínez-Villaseñor et al. (Eds.): MICAI 2019, LNAI 11835, pp. 3–14, 2019.
https://doi.org/10.1007/978-3-030-33749-0_1

citizens. Thus, road maintenance is of paramount importance and many countries have implemented inspection mechanisms and standards to carry out this process.

Nonetheless, both the inspection and journaling processes of road damages remain daunting problems, as government agencies still struggle to maintain accurate and up-to-date databases of such structural damages, making it hard to allocate resources for repair works in an informed manner. The problem is exacerbated as the number of experts that can assess such structural damages is limited, and furthermore, methods typically used to collect data from the field are time-consuming, cost-intensive, require a non-trivial level of expertise, and are highly-subjective and prone to errors. Therefore, both academic endeavors and commercial initiatives have been conducted to facilitate this process, making use of a combination of sophisticated technologies [5]. Most of these approaches combine various sensors (i.e. inertial profilers, scanners), but also imaging techniques, which have demonstrated to be particularly fit for the task. The information gathered by these sensors and cameras can be fed to machine learning algorithms and combined with mobile acquisition systems and cloud computing approaches to automate the process or to create end-to-end solutions.

Such endeavors have demonstrated promising results [6], but many of them have been limited to specific types of road damage classes (cracks, patches, potholes) and relatively small and not sufficiently comprehensive datasets. Furthermore, traditional "AI" systems for road damage classification do not to scale well and are not versatile enough to work in the dire situations usually found by road inspection experts. This has dramatically changed with the advent of the computer vision approaches based on deep learning architectures, which have demonstrated tremendous strides in several computer vision tasks and have slowly made their way into road inspection systems.

Such computer vision-based road detection and classification systems are significantly cheaper than competing technologies and if trained appropriately, they can lead to the implementation of sophisticated and cost-effective acquisition systems. These solutions could be further enhanced if they are implemented on mobile devices for road damage acquisition and stored on cloud computing technologies for further processing and big data analyses. Such an approach could lead to the creation of geo-localized databases containing the current state of the roads and other civil engineering infrastructures, which can be updated and used for forecasting and planning purposes. This is perfectly aligned with the industry 4.0 and digital transformation paradigms and can be easily implemented as business model that can be easily replicated. For instance, the UK has launched the Digital Roads Challenge to attain this goal1.

In this paper, we present an initial approach for a digital asset management tool, geared towards road and street management. Compared to previous works, which concentrated their efforts to specific types damages (potholes [1], cracks [2] and patches [3], to cite a few), our proposal builds upon previous work in this domain, by proposing a large dataset of various types of asphalt damages which is, to the best our knowledge, one of the most comprehensive in the literature. Some of the structural damages typically encountered in the field are depicted on Fig. 1; these images represent structural damages and not blemishes on other infrastructure such as signs and markings.

The proposed road damage dataset has been used to train various machine learning based "object detectors", in which the objects of interest are the structural damages in

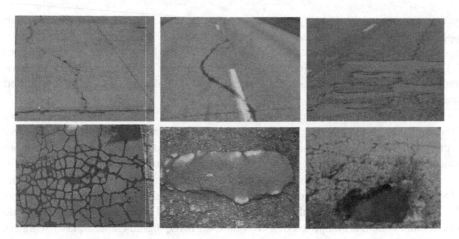

Fig. 1. Examples of structural damages typically found in the literature: (a–b) linear cracks, (c) peeling, (d) alligator cracks, (e) patches and (f) potholes

the dataset. As will be described in more depth in the following section, such systems need to run in real-time to be useful, and therefore, we validated the dataset on lightweight detectors such as LPB cascaded classifiers, and in more recent, deep learning-based Single Shot Detectors (SSD) such as MobileNet and RetinaNet. The two latter were developed so they can run efficiently on mobile devices (i.e. smartphones) in real-time, while achieving high mean average precisions (mAP).

The rest of this paper is organized as follows: in Sect. 2 we further motivate the need for digital asset management systems, specifically for roads and streets. Then, in Sect. 3 we discuss the state of the art in road damage detection using various imaging modalities to provide some context, but we focus our attention to those techniques based on computer vision and modern machine learning approaches. In Sect. 4 we introduce the proposed dataset and an initial approach for road digital asset management, as well as the tools and methods used for validating the proposal. Afterwards, in Sect. 5, we discuss these results with regards with the state of the art and we describe future avenues of research, concluding the article.

2   Motivation

The maintenance of roads and street infrastructure is a major concern, especially in tropical countries where the asphalt and other civil facilities are more prone to suffer structural damages. Nevertheless, this problem is not exclusive of these regions, and the issue is becoming pervasive in developed countries due to the aging of their infrastructure. Thus, in order to cope with these problems, governmental agencies in these countries have developed specific procedures and standards to aid experts in assessing the damage on asphalt and other materials such as concrete.

In the field, the experts have traditionally carried inspections based on these standards following two main approaches: either by direct observations by humans or by quantitative analysis using remote sensing approaches. The visual inspection approach requires experienced road managers, which makes it time-consuming, expensive and prone to errors. Moreover, traditional methods tend to be inconsistent and limited to point observations, making it difficult to scale to large cities or geographical areas, and further, to build and maintain digital corpuses with the acquired data.

The problem is exacerbated as the acquisitions made by traditional inspections are oftentimes not digitally stored, and thus government bodies cannot leverage the power of the digital revolution (i.e. big data analytics) to address these challenges in a more informed and efficient manner. In contrast, more recent quantitative systems, based on large-scale inspection systems using the so-called Mobile Measurement Systems (MMS) or laser-scanning methods have been proposed and deployed in some countries [5]. An MMS can obtain highly accurate geospatial road information using a mobile vehicle; this system is comprised of a GPS unit, an IMU, digital cameras, laser scanners and LIDAR modules. Although these systems are highly accurate, they are considerably more expensive and complex to operate, as well as more difficult to acquire, manage, and maintain by small municipalities lacking the required resources.

In order to alleviate the above-mentioned problems, a great deal of research efforts have been carried out to facilitate and automate the manual inspection process described above. For instance, the civil engineering domain has a long history of using non-destructive sensing and surveying techniques, typically based on computer vision, such as 3D imaging [6] and remote sensing approaches [7] for a variety of applications. The former approach has several advantages over the traditional inspection methods, as well as to other approaches which use solely conventional imagining techniques, as they cope better with changes in illumination and weather conditions.

Although such tools provide an opportunity for frequent, comprehensive, and quantitative surveys of transportation infrastructures, they are costly and difficult to implement and maintain, as such systems typically rely on heavily instrumented vehicles, as depicted on Fig. 2. Therefore, such solutions are is simply not affordable by many countries and even less so for individual municipalities. Thus, researches have sought other methods to reduce the complexity and costs associated with surveying and inspecting road infrastructures, well documented in the literature [7, 8].

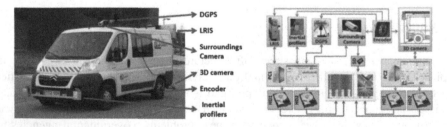

Fig. 2. Example of MMS system, designed by PaveMetrics, analyzed in [5]

As we will see in the next section, such efforts have mainly revolved around image processing and computer vision techniques, as the main information used by inspectors can be obtained from conventional imaging when dealing only with classification problems (and not properly surveying), which have made major strides in this domain due to the combination of efficient and lightweight deep learning-based generic object detectors and mobile computing technologies for inference purposes.

3 Related Works

The automation of road damage inspection generally requires robust computer vision algorithms with a high degree of intelligence, which can be easy to use and run in real-time. However, most the systems in this vein were initially conceived as means for aiding the experts in the field and were limited by the capabilities of the ML algorithms of the time, which were not very reliable and robust, and which were difficult to implement in portable systems. For a thorough state of the art of the various imaging modalities the reader is directed to excellent surveys in 3D imaging [7], remote sensing [8] and computer vision and image processing in general [9, 10].

The biggest challenge for automated road damage detection systems is to consistently achieve high performance, in terms of accuracy, under various complex environments (due to changes in illumination, weather conditions, among other challenges). Despite these problems, several systems for detecting individual structural damages have been proposed in the literature, as described in Sect. 1. However, most of these works have not been able to tackle more challenging scenarios in the development of their machine learning and AI systems, due to the absence of commonly accepted and publicly available datasets. The Kitti dataset [4] could be exploited for such purposes; however, its main purpose is for autonomous driving and using it for road damage detection might prove itself a difficult and ultimately futile endeavor.

Therefore, it was widely recognized by the academic community that there was a need for an extensive dataset specifically designed for road damage assessment, for two main purposes. First, in order to test and perform benchmarks among competing solutions, helping to boost the R&D in the area. Second, to homogenize the data collection process, as such datasets are essential for creating reliable and robust machine learning-based solutions for road and asphalt detection and inspection. This problem has been partially addressed, with some datasets having made available, but much work needs to be done, as roads vary dramatically among countries.

Despite these issues, the available datasets have been exploited over the years to implement machine-learning based solutions, using computer vision-based features and classification algorithms such as SVM for the detection of cracks [11] and potholes [12]. As datasets have become larger, there has been a growing interest in deploying deep learning-based (DL) approaches to the problem of road and asphalt damage detection. It is well known that DL algorithms have demonstrated impressive results in a variety of computer vision-related fields and are behind the autonomous driving revolution. In this sense, several efforts have been conducted to leverage these capabilities in the problem we are tackling, with some very impressive results for certain classes of asphalt damages such as cracks [13].

One advantage of deep learning methods over traditional approaches is that cheaper or less sophisticated imaging devices (i.e. smartphones) can be used for acquiring the training samples, instead of the much more expensive MMS platforms described in the previous section. Approaches based on mobile devices had been explored before, using more traditional CV detectors such as LBP-cascade classifiers [14], but the authors did not compare their results to more recent detectors based on DL. Furthermore, although the results were commendable, they made use of custom datasets and were limited to more "static" analyses. Figure 3 shows a couple of examples of our structural damage detection using the LPB-based approach, using our dataset.

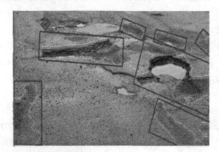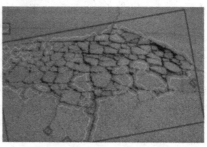

Fig. 3. Detection of alligator cracks and potholes using the most basic ML algorithm explore in this work: an LPB-cascade classifier, note the high number of false positives

On the other hand, recent advances in Generic Object Detection algorithms [15] have now made possible to implement very sophisticated and resource efficient algorithms in constrained devices, such as mobile phones, and some of the recent implementations have started to emerge in various areas and in particular in the field of road inspection and assessment. In this sense, it is also possible now to carry out the deployment phase (acquisition and detection of structural damages) in real time using inexpensive mobile devices as well [17–19], either for individual inspections in situ or mounted on a car, making it an attractive alternative to the expensive MMS platforms.

These advances have been possible due to the development of two-stage detectors such as Fast R-CNN and subsequently single stage detectors like YOLO (for a detailed discussion the reader is directed to an excellent survey [15]). The former category can achieve high accuracies (mean average precision or mAP) but are usually inefficient, as they cannot be deployed in resource constrained devices [16]. The latter category of generic object detectors has steadily improved over time, with new architectures based on Feature Pyramid Networks (i.e. RetinaNet and MobileNet) achieving satisfactory accuracies for challenging problems whilst requiring relatively small footprints, leading to implementations in mobile phones for detecting road damages and collecting geo-referenced information [17–19], as depicted on Fig. 4(a) and (b).

These progresses have also been possible due to the introduction of large-scale datasets required by the data hungry DL algorithms, especially for domain specific problems such as road damages, as the dataset introduced by the University of Tokyo [19]. This dataset contains several types of structural damages (cracks, patches, etc.), but it is still limited, as it presents unbalanced classes, a problem we mitigate in our

Fig. 4. Examples of road damage detection systems running on a smartphone. (a) System by the University of Tokio [19] and (b) Solution by RoadBotics [20]

dataset. In the following sections we will describe the dataset, the initial experiments performed with various algorithms and we will discuss how they compared with the state of the art described above, outlining as well future avenues of research.

4 Proposed Solution

Considering the progresses made in the domain, the integration of the technologies described above into "smart cities" paradigms such as physical asset management systems was only question of time, and some government and private service companies have started to make use of the information collected into road damage databases in various ways. The main idea is to leverage the progresses made in various domains (AI, IoT, mobile and cloud computing) for creating systems that can ease the labor of road inspectors on the one hand, but which can also be used to implement end-to-end solutions for creating a large database of structural damages from individual roads, to streets in medium to large cities, leading to the so-called "digital twins".

These systems could aid in improving the work of the municipalities or governments at the federal level, helping them in managing their assets. Examples of platforms with these capabilities have been deployed in the US (RoadBotics [20]).

4.1 Utilized Dataset

As mentioned previously, the research on road damage detection suffered from a lack of unified datasets. This problem has been partially addressed by the community, with several datasets of various sizes and characteristics; for instance, researchers at the Universita di Roma Tre introduced a dataset [14] with three major structural damage classes (linear and alligator cracks and potholes) and used it for implementing an acquisition system using a mobile phone. More recent efforts have sought to include a broader category of classes, such as the dataset of University of Tokyo [19], which includes 8 types of damages (images of 600×600 pixels), as depicted on Table 1.

The codes in Table 1 are used by the Japanese Government to classify road damages and it was employed by the authors to categorize structural damages in their work. This dataset is the largest currently available and has been extensively used to implement road inspection systems using deep learning architectures, such as SSD like

Table 1. Road damage types in the dataset proposed in [19] and their definitions

Damage type		Description	Class name
Crack	Linear crack	Wheel mark part	D00
		Construction joint part	D01
		Equal interval	D10
		Construction joint part	D11
	Alligator crack	Partial, overall pavement	D20
Other corruption		Rutting, bump, pothole	D40
		White line blur	D43
		Cross walk blur	D44

RetinaNet [17] and MobileNet [18]. Although this dataset is relatively large, some classes or damage instances are poorly represented, such as the potholes class.

However, potholes at various stages of deterioration are one of the most important structural damages that need to me tracked by governmental bodies, and as such, one of the contributions of our work is to include more instances to the classes in the dataset introduced by the authors in [19] to have a more balanced representation, as it can be observed in Table 2. We included more instances of the D00, D10 and D11 classes (longitudinal cracks of various types) and for the D40 (potholes), for which several hundred examples have been added, as shown on the third row of Table 2.

Table 2. Number of damage instances in each class for the original dataset presented in [19] and the one used in this work. Note that the potholes and cracks classes are better represented.

Dataset/Class	D00	D01	D10	D11	D20	D40	D43	D44
Maeda [19]	2,678	3,789	742	636	2,541	409	817	3,733
Modified	**2,978**	3,789	**1042**	**1036**	3,341	**1,609**	817	3733

Using this extended or modified dataset, we have carried out a comparative analysis with previous works in the literature, in order to evaluate if any gains in performance could be achieved, which in most instances was the case. In the next section, we will discuss how the dataset was used for training a set of "generic object detectors", which are the backbone for our acquisition and MMS system. It must be noted that most of the images are taken from "above the road" using mobile devices.

The choice of acquisition system was justified in Sect. 2 from the "technical" perspective, but it should be stressed that in many countries, installing a camera outside the car constitutes a violation of the law [19]. Thus, a great number of solutions are based on inexpensive mobile phone cameras have been proposed and, as mentioned in Sect. 3, they require small footprints and real-time performances, whilst attaining high detection and classification accuracies.

4.2   Training

For the sake of completeness, we have implemented three types of object detectors, concentrating on those amenable for implementation on mobile and embedded platforms: an LBP-cascade classifier (as in [14]) as well more recent, DL-based generic object detectors, specifically MobileNet (as in [17]) and RetinaNet (as in [18]). The latter model can be trained with different backbone DNNs for the feature extraction phase (RestNet or VGG in its various configurations), trading accuracy versus inference time, obtaining in general better results than other popular Single Shot Detectors (SSD) such as YOLO, whilst yielding models amenable for embedded or mobile implementations. For instance, RetinaNet with VGG19 as backbone requires 115.7 MB and can achieve inference times of 0.5 s, fast enough for our purposes.

The labeled dataset is randomly shuffled and separated into training set and validation set, 30% of the images of each class was used for training, taking care that the model did not overfit; for this purpose we have made use of dropout and data augmentation over the original dataset (using various image transformations such as cropping, warping, rotation, among other). Data augmentation is a method for "synthetically" generating more training data from the existing training examples, by submitting the latter to a variety of random transformations that yield believable looking images, which has helped us to move from 18,000 images to over 100,000.

The DNNs description as well as the training phase were implemented with Keras and Tensorflow running on Google Colab with a Tesla K80 GPUs; the models were trained with batch size of 24 and number steps per epoch of 300, using Adam as optimizer, adapting the learning rate as discussed in [19]. As we will see in the next section, the proposed approach obtained improvements over previous works, especially for then underrepresented classes in the original road damages dataset.

5   Results and Discussion

In our experiments, both the training and testing phases were carried out using Google Colab, which enables us to have access to high performance computing (a Tesla K80 GPU and other resources) and to host our dataset (images and videos) on the Google Cloud, all while avoiding any computational burden. In the evaluation phase, we also made use of this tool, importing the trained models and images not seen previously by the models. Furthermore, we carried out experiments on real-time video to test the capabilities of the proposed models in a variety of scenarios, using an open source software for estimating metrics such as IoU (Intersection over Union) and the mAP[2].

Table 3 shows the obtained results for the three "generic object detectors" tested in our experiments. As mentioned before, we decided to implement an LBP-cascaded based classifier to contrast our results with those reported in [14], as we made use of a part of their dataset.

Table 3. Number of damage instances in each class for the original dataset presented in [19] and the one used in this work. Note that the potholes and cracks classes are better represented.

Metric/Class	D01 (Long crack)	D11 (Lat. crack)	D20 (Alligator)	D40 (Pothole)
LPB-cascade	0.7080	0.7182	0.7625	0.7476
MobileNet	0.8124	0.9032	0.9234	0.9675
RetinaNet	**0.9148**	**0.9511**	**0.9522**	**0.9823**

We also report the results for the deep learning approaches reported in the literature, which make use of the MobileNet [17] and RetinaNet [18]. The proposed models achieved consistently better results than those reported in the literature using the same methods ([15, 17, 19], respectively), while achieving higher accuracies and lower inference times, as we will discuss later in this section.

In Table 3, we have decided to show the results only for 4 of the most reported classes (longitudinal and lateral cracks, alligator cracks and potholes), as they are the most prevalent and it makes the comparisons with previous work easier. It should be noted that other works discussed in the state of the art in Sect. 3 have obtained good results for individual road damage classes (even with pixel-level accuracies) but they were not amenable to mobile or embedded vision implementations.

In order to assess the improvements obtained by our extended dataset, we show a comparative analysis between the MobileNet-based classification and detection method [19] and the best of our models, which is shown on Table 4. The SSD detector and classifier performed well, with both high precision and recall, especially compared with the D11 and D40 classes (lateral cracks and potholes, respectively).

Table 4. Number of damage instances in each class for the original dataset presented in [19] and the one used in this work. Note that the potholes and cracks classes are better represented.

Metric	Road damage class							
	D00	D01	D10	D11	D20	D40	D43	D44
Maeda et al. [19]								
Recall	0.40	0.89	0.20	0.05	0.68	0.02	0.71	0.85
Precision	0.73	0.64	0.99	0.95	0.68	0.99	0.85	0.66
Accuracy	0.81	0.77	0.92	0.94	0.83	0.95	0.95	0.81
Best model (ours)								
Recall	0.60	0.90	0.40	0.40	0.76	0.70	0.80	0.70
Precision	0.87	0.70	0.89	0.92	0.92	0.88	0.87	0.82
Accuracy	0.91	0.81	0.92	0.95	0.95	0.98	0.95	0.84

This can be attributed to the larger number of training instances in our dataset, a problem reported by the authors in [19]. The authors mentioned the class D43 (white line blurs) as a counter example, as the number of examples is limited, but we believe that this class is relatively easier to detect, which might explain the results.

The accuracies obtained by our RetinaNet-based model in which, as in the case of the authors in [18], we have used VGG19 as the backbone network. However, the authors in this paper the authors make use of a single metric (a mAP of 0.8279) for reporting their result, without performing a per-class comparison.

In Table 5, we report some of the features of the resultant RetinaNet-based model, compared with other two state of the art models. First, the model size is relatively compact (125.5 MB), while achieving a low inference time (0.5 s) and a higher mean average precision (mAP), making our proposal one of the more.

Table 5. Metrics comparison for our best model against the state of the art

Metric/Model	Model size	Inference time	Best mAP	Type of device
RetinaNet [17]	115.7 MB	0.5 s	0.8279	Mobile
MobileNet [18]	N/A	1.5 s	N/A	Mobile
RetinaNet (ours)	125.5 MB	0.5 s	0.91522	Mobile

6 Conclusions and Future Work

In this study, we have presented the first block for a physical asset management tool, a generic object detector trained to identify and classify road damages from still images or real-time video with high accuracy and low inference time. We have tested different models and approaches to solve this problem, based on traditional computer approaches and on more recent deep learning architectures.

For the training of our models we deployed the relatively large dataset originally introduced by the University of Tokyo, augmenting it with images from Mexican and Italian roads, in order to compensate the disbalance present for some road damages such as potholes. The obtained results clearly show that RetinaNet can outperform other state of the art road damage detectors and it is amenable for a mobile or embedded implementation (i.e. for ADAS applications) while running at acceptable rates (0.5 s in our current implementation), which has been demonstrated to be more than enough for a vehicle with a speed of 40 km/s to avoid information leakage.

As future work, we plan to integrate the model running on a mobile device to a full-fledged Digital Asset Management Asset platform running on Amazon Web Services. The main idea is to leverage the capabilities of the cloud computing system for creating and maintaining a digital twin of the roads of a region or the streets of the city described in Sect. 2. This geo-localized database could be used for monitoring and prognosis purposes, if coupled with a predictive model, leading to a more informed process in the allocation of resources for maintenance, as well as the required periodicity.

Acknowledgements. We thank Prof. Benedetto from University de Roma Tre (Italy) for kindly providing some of the images used to complement the dataset from the University of Tokyo (Japan), along other images obtained by our group in Guadalajara, Mexico. We also thank the people of Vidrona LTD (Edinburgh, UK) for helping us to delimit the problem addressed in this paper, especially to Shailendra and Ashutosh Natraj.

References

1. Koch, C., Asce, A.M., Jog, G.M., Brilakis, I.: Automated pothole distress assessment using asphalt pavement video data. J. Comput. Civ. Eng. **27**, 4 (2013)
2. Oliveira, H., Correia, P.L.: Automatic road crack detection and characterization. IEEE Trans. Intell. Transp. Syst. **14**(1), 155–168 (2013)
3. Radopoulou, S.C., Bralakis, I.: Patch detection for pavement assessment. Autom. Constr. **53**, 95–104 (2015)
4. Geiger, A., Lenz, P., Stiller, C., Urtasun, R.: Vision meets robotics: the KITTI dataset. Int. J. Robot. Res. **32**(11), 1231–1237 (2013)
5. Medina, R., Llamas, J., Zalama E., Gómez-García-Bermejo, J.: Enhanced automatic detection of road surface cracks by combining 2D/3D image processing techniques. In: IEEE International Conference on Image Processing (ICIP), Paris, pp. 778–782 (2014)
6. Ryu, S.K., Kim, T., Kim, Y.R.: Image-based pothole detection system for ITS service and road management system. Math. Probl. Eng. **2015**, 10 (2015)
7. Mathavan, S., Kamal, K., Rahman, M.: A review of three-dimensional imaging technologies for pavement distress detection and measurements. IEEE Trans. Intell. Transp. Syst. **16**(5), 2353–2362 (2015)
8. Schnebele, E., Tanyu, B.F., Cervone, F., Waters, G.: Review of remote sensing methodologies for pavement management and assessment. Eur. Transp. Res. Rev. **7**, 7 (2015)
9. Koch, C., Giorgieva, K., Kasireddy, V., Akinci, B., Fieguth, P.: A review of computer vision based defect detection and condition assessment of concrete and asphalt civil infrastructure. Adv. Eng. Inform. **29**, 196–210 (2015)
10. Mohan, A., Poobal, S.: Crack detection using image processing: a critical review and analysis. Alexandria Eng. J. **57**(2), 787–798 (2018)
11. Hoang, N.D., Nguyen, Q.L.: A novel method for asphalt pavement crack classification based on image processing and machine learning. Eng. Comput. **35**(2), 487–498 (2018)
12. Hoang, N.D.: An artificial intelligence method for asphalt pavement pothole detection using least squares support vector machine and neural network with steerable filter-based feature extraction. Hindawi Adv. Civ. Eng. **2018**, 12 (2018)
13. Cha, Y.J., Choi, W., Büyüköztürk, O.: Deep learning-based crack damage detection using convolutional neural network. Comput.-Aided Civ. Infrastruct. Eng. **32**(5), 361–378 (2017)
14. Tedeschi, A., Benedetto, F.: A real time pavement crack and pothole recognition system for mobile Android-based devices. AEI **32**, 11–25 (2017)
15. Liu, L., Ouyang, W., Wang, X., Fieguth, P., Liu, X., Pietikäinen, M.: Deep learning for generic object detection: a survey. arXiv:1809.02165v2 (2016)
16. Huang, J., et al.: Speed/accuracy trade-offs for modern convolutional object detectors. arXiv: 1611.10012v3 (2018)
17. Ale, L., Zhang, N., Li, L.: Road damage detection using RetinaNet. In: International Conference on Big Data 2018, pp. 5197–5200 (2018)
18. Pereira, V., Tamura, S., Hayamizu, S., Fukain H.: A deep learning-based approach for road pothole detection in Timor Leste. In: 2018 IEEE International Conference on Service Operations and Logistics, and Informatics (SOLI), Singapore, pp. 279–284 (2018)
19. Maeda, H., Sekimoto, Y., Seto, T., Kashiyama, T., Omata, H: Road damage detection using deep neural networks with images captured through a smartphone (2018)
20. RoadBotics (2019). https://www.roadbotics.com/company/. Accessed 01 June 2019

Implementation of Algorithm Recommendation Models for Timetabling Instances

Felipe de la Rosa-Rivera[(✉)] and Jose I. Nunez-Varela

Facultad de Ingeniería, Universidad Autónoma de San Luis Potosí,
Av. Manuel Nava No. 8, Zona Universitaria, 78290 San Luis Potosí, S.L.P., Mexico
fdelarosa@alumnos.uaslp.edu.mx, jose.nunez@uaslp.mx

Abstract. The Curriculum-Based Course Timetabling (CB-CTT) is a problem periodically solved in educational institutions, still, because of the diversity of conditions that define it within different educational contexts, selecting the solution approach that best suits the particular requirements of an instance is a complex task that can be properly formulated as an algorithm selection problem. In this paper, we analyze four selection mechanisms that could be used as algorithms recommendation models. From this analysis, it is concluded that the proposed regression approach exhibited the highest performance. Therefore, it could be applied for algorithm recommendation to solve CB-CTT instances.

Keywords: Educational timetabling · Algorithm selection · Supervised learning

1 Introduction

Educational timetabling is a combinatorial optimization problem that models the assignment of resources and timeslots to a defined set of academic events according to a series of constraints, which can be either hard (mandatory), or soft (optional). Within the educational field, three kinds of timetabling-related problems are distinguished: Examination Timetabling (*Ex-TT*), Post Enrollment Course Timetabling (*PE-CTT*), and Curriculum-Based Course Timetabling (*CB-CTT*). This paper focuses on the third kind (CB-CTT), the most common in Mexican educational models. It consists on scheduling the events in which student groups (i.e., *curriculums*), who share a set of classes, are to be enrolled.

As stated by Bonutti et al. [1], "although CB-CTT is a practically-important and widely-studied problem, it is impossible to write a formulation that suits all cases since every institution has its own rules, features, costs, and constraints". For this reason, it has become relevant to develop an understanding of the generalization performance of solving methods across the CB-CTT problem space. As observed in recent surveys [8,9], the solutions methods proposed to solve

We gratefully acknowledge the support of CONACYT-Mexico (Reg. 618204/461410).

L. Martínez-Villaseñor et al. (Eds.): MICAI 2019, LNAI 11835, pp. 15–27, 2019.
https://doi.org/10.1007/978-3-030-33749-0_2

educational timetabling problems can be grouped into two broad approaches: (i) single-model, and (ii) multi-model.

The single-model approach refers to analytical methods (e.g. linear programming); solution-based heuristics (e.g. tabu search); and population-based heuristics (e.g. genetic algorithms). This approach solves problems based on the implementation of a single solving strategy. On the other hand, the multi-model approach refers to strategies that employ two or more kinds of heuristics (e.g. hybrid-methods), that combine at least two single-models to solve the problem in sequential order; and hyper-heuristics, that iteratively applies a set of low-order heuristics (operators).

A recent approach that, to the best of our knowledge has not yet been implemented, is the concept of an *algorithm recommendation model*, which unlike other multi-model approaches does not apply heuristics to solve sub-parts of an instance, but selects (from the accumulated experience of machine learning methods), the best algorithm to solve an entire instance.

This paper analyzes the suitability of four methodologies that could be applied to construct algorithm recommendation models for the solution of CB-CTT instances, based on the elements of the Algorithm Selection Problem (ASP) framework defined by Rice [11]. Thus, the remainder of the paper is structured as follows. Section 2 defines the basic concepts of the CB-CTT problem, its mathematical formulation and data format. Section 3 describes the framework of the Algorithm Selection Problem. Section 4 presents the collection of meta-heuristics included in the portfolio of algorithms. Section 5 analyzes the performance of the meta-heuristics over a defined collection of CB-CTT instances. Section 6 discusses four selection mechanisms to predict the best meta-heuristic to solve a given instance. Section 7 compares the results of the implemented selection mechanisms, and Sect. 8 discusses conclusions and future work.

2   The Curriculum-Based Course Timetabling Problem

As defined by Di Gaspero et al. [3] for the Second International Timetabling Competition (ITC 2007), the Curriculum-Based Timetabling (CB-CTT) problem consists of the weekly scheduling of lectures for several courses given a number of teachers, rooms, and time periods, in which the conflicts between courses are set according to the curricular plan published by the university. The concept of *curriculum* is what distinguishes the CB-CTT problem from similar educational timetabling problems. It refers to a set of courses that has to be taken together by a group of students. According to this definition, the basic input data required to formulate a CB-CTT problem instance is:

- A set of teaching days D (where a day $d \in D$); and a set of teaching modules per day M_d, (where a module $m_d \in M_d$).
- A set of time slots TS composed of a day and a module $<d, m_d>$.
- A set of teachers T, where each teacher $t \in T$ has a limited workload $w_t \in \mathbb{N}$.
- A set of rooms R, where each room $r \in R$ has a limited availability $a_r \in \mathbb{N}$.

– A set of courses C, where each course $c \in C$ has a total weekly duration $d_c \in$ $\mathbb{N}$, which defines the number of lectures to be scheduled. A course requires at least three resources: a teacher, a room, and a group of students.

– A set of curricula Q, where a curriculum $q \in Q$ is a group of courses that shares a group of students. Therefore, this group of courses cannot be scheduled at the same times.

2.1 Timetabling Data Format

Within the timetabling field, three international competitions have been organized to develop standardized data representations and benchmarking datasets. The third of these competitions (ITC 2011), constitutes a breakthrough in terms of representation of educational timetabling problems. A structured data format was defined that allows the definition of a large set of real-like conditions for instances. The structure of this standardized format is defined by a XML schema (called XHSTT format), composed of four entities [10]:

– *Times*: Set of possible time-slots in which events can be scheduled. These time-slots are often grouped together into *time groups* (e.g. days, weeks).

– *Resources*: Set of available resources that can be assigned to events. Each resource belongs to a specific resource type (e.g. teacher, rooms), and can be grouped together into *resource groups* for administration purposes.

– *Events*: Set of classes to be scheduled. Each event has a duration, that represents the amount of time-slots to be scheduled, and a demand of a set of resources. Events can also be grouped together into *event groups*.

– *Constraints*: Set of constraints that must be fulfilled during the scheduling of events. Each constraint has a cost, that indicates the penalty value of a single violation; and a cost function, that defines how the penalty values are added to the objective function to be minimized.

3 Algorithm Selection Problem

Selecting the best algorithm to solve a particular instance of a problem is a solution approach that Rice [11] anticipated decades ago, when he proposed the framework for the Algorithm Selection Problem (ASP). As defined by Rice, such framework consists of four basic elements:

– *Problem space* ($\mathcal{P}$): A representative set of instances of the given problem.

– *Feature space* ($\mathcal{F}$): A set of features that describes relevant properties of the problem space.

– *Performance space* ($\mathcal{Y}$): A set of metrics that describes the performance of the algorithms (e.g. running time), or its solutions (e.g. value of the objective function) over the problem space.

– *Algorithm space* ($\mathcal{A}$): A set of solution approaches that could be applied to solve the problem.

3.1   ASP Framework for the CB-CTT Problem

The goal of this paper is to analyze different selection mechanisms to build an algorithm recommendation model for the CB-CTT problem by following the ASP framework. The *problem space*, *feature space*, and *performance space*, are defined according to a CB-CTT instance generator [12], and are described next. The *algorithm space* is explained in Sect. 4.

- *Problem space*: Consists of a collection of 6000 instances that models a set of 27 constraints commonly found in educational timetabling problems encoded into XML trees according to the XHSTT format (described in Sect. 2.1).
- *Feature space*: Consists of a set of 30 *complexity metrics* [12], such as number of lectures, number of teachers, rate of available to required rooms; that describe the size, constraint density and solution space of the instances.
- *Performance space*: Is defined with a cost function that sums the violations of hard (mandatory) constraints, with a penalty value of 1000; and violations of soft (optional) constraints, with a penalty value of 1.

The evaluation of the diversity of the described *spaces* was performed based on the *empirical hardness* of the *KHE timetabling engine* [7]. A solver commonly used to produce initial solutions of educational timetabling problems. Each one of the 6000 instances was solved by the KHE engine, and according to the resulting total penalty value of its solution, instances were classified into five categories:

- *Very Easy*: Instances with a resulting penalty value between [0–1,000).
- *Easy*: instances with a resulting penalty value between [1,000–10,000).
- *Medium*: instances with a resulting penalty value between [10,000–50,000).
- *Hard*: instances with a resulting penalty value between [50,000–100,000).
- *Very Hard*: instances with a resulting penalty equal or greater than 100,000.

Instances classified as *Very Easy* had a penalty value very close to its optimal solution (i.e., penalty value of zero) and no hard-constraint violations. In contrast, instances with greater penalty values were difficult enough to require other solving algorithms in order to find *feasible solutions* (with no hard-constraint violations). The KHE engine was able to find optimal solutions for 321 of the *Very Easy* instances. Therefore, a total of 5679 instances were considered to be improved by the set of algorithms (meta-heuristics) described next.

4   Definition of the Algorithm Space

Within the field of combinatorial optimization, algorithms explore solution spaces through different *moves* that permute the order of the elements of an initial solution s, in order to improve it. The neighborhood of a solution $N(s)$, is defined as the set of all solutions which can be reached with the implementation of one type of *move* to a given solution s. Therefore, every time a *move* is applied, a new solution in the neighborhood $N_k(s)$ (where k is the type of *move*) is produced. In this context, the basic version of a solution algorithm starts with an initial solution s that is permuted within a neighborhood $N(s)$ to find a better solution s'. If such solution is found, the current solution is replaced and the search continues on a different neighborhood until a stop condition is met.

The process by which a solution algorithm applies these *moves* to improve the initial solution (s_0) of an instance, significantly varies from algorithm to algorithm according to the searching strategy being used. Therefore, for the definition of the *algorithm space*, we selected four well-known meta-heuristics adapted by the winner of the ITC 2011, the Group of Optimization and Algorithms (GOAL team) of the Federal University of Ouro Preto. This set of meta-heuristics operates based on seven *moves* described in [2], and briefly described next.

Simulated Annealing (SA). As proposed to solve XHSTT educational instances [4], Simulated Annealing (a meta-heuristic that simulates the tempering process of a material), consists of a loop that at each iteration selects a random *move* to be applied to the initial solution. The effect of each move on the penalty function is calculated as $\Delta = f(s') - f(s)$. Successful *moves* (those with $\Delta \leq 0$) are unconditionally accepted, but unsuccessful moves are accepted with some probability $e^{\Delta/T}$, where T is the temperature parameter that defines the probability of accepting worse solutions.

Variable Neighborhood Search (VNS). As implemented by Fonseca and Santos [5], the Variable Neighborhood Search improves the quality of the solution of XHSTT instances by performing a systematic change of neighborhoods. At each iteration, a neighborhood $N_k(s)$ is selected, then a descent method that searches for a local optima in the selected neighborhood is applied. If the solution found by the descent method is better than the current solution, the solution is updated and the neighborhood is set to the first type of *move*. Otherwise, the next *move* is set as the new neighborhood to continue the search process.

Late Acceptance Hill Climbing (LAHC). As implemented by Fonseca et al. [6], Late Acceptance Hill Climbing stores the penalty values of a set of solutions of an instance on a vector $\mathbf{p} = \mathbf{p}_0, \ldots \mathbf{p}_{l-1}$. At each iteration i, a candidate solution s' is generated and it is accepted if its cost is less than or equal to the cost stored on the $i \bmod l$ position of $\mathbf{p}$. Furthermore, if the accepted solution is better than the best solution s^* found so far, its penalty value is stored on the position $i \bmod l$ of vector $\mathbf{p}$.

Iterated Local Search (ILS). As applied to educational timetabling instances [4], Iterated Local Search starts from an initial solution s_0 generated from the implementation of Simulated Annealing. This initial solution s_0 is perturbed through the unconditional acceptance of a distant neighbor, to produce a new candidate solution that is improved by a descent method. The descent method runs until a number of iterations without improvement is reached, producing a solution s' that it is accepted if is better than the best found solution s^*.

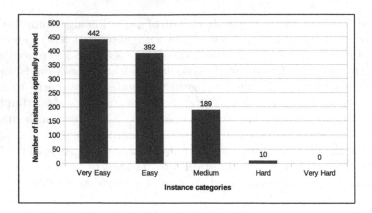

Fig. 1. Number of instances of each CB-CTT category optimally solved by the collection of meta-heuristics.

5   Performance Analysis of the Algorithm Space

As an exploratory analysis of the *performance space*, a solution time of 100 s was set to improve the 5679 non-optimally solved instances (an overall execution time of 6.57 days per meta-heuristic). The collection of meta-heuristics was able to find an optimal solution (with a penalty value of zero) for 1033 instances (i.e. 18.18%), where most of these optimal solutions corresponded to the *categories Very Easy* and *Easy* (as shown in Fig. 1).

To further evaluate the performance of the *algorithm space*, we compared the penalty value of the solutions generated by each meta-heuristic, and defined the *best-known solution* (i.e. the best solution that the collection of meta-heuristics was able to find) for each instance. Based on this comparison, four types of *performance ties* were observed: instances solved to its best-known solution by only one meta-heuristic (*no-tie*), and instances equally solved to its best-known solution by two (*tie-2*), three (*tie-3*), or four (*tie-4*) meta-heuristics. Of course, for instances of type *tie-4*, there is no need of selecting the best algorithm, as any chosen meta-heuristic will equally improve the initial solution of those instances. However, as the number of *ties* decreases, selecting the best algorithm to be applied becomes relevant.

As shown in Fig. 2, the number of instances to which the algorithm selection is trivial (*tie-4*), or to which the random selection of any algorithm has a high probability (of 0.75) to be successful (*tie-3*), corresponds to 61.89% of the 5679 instances defined in the *problem space*. However, they are not equally distributed among the five defined instance *categories*, as, for example, *no-tie* and *tie-2* mainly occur between *Medium*, *Hard*, and *Very Hard* instances. From the analysis of performance ties, we decided to test the effectiveness of recommendation models for instances on which meta-heuristics exhibited a different performance (*no-tie* and *tie-2*), regardless of the type of instance category they belong to. Therefore, the *problem space* was reduced to 2164 instances.

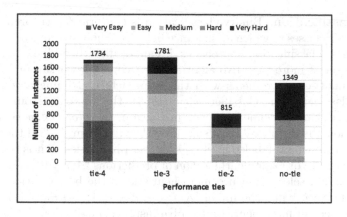

Fig. 2. Distribution of instances according to the number of ties observed in the performance of the meta-heuristics.

6 Selection Mechanisms

The goal of any algorithm recommendation model is choosing the best candidate algorithm to solve a given instance based on the predicted variation of performance in the *algorithm space*. The strategy used to predict this variation has a major role in the effectiveness of the model, and in this paper we refer to it as *selection mechanism*. This section describes four different selection mechanisms that could be applied to solve the Algorithm Selection Problem in the context of the educational timetabling instances and analyze their suitability to build an algorithm recommendation model.

Multi-label Classification. Because of the number of *performance ties* in the *algorithm space*, a straightforward approach to define the *selection mechanism* is formulating the selection task as a multi-label classification problem. Unlike the single-label classification problem, in multi-label classification, there is no limitation on the number of labels that an instance can be assigned. Therefore, it can be applied to predict more than one algorithm for an instance. For example, if an instance (I_i) can be equally solved by the first and the third meta-heuristic of our *algorithm space* (denoted as $\{A_1, A_2, A_3, A_4\}$), then both meta-heuristics must be predicted for that instance as follows, $I_i : \{A_1, A_3\}$.

Multi-class Classification. Multi-class classification refers to the problem of predicting, from a set of more than three classes, the class to which an instance belongs to. Thus, unlike the multi-label problem, only a single class must be predicted for each instance. Considering the same example, where the first and third meta-heuristic exhibit the same performance for a instance I_i, then only one of these predictions: $I_i : \{A_1\}$, or $I_i : \{A_3\}$, would be defined as correct.

Binary Classification. Binary classification is concerned with predicting one of two possible classes to which an instance belongs. Therefore, unlike multi-label and multi-class classification approaches, it cannot directly address the selection task from a set of more than two algorithms. A common workaround, however, to address multi-class problems with this approach, is defining a combination of binary classifiers –one classifier per class. In the context of our ASP, two possible classes can be defined for each instance in the *problem space* according to the question: "Is instance I_i best solved by the algorithm A_n?" If the answer is affirmative, instance i is labeled as class 1 for meta-heuristic i; if it is negative, we label it as class 0. For example, the union of predictions $[A_1i = 0, A_2i = 0, A_3i = 1, A_4i = 0]$ would select the third meta-heuristic as the best solution approach to solve instance i; while the union $[A_1j = 1, A_2j = 1, A_3j = 0, A_4j = 0]$, the first and the second meta-heuristic to solve instance j.

Regression. An alternative *selection mechanism* to classification-based approaches is regression, a supervised-learning used to predict values for continuous variables. Because of its nature, regression methods are not suitable for performing classifications tasks. However, within the context of our ASP, they can be used to predict the performance of each meta-heuristic on a given instance. By following this approach, continuous predicted values can be compared and then transformed into the same classes defined for binary classification: class 1, for the algorithm highest performance algorithm, and class 0 for the others. Unlike binary classification, the continuous nature of the predictions requires the definition of a *comparison threshold* (ct) to consider the possibility of *performance ties* between algorithms. Thus, for example, if the predicted scaled performance of the four meta-heuristics for a given instance I_i is $[A_1i = 1.25, A_2i = 1.16, A_3i = 2.22, A_4i = 2.21]$, then the output of the recommendation model for a $ct = 0$ will be $[A_1i = 0, A_2i = 0, A_3i = 1, A_4i = 0]$; and $[A_1i = 0, A_2i = 0, A_3i = 1, A_4i = 1]$ for a $ct = 0.01$.

6.1   Discussion of Selection Mechanisms

The four *selection mechanisms* described above differ in many dimensions. However, for the purposes of this research, they are compared in two aspects: easiness of implementation, and flexibility to address the set of possible prediction values.

Figure 3 shows the four *selection mechanisms*. Multi-label and multi-class approaches are easy to implement, since they require training a single classifier to predict the best algorithm(s) for a given instance. On the other hand, binary classification requires training a different classifier for each algorithm in the *algorithm space*, to produce a series of $\{0, 1\}$ predictions that are combined into a single output. The more complex *selection mechanism* is regression, which requires a different regressor to predict the performance of each meta-heuristic on a given instance, and a comparison threshold to transform the predictions into a series of $\{0, 1\}$ selection values.

Despite its simplicity, multi-label classification uses a strict multiple assignment of labels, that is not flexible enough to address *performance ties* between

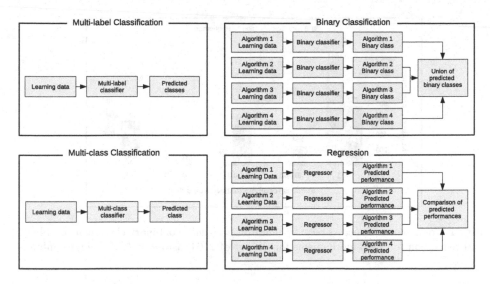

Fig. 3. Set of *selection mechanisms* considered to be used for the algorithm recommendation model.

algorithms. For example, if the algorithms $\{A_1, A_4\}$ are the best to solve an instance I_i, and the prediction obtained with multi-label classifier is $\{A_4\}$, this prediction would be considered as a misclassification error, even though it is partially correct and would finally lead to the best-know solution of instance I_i. Multi-class classification is also not flexible enough to handle *performance ties*, because, it only allows the definition of a single label per instance. Therefore, considering the same example, it would only consider one of these possibilities $I : \{A_1\}$ or $I : \{A_4\}$ as correct for instance I_i.

Due to their structure, that requires using an independent learner for each algorithm in the portfolio, binary classification and regression provides a more flexible approach to address *performance ties*. As each learner is trained with different data, all possible outcomes (*no-tie, tie-2, tie-3, tie-4*) can be predicted, and evaluated at an algorithm level. Considering the same example, if the set $\{A_1i = 1, A_1i = 0, A_3i = 0, A_4i = 1\}$ represents the best algorithms to solve instance I_i, and the prediction obtained with binary classification or regression approaches is $\{A_1i = 1, A_1i = 0, A_3i = 0, A_4i = 0\}$, then it is possible to observe that the prediction is partially correct, since it selected algorithm A_1 as a candidate to solve instance I_1, even though it did not select algorithm A_4.

After analyzing the main advantages and disadvantages of the four described *selection mechanisms*, binary classification and regression approaches were selected as the *selection mechanisms* to be tested in the context of the CB-CTT problem. Their implementation and effectiveness is presented next.

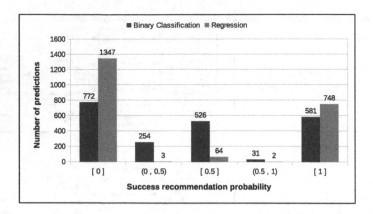

Fig. 4. Comparison of *success recommendation probability* of binary classification (blue) and regression (orange) mechanisms for the set of 2164 instances. (Color figure online)

7   Results

Within the context of the CB-CTT problem, the selection of a meta-heuristic is successful if its application leads to the best-known solution of a given instance. Therefore, to evaluate the performance of both tested approaches with a single metric, we defined the *success recommendation probability* (SRP), calculated as the percentage of meta-heuristics that were accurately recommended (predicted) for a particular instance. This metric was used because of its suitability to assess the three possible prediction cases: *(i)* Number of true meta-heuristics equal to the number of predicted meta-heuristics, *(ii)* Number of true meta-heuristics greater than the number of predicted meta-heuristics, and *(iii)* Number of true meta-heuristics less than the number of predicted meta-heuristics.

To build the selection mechanisms, different machine learning methods were tested, such as, decision trees, gradient boosting trees, support vector machines, and multi-layer perceptrons. Here we only present the results obtained using multi-layer perceptron architectures, since they proved to be the more effective for the classification and regression tasks. For both tasks the same hyper-parameters and layers were used (2 hidden layers of 100 neurons). To estimate the generalization errors of both recommendation models, we obtained the 10-fold cross-validated algorithm predictions for the 2164 instances (i.e. for each instance, the prediction that was obtained for that instance when it was in the test fold), and calculated their SRP.

Because of the adoption of the SRP to assess the global performance of both methodologies, the prediction of the meta-heuristic(s) to be applied to an instance was evaluated from *totally wrong* (SRP = 0) to *totally right* (SRP = 1). Where intermediate values indicated both: *(i)* That a set of algorithms were recommended to solve an instance, and *(ii)* That from this set, only a fraction of the predicted algorithm was correct. Figure 4 shows the distribution

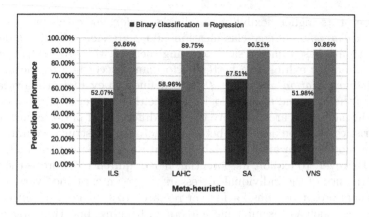

Fig. 5. Accuracy (orange) and explained variance score (blue) of the predictions obtained for each meta-heuristic by the individual classifiers and regressors. (Color figure online)

of the performance of the predictions according to five defined SRP bins. As observed, because of the independence of the predictions of the classifiers, binary classification exhibited a high number of predictions evaluated with a fractional SRP. On the other hand, because of the comparison step, most of the predictions made by the regression approach were evaluated as *totally right* or *totally wrong*, which is the desired behavior of a practical recommendation model.

Both selection mechanisms exhibited a relatively low number of *totally-right* predictions (26.8% for binary classification and 34.5% for regression). Therefore, as further analysis of these results, we evaluated the performance of the individual classifiers and regressors used to build the selection mechanisms. As shown in Fig. 5, the performance of the binary classifiers (measured in terms of accuracy), was not significantly higher than that of a random choice. However, the performance of the regressors (measured in terms of explained variance score), was high for the four meta-heuristics. The fact that the combination of high-performance regressors was not able to produce an accurate recommendation model led us to examine the algorithm recommendation errors, in which we observed that 64.36% of wrong algorithm predictions occurred in instances on which the variation of the solution cost between the best and worst meta-heuristic was low, of less than 2000.

8   Conclusions

In this paper, we present the implementation of algorithm recommendation models for the solution of CB-CTT instances based on the Algorithm Selection Problem framework. To evaluate this multi-model approach, we selected a set of 2164 instances (from an initial set of 6000 instances), that were at most equally solved by two meta-heuristics, and discussed the suitability of four machine learning approaches to be used as *selection mechanisms*.

Because of its higher flexibility to address *performance ties*, we tested two *selection mechanisms*, binary classification and regression. We concluded that despite both are based on the same learning method, the proposed regression-based methodology exhibited a better performance according to the measured *success recommendation probability (SRP)*; defined to evaluate the overall performance of the proposed methodologies despite the number of *performance ties*.

These initial results are indicative that the difference of performance between meta-heuristics could be used as a better predictor to construct accurate recommendation models than algorithm labeling within the context of the CB-CTT problem. However, to exploit its potential, it is required to improve the prediction performance of the individual regressors above an explained variance score of 90%. Therefore, it remains for further research to test more advanced learning approaches such as ensemble methods (e.g., bagging, boosting, stacking), to define the best approach to make use of this data.

Also, as future work, we plan to diversify the difference of performance within the *algorithm space* by: *(i)* Including algorithms of a different nature, that tackle the CB-CTT problem based on mathematical models (such as linear programming), and population-based heuristics (such as evolutionary algorithms); *(ii)* Increasing the diversity of generated CB-CTT instances to be solved; and *(iii)* Increasing the solution running time of the algorithms.

References

1. Bonutti, A., De Cesco, F., Di Gaspero, L., Schaerf, A.: Benchmarking curriculum-based course timetabling: formulations, data formats, instances, validation, visualization, and results. Ann. Oper. Res. **194**(1), 59–70 (2012)
2. Brito, S.S., Fonseca, G.H., et al.: A SA-VNS approach for the high school timetabling problem. Electron. Notes Discrete Math. **39**, 169–176 (2012)
3. Di Gaspero, L., McCollum, B., Schaerf, A.: The second international timetabling competition (ITC-2007): curriculum-based course timetabling (track 3). Technical report, Technical Report QUB/IEEE/Tech/ITC2007/CurriculumCTT/v1.0. Queen's University, Belfast, United Kingdom (2007)
4. da Fonseca, G.H.G., Santos, H.G., et al.: GOAL solver: a hybrid local search based solver for high school timetabling. Ann. Oper. Res. **239**(1), 77–97 (2016)
5. Fonseca, G.H., Santos, H.G.: Variable neighborhood search based algorithms for high school timetabling. Comput. Oper. Res. **52**, 203–208 (2014)
6. Fonseca, G.H., Santos, H.G., Carrano, E.G.: Late acceptance hill-climbing for high school timetabling. J. Sched. **19**(4), 453–465 (2016)
7. Kingston, J.H.: The KHE High School Timetabling Engine (2016). http://www.it.usyd.edu.au/~jeff/khe/
8. MirHassani, S., Habibi, F.: Solution approaches to the course timetabling problem. Artif. Intell. Rev. **39**, 1–17 (2013)
9. Pillay, N.: A survey of school timetabling research. Ann. Oper. Res. **218**(1), 261–293 (2014)

10. Post, G., Kingston, J.H., Ahmadi, S., Daskalaki, S., et al.: XHSTT: an XML archive for high school timetabling problems in different countries. Ann. Oper. Res. **218**(1), 295–301 (2014)
11. Rice, J.R.: The algorithm selection problem. Adv. Comput. **15**, 65–118 (1976)
12. de la Rosa-Rivera, F., Nunez-Varela, J.I., et al.: Measuring the complexity of educational timetabling instances. J. Sched. (in review)

Statistical Approach in Data Filtering for Prediction Vessel Movements Through Time and Estimation Route Using Historical AIS Data

Rogelio Bautista-Sánchez[1]([✉])(iD), Liliana Ibeth Barbosa-Santillán[1,2](iD), and Juan Jaime Sánchez-Escobar[2](iD)

[1] Universidad de Guadalajara, Guadalajara, JAL, Mexico
rogeliobautistasanchez@outlook.com, ibarbosa@cucea.udg.mx
[2] Centro de Enseñanza Técnica Industrial, Guadalajara, JAL, Mexico
jjsanchez@ceti.mx

Abstract. The prediction of vessel maritime navigation has become an interesting topic in the last years, especially in areas of economical commercial exchange and security. Also, vessels monitoring requires better systems and techniques that help enterprises and governments to protect their interests. In specific, the prediction of vessels movements is important concerning safety and tracking. However, the applications of prediction techniques have a high cost of computational efficiency and low resource-saving. This article presents a sample method to select historical data on ship-specific routes to optimize the computational performance of the prediction of ship positions and route estimation in real-time. These historical navigation data can help us to estimate a complete path and perform vessel positions predictions through time. This method works in a vessel tracking system in order to save computational work when predictions or route estimations are in execution. The results obtained after testing the method are almost acceptable concerning route estimation with a precision of 74.98%, and with vessel positions predictions through time a 79% of accuracy.

Keywords: E-Navigation · Neural networks · Vessel prediction · Route selection

1 Introduction

Maritime Navigation is an essential part of international trade. Global maritime exchange increased exponentially in the year 2017 [2], mainly driven by Economies of Asia and Europe since many countries export products around the world in large volumes.

At the beginning of the year 2018, the merchant fleet was estimated to made up of 58,329 vessels [2], and this leads a more commercial exchange.

© Springer Nature Switzerland AG 2019
L. Martínez-Villaseñor et al. (Eds.): MICAI 2019, LNAI 11835, pp. 28–38, 2019.
https://doi.org/10.1007/978-3-030-33749-0_3

Maritime Navigation has taken a boom. One main task is monitoring the seas to describe and predict moving through them, and since e-commerce is exponentially growing, the vessels are the primary transport of products. Today the government and enterprises are more interested in it. Data Mining techniques [5] have been implemented to improve the maritime description such as classification, clustering, and predictions [1].

Today, there are routes of transit established for navigation. Likewise, to find vessel movements and prevent incidents have been born techniques like maritime tracking and vessel monitoring systems. For this last one, in 2002, the IMO (International Maritime Organization) approved the AIS (Automatic Identification System). Now it becomes an indispensable tool in terms of safety and vessel monitoring around the world.

Now, concerning historical vessel positions, a vessel can make use of some routes many times based on an origin and destination. Sometimes ships have to change courses for different reasons such as adverse climatic agents, political disputes, or prohibitions. However, most of the time, their trajectories are similar.

Some systems save historical records to have evidence of the vessels location. Industries such as Marine Traffic are an example of them, whose system manage large amounts of maritime information near to 800 million of position records per month.

One of the principal goals is the prediction and route estimation of the vessel movements but is a difficult task because systems require high-performance computing. Also, it needs to have historical information that can describe patterns in the flow of vessels.

The prediction field of ships trajectory covers different concepts: direction, speed, registered locations, statistical analysis to identify routes, among others. With this information, the model can develop complex algorithms and systems such as Pallotta proposes [11]. Pallotta uses an unsupervised and incremental learning approach to the extraction of maritime movement patterns from raw data to information supporting decisions.

Perera [13] provides an Extended Kalman Filter (EKF) for the estimation of vessel states, and it uses for the prediction of vessel trajectories with the objective to integrating intelligent features into a vessel traffic monitoring and information systems (VTMISs), but with high computational complexity.

In less complicated terms, Zissis [16] proposes a simple system for prediction using a multilayer function for a web-based system capable of real-time learning and accurately predicting any vessels future behavior in low computational time.

Mazzarella [10] proposes a system for the detection and monitoring of multiple vessels. He also shows a proposal for the estimation and prediction of the trajectory in the navigation. Mazzarella uses a Bayesian vessel prediction algorithm based on a Particle Filter (PF) in order to enhance the quality of the vessel position prediction.

The inferential statistic has generated a significant number of tools to contribute to the process of making scientific judgments on the uncertainty data. Besides, localization measures are designed to provide quantitative values of the central location of the sample. These values will be helpful to identify differences between several routes of the vessels. This paper proposes an approach to data selection to reduce computational cost. This work does not focus on precision, but it shows almost acceptable results with a small amount of data.

The paper follows the next organization. Section 2 presents preliminary experiments to show the data behavior and adjust the data before selection. Section 3 describes the operations of selecting routes by clustering using the best statistical values. Section 4 presents the results of these experiments. Finally, Sect. 5 summarizes the conclusions drawn from this work.

2 Data Analysis and Preliminary Experiments

The vessel prediction accuracy depends extensively on the behavior of the existent information, what the process obtains, and mainly the appropriate selection of data. With this, the performance will be acceptable and highly efficient for any system.

2.1 Statistic Analysis

In order to show how the method works, the data used to detail this method are a small sample of routes and their destination. Those come from the port of Lázaro Cárdenas, Michoacán, Mexico, to the port of Balboa in Costa Rica. Besides, it also includes routes of a different route, as is shown in Fig. 1.

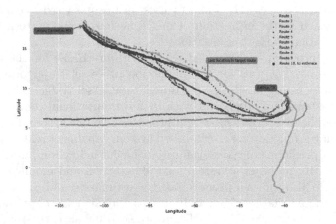

Fig. 1. Routes to the port of Balboa, including different historical routes. At the center, the actual vessel location

As Fig. 1 shows, the route to predict is currently between several others. To be able to select the correct data, the method performed an analysis of the behavior of each route. Another drawback is the number of samples that a vessel can record on a whole journey. For that reason, the process carefully analyzes as much as possible to find patterns. These patterns were used to select routes that perform predictions and route estimation.

The method starts with the statistical analysis identifying the measures of central tendency and dispersion. To know the behavior of data, it searches a gap that can significantly differentiate the routes. The first step is to find the visual differences among each route using the histogram and kernel density estimation (KDE). In this term, it is necessary to consider that if KDE or histogram follows a similar pattern for each route, means that the data would always behave similarly, but that does not occur in real environments.

2.2 Data Adjust

Figure 2 shows the behavior of the sample around its histogram and its KDE. The data of route three and six change around latitude, the data of route nine have another direction. The rest of the data is almost similar to latitude and longitude. This evidence is enough to get the statisticians values and with it, those who help to separate the desired routes from those that are not.

Another important detail is that the information has a different number of observations or small deviations in some routes. At the same time, this historical data contains complete routes. This feature relatively affects finding statistics values that serve as weights to be able to see the appropriate data that will help to predict and estimate routes. In this sample, the actual route objective it is not complete.

In order to adjust the sample routes to the objective route, the goal in this step is to cut the sample data (each route) among the origin and the last actual position values (longitude and latitude approximately) of the target route to estimate as shows Fig. 3.

Once the method cuts the data, it is necessary to compute the statistical values of each route. With the Chi-Squared Selection Method [9], it is possible to find values that have a higher weight to be used for classification. The statistical values for this sample are in Table 1. The choice operation is not strict. It allows having information about routes with different performance and precision to the classification.

As mentioned before, Table 1 shows detailed routes 3, 6, and 9. The data have a marked difference in most of the statistical values, specifically about latitude. The method considers those statistical values that have an extensive range of dispersion to apply the cluster technique that helps us to choose the best routes for prediction. In terms of the visibility of this work, it takes only three statistical values of each route, those that have the broadest range of dispersion.

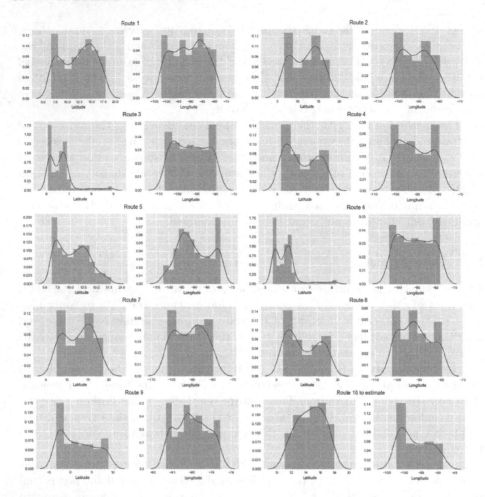

Fig. 2. This image shows Kernel Density Estimation (KDE) and histograms for each sample route in order to visualize differences. Freedman-Diaconis rule was used to calculate bins.

3   Experiments

In this section, after the data analysis and selection of those statistical values that represent in the best way each route. The method uses a clustering technique, and the data selected are evaluated in order to predict.

3.1   Route Selection by Clustering

It is about to apply a Density-Based Spatial Clustering of Applications with Noise (DBSCAN) [6] to discover and select the best data. DBSCAN it was proposed by Albert Ester and can identify clusters and outliers. It can be seen in the sample a clear difference before the application of DBSCAN (Fig. 4).

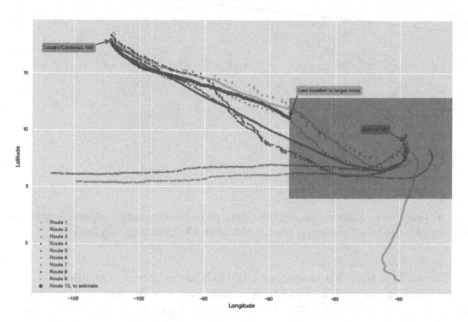

Fig. 3. The data in the representative red section is discarded only for this step. This step helps to approximate the historical data to the actual route in statistic terms. In the case of route nine with a different direction, and similar cases will help to perform the selection of routes in the next step. (Color figure online)

Table 1. Statistic values of the route samples. In bold those selected for clustering.

Route	Mean	SD	Median	Trimmed	MAD	Min	Max	Range	Skew	Kurtosis
R1	−95.7754	4.0476	−95.6280	−95.8105	**5.2224**	−102.1654	−88.5597	13.6057	0.0169	−1.2530
R1	14.8142	1.6970	14.7858	14.7895	**2.0491**	11.9026	17.9070	**6.0044**	0.1057	−1.0275
R2	−96.3409	4.0154	−96.8687	−96.5032	**4.9517**	−102.1421	−88.7607	13.3813	0.2836	−1.1829
R2	14.3558	1.7552	14.3989	14.3369	**1.8985**	11.2068	17.7344	**6.5276**	0.0434	−0.9519
R3	−92.8439	8.6213	−92.8537	−92.9098	**11.5973**	−106.7184	−79.3515	27.3669	0.0591	−1.3124
R3	6.6405	0.5588	6.6110	6.5455	**0.4329**	6.0678	8.9295	**2.8616**	2.0486	5.1606
R4	−97.9075	2.8881	−98.2134	−98.0079	**3.6160**	−102.1575	−92.7202	9.4373	0.2496	−1.2254
R4	14.9484	1.8502	15.0633	15.0308	**2.2380**	11.1500	17.8341	**6.6841**	−0.3252	−1.0109
R5	−95.6835	2.7214	−95.1831	−95.4210	**2.4229**	−102.1772	−91.7679	10.4093	−0.7338	−0.2711
R5	13.3957	1.6398	13.0285	13.2281	**1.4560**	11.0738	17.8367	**6.7629**	0.8153	−0.1128
R6	−90.9273	8.6213	−90.9370	−90.9932	**11.5976**	−104.8000	−77.4350	27.3650	0.0591	−1.3124
R6	5.9164	0.5588	5.8870	5.8214	**0.4330**	5.3437	8.2054	**2.8617**	2.0486	5.1606
R7	−91.1521	7.1799	−90.3865	−91.2039	**9.4471**	−102.0300	−79.5760	22.4540	−0.0273	−1.3422
R7	12.7386	3.4204	13.0450	12.7280	**4.3929**	7.5305	18.6150	**11.0845**	−0.0938	−1.3647
R8	−91.4961	7.0875	−92.0720	−91.6856	**8.9742**	−102.1600	−79.5230	22.6370	0.1990	−1.1234
R8	11.6772	3.9423	10.8310	11.5482	**5.2996**	6.5358	18.4220	**11.8862**	0.2190	−1.4511
R9	−79.9937	0.8074	−80.0350	−80.0011	**0.9539**	−81.3338	−78.5598	2.7740	0.0425	−1.1046
R9	1.8448	4.0131	1.2991	1.6176	**5.3125**	−3.2669	8.9521	**12.2190**	0.3284	−1.2354
R10	−96.6793	4.3768	−97.4817	−96.9322	**5.3426**	−102.2124	−88.5125	13.7000	0.3612	−1.2956
R10	14.6740	1.8548	14.7961	14.7074	**2.2433**	11.0702	17.9470	**6.8768**	−0.1293	−1.0347

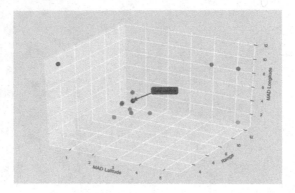

Fig. 4. Features in a 3D vision. Cut the data provides a statistical approximation to the actual route to estimate and predict. All routes help to identify clusters.

The configuration parameters of DBSCAN are related to the minimum distance found in each point, and the minimum elements of clusters were defined by 2. The method applies DBSCAN to see several groups within its routes as it shows in Fig. 5.

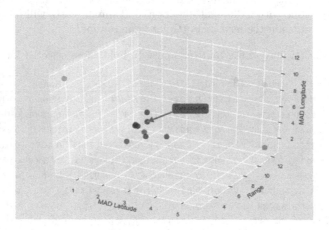

Fig. 5. Cluster discovered using DBSCAN. Those routes in the group will help for prediction and estimation of the objective.

After the application of DBSCAN, the method discards all routes that do not resemble the route to predict. For better results, it is necessary to have enough data to get a faithful approximation of its best statistical values to achieve the performance of the classification according to the theorem of limit central [12]. The algorithm chooses the information that justifies the use of specific routes that share similarity with the target.

In this paper is proposed two techniques for prediction to show the accuracy of prediction and route estimation after the selection of all routes that resemble the current route. As first, the use of an Artificial Recurrent Neural Network (ARNN) [15] with Long Short-Term Memory (LSTM) [7,8] using historical data as continual input streams, as second technique Multivariate Imputation by Chained Equations (MICE), a statistical method for handling missing data [14].

The sample contains almost 17770 records for training in case of the Artificial Neural Network (ANN). For the application of MICE, all records were used, including records of the actual vessel target. Also, for both techniques, it was used only longitude and latitude to save computational power.

3.2   Using an Artificial Neural Network

The type of ANN used before it was an ARNN with a Long Short-Term Memory layer using Keras high-level Framework [4]. For the training data, the filtered historical data it was used, while for the tests, the data corresponding to the current route.

3.3   Using Multivariate Imputation by Chained Equations

This technique highly used in the search for missing values of data-sets provides favorable results [3]. The purpose of this application is the generation of most of the all route, an approximation concerning the prediction of the full path and on it.

For the full application of this technique, it was necessary to carry out a stratified sampling. The algorithm obtains a representative matrix of the data, as shown in Fig. 6, the data is stratified to get the most significant amount of data that contributes to generating a suitable route of estimation.

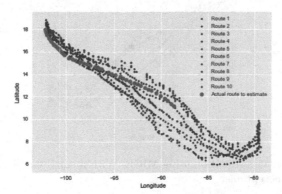

Fig. 6. Routes after stratified sampling. In this form, we can use MICE in order to estimate the rest of the route.

4   Results

Once the experimentation finish, the prediction of a time window for terms of
the ANN and the estimation of the route using the MICE algorithm the method
obtained the following results.

First of all, in Table 2 is compared the actual data of a time window against
which the predictions of the ANN previously trained.

Table 2. Real data contrasted with previously predicted path segment, predicted latitude it has better accuracy than predicted latitude.

Original Lon	Predicted Lon	Original Lat	Predicted Lat
−88.4179687	−87.78852081	11.0005122	**11.1501236**
−88.3146973	−87.64251709	10.9192581	**11.05459881**
−88.2174682	−87.49876404	10.8333059	**10.96898937**
−88.105957	−87.40653992	10.7358156	**10.90005875**
−88.0004882	−87.30580139	10.6390137	**10.81973934**
−87.8862305	−87.21099854	10.5414609	**10.73477745**
−87.8027343	−87.10231781	10.4472987	**10.63841438**
−87.7104492	−86.99958038	10.3361757	**10.5427351**
−87.6187133	−86.88833618	10.2608707	**10.44632149**
−87.5126953	−86.80708313	10.1631997	**10.3532629**

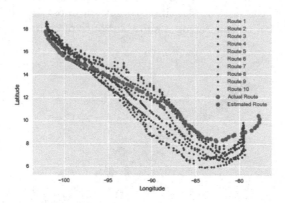

Fig. 7. Results of route estimation using MICE. With a small number of samples, the
results are almost acceptable.

Finally, the prediction does not show excellent results because the accuracy
obtained was 79%. However, it allows approximating the results with few data
(only ten routes as sample).

Concerning the application of the MICE technique as it shows in Fig. 7, the prediction generates almost acceptable results in terms of the route approximation with 74.98% of accuracy using a small sample of routes.

With this, the method can show that the results after select the best routes had an acceptable approximation to the real values in the case of the ANN, and in case of MICE application, it is almost similar.

Compared with other methods cited in this paper, Zissis [16] mention a cloud infrastructure to support scaling on demand (Marine Traffic case) and the system stores the trained vessel ANN and recall it in the near future (24 h) for following predictions. This method is used in real-time and is capable of running on a simple computer with GPU.

5 Conclusions and Future Work

The method in this paper was tested using a small amount of data. The paper shows the application of the method and testing the accuracy using ARNN and MICE techniques. However, the correct selection of data for analysis and prediction in maritime routes is an essential topic before applying some techniques. The impact of the results concerns the protection of the assets found in the Shipments that move in the seas and especially in economic terms. Daily vessels move billions of dollars through the oceans from one country to another, one of the drawbacks of handling all this information as has been mentioned is the profitability of the different projects for this purpose. The computational resources, economic, human and even global infrastructures can be quite high, and now that there are enough techniques, the goal is the viability, the actual application of jobs under a low-cost scheme, but having the same precision as large-scale systems or at least an approximation. This proposal is made under these premises so that it can have application within a monitoring system designed for the Mexican government to have more control in their national seas. It is necessary to mention that some improvements are performed to obtain better results concerning the accuracy and high performance by a low computational cost.

As future work, it is necessary to show how this method works in a real environment and the possible improvements implemented for better performance. This work has been supported by the Sciences Research Council (CONACyT) through the research project number 262756 called "The use of GNSS data for tracking maritime flow for sea security".

Conflicts of Interest. The authors declare that they have no conflicts of interest.

References

1. Alessandrini, A., et al.: Mining vessel tracking data for maritime domain applications (2016). https://doi.org/10.1109/ICDMW.2016.20
2. ANAVE: Merchant marine and maritime transport 2017/2018 (2018)

3. Azur, M.J., Stuart, E.A., Frangakis, C., Leaf, P.J.: Multiple imputation by chained equations: what is it and how does it work? Int. J. Methods Psychiatr. Res. (2011). https://doi.org/10.1002/mpr.329
4. Chollet, F.: Keras Documentation. Keras.Io (2015)
5. Deng, F., Guo, S., Deng, Y., Chu, H., Zhu, Q., Sun, F.: Vessel track information mining using AIS data (2013)
6. Ester, M., Kriegel, H.-P., Sander, J., Xu, X.: A density-based algorithm for discovering clusters a density-based algorithm for discovering clusters in large spatial databases with noise. In: Proceedings of the Second International Conference on Knowledge Discovery and Data Mining, no. 6, pp. 226–231. (1996). http://dl.acm.org/citation.cfm?id=3001460.3001507
7. Gers, F.A., Schmidhuber, J., Cummins, F.:Learning to forget: Continual prediction with LSTM. Neural Comput. (2000). arXiv:1011.1669v3, https://doi.org/10.1162/089976600300015015. ISBN: 0 85296 721 7, ISSN: 08997667
8. Hochreiter, S., Schmidhuber, J.: Long short-term memory. Neural Comput. (1997). https://doi.org/10.1162/neco.1997.9.8.1735
9. Liu, H., Setiono, R.: Chi2: feature selection and discretization of numeric attributes. In: Proceedings of the International Conference on Tools with Artificial Intelligence (1995)
10. Mazzarella, F., Arguedas, V.F., Vespe, M.: Knowledge-based vessel position prediction using historical AIS data. In: 2015 Workshop on Sensor Data Fusion: Trends, Solutions, Applications, SDF 2015 (2015). https://doi.org/10.1109/SDF.2015.7347707
11. Pallotta, G., Vespe, M., Bryan, K.: Vessel pattern knowledge discovery from AIS data: a framework for anomaly detection and route prediction. Entropy (2013). https://doi.org/10.3390/e15062218
12. Peck,   R.,   Devore,   J.L.:   Statistics: The   Exploration   &   Analysis   of   Data.   Cengage   Learning,   Boston   (2011). https://books.google.com.mx/books?id=NsAh3P-WrswC
13. Perera, L.P., Oliveira, P., Soares, C.G.: Maritime traffic monitoring based on vessel detection, tracking, state estimation, and trajectory prediction. IEEE Trans. Intell. Transp. Syst. (2012). https://doi.org/10.1109/TITS.2012.2187282
14. White, I.R., Royston, P., Wood, A.M.: Multiple imputation using chained equations: issues and guidance for practice. Stat. Med. (2011). https://doi.org/10.1002/sim.4067
15. Williams, R.J., Zipser, D.: A learning algorithm for continually running fully recurrent neural networks. Neural Comput. (1989). https://doi.org/10.1162/neco.1989.1.2.270
16. Zissis, D., Xidias, E.K., Lekkas, D.: Real-time vessel behavior prediction. Evolving Syst. (2016). https://doi.org/10.1007/s12530-015-9133-5

Lexical Intent Recognition in Urdu Queries Using Deep Neural Networks

Sana Shams[1]([⊠]), Muhammad Aslam[1],
and Ana Maria Martinez-Enriquez[2]

[1] Department of Computer Science and Engineering,
University of Engineering and Technology, Lahore, Pakistan
2016phdcs2@student.uet.edu.pk, maslam@uet.edu.pk
[2] Department of Computer Science, CINVESTAV-IPN, Mexico, D.F., Mexico
ammartin@cinvestav.mx

Abstract. Recognition of user intent from web queries is required by search engines to improve user experience by adapting search results to the user goals. In this paper we report findings of intent recognition from search queries, using two intent annotated benchmark datasets, ATIS and AOL web query dataset. Both these corpora have been automatically translated from English to Urdu. Through multiple experiments, we analyze and compare performance of four Deep Neural Network (DNN) based models and their architectures, i.e. CNN, LSTM, bi-directional LSTM, and CLSTM (CNN+LSTM). On ATIS dataset, CNN achieves 92.4% accuracy on binary classification. While on AOL dataset, BLSTM performs the best with 83.1% accuracy for 5% test sample proportion for 3 intent classes.

Keywords: User intent · Deep neural network · Convolutional neural network · Long short term memory · BLSTM and CLSTM

1 Introduction

User intent is defined as "the expression of an affective, cognitive, or situational goal in an interaction with a web search engine [1]" In search queries, user's intent can be communicated via multiple semantically similar phrases as shown in the example below.

i.	<u>Short route</u> from <Gulberg> to (Shah Alam)	چھوٹا راستہ <گلبرگ> سے (شاہ عالم) تک	i.
ii.	<u>Fastest way</u> between <Gulberg> and (Shah Alam)	<گلبرگ> اور (شاہ عالم) کے درمیان تیز ترین راستہ	ii.
iii.	<u>Minimal distance</u> from <Gulberg> and (Shah Alam)	<گلبرگ> سے (شاہ عالم) کا کم سے کم فاصلہ	iii.

In this example, all queries describe the same intent of finding an optimal route from one place <Gulberg> to the other (Shah Alam), but the words representing this

L. Martínez-Villaseñor et al. (Eds.): MICAI 2019, LNAI 11835, pp. 39–50, 2019.
https://doi.org/10.1007/978-3-030-33749-0_4

intent are different. Such scenarios pose a significant challenge for intelligent systems to interpret accurate results, for which they must incorporate natural language understanding models to classify both sentences similarly.

Query intent detection from Urdu text is a challenging task. Firstly as search queries are short phrases or keywords, they provide limited contextual information for intent recognition that can perpetuate semantic ambiguity [2]. Secondly, Urdu has a rich morphology, where words have more than one surface form. It is challenging for intent recognition as the same query can be reproduced in a number of different phrases, thus large training corpus must be developed to capture variations maximally.

Previous approaches in intent recognition used feature engineering techniques in which features e.g. n-grams, past user engagements, etc. were used, pruned and given to statistical classifiers like SVM, decision trees, etc. [3–7] for intent recognition. Recent studies have focused on employing deep neural network (DNN) based architectures e.g. convolutional (CNN), feed forward, recurrent neural networks (RNN) and long short term memory networks (LSTM) [8]. As RNN cannot be efficiently trained, due to vanishing point behavior, gated memory units like LSTM have been widely used [9–11]. Combinational DNN architectures e.g. CLSTM, combining the capability of CNN in extracting higher level representation and giving as input to LSTM, are also being used in intent recognition researches [9, 12].

In this study we compare and evaluate the performance of CNN, LSTM, B-LSTM and CLSTM in recognizing intent for Urdu search queries with their accuracies, precision, recall and F1 scores. Due to the unavailability of a corpus of Urdu queries, two benchmark English web search query corpora are used and automatically translated to Urdu for experimentation.

The rest of the paper is organized as follows: In Sect. 2 review of intent recognition studies is presented. In Sect. 3 we discuss deep neural network model used and their architectures. Finally, Sect. 4 presents the results of performance evaluation and Sect. 5 outlines the conclusion and future work.

2   Related Work

There is a vast body of knowledge on domain and intent recognition from written and spoken queries. Earliest works in intent recognition date back to 2003 in which TREC Web Corpus and WT10 g collection was used for recognizing one of the three user intents, defined in Broder's taxonomy [13]. In 2005, newer model for intent recognition was proposed to recognize two of Broder defined user intents [14] from 50 queries with 90% accuracy. With the advent of machine learning (ML) approaches, intent recognition models have been developed using a multitude of ML classifiers reporting varying evaluation results. A large number of researches [3–7] have used SVM for recognizing user intent. In these researches, intent recognition is evaluated across different metrices, number of intent classes and dataset sizes, e.g. 90% accuracy in binary classification (1700 queries), 66.97% accuracy for 7 intents, 90+ F-Score for three intent classes (2000 queries), 60% precision in recognizing 9 intents [15], etc. Neural network based user intent recognition approaches have also been compared with the traditional ML based approaches showing better results when NN classifiers are used [16].

With the adoption of deep learning models in traditional NLP tasks, deep neural network models and architectures have been used in intent recognition giving better prediction accuracy than traditional feature engineered approaches. CNN and recurrent neural networks have proved to be the top performing architectures [8, 10, 17–19]. Single forward layer LSTMs and bi-directional LSTM, with strength to model long distance dependencies, have also been extensively applied in intent detection from queries [20–22]. In more recent studies, CLSTM architecture has also been introduced for intent recognition in which feature map of CNN are organized as sequential window features to serve as input to LSTM [9, 12].

Currently intent recognition for Urdu queries has not been reported [23] though some research regarding other Urdu natural language understanding modules (NLU), e.g. Urdu Semantic Analysis [24]; Urdu Named Entity recognition [25], SVM based domain classification of Urdu documents [26] and SVM based genre identification of Urdu documents [27] has been conducted.

In our work, we report results of intent recognition from two automatically generated web search query datasets in Urdu, using CNN, LSTM, B-LSTM and CLSTM models by comparing the prediction accuracies and F1 scores.

3 Methodology

In this study, classification based approach for user intent recognition is conducted using four deep neural network models that are explained below:

3.1 Convolutional Neural Network (CNN) Based Intent Classifier

CNN were first applied in computer vision, but their vast effectiveness has been evident in a number of natural language processing tasks. In traditional CNN architectures layers with convolving filters are applied to local features e.g. n-gram vector, obtained by concatenating word vectors. These word vectors are projected from a sparse, 1-of-V encoding (where V is the vocabulary size) onto a lower dimensional vector space via a hidden layer, that encodes the semantic features of words in its dimensionality [18]. Through this representation semantically similar words come closer in a lower dimensional space.

The model architecture shown in Fig. 1 is used in the study, which is a simplified version of the CNN architecture proposed in [18]. Here like the traditional CNN architectures, the first layer embeds words into low dimensional vectors. The CNN parameters are learnt in the next layer that performs convolutions over the embedded words using filter sizes 1, 2 and 3 capturing unigram, bi-gram and trigram information of the query. Next, the results are max-pooled into a single feature vector. These features form the penultimate layer, add drop out regularization and are passed to the fully connected softmax layer for classification into the given intent classes. However unlike [18], this network has only one input channel, and as the data is in Urdu, thus pre-trained word2vec vectors for word embedding are not used, instead, word vectors are learnt from the fundamental level.

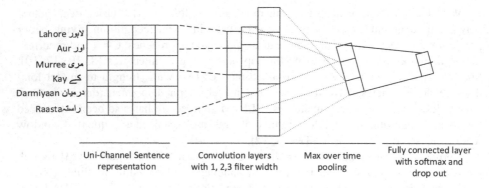

Fig. 1. CNN architecture for Urdu query classification

3.2 Long Short Term Memory (LSTM) Based Intent Classifier

LSTM are a specific type of recurrent neural network that are successfully used in natural language processing tasks due to their capability to model temporal sequences and their long-range dependencies. Unlike traditional RNNs, LSTM employ a different function in hidden state calculations. The memory units in LSTMs are referred to as memory cells, and their parameters comprise the outputs of the N-1 layer and the current layer input. These cells are responsible for deciding what to keep or reset the memory through the added forget gates (f). Lastly output from the input, previous and the current layers are concatenated. At the final classification layer, softmax is applied to the linear classification of the output. LSTM architecture used in this study is unidirectional forward layer with 100 hidden units.

3.3 Bi-directional Long Short Term Memory (BLSTM) Based Intent Classifier

BLSTM extends the unidirectional LSTM by introducing a second hidden layer, where the hidden to hidden connections flow in both backward and forward temporal order. Therefore, the model is able to incorporate context information from both the past and the future.

Figure 2 presents the BLSTM architecture used in the work adapted from [20]. Here W_i denotes the word embedding output of the ith word in the input Urdu query. W_0 and W_n denoted the word embedding output of the beginning BOS and ending EOS of the query. H_if and h_ib denote the LSTM hidden layer outputs in forward and backward directions. I_1 denote the intent output and intent in the final intent classified output of the query.

3.4 C-Long Short Term Memory (CLSTM) Based Intent Classifier

C-LSTM [12] architecture is constructed by feeding the output of a one-layer CNN into LSTM. Here CNN is constructed on top of the pre-trained word vectors, to learn higher-level representations of n-grams. Then to learn sequential correlations from

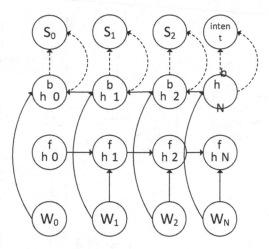

Fig. 2. BLSTM architecture showing intent output layer of the current sentence

higher-level sequence representations, the feature maps of CNN are organized as sequential window features to serve as the input of LSTM. In this way, instead of constructing LSTM directly from the input sentence, each sentence transforms into successive window (n-gram) features to help disentangle factors of variations within sentences. Sequence-based input is used to feed in the neural network, thus there is no dependency on external language, knowledge and complicated pre-processing. The architecture of the CLSTM used in this study is of [12] and is shown in Fig. 3. It uses CNN built in 3.1 and LSTM model built in 3.2 above.

4 Datasets

Corpus of user queries in Urdu is not available. In this study two publically available datasets have been used, the ATIS benchmark evaluation corpus for natural langauge understanding and intent annotated AOL web query log [1]. Both these datasets have been automatically translated from English to Urdu using Google translation toolkit. The translated queries were manually reviewed by two native Urdu speakers in order to ensure that the query phrases were complete and logical. In both the datasets, intent labels were not translated and were used as they were.

4.1 ATIS Corpus

We have used the ATIS corpus setup given in [9, 10, 22]. The training corpus consists of 4,978 utterances and the testing corpus consists of 893 utterances. The corpus is annotated with 26 flight related intents, e.g. flight, airline, ground_services, abbreviation, airfare, quantity, abbreviate, airport, etc. As a large number of queries in training as well as testing belong to the flight intent class therefore all intents have been mapped to only two intents i.e. flight and Others. There are 899 unique running words in the

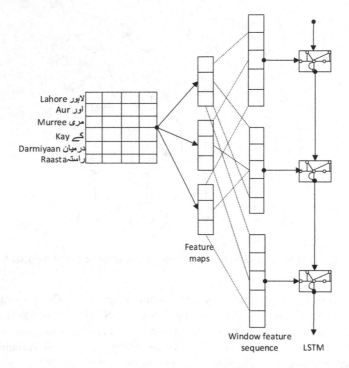

Fig. 3. CLSTM architecture showing intent in the last hidden unit of LSTM

original corpus, which is maintained after Urdu translation as well. Each user query is structured in a consistent format, BOS<user_query>(EOS)<Intent_label>. User query is contained within beginning of statement (BOS) and end of statement (EOS) tags, followed by an Intent_label (Table 1).

Table 1. ATIS web query dataset

ATIS dataset	Count
Training	4978
Testing	893

4.2   AOL Web Query Corpus

The second dataset is drawn from the AOL web query collection [28]. The original web search query corpus consists of more than 21 million query sessions from 650,000 users. In this dataset, 60,000 queries from this collection having click through information has been manually and automatically annotated into three intent classes, navigational, transactional and informational [29]. This corpus has been automatically translated into Urdu and manually cleaned by two native Urdu speakers. In the first set of experiments, 20% random sample has been used for system testing, while 80% of the queries in each intent class have been used in the training set. In the next set of experiments, only 5% randomly selected queries from each intent are used for testing while remaining 95% are used for training (Table 2).

Table 2. AOL web query dataset

Intent	Training	Testing	Total
Navigational	22,123	5,531	27,654
Resource	4,332	1,083	5,415
Informational	21,545	5,386	26,931
Total	48,000	12,000	60,000

5 Experimental Set up

In our experiments, the proposed deep learning models are implemented in Tensorflow. Dataset 1 and Dataset 2 are trained using the separately held training sets. All models are trained using a batch size of 50 for 10 epochs.

5.1 Model Hyper Parameters and Training

In CNN and C-LSTM models we use 3 filters with window sizes of 1, 2 and 3 with 100 feature maps each. The activation function ReLU is used with mini batch size of 50. In LSTM, BLSTM and CLSTM models, 1 LSTM cell layers are used with 100 dimensional hidden layer. Decay rate used is 1 and learning rate decay steps are set to 100,000.

5.2 Regularization

For regularization, we use two techniques; drop out and L2 weight regularization. Firstly, word vectors are normalized after each update, and a drop out layer with keep probability 0.5 between hidden and output layer is used. The L2 regularization of 0.001 is applied to the weights of the softmax layer.

5.3 Model Evaluation

To evaluate the intent recognition results, accuracy, average precision, recall and F-Scores are calculated.

Accuracy is defined as the set of labels predicted for a sample that must exactly match the corresponding set of labels in test_labels.

$$\text{accuracy}(y, \bar{y}) = \frac{1}{n_{\text{samples}}} \sum_{i=0}^{n_{\text{samples}}-1} 1(\bar{y_i} = y_i) \tag{1}$$

If $\bar{y}_i$ is the predicted value of the ith sample and y_i is the corresponding true value, then the fraction of correct predictions over $n_{samples}$ is defined by the above equation. Average precision summarizes a precision-recall curve as the weighted mean of precisions achieved at each threshold, with the increase in recall from the previous threshold used as the weight.

$$\text{Precision} = \sum_n (R_n - R_{n-1})P_n \tag{2}$$

where P_n and R_n are the precision and recall at the nth threshold. Recall is the ratio tp/(tp + fn) where tp is the number of true positives and fn the number of false negatives. The recall is intuitively the ability of the classifier to find all the positive samples. The best value is 1 and the worst value is 0. F1 Score is a weighted average of the precision and recall, where an F1 score reaches its best value at 1 and worst score at 0. The relative contribution of precision and recall to the F1 score are equal.

$$\text{F1 Score} = 2 * (\text{Precision} * \text{Recall})/(\text{Precision} + \text{Recall}) \tag{3}$$

In multi-class and multi-label case, this is the average of the F1 score of each class with weighting depending on the average parameter.

6 Results and Discussion

Complete results of all the models running on both the datasets are shown in Tables 3 and 4 below.

Table 3 shows results for ATIS intent classification for different neural network architectures. Here baseline forward directional, 1 layer LSTM performs poorly than

Table 3. Performance evaluation on translated ATIS dataset. Bold font indicate the best results

Model	Accuracy (%)	Precision	Recall	F-score
LSTM	0.893	0.89	0.89	0.89
B-LSTM	0.899	0.90	0.90	0.90
2B-LSTM	0.904	0.90	0.90	0.90
C-LSTM	0.922	0.92	0.92	0.92
CNN	**0.927**	**0.93**	**0.93**	**0.93**

Table 4. Performance evaluation on translated AOL dataset. Bold font indicate the best results

Model	Accuracy (%)	Precision	Recall	F-score
LSTM	**0.641**	0.66	0.64	0.63
BLSTM	0.639	0.66	0.64	0.63
2BLSTM	0.638	0.66	0.64	0.63
C-LSTM	**0.641**	**0.68**	0.64	0.62
CNN	0.634	0.65	0.63	0.63

the bi-directional models. By comparing the performance of the 1 layer and 2 layer BLSTM, it is evident that increasing layers improves the classification performance. CNN however, shows best results and improves the accuracy further from 2B-LSTM model, i.e. **0.927.** Lastly, CLSTM model employing n gram feature extraction from CNN and capturing long term dependencies over window feature sequences through LSTM, gives comparable results with CNN however took more time to train.

The prediction accuracy on the translated large real life web query dataset (AOL) is reported in Table 4. Here LSTMs including single feed forward and bi-directionals give better and roughly equivalent performances in accuracy, precision and F-score. CLSTM performs best in accuracy **0.641,** along with single layer LSTM but also gives highest precision **0.68.** Unlike ATIS, LSTMs out perform CNN in prediction accuracy on the larger translated AOL dataset.

We further validate our results by randomly drawing out a 5% test set from the AOL dataset and comparing its prediction results with the 20% test set held out earlier. The results are reported in Table 5 above. Results validate that consistently CNN performs worse than the LSTMs, with BLSTM giving the best accuracy **0.831.**

Table 5. Results on 5% and 20% random test set from translated AOL dataset.

Test set	5%	20%
Model	Accuracy (%)	Accuracy (%)
LSTM	0.804	**0.641**
BLSTM	**0.831**	0.639
2BLSTM	0.817	0.638
C-LSTM	0.822	**0.641**
CNN	0.819	0.634

A possible reason for CNN performing better on ATIS and LSTM performing better on AOL dataset might be because the average query length in ATIS is much higher in ATIS than the other larger dataset giving more context for accurate prediction. Secondly the phrase structure of search engine queries (AOL) is also quite different from speech queries (ATIS), where the content in the former is short, noisier and not organized as speech so the model than can map long term dependencies and carry information in both forward and backward directions, would tend to perform better as evident from better accuracies by LSTM and BLSTM models.

Lastly, ATIS data follows binary classification, while on AOL data multi-class (three classes) classification is performed. Further, the size difference in the two datasets also account for the disparate performance. Unknown contexts and words occur more frequently in the AOL dataset than the ATIS dataset.

We also compare our best performing model with other benchmarks reported using ATIS binary classification. The comparative results are presented in Table 6 above. From the results it is evident that although our model did not perform better than the state of the art benchmarks, however the results are still promising and comparable. Firstly all models have benefitted from pre-trained word embeddings made available

Table 6. Comparing classification accuracy on ATIS with prior studies

Model	Accuracy (%)
Ours	92.7
LSTM-GLoVE [22]	93.46
B-LSTM-GLoVE [22]	94.37
LSTM-Enrich [22]	95.08
Joint RNN [30]	95.2
SVM [30]	95.6
B-LSTM-Enrich [22]	96.49
BLSTM [20]	97.31

through training on large language corpora. Thus using embedding or embeddings enriched with linguistic information will significantly improve the reported results.

7 Conclusion

In this paper we have explored lexical user intent recognition specifically in context of search queries, using deep neural networks on two evaluation datasets that have been automatically translated to Urdu. Highest accuracy on ATIS dataset is 92.7 with CNN for binary classification, while on bigger in size AOL dataset accuracy for classifying 3 intents is 0.831 with BLSTM using 5% test set and 0.641 using 20% test set. It is observed that models perform significantly better by using pre trained word embeddings than learning word vectors during training. Majority of the model have used GLoVE and word2vec for english and have reported results. Some studies have enriched baseline embeddings with linguistic knowledge and have produced even better results. Thus to further improve the performance, similar embedding need to be developed and used for Urdu data.

References

1. Jansen, B.J., Booth, D.: Classifying web queries by topic and user intent. In: Extended Abstracts on Human Factors in Computing Systems, CHI 2010, pp. 4285–4290. ACM, Atlanta (2010)
2. Urooj, S., Shams, S., Hussain, S., Adeeba, F.: Sense tagged CLE Urdu digest corpus. In: Proceedings of Conference on Language and Technology (CLT 14), Karachi, Pakistan (2014)
3. Ashkan, A., Clarke, C.L.A., Agichtein, E., Guo, Q.: Classifying and characterizing query intent. In: Boughanem, M., Berrut, C., Mothe, J., Soule-Dupuy, C. (eds.) ECIR 2009. LNCS, vol. 5478, pp. 578–586. Springer, Heidelberg (2009). https://doi.org/10.1007/978-3-642-00958-7_53
4. Mendoza, M., Zamora, J.: Identifying the intent of a user query using support vector machines. In: Karlgren, J., Tarhio, J., Hyyrö, H. (eds.) SPIRE 2009. LNCS, vol. 5721, pp. 131–142. Springer, Heidelberg (2009). https://doi.org/10.1007/978-3-642-03784-9_13

5. Calderón-Benavides, L., González-Caro, C., Baeza-Yates, R.: Towards a deeper understanding of the user's query intent. In: Workshop on Query Representation and Understanding, SIGIR 2010, Geneva, Switzerland (2010)
6. González-Caro, C., Baeza-Yates, R.: A multi-faceted approach to query intent classification. In: Grossi, R., Sebastiani, F., Silvestri, F. (eds.) SPIRE 2011. LNCS, vol. 7024, pp. 368–379. Springer, Heidelberg (2011). https://doi.org/10.1007/978-3-642-24583-1_36
7. Ren, P., Chen, Z., Song, X., Li, B., Yang, H., Ma, J.: Understanding temporal intent of user query based on time-based query classification. In: Zhou, G., Li, J., Zhao, D., Feng, Y. (eds.) NLPCC 2013. CCIS, vol. 400, pp. 334–345. Springer, Heidelberg (2013). https://doi.org/10.1007/978-3-642-41644-6_31
8. Hashemi, H.B., Asiaee, A.H., Kraft, R.: Query intent detection using convolutional neural networks (2016)
9. Shi, Y., Yao, K., Tian, L., Jiang, D.: Deep LSTM based feature mapping for query classification. In: North American Chapter of the Association for Computational Linguistics: Human Language Technologies, pp. 1501–1511. Association of Computational Linguistics, San Diego (2016)
10. Ravuri, S., Stolcke, A.: Recurrent neural network and LSTM models for lexical utterance classification. In: INTERSPEECH (2015)
11. Ravuri, S., Stolcke, A.: A comparative study of neural network models for lexical intent classification, pp. 368–374 (2015)
12. Zhou, C., Sun, C., Liu, Z., Lau, F.: A C-LSTM neural network for text classification. CoRR, abs/1511.08630 (2015)
13. Broder, A.: A taxonomy of web search. SIGIR Forum 36(2), 3–10 (2002)
14. Lee, U., Liu, Z., Cho, J.: Automatic identification of user goals in web search. In: Proceedings of the 14th International Conference on World Wide Web, pp. 391–400. ACM, Chiba (2005)
15. Carlos, C.S., Yalamanchi, M.: Intention analysis for sales, marketing and customer service. In: COLING (2012)
16. Song, I., Diederich, J.: Intention extraction from text messages. In: Wong, K.W., Mendis, B. S.U., Bouzerdoum, A. (eds.) ICONIP 2010. LNCS, vol. 6443, pp. 330–337. Springer, Heidelberg (2010). https://doi.org/10.1007/978-3-642-17537-4_41
17. Zhang, H., Song, W., Liu, L., Du, Ch., Zhao, X.: Query classification using convolutional neural networks. In: 10th International Symposium on Computational Intelligence and Design (ISCID), pp. 441–444 (2017)
18. Kim, Y.: Convolutional neural networks for sentence classification. In: Proceedings of the 2014 Conference on Empirical Methods in Natural Language Processing (EMNLP), pp. 1746–1751. Association for Computational Linguistics, Doha (2014)
19. Collobert, R., Weston, J., Bottou, L., Karlen, M., Kavukcuoglu, K., Kuksa, P.: Natural language processing (almost) from scratch. CoRR, abs/1103.0398 (2011)
20. Kim, J., Tur, G., Celikyilmaz, A., Cao, B., Wang, Y.: Intent detection using semantically enriched word embeddings. In: 2016 IEEE Spoken Language Technology Workshop (SLT), San Diego, CA, pp. 414–419 (2016)
21. Fang, I.-T.: Deep learning for query semantic domains classification. In: Annual Conference on Neural Information Processing Systems (NIPS). Microsoft, (2017)
22. Sreelakshmi, K., Rafeeque, P.C., Sreetha, S., Gayathri, E.S.: Deep bi-directional LSTM network for query intent detection. Proc. Comput. Sci. 143, 939–946 (2018)
23. Syed, A.Z., Aslam, M., Martinez-Enriquez, A.M.: Associating targets with SentiUnits: a step forward in sentiment analysis of Urdu text. Artif. Intell. Rev. 41(4), 535–561 (2014)

24. Basit, R.H., Aslam, M., Martinez-Enriquez, A.M., Syed, A.Z.: Semantic similarity analysis of Urdu documents. In: Carrasco-Ochoa, J.A., Martínez-Trinidad, J.F., Olvera-López, J.A. (eds.) MCPR 2017. LNCS, vol. 10267, pp. 234–243. Springer, Cham (2017). https://doi.org/10.1007/978-3-319-59226-8_23
25. Malik, M.K.: Urdu named entity recognition and classification system using artificial neural network. ACM Trans. Asian Low-Resour. Lang. Inf. Process. 17(1), 1–13 (2017)
26. Ali, A.R., Ijaz, M.: Urdu text classification. In: Proceedings of the 7th International Conference on Frontiers of Information Technology, pp. 1–7. ACM, Abbottabad (2009)
27. Adeeba, F., Hussain, S., Akram, Q.: Urdu text genre identification. In: Conference on Language and Technology (CLT 2016), Lahore, Pakistan (2016)
28. Pass, G., Chowdhury, A., Torgeson, C.: A picture of search. In: Proceedings of the 1st International Conference on Scalable Information Systems, p. 1. ACM, Hong Kong (2006)
29. Figueroa, A.: Exploring effective features for recognizing the user intent behind web queries. Comput. Ind. 68(C), 162–169 (2015)
30. Yao, K., Peng, B., Zhang, Y., Yu, D., Zweig, G., Shi, Y.: Spoken language understanding using long short-term memory neural networks. In: 2014 IEEE Spoken Language Technology Workshop (SLT), South Lake Tahoe, NV, pp. 189–194 (2014)

A Simple but Powerful Word Polarity Classification Model

Omar Rodríguez López[✉] and Guillermo de Jesús Hoyos Rivera

Centro de Investigación en Inteligencia Artificial, Universidad de Veracruz,
Sebastián Camacho 5, Col. Centro, 91000 Xalapa Enríquez, Mexico
lopez.osrIA@gmail.com, ghoyos@uv.mx

Abstract. Polarity lexicons have largely been used for opinion mining, also known as sentiment analysis. Their high relevance has made them invaluable when it comes to classifying the opinions originated by digital platforms users. However, there is a great dependence on resources developed in other languages, in special English, to create a lexicon in Spanish. In this work we develop a polarity lexicon for Mexican Spanish from a thesaurus and two *seed words* sets inside it that we use to assign polarity values to words, from a frequentist treatment, and taking into account the assumption that synonymous words have similar polarities.

Keywords: Polarity lexicon · Mexican Spanish · Thesaurus · Seed words

1 Introduction

The creation of polarity lexicons[1] for opinion mining has proved to be a defying task which, even if it has been studied for several years, still offers considerable challenges. Polarity lexicons are intended to offer information to the opinion classification systems by providing numerical values associated with the words they contain, so that the opinions under study can be classified based on the calculations made with these values.

However, much of the work done so far regarding the development of polarity lexicons concentrates its efforts in the English language [2,3,10,13,15,21] and although there are different works that generate lexicons for other languages [1,4,6,8,14], the dependence on these approximations of the resources generated for English still exists. In this work we present the creation of a lexicon for Mexican Spanish, based on a frequentist approach that uses a general purpose Spanish thesaurus and two sets of *seed words*, created from the terms contained in the thesaurus, as starting point.

Our approach is based on basic assumptions from which the creation of the polarity lexicon is tackled, so this work has not included any external tool to

---

[1] A polarity lexicon is a list of words, of a particular language, classified according to a multiple categories. In some cases a numerical value is associated with each word indicating its sentimental orientation.

© Springer Nature Switzerland AG 2019
L. Martínez-Villaseñor et al. (Eds.): MICAI 2019, LNAI 11835, pp. 51–62, 2019.
https://doi.org/10.1007/978-3-030-33749-0_5

the aforementioned. We believe that starting the construction of a lexicon from the basics is crucial for the future understanding of its performance, therefore, this article focuses on showing the creation process. On the other hand, making a fair comparison of the lexicon obtained here with others previously developed for Spanish is impossible given the difference not only in approach but also in methodology in the creation of each lexical resource.

The rest of the article is organized as follows: Sect. 2 shows the work related to the creation of polarity lexicons. Section 3 is divided into three parts; the first part explains the creation of the two *seed words* sets; the second part contains the polarity scale selected as well as the interpretation of the thesaurus as a graph, and finally, the third part describes the creation of the lexicon in Spanish. Section 4 shows the results obtained and Sect. 5 presents the discussion and future work.

2   Related Work

There are many works focused on the construction of polarity lexicons, each of them offering a different approach depending on the intended use of the tagged words. Among the most cited lexicons in the literature, all of them developed for the English language, the following can be mentioned: The General Inquirer Lexicon [21] is a lexicon equipped with an interface for the user that contains words labeled according to a certain number of categories. MPQA Subjectivity Cues Lexicon [22], classifies the words as positive and negative, adding their intensity for each one, that is, if they are *strong* or *weak* words. SentiWordNet [3], assigns to each WordNet *synset*[2] values of positivity, negativity and objectivity. SenticNet3 [5], is a semantic and affective resource for concept-level sentiment analysis. Liu's [13] lexicon, on the other hand, labels the words contained as positive or negative, without assigning them any extra numerical value.

Regarding the development of lexicons for other languages, several approaches can be found in the literature, including Arabic [1], Chinese [14], Romanian [4] and Spanish. Specifically in the latter there exist different approaches to the construction of a lexicon: In [16] the iSOL lexicon is created from a translation of the Bing Liu's lexicon and a subsequent manual refinement to detect errors in the translation. In [19], on the other hand, a lexicon of words labeled by six basic emotions is developed from WordNet-Affect. A similar approach to that shown in the creation of SentiWordNet is presented in [7], where the authors add elements to the original process to create a lexicon for Spanish. In [18] a framework is presented to generate lexicons, in a *target* language, from data previously labeled in a *source* language. In [20] a semi-automatic approach is shown to create sentiment dictionaries in multiple languages, this by means of the translation of two dictionaries, in the *source* language, to the *target* language. In [17], on the other hand, a lexical resource is developed from an adaptation of WordNet 3.0 to Spanish and in [11] the authors present *Elsa*, a special Spanish lexicon for Augmentative and Alternative Communication.

---

[2] A WordNet *synset* is a set of synonyms that share a common meaning.

However one of the main problems that arise at creating polarity lexicons is that the dependence on resources generated for another language is still considerable. In this work we propose a way to develop a lexicon for Mexican Spanish, starting from a two sets of *seed words* and a thesaurus of Spanish words. The use of these sets for the construction of lexical resources has been seen in previous works [9,12,20], whose approach varies in terms of their construction as well as their subsequent application. Our approach does not carry out any translation of others lexical resources, which seeks to eliminate the corresponding loss of information, and starts with the assumption that from basic mathematical calculations it is possible to create a lexicon, as starting point, for the analysis of opinions in Mexican Spanish.

3   Lexicon Creation

3.1   Creating *Seed Words* Sets

Normally in a polarity lexicon the positive, negative and neutral categories are used, but it is possible to find lexicons that make use of some previously established emotional scale. In addition, it is possible to create lexicons from a manual labeling of words, with a set of experts for example, or using dictionaries or other resources. In this work we use the OpenOffice thesaurus for Spanish, from now referred as $\mathbb{T}$, because its general purpose. This is a thesaurus made up of words from Spanish and not by terms corresponding to a specific area, and which appear together with their synonyms, divided according to their possible uses.

Before continuing, however, it is important to mention that we only consider the words appearing in the thesaurus and no other words. So we assume a closed world hypothesis for our work. Table 1 shows a quick query to $\mathbb{T}$ with the words related to *dichoso*, a Spanish word used to indicate happiness or joy but which can also appear in contexts where there is a certain degree of irritation. Each of the rows corresponds, therefore, to a different context in which the contained words can be used. While the first lines refer to words like *afortunado*, (*lucky*), and *feliz* (*happy*), the last one shows the *negative* side of the word *dichoso* when relating it to *maldito*, (*damned*).

Starting from this lexical resource two *seed words* sets are created and used to develop a lexicon in Mexican Spanish. We extend both sets by establishing the concept of **base polarity**, which, as far as we know, has not been defined as such, described in Definition 1.

Definition 1. *Base polarity is the polarity that has a word out of any specific context, originated by its meaning and that can be identified without ambiguity by the word itself.*

The idea behind the use of $\mathbb{T}$ is to take advantage of the synonymity relations established in it, to identify, according to the base polarity, those words that can be labeled as undeniably positive or negative, respectively, that is, those words whose meanings in the Spanish dictionary have a positive or negative polarity.

Table 1. The words related with *dichoso* appear grouped in rows that represent their semantic fields.

Semantic fields	Words
Field 1	gozoso, **dichoso**, feliz, afortunado, alborozado, complacido, encantado, radiante, alegre, jubiloso
Field 2	eufórico, entusiasmado, jubiloso, alegre, **dichoso**, radiante
Field 3	devoto, bonachón, ferviente, bueno, religioso, **dichoso**, bendito, beatífico, piadoso
Field 4	fausto, afortunado, feliz, alegre, **dichoso**, propicio, venturoso, satisfecho, risueño
Field 5	bendito, feliz, **dichoso**, contento, satisfecho
Field 6	boyante, próspero, feliz, **dichoso**, acomodado, fastuoso, rico, poderoso, potentado, afortunado, acaudalado
Field 7	empecatado, **dichoso**, maldito, condenado, endemoniado, endiablado

So, for example, words like *belleza* (*beauty*) and *repugnante* (*disgusting*), will be positive and negative respectively.

The application of base polarity to the words of the thesaurus to create the sets of *seed words*, from now referred to as $\mathbb{PBL}$ and $\mathbb{NBL}$, namely *Positive Base Lexicon* and *Negative Base Lexicon*, respectively, starts with a revision of the meanings of each word according to the following points:

– If every meaning of the word can be identified with a positive *intention*, then this word will be included in the list of clearly positive words, in the opposite case the word will belong to the list of clearly negative words. For positive labeling the assigned value is 1, while for the negative it will be −1.
– If at least one of the meanings of the word under review cannot be assigned to a *intention* that corresponds to the rest, then the word cannot be labeled in any way, that is, its polarity value will remain as an incognita.

As a result of the manual process described above, which took about eight months to complete, $\mathbb{PBL}$ and $\mathbb{NBL}$ contain a total of 548 and 1,331 words respectively. It is important to mention that these basic lexicons are perfectible and therefore need constant revisions,[3] however for our purposes they work correctly. Then to continue the process of creating the lexicon it is necessary to establish a numerical scale to assign values to the rest of words and to interpret $\mathbb{T}$ as a graph whose nodes are represented by the words contained in it and with the arcs indicating the existence of a relation between two words p_i and p_j.

---

[3] New words may arise or other language terms may be adopted by Spanish users.

3.2   Polarity Scale and Interpretation of $\mathbb{T}$ as a Graph for the Assignment of Polarity Values

The functioning of language goes beyond a model that attempts to label any word according to a disjoint binary or ternary polarity scale, as several of the works cited above have shown. The variability of use not only of the words of a language but also of the expressions transcends any discrete scale that searches to translate the emotions inherent in an opinion to an analytical framework.

In this work we choose the interval $[-1, 1]$, as an attempt to condense all the information of the word in a single number. So we use the traditional representation of positive and negative to subsequently extend the numerical range up to the mentioned real interval.

Figure 1 shows the representation selected in this work, where the values of 1 and -1 are assigned to the positive and negative words, hence the values for the words in $\mathbb{PBL}$ and $\mathbb{NBL}$ were 1 and -1, respectively, and 0 for those whose polarity is neutral. This model only deals with one real number from which the necessary information can be obtained. Moreover it can be chosen any numerical scale that fits the needs of the lexicon or the approach that is given, and can then be a line, for example, in $\mathbb{Z}$, for simplicity sake for human interpretation.

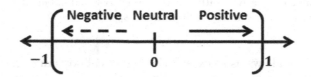

Fig. 1. Geometric representation for the polarity of the words.

The interpretation of $\mathbb{T}$ as a graph then starts from Definitions 2 to 4, presented next, that establish what should be understood by a node, arcs and under what condition they can be related.

Definition 2. *Let p_i be the word to which we want to calculate its polarity value and be $\mathbb{S}_{p_i} = \{s_{p_i 1}, s_{p_i 2}, \ldots, s_{p_i k}\}$, with $k = 1, 2, \ldots, n$, the set of synonyms of p_i, divided into groups.[4] It follows that $s_{p_i k} = \{p^k_{1 p_i}, p^k_{2 p_i}, \ldots, p^k_{j p_i}\}$, for $j = 1, \ldots, m$. $S = \bigcup_i \mathbb{S}_{pi}$ will be the set of all groups and $P = \bigcup_i p_i$ will be the set of all words, contained in $\mathbb{T}$.*

Definition 3. *Given p_i, for any other word p_j, with $p_j \in \mathbb{S}_{p_i}$, exists an arc $a_{i,j}$ between p_i y p_j. Let $\mathbb{A}_{p_i}$ be the set of all the arcs that come out of p_i and $A = \bigcup_i \mathbb{A}_{pi}$ the set of all the arcs between words.*

Definition 4. *$\mathbb{T}$ is defined as the graph determined by the set of nodes P and the set of arcs A which we write as $\mathrm{M} = (P, A)$.*

---

[4] Here the term group does not refer to the concept of abstract algebra.

The assignment of polarity of the remaining words, that is, those whose polarity value could not initially be determined, takes as an inspiration what is seen in [12] and it is shown in the Algorithm 1 (Fig. 2).

Algorithm 1: Assigning polarity to the rest of words

```
for each p in T
    positive = 0
    negative = 0
    for each s_{p_i} ∈ S_{p_i}
        s_{p_i} = s_{p_i}\p
        for each s_{p_ik} ∈ s_{p_i}
            if s_{p_ik} ∈ PBL
                positive ++
            if s_{p_ik} ∈ NBL
                negative ++
    polarity(p) = (positive - negative)/∑_{r=1}^{r=k} #s_{p_ir}
```

Fig. 2. Polarity assignment to the rest of words using the base lexicons. $\mathbb{T}$ = thesaurus. Positive = number of clearly positive words. Negative = number of clearly negative words. $\sum_{r=1}^{r=k} \#s_{p_ir}$ = the sum of cardinalities of s_{p_ir}

This procedure allows us to extend the numerical domain of the classes considered towards the continuum of the interval $[-1, 1]$, so that it is possible to speak of *degrees* of negativity and positivity being the neutrality the balance between both. Unfortunately, the described process produces, as a side effect of the use of the positivity and negativity ratios, many words for which the assigned polarity value is zero. The total number of words within $\mathbb{T}$ labeled as neutral, is $14,127$ while the number of words with a certain degree of positiveness and negativeness detected is $2,444$ and $3,632$ respectively, which means, in terms of the number of words contained in $\mathbb{PBL}$ and $\mathbb{NBL}$ an increase of 1896 (approximately 450%) and 2301 (approximately 300%) positive and negative words.

Figure 3 shows the distribution of the polarity values assigned to the rest of the words. Although we consider neutrality as a valid label, it is certainly necessary to examine those words that are neutral because they are not related to any positive or negative word and to distinguish them from those that are related to labeled words but whose polarity ratios, positive and negative, are neutralized when adding them in the final step of assigning values.

3.3   Depth Levels in Polarity Calculations

To solve the problem described in the previous section, the graph $\mathbb{M}$ is used to model the *influence* that one word, p_i, can have on another, p_j, considering the number of arcs needed to go from p_i to p_j. This interpretation suggests the

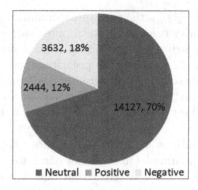

Fig. 3. Distribution of the polarity values obtained for the words and their approximate percentages.

use of *depth levels* that represent the *influence loss* between both words which grows as the *path* between them becomes larger. It is from this moment that the selection of numeric successions to model this situation becomes evident. Each term of the succession will then correspond to a certain depth level and these, in turn, will represent the number of traversed groups.

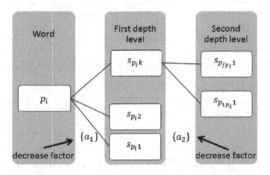

Fig. 4. The depth levels are represented by the synonyms of the word p_i and the loss of *influence* between them by the terms of the sequence. Thus, for example, the polarity values obtained for words at a second depth level will be affected by the second term of the selected sequence.

Figure 4 schematizes the described procedure. In this way, to calculate the polarity of a word, p_i, its synonyms, $\mathbb{S}_{p_i}$, are taken, which are the first level of depth. Subsequently, the synonyms of each of the words contained in $\mathbb{S}_{p_i}$ are taken, thus reaching the second level of depth, and where the next calculations can be made to corroborate whether the polarity value assigned to p_i is still 0. Let $h_j \in s_{p_i m}$ for some m and j, then the polarity of p_i will be given by $\frac{positive+negative}{\mathbb{A}} * a_2$, where a_2 is the second term of the previously selected succession and $\mathbb{A} = \sum_{r=1}^{r=k} \#s_{h_j r}$ the sum of cardinalities of $s_{h_j r}$ for some k. In this way, during the polarity calculation for p_i, now each of the words, h_i, in its synonyms will have a polarity value resulting from a *deeper* revision. Each of these values will accumulate to create the polarity value.

The five sequences selected in this paper are presented in Fig. 5. In particular, we are interested in using the first terms of each succession, considering that these are the ones that best represent the *influence* of the words. The similar decreasing behavior of the successions makes the rest of the terms irrelevant when calculating the polarities of the words at those depth levels because the numerical differences are minimal. On the other hand, for some of the successions there is a certain growth in the first terms that does not correspond to the loss of mentioned *influence*, so in such cases these terms are ignored and work is done with the succession from the moment in which its behavior is monotonous decreasing.

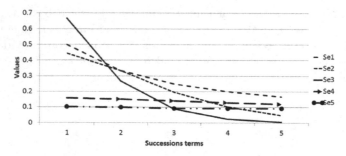

Fig. 5. The selected successions for model depth levels. Se1 $= \{\frac{1}{n}\}_{n=2}$, Se2 $= \{\frac{n^2}{3^n}\}_{n=2}$, Se3 $= \{\frac{2^n}{n!}\}_{n=4}$, Se4 $= \{\frac{log(n)}{n}\}_{n=2}$, Se5 $= \{\frac{(log(n))^2}{n}\}_{n=10}$

4   Results

Table 2 contains the assigned polarity values, by succession and depth level, for some representative words that serve as an example to show the potential of the process explained in Sect. 4. It is necessary to mention that these words do not belong to PBL or NBL because not all their meanings could correspond with a positive or negative intention. *Sobresaltar (shock)*, *damnificar (damage)* and *reprobable (reprehensible)*, are three Spanish words that indicate negative aspects of a situation and its polarity value reflects it. On the other hand, the terms *lindo (cute)*, *entrañable (endearing)* and *galanería (gallantry)*, denote positive feelings and that is why their values are above zero. As can be seen, counting the ratios for positivity and negativity when reviewing the synonyms of the words offers useful information to determine polarity.

The results obtained after using the $\mathbb{PBL}$ and $\mathbb{NBL}$ and different depth levels to assign polarity values to the rest of the words in $\mathbb{T}$ are shown in Fig. 6.

Table 2. Some words and their polarity values.

Word	L1	L2Se1	L2Se2	L2Se3	L3Se1	L3Se3
sobresaltar	−0.857	−0.9027	−0.9001	−0.9259	−0.8964	−0.8929
damnificar	−0.8333	−0.8689	−0.8670	−0.8888	−0.8586	−0.8509
reprobable	−0.7144	−0.7777	−0.7654	−0.8130	−0.7530	−0.7455
lindo	0.5	0.5762	0.5677	0.6018	0.5605	0.5512
entrañable	0.5833	0.6743	0.6661	0.6982	0.6562	0.6466
galanería	0.8571	0.9017	0.8988	9131	0.8948	0.8914

Grouped bars correspond to the values, within an interval, generated by each of the successions. On the other hand, the line on each bar indicates the average of words tagged within the corresponding interval for each sequence and level of depth. For legibility reasons of the graph, some of the successions, at a second and third level of depth, were not included.

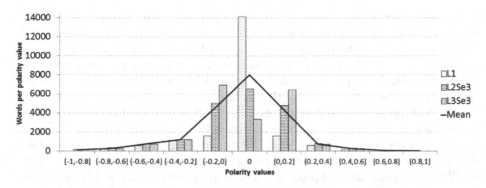

Fig. 6. Proportion of the polarity values for the words according to their label obtained by the proposed method. L1 = Depth level 1, L2Se1 = Depth level 2 Succession 1, L2Se2 = Depth level 2 Succession 2, L2Se3 = Depth level 3 Succession 3, L3Se1 = Depth level 3 Succession 1, L3Se3 = Depth level 3 Succession 3. The sequences used, denoted as Se, correspond to those described in Fig. 5

According to the obtained results, the best succession, in terms of polarity values, number of neutral words, behavior and information obtained, turned out to be Se3, for which not only a better distribution of words per label is achieved but also the polarity values they are *amplified* for each word.

A considerable decrease in the number of words labeled as neutral can be observed, in Fig. 6, as the level of depth in the calculations increases. It can then be said with certainty that the problem of the premature classification of those words is solved with satisfactory results. While at a first level of depth the total number of neutral words was 14, 127, and the number of words with a certain degree of positiveness and negativeness was $2,444$ and $3,632$, respectively, for a third level, considering the succession Se3, the total number of neutral words is $3,344$, and the number of positive and negative terms is $7,596$ and $9,263$, respectively.

On the other hand it is important to note that our proposal, with the gradual emotional distinction that implies, allows to give a functional treatment to the assignment of polarities, in such way that a word will have one and only one associated value, thus serving as starting point to standardize the calculations.

However, it is important to note that although a decrease in neutral words is achieved depending on the chosen depth level, the fact is that many of the polarity values are too close to 0, which could suggest that the values obtained do not adequately represent the polarity variations between the words. It is curious, on the other hand, how the polarity values have a greater number of words with a certain degree of negativity than positivity, which seems to suggest a negative trend in the way in which the language is used.

5   Conclusions and Future Work

In this work we have presented the development of a polarity lexicon for Mexican Spanish that starts from two *seed words* sets and a thesaurus. It has been shown that from a frequentist approach, numerical values that capture the positivity, negativity or neutrality of the words can be obtained. Of course, more work is required to refine the polarity values, but as an approach that starts from the simple to the complex, we believe that it offers good research opportunities.

The inclusion of bigrams, trigrams and negation markers in the calculations as well as their representation will help the refinement of the polarity values to be able to work with typical phrases of the language that undoubtedly affect the polarity assignment. The use of machine learning algorithms, corresponding to different classification approaches, will help to improve the obtained values, with which it is also expected to achieve a better distribution in them, leaving behind the great concentration that currently exists around zero. In addition, it is intended to carry out a sentence analysis taking as starting point what is stated in this article, together with its possible improvements, and to help obtain more information for the analysis of opinion, in Mexican Spanish, of social networks.

The current dependence on tools and lexical resources generated for other languages increases the need to experiment with different ideas that allow a greater development of current opinion classification systems in Spanish. The number of digital users and the amount of textual data they generate strongly invites us to carry out efforts that seek to break the mold of what has been used so far.

References

1. Abdul-Mageed, M., Diab, M.T., Korayem, M.: Subjectivity and sentiment analysis of modern standard Arabic. In: Proceedings of the 49th Annual Meeting of the

Association for Computational Linguistics: Human Language Technologies: Short Papers-Volume 2, pp. 587–591. Association for Computational Linguistics (2011)

2. Almatarneh, S., Gamallo, P.: Automatic construction of domain-specific sentiment lexicons for polarity classification. In: De la Prieta, F., et al. (eds.) PAAMS 2017. AISC, vol. 619, pp. 175–182. Springer, Cham (2018). https://doi.org/10.1007/978-3-319-61578-3_17

3. Baccianella, S., Esuli, A., Sebastiani, F.: SentiWordNet 3.0: an enhanced lexical resource for sentiment analysis and opinion mining. In: LREC, vol. 10, pp. 2200–2204 (2010)

4. Banea, C., Mihalcea, R., Wiebe, J.: A bootstrapping method for building subjectivity lexicons for languages with scarce resources. In: LREC, vol. 8, pp. 2–764 (2008)

5. Cambria, E., Olsher, D., Rajagopal, D.: SenticNet 3: a common and common-sense knowledge base for cognition-driven sentiment analysis. In: Twenty-Eighth AAAI Conference on Artificial Intelligence (2014)

6. Clematide, S., Klenner, M., Montoyo, A., Martínez-Barco, P., Balahur, A., Boldrini, E.: Evaluation and extension of a polarity lexicon for German (2010)

7. Cruz, F.L., Troyano, J.A., Pontes, B., Ortega, F.J.: Ml-SentiCon: un lexicón multilingüe de polaridades semánticas a nivel de lemas. Procesamiento del Lenguaje Natural **53**, 113–120 (2014)

8. Dehkharghani, R., Saygin, Y., Yanikoglu, B., Oflazer, K.: SentiTurkNet: a Turkish polarity lexicon for sentiment analysis. Lang. Resour. Eval. **50**(3), 667–685 (2016)

9. Esuli, A., Sebastiani, F.: SentiWordNet: a publicly available lexical resource for opinion mining. In: LREC, vol. 6, pp. 417–422. Citeseer (2006)

10. Gamallo, P., Garcia, M.: Citius: A Naive-Bayes strategy for sentiment analysis on English tweets. In: Proceedings of the 8th international Workshop on Semantic Evaluation (SemEval 2014), pp. 171–175 (2014)

11. García-Méndez, S., Fernández-Gavilanes, M., Costa-Montenegro, E., Juncal-Martínez, J., González-Castaño, F.J.: Lexicon for natural language generation in Spanish adapted to alternative and augmentative communication. In: Proceedings of the Linguistic Resources for Automatic Natural Language Generation-LiRA@NLG, pp. 11–15 (2017)

12. Kim, S.M., Hovy, E.: Determining the sentiment of opinions. In: Proceedings of the 20th International Conference on Computational Linguistics, p. 1367. Association for Computational Linguistics (2004)

13. Liu, B.: Sentiment analysis and opinion mining. Synth. Lect. Hum. Lang. Technol. **5**(1), 1–167 (2012)

14. Lu, B., Song, Y., Zhang, X., Tsou, B.K.: Learning Chinese polarity lexicons by integration of graph models and morphological features. In: Cheng, P.-J., Kan, M.-Y., Lam, W., Nakov, P. (eds.) AIRS 2010. LNCS, vol. 6458, pp. 466–477. Springer, Heidelberg (2010). https://doi.org/10.1007/978-3-642-17187-1_45

15. Mihaylov, T., Balchev, D., Kiprov, Y., Koychev, I., Nakov, P.: Large-scale goodness polarity lexicons for community question answering. In: Proceedings of the 40th International ACM SIGIR Conference on Research and Development in Information Retrieval, pp. 1185–1188. ACM (2017)

16. Molina-González, M.D., Martínez-Cámara, E., Martín-Valdivia, M.T., Perea-Ortega, J.M.: Semantic orientation for polarity classification in Spanish reviews. Expert Syst. Appl. **40**(18), 7250–7257 (2013)

17. Montraveta, A.F., Vázquez, G.: La construcción del WordNet 3.0 en español. In: La lexicografía en su dimensión teórica, pp. 201–220. Universidad de Málaga (UMA) (2010)

18. Perez-Rosas, V., Banea, C., Mihalcea, R.: Learning sentiment lexicons in Spanish. In: LREC, vol. 12, p. 73 (2012)
19. Rangel, I.D., Guerra, S.S., Sidorov, G.: Creación y evaluación de un diccionario marcado con emociones y ponderado para el español. Onomázein: Revista de lingüística, filología y traducción de la Pontificia Universidad Católica de Chile (29), 31–46 (2014)
20. Steinberger, J., et al.: Creating sentiment dictionaries via triangulation. In: Proceedings of the 2nd Workshop on Computational Approaches to Subjectivity and Sentiment Analysis, pp. 28–36. Association for Computational Linguistics (2011)
21. Stone, P.J., Dunphy, D.C., Smith, M.S.: The general inquirer: a computer approach to content analysis (1966)
22. Wiebe, J., Wilson, T., Cardie, C.: Annotating expressions of opinions and emotions in language. Lang. Resour. Eval. 39(2–3), 165–210 (2005)

Mineral Classification Using Machine Learning and Images of Microscopic Rock Thin Section

Henrique Pereira Borges[✉] and Marilton Sanchotene de Aguiar

Research Group on Cyber-Physical Systems Engineering,
Technology Development Center,
Federal University of Pelotas, Pelotas, RS, Brazil
{hpborges,marilton}@inf.ufpel.edu.br

Abstract. The most widely used method for mineral type classification from a rock thin section is done by the observation of optical properties of a mineral in a polarized microscope rotation stage. Several studies propose the application of digital image processing techniques and Neural Networks to automate this task. This study uses simpler and more scalable machine learning techniques, being nearest neighbor and decision tree, and adds new optical properties to be extracted from the digital images. Two datasets are used, one provided by Ferdowsi University of Mashhad, with 17 different minerals, and another built from scratch in the geology department of Federal University of Pelotas, containing 4 different minerals. The datasets are composed of mineral images captured under cross and plane polarized light from different rock thin sections. For each dataset used, we took a pair of images of the same mineral taken on different lights, extracted optical properties of color and texture, applied a machine learning algorithm and provided the results. At the end of this study, we demonstrate it is possible to achieve high accuracy as Neural Networks with more simple machine learning algorithms as the our dataset showed average results as high as 97% and Mashhad's as high as 93%.

Keywords: Image processing · Machine learning · Mineralogy

1 Introduction

Correct mineral identification is an essential and recurring task in mineralogy, and there are many techniques that depend on the type of mineral or specialized equipment such as x-ray and spectrograms [7,8]. This study's chosen technique is using rock thin sections in a microscope with polarized light, which is also the most embracive, low cost, fast and practical method of identification [2].

This technique is the most explored in studies that address the task of identifying minerals with artificial intelligence. To identify a mineral, a mineralogist places the rock thin section in a polarized microscope and observes the optical

© Springer Nature Switzerland AG 2019
L. Martínez-Villaseñor et al. (Eds.): MICAI 2019, LNAI 11835, pp. 63–76, 2019.
https://doi.org/10.1007/978-3-030-33749-0_6

properties of the desired mineral in both plane and cross polarized lights. Such task may take years of experience of a professional [2,5]. It is of great value to automate this task using a machine, it would allow a mineralogist to spend more time in another task. This issue may be easy enough to be transformed in a computational classification problem using the mineral images taken from the rock thin section. In order to solve it, we propose to use computer vision techniques to extract the optical properties, and machine learning to classify them. This combination is already successfully applied in many areas of knowledge including mineral classification, but the general application in geology is limited [6].

Related studies that contemplate such techniques are limited to those that classify minerals from digital images of rock thin sections, taken from a polarized microscope. All the related studies used optical properties of the mineral varying the number of properties taken. Most studies take the generic digital image properties, such as color and texture, and only one study made a parallel between the techniques of a professional and how to extract them from an image [5]. The latter does not use machine learning but its own technique to classify the minerals, and we used that study as a guide to extract the optical parameters for this classification.

In such a context, the motivation of this paper is to show a counterpoint with simpler machine learning techniques to perform such task. The motivation started with the alumni of the Geology department of the Federal University of Pelotas wondering whether it was possible to automate this task, as it is considered to be of great complexity for a human to perform. This problem was already addressed by the literature but most studies use Neural Networks as a machine learning technique, with a few exceptions being [2,5]. A state-of-the-art analysis, we came across of a study [6] that uses kNN and ID3, among others, for rock classifications, a very similar problem. The best results showed an accuracy of 100% with certain rock types. We believe that the task to classify minerals must be easy for a computer to perform, and with the most basic techniques it should achieve good accuracy. The results are optimistic (above 90% of accuracy), and new techniques were applied and documented to create the dataset for this task. This paper is organized as follows: in Sect. 2, we discuss the general guidelines that most studies use, and our own technique employed. In Sect. 3, we discuss related studies in more detail, and in Sect. 4 we discuss and compare our results.

2   Methodology

In this Section, we propose a generic method to address the problem that closely approximates to a generic method of data mining or machine learning. In other words, we propose a method to capture, elaborate, and apply a machine learning algorithm on a dataset. In the case of the specific task there are some inherent problems such as maintaining the spatial location of the minerals in the images and cropping out the body of the minerals. For the professional, the task is carried out in this form: a rock thin section of interest is taken, placed on a polarized microscope and the optical properties of the specific mineral are observed by changing the angle of the polarized light, which is achieved by rotating the stage that the thin section is on. Figure 2 shows a standard microscope for such a task.

We will also detail our own methodology and how we built our own dataset, which will be referenced as GEO Dataset in this paper. Also, we kindly received a dataset from the authors Aligholi et al. [5], and it will be referenced as MAS Dataset. We detail how we sampled our datasets and show a comparison between them on Table 1.

2.1 Gather

The step of capturing the images of the rock thin section in the microscope with simple or crossed polarized light depends largely on the available microscope. If it is digital, it is sufficient to extract the enlarged images of the microscope plate, but if it is analog, one must attach a digital camera to the lens of the microscope and take photos of the zoomed in image. Images must be taken from different polarized light angles to show the optical properties of the mineral. Figure 1 shows the difference between plane and cross polarized light.

(a)   (b)

Fig. 1. Mineral under (a) cross polarized light and (b) plane polarized light.

The Geology department of our Federal University of Pelotas gathered images of rock thin section on a microscope with polarized light and a rotating stage. Figure 2 shows the microscope used and its parts: (A) adapted camera support; (B) binocular tube; (C) analyzer; (D) objective revolver; (E) objective 4×; (F) rotating stage; (G) condenser and analyzer; (H) coarse and fine focus knob; and, (I) blue light illumination system.

The method consists of attaching a digital camera on the microscope's lens and taking a photo of the rock thin section at angles of 10°, 30°, 45°, 90° and 180° on both light types.

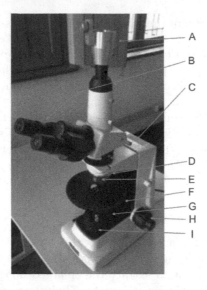

Fig. 2. Polarized microscope with rotation stage used for image gathering. (Color figure online)

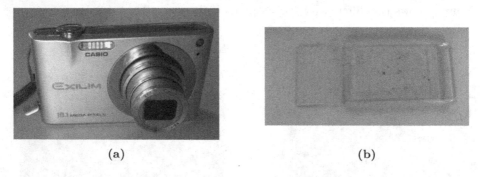

(a)   (b)

Fig. 3. Images of (a) the camera used for capturing and (b) a rock thin section.

Figure 3(a) shows the camera used, a 10.1 mega-pixel Casio Exilim. All photos used the maximum resolution of the camera. Figure 3(b) shows a rock thin section of approximately 30 μm annexed to a glass base. Images of 6 different rock thin sections were gathered for GEO dataset. As aforementioned, the same thin section at different angles shifts the spatial location of the minerals within the image, what it is evident on Fig. 5.

2.2 Segment

Here, a problem related to the type of microscope is presented. To change the polarized light angle, the mineral must be rotated on the microscope stage, compromising the spatial location of the mineral. The image, as shown on Fig. 1, is a collection of minerals and the task is to classify just one of those at a time. It is a challenge to select one mineral body from the image. Some studies have automated this step, as explained in Sect. 3, but the majority performed this manually, and for each image the region of the mineral of interest was selected.

The segmentation for GEO dataset was conducted by hand by geologist experts. They selected the body of the mineral and did a grid crop of 50×50 pixels for each cell. In that way, a single mineral body resulted in several cropped images. Those experts identified and cropped four types of minerals, namely: quartz, biotite, microcline and plagioclase (Fig. 4).

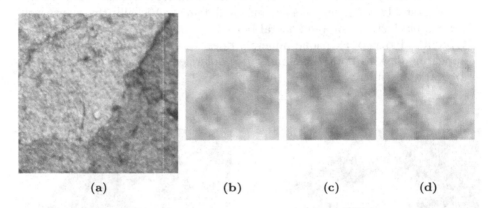

(a)   (b)   (c)   (d)

Fig. 4. An example of (a) a mineral body under plane polarized light and (b–d) its cropped body images.

2.3   Extraction

This is the step to extract the optical properties of the images. It is important to note that the sample size of the related studies is not constant. In [2], the authors only take into account a single image whereas others take into account several images of the same mineral. Some optical properties can only be properly extracted with a collection of images as it shows the color transformations with different polarized light angles. Also, it is important to note that the color space RGB (standard for most digital cameras) is not well suited for this problem, as it is very sensitive for white color (brightness) variations. To rectify, there should be used a color space that isolates brightness to a single channel such as V in HSV (Hue, Saturation, Value). Here follows an overview of documented mineral optical properties that can be extracted from an image:

Color: The average color shown from a mineral on a cross polarized light or plane polarized light. Some studies apply a filter, such as the median filter used on [3] for noise reduction.

Pleochroism and Birefringence: The optical property of color change under plane polarized light (pleochroism) or cross polarized light (birefringence). This property takes into account images with different polarized light angles.

Texture: Not only color fully demonstrates the optical properties of the mineral, the professional observes subtle color-independent features such as undulatory extinction or small amounts of alteration without having to resort to specialized tests [2]. Minerals under specific cross polarized light angles appear in their darkest, almost totally black, and this is called extinction angle. Figure 5 shows a mineral at an extinction angle.

According to the work of [2], undulatory extinction, which results from a bend lattice and produces a series of dark bands crossing the crystal during rotation, can be quantified by textural parameters. Another texture parameter is twinning, which occurs when two separate crystals share some of the same crystal lattice points in a symmetrical manner. Visually, this shows well defined black stripes on the mineral body.

Opacity, Isotropy: Opaque minerals does not allow light to go through, appearing dark as both plane and cross polarized lights. Isotropic minerals are dark only in cross polarized light.

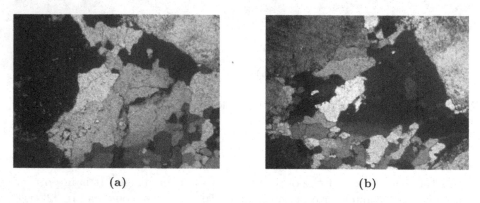

(a)   (b)

Fig. 5. Mineral at the center (a) on a non-extinction angle of polarized light and (b) at its extinction angle.

Sampling. In both GEO & MAS datasets, the images taken under plane or cross polarized light are well defined. Thus, we iterated the minerals and made every possible pair of a cross polarized image and a plane polarized image. Then, if a mineral has N images under cross polarized light and M under plane polarized light, we created $N \times M$ samples from it. This decision was made to generate the highest number of possible samples.

Even though every pair of images is unique, a single image is repeated several times and, to address that, we used image augmentation techniques better explained below. On Table 1 we compare the datasets used in our experimentation. The one created in our Geology Department is more limited in number of different mineral types, but it has a greater number of minerals per type. Lastly, MAS Dataset has a well defined number of images. Therefore, for every mineral we extracted 361 samples (19×19), whereas in GEO Dataset there were a large amount of images so number of samples easily reached six digits per mineral. All images used RGB color space.

Table 1. Comparative of the used datasets

	GEO Dataset	MAS Dataset
Mineral types	4	17
Total number of minerals	76	81
Number of crops per mineral	>1000	38
Crop resolution	50×50	86×171
Total size	2.22 GB	0.18 GB

Process. In this step, we processed those samples. All the implementation was done in python language, using *OpenCV* and *Scikit-learn* as main libraries. As RGB color space is undesirable for this task as discussed, we opted to transform to LAB color space, the same used in [5]. The equation used by *OpenCV* is described on Eq. 1.

$$
\begin{bmatrix} X \\ Y \\ Z \end{bmatrix} \leftarrow \begin{bmatrix} 0.412453 \ 0.212671 \ 0.019334 \\ 0.357580 \ 0.715160 \ 0.119193 \\ 0.180423 \ 0.072169 \ 0.950227 \end{bmatrix} \bullet \begin{bmatrix} R \\ G \\ B \end{bmatrix}
$$

$$X \leftarrow X/X_n, \text{ where } X_n = 0.950456$$

$$Z \leftarrow Z/Z_n, \text{ where } Z_n = 1.088754$$

$$[b!] \quad L \leftarrow \begin{cases} 116 * Y^{1/3} - 16 & \text{for } Y > 0.008856 \\ 903.3 * Y & \text{for } Y \leq 0.008856 \end{cases} \tag{1}$$

$$a \leftarrow 500(f(X) - f(Y))$$

$$b \leftarrow 200(f(Y) - f(Z))$$

where

$$f(t) = \begin{cases} t^{1/3} & \text{for } t > 0.008856 \\ 7.787t + 16/116 & \text{for } t \leq 0.008856 \end{cases}$$

All samples went through Image Augmentation shuffling. This is needed to shuffle the samples because, as discussed, one image may be repeated in a large number of samples. We used a python library from a github repository named *aleju/imgaug* that uses *OpenCV* as a base for its operations. A small sample of augmented images compared to their original image can be found in Fig. 6. The random number generator used was from the standard Python library *random*. These operations were also applied in a random order.

Rotate: It rotates the image at any angle using its center as a pivot. This rotation might place some pixels outside the image frame. In this case, that information is lost and the missing pixels are painted black on the image, as it can be seen in Fig. 6.

Gaussian blur: it applies the standard technique to make a blur effect on the image. The parameters for the Gaussian blur with sigma value ranges from [0, 3].

Flip: It flips the image entirely by one or both x and y axis.

Crop: It crops columns or rows from the bottom, top, right or left, which is randomly chosen. The value ranges from [0, 16].

Zoom: It zooms in the image with a value higher than one, else zooms out the image. If an image is zoomed in, its peripheral region is lost. Zoom value ranges from [0.8, 1.2].

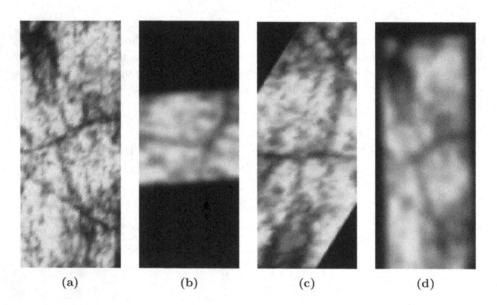

(a)   **(b)**   **(c)**   **(d)**

Fig. 6. An example of (a) an image sample and (b–d) its augmented results.

For the parameters, as our sample is only a single image of each polarized light type, the properties that required a set of images could not be processed. Those are the parameters extracted from each sample:

Color: We extracted the average LAB values of the images taken under cross polarized light and plane polarized light, respectively.

Texture: As detailed in [2], texture parameters were calculated using a co-occurrence matrix that was calculated for each grain. A co-occurrence matrix, representing a two-dimensional histogram, defines a $P[i, j]$ value which corresponds to the number of pixels with the values i and j separated by the displacement vector $(1,1)$. This displacement expressed as an image mask is the 2×2 identity matrix. With the normalized matrix P the following measurements are calculated (as shown in Eq. 2) for images taken under cross polarized light.

$$
\begin{aligned}
Contrast &= \sum\sum (i-j)^2 P[i,j] \\
Entropy &= -\sum\sum P[i,j]log(P[i,j]) \\
Energy &= \sum\sum P^2[i,j] \\
homogeneity &= \sum\sum P[i,j]/(1+|i-j|)
\end{aligned}
\tag{2}
$$

The result was an integer with high positive range values. To improve the accuracy of the machine learning algorithms, we normalized that integer using Eq. 3.

$$
normalize(x) = \begin{cases} 0, & \text{if } x = 0 \\ log_{10}(x), & \text{otherwise} \end{cases}
\tag{3}
$$

2.4   Classify

In this broad step, processed data were used to train and evaluate a machine learning algorithm. There is no documented standard to be applied in this step. As explained in more detail in Sect. 3, different evaluations methods were used, but for those that used machine learning, all of them were supervised.

Experimental Results. We applied both datasets on Nearest Neighbor ($n = 1$) and Decision Tree algorithms (*ID3*). Our evaluation method was the k-fold algorithm also known as cross validation with $k = 10$. We conducted two experiments with both datasets: one using only the color parameter, and the other using the parameters color and texture. The purpose was to verify if with the simplest descriptors and machine learning the results were high, and if texture made any difference in classification. Table 2 shows the overall results for both datasets using Color (C) and Color & Texture (C&T). Table 3 shows the results for GEO Dataset and Table 4 shows MAS Dataset results.

Table 2. Experimental results

	Dataset GEO		Dataset MAS	
	C&T	C	C&T	C
KNN	97.71%	97.65%	93.65%	92.36%
DTREE	97.31%	96.36%	94.23%	87.50%

Table 3. Individualized results for GEO Dataset.

	KNN		DTREE	
	C&T	C	C&T	C
Biotite	99.92%	99.92%	99.86%	99.87%
Microcline	97.07%	96.98%	95.96%	96.13%
Plagioclase	96.81%	96.73%	96.67%	96.66%
Quartz	97.05%	96.98%	96.76%	96.80%
AVERAGE	97.71%	97.65%	97.31%	97.36%

Table 4. Individualized results for MAS Dataset.

	KNN		DTREE	
	C&T	C	C&T	C
Anthophyllite	85.65%	85.32%	86.81%	76.23%
Apatite	98.89%	98.89%	96.40%	93.63%
Augite	97.23%	96.72%	93.44%	89.52%
Biotite	93.17%	92.68%	94.99%	91.49%
Calcite	93.91%	92.52%	98.01%	86.54%
Chlorite	98.15%	97.69%	95.84%	89.57%
Garnet	99.72%	99.86%	99.03%	98.48%
Hornblende	95.22%	94.44%	94.92%	89.46%
Lucite	99.03%	98.89%	97.09%	96.81%
Microcline	92.24%	86.98%	90.86%	78.67%
Muscovite	97.23%	97.69%	96.31%	94.46%
Olivine	94.78%	93.21%	93.03%	87.03%
Orthoclase	92.63%	87.26%	95.12%	82.38%
Opx	99.58%	99.58%	93.49%	88.92%
Plagioclase	91.62%	90.65%	89.54%	79.57%
Quartz	89.16%	87.93%	94.86%	85.12%
Sanidine	81.58%	70.08%	91.83%	73.41%
AVERAGE	94.11%	92.38%	94.21%	87.13%

3   Related Work

Thompson et al. [1] used a fully automated rotating polarized stage that allows the thin section to remain fixed at different polarized light angles, in a way that there is no spatial dislocation of the minerals. They took photos of each thin section 200 times (0 to 180° in 0.9 steps) under cross and plane polarized light. From them, they constructed two images where one contains pixels when they were in their brightest (maximum intensity image) and lowest (minimum intensity image) for each polarized light type in HSV color space. To segment the minerals, they used an edge detection algorithm and identified each mineral manually. The properties taken were pleochroism (maximum minus minimum intensity images), color and image texture from maximum and minimum intensity images. They applied their dataset in an artificial neural network and as it had a large input parameter set, they used a genetic algorithm to select only useful parameters. They used a fixed number of samples per mineral, which roughly translates to 22% of the dataset for training. Their average accuracy for 11 different minerals was 93.53%.

The work of Ross et al. [2] shares the same technique of Thompson et al. [1] to gather, segment and extract the optic parameters from the digital images. The only difference is that the HSI color space was used instead of HSV. They used a large parameter set for a genetic algorithm that selects the best decision tree for each mineral type. The results were individualized for each mineral type and the results ranged from 86% to 98%.

Baykan and Yilmaz [3] used a rotating polarizer stage and took the images at an interval of $1°$. They chose the images that showed maximum and minimum intensity overall and manually segmented each mineral region from the image. The parameter input was the value of the pixel itself of the plane and cross polarized light; therefore, this study used only color as parameter for the artificial neural network in both RGB and HSV color spaces. To train the artificial neural network, they used a fixed number of pixels for each mineral and their best result was an average of 89.53% of accuracy.

Izadi et al. [4] did not define how the images were taken. They used a clustering algorithm to identify different mineral regions for segmentation. For each region, the average color in RGB and HSV color spaces were taken from both polarized light types and used as parameter input for a neural network. They used 20% for test and 80% for training, resulting in an average accuracy of 95.4%. The authors published another work on [9] where they do not detail how the images were retrieved, only that they were taken at the maximum intensity of polarizing colors. They also used a clustering technique to identify mineral regions. A cascade approach was used for this problem: first, they divided the minerals types in two groups A and B; where group A was classified using only color, and group B using color and texture. Then, to apply, they trained an ANN using only colors as input for each pixel, namely the HSI and RGB values. If it classified any cluster as group A, the classification was final, otherwise it was evaluated in another ANN. This other ANN used as input the texture parameters, such as correlation, energy, homogeneity, maximum probability and entropy, and the output classified the cluster for mineral type in group B. The overall accuracy achieved is 94.99%.

According to Aligholi et al. [5] a digital camera on a rotating polarized stage microscope was used to capture images from 0 to $90°$ in a 5-degree interval. The images were rotated to rectify the spatial location of the minerals. The parameters extracted were all of those described in Sect. 2.3 and they used their own classification algorithm with results above 96.8%. Their dataset, which contains the highest number of different minerals, was made available for this study. The authors published another study on [10], where they still do not employ a direct approach of machine learning. However, they used an advanced color technique in a scheme that resembles a kNN method. They extracted the color vector for the set of images taken of a mineral on plane and cross polarized lights, and in a new entry, they compared the Hausdorff distance between the vectors. If the vector fell on an acceptable range, it was classified as the same as the nearest vector. They achieved the highest results documented with an average accuracy off 98.3%, proving that color by itself is very distinctive for a machine to perform mineral identification.

Table 5. Accuracy across related studies and Dataset MAS.

	(KNN C&T)	[1] (ANN)	[3] (ANN)	[4] (ANN)	[5] (ESP)
Biotite	93.17%	95.95%	98.11%	95.00%	98.50%
Calcite	93.91%	95.39%			95.00%
Chlorite	98.15%		89.58%		
Garnet	99.72%	95.50%		95.50%	
Hornblende	94.72%	95.35%			98.00%
Muscovite	97.23%		84.69%		
Olivine	94.78%	91.39%			
Plagioclase	91.62%	89.94%			
Quartz	89.16%	95.30%	81.55%	95.00%	96.00%

Table 6. Summary of comparison of related studies.

	Segment	Extract	Classify	Result
kNN (C&T)	Manual	Color Texture	kNN	97.71%
Thompson et al. [1]	Edge detection	Color Texture Pleochroism Birefringence	ANN	93.53%
Baykan and Yilmaz [3]	Manual	Color	ANN	89.53%
Izadi et al. [4]	Clustering	Color	ANN	95.4%
Izadi et al. [9]	Clustering	Color Texture	ANN	94.99%
Aligholi et al. [5]	Manual	Color Texture Birefringence Pleochroism ...	ESP	96.8%
Aligholi et al. [10]	Manual	Adv color	ESP	98.3%

4   Conclusion

We do prove that such a task, which may be complex for a human to execute, is easier for a machine to perform. As it can be seen in Sect. 2.4, even with the simplest descriptor of color and machine learning algorithms, an accuracy as high as 99% was achieved. With those results, one of our objectives was to demonstrate that this is a simple task for a computer to achieve, thus, to apply such a complex method of artificial neural networks may be an exaggeration. Also, our study suggests that more descriptors are needed for some mineral types, as affirmed by [9], being the image texture. The presence of texture parameter, notably on Sanidine, Orthoclase and Microcline, made a significant difference on both classification algorithms. This implies that more elaborated descriptors are needed for specific cases, but for the majority, color is a sufficient descriptor.

We compare our numbers with the highest documented accuracy in state of the art studies, only to show that, in accuracy, our method is within the same level as artificial neural networks. However, we cannot make a direct comparison due to great divergences between our applied methods, as seen in Sect. 3. Also, we contemplated the new technique of image augmentation which created a diverse and high number of samples. We compiled a summary comparing our overall accuracy in Table 6. In Table 5 we specified those studies that used Artificial Neural Networks (ANN) and (ESP), and the one that did not use a machine learning technique. We also listed only the common minerals between related studies and MAS Dataset, as it had the highest number of mineral types.

Acknowledgments. We would like to send a special thanks for the UFPEL Geology Department and the authors Aligholi et al. [5] for providing the dataset for our experiment.

This study was financed in part by the Coordenação de Aperfeiçoamento de Pessoal de Nível Superior - Brasil (CAPES) - Finance Code 001.

References

1. Thompson, S., Fueten, F., Bockus, D.: Mineral identification using artificial neural networks and the rotating polarizer stage. Comput. Geosci. **27**(9), 1081–1089 (2001)
2. Ross, B.J., Fueten, F., Yashkir, D.Y.: Automatic mineral identification using genetic programming. Mach. Vis. Appl. **13**(2), 61–69 (2001)
3. Baykan, N.A., Yilmaz, N.: Mineral identification using color spaces and artificial neural networks. Comput. Geosci. **36**(1), 91–97 (2010)
4. Izadi, H., Sadri, J., Mehran, N.: Intelligent mineral identification using clustering and artificial neural networks techniques. In: 2013 First Iranian Conference on Pattern Recognition and Image Analysis (PRIA), pp. 1–5. IEEE, Birjand (2013)
5. Aligholi, S., Khajavi, R., Razmara, M.: Automated mineral identification algorithm using optical properties of crystals. Comput. Geosci. **85**, 175–183 (2015)
6. Mlynarczuk, M., Górszczyk, A., Slipek, B.: The application of pattern recognition in the automatic classification of microscopic rock images. Comput. Geosci. **60**, 126–133 (2013)

7. Rinnen, S., Stroth, C., Riße, A., Ostertag-Henning, C., Arlinghaus, H.F.: Characterization and identification of minerals in rocks by ToF-SIMS and principal component analysis. Appl. Surf. Sci. **349**, 622–628 (2015)
8. Akkaş, E., Akin, L., Çubukçu, H.E., Artuner, H.: Application of Decision Tree Algorithm for classification and identification of natural minerals using SEM–EDS. Comput. Geosci. **80**, 38–48 (2015)
9. Izadi, H., Sadri, J., Bayati, M.: An intelligent system for mineral identification in thin sections based on a cascade approach. Comput. Geosci. **99**, 37–49 (2017)
10. Aligholi, S., Lashkaripour, G.R., Khajavi, R., Razmara, M.: Automatic mineral identification using color tracking. Pattern Recogn. **65**, 164–174 (2017)

Lexical Function Identification Using Word Embeddings and Deep Learning

Arturo Hernández-Miranda[1], Alexander Gelbukh[1],
and Olga Kolesnikova[2(✉)]

[1] Centro de Investigación en Computación, Instituto Politécnico Nacional,
07738 Mexico City, Mexico
arturhm@ciencias.unam.mx
[2] Escuela Superior de Cómputo, Instituto Politécnico Nacional,
07738 Mexico City, Mexico
kolesolga@gmail.com
https://www.gelbukh.com

Abstract. In this work, we report the results of our experiments on the task of distinguishing the semantics of verb-noun collocations in a Spanish corpus. This semantics was represented by four lexical functions of the Meaning-Text Theory. Each lexical function specifies a certain universal semantic concept found in any natural language. Knowledge of collocation and its semantic content is important for natural language processing, as collocation comprises the restrictions on how words can be used together. We experimented with a combination of GloVe word embeddings as a recent and extended algorithm for vector representation of words and a deep neural architecture, in order to recover most of the context of verb-noun collocations in a meaningful way which could discriminate among lexical functions. Our corpus was a collection of 1,131 Excelsior newspaper issues. As our results showed, the proposed deep neural architecture outperformed state-of-the-art supervised learning methods.

Keywords: Word embeddings · Deep learning · Lexical function · Meaning-Text Theory

1 Introduction

Human language is a highly ambiguous system, thus presenting a big challenge for natural language processing (NLP) by a machine. In spite of ambiguity, human speakers are able to produce and understand text messages in natural language, so NLP as an area of Artificial Intelligence (AI) has been trying to develop formal models to be implemented in machine text generation and comprehension.

As many other formal models proposed up to date, the formal model of lexical functions developed within the Meaning-Text Theory [6] aims at resolving language ambiguity. In doing so, it created a taxonomy of lexical functions that in a non-ambiguous way represent basic semantic and syntactic properties of collocations, defined as phrases whose meaning cannot be derived from the meanings of their constituent words, for example, *take a step*. This collocation does not mean 'grab a step', but 'perform the action of stepping'. As opposed to collocations, the meaning of

L. Martínez-Villaseñor et al. (Eds.): MICAI 2019, LNAI 11835, pp. 77–86, 2019.
https://doi.org/10.1007/978-3-030-33749-0_7

free word combinations is compositional, e.g., the semantics of *take a book* is transparent and easily interpreted as the union of the meanings of individual words. Thus, collocations are a particular case of word ambiguity. However, being a particular case, it is not a small case, since collocations may comprise up to 70% of text depending on text theme and style.

Most collocations include two words called the base and the collocate. The lexical choice of the collocate depends on the base. In the example *take a step*, the base is *a step* and the collocate is *take*. In order to lexicalize the meaning of 'perform the action expressed by the base', *a step* chooses *take* but not any of its synonyms, for example, *perform, realize, carry out*, etc. Such selectional preference of the base is characteristic of collocations.

Lexical functions (LFs) capture selectional preferences of words as mappings from the base, which is the LF argument, to a set of other words, or collocates, which is the LF meaning. For example, we can generally represent *take as step* as LF(*step*) = *take*. However, each lexical function has its meaning and syntactic pattern, in fact, the specific notation for *take a step* is Oper1(*step*) = *take*. Oper1 is one of about 60 LFs described in [6], its name comes from the Latin word *operari* 'do, carry out', and its semantics is 'perform the action given by the noun' as in the collocations *make a decision, take a walk, do an exercise, give a smile, pay a visit*. Although in all these collocations the verbs vary, all of them convey the meaning of 'performing' the action lexicalized by the respective noun.

Integers in the LF notation capture the predicate-argument structure typically used to express the LF meaning in sentences. In Oper1, 1 means that the action is performed by the agent, the first argument of the verb; therefore, Oper1 represents the pattern 'the agent performs what is expressed by the noun'. Consider, for example, *the president made a decision to continue the discussion*. Here, *the president* is the agent of the action *made (a decision)*.

Other common LFs found in collocations, in particular, in verb-noun collocations, are Real1, CausFunc0, and CausFunc1, we explain them in what follows.

Real1, Latin *realis* 'real', conveys the meaning of fulfilling a requirement imposed by the noun or performing an action typical for the noun: *drive a bus, follow advice, spread a sail, prove an accusation, succumb to illness, turn back an obstacle*.

Oper1 and Real1 are simple LFs, they formalize a single semantic unit. A combination of more than one semantic units is denoted by a complex lexical function, for example, CausFunc0 and CausFunc1.

Caus, from Latin *causare* 'cause', formalizes the pattern 'do something so that the event denoted by the noun starts occurring'. Func0, from Latin *functionare* 'function', represents the meaning 'happen, occur'. Making the union of these two concepts, we obtain the function CausFunc0 meaning 'the agent does something so that the event denoted by the noun occurs', some examples are *bring about the crisis, create a difficulty, establish a system, produce an effect*.

Another complex LF, CausFunc1, formalizes the construction 'the non-agentive participant does something such that the event denoted by the noun occurs', for example, *open a perspective, raise hope, cause damage*.

In this work, our objective was to identify lexical functions typical for Spanish verb-noun collocations in a corpus automatically. We developed three methods based on different deep neural network configurations to distinguish among various LFs in texts and obtained experimental results which are higher than state of the art results.

The rest of the paper is organized as follows. Section 2 presents related work, in Sect. 3 we explain the proposed methods and give a brief description of our dataset and the corpus. In Sect. 4 we discuss the results, and Sect. 5 includes conclusions and future work.

2 Related Work

It is not a trivial task to detect fine-grained semantic differences represented by lexical functions automatically, so more research has been so far accomplished on manual methods of annotating collocations with lexical functions and consequently building collocation dictionaries enriched by LFs or semantic networks and ontologies incorporating LFs in them. One of such projects is French Lexical Network (FLN) [5] created based on the LF taxonomy and available for download in the XML format; connections between words in the network are tagged with syntagmatic relations corresponding to LFs. Such annotation, absent in WordNet [7], another popular and widely used semantic network, makes FLN a unique repository of lexical semantic data existing up to date. Fonseca, Sadat, and Lareau [2] developed a Java API in order to retrieve data from FLN which they used to detect collocations in a textual corpus with an overall precision of 76.30% and to produce semantic classification of the identified collocations.

A few works have been done on LFs automatic detection. Wanner [12], Wanner, Bohnet, and Giereth [13] experimented with nine LFs in Spanish verb-noun collocations, representing each collocation by a vector whose features were hypernyms of the noun and the verb. In the experiments, an average F1–measure of about 70% was obtained. The highest results were shown by the ID3 algorithm with an F1–measure of 76% and by the Nearest Neighbor technique with an F1–measure of 74%.

Tutin [10] took advantage of the database of French collocations described by Polguère [9], syntactic patterns, and finite-state transducers associated with metagraphs for labeling collocations with LFs in corpora. In the experiments, a precision of 90% and a recall of 86.20% were archived.

Enikeeva and Popov [1] applied Affinity Propagation algorithm to cluster collocations using word embeddings [8] of the collocation constituents. Clusters were expected to contain different semantic classes of collocations, each with respect to a particular lexical function. A precision of 64% was obtained on LFs for verb-noun collocations, which is the collocation type we experimented on in this work.

In our previous work [3], an average F1–measure of 74% was achieved on a Spanish verb-noun LFs applying all relevant supervised learning methods implemented in Weka software [14]; collocations were represented as vectors of Spanish WordNet

[11] hypernyms of the constituent words. We also studied how LFs can be detected by their context words using supervised learning in [4]. The best F1-measure was 50% using tf-idf of context words as features and support vector machine with a linear kernel.

3 Data and Method

In our experiments, we used a dataset of Spanish verb-noun collocations labeled manually with lexical functions compiled by us in previous work [3]; Table 1 give some examples of our data. The corpus used in our experiments is a collection of 1,131 issues of the Excelsior newspaper in Spanish from April 1, 1996 to June 24, 1999.

Table 1. Examples of data used in our experiments

Lexical function and its meaning	Vern-noun collocations	
	Spanish	English translation
Oper1 perform an action given by the noun	*realizar un estudio* *cometer un error* *dar un beso*	do a study make an error give a kiss
Real1 fulfill the requirement of the noun	*alcanzar el nivel* *utilizar recurso* *cumplir la función*	reach a level use a resource fulfill the function
IncepOper1 begin to perform an action given by the noun	*iniciar un proceso* *tomar la palabra* *adoptar la actitud*	begin a process take the floor adopt the attitude
ContOper1 continue to perform an action given by the noun	*seguir un curso* *mantener un contacto* *guardar silencio*	follow a course keep in touch keep silent
CausFunc0 the agent does something so that the event denoted by the noun occurs	*crear una cuenta* *formar un grupo* *hacer ruido*	create an account form a group make noise
CausFunc1 the non-agentive participant does something such that the event denoted by the noun occurs	*ofrecer una posibilidad* *causar un problema* *crear una condición*	offer a possibility cause a problem create a condition

Our objective was to identify lexical functions in a Spanish corpus using one part of our dataset of collocations tagged with LFs as a training set, and the other part as a test set. Words in the context of verb-noun collocations were represented by Spanish GloVe word embeddings which were input to three configurations of neural networks: multilayered perceptron (MP), concatenated input embeddings perceptron (CP), and the model designed in [15] for text summarization, here we adapted it to our task and called this model as Extract for Autoencoder (EXA).

In each configuration, the input word embeddings were submitted to a different operation: in the first configuration with MP, the input of the three embeddings, generated for each collocation, was their arithmetic mean. The three embeddings were for the central word W_k (the noun as the base of a verb-noun collocation), the word on the left in the corpus W_{k-1}, and the work on the right W_{k+1}, see Fig. 1.

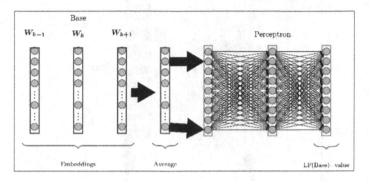

Fig. 1. MP

In the second configuration with CP, W_{k-1}, W_k, and W_{k+1} were concatenated and the resulting vectors were fed into a multilayered perceptron, see Fig. 2.

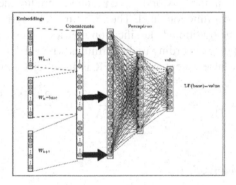

Fig. 2. CP

In the third configuration, the network was trained using the embedding of the base of each collocation concatenated with arbitrarily chosen context words on one hand (noise), and the concatenated input for the base with the left and right context word, as in the second configuration of CP, was applied, see Fig. 3.

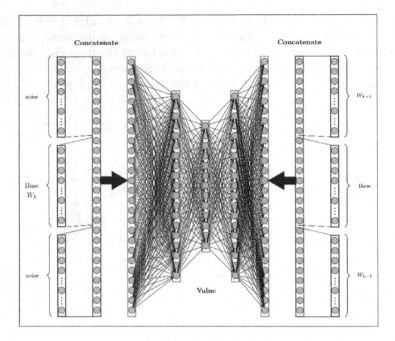

Fig. 3. EXE

For each configuration, the networks were trained to predict the collocates of nouns with the respective lexical function label. The learnt models were tested on the test set and evaluated using three traditional classification metrics: precision (P), recall (R), and F1-measure (F1), computed according to the formulas where TA is true acceptance, TR is true rejection, FA is false acceptance, and FR is false rejection:

$$P = \frac{TR}{TR+FR}, \ R = \frac{TR}{TR+FA}, \ F1 = \frac{2 \times P \times R}{P+R}$$

4 Results and Discussion

Table 2 presents the results of lexical functions' identification in terms of F1-measure (F1) for three experimental configurations, respectively. The best result for each configuration is highlighted in boldface. We experimented with different number of epochs, so the results in Table 2 are given with respect to the number of epochs. Figure 4 visualizes the results for convenient comparison of the three configurations.

Table 2. Lexical function detection using three neural network configurations

# of epochs	F1, MP	F1, CP	F1, EXA
20	35.83%	43.46%	52.5%
30	44.65%	51.70%	53.1%
40	50.78%	58.06%	53.6%
60	51.59%	58.29%	53.6%
80	51.57%	**58.44%**	54.1%
100	50.99%	57.71%	53.4%
120	50.64%	57.58%	53.9%
150	**51.77%**	58.37%	53.7%
170	51.39%	58.09%	52.7%
190	50.40%	57.10%	52.4%
200	50.36%	57.05%	53.4%
210	50.31%	57.13%	**54.2%**
250	50.17%	56.90%	53.2%
280	50.17%	56.77%	53.4%

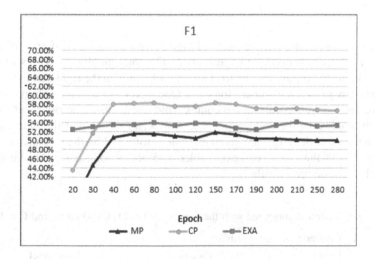

Fig. 4. Graphs of F1-measure for three neural network configurations

As it can be observed in Table 2 and also in the graphs in Fig. 4, the best F1-measures are as follows: 51.77% for the MP configuration after 150 epochs, 58.44% for the CP network after 80 epochs, and 54.2% for the EXA configuration after 210 epochs. The network CP, with concatenated word embeddings, produced the best result, an F1-measure of 58.44%, and achieved it faster, after only 80 epochs.

It is important to note, that all best F1-measure values surpass the state of the art F1-measure value of 50% shown by support vector machine with a linear kernel and reported in [4]. The experiments in [4] was performed on the same Excelsior corpus and with the same set of verb-noun collocations, so this comparison is perfectly fair and demonstrates the power of word embeddings and neural networks to discriminate among contexts of different lexical functions. In fact, it is an outstanding result because there is a lot of similarity among the contexts of lexical functions. To show this similarity, we chose four lexical functions as examples: Oper1, Real1, CausFunc0, and CausFunc1.

Table 3. Oper1 context compared with the context of Real1, CausFunc0, and CausFunc1

Oper1	Common context words					
	Real1		CausFunc0		CausFunc1	
	# of common words	% of common words	# of common words	% of common words	# of common words	% of common words
2,605 words in the left context	839	32.21%	750	28.79%	950	36.47%
1,592 words in the right context	593	37.25%	521	32.73%	573	35.99%

In Table 3, we compare the context of Oper1 with the context of each of the rest three LFs: Real1, CausFunc0, and CausFunc1. The total number of words in the left context found in the corpus, and the total number of words in the right context of Oper1 collocations are given, remember, for each Oper1 verb-noun collocation, only one word to the left was retrieved as a left context, and one word to the right was retrieved for the right context of the collocation. The number of words that the Oper1 context shares with the other three LFs are given in Table 3 followed by the percentage of these common words in the Oper1 context. Tables 4, 5 and 6 for Real1, CausFunc0, and CausFunc1 are structured similarly.

Table 4. Real1 context compared with the context of Oper1, CausFunc0, and CausFunc1

Real1	Common context words					
	Oper1		CausFunc0		CausFunc1	
	# of common words	% of common words	# of common words	% of common words	# of common words	% of common words
1,710 words in the left context	839	49.06%	587	34.33%	719	42.05%
1,576 words in the right context	593	37.63%	488	30.96%	526	33.38%

Table 5. CausFunc0 context compared with the context of Oper1, Real1, and CausFunc1

CausFunc0	Common context words					
	Oper1		Real1		CausFunc1	
	# of common words	% of common words	# of common words	% of common words	# of common words	% of common words
1,486 words in the left context	750	50.47%	587	39.50%	637	42.87%
1,160 words in the right context	521	44.91%	488	42.07%	458	39.48%

Table 6. CausFunc1 context compared with the context of Oper1, Real1, and CausFunc0

CausFunc1	Common context words					
	Oper1		Real1		CausFunc0	
	# of common words	% of common words	# of common words	% of common words	# of common words	% of common words
2,065 words in the left context	950	46.00%	719	34.82%	637	30.85%
1,246 words in the right context	573	45.99%	526	42.22%	458	36.76%

5 Conclusions and Future Work

In this work, we applied word embeddings and three configurations of neural networks to the task of identifying lexical functions in Spanish verb-noun collocations. Our best result is an F1-measure of 58.44% achieved by a neural network using concatenated word embeddings for three words as an input: the embedding of the central word, which was the noun in a verb-noun collocation, the embedding of the word to the left in the context of the noun, and the embedding of one word to the right in the context of the noun. This result was showed after 80 epochs demonstrating speedy and efficient learning. Our result surpassed the best state of the art result, an F1-measure of 50% showed by support vector machine with a linear kernel.

In future, we plan to experiment with other configurations of the input and the neural network.

Acknowledgements. The research was done under partial support of Mexican Government: SNI, BEIFI-IPN, and SIP-IPN grants 20196021, 20196437.

References

1. Enikeeva, E., Popov, A.: Developing a Russian database of regular semantic relations based on word embeddings. In: Krek, S., Cibej, J., Gorjanc, V., Kosem, I. (eds.) Proceedings of the XVIII EURALEX International Congress: Lexicography in Global Contexts, Ljubljana, Slovenia, pp. 799–809 (2018)
2. Fonseca, A., Sadat, F., Lareau, F.: Retrieving information from the French lexical network in RDF/OWL format. In: Calzolari, N., et al. (eds.) Proceedings of the 11th International Conference on Language Resources and Evaluation, Miyazaki, Japan (2018)
3. Gelbukh, A., Kolesnikova, O.: Supervised learning for semantic classification of Spanish collocations. In: Martínez-Trinidad, J.F., Carrasco-Ochoa, J.A., Kittler, J. (eds.) MCPR 2010. LNCS, vol. 6256, pp. 362–371. Springer, Heidelberg (2010). https://doi.org/10.1007/978-3-642-15992-3_38. The complete list of 737 Spanish verb-noun collocations annotated with 36 lexical functions can be accessed at http://148.204.58.221/okolesnikova/index.php?id=lex/ or http://www.gelbukh.com/lexical-functions
4. Kolesnikova, O., Gelbukh, A.: Exploring the context of lexical functions. In: Batyrshin, I., Martínez-Villaseñor, L., Ponce Espinosa, H.E. (eds.) MICAI 2018. LNCS (LNAI), vol. 11289, pp. 57–69. Springer, Cham (2018). https://doi.org/10.1007/978-3-030-04497-8_5
5. Lux-Pogodalla, V., Polguère, A.: Construction of a French lexical network: methodological issues. In: First International Workshop on Lexical Resources, Ljubljana, Slovenia, pp. 54–61 (2011)
6. Mel'čuk, I.A.: Lexical functions: A tool for the description of lexical relations in a lexicon. In: Wanner, L. (ed.) Lexical Functions in Lexicography and Natural Language Processing, pp. 37–102. Benjamins Academic Publishers, Amsterdam (1996)
7. Miller, G.A., Leacock, C., Tengi, R., Bunker, R.T.: A semantic concordance. In: Proceedings of the Workshop on Human Language Technology Association for Computational Linguistics, Stroudsburg, PA, pp. 303–308 (1993)
8. Mikolov, T., Sutskever, I., Chen, K., Corrado, G.S., Dean, J.: Distributed representations of words and phrases and their compositionality. In: Advances in Neural Information Processing Systems, pp. 3111–3119. Neural Information Processing Systems Foundation, Inc. (2013)
9. Polguère A.: Towards a theoretically-motivated general public dictionary of semantic derivations and collocations for French. In: Proceedings of EURALEX 2000, Stuttgart, Germany, pp. 517–527 (2000)
10. Tutin, A.: Annotating lexical functions in corpora: showing collocations in context. In: Apresjan, Y., Iomdin, L. (eds.) Proceedings of the Second International Conference on the Meaning-Text Model, pp. 498–510. Slavic Culture Languages Publishing House, Moscow (2007)
11. Vossen, P.: EuroWordNet: a multilingual database of autonomous and language-specific wordnets connected via an inter-lingual-index. Int. J. Lexicography 17(2), 161–173 (2004)
12. Wanner, L.: Towards automatic fine-grained classification of verb-noun collocations. Nat. Lang. Eng. 10(2), 95–143 (2004)
13. Wanner, L., Bohnet, B., Giereth, M.: What is beyond collocations? Insights from machine learning experiments. In: Proceedings of the 12th EURALEX International Congress, Turin, Italy, pp. 1071–1084 (2006)
14. Witten, I.H., Frank, E.: Data Mining: Practical Machine Learning Tools and Techniques. Morgan Kaufmann, San Francisco (2005)
15. Yousefi-Azar, M., Hamey, L.: Text summarization using unsupervised deep learning. Expert Syst. Appl. 68, 93–105 (2017)

A Deep Learning Approach for Hybrid Hand Gesture Recognition

Diego G. Alonso$^{(\boxtimes)}$, Alfredo Teyseyre, Luis Berdun, and Silvia Schiaffino

ISISTAN (CONICET-UNCPBA), Campus Universitario, Tandil, Argentina
{diego.alonso,alfredo.teyseyre,luis.berdun,
silvia.schiaffino}@isistan.unicen.edu.ar

Abstract. Emerging depth sensors and new interaction paradigms enable to create more immersive and intuitive Natural User Interfaces by recognizing body gestures. One of the vision-based devices that has received plenty of attention is the Leap Motion Controller (LMC). This device models the 3D position of hands and fingers and provides more than 50 features such as palm center and fingertips. In spite of the fact that the LMC provides such useful information of the hands, developers still have to deal with the hand gesture recognition problem. For this reason, several researchers approached this problem using well-known machine learning techniques used for gesture recognition such as SVM for static gestures and DTW for dynamic gestures. At this point, we propose an approach that applies a resampling technique based on fast Fourier Transform algorithm to feed a CNN+LSTM neural network in order to identify both static and dynamic gestures. As far as our knowledge, there is no full dataset based on the LMC that includes both types of gestures. Therefore, we also introduce the Hybrid Hand Gesture Recognition database, which consists of a large set of gestures generated with the LMC, including both type of gestures with different temporal sizes. Experimental results showed the robustness of our approach in terms of recognizing both type of gestures. Moreover, our approach outperforms other well-known algorithms of the gesture recognition field.

Keywords: Hand Gesture Recognition · Deep Learning · Natural User Interfaces · Leap Motion Controller

1 Introduction

During the last decade, emerging technologies and new interaction paradigms motivated the creation of several commercial depth sensors such as Kinect, Real Sense, and Xtion. These devices enable the recognition of body gestures, which strongly enhances Human-Computer Interaction (HCI). In particular, the ability of understanding hand gestures has become a crucial component for the development of more immersive and intuitive Natural User Interfaces (NUIs) in many domains including virtual reality gaming, physical rehabilitation, and sign language recognition. At this point, one of the vision-based devices that has received

© Springer Nature Switzerland AG 2019
L. Martínez-Villaseñor et al. (Eds.): MICAI 2019, LNAI 11835, pp. 87–99, 2019.
https://doi.org/10.1007/978-3-030-33749-0_8

plenty of attention is the Leap Motion Controller (LMC), which captures the movements of human hands creating a virtual representation of them.

The LMC is a small sensor consisting of two monochromatic cameras and three infrared LEDs. It models the 3D position of hands and fingers and provides more than 50 features such as palm center, fingertips, finger bones, and hand orientation. Nevertheless, its Application Programming Interface (API) only provides support for recognizing three gestures. For this reason, in spite of the fact that the LMC provides such useful information, developers still have to deal with the tedious and difficult task of recognizing gestures. Thus, several researchers approached this issue of increasing the LMC gesture recognition capabilities by using machine learning techniques. These hand gesture recognition approaches can be grouped into two main categories: static and dynamic [3]. In brief, static hand gesture recognition considers single frames of data and dynamic hand gesture recognition considers sequences of frames of data.

For dynamic hand gesture recognition most commonly used techniques are Dynamic Time Warping (DTW) and Hidden Markov Models (HMM), while for static hand gesture recognition the conventional method is Support Vector Machines (SVM) [2]. However, the studies in the current state-of-art do not addressed the hybrid hand gesture recognition problem, which considers both static and dynamic gestures together. In addition, as far as our knowledge, there is no dataset generated with the LMC that contains both static gestures and dynamic gestures.

In this context, this paper presents a robust approach for hybrid hand gesture recognition with LMC using deep learning. We propose a neural network architecture that involves using a Convolutional Neural Network (CNN) for extracting features from the 3D data provided by the LMC, combined with a Long Short-Term Memory (LSTM) recurrent network for supporting the temporal dimension of the 3D data. It is important to clarify that, we consider real time scenarios in which the sequences of each gesture have not necessarily the same size. For this purpose, before feeding our CNN+LSTM model we augment the 3D data provided by the LMC with a resampling technique based on Fast Fourier Transform (FFT) algorithm. Thus, our approach is able to classify 3D data sequences of different sizes. It is noteworthy that, we also applied a centering transformation in order to make the sequences suitable for comparison. In short, we move the hand joints regarding the palm position so as to avoid heterogeneous hand part locations within the LMC detection field.

To evaluate our approach, we generated a balanced dataset consisting of 20 gestures including both static and dynamic types, and we performed a cross-validation scheme. Experimental results showed the robustness of the approach in terms of recognizing both types of gestures. Furthermore, our approach achieved higher accuracy rates than other well-known algorithms proposed in the current state-of-art for hand gesture recognition.

The remainder of this paper is organized as follows. Section 2 describes relevant related works of the current state-of-art. Section 3 introduces our proposed approach. Section 4 discusses the experiments and results along with the lessons learned. Finally, Sect. 5 presents the conclusions and future work.

2   Related Work

In this section, we review relevant works of the current state-of-art of hand gesture recognition with LMC. In Subsect. 2.1, we focus on the approaches that tackle static hand gesture recognition. In Subsect. 2.2, we analyze the approaches that address dynamic hand gesture recognition.

2.1   Static Hand Gesture Recognition

A static gesture, also known as pose or posture, refers to only a single image or a single frame of data corresponding to one command such as stop [14]. However, we adapt this definition to the context of real-time HCI scenarios. In these scenarios, the devices establish a stream where the input data is provided continuously. Under this condition, we determine that a static gesture is one that given a sequence of frames could be identified by individually taking any frame of that sequence. Chuan et al. [4], recognized 26 letters of the American Sign Language (ASL), which were single-framed gestures, using a K-Nearest Neighbor (KNN) classifier and a Support Vector Machine (SVM) classifier. In particular, they extracted 9 features from the raw data of the LMC and performed a 4-fold cross-validation test obtaining an average recognition rate of 72.78% and 79.83% by KNN and SVM respectively. Similarly, Mohandes et al. [12] identified 28 letters of the Arabic Sign Language (ArSL). Their approach preprocessed the raw data and extracted 12 features in order to feed a Multilayer Perceptron neural network (MLP) and a Naive Bayes Classifier (NBC). The authors reported an average recognition accuracy of 98.3% for the NBC and 99.1% for the MLP technique in a 5-fold cross-validation test. Khelil and Amiri [6] trained a SVM for recognizing static gestures of the ArSL too, achieving a recognition accuracy of 91.3%.

Other approaches proposed using multiple sensors working together. For example, Marin et al. [9] analyzed the use of LMC and Microsoft Kinect, both individually and in joint, for 10 static gestures of the ASL. In particular, they trained a SVM classifier using three feature vectors for the LMC and two for the Kinect. Experimental results showed that better recognition accuracy is achieved by combining data from both devices. Later, the authors extended their work by proposing new features that improved the recognition accuracy [10]. Fok et al. [5] combined two LMCs for the recognition of 10 digits of the ASL. The authors proposed a Hidden Markov Model (HMM) of 9 states, which were empirically determined. Experimental results evidenced that the multi-sensor approach (accuracy: 93.14%) can deliver higher recognition accuracy than a single-sensor system (accuracy: 87.39%).

2.2   Dynamic Hand Gesture Recognition

Unlike previous works, in which the authors experimented with static gestures, other researchers evaluated their approaches analyzing dynamic gestures. A dynamic gesture, also known as move, is a temporal and spatial sequence of postures [15]. López (et al.) [7] introduced an approach for manipulating augmented objects based on a SVM classifier, which was trained with only a set of features provided by the LMC. Their approach was tested with 8 dynamic gestures performed by 12 participants and achieved an average recognition accuracy of roughly 80%. Chen et al. [1] took the projection of the palm position directly obtained from the LMC and trained a SVM classifier and a HMM. The authors built a dataset of 3600 samples for 36 dynamic gestures of the ArSL. The results showed that SVM outperformed HMM in recognition accuracy and recognition time. In addition, the authors obtained encouraging results for early gesture recognition. McCartney et al. [11] processed a sequence of frames with positional data and summarize it to a shorter sequence of lines and curves. With these new sequences they fed a HMM in order to detect start and stop points for dynamic gestures. A dataset of 9600 samples of 12 dynamic gestures was performed for the experiments. The obtained results with the introduced method were not as well as expected. However, the authors also proposed an approach based on image processing that consists on training CNNs. They achieved an accuracy rate of 92.4% using only samples corresponding to 5 of the 12 gestures. Lu et al. [8] fed a Hidden Conditional Neural Field (HCNF) classifier with single finger and double finger features extracted from the LMC. The authors generated two different datasets with dynamic gestures performed by 10 participants. The experimental results showed that the proposed approach achieved an average recognition accuracy of 95% for one dataset and 89.5% for the other.

This analysis of the current state-of-art provides evidence that these approaches, both those for static gestures and those for dynamic gestures, allow developers to create different ways of interacting through the LMC. Nevertheless, to the best of our knowledge, no approach considers simultaneously recognizing both types of hand gestures. In addition, although neural networks have been used for gesture recognition, no approach considers using a CNN+LSTM architecture for hand gesture recognition with the LMC.

3   Our Approach for Hybrid Hand Gesture Recognition

In general terms, we propose a 3-step pipeline that consists in Data Acquisition, Data Preprocessing, and Gesture Classification based on a Deep Learning Model. As it is shown in Fig. 1, once a user performs a gesture in the interaction field of the LMC the Data Acquisition step begins. In short, the tracking software of the LMC reads the sensor data and combines it with a skeletal model of the human hand. The data is assembled in the form of frames, which contain the information of several hand joints including fingers, palm, and wrist. Thus, a gesture is interpreted as a sequence of frames that describes the overall movement of the different hand joints over time. The gesture data provided by the LMC is collected by our tool and passed as raw data to the next step of the pipeline.

The Data Preprocessing step aims to make the raw data suitable for comparison. As mentioned before, in real-time scenarios the gestures have different temporal sizes, that is why our approach resamples the sequence of frames to a predefined number of frames by using the Fast Fourier Transform (FFT) algorithm. Afterwards, our approach proceeds to crop some percentage of the beginning and the ending of the resampled sequence to avoid noisy data corresponding to the positions of the hand both before performing the gesture and after completing the gesture. This is an important step, particularly, when analyzing an stream with several gestures. Another crucial preprocessing transformation is centering, which consists in moving the trajectories of the hand joints regarding the palm position. This is applied because heterogeneous joint locations within the LMC interaction field negatively affect the recognition accuracy.

The gesture representation delivered by the Data Preprocessing step is used to feed a neural network classifier. In brief, the network architecture of our approach consists in a Convolutional layer for extracting meaningful features of the frames, a Long Short-Term Memory layer for modelling the temporal dimension of the data, and two fully connected layers for making easier the classification task. This architecture is also known as CLDNN [13]. Finally, our approach indicates the predicted gesture.

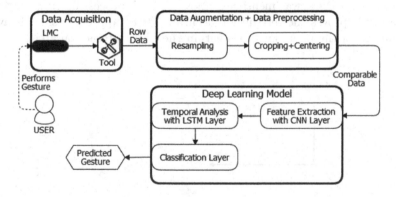

Fig. 1. Our Deep Learning approach for Hybrid Hand Gesture Recognition with LMC.

In the next subsections, we delve into each step of the proposed pipeline. In Subsect. 3.1, we describe the Data Acquisition with LMC and its features. In Subsect. 3.2, we explain the transformations applied in the Data Preprocessing step. In Subsect. 3.3, we introduce our Deep Learning Model architecture.

3.1 Data Acquisition with Leap Motion Controller

As mentioned before, the LMC is a vision-based device that consists of two cameras and three infrared LEDs. Among the vision-based approaches for data acquisition, it is considered an active technique since it uses the projection of structured light [3]. The LMC interaction area is like an inverted pyramid because of the intersection of the binocular cameras' fields of view and its viewing range is about 2.6 ft. In short, the LMC's USB controller reads the sensor data into its own local memory, performs resolution adjustments, and streams it to the tracking software. Afterwards, the LMC applies advanced algorithms to the raw sensor data in combination with a model of the human hand for inferring the 3D positions and directions of the different joints. Some of these joints are the fingertips, the finger bones (distal, intermediate, proximal, metacarpal), the palm, the wrist, among others. For more details about the LMC see here[1].

3.2   Data Preprocessing

At first, considering the variations in the temporal sizes of the gestures, our approach resamples the gesture data. At this point, it uses a well-known resampling technique based on the FFT algorithm, which efficiently computes the Discrete Fourier Transform (DFT) of a sequence. Figure 2a shows a handwaving gesture consisting of five frames being resampled, in this case, up-sampled to nine frames. Then, our approach crops a percentage of the beginning and the ending of the resampled gesture. We empirically determined cropping 10% of the beginning and 10% of the ending of the gesture. Moreover, our approach centers the trajectories of the different hand joints regarding the palm position as it is shown in Fig. 2b. As it was mentioned above, this preprocessing transformation significantly improves the recognition accuracy of the approach, since it avoids the variations of the joints locations within the LMC interaction area.

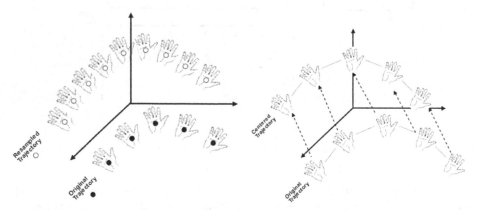

(a) Resampling of a handwaving gesture   (b) Centering of a handwaving gesture

Fig. 2. Data Preprocessing applied techniques.

---

[1] http://blog.leapmotion.com/hardware-to-software-how-does-the-leap-motion-contro ller-work/.

3.3   Deep Learning Architecture

Once the comparable data is available, our approach delivers it to a neural network classifier based on a CNN+LSTM architecture (see Fig. 3). First, the input data is divided in a predefined number of steps and passed to a Convolutional 2D layer that works as a feature extractor. Shortly, this layer applies a specified number of filters that scan the input by subregions and perform a set of mathematical operations, also known as convolutions, to generate convolved feature maps. After performing several tests we decided to use 64 filters of 2×2 size. This layer intends to learn complex feature representations from raw data. Since our input data are 1D signals, our approach transforms them to 2D virtual images. Then, a pooling layer summarizes the outputs of neighboring groups of neurons in the same kernel map reducing its dimensionality by performing a basic downsampling operation along the spatial dimensions. Since CNNs learn so fast, our approach has a Dropout layer (in our case of 0.3) that aims to improve the learning process by slowing it down. In order to pass the CNN feature outputs to the LSTM, our approach also has a Flatten layer that represents the features as one long vector. LSTM is a type of Recurrent Neural Networks (RNNs), which is specifically designed to maintain long-term dependencies. The LSTM (in our case of 256 units) can model the temporal structure of the input data being crucial for sequential prediction. Finally, our approach has two fully connected layers. The first one (in our case of 128 neurons) for reducing variation in the hidden states and the second one for the classifying task (in our case of 20 classes). It is important to note that, for the experiments, the batch size was set to 32 and the number of epochs was set to 30.

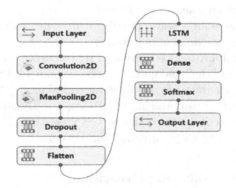

Fig. 3. Deep Learning Model Architecture.

4   Experiments

As mentioned before, to the best of our knowledge, no study considers simultaneously recognizing static and dynamic hand gestures. Therefore, we generated a balanced dataset with the LMC containing both static and dynamic hand gestures. In order to validate our proposal, we compared its recognition accuracy with the recognition accuracy of three well-known algorithms of the hand gesture recognition field. In Subsect. 4.1, we describe the generated dataset and the selected techniques for comparison. In Subsect. 4.2, we present the experimental results and discussion.

4.1   Experimental Setup

For generating the dataset, we implemented a prototype tool that allows us to collect data directly from the LMC. In addition, this tool also has support for incorporating new recognition techniques and preprocessing capabilities. Thus, we created our dataset by using this tool. In short, as a trainer places his/her hand in the interaction area of the LMC and performs a gesture, our tool stores the movements as a sequence of frames by using the LMC SDK.

In order to evaluate the robustness of our approach, we collected samples for 10 static hand gestures (see Fig. 4a) and 10 dynamic hand gestures (see Fig. 4b). In particular, we recorded 30 samples for each gesture, thus, generating a dataset of 600 hand gesture samples. It should be noted that, both static and dynamic hand gestures vary in a range between 6 and 181 frames. This means that the samples do not have the same temporal sizes and they are not of a single frame as typically static gestures are described. As mentioned before, we decided to record the samples this way because in real-time scenarios, the hand gestures, even the poses, are not of a single frame, since it is not possible to maintain the hand completely immobile (considering that, for example, the LMC provides 30 frames per second). It is important to note that the error rate of the camera causes variations between frames too. Therefore, is really important to consider more than a single frame for a static hand gesture when working with real-time scenarios. The dataset is available online here[2].

For validating our approach we compared its recognition accuracy with some well-known algorithms of the hand gesture recognition field. Particularly, we analyzed the recognition accuracy of the following techniques: (a) our CNN+LSTM approach; (b) Support Vector Machines (SVM); (c) Dynamic Time Warping (DTW); and Human Activity Recognition CNN (HAR-CNN). For the experiments we performed a 10-fold cross-validation scheme.

4.2   Experimental Results and Discussion

Our approach reached the higher average recognition accuracy both for static gestures and for dynamic gestures. Hence, our CNN+LSTM approach obtained the higher overall recognition accuracy which value was 0.9883. These results demonstrated the robustness of our approach considering both types of gestures in real-time scenarios. Another technique that obtained a high average recognition accuracy was the HAR-CNN, which reached 0.98. Figure 5 shows

---

[2] http://si.isistan.unicen.edu.ar/bemyvoice/datasetdownload.html.

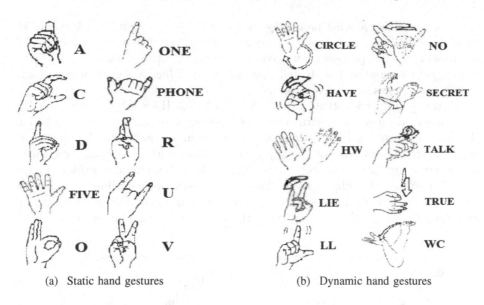

(a) Static hand gestures   (b) Dynamic hand gestures

Fig. 4. List of gestures of our hybrid hand gesture recognition dataset.

the confusion matrices generated after performing the cross-validation test on all the evaluated techniques.

By analyzing the confusion matrices, we identified that our approach confused 7 samples with very similar gestures. In particular, it confused: two samples of the 'FIVE' gesture and one sample of the 'HANDWAVING' gesture with the 'CIRCLE' gesture, which the three of them consist in moving the hand with the five fingers extended; one sample of the 'U' gesture with the 'LIE' gesture, which basically consist in shaking the hand with the same shape of the 'U' gesture; one sample of the 'NO' gesture with the 'ONE' gesture, in which the former gesture consists in shaking the hand with the shape of the latter; and one sample of the 'HAVE' gesture with the 'A' gesture whose hand shapes are very similar. It should be noted that, these samples were confused by the other techniques as well. The HAR-CNN approach confused 12 samples, among which we identified three non-similar classification mistakes: a sample of the 'SECRET' gesture with the 'HANDWAVING' gesture; a sample of the 'R' gesture with the 'HANDWAVING' gesture; and one sample of the 'TRUE' gesture with the 'HAVE' gesture. The DTW, which is a well-known technique of the dynamic hand gesture recognition field, reached an overall recognition accuracy of 0.8767. Regarding the SVM, which is a frequently used technique in the static hand gesture recognition field, reached an overall recognition accuracy of 0.8333, being the lowest value achieved of the evaluated techniques. It is important to note that, we evaluated the SVM technique varying the number of clusters but the best result was obtained by setting it with one cluster.

In order to be able to perform a deeper analysis, we reduced the confusion matrices to the misclassification rates of static and dynamic labels. In particular, we desired to observe what percentage of the misclassified samples was confused with the same type of gesture (e.g. static gestures confused with other static gestures) and what percentage was confused with the other type of gesture (e.g. static gestures confused with dynamic gestures). Thus, we generated a 2×2 matrix that shows these percentages (see Fig. 6).

At this point, we identified that CNN+LSTM and HAR-CNN approaches did not confuse static gestures with other static gestures. In addition, we noted that the HAR-CNN recognized static gestures with a higher accuracy than dynamic gestures, while our CNN+LSTM approach obtained a higher accuracy recognizing dynamic gestures than static ones. Although both techniques achieved high precision values, this observation allows us to show the contribution made by the LSTM layer that, in short, analyzes the temporal evolution of the features extracted by the CNN, thus improving the analysis of dynamic gestures.

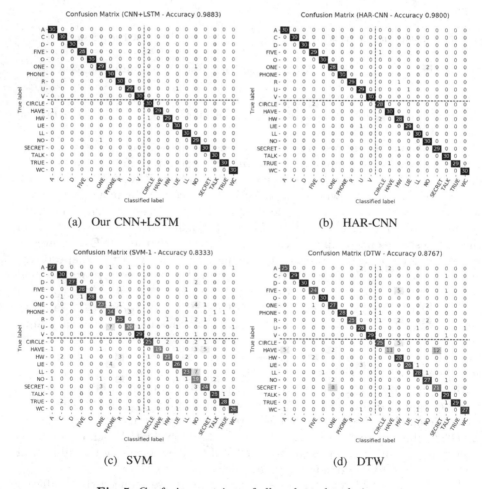

(a) Our CNN+LSTM

(b) HAR-CNN

(c) SVM

(d) DTW

Fig. 5. Confusion matrices of all evaluated techniques.

The SVM technique reached a higher recognition accuracy when classifying static gestures than classifying dynamic ones. This decrease in the recognition accuracy can be understood due to the nature of the SVM technique, which looks for the hyperplane that best separates the classes. Therefore, the SVM benefits when the points of the trajectories are concentrated, which is the case of static gestures, and not when the points are dispersed in a non-linear or non-parametric way, which can be the case of dynamic gestures. In contrast to expectations, the DTW algorithm reached higher accuracy recognizing static gestures than dynamic ones. However, we identified similar behaviors to our CNN+LSTM approach regarding the distribution of misclassified samples.

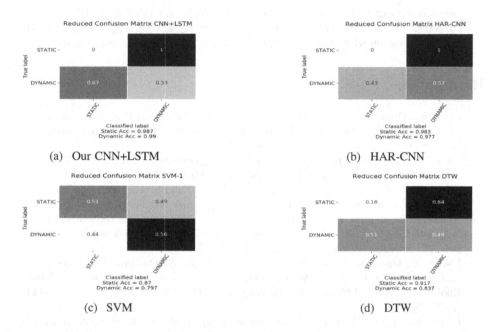

(a) Our CNN+LSTM

(b) HAR-CNN

(c) SVM

(d) DTW

Fig. 6. Reduced confusion matrices of all evaluated techniques.

5 Conclusions and Future Work

In this paper, we have presented a deep learning approach for hybrid hand gesture recognition. The main contribution of this work is a robust approach based on a CNN+LSTM architecture that enables to simultaneously classify both static and dynamic gestures. Moreover, we proposed a data preprocessing step before feeding the neural network that allows us to compare gestures of varied temporal sizes, which is a valuable factor considering real-time scenarios. Furthermore, for the experiments, we generated a hybrid hand gesture dataset with the LMC. This dataset is easy to reproduce with the LMC SDK and we published it online to contribute to this topic. Other contribution is the comparison of our approach, regarding the recognition accuracy, with other well-known techniques of the gesture recognition field such as SVM and DTW.

The encouraging results obtained suggest that static and dynamic hand gestures, even of different temporal sizes, can be recognized with the same approach. At this point, one of our future works is using this approach for addressing the continuous hand gesture recognition problem. In short, it consists in segmenting a stream containing several hand gestures and classifying them. Moreover, it would be interesting to analyze the performance of the approach in low processing capabilities scenarios such as mobile.

Acknowledgements. This work has been supported by CONICET PIP No. 112-201501-00030CO (2015–2017). In addition, we gratefully acknowledge the support of NVIDIA Corporation with the donation of the Titan GPU used for this research.

References

1. Chen, Y., Ding, Z., Chen, Y.L., Wu, X.: Rapid recognition of dynamic hand gestures using leap motion. In: 2015 IEEE International Conference on Information and Automation, pp. 1419–1424. IEEE (2015)
2. Cheng, H., Yang, L., Liu, Z.: Survey on 3D hand gesture recognition. IEEE Trans. Circuits Syst. Video Technol. **26**(9), 1659–1673 (2015)
3. Cheok, M.J., Omar, Z., Jaward, M.H.: A review of hand gesture and sign language recognition techniques. Int. J. Mach. Learn. Cybernet. **10**(1), 131–153 (2019)
4. Chuan, C.H., Regina, E., Guardino, C.: American sign language recognition using leap motion sensor. In: 2014 13th International Conference on Machine Learning and Applications (ICMLA), pp. 541–544. IEEE (2014)
5. Fok, K.Y., Ganganath, N., Cheng, C.T., Chi, K.T.: A real-time ASL recognition system using leap motion sensors. In: 2015 International Conference on Cyber-Enabled Distributed Computing and Knowledge Discovery (CyberC), pp. 411–414. IEEE (2015)
6. Khelil, B., Amiri, H.: Hand gesture recognition using leap motion controller for recognition of Arabic sign language. In: 3rd International conference ACECS 2016 (2016)
7. López, G., Quesada, L., Guerrero, L.A.: A gesture-based interaction approach for manipulating augmented objects using leap motion. In: Cleland, I., Guerrero, L., Bravo, J. (eds.) IWAAL 2015. LNCS, vol. 9455, pp. 231–243. Springer, Cham (2015). https://doi.org/10.1007/978-3-319-26410-3_22
8. Lu, W., Tong, Z., Chu, J.: Dynamic hand gesture recognition with leap motion controller. IEEE Signal Process. Lett. **23**(9), 1188–1192 (2016)
9. Marin, G., Dominio, F., Zanuttigh, P.: Hand gesture recognition with leap motion and kinect devices. In: 2014 IEEE International Conference on Image Processing (ICIP), pp. 1565–1569. IEEE (2014)
10. Marin, G., Dominio, F., Zanuttigh, P.: Hand gesture recognition with jointly calibrated leap motion and depth sensor. Multimed. Tools Appl. **75**(22), 14991–15015 (2016)
11. McCartney, R., Yuan, J., Bischof, H.P.: Gesture recognition with the leap motion controller. In: Proceedings of the International Conference on Image Processing,

Computer Vision, and Pattern Recognition (IPCV). p. 3. The Steering Committee of The World Congress in Computer Science, Computer Engineering and Applied Computing (WorldComp) (2015)

12. Mohandes, M., Aliyu, S., Deriche, M.: Arabic sign language recognition using the leap motion controller. In: 2014 IEEE 23rd International Symposium on Industrial Electronics (ISIE), pp. 960–965. IEEE (2014)

13. Sainath, T.N., Vinyals, O., Senior, A., Sak, H.: Convolutional, long short-term memory, fully connected deep neural networks. In: 2015 IEEE International Conference on Acoustics, Speech and Signal Processing (2015)

14. Sarkar, A.R., Sanyal, G., Majumder, S.: Hand gesture recognition systems: a survey. Int. J. Comput. Appl. 71(15), 25–37 (2013)

15. Wang, Q., Xu, Y., Chen, Y.L., Wang, Y., Wu, X.: Dynamic hand gesture early recognition based on hidden semi-markov models. In: 2014 IEEE International Conference on Robotics and Biomimetics. IEEE (2014)

Feed Forward Classification Neural Network for Prediction of Human Affective States Using Continuous Multi Sensory Data Acquisition

Andrés Rico$^{(\boxtimes)}$ and Leonardo Garrido$^{(\boxtimes)}$

Tecnologico de Monterrey, Writing Lab, TecLabs,
Vicerrectoría de Investigación y Transferencia de Tecnología,
Eugenio Garza Sada 2501 Sur, Col. Tecnológico, 64849 Monterrey, NL, Mexico
`aricom@mit.edu,leonardo.garrido@tec.mx`

Abstract. Machines that are able to recognize and predict human affective states or emotions have become increasingly desirable over the last three decades [10]. This can be attributed to their relevance to human endeavors accompanied by the ubiquity of computing devices and an increasing trend for technology to be ever more present and engrained in people's daily lives. There have been advancements in AI applications that are able to detect a person's affective states through the use of machine learning models. These advancements are mostly based on architectures that take as inputs facial expression image data instances or highly specific sensor data, such as ECG or skin conductivity readings. The problem with these approaches is that models are not being designed with capabilities to receive, and modularly add multiple sensory inputs, therefore failing to operate and deal with the differences that exist on how individuals experience emotions. The present publication proposes a methodology consisting of a continuous multi sensory data acquisition process, and the construction of a feed forward classification neural network with three, 200 neuron, hidden layers. Experimentation was carried out on six different subjects, collecting over 100 h of data points containing environmental and personal variables such as activity (accelerations), light exposure, temperature and humidity. A different model was trained for each one of the subjects for 60–1500 epochs, yielding individual prediction accuracies, on test sets, of 82(%)–95(%).

Keywords: Affective states · Neural networks · Affective computing · Multi sensory inputs · Educational innovation · Tec-21 · Higher education

1 Introduction

With the rise of ubiquitous computing, artificial intelligence and robotics, it has become of great interest to create computer programs that are able to understand

© Springer Nature Switzerland AG 2019
L. Martínez-Villaseñor et al. (Eds.): MICAI 2019, LNAI 11835, pp. 100–111, 2019.
https://doi.org/10.1007/978-3-030-33749-0_9

human affective states. These emotional programs promise to promote Human - Computer Interaction (HCI) to a new level in which humans and technology can start to function as a well orchestrated and natural symbiosis [10]. Machines that are able to understand emotions can improve human - computer interactions with automation in industries like mobility (autonomous vehicles), health care, education (educational innovation endeavors), security and general consumer products.

Modern systems that are capable of understanding emotions or affective states are mostly based on face recognition architectures and specific sensor input. These systems help computers identify a subject's emotional state by analyzing data generated by images containing tagged face expressions or by processing different inputs coming from a highly specific bio sensor measuring ECG readings, skin conductivity or brain activity [1,6,9,14].

There are several problems associated with these approaches. The first problem is that the data acquisition process can be tedious and costly, as seen in [9], due to the fact that data sets need to be large, continuous, labeled and user specific for the implementations to work. In addition to the problems generated by the collection of data, scientific evidence shows that emotional or affective states depend on a much larger set of variables than the ones that are currently being used by state of the art systems, such as contextual and environmental variables [2]. The theory of constructed emotion, described in [3], states that emotions are generated by a diverse combination of variables that are not controlled by the individual nor fully expressed through face gestures or specific body states.

The proposed methodology solves these problems through the use of a multi sensory input as well as a continuous user monitoring system for data collection. The multi sensory input is based on the assumption that humans have specific emotion generators that are responsible for the modulation and creation of emotions, accounting to the complexity of emotional states exposed in [3].

This generators are represented in a broad sense by variables that are part of a human's memories, inner states (Bio-metrics), external states (Environmental states), and social context. The described generators help us underlay a framework in which we can predict an affective state through the acquisition of data points collected from variables that can be found within the broad definitions stated above, see Fig. 1.

The described implementation only takes into account variables that characterize a human's external state or environmental state meaning that we see room for improvement of the system through the addition of data points coming from other emotional generators. With this in mind, we chose to use an MIT terMITe [15] as the primary generator for our model. The MIT terMITe is a compact, lightweight board with internet connectivity capable of sensing variables like 3 axis acceleration, temperature, humidity, light intensity, atmospheric pressure and proximity, the board was developed at the MIT Media Lab's City Science Research Group.

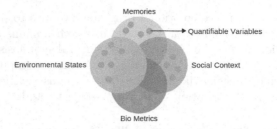

Fig. 1. Emotion Generators Framework Diagram. The framework specifies the different global variables that can be taken into account to construct an emotional or affective state. The green outline on environmental state variables specifies the variables on which this implementation focused on, including user activity. Future implementations on the model will explore sensory acquisition of variables from other generators such as Bio Metrics and Social Context. (Color figure online)

2   Continuous Multi Sensory Data Acquisition

Supervised machine learning techniques require data sets that have examples of the input data as well as examples of the class that each data point belongs to. For this implementation, the input data (X) is obtained using an environmental sensor (MIT terMIte) mounted on the user's chest, see Fig. 2. The environmental sensor gathers data points of three axis acceleration (user activity), temperature, humidity and light intensity one time every second and a half. Affective state class labels (Y) are collected by using a mobile application (Android) in which users can continuously indicate how they feel. The mobile app, which was built specifically for experimentation of the proposed model, uses an affective diagram based on the circumplex model of affect, shown in [12], that allows users to easily switch between feelings, see Fig. 3.

Communication between the sensor and mobile app is done through user datagram protocols (UDP). Data from the environmental sensor is sent to a smart phone, with the mobile app installed, so that the application can label the received data string with the current affective state selected on the user interface. Completed data strings (environmental variables along with affective state labels) are then stored on the smartphone's internal memory as a CSV text file. The CSV file is later processed and used for training of the neural network on an external computer, see Fig. 4.

Batteries used during experimentation allowed for three hour intervals of data acquisition. During each interval a subject would mount the termite on their body and choose affective states from the UI on the mobile app, see Fig. 2. Each one of the six Subjects gather data points for an average of four hours per day. Data obtained from experiments contains around 350,000 data points in total.

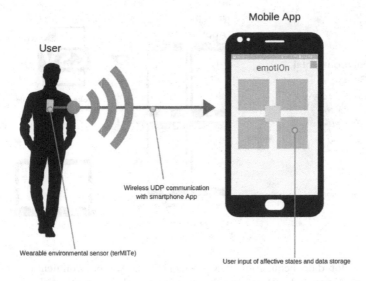

Fig. 2. Data collection system setup. MIT terMITe (environmental sensor) wearable placement on subject's chest through magnetic components attached to case. The sensor is designed to be mounted in a minimally invasive way so that users can carry out activities in a normal way while gathering data. The environmental sensor communicates with mobile app, using UDP, to collect and store data.

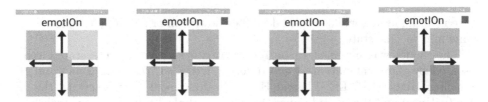

Fig. 3. UI Screenshots with activation of different affective states. The user continuously specifies his affective state for the mobile app to attach labels onto environmental sensor information. Labels activated on images from left to right correspond to LH, HH, LL and HL respectively.

2.1 Units for Environmental, Activity and Affective State Variables

The termite's output variables have standard metric units. User activity is measured by three axis acceleration represented in m/s^2, temperature is measured in Degrees Celsius, the value for humidity represents a percentage describing Relative Humidity in the environment, and light intensity is measured in lux (lx).

Affective state variables are measured and labeled based on the circumplex model of affect proposed in [12]. This model measures affective states based on a two variable coordinate system (x, y) were x refers to the description of valence and y is used to describe arousal. Valence is how pleasant or unpleasant a certain

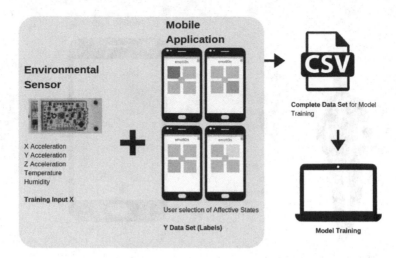

Fig. 4. Steps for data acquisition. Data is sent from the environmental sensor to a mobile phone through UDP communication. The mobile phone, with the emotIOn mobile app installed, receives the data packet and adds the affective state label to complete an entire data string composed of environmental variables and user affective state labels. The data is then stored on the device's internal memory as a csv file for later processing by an external computer.

state is for a human, while arousal describes how calm or agitated a person feels while in a specific state.

The model was modified to be represented with five discrete states, represented by the combination of two different letters; L (meaning Low) and H (meaning High) (HH, LH, LL and HL). The first index is linked with the X axis (valence) and the second index of the pair is linked to the Y axis (arousal), see Fig. 5. In addition to the four combinations of valence and arousal, a fifth state was added to represent a neutral state (N), meaning that the user is not feeling pleasant, unpleasant, agitated nor calm. The five different states were then linked to discrete numbers from one to five with representation shown in Table 1.

Table 1. Codification of affective states with letter index and discrete number representation.

Affective state	Letter index	Discrete number representation
Neutral	N	1
Pleasant and Agitated	HH	2
Unpleasant and Agitated	LH	3
Unpleasant and Calm	LL	4
Pleasant and Calm	HL	5

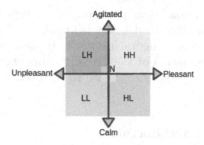

Fig. 5. Modified circumplex model of affect. The model is composed by a two variable coordinate system, were x refers to the description of valence and y is used to describe arousal, composed of five discrete regions (N, HH, LH, LL and HL).

Data Structuring. Data points were structured as matrices containing seven columns and n rows where n is the number of data points obtained for each individual user. The first six columns of the matrix are the variables obtained by the terMITe describing the users environment and activity. The last column of the set is the column that indicates the affective state in which the subject is in. An input (X) matrix was created using the first six columns containing variables of three axis acceleration, temperature, humidity and light intensity, see Table 2. An individual class vector (Y) was created using only the seventh data point of each row where each affective state was labeled with an integer within the range 1–5 ($1 = N$, $2 = HH$, $3 = LH$, $4 = LL$, $5 = HL$).

Table 2. Data structure table for X inputs

X Accel m/s^2	Y Accel m/s^2	Z Accel m/s^2	Temperature C	Light lx	Humidity %
−1.32	−10.3	0.56	34.64	365.75	45.35
0.19	−9.56	1.17	28.30	331.25	43.52
0.19	−9.56	1.17	28.30	331.25	43.52
−0.33	−9.62	1.49	31.34	250	37.94
⋮	⋮	⋮	⋮	⋮	
nth point	nth point	nth point	nth point	nth point	nth point

Data Randomization. Given that emotions don't have drastic changes in time and that new data points were generated every second and a half, the data sets obtained showed uniformity and a slow variation in terms of the seventh column labels (Affective state labels). This uniformity is not desired when training machine learning models so all of the data files' rows were randomly shuffled, as suggested in [4], fifty times to create non uniform labels along all rows before feeding the data into the learning algorithm.

3 Feed Forward Classification Neural Network

Emotions show complex, non linear patterns. These types of patterns are best learned by a machine learning model that is able to deal with non linear functions. Backpropagation allows neural networks to deal with non linear functions [11] so the implementation of a classifying neural network with backpropagation was the evident algorithm to choose to start learning from the gathered data.

3.1 Neural Network Architecture

A highly dense interconnected classifying neural network, see Fig. 6, was built using the high level programming language, Python, with support from the TensorFlow Library [13] and the Keras API [7]. The neural network's architecture consists of an input layer with six neurons, these six neurons copy each one of the environmental sensor data points and passes them directly to the hidden layers.

The network has three hidden layers of 200, densely interconnected, rectifier linear units. Linear rectifying units are artificial neurons with an activation function that can mimic a biological neuron in a more precise way than sigmoid or hyperbolic tangent activated neurons can, yielding better results for complex, non linear problems [5,8]. The rectifier function is defined as $f(x) = max(0, x)$ where x is the input to the function, meaning that every neuron will output the same value that enters it as long as it is above zero. If the input value is equal to, or below zero, the output will be zero.

Lastly, the output layer is made up by five neurons with softmax activation functions. The softmax function is defined as:

$$\sigma(z) : \mathbb{R}^K \to [0, 1]^K \tag{1}$$

$$\sigma(z)_j = \frac{e^z_j}{\sum_{k=1}^{K} e^{z_k}} for j = 1, ..., K. \tag{2}$$

In Eq. 2, z is an input vector for the function made up of the five output neuron values, j is the specific neuron that is being normalized, K is the number of output neurons and $\sigma(z)$ equals a vector with normalized values within the range of $[0, 1]$ representing the probability of an output neuron being chosen as a prediction.

The network classifies an example using the highest output obtained within the five output neurons. The softmax function outputs values between 0 and 1 to the output layers, if you sum the values obtained for each neuron on each training example you get a total value of 1 meaning that the values could also be used to express the model's confidence in the prediction that its making.

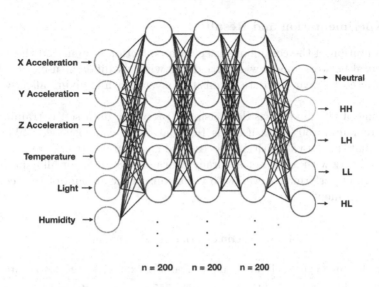

Fig. 6. Neural network architecture diagram showing six neuron input layer (green) along with three, 200 neuron, hidden layers with rectifying linear units (blue) and a five neuron output layer that uses a softmax function for classification (multicolor). (Color figure online)

3.2   Model Training

The environment has different effects on affective states for every individual, some people may be more sensible or less sensible than others to changes in their environment. Taking this fact into account, the neural network was trained using individual data sets, this means that each model can be specifically personalized to the patterns exposed by its user. Training a different model for each user is important because it is the way we can assure that the model learns unique patterns belonging to each individual user.

The model was trained using the complete data set collected for each subject composed of a varied amount of examples specified in Table 3. Each model was trained for an average of 1,500 epochs with the aim of minimizing the error of each specific class by using a sparse categorical cross entropy loss function defined as:

$$(\widehat{y}, y) = -\sum_{j} y_j ln(\widehat{y}_j) \tag{3}$$

In Eq. 3, $\widehat{y}$ is the probability vector that is outputed by the softmax function, j represents each element of the vector and y is a binary vector with a value of 1 for the highest element of $\widehat{y}$ and zeros on the rest of its elements.

3.3 Experimentation and Results

Experimentation of the continuous user data collection system and the training of the neural network model was carried out with six different users. Each user was instructed to wear the data acquisition system while giving affective state inputs.

Training of the model was done using 70% of the data set as training data and the remaining 30% was used as test data. We can visualize Table 3 and conclude that the data acquisition process and the neural network are performing in a desired way with a test set accuracy average of 89.11% for all experiments, keeping a good performance even with variations in the amount of data collected for each experiment.

Table 3. Experimentation results summary

User	Training epochs	Hours of data	Training examples	Test set accuracy
U1	60	141.14	338,757	92.54%
U2	1,500	6.17	14,825	95.08%
U3	1,500	3.71	8,913	92.98%
U4	1,500	4.22	10,129	85.29%
U5	1,500	6.16	14,798	86.75%
U6	1,500	1.66	3,988	82.02%

The learning accuracy curves (test and training) show that the model behaves in a smooth, predictable and desirable manner due to the fact that they show steady changes as training iterates through epochs, see Fig. 7. We can also infer that the model is not overfitting the data because it keeps a high performance on test sets, concluding that our model can generalize to predict new affective states in a reliable manner.

Accuracies shown by the model are promising results for this affective state prediction methodology. While using only one type of sensor can mean that the model is not as robust as it could be, the framework proves to be of interest for further exploration and the addition of new data points to the system will help us build a more robust classification algorithm.

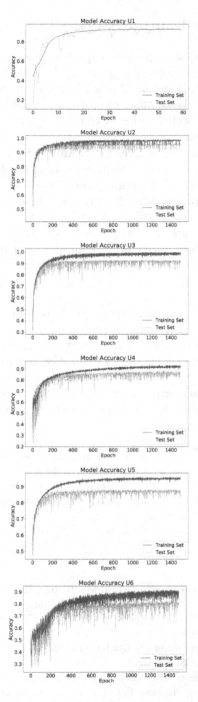

Fig. 7. Figures representing test set and training set accuracies of model on each training epoch for each user (six). Each curve represents training of individual users with their collected data. As users gather more data, the curves become more smooth and stable. We can clearly see that the model is performing as it is expected in terms of accuracy achieves on training and test sets.

4   Conclusions and Future Work

Using a continuous multi sensory data acquisition process allows for the development of data sets that contain more labeled variables that are capable of describing specific affective states. This will help to create systems that do not fail to take into account the complex mixture of variables that are involved in a specific affective state as well as being flexible enough to adapt to the differences that each individual presents.

The model can be made stronger with the integration of emotional generator variables that describe memories, internal states and social context. The addition of reliable sensors capable of detecting more emotional generators would help the model train on a more realistic description of how emotions in humans are generated.

The neural network architecture exposed is flexible enough to integrate a larger number of describing variables without the need to radically change the model, only an increment of input neurons would be necessary to add new sensory inputs, meaning that further developments in sensors can be easily integrated to the exposed system.

Future work will focus on the addition of more input variables through the development of new wearable sensors that are as easy to mount and as non intrusive as the environmental sensor used in this case. Another path that will be taken is a scaling project for educational innovation scenarios to understand how the model behaves when data sets are gathered by using the environmental sensor for significantly larger amounts of time than the times used for this publication and how it can be applied to the improvement of learning through emotion understanding of students.

Acknowledgment. The authors would like to acknowledge the financial support of Writing Lab, TecLabs, Tecnologico de Monterrey as well as the MIT Media Lab's City Science Group, specifically Carson Smuts, Jason Nawyn and Kent Larson, for the technical development and facilitation of the environmental sensors used for this publication's data acquisition process.

References

1. Amores, J., et al.: BioEssence: a wearable olfactory display that monitors cardio-respiratory information to support mental wellbeing. In: 2018 40th Annual International Conference of the IEEE Engineering in Medicine and Biology Society (EMBC). IEEE (2018)
2. Barrett, L.F.: How Emotions are Made: The Secret Life of the Brain. Houghton Mifflin Harcourt, New York (2017)
3. Barrett, L.F.: The theory of constructed emotion: an active inference account of interoception and categorization. Soc. Cogn. Affect. Neurosci. **12**(1), 1–23 (2017)
4. Dietterich, T.G.: Ensemble methods in machine learning. In: Kittler, J., Roli, F. (eds.) MCS 2000. LNCS, vol. 1857, pp. 1–15. Springer, Heidelberg (2000). https://doi.org/10.1007/3-540-45014-9_1

5. Glorot, X., Bordes, A., Bengio, Y.: Deep sparse rectifier neural networks. In: Proceedings of the Fourteenth International Conference on Artificial Intelligence and Statistics (2011)
6. Hernandez, J., Hoque, M.E., Picard, R.W.: Mood meter: large-scale and long-term smile monitoring system (2012)
7. Keras Documentation. https://keras.io/. Accessed 05 May 2019
8. Maas, A.L., Hannun, A.Y., Ng, A.Y.: Rectifier nonlinearities improve neural network acoustic models. In: Proceedings ICML, vol. 30, no. 1 (2013)
9. Mollahosseini, A., Hasani, B., Mahoor, M.H.: Affectnet: a database for facial expression, valence, and arousal computing in the wild. IEEE Trans. Affect. Comput. **10**, 18–31 (2017)
10. Picard, R.W.: Affective Computing. MIT Press, Cambridge (2000)
11. Rumelhart, D.E., et al.: Backpropagation: the basic theory. In: Backpropagation: Theory, Architectures and Applications, pp. 1–34 (1995)
12. Russell, J.A.: A circumplex model of affect. J. Pers. Soc. Psychol. **39**(6), 1161 (1980)
13. Tensor Flow Documentation. http://tensorflow.org/api_docs/. Accessed 05 May 2019
14. Teo, J., et al.: Classification of affective states via EEG and deep learning. Int. J. Adv. Comput. Sci. Appl. **9**(5), 132–142 (2018)
15. TerMITes Homepage. http://termites.synthetic.space/. Accessed 05 May 2019

Advanced Transfer Learning Approach for Improving Spanish Sentiment Analysis

Daniel Palomino$^{(\boxtimes)}$ ⓘ and José Ochoa-Luna ⓘ

Department of Computer Science,
Universidad Católica San Pablo, Arequipa, Peru
{daniel.palomino.paucar,jeochoa}@ucsp.edu.pe

Abstract. In the last years, innovative techniques like Transfer Learning have impacted strongly in Natural Language Processing, increasing massively the state-of-the-art in several challenging tasks. In particular, the Universal Language Model Fine-Tuning (ULMFiT) algorithm has proven to have an impressive performance on several English text classification tasks. In this paper, we aim at developing an algorithm for Spanish Sentiment Analysis of short texts that is comparable to the state-of-the-art. In order to do so, we have adapted the ULMFiT algorithm to this setting. Experimental results on benchmark datasets (InterTASS 2017 and InterTASS 2018) show how this simple transfer learning approach performs well when compared to fancy deep learning techniques.

Keywords: Sentiment analysis · Natural Language Processing · Language Model · Transfer learning

1 Introduction

Sentiment analysis allows us to perform an automated analysis of millions of reviews. With the rapid growth of Twitter, Facebook, Instagram and online review sites, sentiment analysis draws growing attention from both research and industry communities [17]. While it has been extensively researched since 2002 [14], it is still one of the most active research areas in Natural Language Processing (NLP), web mining and social media analytics [27].

Polarity detection is the basic task in sentiment analysis. This task allows us to determine whether a given opinion is positive, negative or neutral. Currently, this text classification problem is usually addressed by machine learning methods. Thus, training data and labeled reviews are used to build a classifier [14]. This machine learning approach used to rely heavily on feature engineering.

Nowadays, in NLP it is common to use text input encoded as word embeddings. Those embeddings, which allow us to encode semantic similarities among words, can be defined using several approaches such as Word2vec [19], Glove [24]

This work was funded by CONCYTEC-FONDECYT under the call E041-01 [contract number 34-2018-FONDECYT-BM-IADT-SE].

and FastText [2], to name a few. When we reuse pre-trained word embeddings in several tasks, we are indirectly employing a transfer learning scheme. In our work, we focus on another transfer learning approach: by pre-training a complete language model for a given language and then use it in text classification, we expect to transfer "knowledge" about the language that allow us to improve the task at hand.

Consequently, in this paper we tackle the polarity detection task using a transfer learning approach based on language modelling. Moreover, we apply this approach on automated classification of Twitter messages in Spanish and its variant Spanish-PE (Peruvian Spanish language). In particular, our approach is based on the Universal Language Model Fine-Tunning (ULMFiT) algorithm [12]. We have chosen ULMFiT because it has proven to have an impressive performance on several English text classification tasks. This kind of transfer learning scheme is novel for Spanish sentiment analysis and could be useful in several domains. Overall, our goal is to provide a general procedure that can be applied with less effort in other text classification works.

Our Spanish sentiment analysis algorithm allows us to obtain comparable state-of-the-art results, in terms of F1, over the InterTASS 2017 benchmark dataset [16] and competitive results over InterTASS 2018 benchmark [15].

In addition, we have compared our proposal against several combinations of neural language model embeddings and deep learning algorithms. Moreover, we have also compared our proposal against several combinations of ELMo [25] language model and deep neural networks. In both cases, the best performance is achieved by our setting which is based on ULMFiT.

The remainder of the paper is organized as follows. In Sect. 2, related works are explained. Background concepts are given in Sect. 3. Our methodology is presented in Sect. 4. Experiments and Results are described in Sect. 5. Conclusions and Future work are given in Sects. 6 and 7.

2   Related Work

There is a plethora of related works regarding sentiment analysis. However, in this section we are only concerned with contributions for the Spanish language. Arguably, one of the most complete Spanish sentiment analysis systems was proposed by Brooke et al. [3], which had a linguistic approach. Recent successful approaches for Spanish polarity classification have been mostly based on machine learning [8].

In the last seven years, the TASS at SEPLN Workshop has been the main source for Spanish sentiment analysis datasets and proposals [9,15,16]. Benchmarks for both the polarity detection task and aspect-based sentiment analysis tasks have been proposed in several editions of this Workshop (Spanish Tweets have been emphasized).

During the last TASS 2018 [15] three deep learning proposals were presented. First, Gonzales et al [10] used CNN, Attention Bidirectional Long Short Term Memory (Att-BLSTM) and Deep Averaging Networks (DAN) which allowed to get the best results on InterTASS-ES. Second, Chiruzzo and Rosa [4] tested several setups of word embeddings, CNN and Long Short Term Memory (LSTM). They obtained good results over InterTASS-ES and InterTASS-CR, their focus was on improving the recognition of neutral tweets by using a mixed-balanced training method for the LSTM. Finally, CNNs, LSTMs, Bidirectional LSTM (BiLSTM) and a hybrid approach between CNN and LSTM were tested by Montanes et al. [20]. We refer to [21] in order to get an in-depth review of several deep Learning approaches for the Spanish language before 2018.

Our proposal is a deep learning approach but, unlike previous approaches, it uses a pre-trained language model to improve the polarity detection task. This setup is novel for the Spanish language.

3 Background

In this section we are interested in defining concepts which allow us to understand how sentiment analysis is approached using Deep Learning and transfer learning.

3.1 Word Representations and Language Modelling

A traditional way to encode words in order to be used for Machine Learning algorithms has evolved from one-hot to word representations. One-hot encodings provide no useful information to a classifier regarding the relationships that may exist between symbols. In fact, if we perform a dot product between two semantically similar words, the result will be a vector of zeros. In contrast, a word representation paradigm proposes to represent a word by means of its neighbours, i.e., its context.

In the last six years, there were several proposals for better symbols encodings. By examining large corpus it is possible to learn word vectors that are able to capture the relationships between words in a surprisingly expressive way. Neural networks and co-occurrence approaches were explored with great success; Characters and sentence embeddings were also tested. Nowadays, word embeddings are ubiquitous and used as input in several NLP tasks.

Recently, word encoding has also been tackled by language modelling. This idea, borrowed from computer vision, is to transfer knowledge from a general language model to a specific NLP task. To do so, several approaches have been proposed so far.

As stated by Devlin et al. [5] there are two strategies for applying pre-trained language representations to downstream tasks: feature-based and fine-tuning. The first approach uses task-specific architectures that include the pre-trained representations as additional features. For instance in ELMo [25], word vectors are learned functions of the internal states of a deep bidirectional language model (biLM), which are pre-trained on a large text corpus. They can be added to existing models. The second approach, fine-tuning, introduces minimal task-specific parameters, and is trained on the downstream tasks by simply fine-tuning all pre-trained parameters. For instance, BERT [5] is designed to pre-train deep bidirectional representations (Transformer architecture) from unlabeled text by jointly conditioning on both left and right context in all layers. Then, the pre-trained BERT model can be fine tuned with just one additional output layer, without substantial task specific architecture modifications. Another fine-tuning example is the Universal Language Model Fine-tuning (ULMFiT) framework [12]. ULMFiT enables robust inductive transfer learning for any NLP task, akin to fine-tuning ImageNet model. To do so, discriminative fine-tuning, slanted triangular learning rates and gradual unfreezing are used. In addition, techniques to retain previous knowledge and avoid catastrophic forgetting during fine-tuning are proposed.

In this paper we follow the ULMFiT approach and to the best of our knowledge, using this kind of inductive transfer learning approach is novel for the Spanish language.

3.2   Sentiment Analysis Using Deep Learning

Given a encoded input based on either word embedding or language models, several Deep Learning algorithms have been proposed for text classification in the past [11,13].

Sentiment Analysis using Convolutional Neural Networks (CNNs) can be approached by using either 2D or 1D architectures. When using a 2D architecture, a sentence can be represented as a matrix. Thus, the sentence length denotes the number of rows and the word embedding dimension denotes the number of columns. This allows us to perform discrete convolutions. However, one must be careful when defining filter sizes, which usually have the same width as word embeddings [13]. In contrast, when working with 1D representation, several word embeddings in a long vector are concatenated and then several convolution layers are applied.

On the other hand, Recurrent Neural Networks (RNNs) are best suited for tasks that involve sequential inputs such as speech and language [11]. These networks process an input sequence one element at a time, maintaining in their hidden units a state vector that implicitly contains information about the history of all the past elements of the sequence. In the context of Sentiment Analysis, an opinionated sentence is a sequence of words. Thus, each word is mapped to a word embedding which is the input at every time step of the RNN. The maximum sequence length denotes the length of the recurrent neural network. Each hidden state models the dependence among a current word and all the precedent words. Usually, the final hidden state, which ideally denotes all the encoded sentence, is connected to a dense layer so as to perform sentiment classification.

4   Methodology

As discussed above, the word embedding and language modelling approaches are the core of modern techniques for text classification which are included into the group of transfer learning methodology. A general transfer learning approach is comprised by two steps:

- The training of a first model on a source domain.
- The reuse or adaptation of the last one within a second model for training on a target domain.

For a complete review of transfer learning methodology, we refer to Pan et al. [23] which describe in detail this approach and their sub-categories.

Recent works on text classification [12] highlight the use of an intermediate step which re-trains the first model using phrases of the target domain or a similar one. This new process, called Fine-Tuning, is inserted in the general pipeline as follows:

- A first model for learning a Language Model (LM) which will be trained using sentences from the source domain. The aim of this step is to learn language essence and to extract deep information about sentence's composition.

  Also, due to the sequential nature of this task [26], a good choice for learning the language model is resort to a Recurrent Neural Network (RNN) architecture. In particular, a suitable model is the weight-dropped AWD-LSTM [18]. It is an architecture of stacked multi-layer LSTM which uses DropConnect on hidden-to-hidden weights so as to perform a recurrent regularization. In addition, a variation of the averaged stochastic gradient method, called NT-ASGD, is used.
- An intermediate step for fine-tuning the language model which re-trains its parameters using the target domain.
- A second model which will be adapted from of the first one, adding two layers for classification. This model takes advantage of the knowledge learned and will be trained on the labeled target domain.

This methodology to address general text classification problems is presented by Howard et al. [12]. The authors also propose techniques to perform fine-tuning and avoid overfitting such as gradual unfreezing, discriminative fine-tuning (Discr), and slanted triangular learning rate (STLR). The overall process is called: Universal Language Model Fine-Tuning (ULMFiT).

The updated pipeline, using ULMFiT, is shown in Fig. 1. The next three stages have been tailored to the Spanish Sentiment Analysis task as follows:

(a) The language model (LM) is trained on a general domain corpus to capture general features of the language in different layers. To do so, we have learned a LM for the Spanish language using Wikipedia data.
(b) The full LM is fine-tuned on target task data using discriminative fine-tuning (Discr) and slanted triangular learning rates (STLR) to learn task-specific features. In our case, the target task is Spanish sentiment analysis from Tweets thus, fine-tuning of the LM is performed using unlabeled Spanish Tweets.
(c) The classifier is fine-tuned on the target task using gradual unfreezing, Discr, and STLR to preserve low-level representations and adapt high-level ones (shaded: unfreezing stages; black: frozen). In our context, the sentiment analysis classifier is fine-tuned using labeled Spanish tweets.

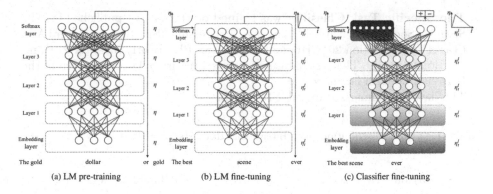

(a) LM pre-training   (b) LM fine-tuning   (c) Classifier fine-tuning

Fig. 1. Stages of updated pipeline using ULMFiT [12].

We have adapted the ULMFiT pipeline for Sentiment Analysis on Spanish tweets datasets and experiments (next section) show effectiveness of this approach in contrast to other modern transfer learning techniques.

5   Experiments

A complete description about the hardware and software requirements for reproducing this paper are described in this section. In addition, we show the hyperparameters tuned during experimentation by picking a learning rate that lead to convergence without overfitting and regularization.

5.1   Technical Resources

All experiments were carried out on Jupyter Notebooks running Python 3.6 kernel and PyTorch 0.3.1.

For a complete detail about dependencies, the repository of the project is available at [22]. All models were trained on a Google Cloud VM with 2 vcpu, 13 GB of RAM and GPU K80 with 12 GB GDDR5.

5.2   Datasets

To train the entire model end to end, three data sources were used:

– **The General Language Model** was trained on a dump of the entire Spanish Wikipedia. The top 100 million articles were only kept and the vocabulary was limited to 60,000 tokens in accordance to the English setting approach.
– **The Specific Language Model** was trained using 140,000 unlabeled tweets for the Spanish language that were collected from Twitter API using Tweepy (3.7.0).

– **The Specific Task Classifier** was trained on the dataset published by The Spanish Society for Natural Language Processing (SEPLN) for InterTASS (Task1) Competition 2017 [16] and InterTASS-PE (Task1/Sub-task 2) Competition 2018 [15]. This last dataset was extracted from Tweets written in the Peruvian Spanish language.
The data is summarized in Table 1a and b.

Table 1. Tweets distribution over InterTASS datasets (P = Positive, N = Negative, NEU = Neutral).

	(a) InterTASS 2017.		
	Training	Development	Test
P	317	156	642
NEU	133	69	216
N	416	219	767
NONE	138	62	274
Total	1008	506	1899

	(b) InterTASS-PE 2018.		
	Training	Development	Test
P	231	95	430
NEU	166	61	367
N	242	106	472
NONE	316	238	159
Total	1000	500	1428

5.3 Pre-processing

Each corpus was pre-processed as follows:

– Twitter user references were replaced by the token "user_ref".
– URL references were replaced by the token "hyp_link".
– Hashtags comments were replaced by the token "hash_tag".
– Slang words were replaced by their formal equivalent, for example, "q" and "k" were replaced by the correct word "que".
– Interjections denoting laughter ("jaja", "jeje", "jiji", "jojo") were replaced by the token "risa_ja", "risa_je", "risa_ji", "risa_jo".
– Any other character like "\n", "&lt", "&gt", "\xa0" were replaced by a space character.
– Redundant space character were removed.
– The text was converted to lowercase.

5.4 Architecture

The architecture for the General Language Model as well as for the Specific Language Model are based on the AWD-LSTM model [18]. The model is comprised by a three stacked layer LSTM model with 1150 units in the hidden layer and a embedding of size 400.

The classifier layer has two linear blocks with batch normalization and dropout. Rectified linear unit activations are used in the intermediate layer and a softmax function in the last layer.

5.5   Hyperparameters

For both training datasets, InterTASS (Task1) Competition 2017 [16] and InterTASS-PE (Task1/Sub-task 2) Competition 2018 [15], the hyperparameters are similar across all stages of the ULMFiT method.

The main hyperparameters shared for all models were:

- Backpropagation Through Time (BPTT): 70
- Weight Decay (WD): $1e{-}7$
- The batch size (BS) was limited by the available GPU memory.

Besides these parameters, the models used different configurations for the learning rate (LR), dropouts, cyclical learning rate (CLR) and slanted triangular learning rates (STLR). Additionally, gradient clipping (CLIP) was applied to the models.

Two configurations of dropout were used (see Table 2).

Table 2. Dropout configurations.

Dropout	ULMFiT [12]	AWD-LSTM [18]
Embedding Dropout	0.02	0.10
Input Dropout	0.25	0.60
Weight Dropout	0.20	0.50
Hidden Dropout	0.15	0.20
Output Dropout	0.10	0.40

General Language Model. The hyperparameters for this model were directly transferred from [12] without changes and scripts used were taken from the official Fastai [6] and ULMFiT [7] repositories.

Specific Language Model. A graphic learning rate finder (LRF) was used to determine suitable candidate learning rates. With the information extracted from this, a suitable learning rate (LR) was set to 12 for InterTASS 2017 and 5 for InterTASS-PE 2018 dataset.

Also, the gradient clipping (CLIP) was set to 0.25 and the dropout configuration (Table 2) was set to 0.8*ULMFiT.

Specific Task Classifier. Similar to the previous model, a graphic learning rate finder (LRF) was used to determine suitable candidate learning rates. A suitable LR was set to $3e{-}3$ for InterTASS 2017 and $2.5e{-}3$ for InterTASS-PE 2018 dataset.

Also, the gradient clipping (CLIP) was set to 0.25 and the dropout configuration (Table 2) was set to 1.0*ULMFiT.

5.6   Results

The results for InterTASS (Task1) Competition 2017 [16] were better than expected as shown in Table 3a, achieving the second best result, according to M-F1 metric (the ELiRF-UPV team reached a M-F1 score of 0.493).

Furthermore, results on InterTASS-PE (Task1/Sub-task 2) Competition 2018 [15] are shown in Table 3b. While they weren't the best, they are within the best eight results of the competition.

Table 3. Results over InterTASS Test datasets.

(a) InterTASS 2017.

Team	M-F1	Acc.
ELiRF-UPV-run1	0.493	0.607
Our proposal	**0.481**	**0.567**
RETUYT-svm_cnn	0.471	0.596
ELiRF-UPV-run3	0.466	0.597
ITAINNOVA-model4	0.461	0.476
jacerong-run-2	0.460	0.602
jacerong-run-1	0.459	0.608
INGEOTEC-evodag001	0.457	0.507
RETUYT-svm	0.457	0.583
tecnolengua-sentonly	0.456	0.582

(b) InterTASS-PE 2018.

Team	M-F1	Acc.
retuyt-cnn-pe-1	0.472	0.494
atalaya-pe-lr-50-2	0.462	0.451
retuyt-lstm-pe-2	0.443	0.488
retuyt-svm-pe-2	0.441	0.471
ingeotec-run1	0.439	0.447
elirf-intertass-pe-run-2	0.438	0.461
atalaya-mlp-sentiment	0.437	0.520
retuyt-svm-pe-1	0.437	0.474
Our proposal	**0.436**	**0.463**
elirf-intertass-pe-run-1	0.435	0.440

When training the specific language model (fine-tuning the specific LM in the step 2 of the general pipeline) an interesting evolution of results is observed, Fig. 2a and b show these insights. The first 5 experiments on both benchmarks, which use only the train and development datasets for training the specific language model, turned out poor results. Conversely, the next 5 experiments that included unlabeled tweets extracted using the Twitter API yielded better results.

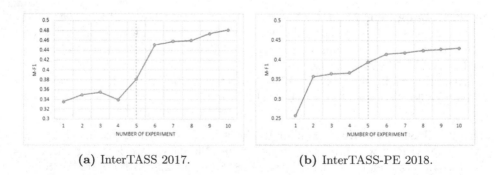

(a) InterTASS 2017.   **(b)** InterTASS-PE 2018.

Fig. 2. Evolution of results over InterTASS Test datasets.

We have performed additional experiments using word embeddings trained with the ULMFiT language model (the word embeddings built from AWD-LSTM model) and other classifiers. Thus, CNN, Multi-layer Perceptron (MLP), Support Vector Machine (SVM) and Gaussian Naive Bayes (GNB) have been tested. We have also used a high performance method for building sentence embeddings [1] called Sentence Inverse Frequency (SIF). As shown in Table 4a, none of those combinations show promising results, the ULMFiT approach (Sect. 4) performed better.

Table 4. Our proposal against other approaches

(a) ULMFiT vs different classifiers using the same AWD-LSTM word embedding.

	M-F1
ULMFiT	0.481
AWD-LSTM + CNN	0.448
AWD-LSTM + MLP	0.338
AWD-LSTM + SIF + SVM	0.385
AWD-LSTM + SIF + GNB	0.257

(b) ULMFiT vs different classifiers using the same modern ELMo word embedding.

	M-F1
ULMFiT	0.481
ELMo + CNN	0.321
ELMo + MLP	0.284
ELMo + SIF + SVM	0.396
ELMo + SIF + GNB	0.376

We have also performed comparisons against other transfer learning approaches based on language modelling. Results using the state-of-the-art method Deep Contextualized word representation [25], also called Embeddings from Language Models (ELMo), are shown in Table 4b. These results demonstrate that ULMFiT is the best choice.

6   Conclusions

We have adapted an inductive transfer learning approach called ULMFiT in order to perform sentiment analysis on Spanish Tweets. To the best of our knowledge this is a novel approach for this language. We have also demonstrated that such design choice is the best in comparison to other classifiers like Convolutional Neural Networks, Support Vector Machine, Gaussian Naive Bayes and other state-of-the-art transfer learning approaches such as ELMo.

Our best result, which is comparable to the state-of-the-art, was obtained on the InterTASS 2017 dataset [16]. Furthermore, we have obtained competitive results over the InterTASS-PE 2018 dataset which is composed by Tweets in Spanish from the Peruvian dialect [15].

7   Future Work

Recently, another transfer learning approach, called Bidirectional Embedding Representations from Transformers (BERT) [5], has emerged as the state-of-the-art in many NLP tasks. The use of this language model could enhance the performance of the pipeline presented in this work.

Also, there is a room for improvement if the language model approach is combined with data augmentation techniques. In this sense, new approaches for data augmentation such as the "BERT contextual augmentation" algorithm [28] could help us to improve our results if applied to our smalls datasets.

References

1. Arora, S., Liang, Y., Ma, T.: A simple but tough-to-beat baseline for sentence embeddings. In: International Conference on Learning Representations (2017)
2. Bojanowski, P., Grave, E., Joulin, A., Mikolov, T.: Enriching word vectors with subword information. Trans. Assoc. Comput. Linguist. 5, 135–146 (2017)
3. Brooke, J., Tofiloski, M., Taboada, M.: Cross-linguistic sentiment analysis: From English to Spanish. In: Proceedings of RANLP, vol. 2009, pp. 50–54 (2009)
4. Chiruzzo, L., Rosá, A.: RETUYT-InCo at TASS 2018: sentiment analysis in Spanish variants using neural networks and SVM. In: Proceedings of TASS 2018: Workshop on Sentiment Analysis at SEPLN, pp. 57–63 (2018)
5. Devlin, J., Chang, M., Lee, K., Toutanova, K.: BERT: pre-training of deep bidirectional transformers for language understanding. CoRR abs/1810.04805 (2018)
6. Fastai: Fastai, May 2019. https://github.com/fastai/fastai
7. Fastai: ULMFiT, May 2019. https://github.com/fastai/fastai/tree/master/courses/dl2/imdb_scripts
8. Garcia, M., Martinez, E., Villena, J., Garcia, J.: Tass 2015 - the evolution of the spanish opinion mining systems. Procesamiento de Lenguaje Natural 56, 33–40 (2016)
9. Garcia-Cumbreras, M.A., Villena-Roman, J., Martinez-Camara, E., Diaz-Galiano, M., Martin-Valdivia, T., Ureña Lopez, A.: Overview of TASS 2016. In: Proceedings of TASS 2016: Workshop on Sentiment Analysis at SEPLN, pp. 13–21 (2016)
10. Gonzalez, J.A., Hurtado, L.F., Pla, F.: ELiRF-UPV at TASS 2018: sentiment analysis in twitter based on deep learning. In: Proceedings of TASS 2018: Workshop on Sentiment Analysis at SEPLN, pp. 37–44 (2018)
11. Graves, A.: Supervised Sequence Labelling with Recurrent Neural Networks. Studies in Computational Intelligence. Springer, Berlin (2012). https://doi.org/10.1007/978-3-642-24797-2. https://cds.cern.ch/record/1503877
12. Howard, J., Ruder, S.: Universal language model fine-tuning for text classification. In: Proceedings of the 56th Annual Meeting of the Association for Computational Linguistics (Volume 1: Long Papers), pp. 328–339. Association for Computational Linguistics, Melbourne, July 2018. https://www.aclweb.org/anthology/P18-1031
13. Kim, Y.: Convolutional neural networks for sentence classification. In: Proceedings of the 2014 Conference on Empirical Methods in Natural Language Processing, EMNLP 2014, 25–29 October 2014, Doha, Qatar, A meeting of SIGDAT, a Special Interest Group of the ACL, pp. 1746–1751 (2014). http://aclweb.org/anthology/D/D14/D14-1181.pdf
14. Liu, B.: Sentiment Analysis and Opinion Mining. Morgan and Claypool Publishers, San Rafael (2012)
15. Martinez-Camara, E., et al.: Overview of TASS 2018: opinions, health and emotions. In: Proceedings of TASS 2018: Workshop on Sentiment Analysis at SEPLN, pp. 13–27 (2018)

16. Martinez-Camara, E., Diaz-Galiano, M., Garcia-Cumbreras, M.A., Garcia-Vega, M., Villena-Roman, J.: Overview of TASS 2017. In: Proceedings of TASS 2017: Workshop on Sentiment Analysis at SEPLN, pp. 13–21 (2017)
17. McGlohon, M., Glance, N., Reiter, Z.: Star quality: aggregating reviews to rank products and merchants. In: Proceedings of Fourth International Conference on Weblogs and Social Media (ICWSM) (2010)
18. Merity, S., Keskar, N.S., Socher, R.: Regularizing and optimizing LSTM language models. CoRR abs/1708.02182 (2017). http://arxiv.org/abs/1708.02182
19. Mikolov, T., Sutskever, I., Chen, K., Corrado, G.S., Dean, J.: Distributed representations of words and phrases and their compositionality. In: Burges, C.J.C., Bottou, L., Welling, M., Ghahramani, Z., Weinberger, K.Q. (eds.) Advances in Neural Information Processing Systems 26, pp. 3111–3119. Curran Associates, Inc. (2013). http://papers.nips.cc/paper/5021-distributed-representations-of-words-and-phrases-and-their-compositionality.pdf
20. Montañes, R., Aznar, R., del Hoyo, R.: Application of a hybrid deep learning model for sentiment analysis in Twitter. In: Proceedings of TASS 2018: Workshop on Sentiment Analysis at SEPLN, pp. 51–56 (2018)
21. Ochoa-Luna, J., Ari, D.: Deep neural network approaches for spanish sentiment analysis of short texts. In: Simari, G.R., Fermé, E., Gutiérrez Segura, F., Rodríguez Melquiades, J.A. (eds.) IBERAMIA 2018. LNCS (LNAI), vol. 11238, pp. 430–441. Springer, Cham (2018). https://doi.org/10.1007/978-3-030-03928-8_35
22. Palomino, D.: ULMFit implementation for TASS dataset evaluation, May 2019. https://github.com/dpalominop/ULMFit
23. Pan, S.J., Yang, Q.: A survey on transfer learning. IEEE Trans. Knowl. Data Eng. 22(10), 1345–1359 (2010). https://doi.org/10.1109/TKDE.2009.191
24. Pennington, J., Socher, R., Manning, C.D.: Glove: global vectors for word representation. In: Empirical Methods in Natural Language Processing (EMNLP), pp. 1532–1543 (2014). http://www.aclweb.org/anthology/D14-1162
25. Peters, M., et al.: Deep contextualized word representations. In: Proceedings of the 2018 Conference of the North American Chapter of the Association for Computational Linguistics: Human Language Technologies, Volume 1 (Long Papers). pp. 2227–2237. Association for Computational Linguistics, New Orleans, Louisiana, June 2018. https://doi.org/10.18653/v1/N18-1202, https://www.aclweb.org/anthology/N18-1202
26. Rother, K., Rettberg, A.: ULMFiT at GermEval-2018: a deep neural language model for the classification of hate speech in German Tweets. In: Proceedings of the GermEval 2018 Workshop, pp. 113–119 (2018)
27. Tang, D., Wei, F., Qin, B., Yang, N., Liu, T., Zhou, M.: Sentiment embeddings with applications to sentiment analysis. IEEE Trans. Knowl. Data Eng. 28(2), 496–509 (2016)
28. Wu, X., Lv, S., Zang, L., Han, J., Hu, S.: Conditional BERT contextual augmentation. CoRR abs/1812.06705 (2018). http://arxiv.org/abs/1812.06705

AE-CharCNN: Char-Level Convolutional Neural Networks for Aspect-Based Sentiment Analysis

Ulisses Brisolara Corrêa[1,2]([⊠]) [iD] and Ricardo Matsumura Araújo[2] [iD]

[1] Computer Science Program (PPGC), Center for Technological Advancement (CDTec), Federal University of Pelotas (UFPel), Pelotas, RS 96010-610, Brazil
{ub.correa,ricardo}@inf.ufpel.edu.br
[2] Sul-rio-grandense Federal Institute of Education, Science, and Technology (IFSul), Charqueadas, RS 96745-000, Brazil
ulissescorrea@charqueadas.ifsul.edu.br

Abstract. Sentiment Analysis was developed to support individuals in the harsh task of obtaining significant information from large amounts of non-structured opinionated data sources, such as social networks and specialized reviews websites. A yet more challenging task is to point out which part of the target entity is addressed in the opinion. This task is called Aspect-Based Sentiment Analysis. The majority of work focuses on coping with English text in the literature, but other languages lack resources, tools, and techniques. This paper focuses on Aspect-Based Sentiment Analysis for Accommodation Services Reviews written in Brazilian Portuguese. Our proposed approach uses Convolution Neural Networks with inputs in Character-level. Results suggest that our approach outperforms lexicon-based and LSTM-based approaches, displaying state-of-the-art performance for binary Aspect-Based Sentiment Analysis.

Keywords: Aspect-Based Sentiment Analysis · Convolutional Neural Networks · Char-level embedding

1 Introduction

We are living in the social media era. People's opinions about a plethora of topics can be abundantly found on the Internet. This kind of information is extremely valuable to other individuals, organizations, and government entities.

According to Liu [12], whenever people have to make decisions they seek out others' opinions, usually friends and family, to support their choices. Social networks allows for opinions to be more easily accessible. Now one can easily get opinions directly from users that already have bought a product or from some experts in this kind of product. Thus individuals can take advantage of the experiences of others. But the amount of opinionated content generated by users

© Springer Nature Switzerland AG 2019
L. Martínez-Villaseñor et al. (Eds.): MICAI 2019, LNAI 11835, pp. 124–135, 2019.
https://doi.org/10.1007/978-3-030-33749-0_11

on the Internet day by day makes it too difficult to manually distill significant information, even for big organizations.

Sentiment Analysis is the Computer Science response to this problem. This research area, also known as Opinion Mining, was developed to support individuals in the harsh task of obtain significant information from large amounts of non-structured opinionated data sources, like social networks and specialized reviews websites (such as: IMDB, Rotten Tomatoes, Metacritic, etc.).

Extract significant information about opinions from raw text is a hard task. Opinionated text can present opinions towards different entities, or conflicting opinions about same entity. Correctly address the target of an opinion is crucial to ensure the perfect understanding of the expressed sentiment. Aspect-based Sentiment Analysis (ABSA) is a sentiment analysis process that is done paying particular attention to the aspect to which the sentiment is addressed.

Opinion Mining research focuses on tasks related to: sentiment classification, subjectivity detection, sentiment orientation detection, etc. Works in this research area usually apply techniques based on classical Natural Language Processing (NLP), such as: hand-crafted linguistic feature extraction, structural pattern detection, and shallow models (e.g. Support Vector Machines and Logistic Regression) [21].

Deep Learning architectures and algorithms are getting significant results in several Computer Science problems. Computer vision is clearly the field where Deep Learning (DL) application has displayed more significant gains, mostly with Convolutional Neural Networks (CNN), starting with the work of Krizhevsky et al. [11]. Based on these good results in computer vision and pattern recognition, NLP researchers have been trying to apply Deep Learning on textual input. Recently, NLP research has been gradually adopting more complex and flexible models, based on Deep Learning, as can be seen in recent top conferences [21].

Sentiment Analysis, as an NLP task, has also been taking advantage of these techniques [17]. Works based on character-level convolutional networks have achieved promising results in text classification and document-level sentiment analysis [19,20,23]. This kind of approach deals naturally with typos, encoding errors, and rare words. Moreover, they are less susceptible to external resources influence on performance, when comparing with lexicon-based sentiment classifiers, which are highly dependent of those resources [8].

Works focused in dealing with English text are plenty in the literature, however other languages lack good tools and techniques to NLP and Sentiment Analysis [6,7]. Because of this disparity some authors tried approaches based on language translation with reasonable results [1,15], but making the approach dependant of the translation tool.

This work aims to apply Aspect-Embedding to make Character-level Convolution Neural Networks compliant with sentiment classification in ABSA. Previous works used Char-level CNNs to classify sentiment in document-level. But, following Chaves et al. [3], up to 86% of hotel's reviews present both positive and negative opinions about different hotel's aspects (parts or attributes of the hotel). Then document-level sentiment analysis will have limited performance in this domain. In our approach, the network receives the review and the aspect to be assessed in Brazilian Portuguese. We evaluate our approach against two state-of-art approaches [7,18].

The remaining of this text is organized as follow. A succinct overview about Sentiment Analysis is shown in Sect. 2. Section 3 discusses relevant related work. Next, Sect. 4 presents our proposed approach. Experimental methodology and results are shown and analyzed in Sect. 5. Finally Sect. 6 summarizes our contributions and future work.

2   Sentiment Analysis

2.1   Opinion Definition

Liu [12] proposes a taxonomy for opinions. Two main classes are highlighted: regular and comparative opinions. *Regular Opinions* refers a entity directly or indirectly, while *Comparative Opinions* expresses relations between two or more entities, focusing on their similarities or differences.

Most works in Sentiment Analysis deal with Regular Opinions, frequently referenced simply as *Opinions*. Liu [12] formally defines an opinion as a quadruple,

$$Opinion : (g, s, h, t),\tag{1}$$

where:

- g – entity towards sentiment is addressed;
- s – sentiment of the opinion;
- h – opinion holder, the person or organization who holds the opinion;
- t – time when the opinion was expressed.

The full understanding of all these elements is crucial to ensure a Sentiment Analysis system with the best results. In a more fine grained way we can decompose g to discover the specific *aspect* towards which the opinion is targeted. Aspects can be parts or attributes of entities, e.g. room and comfort are aspects of hotel.

Liu [12] states that an entity (e) can be a product, service, topic, person, organization, issue, or event. Entities can be described as pairs:

$$e : (T, W),\tag{2}$$

where:

- T – hierarchy of parts, subparts, and so on;
- W – set of attributes of e.

Sentiment Analysis can be done at different levels of granularity. Some works assign a single sentiment orientation to a whole document. Other works break documents in finer grained pieces (such as: blocks, sentences or paragraphs), then extract their sentiment orientation. Both approaches suppose that the text being analyzed has an opinion about an entity chosen previously. This assumption can lead the classifier to high error rates by assigning sentiment orientation to the wrong target entity.

A more precise Sentiment Analysis approach is aspect-based. Aspect-Based Sentiment Analysis (ABSA) summarizes the sentiment orientation towards each entity's aspects. These fine-grained results are more meaningful, enabling a better understanding of the entity pros and cons.

According to Pang et al. [13], ABSA should be split in two subtasks:

1. the identification of product aspects (features and subparts), and
2. extraction of the sentiment orientation (opinions) associated with these aspects.

This work proposes a novel convolutional network architecture to tackle with the last subtask.

3   Related Works

Aspect-Based Sentiment Analysis is crucial to ensure that companies, governments, or even individuals get adequate information from large data sets of opinionated text. Liu [12] states that traditional ML methods, such as Support Vector Machines or Naïve Bayes, are inadequate to deal with ABSA. Currently, just a few works in literature deals with Portuguese texts in aspect-level [7].

Freitas [7] proposes a novel lexicon-based approach to sentiment analysis in aspect-level. Proposed approach comprises four steps: pre-processing, feature identification (aspect extraction), polarity identification, and polarity summarizing. Work was evaluated over a data set of accommodation sector. Author made a fine-grain analysis, at aspect-level, where explicit and implicit references to features were recognized using a domain ontology. The best results were obtained using POS-tagging extracted with TreeTagger, sentiment lexicon synsets with polarities from Onto.PT, and syntactic pattern detection, adjective position rule for negative polarity identification and presence or absence of polarity words in surrounding window for positive polarity identification.

Research from Blaz and Becker [1] proposes a hybrid approach, where the sentiment classification is made using both Lexicon-based and Machine Learning (ML) based approaches. They propose the automatically creation of a Domain Dictionary with opinionated terms in the Information Technology (IT) domain. Then they use these terms to filter ticket for sentiment analysis. For evaluate the work, the authors propose 3 approaches (one based on dictionary and two based on position of tokens in tickets) to calculating the polarity of terms in tickets. The study was developed using 34,895 tickets from 5 organizations, from which 2,333 tickets were randomly selected to compose a Gold Standard. The best results display an average precision and recall of 82.83% and 88.42%, which outperforms the compared sentiment analysis solutions.

Carvalho et al. [2] investigate the expression of opinions about human entities in UGC. A set of 2,800 online comments about news was manually annotated, following a rich annotation scheme designed for this purpose. The authors conclude that it is difficult to correctly identify positive opinions because they are much less frequent than negative ones and particularly exposed to verbal irony. The human entities recognition is also a challenge because they are frequently mentioned by pronouns, definite descriptions, and nicknames.

When analyzing works focused on other languages, we can find approaches based on newer techniques, such as Convolutional Neural Networks, Recurrent Networks, and Attention Mechanisms.

Convolutional Neural Networks already have been used to infer sentiment present on microblogs' posts [5,14,16,17,19,20,23]. Commonly using word-embeddings as input for Document-Level Sentiment Analysis, mainly over microblogs' posts. This kind of approach lacks support for words unseen on training, demanding extra pre-processing steps. For instance, input texts can be pre-processed with stemming or lemmatization to group words, reducing the effect of absent words in the *corpus* training set.

FastText word embedding method proposes to look at words as sets of n-grams, what can reduce this kind of problem, since the unknown word can be created by a composition of trained n-grams [10]. One can argues that word embeddings pre-trained over large data sets, like Wikipedia, are available, notwithstanding Sentiment Analysis is highly dependent on the text domain. Thus, this kind of approach tends to be hampered by the usage of domain bias and jargon.

In the other hand, Character-Level models cope with text in a smaller granularity, intrinsically dealing with typos and enabling a behaviour similar to stemming [23]. CharCNN [23], Conv-Char-S [19], and NNLS [20] exploit these advantages to text classification, including Document-Level Sentiment Analysis.

Wang et al. [18] propose a novel approach to ABSA using Long Short-Term Memories (LSTM) with Attention Mechanism. Their network has two inputs, one representing the text to gauge sentiment and another to represent which aspect we want the network to pay attention to.

Authors claim that it's the first approach to generate distinct embeddings for each input, one for aspects and another for reviews. Aspect-Embeddings (AE) differs from the embedding used to represent words in the networks' input. Wang et al. [18] evaluate three different approaches: AT-LSTM, AE-LSTM, and ATAE-LSTM. *AT* denotes approaches that employ Attention mechanism, while *AE* denotes approaches that use Aspect Embedding.

We propose approaches that differs from early work by applying char-level CNNs to evaluate sentiment in Aspect-level. In order to do so, we added an extra input to CharCNN [23] and NNLS [20] models. This extra input is an Aspect-Embedding, based on the one proposed by Wang et al. [18]. As far as we know, there's no work using char-level CNNs with an extra input representing aspects in an ABSA approach. A more detailed explanation is given in Sect. 4.

4   Proposed Approach

This work proposes an Aspect-Based Sentiment Analysis approach based on Character-level Convolutional Neural Networks, with an additional Aspect Embedding input.

ABSA is a specific kind of text classification problem. To extract the sentiment orientation of an opinionated text towards a specific entity's aspect demands an extra input, addressing the aspect of interest or a model that predicts both sentiment orientation and target aspect.

Our approach takes advantage of the concepts of different approaches. We adopted Aspect-Embedding idea from Wang et al. [18] and applied in a Character-Level Convolutional Neural Networks, CharCNN [22]. Besides that, we tried a shallower char-level architecture, NNLS, which is smaller and presents better results than CharCNN on Document-Level Sentiment Analysis [20].

We call our approach Aspect-Embedding Character-Level Convolutional Neural Network (shortened as AE-CharCNN). AE-CharCNN takes advantage of the character-level CNN approach, avoiding complex pre-processing because it copes with text in a smaller granularity, intrinsically dealing with typos, encoding errors, and enabling a behaviour similar to stemming and making it easy to train a method tolerant to typos and encoding errors [19,20,23].

Figures 1 and 2 presents the two char-level CNN architectures we propose to solve ABSA. Figure 1 presents the architecture of AE-CharCNN-v1, based on the CharCNN model [23]. Figure 2 presents the AE-CharCNN-v2, based on the NNLS-v2 model [20]. Green blocks represent original model's flow, while red blocks represent the flow we added to deal with aspects.

Both models are fed with char-level embeddings, starting the green flow. Aspect-embedding also is a char-level embedding, but does not share information with the embedding used to reviews. The features at the end of both flows are concatenated in a single input to the classifying stage, composed of three dense (fully connected) layers in AE-CharCNN-v1 and a single dense layer in AE-CharCNN-v2.

As can be seen in Figs. 1 and 2, we have two flows in ours network architectures, one for aspects and another for the reviews. Both flows receive a character-level input. Features generated by these flows are concatenated before the application of the fully connected (dense) layers.

In our approaches, aspect-embedding inputs cannot exceed 100 characters. Review inputs are set to 2204 characters, length of the longest review in the corpus. In both cases, if bigger inputs are fed they are cut in the limit length. Otherwise, if smaller inputs are given, they are padded to the dimensions aforementioned.

Both architectures weights were adjusted using Adam optimizer, during 20 epochs, 32 samples batch size, and with a learning rate set to $10e^{-3}$. All hidden layers use ReLU activation function. The kernel size of feature extraction layers can be seen in Figs. 1 and 2.

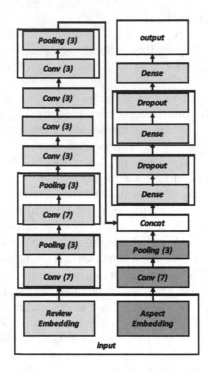

Fig. 1. Aspect-Embedding CharCNN (AE-CharCNN). (Color figure online)

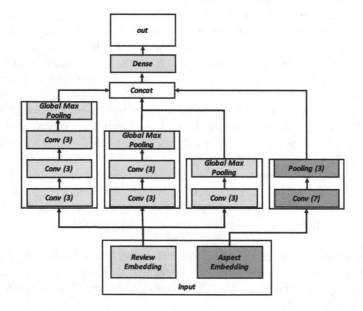

Fig. 2. Aspect-Embedding CharCNN v2 (AE-CharCNN-v2). (Color figure online)

Our model was trained with Cross Entropy Loss, which combines a LogSoftmax with Negative Log Likelihood Loss (NLLLoss)[1]. Original work from LeCun [22] was developed using torch library and uses NLLLoss and an additional LogSoftmax layer at the end of network architecture. Weights were initialized using a Gaussian distribution. The mean and standard deviation used for initializing the large model is (0, 0.02) and small model (0, 0.05).

5   Experiments and Results

This Section presents our experiments over the proposed approach, as well as the comparison with two state-of-the-art approaches: Lexicon-based for Portuguese [7] and LSTM-based with Attention Mechanism adapted from English [18]. All approaches were tested over the same *corpus*. Source code for experiments presented here is available in https://github.com/ulissesbcorrea/ae-charcnn.

5.1   *Corpus* – TripAdvisor's Reviews About Porto Alegre Accommodation Services

Our experiments were conducted over a *corpus* of reviews about Porto Alegre Accommodation Services extracted from TripAdvisor. Freitas [7] created that *corpus* manually annotated with aspect level sentiment orientation.

The *corpus* contains all TripAdvisor's reviews about hotels located in Porto Alegre until May 2014. There are 987 entries with opinions about hotel's aspects. A total of 194 hotel reviews were manually annotated, assigning polarity to opinions targeted to every hotel aspect directly or indirectly referenced in the review.

Each data set entry links one entity's aspect with one concept from a domain ontology (HOntology [4]). The annotation process collected explicit references to hotel's aspects, the data set contains 987 explicit opinions about HOntology concepts, we use this entries as input to out model. Besides that, annotators also collected implicit and explicit references to TripAdvisor's categories (Localization, Room, Service, Value, and Cleanliness). There are 269 explicit and 71 implicit mentions to these categories.

5.2   Baselines

ATAE-LSTM [18]. Our first baseline is an implementation of ATAE-LSTM from Wang et al. [18], detailed in Sect. 3.

This approach depends on word embedding. Authors claim that they have used pre-trained Glove word vectors, obtained from Stanford[2] repository.

---

[1] This work was developed using PyTorch 1.0.
[2] Pre-trained English Glove models can be obtained from http://nlp.stanford.edu/projects/glove/.

Glove models for Brazilian Portuguese are not available in Stanford's repository. Then we adapted the code to use Glove word embedding trained to Brazilian Portuguese[3] [9].

Results presented in this Section were obtained by executing authors code as is, except by the exchange of Glove pre-trained model.

Lexicon-Based ABSA Approach [7]. We also tried the lexicon-based method proposed by Freitas [7], the only approach for ABSA fully developed focusing only on Brazilian Portuguese, as far as we know.

This approach was proposed in the same work were the TripAdvisor's Corpus was created. This is a knowledge-based model, fully based on linguistic rules to detect opinions and lexicons to obtain sentiment orientation.

Results presented here were obtained by modifying authors code to calculate overall accuracy. Freitas [7] code calculated other metrics per aspect (ontology's concepts).

5.3 Results

This Section presents a performance comparison between baselines and CharCNN approaches. Table 1 summarizes accuracies obtained by the approaches tested. Both binary (positive/negative) and three-way (positive/neutral/negative) accuracies were assessed. As one can see, the best results are presented by the CharCNN-v2.

Accuracy values presented for ATAE-LSTM and AE-CharCNN were obtained from the mean of 10 executions. For each execution we randomly split the *corpus* in train and test sets, in a 70/30 proportion. Accuracy values in Table 1 were assessed on test set.

Table 1. Test accuracy

	Binary (+, −)	Three-way (+, Neutral, −)
Large AE-CharCNN-v1 (ours)	0.69 ± 0.02	0.54 ± 0.03
Small AE-CharCNN-v1 (ours)	0.68 ± 0.03	**0.55 ± 0.03**
Large AE-CharCNN-v2 (ours)	**0.71 ± 0.03**	**0.55 ± 0.04**
Small AE-CharCNN-v2 (ours)	**0.71 ± 0.02**	**0.55 ± 0.02**
ATAE-LSTM	0.69 ± 0.19	0.49 ± 0.13
Lexicon-Based*	0.66 ± 0.00	**0.55 ± 0.00**

*Freitas [7] approach is deterministic, resulting in no standard deviation

It is important to notice that the Lexicon-Based approach is a knowledge-based approach developed by the author of the *corpus* used in our experiments.

---

[3] Pre-trained Brazilian Portuguese Glove models can be obtained from http://nilc.icmc.usp.br/embeddings.

Besides that, this method is highly dependent of external resources, such domain ontology, sentiment lexicon, and PoS-Tagger. These external resources demands a lot of effort to be created. Moreover, all external resources have an important impact on lexicon-based sentiment classifiers, as can be seen on the work of Freitas and Vieira [8].

6   Conclusion and Further Works

This work presented results about the application of character-level approaches to ABSA focused on Brazilian Portuguese. Results showed that data-driven approaches can perform better than knowledge-based (lexicon-based) approach, without the high dependence of additional external resources [8].

AE-CharCNN takes advantage of the character-level approach, avoiding complex pre-processing and making it easy to train a method tolerant to typos, rare or absent words during training, and encoding errors.

There are several possible paths for further works. For instance, to test the proposed approach with other *corpora* should bring more clarity about the performance difference between the work of Freitas [7] and ML approaches. Since there is a possibility that their results are biased by the rules created with those TripAdvisor's Reviews in mind.

We are also working on expanding TripAdvisor's data set. All reviews written in Portuguese were collected and are being annotated with the same protocol proposed by Freitas [7]. It should improve the performance of data-driven models.

Besides that, data-driven models are sensitive to data set where they were trained. Our experiments were done with hyperparameter proposed in earlier works, applied to other corpora. A grid search of hyperparameters can improve the AE-CharCNN performance over TripAdvisor's data set.

Acknowledgments. This study was financed in part by the Coordenação de Aperfeiçoamento de Pessoal de Nível Superior - Brasil (CAPES) - Finance Code 001. We gratefully acknowledge the support of NVIDIA Corporation with the donation of the Titan X GPU used for this research.

References

1. Blaz, C.C.A., Becker, K.: Sentiment analysis in tickets for it support. In: 2016 IEEE/ACM 13th Working Conference on Mining Software Repositories (MSR), pp. 235–246, May 2016. https://doi.org/10.1109/MSR.2016.032
2. Carvalho, P., Sarmento, L., Teixeira, J., Silva, M.J.: Liars and saviors in a sentiment annotated corpus of comments to political debates. In: Proceedings of the 49th Annual Meeting of the Association for Computational Linguistics: Human Language Technologies: short papers-Volume 2, pp. 564–568. Association for Computational Linguistics (2011)
3. Chaves, M.S., de Freitas, L.A., Souza, M., Vieira, R.: PIRPO: an algorithm to deal with polarity in Portuguese online reviews from the accommodation sector. In: Bouma, G., Ittoo, A., Métais, E., Wortmann, H. (eds.) NLDB 2012. LNCS,

vol. 7337, pp. 296–301. Springer, Heidelberg (2012). https://doi.org/10.1007/978-3-642-31178-9_37

4. Chaves, M.S., Freitas, L.A., Vieira, R.: Hontology: a multilingual ontology for the accommodation sector in the tourism industry. In: 4th International Conference on Knowledge Engineering and Ontology Development, pp. 149–154 (2012)

5. Dos Santos, C., Gatti, M.: Deep convolutional neural networks for sentiment analysis of short texts. In: Proceedings of COLING 2014, the 25th International Conference on Computational Linguistics: Technical Papers, pp. 69–78 (2014)

6. Fernandes, A.A., de Freitas, L.A., Corrêa, U.B.: Minerando tweets. In: Pesquisas e Perspectivas em Linguística de Corpus, pp. 283–302. Mercado de Letras (2015)

7. Freitas, L.A.: Feature-level sentiment analys is applied to Brazilian Portuguese reviews. Ph.D. thesis, Programa dePós-Graduação em Ciência da Computação. Pontifícia Universidade Católica do Rio Grande do Sul, Porto Alegre (2015)

8. de Freitas, L.A., Vieira, R.: Exploring resources for sentiment analysis in portuguese language. In: 2015 Brazilian Conference on Intelligent Systems (BRACIS), pp. 152–156, November 2015. https://doi.org/10.1109/BRACIS.2015.52

9. Hartmann, N., Fonseca, E., Shulby, C., Treviso, M., Rodrigues, J., Aluisio, S.: Portuguese word embeddings: evaluating on word analogies and natural language tasks. arXiv preprint arXiv:1708.06025 (2017)

10. Joulin, A., Grave, E., Bojanowski, P., Mikolov, T.: Bag of tricks for efficient text classification. In: Proceedings of the 15th Conference of the European Chapter of the Association for Computational Linguistics: Volume 2, Short Papers, pp. 427–431. Association for Computational Linguistics, April 2017

11. Krizhevsky, A., Sutskever, I., Hinton, G.E.: Imagenet classification with deep convolutional neural networks. In: Proceedings of the 25th International Conference on Neural Information Processing Systems - Volume 1, pp. 1097–1105, NIPS'12, Curran Associates Inc., USA (2012). http://dl.acm.org/citation.cfm?id=2999134.2999257

12. Liu, B.: Sentiment Analysis: Mining Opinions, Sentiments, and Emotions. Cambridge University Press, Cambridge (2015)

13. Pang, B., Lee, L., et al.: Opinion mining and sentiment analysis. Found. Trends®Inf. Retrieval **2**(1–2), 1–135 (2008)

14. Severyn, A., Moschitti, A.: Twitter sentiment analysis with deep convolutional neural networks. In: Proceedings of the 38th International ACM SIGIR Conference on Research and Development in Information Retrieval, pp. 959–962. ACM (2015)

15. Singhal, P., Bhattacharyya, P.: Borrow a little from your rich cousin: using embeddings and polarities of English words for multilingual sentiment classification. In: Proceedings of COLING 2016, the 26th International Conference on Computational Linguistics: technical papers, pp. 3053–3062 (2016)

16. de Souza, J.G.R., de Paiva Oliveira, A., de Andrade, G.C., Moreira, A.: A deep learning approach for sentiment analysis applied to hotel's reviews. In: Silberztein, M., Atigui, F., Kornyshova, E., Métais, E., Meziane, F. (eds.) NLDB 2018. LNCS, vol. 10859, pp. 48–56. Springer, Cham (2018). https://doi.org/10.1007/978-3-319-91947-8_5

17. Tang, D., Zhang, M.: Deep learning in sentiment analysis. In: Deng, L., Liu, Y. (eds.) Deep Learning in Natural Language Processing, pp. 219–253. Springer, Singapore (2018). https://doi.org/10.1007/978-981-10-5209-5_8

18. Wang, Y., Huang, M., Zhao, L., et al.: Attention-based LSTM for aspect-level sentiment classification. In: Proceedings of the 2016 Conference on Empirical Methods in Natural Language Processing, pp. 606–615 (2016)

19. Wehrmann, J., Becker, W., Cagnini, H.E.L., Barros, R.C.: A character-based convolutional neural network for language-agnostic twitter sentiment analysis. In: 2017 International Joint Conference on Neural Networks (IJCNN), pp. 2384–2391, May 2017. https://doi.org/10.1109/IJCNN.2017.7966145

20. Wehrmann, J., Becker, W.E., Barros, R.C.: A multi-task neural network for multilingual sentiment classification and language detection on twitter. Mach. Translation **2**(32), 37 (2018)

21. Young, T., Hazarika, D., Poria, S., Cambria, E.: Recent trends in deep learning based natural language processing. CoRR abs/1708.02709 (2017). http://arxiv.org/abs/1708.02709

22. Zhang, X., LeCun, Y.: Text understanding from scratch. arXiv preprint arXiv:1502.01710 (2015)

23. Zhang, X., Zhao, J., LeCun, Y.: Character-level convolutional networks for text classification. In: Advances in Neural Information Processing Systems, pp. 649–657 (2015)

Understanding the Criminal Behavior in Mexico City through an Explainable Artificial Intelligence Model

Octavio Loyola-González[(✉)] [iD]

Tecnologico de Monterrey, Vía Atlixcáyotl No. 2301,
Reserva Territorial Atlixcáyotl, 72453 Puebla, Mexico
octavioloyola@tec.mx

Abstract. Nowadays, the Mexican government is showing a great interest in decreasing the crime rate in Mexico. A way to carry out this task is to understand criminal behavior in each Mexico states by using an eXplainable Artificial Intelligence (XAI) model. In this paper, we propose to understand the criminal behavior of the Mexico city by using an XAI model jointly with our proposed feature representation based on the weather. Our experimental results show how our proposed feature representation allows for improving all tested classifiers. Also, we show that the XAI-based classifier improves other tested state-of-the-art classifiers.

Keywords: Criminal behavior · Explainable artificial intelligence · Contrast Patterns

1 Introduction

Nowadays, the crime rate is growing in several countries; as a consequence, all governments are creating strategies for decreasing the crime rate in their countries, such as more controlled human migration, creating jobs, and increasing citizen vigilance; among others [3,10]. Although these strategies are helping to down the crime rate in several countries, an important factor is to understand the criminal behavior for creating more accurate strategies focused on the characteristics of each country.

Mexico is one of the countries presenting high-growth criminal rate. Based on reports issued by the United Nations Office on Drugs and Crime (UNODC), Mexico is into the top-20 countries presenting a high criminal rate from 230 analyzed countries [19]. In addition, official figures suggest that during the first three months of 2019 have seen a 9.6% increase in murders in Mexico [4].

Figure 1 shows a map of homicides in Mexico from October 2018 to March 2019 taken from the www.elcri.men Website. The color of the circles corresponds to the homicide rate[1] (from white to red, intense red means high values), and

---

[1] Homicide rate is computed per year per 100,000 inhabitants.

© Springer Nature Switzerland AG 2019
L. Martínez-Villaseñor et al. (Eds.): MICAI 2019, LNAI 11835, pp. 136–149, 2019.
https://doi.org/10.1007/978-3-030-33749-0_12

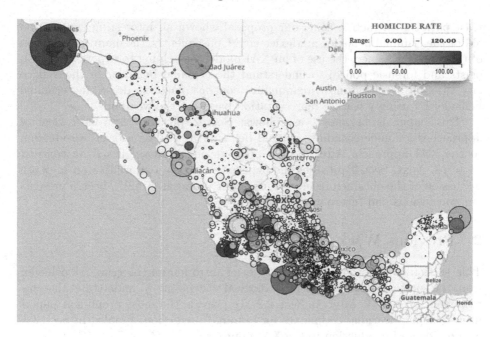

Fig. 1. Map of homicides in Mexico from October 2018 to March 2019. (Color figure online)

the size of the circles corresponds to the number of homicide reported. From this figure, we can see that there is a high level of crimes throughout Mexico. Notice that those states containing a border with the United States of America (northern border) or touristic places are presenting high crime rates. Two of the factors inciting these high crime rates are: the human migration and drug trafficking [8,15]. However, official figures suggest that the number of crimes in the capital of Mexico (Mexico City) is growing significantly [4,19]. Hence, it is important to know what type of factors is propitiating that the number of crimes is high in Mexico city when it is far away from a border.

A way to know what factors are inciting to obtain a high crime rate in Mexico city is by using an eXplainable Artificial Intelligence (XAI) model. XAI models have reported accurate classification results, and also, experts in the application area can understand these models [13,17]. Also there are practical problems where an XAI model is mandatory, such as the Equal Credit Opportunity Act of the US [14], healthcare, biotechnology, and military; among others [17].

Based on mentioned above, in this paper, we introduced a feature representation by using information from the weather for forecasting crime behavior in Mexico city. Our feature representation allows improving the classification results for all the tested classifiers. Also, we propose to understand the criminal behavior of the Mexico city by using an XAI model, which is based on contrast patterns extracted from a public crime database. From our results, we can notice that the XAI-based classifier improves other state-of-the-art classifiers. The contrast patterns extracted, using our proposal, shown an interesting explanation about the criminal behavior in Mexico city. Consequently, the main contribution of this paper is, hence, the use of an XAI model for helping to experts (psychologists and forensic police) to understand the criminal behavior in the Mexico city through a collection of high-quality contrast patterns describing criminal behavior by using a feature representation based on the weather.

This paper is organized as follows: Sect. 2 provides a brief review of approaches for understanding criminal behavior as well as a brief introduction to the XAI approach. After, Sect. 3 presents our proposal based on contrast patterns. Next, Sect. 4 provides the experimental setup as well as an in-depth discussion of the obtained results by using our proposal. Finally, Sect. 5 presents our conclusions and future work.

2   Previous Work

This section is devoted to showing a brief introduction to criminal behavior from the social, biological, and psychological viewpoints to understand the phenomenon (Sect. 2.1). After, in Sect. 2.2, we provide the most prominent papers using machine learning techniques for criminal prediction. Finally, in Sect. 2.3, we provide an introduction to the XAI approach.

2.1   Main Factors for Perpetrating Crimes

According to [11], persons suffering from mental disorders, schizophrenia, bipolar affective disorder, aggression, depression, adjustment disorders, and sexual disorders are prone to show criminal behavior. However, people can also show criminal behavior or illegal conducts because they are suffering from drug- or alcohol-induced psychosis or conditions caused by a traumatic procedure [11].

While each person who perpetrates a crime has its reasons and life situation, there exist a few overarching factors criminologists believe can contribute to criminal behavior [11]. The most relevant factors are [20]:

Biological Risk Factors: the variances in autonomic arousal, neurobiology, and neuroendocrine functioning have been shown to increase the likelihood that people might perpetrate criminal acts.

Adverse Childhood Experiences: persons were raised in particularly bad situations are at an increased risk for criminal behavior in both their juvenile and adult years. Researches show that convicted criminals have experienced four times as many adverse childhood events than non-criminals people.

Negative Social Environment: people around can influence who we are. A high-crime neighborhood can increase the probabilities of turning us in criminal. However, being in the presence of criminals is not the only way our environment can affect our behaviors. Official figures suggest that people simply living in poverty increase the likelihood of being incarcerated by some illegal conduct.

Substance Abuse: some drugs, such as alcohol, lower our inhibitions, while others, such as cocaine, overexcite the nervous system. For all cases, the physiological and psychological changes caused by intoxicants provide a negatively impact in the brain for good self-control and decision-making. People under the effects of some drug present an altered state, which can lead directly to perpetrate a criminal act. Even, some data figure that those addicted to drugs could turn to crime to pay for their drug consume.

2.2 Machine Learning for Forecasting Crime Behavior

The technology revolution has facilitated the generation of several data using digital devices, resorting to machine learning techniques for obtaining good classification results, and knowledge discovering. Researching on criminal behavior is an active topic attracting a tremendous amount of interest from both experts in the application area (forensic, police, politicians, and psychologists) and machine learning researchers. Consequently, several authors [1,2,5,6,9,18,21,22] have proposed machine learning models for forecasting criminal behavior.

In [21], the authors propose to use a support vector machines (SVM) model to predict the probability of re-incarceration. The authors used two no-public databases (Data1978 and Data1980), which were retrieved from the National Archive of Criminal Justice Data of the Inter-University Consortium for Political and Social Research. Their experimental results show that the author's proposal is better than other state-of-the-art proposals such as neural networks and logistic regression, but the authors did not compare their results against an understandable model.

In [2], a Bayesian Network (BN) model of criminal behavior is obtained linking the action of an offender on the scene of the crime to its psychological profile. The authors used a database containing both crime scene and offender features from homicide cases solved by the British police from the 1970s to the early 1990s. Their proposal shows a 15% improvement with respect to a previous BN model obtained from the same data. This model was not compared against other state-of-the-art proposals designed for forecasting criminal behavior.

In [1], the authors proposed a machine learning ensemble-based algorithm for crime prediction through urban metrics and statistical learning. The authors used several features coming from different public databases of Brazil (urban indicators, public health, Brazilian national census), taking into account the years 2001 to 2010. The authors applied a random regression forest tuned to 200 regression trees and 100 level of depth. Their experimental results show that the proposed model has a 39% of accuracy, and the authors did not compare their results against other popular state-of-the-art machine learning approaches. Also, it is very hard to understand the 200 regression trees with 100 level of depth.

In [9], an approach using a cascaded network of Kohonen neural networks followed by heuristic processing of the network's outputs is proposed. First, the Kohonen network is used to build a clustering for recognizing and grouping potential serial crimes. After, a heuristic procedure is applied to obtain a classification result. Some of the used heuristics are grouping crimes by day; authors did not group crimes that occurred before midnight with those that occurred after midnight. Grouping by distance, If the difference between the two actual times for the crimes is not higher than the time needed to move between the two crimes' locations, then the two crimes do not belong to the same class. This proposal shows 84% of accuracy; however, authors did not compare their results against other state-of-the-art machine learning models.

In [22], the authors proposed a machine learning approach for detecting specific patterns of crime that are committed by the same offender or group of offenders. The authors used a database from 4855 housebreaks in Cambridge between 1997 and 2006 recorded by the Crime Analysis Unit of the Cambridge Police Department. The authors used a hierarchical agglomerative clustering and an iterative nearest neighbor algorithm as the proposed method. The authors proposed a new metric for the nearest neighbor used according to the input data. The experimental results were carried out by using an external validation, and the authors did not show accuracy results. Also, this model did not compare against other state-of-the-art models designed for forecasting criminal behavior.

2.3   Explainable Artificial Intelligence Approach

Several of the proposal stated in Sect. 2.2 are using models based on a complex mathematical function (like SVM) or they need a deep understanding of the distance function and the representation space (like kNN), and consequently it is rather incomprehensible for experts in practical applications [13]. Hence, there has been a trend of moving away from black-box AI models towards XAI models, particularly for critical industries such as healthcare, security, and military [17]. In other words, there has been a focus to obtain XAI models, as well as fusing understandable and black-box models for explaining to both experts and the intelligent lay audience the results obtained by the applied model.

There are two main approaches used to develop explainable systems, namely: ante-hoc and post-hoc [17]. Ante-hoc approach entails the building on explainability into a model from the very beginning (analogous to secure-by-design), while post-hoc approach typically trains models, with explainability only being incorporated during testing. Both approaches are useful for different settings, and hence they are suitable for helping the experts in the practical application.

Contrast pattern-based classification is a family of classifiers following the XAI approach. It uses a collection of contrast patterns to create a model that classifies a query object in a predefined class [13]. A *pattern* is an expression defined in a certain language that describes a collection of objects. Usually, a pattern is represented by a conjunction of relational statements (a.k.a *items*), each with the form: $[f_i \# v_j]$, where v_j is a value in the domain of feature f_i, and $\#$ is a relational operator from the set $\{\in, \notin, =, \neq, \leq, >\}$ [13]. For example, $[crime\_time \in [2,6]] \land [Number\_of\_offenders > 2] \land [type\_of\_crime =$ "$Robbery$"] is a pattern describing a collection of crimes. A *contrast pattern* (cp) for a class C_i is a pattern p where the number of objects covered by p in C_i is significantly higher than any cover of p for every class other than C_i [13].

For building a cp-based classifier, there are three main phases: Mining, Filtering, and Classification [13]. Mining is dedicated to finding a set of candidate patterns by an exploratory analysis using a search-space; using a set of inductive constraints provided by the user. Filtering is devoted to obtain a small collection of high-quality patterns by using all patterns extracted in the previous stage. Classification is responsible for searching the best strategy for combining the information provided by a subset of patterns and so builds an accurate model based on patterns.

Cp-based classification has shown both accurate classification results and understandable models in many practical contexts, such as gene expression profiles, characterization for subtypes of leukemia, microarray concordance analysis, classification of spatial and image data, structural alerts for computational toxicology, and prediction of heart diseases [13]; among others. However, cp-based classification have not been used to extract patterns for understanding the criminal behavior. Therefore, in this paper, we will propose a cp-based classifier for understanding the criminal behavior in Mexico city.

3   Our Proposal

In this section, firstly, we show characteristic of the public crime data to be used and how we increased this database by using additional information coming from the weather (Sect. 3.1). After, in Sect. 3.2, we explain the cp-based approach to be used to extract all the patterns describing crime behavior in Mexico city.

3.1   Feature Representation

We use a public crime database coming from the attorney general's office (PGJ, by its initials in Spanish), which are available for downloading at https://datos.cdmx.gob.mx. This database has the following 16 features: year, month, town hall, crime category, specific crime, agency, attorney general, investigation office, start date, street1, street2, colony, latitude, longitude, year and month, and geolocation. From these features, we can notice that there are repetitive features such as geolocation, year, and month. This database contains 766,303 objects from January 2016 to March 2019 distributed as follow: 197,913 in 2016; 228,323 in 2017; 255,313 in 2018; and 84,754 in 2019.

As was stated by other authors [7, 16], the weather has a significant effect on criminal behavior; for example, the temperature can change the crime rate. Consequently, we have added weather features to the public crime database by using the API provided by the website: www.worldweatheronline.com.

Table 1 shows each feature proposed in our weather feature representation. We have provided a brief description for each feature. Finally, we have proposed a new feature representation based on 209 characteristics coming from the weather.

Table 1. Weather features proposed in our feature representation.

Feature	Description	Feature	Description
sunrise	The time in the morning when the sun appears or full daylight arrives	sunset	The time in the evening when the sun disappears or daylight fades
moonrise	The time in the night when rising of the moon above the horizon	moonset	The time in the early morning when the moon below the horizon
moon phase	It is the shape of the directly sunlit portion of the Moon as viewed from Earth	moon illumination	It is defined as the fraction of the lunar disk that is illuminated at local civil midnight, where 1.0 is fully illuminated
max temp	It is expressed in Celsius and it means what it the maximum temperature in a day	min temp	It is expressed in Celsius and it means what it the minimum temperature in a day
UV Index	It is an international standard measurement of the strength of sunburn-producing ultraviolet (UV) radiation at a particular place		
The features related below contain values for the following hour intervals: 0, 3, 6, 9, 12, 15, 18, and 21			
max temp	It is expressed in Celsius and it means what it the maximum temperature in a day	wind speed	It is caused by air moving from high to low pressure; it is measured in Miles
win dir degree	It is reported by the direction from which it originates; It is measured in degrees clockwise from due north	win dir 16 points	It is reported by the direction from which it originates; It is indicated in point, which is divided into 16 cardinal point
precip	It is measure in mm, referring to the amount of rain per square meter in one hour	humidity	It measures the amount of water vapour present in air
humidity	It is a measure of the distance at which an object or light can be clearly discerned	pressure	It is the force per unit of area exerted on the Earth's surface by the weight of the air above the surface
cloud cover	It refers to the fraction of the sky obscured by clouds when observed from a particular location	heat index	It is a measure of how hot it really feels when relative humidity is factored with the actual air temperature
dew point	It is the term that most meteorologists use to describe the amount of moisture in the air	wind chill	It is the lowering of body temperature due to the passing-flow of lower-temperature air
wind gust	It measure a brief increase in the speed of the wind, usually less than 20 s	feels like	It is our "feels like" temperature that gives you a better idea about how the weather will actually feel when you step outdoors
chance of Rain	If the forecaster is only 50% sure that precipitation will occur, and expects that, if it does occur, it will produce measurable rain over about 80% of the area, the chance of rain is 40%	chance of from dry	It means that out of 100 situations with similar weather, it should rain on 20 of those, and not rain on 80
chance of windy	It means that out of 100 situations with similar weather, it should change the wind on 20 of those, and not wind on 80	chance of overcast	It means that out of 100 situations with similar weather, it should change the overcast on 20 of those, and not overcast on 80
chance Of Sunshine	It measures the probability that the direct sunlight unbroken by cloud, especially over a comparatively large area	chance of frost	It measures the probability about the chance of frost for a given date at each tracked location
chance of high temp	It measures the probability about the chance of high temp for a given date at some location	chance of fog	It measures the probability about the chance of fog for a given date at some location
chance of snow	It measures the probability about the chance of snow for a given date at some location	chance of thunder	It measures the probability about the chance of thunder for a given date at some location
UV Index	It is an international standard measurement of the strength of sunburn-producing ultraviolet (UV) radiation at a particular place		

3.2   Contrast Pattern-Based Classification

As was stated in Sect. 2.3, cp-based classifiers are used in various real-world applications, in which they have reported effective classification results [13]. Nevertheless, to our knowledge, cp-based approach has not been used for understanding crime behavior.

There are two approaches for mining contrast patterns: exhaustive search and based on decision trees. The approach based on decision trees has two advantages against the exhaustive search approach: (i) the local discretization performed by decision trees with numeric features avoids doing an "a priori" global discretization, which might cause information loss; (ii) decision trees provide a significant reduction of the search space of potential patterns [13].

There are several algorithms for mining contrast patterns based on decision trees, but those following the diversity approach has shown better results than other approaches. In [13], the authors have shown that Random Forest miner (RFm) is a CP mining model that allows obtaining a collection of high-quality patterns, which produce better classification results than other cp-based solutions. RFm builds 100 decision trees by using a random subset of the features for each induction. After, patterns are extracted from the paths from the root node to the leaves. Next, for each pattern, the class with the highest support determines the pattern's class. At the end stage, RFm uses a filtering stage where a small collection of high-quality patterns are selected for the classification stage.

On the other hand, there are several cp-based classifiers but PBC4cip [13] has reported good classification results; including class imbalance problems. PBC4cip weights the sum of supports in each class, for all patterns covering a query object, taking into account the class imbalance level.

Based on the above mentioned, we select RFm as cp mining for extracting all the contrast patterns describing crime behavior in Mexico city and PBC4cip as the cp-based classifier for the classification stage.

4   Experimental Results

This section is devoted to showing the experimental setup (Sect. 4.1) as well as an in-depth discussion of the obtained results (Sect. 4.2).

4.1   Experimental Setup

For our experiments, we split the public crime database, stated in Sect. 3.1, in four databases, each one containing crimes for a specific year (i.e., one database for crimes issued in 2016, other for crimes issued in 2019, and so on). All databases contain the 209 mixed features stated in Sect. 3.1 and other six features from the original database such as day, month, latitude, longitude, colony, and crime category. As we need to understand criminal behavior, we select the feature crime category as the class. For each crime category, we use a one vs. all strategy for helping to the contrast pattern mining algorithm to extract better high-quality patterns.

All databases were partitioned using 5-fold-cross-validation and Distribution Optimally Balanced Stratified Cross-Validation (DOB-SCV) for avoiding problems into data distribution on class imbalance problems [13].

As we stated in Sect. 3, RFm allows obtaining a set of patterns which produce better classification results than other pattern-based solutions reported in the literature. For this reason, we selected this miner in our experimental setup. Also, we selected PBC4cip [13] as the pattern-based classifier because it has reported better classification results than other state-of-the-art classifiers.

We compare the classification results obtained by the different tested pattern-based classifiers against other nine state-of-the-art classifiers, such as k-Nearest Neighbor with k = 3 (**3NN**), Bagging using C4.5 (**Bag_DT**), Bayesian network (**BN**), C4.5 (**J48**), Logistic Regression (**Log**), Multilayer Perceptron (**MLP**), Naïve Bayes (**NaiveBayes**), Random Forest (**RF**), and Support Vector Machine (**SVM**); all these were executed using the WEKA Data Mining tool [12], using the parameter values recommended by their authors.

To evaluate the performance of supervised classifiers, we used Area Under the receiver operating characteristic Curve (AUC) [13], which evaluates the true positive rate (TP_{rate}) versus the false positive rate (FP_{rate}). Finally, we used the Friedman's test and the Finner's dynamic post-hoc procedure to statistically compare our results. Both test and procedure are used by [13] for their experimental setup; which is similar to our experimentation setup.

4.2   Results and Discussion

In this section, we discuss the results in two parts: first, we show the classification results obtained for all tested classifiers by using the original feature representation, and after that, we show the classification results of the same tested classifiers but using our feature representation.

Table 2 shows all the results of average AUC for all tested classifiers on the tested databases using the original feature representation. From this table, we can see that all tested classifiers obtained classification results lower than 0.67 of AUC for all tested databases. The best classifiers were BN and RFm+PBC4cip, which attained 0.66 of AUC for the tested databases using the original feature representation. From these results, we can conclude that the original feature representation leaves a room for improving the obtained classification results.

Table 3 shows all the results of average AUC for all tested classifiers on the tested databases using our feature representation. From this table, we can see how the new feature representation allows improving the classification results of all tested classifiers in a significant way. From these results, we can notice that RFm+PBC4cip obtain the best results for three from four tested databases and it shows the best results of average AUC with the lower standard deviation.

Table 4 shows the result of average AUC (Average AUC), the standard deviation (SD), the average ranking according to the Friedman's test, and the adjusted p-value of the Finner's procedure for all tested classifiers, considering all the tested databases by using our feature representation. This table is ordered according to the average of the Friedman's ranking value and the thin horizontal line indicates the point after which there is a statistically significant difference with the best result in the Friedman ranking (unadjusted p-value $\leq$ 0.033617).

Table 2. Results of average AUC for all compared classifiers on the tested databases using the original feature representation. The best results appear boldface and those results not available because of a lot of delay during execution time appear as N/A.

Classifiers/databases	2016	2017	2018	2019	Avg	SD
3NN	0.5787	0.6819	0.5416	0.5652	0.5919	0.0537
Bag_DT	0.5764	0.5792	0.5811	0.5713	0.5770	**0.0037**
BN	0.5629	0.6597	0.6813	0.7643	**0.6671**	0.0717
J48	0.5212	0.6255	0.6129	0.6144	0.5935	0.0420
Log	N/A	N/A	0.6885	0.5928	0.3203	0.3221
MLP	N/A	N/A	**0.6912**	**0.7675**	0.3647	0.3657
NaiveBayes	0.6211	0.6300	0.6741	0.6605	0.7811	0.0150
RF	**0.6801**	0.5901	0.6393	0.7240	0.6584	0.0495
SVM	N/A	N/A	N/A	0.7231	0.1808	0.3131
RFm+PBC4cip	0.5923	**0.6851**	0.6756	0.6943	0.6618	0.0407
Average	0.5904	0.6359	0.6428	**0.6677**	–	–
SD	0.0461	0.0388	**0.0505**	0.0739	–	–

From Table 4, we can conclude that the results of RFm+PBC4cip against RF, Bag_DT, and BN are not statistically different, but these results are statistically better than the results obtained by the remaining tested classifiers. Also, it can be noticed that RFm+PBC4cip obtained the best average AUC results and lowest standard deviation among all the tested classifiers.

It is important to highlight that in Tables 2 and 3 the classifiers MLP, Log and SVM continues executing, after three months, the experiments for the tested databases. This is because MLP takes as an input numerical data, and to convert the attributes of these databases from categorical to numerical, we use one-hot encoding. The length of the encoded feature vector heavily affects the execution time, making MLP unsuitable for this problem. In a similar way, As a consequence, these results appear as NA in Tables 2 and 3.

Table 5 shows five pure[2] patterns describing each one a single crime category. For each pattern, we show its index (No.), items describing the pattern (description), the class associated with that pattern, and its support (Supp.). From this table, we can see that for the class "Low impact crime" the pattern has higher support than those patterns describing other classes (e.g., violation). This would be produced by the effect of the class imbalance problem because there exist significantly lower objects for these classes than the remaining ones.

---

[2] A pattern is considered a *pure pattern* when it covers objects for only one class.

Table 3. Results of average AUC for all compared classifiers on the tested databases using our feature representation. The best results appear boldface and those results not available because of a lot of delay during execution time appear as N/A.

Classifiers/databases	2016	2017	2018	2019	Avg	SD
3NN	0.8587	0.8488	0.8294	0.8652	0.8505	0.0135
Bag_DT	0.8764	0.8792	0.8801	0.8713	0.8768	**0.0034**
BN	0.8699	0.8597	0.8827	0.8633	0.8689	0.0088
J48	0.8312	0.8255	0.8199	0.8144	0.8228	0.0063
Log	N/A	N/A	0.7885	0.7988	0.3968	0.3968
MLP	N/A	N/A	0.8211	0.8675	0.4222	0.4225
NaiveBayes	0.7997	0.7899	0.7741	0.7605	0.7811	0.0150
RF	0.8801	**0.8901**	0.8893	0.8240	0.8709	0.0273
SVM	N/A	N/A	N/A	0.8631	0.2158	0.3737
RFm+PBC4cip	**0.8912**	0.8851	**0.8882**	**0.8943**	**0.8897**	**0.0034**
Average	**0.8582**	0.8540	0.8415	0.8422	–	–
SD	**0.0207**	0.0336	0.0422	0.0391	–	–

Table 4. Statistical results for the tested classifiers by using our feature representation.

Classifier	Average AUC	SD	Ranking	Unadjusted p-value
RFm+PBC4cip	0.8897	0.0034	1.5	–
RF	0.8709	0.0273	2.75	0.05
Bag_DT	0.8768	0.0034	3	0.04457
BN	0.8689	0.0088	4	0.039109
3NN	0.8505	0.0135	4.5	0.033617
MLP	0.4222	0.4225	6.75	0.028094
J48	0.8228	0.0063	6.75	0.022539
NaiveBayes	0.7811	0.0150	8.25	0.016952
SVM	0.2158	0.3737	8.5	0.011334
Log	0.3968	0.3968	8.75	0.005683

All extracted patterns are expressed in a suitable language for experts in the application area, which can help to understand the criminal behavior in Mexico city through our feature representation based on the weather.

From all our results, we can conclude that our feature representation using weather data allows improving the results of all tested classifiers. Also, we can conclude that our proposal provides an explanatory model, which is helpful for experts in the application area. Although BN obtains similar classification results than our proposal, it is very hard to be analyzed by experts. On the other hand, RF and Bag_DT provide models that could be converted into rules, but they contain significantly more rules than those extracted from the model provide by RFm. Therefore, we conclude that our feature representation and our proposal based on patterns is the best solution for understanding crime behavior in Mexico city.

Table 5. Some extracted contrast patterns describing crime behavior in Mexico city.

No.	Description	Class	Supp.
P_1	$W\_hour300\_feelsLikeC > 12.50 \wedge W\_hour2100\_dewPointC > 9.00$	Low impact crime	0.83
P_2	$W\_hour900\_heatIndexC > 12.50 \wedge W\_hour1200\_windChillC > 21.50 \wedge W\_hour0\_heatIndexC > 27.50$	Homicide	0.66
P_3	$W\_mintempC > 12.50 \wedge W\_hour1800\_visibility > 18.00 \wedge W\_hour900\_chanceOfSunShine <= 82.00$	Kidnapping	0.57
P_4	$W\_moon\_illumination <= 23.00 \wedge W\_hour1200\_chanceOfOverCast > 38.50 \wedge W\_hour600\_windChillC > 20.50$	Violation	0.31
P_5	$W\_moonrise \leq 10.50 \wedge W\_hour0\_cloudCover > 4.50 \wedge W\_hour900\_windChillC > 21.00 \wedge W\_moon\_illumination > 8.00$	Injuries by firearm shot	0.30

5   Conclusions and Future Work

Nowadays, all countries are showing a great interest in decreasing the crime rate in the world. A suitable way is to understand criminal behavior by using an XAI model. In this paper, we use an XAI model for helping to experts to understand the criminal behavior in the Mexico city through a collection of high-quality contrast patterns describing criminal behavior by using a feature representation based on the weather.

From our classification results, we can conclude that our proposed feature representation based on the weather allows improving all the tested classified, both black-box and XAI models. Also, we have shown that our proposal, of using the Random Forest miner for extracting the contrast patterns and after using PBC4cip for the classification stage, obtains significantly better classification results than six of the 10 tested classifiers. However, among those classifiers where our proposal does not obtain significant differences, we can conclude that our proposal obtains the best position into the Friedman's ranking and our proposal obtains fewer patterns regarding the other tested XAI models reporting similar classification results.

As every paper, this one has some limitations. First, results could not be corroborated by using the experts in the application area. Nevertheless, the XAI model used has shown suitable results for experts in other application areas. Second, our feature representation based on the weather could be improved by using feature selection methods. Similarly, other feature representation based on social networks could be proposed. Finally, since the feature representation proposed has several features, the extracted patterns contain several items.

Based on the limitations above mentioned, as future work, we plan to add new features to the public Mexican crime database by using information extracted from the tweets posted taking into account the date, time, and geolocation reported by the criminal database. Also, we plan to use several feature selection methods for obtaining the best subset of features describing the problem. Finally, we plan to fuzzy the numerical features and after to use a fuzzy pattern classification. In this way, we hope to find new discriminative patterns, which help to understand, in a better way, the criminal behavior in Mexico city.

Acknowledgments. Author is thankful to Prof. Miguel Angel Medina-Pérez, PhD; for his valuable contributions improving the grammar and style of this paper.

References

1. Alves, L.G., Ribeiro, H.V., Rodrigues, F.A.: Crime prediction through urban metrics and statistical learning. Phys. A Stat. Mech. Appl. **505**, 435–443 (2018)
2. Baumgartner, K.C., Ferrari, S., Salfati, C.G.: Bayesian network modeling of offender behavior for criminal profiling. In: Proceedings of the 44th IEEE Conference on Decision and Control, pp. 2702–2709, December 2005
3. BBC News: InSight crimes 2018 homicide round-up. https://www.insightcrime.org/news/analysis/insight-crime-2018-homicide-roundup/ (2019). Accessed 21 May 2019
4. BBC News: Mexico murder rate rises in first three months of 2019. https://www.bbc.com/news/world-latin-america-48012923 (2019). Accessed 21 May 2019
5. Berk, R., Hyatt, J.: Machine learning forecasts of risk to inform sentencing decisions. Fed. Sentencing Reporter **27**(4), 222–228 (2015)
6. Berk, R.A., Sorenson, S.B., Barnes, G.: Forecasting domestic violence: a machine learning approach to help inform arraignment decisions. J. Empirical Legal Stud. **13**(1), 94–115 (2016)
7. Chen, X., Cho, Y., Jang, S.Y.: Crime prediction using twitter sentiment and weather. In: 2015 Systems and Information Engineering Design Symposium, pp. 63–68 (2015)
8. CNN: Mexico drug war fast facts. https://edition.cnn.com/2013/09/02/world/americas/mexico-drug-war-fast-facts/index.html (2019). Accessed 21 May 2019
9. Dahbur, K., Muscarello, T.: Classification system for serial criminal patterns. Artif. Intell. Law **11**(4), 251–269 (2003)
10. Farrington, D.P., Welsh, B.C.: The Oxford Handbook of Crime Prevention. Oxford University Press, Oxford (2012). https://www.oxfordhandbooks.com/view/10.1093/oxfordhb/9780195398823.001.0001/oxfordhb-9780195398823
11. Guze, S.B., Woodruff, R.A., Clayton, P.J.: Psychiatric disorders and criminality. JAMA **227**(6), 641–642 (1974)
12. Hall, M., Frank, E., Holmes, G., Pfahringer, B., Reutemann, P., Witten, I.H.: The WEKA data mining software: an update. SIGKDD Explor. **11**(1), 10–18 (2009)
13. Loyola-González, O., Medina-Pérez, M.A., Martínez-Trinidad, J.F., Carrasco-Ochoa, J.A., Monroy, R., García-Borroto, M.: PBC4cip: a new contrast pattern-based classifier for class imbalance problems. Knowl.-Based Syst. **115**, 100–109 (2017)
14. Martens, D., Baesens, B., Gestel, T.V., Vanthienen, J.: Comprehensible credit scoring models using rule extraction from support vector machines. Eur. J. Oper. Res. **183**(3), 1466–1476 (2007)

15. Mexico News Daily: Mexico getting tougher on migrants as thousands wait for visas in Chiapas. https://mexiconewsdaily.com/news/mexico-getting-tougher-on-migrants/ (2019). Accessed 21 May 2019
16. Ranson, M.: Crime, weather, and climate change. J. Environ. Econ. Manag. **67**(3), 274–302 (2014)
17. Rudin, C.: Stop explaining black box machine learning models for high stakes decisions and use interpretable models instead. Nat. Mach. Intell. **1**(5), 206–215 (2019)
18. Saeed, U., Sarim, M., Usmani, A., Mukhtar, A., Shaikh, A.B., Raffat, S.K.: Application of machine learning algorithms in crime classification and classification rule mining. Res. J. Recent Sci. **2277**, 106–114 (2015)
19. United Nations Office on drugs and crime: statistics and data. https://dataunodc.un.org/crime/intentional-homicide-victims (2019). Accessed 21 May 2019
20. Walden University: What influences criminal behavior? https://www.waldenu.edu/online-bachelors-programs/bs-in-criminal-justice/resource/what-influences-criminal-behavior (2019). Accessed 21 May 2019
21. Wang, P., Mathieu, R., Ke, J., Cai, H.J.: Predicting criminal recidivism with support vector machine. In: International Conference on Management and Service Science, pp. 1–9 (2010)
22. Wang, T., Rudin, C., Wagner, D., Sevieri, R.: Learning to Detect Patterns of Crime. In: Blockeel, H., Kersting, K., Nijssen, S., Železný, F. (eds.) ECML PKDD 2013. LNCS (LNAI), vol. 8190, pp. 515–530. Springer, Heidelberg (2013). https://doi.org/10.1007/978-3-642-40994-3_33

Improving Hyper-heuristic Performance for Job Shop Scheduling Problems Using Neural Networks

Erick Lara-Cárdenas(✉) [iD], Xavier Sánchez-Díaz[iD], Ivan Amaya[iD],
and José Carlos Ortiz-Bayliss[iD]

School of Engineering and Sciences, Tecnologico de Monterrey,
Ave. Eugenio Garza Sada 2501, 64849 Monterrey, NL, Mexico
a00398510@itesm.mx, {sax,iamaya2,jcobayliss}@tec.mx

Abstract. Job Shop Scheduling problems have become popular because of their many industrial and practical applications. Among the many solving strategies for this problem, selection hyper-heuristics have attracted attention due to their promising results in this and similar optimization problems. A selection hyper-heuristic is a method that determines which heuristic to apply at given points of the problem throughout the solving process. Unfortunately, results from previous studies show that selection hyper-heuristics are not free from making wrong choices. Hence, this paper explores a novel way of improving selection hyper-heuristics by using neural networks that are trained with information from existing selection hyper-heuristics. These networks learn high-level patterns that result in improved performance concerning the hyper-heuristics they were generated from. At the end of the process, the neural networks work as hyper-heuristics that perform better than their original counterparts. The results presented in this paper confirm the idea that we can refine existing hyper-heuristics to the point of being able to defeat the best possible heuristic for each instance. For example, one of our experiments generated one hyper-heuristic that produced a schedule that reduced the makespan of the one obtained by a synthetic oracle by ten days.

Keywords: Job shop scheduling · Hyper-heuristics · Neural networks

1 Introduction

When solving a job shop scheduling problem (JSSP), the task is to schedule a set of jobs on a set of machines, subject to two constraints: each machine must handle at most one job at a time, and each job must respect a specified processing order throughout the machines. Thus, solving a JSSP requires to find a schedule for the jobs that minimizes the time required to complete all of them (the makespan). Since JSSPs become quite challenging to handle in real-world applications (they belong to the NP-hard problem class), finding more reliable methods to solve JSSPs is an essential topic of study.

© Springer Nature Switzerland AG 2019
L. Martínez-Villaseñor et al. (Eds.): MICAI 2019, LNAI 11835, pp. 150–161, 2019.
https://doi.org/10.1007/978-3-030-33749-0_13

Many methods to solve JSSPs have been proposed [1]. Among them, exact ones produce optimal results but are limited to the instance size. As a response, metaheuristics have commonly been used for solving the JSSP. Some examples include the use of simulated annealing [2–4], tabu search [5–7] and genetic algorithms [8–10], just to mention a few.

In addition to metaheuristics, recent research has also focused on heuristics specifically designed for this problem. Heuristics work by generating approximate solutions in a short time and with few computational resources. Some examples of this approach include dispatching rules [11] and the shifting bottleneck procedure [12]. Heuristics cannot guarantee the quality of the solutions, and there is no single one that performs best on every instance of the problem. For this reason, we sometimes rely on methods that combine the strengths of such heuristics in some intelligent fashion, in order to obtain a more stable performance for a broader range of instances.

The problem of selecting the most suitable algorithm or solving strategy for one particular situation is usually referred to as the algorithm selection problem. Examples of algorithm selection strategies include, but are not limited to: algorithm portfolios [13–15], selection hyper-heuristics [16,17] and instance-specific algorithm configuration [18]. In general, all these methods manage a set of solving strategies and apply one that is suitable for the current problem state of the instance being solved. Striving to unify terms, from this point on, we will use selection hyper-heuristic to refer to the methods proposed in this paper.

The remainder of this document is organized as follows. Section 2 presents the most relevant concepts and literature related to this work. Section 3 describes the proposed solution model. The reader will find the experiments and their corresponding analysis in Sect. 4. Finally, Sect. 5 presents the conclusion and future work derived from this investigation.

2   Background and Related Work

A JSSP is formally defined as a set of jobs $J = \{1, \ldots, n\}$ and a set of machines $M = \{1, \ldots, m\}$. The order in which each job $j \in J$ must be processed through the machines is specified by a permutation $\sigma_j = (\sigma_j^1, \ldots, \sigma_j^m)$. For each job $j \in J$, a non-negative integer $p_{j,i}$ represents the processing time of job j on machine i. The time in which job j exits the system (i.e. the makespan of such a job), is denoted by C_j, while $C_{i,j}$ denotes the completion time of job j on machine i. The objective in this work is to minimize the total makespan (i.e. the summation over the makespan of all jobs).

Recently proposed solving strategies for JSSPs include the improved shuffled complex evolution [19], tabu search/path relinking (TS/PR) [20], evolutionary computation [1,21], and particle swarm optimization [22]. Even so, recent studies [23,24] encourage the generalization capabilities of neural networks. So, in order to take advantage of such a capability, we propose using neural networks as a way to generalize and improve upon existing selection constructive hyper-heuristics. The current literature already contains a few works where neural networks have been used within the field of hyper-heuristics. Some works have explored the idea of learning patterns in the performance of different heuristics for constraint satisfaction problems [25]. Other authors, such as Tyasnurita et al., have focused on learning heuristic selection for vehicle routing by using time-delay neural networks [26]. Similarly, some works have combined neural networks with other techniques to produce hyper-heuristics. For example, authors have combined neural networks with logistic regression to produce hyper-heuristics for educational timetabling [27]. The evolution of neural network topologies to construct hyper-heuristics for constraint satisfaction problems has also been explored [28]. To the best of our knowledge, there is no previous study where neural networks are used to improve the behavior of existing hyper-heuristics, as depicted in this work.

2.1   Instance Features

The features considered to characterize the problem state in this investigation are divided into two types. The first one characterizes the schedule (i.e. the solution found so far), and we consider three of them:

- **Average processed times (APT).** APT expresses the ratio between the sum of the processing times of the previously processed activities and the sum of the processing times of the complete list of activities. This feature estimates how advanced the scheduling process is with respect to the initial conditions of the instance.
- **Dispersion of processing time index for scheduled activities (DPT).** DPT is calculated as the ratio between the standard deviation of the processing times and the mean of the processing times.
- **Percentage of slack in makespan (SLACK).** This feature refers to the ratio between the amount of available machine time (slack) in the whole schedule and the current makespan of the schedule. The larger the slack, the fewer the activities are, but also the more space where similar activities can be allocated.

The second type describes the problem state (i.e. the remaining/unscheduled part of the instance), and we also consider three of them:

- **Dispersion of processing time index for pending jobs (DNPT).** For unscheduled activities: the ratio between the standard deviation of processing times and the mean of processing times.
- **Average non processed times (NAPT).** NAPT is the complement of the APT. It is calculated as the ratio between the sum of processing times of pending activities and the sum of processing times of the whole list of activities.
- **Average pending processing times per job (NJT).** NJT calculates, for all the pending activities, the sum of the processing times normalized for each job. Then, it divides such an amount by the number of pending jobs.

2.2   Heuristics

All heuristics considered in this work are constructive. So, they build a solution iteratively, i.e. taking one decision at the time. For their definition, let U_a be the list of pending activities, i.e. the ones to be scheduled. Let $S_i = (a_{j,i}, t_{a_j})$ be a list of tuples where i represents the machine number, $a_{j,i}$ is an activity of job j that has to be processed in machine i, and t_{a_j} is the time where activity a is being scheduled in job j. Thus, the considered heuristics for this investigation are the following:

- **Shortest Processing Time (SPT).** From U_a select the activity $a_{j,i}$ with the shortest p_{ij}.
- **Longest Processing Time (LPT).** From U_a select the activity $a_{j,i}$ with the longest p_{ij}.
- **Maximum Job Remaining Time (MRT).** From U_a select the job that needs the most time for it to finish. It returns the first possible activity (in precedence order) that corresponds to said job in the first available time.
- **Most Loaded Machine (MLM).** In U_a find the machine i which has maximum total processing time. The heuristic will return the activity a_j that has the lowest possible t_{a_j} if scheduled in machine i. If no activity is possible, then for the set of machines minus machine i, it selects the next machine with maximum total processing time until a suitable activity is found.
- **Least Loaded Machine (LLM).** In U_a find the machine i which has minimum total processing time. The heuristic will return the activity a_j that has the lowest possible t_{a_j} if scheduled in machine i. If no activity is possible, then for the set of machines minus machine i, select the next machine with minimum total processing time until a suitable activity is found.
- **Earliest Start Time (EST).** For U_a, get the activities which can be scheduled at a given state, this represents the possible activities. And, find the job that has the earliest possible starting time at the current problem state, and select the activity that corresponds to said job from the list of possible activities.

2.3   JSSP Instances

All the instances considered for this investigation were synthetically generated by using one algorithm taken from the literature [29]. The algorithm produces scheduling problems with a random distribution of the numbers for the machines and the completion times for each job. All the instances generated contain 15 machines and 15 jobs. In total, we generated 60 instances, where half of them are considered for training and the remaining half, for testing purposes.

3   Solution Model

The solution model proposed takes one selection constructive hyper-heuristic as input. This hyper-heuristic can be generated by using any selection hyper-heuristic generation method available. To clarify the terminology, from now on, we will refer to the hyper-heuristics used as input simply as input hyper-heuristics. By using these input hyper-heuristics, we solve the instances used for training and all the points in the instance space visited throughout the solving process (with their respective recommended heuristics) are recorded for further use. Then, the model focuses on refining the decisions made by the input hyper-heuristics by using neural networks.

The solution model first goes through a training stage where the neural network learns to behave as an improved version of the input hyper-heuristic. Information from the input hyper-heuristic is used to create a set of training examples for the neural network. In the second stage, the one devoted to testing, the neural network (the improved hyper-heuristic) is used to solve a set of unseen JSSP instances. The neural network receives a JSSP instance and decides, based on the problem state, the most suitable heuristic to apply to produce a good quality schedule.

The basic topology of the neural networks used in this investigation consists of at least three layers. Both the input and the output layers contain six neurons: one neuron per feature in the case of the input layer and one neuron per heuristic in the case of the output one. For these networks to be able to work as hyper-heuristics, they receive the features that characterize a JSSP instance, and only one of the output neurons must fire (the one that corresponds to the heuristic to apply). The number of hidden layers, as well as the number of neurons in each of these layers, is defined for each particular experiment.

4   Experiments

This section presents the experiments conducted in this investigation, where we use the makespan as a performance indicator (the lower, the better). Bear in mind that the makespan on a given instance serves the purpose of identifying its best solver, and that total makespan (i.e. the summation across all instances) indicates overall performance. All data are given for the test set.

4.1   Improving Hyper-heuristics Through Neural Networks: A Preliminary Approach

All the input hyper-heuristics used in this work were generated by using a recently proposed method that relies on simulated annealing for producing hyper-heuristics for JSSPs [30]. The hyper-heuristics produced by this method consists of a series of rules in the form (condition ← action). The condition of these rules contains the values for each feature that make a heuristic (condition) more suitable than others at a particular moment in the construction of the schedule. Given one problem instance, the hyper-heuristic calculates the values of the features that characterize the current problem state. Then, it calculates the Euclidean distance between the condition of every rule in the hyper-heuristic and the current problem state. The rule which condition is closest to the problem state fires and, as a consequence, its corresponding heuristic is applied to the problem. The parameters used for running the simulated annealing hyper-heuristic generator include a minimum and maximum temperature of 1 and 100, respectively, and 150 steps.

As stated before, the result of the hyper-heuristic generation process is a collection of heuristic rules that map some regions of the instance space to specific heuristics. When a hyper-heuristic is used to solve an instance, it must decide which heuristic to use at given steps throughout the process. We refer to such steps as decision points. If we use a hyper-heuristic to solve an instance and record, for each decision point, the recommended heuristic, we can get a more detailed overview of the solving process. We call the set of decision points and their corresponding recommended heuristic, extended heuristic rules.

As a first experiment, we produced four hyper-heuristics by using the simulated annealing generation model (SAHH01 to SAHH04) on the training set. We then used the heuristic rules from each of these hyper-heuristics to train, for each SAHH, three improved hyper-heuristics by using neural networks (NNHH). Each one of the NNHHs incorporated slight changes on its topology, resulting in 12 different NNHHs. As aforementioned, the SAHHs make their decisions based on the Euclidean distances between the problem states and the conditions in the heuristic rules. On the other hand, the NNHHs decide which heuristics to apply at a given moment by using the weights in the network.

The topologies used for these experiments are defined by the number of layers and neurons in such layers (in the form 1 Input-N Hidden-1 Output). Then, topologies A, B, and C are, 6-64-64-18-6, 6-64-48-32-6, and 6-64-48-32-16-6, respectively. In all cases, a learning rate of 0.014 and a momentum of 0.87 were used. These parameters were set based on preliminary experimentation.

Table 1 shows the total makespan of the four hyper-heuristics produced through the simulated annealing method (second column). Time differences (expressed in hours) of the total makespan between each NNHHs and their corresponding SAHH are also shown (columns three to five). Here, a negative result indicates that a reduction in the total makespan was achieved by the improved hyper-heuristic. On the contrary, a positive result indicates that no improvement was obtained (and the schedule produced by the corresponding NNHH increases the makespan of the input hyper-heuristic). For simplicity, the cells in this table are referred to by a name resulting from the combination of the row and column. Hence, NNHH02B corresponds to the value 3,221. This indicates that using SAHH02 as input while considering topology B for the network, increases the schedule by 3,221 h.

In the case of SAHH01, NNHH01A was able to reduce the makespan in just 30% of the instances of the test set. NNHH01B and NNHH01C showed better performance, reducing the makespan of SAHH01 in 63% of the instances. Similarly, NNHH02A and NNHH02B reduced the makespan produced by SAHH02 in 23.33% of the cases, while NNHH02C did so in 73.33% of them.

A similar analysis was conducted on SAHH03. Here, all topologies yielded the same performance improvement: 33.33% of the cases. Nonetheless, NNHHs generated from SAHH04 improved on 50%, 30%, and 73.33% of the cases, respectively.

Table 1. Comparison of four SAHHs versus the NNHHs trained with heuristic rules. Best results are highlighted in bold.

Input hyper-heuristic	Total makespan	Topology A	Topology B	Topology C
SAHH01	40,538	1,596	**−1,387**	**−1,387**
SAHH02	40,748	3,221	3,221	**−2,597**
SAHH03	**41,299**	2,670	2,670	2,670
SAHH04	42,297	**−163**	1,672	**−3,146**

The most relevant information obtained from this first experiment is the evidence that a considerable reduction of hours in the total makespan of the schedules can be obtained by some of the neural network hyper-heuristics, concerning the original hyper-heuristics provided as input. For example, in cases like NNHH01C, the total time reduction (1,387 h) accounts for almost two months. Similarly, NNHH04C offered an improvement of almost four months (3,146 h). Of course, results were not always satisfactory and approaches like NNHH01A and NNHH04B actually require more time (1,596 and 1,672 additional hours, respectively).

4.2 Extended Heuristic Rules

In this experiment, we repeated the experimental methodology from Sect. 4.1 but this time, we used the extended heuristic rules to train the neural networks. With this experiment, we want to explore the behavior of the neural network hyper-heuristics when the number of training cases increases. We used SAHH01 to SAHH04, along with the three topologies used in the previous experiment to produce three neural network hyper-heuristics for each SAHH. The results from this experiment are depicted in Table 2.

Table 2. Comparison of four SAHHs versus the NNHHs trained with extended heuristic rules. Best results are highlighted in bold.

Input hyper-heuristic	Total makespan	Topology A	Topology B	Topology C
SAHH01	40,538	**−938**	1,759	1,759
SAHH02	40,748	**−191**	**−1,597**	1,386
SAHH03	**41,299**	967	835	835
SAHH04	42,297	325	**−163**	**−163**

As shown in Table 2, in all the cases, except for SAHH03, at least one of the neural network hyper-heuristics created using the extended heuristic rules reduced the total makespan achieved by the corresponding SAHH from which they were created. In the case of NNHH01A-EXT, it reduced the total makespan obtained by SAHH01 by 938 h and performed better or equal than SAHH01 in 22/30 instances. However, NNHH01B-EXT and NNHH01C-EXT were unable to reduce the total makespan and were capable of improving the solution obtained by SAHH01 in only 36.66% of the instances.

Similarly, NNHH02A-EXT improved the schedules generated by SAHH02 in 191 h (70% of the instances). Even so, NAHH02B obtained a more significant reduction in the total makespan (1,597 h), while slightly improving the ratio of instances (73.33%). Hence, the reason falls to extensive individual improvements per instance for those instances where it is better than SAHH02. However, NNHH02C-EXT required 1,386 more hours to solve the test set, even when it performed better than SAHH02 in 33.33% of the instances.

Unfortunately, the neural network model was unable to improve the total makespan obtained from the schedules produced with SAHH03. Although no improvement in the overall makespan was obtained, NNHH03A-EXT outperformed SAHH03 in 43.33% of the instances, while NNHH03B-EXT and NNHH03C-EXT performed better than SAHH03 in 40% of the instances.

Lastly, NNHH04A-EXT performed at least as well as SAHH04 in 53.33% of the instances, but it was not enough to reduce the total makespan obtained by SAHH04. In contrast, NNHH04B-EXT and NNHH04C-EXT reduced the total makespan obtained by SAHH04 in 163 h, demonstrating a performance improvement in most of the cases when compared to SAHH04.

4.3   Confirmatory Experiments with Extended Heuristic Rules

The rationale behind this experiment is to explore if using a better input hyper-heuristic can also improve the performance of the neural network hyper-heuristics. Thus, we produced 40 new SAHHs (by using the methodology described in Sect. 4.2) and ranked them according to their overall performance in the training set. We then selected the best SAHH and used it for generating three NNHHs (by using the same topologies described in Sect. 4.1).

Table 3 shows the resulting data. NNHHBestA-EXT and NNHHBestB-EXT were able to reduce total makespan by 286 and 806 h, respectively. Also, they improved the solution of 67% and 63% of the instances, respectively. Nonetheless, and even though NNHHBestC-EXT improved the results for 80% of the instances, it worsened the overall result by 121 h.

So far, we have compared the performance of the improved heuristic versus their original counterparts. For this last experiment, we aim at exploring the performance of the hyper-heuristic when compared against the best result the heuristics can produce: a synthetic oracle. Hence, ORACLE represents the makespan of the schedule obtained by the best heuristic for each particular instance in the test set.

ORACLE performs better than SAHHBest and NNHHBestC-EXT, by 43 and 164 h, respectively. On the other hand, NNHHBestA-EXT outperforms both SAHHBest and ORACLE in 50% of the instances, resulting in a total reduction of the makespan by 286 and 243 h, respectively. NNHHBestB-EXT significantly reduces the total makespan of both SAHHBest and ORACLE, since it requires

806 and 763 fewer hours to solve the test set, respectively. The reduction in the overall makespan corresponds, on average, to 25 less hours per instance (more than a day saved per instance).

Table 3. Comparison of the SAHH-B, and the NNHHs trained with its extended heuristic rules.

Method	Total makespan	Topology A	Topology B	Topology C
SAHHBest	38,288	−286	−806	121
ORACLE	38,245	−243	−763	164

4.4 Analysis of the Hyper-heuristics

When the 40 SAHHs generated in Sect. 4.3 were analyzed in a more detailed fashion, we observed that they produced contrasting results. For example, the difference in the total makespan between the best and worst SAHHs is 8,714 h, which exposes the variation of simulated annealing for producing hyper-heuristics, even under similar conditions.

On this regard, the proposed improvement method is independent of the strategy used to produce the input hyper-heuristics to be improved. The only requirement for our model to work is that the hyper-heuristics used as input can be represented as heuristic rules or that they can be used to produce the extended heuristic rules.

To support the previous statement, a Principal Component Analysis (PCA) was conducted to map the decisions taken by two selected hyper-heuristics into a 2D space, as illustrated in Fig. 1.

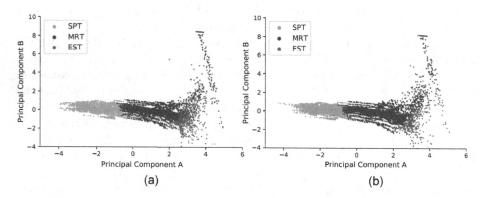

Fig. 1. PCA for extended heuristic rules and selected heuristic on each point by (a) the best generated SAHHBest and (b) NNHHBestB-EXT.

We obtained some relevant findings from this analysis. If the bottom right regions of the figures are compared, it can be appreciated in Fig. 1(b) that the action area of the heuristics is delimited by an almost straight line. Similarly, the central sections of Fig. 1(b) show the order given to the heuristic rules (straight lines) in comparison with those present in Fig. 1(a).

5   Conclusion

This paper presents the first ideas on how to improve the performance of existing heuristics by using neural networks. Although hyper-heuristics, in general, produce competent results, the differences in performance between two hyper-heuristics (generated with the same model and parameters) might sometimes be contrasting. This may happen because of the many decisions in the generation process. Then, by using the proposed approach, we can try to improve such hyper-heuristics to reduce the performance gap between most of them. It is important to mention that, in some cases, the little time investment to try to improve an existing heuristic (a few minutes) can represent several weeks of time savings.

The hyper-heuristic improvement model described in this document seems to be independent of the way the input hyper-heuristics are produced as long as we can extract the training data from the input hyper-heuristic. The fact that the model is independent of the way the input hyper-heuristics are produced has another significant benefit: the model is also domain independent. Then, we expect that applying this improvement strategy on hyper-heuristics produced for other problem domains is likely to succeed. Of course, further experimentation that involves more problem domains is a must for future work. Some other ideas remain unexplored and should also be addressed as future work. For example, more extensive experimentation that includes different neural network topologies as well as the potential exploitation of past decisions (the use of a memory module) to decide the heuristic to apply.

Acknowledgment. This research was partially supported by CONACyT Basic Science Project under grant 287479 and ITESM Research Group with Strategic Focus on Intelligent Systems.

References

1. Kurdi, M.: An effective new island model genetic algorithm for job shop scheduling problem. Comput. Oper. Res. **67**, 132–142 (2016)
2. Hernández-Ramírez, L., Frausto Solís, J., Castilla-Valdez, G., González-Barbosa, J.J., Terán-Villanueva, D., Morales-Rodríguez, M.L.: A hybrid simulated annealing for job shop scheduling problem. Int. J. Comb. Optimiz. Probl. Inform. **10**, 6–15 (2018)
3. van Laarhoven, P.J.M., Aarts, E.H.L., Lenstra, J.K.: Job shop scheduling by simulated annealing. Oper. Res. **40**, 113–125 (1992)
4. Satake, T., Morikawa, K., Takahashi, K., Nakamura, N.: Simulated annealing approach for minimizing the makespan of the general job-shop. Int. J. Prod. Econ. **60–61**, 515–522 (1999)

5. Bozejko, W., Gnatowski, A., Pempera, J., Wodecki, M.: Parallel tabu search for the cyclic job shop scheduling problem. Comput. Ind. Eng. **113**, 512–524 (2017)
6. Nowicki, E., Smutnicki, C.: A fast taboo search algorithm for the job shop problem. Manag. Sci. **42**, 797–813 (1996)
7. Zhang, C., Li, P., Guan, Z., Rao, Y.: A tabu search algorithm with a new neighborhood structure for the job shop scheduling problem. Comput. Oper. Res. **34**, 3229–3242 (2007)
8. Bhatt, N., Chauhan, N.R.: Genetic algorithm applications on job shop scheduling problem: a review. In: International Conference on Soft Computing Techniques and Implementations (ICSCTI), pp. 7–14 (2015)
9. Ghedjati, F.: Genetic algorithms for the job-shop scheduling problem with unrelated parallel constraints: heuristic mixing method machines and precedence. Comput. Ind. Eng. **37**, 39–42 (1999)
10. Hou, S., Liu, Y., Wen, H., Chen, Y.: A self-crossover genetic algorithm for job shop scheduling problem. In: IEEE International Conference on Industrial Engineering and Engineering Management, pp. 549–554 (2011)
11. Blackstone, J.H., Phillips, D.T., Hogg, G.L.: A state-of-the-art survey of dispatching rules for manufacturing job shop operations. Int. J. Prod. Res. **20**, 27–45 (1982)
12. Adams, J., Balas, E., Zawack, D.: The shifting bottleneck procedure for job shop scheduling. Manag. Sci. **34**, 391–401 (1988)
13. Epstein, S.L., Freuder, E.C., Wallace, R., Morozov, A., Samuels, B.: The adaptive constraint engine. In: Van Hentenryck, P. (ed.) CP 2002. LNCS, vol. 2470, pp. 525–540. Springer, Heidelberg (2002). https://doi.org/10.1007/3-540-46135-3_35
14. Petrovic, S., Qu, R.: Case-based reasoning as a heuristic selector in a hyper-heuristic for course timetabling problems. In: Proceedings of the 6th International Conference on Knowledge-Based Intelligent Information Engineering Systems and Applied Technologies, KES 2002, vol. 82, pp. 336–340 (2002)
15. O'Mahony, E., Hebrard, E., Holland, A., Nugent, C., O'Sullivan, B.: Using case-based reasoning in an algorithm portfolio for constraint solving. In: Irish Conference on Artificial Intelligence and Cognitive Science, pp. 210–216 (2008)
16. Ortiz-Bayliss, J.C., Terashima-Marín, H., Conant-Pablos, S.E.: Combine and conquer: an evolutionary hyper-heuristic approach for solving constraint satisfaction problems. Artif. Intell. Rev. **46**, 327–349 (2016)
17. Sim, K., Hart, E., Paechter, B.: A lifelong learning hyper-heuristic method for bin packing. Evol. Comput. **23**, 37–67 (2015)
18. Malitsky, Y.: Evolving instance-specific algorithm configuration. In: Malitsky, Y. (ed.) Instance-Specific Algorithm Configuration, pp. 93–105. Springer, Cham (2014). https://doi.org/10.1007/978-3-319-11230-5_9
19. Zhao, F., Zhang, J., Zhang, C., Wang, J.: An improved shuffled complex evolution algorithm with sequence mapping mechanism for job shop scheduling problems. Expert Syst. Appl. **42**, 3953–3966 (2015)
20. Peng, B., Lü, Z., Cheng, T.: A tabu search/path relinking algorithm to solve the job shop scheduling problem. Comput. Oper. Res. **53**, 154–164 (2015)
21. Cheng, T.C.E., Peng, B., Lü, Z.: A hybrid evolutionary algorithm to solve the job shop scheduling problem. Ann. Oper. Res. **242**, 223–237 (2016)
22. Gao, L., Li, X., Wen, X., Lu, C., Wen, F.: A hybrid algorithm based on a new neighborhood structure evaluation method for job shop scheduling problem. Comput. Ind. Eng. **88**, 417–429 (2015)
23. Neyshabur, B., Bhojanapalli, S., McAllester, D., Srebro, N.: Exploring generalization in deep learning. In: Advances in Neural Information Processing Systems, pp. 5947–5956 (2017)

24. Olson, M., Wyner, A., Berk, R.: Modern neural networks generalize on small data sets. In: Advances in Neural Information Processing Systems, pp. 3619–3628 (2018)
25. Ortiz-Bayliss, J.C., Terashima-Marín, H., Conant-Pablos, S.E.: Neural networks to guide the selection of heuristics within constraint satisfaction problems. In: Martínez-Trinidad, J.F., Carrasco-Ochoa, J.A., Ben-Youssef Brants, C., Hancock, E.R. (eds.) MCPR 2011. LNCS, vol. 6718, pp. 250–259. Springer, Heidelberg (2011). https://doi.org/10.1007/978-3-642-21587-2_27
26. Tyasnurita, R., Özcan, E., John, R.: Learning heuristic selection using a time delay neural network for open vehicle routing. In: IEEE Congress on Evolutionary Computation (CEC), pp. 1474–1481 (2017)
27. Li, J., Burke, E.K., Qu, R.: Integrating neural networks and logistic regression to underpin hyper-heuristic search. Knowl.-Based Syst. **24**, 322–330 (2011)
28. Ortiz-Bayliss, J.C., Terashima-Marín, H., Conant-Pablos, S.E.: A neuro-evolutionary hyper-heuristic approach for constraint satisfaction problems. Cogn. Comput. **8**, 429–441 (2016)
29. Taillard, E.: Benchmarks for basic scheduling problems. Eur. J. Oper. Res. **64**, 278–285 (1993)
30. Garza-Santisteban, F., et al.: A simulated annealing hyper-heuristic for job shop scheduling problems. In: 2019 IEEE Congress on Evolutionary Computation (CEC), pp. 57–64 (2019)

Early Anomalous Vehicular Traffic Detection Through Spectral Techniques and Unsupervised Learning Models

Roberto Carlos Vazquez-Nava[1(✉)], Miguel Gonzalez-Mendoza[1(✉)],
Oscar Herrera-Alacantara[2(✉)], and Neil Hernandez-Gress[1(✉)]

[1] School of Engineering and Sciences, Tecnologico de Monterrey, Monterrey, Mexico
{A01746886,ngress}@itesm.mx, mgonza@tec.mx
[2] Universidad Autonoma Metropolitana, Mexico City, Mexico
oha@azc.uam.mx

Abstract. Smart Mobility seeks to meet urban requirements within a city and solve the urban mobility problems, one of them is related with vehicular traffic. The anomalous vehicular traffic is an unexpected change in the day-to-day vehicular traffic caused by different reasons, such as an accident, an event, road works or a natural disaster. An early detection of anomalous vehicular traffic allows to alert drivers of the anomaly and can make better decisions during their journey. The current solutions for this problem are mainly focused on the development of new algorithms, without giving enough importance to the extraction of underlying information from vehicular traffic, and even more, when this is a univariate time series and it is not possible to obtain other context features that describes its behavior. To address this issue, we propose a methodology for temporary, spectral and aggregation features and an unsupervised learning model to detect anomalous vehicular traffic. The methodology was evaluated in a real vehicular traffic database. Experimental results show that by using spectral attributes the detection of anomalous vehicular traffic, the Isolation Forest obtains the best results.

Keywords: Anomalous vehicular traffic · Smart Mobility · Digital filters · Unsupervised models

1 Introduction

Nowadays, urban mobility involves most of the activities that take place within a city. However, poorly managed transport has a negative impact in cities, because it increases [4]: air and noise pollution, trip times for drivers, energy consumption and the vehicular congestion, the most common worldwide. These problems cause an imbalance in the daily life of the inhabitants in the city. To solve them, Smart Mobility (SM) is key, because it seeks to meet urban requirements within a city for a safer, more efficient and sustainable urban mobility [19].

© Springer Nature Switzerland AG 2019
L. Martínez-Villaseñor et al. (Eds.): MICAI 2019, LNAI 11835, pp. 162–175, 2019.
https://doi.org/10.1007/978-3-030-33749-0_14

Anomalous vehicular traffic (AVT) is an unexpected change in the day-to-day vehicular traffic, this can be caused by different reasons: an accident, an event, road works or a natural disaster [24]. The detection of AVT is a problem that SM must solve, because it plays an important role in a city by reducing costs, taking short-term and long-term decisions, and identifying problems with critical infrastructure.

Previous researches on the detection of AVT base their solutions on using inductive loop sensors, video surveillance and crowdsourcing systems. However, these solutions are limited in the sense that they focus mainly on creating new algorithms, and do not pay attention to the underlying information that can be extracted from vehicular traffic.

In this work, vehicular traffic is cataloged as a univariate time series, where the unique feature is the cars counted and implicitly the time. Therefore, the feature extraction is relevant in this type of problem where information is scarce, since by having new features there is a significant contribution of information to anomaly detection models, by facilitating their learning process and improving its performance. In this research, we propose to develop a methodology for the extraction of spectral, temporary and aggregation features of the vehicular traffic and through unsupervised learning models to perform the early detection of AVT.

The rest of this document is organized as follows. In the next section, the related work is explained. In Sect. 3, the problem statement is presented. Then, in Sect. 4, the proposed methodology is described, followed by the experimentation carried out and the results in Sect. 5. While in Sect. 6 the conclusions are presented.

2   Related Work

Solutions that allow the AVT detection acquired information from different devices, for example, with the use of the GPS and smartphones, vehicles trajectory can be shared, also, with social media platforms, people tend to post messages related to vehicular traffic problems. Based on GPS devices, Kuang et al. [16] propose a solution using wavelets and PCA, meanwhile using twitter as a source of information, D'Andrea et al. [8], present a real-time monitoring system for traffic event detection. The system fetches tweets and processes them to assign the appropriate class label as event or not. However, these solutions involve problems with privacy if there are not the correct licenses. Also, if there is not information from all the actors related with vehicular traffic, the data can not be representative.

Zameni et al. [24] propose a *City Traffic Event Detection* method that is able to detect anomalous local events while ignoring the so-called *legitimate global traffic* changes as anomalous. However, these solutions are dependent on vehicular traffic registered by other points in a city to detect AVT.

Visual data contains rich information, and it can play a vital role by detecting AVT. Solutions based on video surveillance system are proposed by Babaei

[3] and Singh et al. [23], who use trajectories of vehicles, the first one by combining multi-view monitoring with Support Vector Machines, while the second one base their solution on neural networks which learns feature representation from volumes of raw pixel intensity of surveillance videos. The work proposed by Farooq et al. [11], explores multidimensional data by using a single camera and features like objects position, trajectory, orientation, visible age in the scene and invisible count, and with DBSCAN model detect AVT. However, surveillance cameras involve huge computing resources consumption and their infrastructure may not cover the whole city.

The inductive loop sensor is used to count cars that circulate in a road. With data acquired by this device, Hutchins et al. [13] perform anomaly detection, using Markov-modulated Poisson processes. While Jawad et al. [14] perform anomaly detection using biological sequence and profile hidden Markov models too. When using this type of sensors, features such as those extracted by surveillance, GPS or social media are not possible. Therefore, feature extraction becomes relevant when information is scarce and it ins necessary to improve anomaly detection algorithms performance.

3   Anomalies Detection

3.1   Problem

An anomaly in the field of vehicular traffic is a pattern that deviates significantly from the flow established as normal; an example of this concept is shown in Fig. 1. In the anomalies detection problems, generally there is not knowledge of those observations classified as anomalous. However, in the literature these types of problems are divided into three categories [1]:

1. *Supervised:* These techniques have prior knowledge of normal and anomalous observations.
2. *Semi-supervised:* It is assumed that all training observations belong to normal class.
3. *Unsupervised:* In these techniques do not require training data, since they assume the normal instances are much more frequent than anomaly ones.

In this research two approaches are studied: semi-supervised and unsupervised learning.

3.2   Unsupervised Anomaly Detection Algorithms

In this work, three well-known anomaly detection algorithms are used. A brief description of them is listed below [1]:

- *Isolation Forest (iF)* [17]. This algorithm classifies an observation as outlier if it is easily isolated by random divisions.

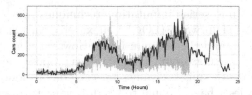

Fig. 1. Anomalous vehicular traffic example indicated in red. (Color figure online)

- *One-Class SVM (OCSVM)* [22]. This method is based on support vector machines, which seeks to define a decision boundary in the kernel space that separates normal observations from anomalies.
- *Local Outlier Factor (LOF)* [6]. Compute the score of how abnormal a point x_i is when calculating its average distance to its nearest k neighbors. A point is more anomalous if it is significantly further from its neighbors than from the others.

4   Proposed Methodology

4.1   Methodology Overview

The methodology proposed in this work is depicted in Fig. 2. In the following sections, the imputation algorithm is detailed, followed by the explanation of how the temporary, spectral and aggregation features are computed. Finally, the feature selection process is explained. This methodology is for vehicular traffic signal whose time sampling is 5 min.

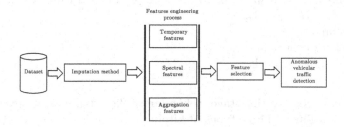

Fig. 2. Steps of the proposed methodology.

4.2   Imputation Method

The missing values problem is common in almost all researches, to delete them can have a significant effect on both conclusions and quality of models that are used [15]. Therefore, missing values must be imputed with reasonable values [18].

Some univariate time series imputation techniques are [18]: overall mean, last observation carried forward (LOCF), next observation carried backward (NOCB), interpolation and the Kalman filter. However, for contiguous missing values, these methods are not useful. Therefore, we propose the imputation Algorithm 1, which imputes the missing values for each day as long as the amount of its missing values is less than or equal to the following threshold:

$$thr = \lceil n(1 - Pr_\sigma) \rceil \tag{1}$$

Where n is the number of observations that one day has, and Pr_σ is 0.6827 which represents the percentage of data that should fall within a normal distribution with one standard deviation from the mean.

A missing value will be imputed with the average of the non-missing values cars count with the days of the other weeks, and that coincide with the time and day in which the missing value was recorded. An example of the proposed imputation algorithm application is illustrated in Fig. 3.

4.3   Feature Engineering

In this section it is explained how the different features are computed. The only feature available is vehicular traffic, which will be called *cars* from now on. At the end of feature engineering process, there are 268 features for each of the time aggregations: 5, 15, 20, 30 and 40 min, also 1, 1.5, 2, 2.6, 3, 6, 8, 12 and 24 h.

Temporary Features. These attributes are based on the date and time at which an observation was recorded. They are listed below:

- Hour of day (H): corresponding to the time (hh:mm) in which the observation was detected, $H \in [0, 24)$.
- Month Number.
- Day number of the year.
- Day number of the week.

Spectral Features. In this stage, vehicular traffic attributes are extracted by applying digital filters. Three types of filters are used: low-pass, band-pass and high-pass [21], all of them Chebychev Type I. For the filters design, the bilinear transformation procedure explained by Parks [20] was followed.

A scalogram was built with wavelet Morlet [9] to determine the cutoff frequencies of the different filters implemented. In Fig. 4 is depicted the scalogram of a vehicular traffic signal sampled at 5 min. Indicated by dotted lines, the bandpass frequencies are located, which delimit the ranges of the frequencies in which the new signals will be bounded. To refer to each of the filtered signals, from now on, the term *Band i* will be used, where $i \in [1, 5]$.

To obtain the bands, we use 5 filters: 1 low-pass, 1 high-pass and 3 pass-band. The selection of all bands has two-fold: the first one is include the entire range of

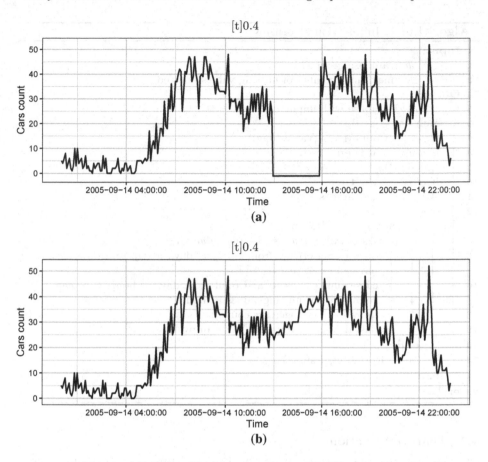

Fig. 3. It is shown both the day with missing values (a) and the same day with missing values imputed (b).

the signal frequency in a range $f \in [0, f_N]$, where f_N is the Nyquist frequency, and the second one, is to separate those bands where the signal presents more energy. The specifications of implemented filters are detailed in Table 1. To avoid the lag between the original signal and the bands, zero-phase filters were used [2].

Aggregation Features. In this stage, 43 new features are extracted from both cars and the 5 bands. Those features only are extracted from different time aggregations. In Table 2 the 43 features are mentioned and the way to calculate them is found in more detail in [7]. The sum was used as aggregation function to compute the representative values of spectral and cars features, and for temporary ones, the lowest value is selected, when time aggregations are used. Meanwhile, for the time of 5 min, 3 consecutive observations were used to calculate this type of features.

Algorithm 1. Imputation algorithm.

```
 1 Input:
 2          db: Database grouped by days.
 3          thr: maximum number of missing values allowed.
 4 Output:
 5          db: Database with imputed values.
 6 foreach day ∈ db do
 7 │  qty_mv ← CountMissingValues(day);
 8 │  if qty_mv = 0 then
 9 │  │  NextDay;
10 │  if qty_mv ⩾ thr then
11 │  │  DeleteDayDatabase(day);
12 │  else
13 │  │  foreach hour ∈ day do
14 │  │  │  if cars count at hour is missing value then
15 │  │  │  │  days ← SelectDays from db ⟺ days = day and days do not
       │  │  │  │  have an event registered;
16 │  │  │  │  cars count ← SelectCarsCount from days at hour ⟺ cars
       │  │  │  │  count are not missing values at hour;
17 │  │  │  │  impval ← Average(cars count);
18 │  │  │  │  day at hour ← ImputateValue(impval);
19 │  │  end
20 │  │  db ← UpdateValues(day)
21 │  end
22 end
```

4.4 Feature Selection

The features obtained are normalized. The feature selection has two phases. The first one, those features which variance is zero and with indeterminate values are excluded. In the second phase, the Mann-Whitney-U and Fisher's Exact statistical tests were used, the first one is applied to features with real values, and the second to features with binary values. These statistical tests calculate the degree of significance of a feature with the target class (ground truth) as a $p-value$. After calculating the $p-value$ for each feature, the Benjamini-Yekutieli procedure is used [5], which decides which features to keep. The null hypothesis H_0, establishes that the selected feature has no influence on the target class. If H_0 is rejected, the feature is kept. The implementation of this feature selection procedure is in [7].

5 Experiments

5.1 Database

A real vehicular traffic database was used. It consists of estimated vehicle counts every 5 min over 175 days from an inductive loop sensor located on the Glendale

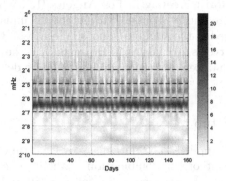

Fig. 4. Vehicular traffic scalogram with a time sampling of 5 min. The band frequencies bounded by dotted lines are shown. In total there are 5 bands, Band 1 corresponds to lowest frequencies, and Band 5 to highest ones.

Table 1. Parameters of the digital filters implemented.

Band	Filter type	f_p (mHz)	f_s (mHz)	R_p (dB)	R_s (dB)	Order
1	Low-pass	2^{-7}	2^{-6}	2	30	4
2	Pass-band	$2^{-6}\ 2^{-5}$	$2^{-7}\ 2^{-4}$	2	30	3
3	Pass-band	$2^{-4}\ 2^{-3}$	$2^{-3}\ 2^{-2}$	2	30	3
4	Pass-band	$2^{-2}\ 2^{-1}$	$2^{-1}\ 2^{-0}$	2	30	3
5	High-pass	2^{-1}	$2^{-0.5}$	2	30	3

Table 2. Aggregation features.

Feature	Feature	Feature
Absolute energy	Absolute sum of changes	Aggregation function
Approximate entropy	Autocorrelation	Binned entropy
Non-linearity measure (c3)	Complexity-invariant distance	Count above mean
Count below mean	Energy ratio by chunks	FFT aggregated by mean
FFT aggregated by var.	FFT aggregated by skew	FFT aggregated by kurtosis
FFT first coefficient	First location of max. value	First location of min. value
Has duplicate max value	Has duplicate min value	Kurtosis
Large standard deviation	Last location of Maximum	Last location of minimum
Linear trend	Longest strike above mean	Longest strike below mean
Maximum value	Mean value	Mean abs change
Mean change	Mean second derivative central	Median value
Minimum value	Number of peaks	Partial autocorrelation
Quantile	Skewness	Standard deviation
Sum values	Time reversal	Variance
Variance larger than std		

on-ramp to the 101-North Freeway in Los Angeles [13], which is close enough to the Dodgers Stadium and it is possible to detect the unusual vehicular traffic due to the games played in the stadium. There is record of 81 games at Dodgers Stadium which will serve as ground truth. However, 3 of the 81 days do not have enough observations and were discarded. AVT should be detected as soon as the game ends.

5.2   Experiment Setup

The methodology was applied to 32 databases by each time aggregation. These databases are the result of the combination without repetition of the bands from 0 to 5 bands. The total databases created are 480 and are in google drive repository[1]. The models were used as both semi-supervised and unsupervised learning. In the semi-supervised learning, 5-fold cross-validation was used. The anomalies were introduced in the validation process. The performance of the 3 algorithms were evaluated by computing the Area Under the ROC Curve (AUC) metric. For semi-supervised learning, the 5 different values of AUC obtained are averaged.

Table 3. AUC values by using all the bands and none of them in semi-supervised learning. The best AUC values are remarked in bold.

Time	Non-Bands			All Bands		
	LOF	OCSVM	iF	LOF	OCSVM	iF
5 min	0.4607	**0.8051**	0.7972	0.7587	0.8820	**0.9344**
15 min	**0.8319**	0.7901	0.7325	0.8755	0.8857	**0.9334**
20 min	**0.8019**	0.7592	0.6779	0.8121	0.8799	**0.9353**
30 min	**0.8339**	0.8084	0.7731	0.7952	0.8840	**0.9398**
40 min	**0.8569**	0.8185	0.8018	0.8338	0.9104	**0.9322**
1 h	0.8695	0.8624	**0.8755**	0.8914	0.8975	**0.9468**
1.5 h	**0.9087**	0.7831	0.8235	0.9184	0.8758	**0.9235**
2 h	**0.8940**	0.7756	0.8679	0.9008	0.8723	**0.9424**
2.6 h	**0.9389**	0.8241	0.8966	0.9201	0.8542	**0.9400**
3 h	**0.9559**	0.8680	0.9232	0.9320	0.8837	**0.9491**
4 h	**0.9377**	0.5527	0.8991	0.9553	0.8435	**0.9559**
6 h	0.8721	0.7421	**0.9108**	0.9550	0.9171	**0.9693**
8 h	0.7758	0.6589	**0.7809**	0.9153	0.8565	**0.9401**
12 h	0.7286	0.7991	**0.8983**	0.8629	0.9128	**0.9531**
24 h	0.8139	0.7832	**0.8202**	0.9055	0.9204	**0.9477**

---

[1] https://drive.google.com/drive/folders/1Noqgm1PXNg-qmjuP0GQtnkV918JWIKMq?usp=sharing.

The experimentation was carried out on a PC with an AMD Ryzen 3 2200g processor and 16 GB of RAM. The programming language used for the implementation of the imputation algorithm and the filters was python. We used the Scikit-Learn library which contains the 3 algorithms, their default parameters were used.

5.3 Results

In Tables 3 and 4 are depicted the AUC values for each model in both semi-supervised and unsupervised learning respectively, when all the bands and none of them are used. These results are upper and lower limits. Meanwhile, in the Table 5 are depicted the best AUC values. In the following sections an analysis of the time aggregations, the most relevant features and the models used in the experimentation is carried out.

5.4 Time and Features Analysis

First off, the Band 1 and the aggregation features generated from it were discarded in the feature selection process. Band 1 corresponds to small frequencies and does not present much variability over time compared with the other bands. From Tables 3 and 4, it is observed that the use of bands as features increase

Table 4. AUC values by using all the bands and none of them in unsupervised learning. The best AUC values are remarked in bold.

Time	Non-Bands			All Bands		
	LOF	OCSVM	iF	LOF	OCSVM	iF
5 min	0.4477	**0.8041**	0.7917	0.7037	0.8809	**0.9302**
15 min	**0.8068**	0.7876	0.7427	0.8399	0.8829	**0.9312**
20 min	0.7516	**0.7561**	0.7134	0.7612	0.8771	**0.9308**
30 min	**0.8250**	0.8041	0.7321	0.7193	0.8788	**0.9273**
40 min	**0.8332**	0.8119	0.7960	0.7485	0.9049	**0.9399**
1 h	0.8192	**0.8541**	0.8491	0.6988	0.8870	**0.9407**
1.5 h	**0.8418**	0.7673	0.8263	0.6773	0.8543	**0.9235**
2 h	0.7141	0.7481	**0.8387**	0.6712	0.8449	**0.9375**
2.6 h	0.8016	0.7834	**0.8758**	0.5903	0.8134	**0.9084**
3 h	0.8100	0.8260	**0.8808**	0.5707	0.8340	**0.9314**
4 h	**0.8001**	0.5006	0.7980	0.6163	0.7835	**0.9155**
6 h	0.6000	0.6262	**0.7771**	0.5515	0.8263	**0.8561**
8 h	**0.6234**	0.5552	0.5931	0.6839	0.7438	**0.8391**
12 h	0.6375	0.6377	**0.6708**	0.5729	0.7202	**0.7636**
24 h	0.6504	**0.6685**	0.6583	0.6374	0.5609	**0.6833**

the AUC values in both semi-supervised and unsupervised learning in most time aggregations, only the best AUC value obtained by using non-bands is at 3 h time in semi-supervised learning.

It is shown in Table 5 the highest AUC values. The maximum values are observed at 6 and 1 h with semi-supervised and unsupervised learning respectively. However, to perform the early detection of AVT, we choose the time aggregations less than or equal to 1 h since the AUC results are acceptable in both learnings.

The most relevant features when the algorithms get the best AUC values in both learnings are vehicular traffic (cars), regarding with spectral features are Band 3 and Band 4. The temporary feature is Hour of day, and the aggregation features are Maximum value, FFT mean, Minimum value, Absolute energy, Absolute sum of changes, Mean abs of changes, Mean abs change, Standard deviation, Variance, FFT variance and C3.

Table 5. The maximum AUC values obtained (remarked in bold) in both semi-supervised and unsupervised learning. Also, the bands most relevant in the databases are shown. NB refers to Non-Bands.

	Semisupervised						Unsupervised					
Time	LOF	Bands	OCSVM	Bands	iF	Bands	LOF	Bands	OCSVM	Bands	iF	Bands
5 min	0.8300	(3,4,5)	0.9223	(3,4)	**0.9537**	(3)	0.8099	(4)	0.9217	(3,4)	**0.9532**	(3)
15 min	0.9022	(3,4)	0.9240	(3,4)	**0.9552**	(3,4)	0.8872	(3,4,5)	0.9220	(3,4)	**0.9529**	(3)
20 min	0.9019	(2,4)	0.9184	(3,4)	**0.9482**	(3,4,5)	0.8790	(2,4)	0.9166	(3,4)	**0.9464**	(3,4,5)
30 min	0.8945	(2,4)	0.9183	(3,4)	**0.9556**	(3,4)	0.8756	(2,4)	0.9147	(3,4)	**0.9509**	(3,4)
40 min	0.9052	(3)	0.9428	(3,4)	**0.9509**	(3)	0.8697	(3,4)	0.9397	(3,4)	**0.9514**	(3,4)
1h	0.9109	(2)	0.9468	(3,4)	**0.9658**	(3)	0.8563	(4)	0.9398	(3,4)	**0.9619**	(3,4)
1.5 h	0.9403	(2)	0.9256	(3,4)	**0.9528**	(3,4)	0.8725	(4,5)	0.9130	(3,4)	**0.9407**	(3,4)
2 h	0.9218	(3,4,5)	0.9171	(3,4,5)	**0.9600**	(3,5)	0.8285	(4)	0.8971	(3,4,5)	**0.9474**	(3,4)
2.6 h	0.9436	(3)	0.9105	(3,4)	**0.9593**	(3)	0.8318	(4)	0.8824	(3,4)	**0.9460**	(3,4)
3 h	0.9559	(NB)	0.9271	(3,4)	**0.9616**	(3,4)	0.8501	(4)	0.8965	(3,4)	**0.9506**	(3,4,5)
4 h	0.9572	(3,4)	0.8852	(3,4)	**0.9575**	(3)	0.8124	(5)	0.8165	(3,4)	**0.9192**	(3,4)
6 h	0.9550	(2,3,4,5)	0.9371	(3,4)	**0.9820**	(2,3,4)	0.6420	(4)	0.8387	(3,4)	**0.9120**	(3,4,5)
8 h	0.9207	(3,4)	0.8752	(2,3,4)	**0.9570**	(2,3,4)	0.7462	(4,5)	0.7571	(2,3,4)	**0.8829**	(2,3,4)
12 h	0.8629	(2,3,4,5)	0.9155	(2,3,4)	**0.9718**	(2,3,4)	0.6887	(2,4,5)	0.7202	(2,3,4,5)	**0.8196**	(2,3,4)
24 h	0.9068	(2,3,4,5)	0.9204	(2,3,4,5)	**0.9517**	(3,4,5)	**0.8278**	(4,5)	0.7072	(NB)	0.7217	(2,4,5)

5.5 Models Analysis

From Table 3, the models used as semi-supervised approach without any band, LOF gets the best AUC values in most of the time aggregations, followed by iF. While using all the bands, iF obtains the best AUC values. The unsupervised approach showed in Table 4, when bands are not used, there is not an algorithm that stands out, while using all the bands, the iF obtains the best AUC values. An advantage of this algorithm is that it works with high-dimensional data.

From Table 5, the algorithm that obtains the best values in both semi-supervised and unsupervised learning is iF algorithm, except in a 24-h time aggregation, where LOF has the best result in unsupervised learning.

The iF algorithm obtains the best AUC values, but to know if there is a significant difference between algorithms, we applied the Friedman test and the Bergmann-Hommel dynamic post-hoc [12]. We consider a level of significance of $\alpha = 0.05$. To show the post-hoc results, we used Critical Difference diagrams (CD diagrams) [10]. In a CD diagram, the rightmost algorithm is the best one, while the algorithms sharing a thick line have statistically similar behaviours. CD diagrams are shown in Fig. 5, in both semi-supervised and unsupervised learning the Isolation Forest is the best model.

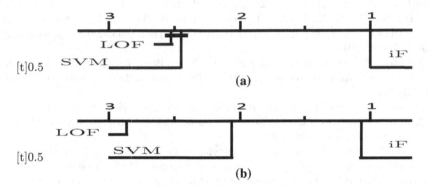

Fig. 5. CD diagrams with the statistical comparisons of LOF, OCSVM and iF. (a) Semisupervised learning and (b) Unsupervised learning

6 Conclusions

In this paper, we proposed a new methodology for features extraction based on spectral techniques to detect early anomalous vehicular traffic with an unsupervised algorithms. The best results was obtained using Isolation Forest, in both semi-supervised and unsupervised learning, which is an algorithm easy to understand. The relevant time aggregation for the early detection of AVT are all those less than or equal to 1 h in both learning methods studied, meanwhile Bands 3 and 4 turned out to be those spectral features that provide more information about the vehicular traffic. The most relevant temporary feature is Hour of day. Also, aggregation features play a important role to enrich vehicular traffic database. As future work, we are interested to create an heterogeneous ensemble with unsupervised algorithms to enhance the AVT detection.

References

1. Aggarwal, C.: Outlier analysis. In: Aggarwal, C.C. (ed.) Data Mining, pp. 237–263. Springer, Cham (2015). https://doi.org/10.1007/978-3-319-14142-8_8
2. Antoniou, A.: Digital Signal Processing. McGraw-Hill, New York (2016)
3. Babaei, P.: Vehicles behavior analysis for abnormality detection by multi-view monitoring. Int. Res. J. Appl. Basic Sci. **9**(11), 1929–1936 (2015)
4. Benevolo, C., Dameri, R.P., D'Auria, B.: Smart mobility in smart city. In: Torre, T., Braccini, A.M., Spinelli, R. (eds.) Empowering Organizations. LNISO, vol. 11, pp. 13–28. Springer, Cham (2016). https://doi.org/10.1007/978-3-319-23784-8_2
5. Benjamini, Y., Yekutieli, D., et al.: The control of the false discovery rate in multiple testing under dependency. Ann. Stat. **29**(4), 1165–1188 (2001)
6. Breunig, M., Kriegel, H.P., Ng, R., Sander, J.: LOF: identifying density-based local outliers. ACM SIGMOD Rec. **29**(2), 93–104 (2000)
7. Christ, M., Braun, N., Neuffer, J., Kempa-Liehr, A.: Time series feature extraction on basis of scalable hypothesis tests (tsfresh-a Python package). Neurocomputing **307**, 72–77 (2018)
8. D'Andrea, E., Ducange, P., Lazzerini, B., Marcelloni, F.: Real-time detection of traffic from twitter stream analysis. IEEE Trans. Intell. Transp. Syst. **16**(4), 2269–2283 (2015)
9. Debnath, L.: Wavelets and Signal Processing. Springer, New York (2012)
10. Demšar, J.: Statistical comparisons of classifiers over multiple data sets. J. Mach. Learn. Res. **7**(Jan), 1–30 (2006)
11. Farooq, M., Khan, N., Ali, M.: Unsupervised video surveillance for anomaly detection of street traffic. Int. J. Adv. Comput. Sci. Appl. (IJACSA) **8**, 270–275 (2017)
12. Garcia, S., Herrera, F.: An extension on statistical comparisons of classifiers over multiple data sets for all pairwise comparisons. J. Mach. Learn. Res. **9**(Dec), 2677–2694 (2008)
13. Hutchins, J.: Dodgers loop sensor dataset. UCI Machine Learning Repository (2006)
14. Jawad, A., Kersting, K., Andrienko, N.: Where traffic meets DNA: mobility mining using biological sequence analysis revisited, pp. 357–360 (2011)
15. Kang, H.: The prevention and handling of the missing data. Korean J. Anesthesiol. **64**(5), 402 (2013)
16. Kuang, W., An, S., Jiang, H.: Detecting traffic anomalies in urban areas using taxi GPS data. Math. Probl. Eng. **2015**, 13 (2015)
17. Liu, F., Ting, K., Zhou, Z.H.: Isolation forest, pp. 413–422 (2008)
18. Moritz, S., Sardá, A., Bartz-Beielstein, T., Zaefferer, M., Stork, J.: Comparison of different methods for univariate time series imputation in R. arXiv preprint arXiv:1510.03924 (2015)
19. Moustaka, V., Vakali, A., Anthopoulos, L.G.: A systematic review for smart city data analytics. ACM Comput. Surv. **51**(5), 103:1–103:41 (2018)
20. Parks, T., Burrus, C.: Digital Filter Design. Topics in Digital Signal Processing. Wiley, New York (1987)
21. Proakis, J.: Digital Signal Processing: Principles Algorithms and Applications. Pearson Education India (2001)
22. Schölkopf, B., Platt, J., Shawe-Taylor, J., Smola, A., Williamson, R.: Estimating the support of a high-dimensional distribution. Neural Comput. **13**(7), 1443–1471 (2001)

23. Singh, D., Mohan, C.K.: Deep spatio-temporal representation for detection of road accidents using stacked autoencoder. IEEE Trans. Intell. Transp. Syst. **20**(3), 879–887 (2019)
24. Zameni, M., et al.: Urban sensing for anomalous event detection: In: Brefeld, U., et al. (eds.) ECML PKDD 2018. LNCS (LNAI), vol. 11053, pp. 553–568. Springer, Cham (2019). https://doi.org/10.1007/978-3-030-10997-4_34

ADSOA - Fault Detection and Recovery Technology Based on Collective Intelligence

Juan Sebastián Guadalupe Godínez Borja,
Marco Antonio Corona Ruiz, and Carlos Pérez Leguízamo$^{(\boxtimes)}$

Central Bank of Mexico (Banco de México), Av. 5 de Mayo #2,
06059 Mexico City, Mexico
{jgodinez, macorona, cperez}@banxico.org.mx

Abstract. Mission Critical Systems (MCS) require continuous operation since a failure might cause economic or human losses. Autonomous Decentralized Service Oriented Architecture (ADSOA) is a proposal to design and develop MCS in which the system functionality is divided into service units in order to provide functional reliability and load balancing; on the other hand, it offers high availability through distributed replicas. A fault detection and recovering technology has been proposed for ADSOA based on collective intelligence. In this technology, an operation service level degradation should be detected autonomously by the service units at a point in which the continuity of the service may be compromised. Once a failure of this type is detected, each service unit analyses the system's state and collectively decide the strategy to recover itself. The recovery technology instructs those selected service units to be gradually cloned in order to get the operational service level.

Keywords: Service continuity · Fault tolerance · Service-oriented architecture · Autonomous Decentralized Systems · Fault detection · Fault recovery

1 Introduction and Motivation

In the presence of a failure, most of the conventional systems implement reactive fault detection and recover mechanisms either automatically or manually. In both cases, the aim is to switch to a redundant or standby computer server upon the failure or abnormal termination of the previously active system. In some cases, the Mean Time to Recovery (MTTR) [15] of these technologies may represent a low risk for the service that the system offers. However, since a failure in MCS may provoke fatal consequences, it is important to reduce the MTTR to a value near to zero.

In this paper, we briefly present ADSOA [4–6], which has been proposed as a service-oriented architecture for designing MCS, and it has been mainly utilized in financial sector applications. This architecture provides high functional reliability since it is possible to distribute and replicate the functionality of a system in specialized service units. One of the main technologies of ADSOA, called Loosely Coupled Delivery Transaction and Synchronization Technology [6], allows the system to detect

L. Martínez-Villaseñor et al. (Eds.): MICAI 2019, LNAI 11835, pp. 176–186, 2019.
https://doi.org/10.1007/978-3-030-33749-0_15

when the provision of a service has reached a point in which the continuity of the service may be compromised and it sends a signal alarm to a monitor. This approach may represent a risk for a MCS since it depends on human intervention for taking the necessary actions to repair the system.

This has motivated this paper which presents a technology to autonomously detect and recover gradually all the unit services required for the operational service level in ADSOA. This technology is based on a cloning mechanism that is activated once the operational service level has been compromised due to some failed services units. We describe the protocol and algorithms that the healthy services units utilize in this cloning mechanism and show how they coordinate among them in order to avoid a massive creation of replicas. We developed a prototype in order to illustrate this approach.

The rest of this paper is organized as follows: In Sect. 2, we show the related work. In Sect. 3, we give a view of ADSOA concept and architecture. In Sect. 4, we present the proposed technology. In Sect. 5, we show a prototype, and finally, in Sect. 6, the conclusion and future work.

2   Related Work

Cloning technologies have been widely used in different technological areas for providing high reliability to the system in which it is applied. In Optical Burst Switching (OBS) Networks, burst cloning has been proposed as a proactive loss recovery mechanism that attempts to prevent burst loss by sending two copies of the same burst, if the first copy is lost, the second copy may still be able to reach the destination [9, 10]. When designing cloning technologies one relevant issue that has to be considered is the resource utilization by the new clones. In this sense, in OBS Networks some technologies have been proposed for optimizing such resource utilization and maintaining a QoS [11, 12]. In Multi Agents Systems (MAS), a frequently proposed solution to avoid performance bottlenecks due to insufficient resources is cloning an agent and migrate it to remote hosts [13, 14].

Our approach is also comparable to the existing work on cloning technologies in terms of concept and objectives but applied to a novel service-oriented architecture for MCS. The main contribution of the proposed cloning technology are the protocol and algorithms that services units utilize to detect some failures in the service provision and the way they coordinate themselves to recover gradually the operation of that damaged part of the system.

3   Autonomous Decentralized Service Oriented Architecture

3.1   ADSOA Concept

A proposal used to implement MCS in financial sector is ADSOA [4–6], it provides load balancing and functionality, high availability and service-oriented modeling. ADSOA is based on Autonomous Decentralized Systems (ADS) [1–3] and Service Oriented Architecture (SOA) [7, 8].

ADS is based in the concept of analogizing living things. The living body is built of numerous cells, each growing up independently, maintaining by body metabolism, and going on living. Depending on concept of perceiving the system that it is consisted by autonomous controllability and autonomous coordinability, ADS technology achieves fault tolerance, on-line maintenance and on-line expansion of the computer system. On the other hand, SOA offers a system modeling oriented to services and allows composition and reusability. ADSOA is the combination of SOA concept with ADS characteristics.

The ADSOA conceptual model, shown in Fig. 1, is composed of autonomous entities that offers or requests services via messages. Each entity is formed by several instances fully independent. Each instance has the same functionality that its entity represents. A subsystem can be formed by a group of entities and in the same sense a business may be formed by a group of subsystems. This is similar to a living organism where an instance is like a cell, a subsystem could be an organ and the business is like a living organism.

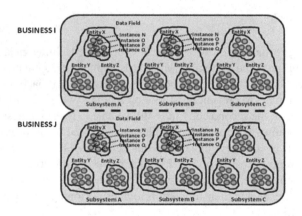

Fig. 1. ADSOA conceptual model

In order to model a MCS using ADSOA, it is necessary to have a service-oriented thinking. At the beginning the system architect identifies the businesses involved in the process and then models the sub-systems in a business according to their responsibility. Finally, entities are modeled according to their atomic functionality. This modeling will allow to the system to grow, evolve, do composition and reuse the components. The next phase is to develop the services entities.

All the systems immersed in ADSOA are able to configure according to physical resources and criticality level. To offer high service availability, it is necessary to have a distributed environment and put on replicated entities. On the other hand, for load balancing it is necessary to divide the functionality in the entities, in such a way that the work be split without a coordinator. The challenge is to provide auto-coordination and auto-control to the system. In this sense, the Autonomous Processing Entity (APE) was proposed; it implements the communication protocol, manages the control instance messages and the services execution. Also, it is possible to define in each service (offered or requested) of the APE its criticality. All these elements form a technology denominated "Loosely Coupling Synchronization and Transactional Delivery Technology".

3.2 Loosely Coupling Synchronization and Transactional Delivery Technology

In this technology, we define the concept of transaction in the scenario in which an entity requests a service to another and requires knowing if it has been received. The requesting entity must maintain this request in pending processing state until it receives an acknowledgement from receiving entity. Also, we define sequential order in the sense that the entity requester must receive a minimum number of acknowledgments from receiving entities in order to send the next service request, for example, a X + 1 request should not be sent until it receives the minimum number of acknowledgments of the X request.

The service request information structure should include the following elements: Content Code, Foliated Structure and Request Information.

The Content Code specifies the content and defines the requested service.

The foliated structure identifies the transaction. This structure is based on:

1. Requester id,
2. Specialized task id for that request (Pivot),
3. A sequence number,
4. A generated id based on the original request information (event number) and
5. A dynamic and unique id for the instance of the entity (instprintid).

With these elements the identification of acknowledgments received by the entity is guaranteed. We can also ensure the sequence of multiple requests, as shown in Fig. 2.

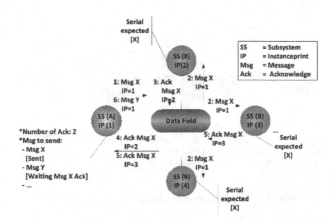

Fig. 2. Sequentiality and transactionality

If an instance receives a service request with a sequence number greater than expected, then by the principle of sequential order, knows that another instance of its entity will have the missing messages. In this case, the receiver instance asks to his entity the missed messages, that is, the other instances of the same entity. This idea is represented in Fig. 3.

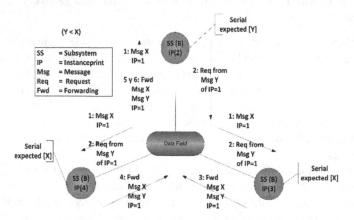

Fig. 3. Synchronization with other instances

On the other hand, if an entity receives several times the same service request, this can be distinguished by the instprintid if this request belongs to the same requester instance or from a different instance of the same entity. According to this, the receiver entity can determine whether requests received are in accordance with the minimum number of requests that the requester entity are required to send, as shown in Fig. 4.

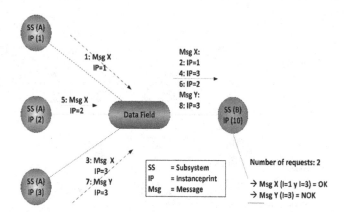

Fig. 4. Receiving multiple requests from an entity

In summary, the communication among the elements and its instances is based on an asynchronous and event-driven message protocol. This technology detects if an entity does not provide the service level required. It occurs when an instance sends a service request to an entity and each entity instance receives it and send back an acknowledge message, then sender registers how many acknowledges have received and evaluates if it covers the criticality level, if it is not proper, the sender repeats the sending process. E.g. consider a service with a criticality level equals to 3, its means that this business requires at least three distributed instances; when another instance requests a service to them, it expects at least three acknowledges to satisfy the criticality level, if it is not satisfied the entity will send the request of service again. When the sender detects that the maximum number of retries has reached, it triggers the alert process, which consists in sending an alert message that could be processed by a monitor element. This monitor alerts ADSOA infrastructure managers to perform the necessary activities and recover service continuity (creating new instances required to reach the criticality level). Unfortunately, this goes against MCS's principles since manual intervention is required thereby MTTR becomes dependent on operator's reaction.

In the next section, we present a technology that allows ADSOA subsystems to autonomously detect and recover for a failure in a replicated entity by cloning one by one an operational entity until the system reaches the criticality level required.

4   Fault Detection and Recovery Technology Based on Collective Intelligence

This technology is created to allow an MSC that uses an ADSOA infrastructure to self-recover automatically. This basic operation is to use the current self-monitoring scheme and instead of sending alerts to the operator when the service level is not appropriate, it instructs one entity of the degraded group to clone itself (functionality and state). An important challenge in the cloning process is to avoid the generation of multiple indiscriminate copies, which in a living organism would be a cancer. To ensure the healthy recovery, the entity selected to recover the system, generates a cloning-key with information of the times it has been cloned, its id, its instprintid and the requested entity id; this information is introduced into the algorithm to generate the cloning-key, that will be unique to only one cloning process between this entity and the requested id.

In this architecture, all the entities offer and request services, one of these services are the fault detection and the recovering by cloning an entity. In this technology at least two entities are involved; to explain the protocol let's imagine a group of entities ("A subsystem"), which request a service to other group of entities ("B subsystem"). In Fig. 5, "A subsystem" is requesting a service to "B subsystem", the message exchange is carried out in compliance with ADSOA Loosely Coupling Synchronization and Transaction Delivery Technology, with the number of acknowledgments needed to ensure that the level of service is appropriate for. In this example, the "A subsystem", requires 3 acknowledgments by "B subsystem", and the "B subsystem" needs 2 service requests by "A subsystem"; when the number of acknowledgments is complying, "B subsystem" attends "A subsystem".

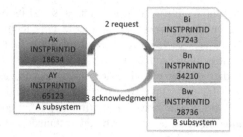

Fig. 5. Normal operation cycle

If the number of the entities of the "B subsystem" is decreased because of a failure in the process or the server, the "A entities" detects that the service level is not complying within "B subsystem", since the minimum number of acknowledgments, 3 for this example, cannot be reached within a specific period of time. Thus, the "A entities" starts the recovery mechanism instead.

Figure 6 shows the first steps in the recovery protocol. Firstly, the "A subsystem" receives the acknowledgments from "B subsystem". Secondly, based in collective intelligence the "A subsystems" selects the lowest "B"'s instprintid, which will be responsible for cloning itself. Thirdly, all the "A entities" request the "Auto-Cloning Service (reqidclon)", with the instprintid of the "B entity" selected for auto-cloning. In this example the "Bi entity" will be the responsible for cloning itself; although the "Bn entity" received the same request, only the "Bi entity" will clone. Fourthly, when the "Bi entity" receives the reqidclon request, it generates a cloning-key and sends both this cloning–key and its instprintid as a "Send the key (sendkey)" request service message. By sending its instprintid it can be ensured that the "A subsystem" will instruct to only the selected "B entity" to continue with the cloning process. Fifthly, when the "A subsystem" receives the sendkey service request, it takes the cloning-key in the message and sends it by the "Automatic recovery (autrecov)" request service message to the "B subsystem", it also attaches to this message the instprintid selected in the second step of this protocol.

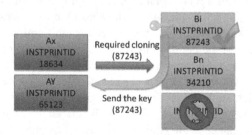

Fig. 6. Start up the cloning mechanism

Figure 7 shows the final step of the protocol. When the "B subsystem" receives the autrecov request service message, as it occurs in the third step of this protocol, only the "Bi entity" will attend it, since its instprintid is in the received service message. "Bi entity" will validate if the cloning-key in the message is still valid and if so it will make a cloning of itself. During this process, "Bi entity" will close all the communication with outside and generate a new element in the same state like itself; once the cloning process is finished, it will open the communication again. Otherwise, if the cloning-key is not longer valid because the cloning process has already been completed, the message is ignored. It is important to notice, that the others "A entities" also send this final request service message, but only the first message which reaches "Bi entity" will be processed.

Fig. 7. Cloning phase

In this sense, this technology will autonomously maintain the operational service level without human intervention.

5 Prototype

A prototype which implements this technology has been developed, as shown in Fig. 8. This prototype consists of two subsystems with one entity each one, the Requester subsystem/entity, which is shown in blue color, and the Counter subsystem/entity, which is shown in orange color. The Requester demands a service to the Counter for providing a number which later it will be displayed in its screen. When the Counter receives this service request, it will increase by one the previous sent number and send it into a service request message to the Requester. For this example, the service level operation was set to 1 to the Requester and 3 to the Counter; it means that there will be only 1 instance of the Requester and 3 instances of the Counter. On the other hand, the Requester will send its next service request only if it receives from the Counter instances 3 acknowledges for the current request. In order to simulate a failure in a Counter instance, a PAUSE button has been implemented.

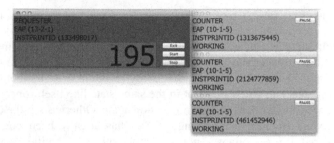

Fig. 8. Normal operation cycle I (Prototype)

In Fig. 9, it is shown that when the entity "2124777859" is stopped, the cloning-mechanism detects such failure and selects entity "1313675445" to repair the system. The reqidclon service request message is sent from the Requester to the Counter with instprintid "1313675445". This entity generates the cloning-key and then it sends the sendkey service request message to the Requester.

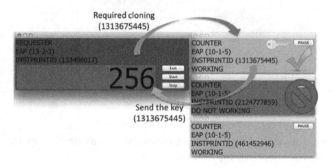

Fig. 9. Start up the cloning mechanism (Prototype)

In Fig. 10, the final part of the mechanism is shown. The Requester processes the sendkey service request message and sends to the selected entity the autrecov service request message. The "1313675445" entity starts the cloning process; firstly it closes the communication with outside, then it clones itself, and when the entity "191232582" is started, the "1313675445" entity finally opens the communication. In this sense, the system has repaired autonomously the damaged part and it can continue its normal operation.

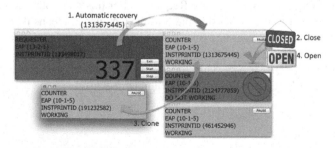

Fig. 10. Normal operation cycle II (Prototype)

6 Conclusion and Future Work

In this paper, we briefly presented ADSOA, which has been proposed as a service-oriented architecture for designing MCS, which has been mainly utilized in financial sector applications. We have proposed a cloning mechanism based on collective intelligence to detect an operational failure and to recover smartly, quickly and efficiently the operational service level when a decrease on it is detected. We have built a prototype to verify the feasibility of this technology.

Besides the ongoing development efforts to complete the cloning prototype implementation, future work in this area focuses on get some metrics about resource utilization, network partition and multiple clones' coexistence. We will also compare the proposed technology with others such as those mentioned in Sect. 2.

References

1. Mori, K., Miyamoto, S., Ihara, H.: Proposition of autonomous decentralized concept. J. IEEE Japan **104**(12), 303–310 (1994)
2. Ihara, H., Mori, K.: Autonomous decentralized computer control systems. IEEE Comput. **17** (8), 57–66 (1984)
3. Mori, K.: Autonomous decentralized computer control systems. In: First International Symposium on Autonomous Decentralized Systems, ISADS 1993, Kawasaki, Japan, pp. 28–34 (1993)
4. Coronado-García, L.C., Pérez-Leguízamo, C.: A mission-critical certification authority architecture for high reliability and response time. IJCCBS Spec. Issue Auton. Decent. Syst. Web Comput. **2**(1), 6–24 (2011)
5. Coronado-García, L.C., Hernández-Torres, P.J., Pérez-Leguízamo, C.: An autonomous decentralized system architecture using a software-based secure data field. In: The 10th International Symposium on Autonomous Decentralized Systems, ISADS 2011, Kobe, Japan (2011)
6. Coronado-García, L.C., Hernández-Torres, P.J., Pérez-Leguízamo, C.: An autonomous decentralized service oriented architecture for high reliable service provision. In: The 10th International Symposium on Autonomous Decentralized Systems, ISADS 2011, Kobe, Japan (2011)
7. Erl, T.: Service-Oriented Architecture (SOA): Concepts, Technology, and Design. Prentice Hall, Upper Saddle River (2005)
8. Josuttis, N.M.: SOA in Practice: The Art of Distributed System Design. O'Reilly Media, Newton (2007)
9. Xiaodong, H., Vokkarane, V.M., Jue, J.P.: Burst cloning: a proactive scheme to reduce data loss in optical burst switched networks. In: IEEE International Conference on Communications, ICC 2005, Seoul, Korea (2005)
10. Riadi, S., Mohammed, V.-A.: A decision algorithm for efficient hybrid burst retransmission and burst cloning scheme over star OBS networks. In: Second International Conference on Innovating Computing Technology, INTECH 2012, Casablanca, Morocco (2012)
11. Ji, L., Yeung, K.L.: Burst cloning with load balancing. In: Optical Fiber Communication Conference, OFC 2006, Anaheim, California (2006)

12. Askar, S., Zervas, G., Hunter, D.K., Simeonidou, D.: Classified cloning for QoS provisioning in OBS networks. In: The 36th European Conference and Exhibition on Optical Communication, ECOC 2010, Turin, Italy (2010)
13. Shehory, O., Sycara, K., Chalasani, P., Jha, S.: Agent cloning: an approach to agent mobility and resource allocation. IEEE Commun. **36**(7), 63–67 (1998)
14. Ye, D., Zhang, M., Sutanto, D.: Cloning, resource exchange and relation adaptation: an integrative self-organisation mechanism in a distributed agent network. IEEE Trans. Parallel Distrib. Syst. **PP**(99), 1 (2013)
15. Laplant, P.A., Ovaska, S.J.: Real Time Systems Design and Analysis. Wiley-IEEE Press, Hoboken (2011)

Gentrification Prediction Using Machine Learning

Yesenia Alejandro[1] and Leon Palafox[2]([⊠]) [iD]

[1] Universidad Nacional Autónoma de México, Mexico City, Mexico
act.yac@ciencias.unam.mx
[2] Universidad Panamericana, Mexico City, Mexico
lpalafox@up.edu.mx

Abstract. Gentrification is a problem in big cities that confounds economic, political and population factors. Whenever it happens, people in the higher brackets of income replace people of low income. This replacement generates population displacement, which force people to change their lives radically.

In this work, we use Classification Trees to generate an index, which will indicate the likelihood for a neighborhood to gentrify. This index uses many population variables that include things like age, education and transportation.

This system can be used later to inform decisions regarding urban housing and transportation. We can prevent areas of the city of overflowing with private investment in lieu of public housing policy that allows people to stay in their places of living.

We expect this work to be a stepping zone on working towards a generalization of gentrification effects in different cities in the world.

Keywords: Gentrification · Machine learning · Decision trees

1 Introduction

In recent years, we have had an explosion of available data in many fields of knowledge. We have companies like Facebook that collect different kinds of information from users.

Some of the data that has been collected in the last years has been geographical and demographic data, from income to number of people living in a single room; we can access vast amounts of information regarding the social fabric of different places.

One of the problems most commonly associated with habitability and social justice is the displacement of people by the effects of the markets. When a neighborhood vastly changes its face to give rise to new business and a new breed of inhabitants, we call this process Gentrification [7].

© Springer Nature Switzerland AG 2019
L. Martínez-Villaseñor et al. (Eds.): MICAI 2019, LNAI 11835, pp. 187–199, 2019.
https://doi.org/10.1007/978-3-030-33749-0_16

Gentrification is a phenomenon that happens in many cities in the world. One of the prime examples of gentrification is San Francisco [9], where the people that provides services are no longer capable of living in the city and are in turn displaced to other cities far away from the urban center.

It is difficult to create generic models to predict and analyze gentrification. First, the gentrification effects can be vastly different depending on the city. Where in New Orleans gentrification can happen near the French Quarters, in Mexico City, gentrification happens near the zoo.

In this work, we test different Machine Learning models to predict which places gentrification in a narrow period. The applications of this work may vary from profitable real estate developments to create new public housing policy to accommodate the people that loses their homes due to the gentrification.

1.1   Gentrification

Population displacement is an important issue in cities and/or knowledge centers, where the pressure for urban life is accelerating. These cities attract new businesses, highly skilled workers and large corporations. Generally, in the popular neighborhoods of these cities a process of transformation arises where the medium and high-income replaces the low-income population living in some area. This population is responsible for renovating the houses on their own account or private investment (real estate agencies and banks). All this drives supply, demand and the cost of housing. As a result, residents may feel pressured to move to more affordable locations. This process is defined under the term of *gentrification* [1].

There are generally three dynamic factors that relevant for gentrification: (a) movement of people, (b) public policies and investments and (c) private capital flows. These elements are by no means exclusive - they are very dependent on each other - and each of them is mediated by conceptions of class, place and scale [1].

Gentrification is typically the result of investment in a community by local government, community activists, or business groups, and can often stimulate economic development, attract business, and reduce crime rates [4].

Several studies analyze gentrification. Mainly, they focus on analyzing the advantages and disadvantages from a social perspective and its impact on the communities affected by this phenomenon.

Because there is no universally accepted definition of gentrification, that is why in this work we consider the following elements as an integral part of the gentrification process [1]:

- Population movements, being able to present as direct or indirect displacement. The direct displacement is that in which the people are forced to leave their homes through violent actions, known as compulsive evictions. Indirect displacement would be from socioeconomic factors; old residents are forced to leave their homes because rent increases or because real estate taxes increased when the market value of the property increases. Alternatively, because the transformations make the old residents no longer feel comfortable being in their neighborhood.

- Degraded, or non-degraded dwellings are usually rehabilitated, renovated or change their land use.
- Commercial businesses such as restaurants, aesthetics, art galleries and bars are established in spaces previously occupied by a traditional family business.
- Old facilities (warehouses, factories, railway stations, commercial ports) are converted into facilities of different use (commercial, housing, offices and services) for medium and high-income social groups.

1.2   Gentrification in Mexico City

The effects of gentrification in Mexico City (CDMX) have been cited in some newspapers. Such is the case of [3], where he cites the neighborhoods **Doctores, Obrera, Tabacalera and Alamos** as neighborhoods that are undergoing through a gentrification process due to their commercial offer, service offer and commuting convenience.

On the other hand [2] cites the neighborhoods **Condesa, Cuauhtemoc, Hipodromo de la Condesa, Roma Sur, Roma Norte, Juarez, Doctores, Guerrero, Santa Maria La Ribera and Centro** as undergoing a gentrification process due to an increase of annual property taxes, increase in rents and sale prices of real estate.

According to Forbes [5], the neighborhoods that have potential because of their geographical position, transportation services, entertainment and gastronomy offerings are **Juarez, Doctores, San Rafael, Santa Maria La Ribera, Irrigacion y and Escandon**.

1.3   Machine Learning and Gentrification

Due to the nature of Machine Learning and Gentrification, there has not been many works using Machine Learning to predict or analyze gentrification. Recently, Reades et al. [8] used a Machine Learning algorithm to predict Gentrification in London. However, they acknowledged the limitation of their work. Furthermore, variables, which are important to predict gentrification in one city, might be useless in a different setting. In New Orleans, the gentrified neighborhoods are near the ocean [6], while Mexico City doesn't have an ocean, or other coastal cities might have different water front's not prone for gentrification.

To our knowledge, this is the first time that Machine Learning algorithms have been used to predict and analyze gentrification in Mexico City, and as such, is still a work in progress as gentrification is an undergoing phenomenon, and new governmental policies might induce gentrification in other areas which had not been considered before.

2   Methodology

In this work, we extracted data from different sources of information, once we had all the data, we tested multiple Machine Learning algorithms to compare their metrics and in such a way decide which is better suited to analyze the problem of gentrification with the data that we have.

2.1   Data Sources

As we mentioned before, the geographical coverage of this work is limited to Mexico City, the most populated city in Mexico. Mexico City has enough studies done in gentrification and plenty of data associated with commerce and social fabric. This availability of data will allow us to model the city in the most accurate way.

Fig. 1. CDMX neighborhoods

The Fig. 1 shows the 1,436 neighborhoods of the CDMX that are handled in the present work.

The data that we use was recollected in 2000, 2010 and 2016, which mostly comes from the Population and Housing Censuses conducted by INEGI, Mexico's geographical institute.

Table 1 shows the neighborhoods that are defined as gentrified in the present work ([3,5]).

Figure 2 shows the location of the gentrified neighborhoods on a Google map. The gentrified neighborhoods are in the center of Mexico City. In the delegations Cuauhtemoc, Miguel Hidalgo and Benito Juarez.

Table 1. Gentrified neighborhoods

1. Alamos	9. Irrigacion
2. Centro	10. Juarez
3. Condesa	11.Obrera
4. Cuauhtemoc	12. Roma Norte
5. Doctores	13. Roma Sur
6. Escandon	14. San Rafael
7. Hipdromo	15. Santa Maria la Ribera
8. Hipodromo de la Condesa	16. Tabacalera

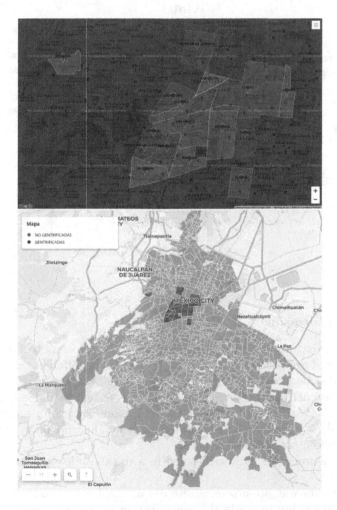

Fig. 2. Gentrified neighborhoods

2.2   Data

The different data sources we used are referenced in the Fig. 3.

- Inventario Nacional de Viviendas 2016: National inventory of living quarters.
- Censo de Población y Vivienda: national census in Mexico.
- SCINCE: System to query the census information.
- DENUE: National directory of economic activities.
- Softec: Private database with information regarding the cost of the square meter.
- Shapefiles: Different shapefiles for the geographical units in Mexico City.

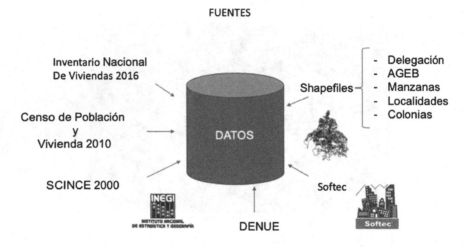

Fig. 3. Data sources

2.3   Data Processing

Since the data that we used comes from a variety of sources, we had to undergo a heavy process of pre-processing to be able to match the different tables in terms of having the same locations coincide in the different sources.

In some case neighborhoods were named different and we did not have a unification code for the different neighborhoods. In some other, for temporal data, neighborhoods ceased to exist or altogether new neighborhoods were created in the years between the different census.

All the pre-processed data was stored in a database located in an Amazon DB.

Once the data was pre-processed, we did an exploratory analysis, and then we used the algorithm to create the gentrification indicator number.

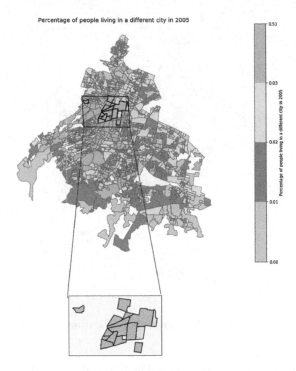

Fig. 4. Percentage of people living in a different city in 2005

2.4   Exploratory Analysis

Since we had many sources of information, we created different graphs, we put in this work what we considered are the most important to represent the problem of gentrification.

These are not the only variables we used, but the ones we chose to represent in this paper, for further analysis, please contact any of the corresponding authors.

In Fig. 4 we indicate how many people in the past census were living in a different state. It shows us how popular are these areas among new comers. The map clearly shows that gentrified neighborhoods are rather popular for people who recently moved to Mexico City.

In Fig. 5 we show the average education in those areas. Gentrified areas attract people whose education is higher, which means these people may have higher incomes and go in line with the classic gentrification analyses usually given in the literature.

3   Algorithm Description

In this section we describe the modeling process based on the data defined in the last section. The type of problem, the target variable and the evaluation of the model are defined.

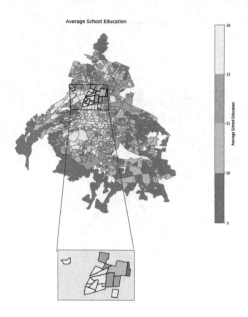

Fig. 5. Average school education

We want to estimate the target variable "Gentrified" and "Not Gentrified", that is, a binary categorical variable.

The solution to the problem is addressed by fitting a Random Forest Classifier model.

3.1   Random Forest Classifier

By adjusting the Random Forest Classifier (RFC) model, we estimate the probability of belonging to each neighborhood from Mexico City to class 1: "Gentrified" or 0: "Not Gentrified" given the values of the variables used for the regression, which we will denote by X.

The expression 1 denotes the probability of belonging to class 1 given X and the expression 2 denotes the probability of belonging to class 0.

$$P(X) = Pr(Y = 1|X) \tag{1}$$

$$P(X) = Pr(Y = 0|X) \tag{2}$$

In the data set we have 16 observations with label 1 and 1,420 observations with label 0.

In the adjustment of the model there are two stages (a) Training and (b) Testing. As a first step, the data is divided into two sets that are used in the two stages mentioned: training set and test set. The training set is used to adjust the model and estimate the parameters that will allow estimates to be made on new data. The test set is used to adjust the model on data that the model has never seen and the accuracy of the model is estimated by comparing the estimate with the real value of the target variable. The division of the data of the training set and test set is done under the proportion 80% and 20% of the data, respectively.

We fit a Random Forest Classifier model with 45 trees. Next we present the metrics that allow to measure the precision of the model.

3.2   Model Evaluation

In Fig. 6 the confusion matrix is shown, as well as the adjustment error and the prediction error.

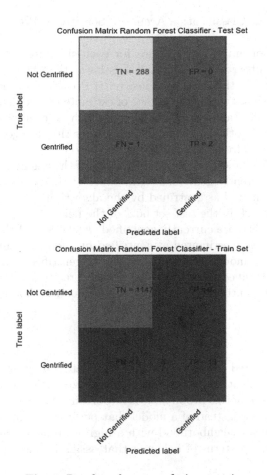

Fig. 6. Random forest confusion matrix

In the inverse diagonal the errors of the model are shown, FP are the values where the model classifies as Gentrified some neighborhood that is not and the FN happens when the model estimates as non-Gentrified a neighborhood that is gentrified.

Table 2. Detail of precision metrics

Set	Classification accuracy	Sensitivity	Precision	F1 score
Train	100%	100%	100%	100%
Test	99.65%	66%	100%	80%

Table 2 shows the Classification Accuracy, Sensitivity, Precision and F1 Score metrics.

Since the proportion of observations for each class are not similar, that is, the proportion of observations with tag 1 is lower than those with tag 0. The metrics that matter in this case are Sensitivity, Precision and F1 Score.

The Precision shows which percentage of estimated Gentrified neighborhoods are currently gentrified and Sensitivity shows which percentage of total observations were estimated with the Gentrified label since they are gentrified. F1 Score is a metric calculated from Sensitivity and Precision.

According to these metrics, in training, 100% of the neighborhoods estimated as gentrified are currently gentrified. And 100% of the neighborhoods that are gentrified were estimated as gentrified by the algorithm.

On the other hand, in the test set 66% of the neighborhoods that have been estimated as gentrified are currently gentrified. And 100% of the neighborhoods that are gentrified were estimated as gentrified by the algorithm.

In summary, the model learned to identify a gentrified neighborhood 100% of the time and classified it as gentrified with a precision of 100%. In the test 66% of the time It identifies a gentrified neighborhood with a precision of 100%.

4   Results

Once we have evaluated the model, is time to create a map, where we show the probability of gentrification for the different analyzed neighborhoods.

Due to the nature of this problem, it is important to analyze the probabilities of belonging to class 1 instead of a model that perfectly estimates the classes. If the model estimates a neighborhood with a high probability of being gentrified it is because it finds patterns of behavior that assign it this probability.

Table 3. Gentrifiable colonies

Colonia	Probability	Colonia	Probability
Roma Norte	0.93	Los Morales Secc Palmas	0.13
Hipodromo	0.89	San Rafael	0.13
Countess	0.84	Lomas Altas	0.13
Santa Maria La Ribera	0.82	Granada	0.11
Hipodromo De La Condesa	0.78	Fracc Res Emperors	0.11
Juarez	0.71	Villa Azcapotzalco	0.09
Alamos	0.71	Tacuba	0.09
Cuauhtemoc	0.71	University City	0.09
Escandon	0.67	Industrial	0.07
Doctors	0.67	Argentina Antigua	0.07
Irrigacion	0.67	Moctezuma 2Da Secc	0.07
Obrera	0.64	Agricola Oriental	0.07
Centro	0.64	Guadalupe Inn	0.07
Tabacalera	0.64	Insurgentes Mixcoac	0.07
Roma Sur	0.62	Ciudad De Los Deportes	0.07
Veronica Anzures	0.47	Algarin	0.07
Chapultepec Morales	0.42	Actipan	0.07
Del Valle	0.29	Nonoalco	0.07
Noche Buena	0.27	Las Americas	0.07
Napoles	0.24	San Miguel Chapultepec	0.07
Del Valle Sur	0.22	Pedregal Del Maurel	0.07
Polanco Reforma	0.18	Anzures	0.07
Center	0.16	Morelos	0.07
The Alps	0.13	Jamaica	0.07

The group of "gentrifiable" neighborhoods is defined as those colonies that have a probability greater than 5% of gentrification. Analyzing the probabilities of belonging to class 1, the class of the label Gentrified. The table 3 shows the list of gentrifiable neighborhoods ordered by their probability.

The map of Fig. 7 shows the probability map of gentrification showing with wine color those with the highest probability and in pink those with less probability.

This is the first time that such map has been created for Mexico City, and it shows quite reliably some of spots where inhabitants of the city "feel" like the city is becoming gentrified.

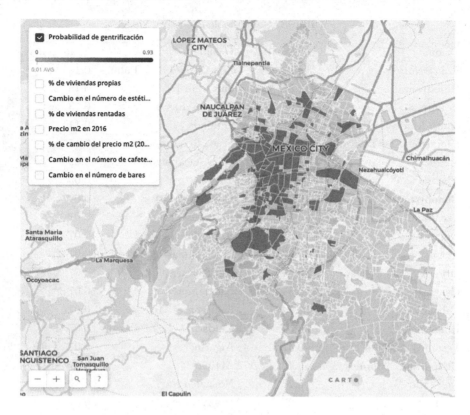

Fig. 7. Gentrification map

5   Conclusions and Future Work

After creating the model, and analyzing all the data, we predict the moment when a neighborhood is going to become gentrified. Several variables become of importance once we run the Random Forest, and these variables can be used for later social studies in creating new housing policies regarding gentrification in other neighborhoods.

In our future work, we will create a mapping between cities to bring the learning of a model to a different city, and in such a way, even if we do not know if a city has gentrified neighborhoods, we can create estimators to calculate an index for previously unknown places.

References

1. Salinas-Arreortua, L.A.: La gentrificación de la colonia condesa, ciudad de méxico. aporte para una discusión desde latinoamérica. Revista Geográfica de América Central **II**, 145–167 (2013)

2. Camhaji, E.: La santa que ahuyenta a los 'hipsters' del corazón de la ciudad de méxico (2017)
3. Cantera, S.: Gentrificación: las colonias de cdmx que se "aburguesan" (2017)
4. Clark, E.: The order and simplicity of gentrification: a political. Revista Geográfica de América Central 256–264 (2004)
5. Forbes: 5 colonias con potencial en el df (2014)
6. Gotham, K.F.: Tourism gentrification: the case of new Orleans' vieux carre (French quarter). Urban Stud. 42(7), 1099–1121 (2005)
7. Lees, L., Slater, T., Wyly, E.: Gentrification. Routledge, Abingdon (2013)
8. Reades, J., De Souza, J., Hubbard, P.: Understanding urban gentrification through machine learning. Urban Stud. 56(5), 922–942 (2019)
9. Stehlin, J.: Cycles of investment: bicycle infrastructure, gentrification, and the restructuring of the San Francisco bay area. Environ. Plann. A 47(1), 121–137 (2015)

Pulsed Neural Network Plus Parallel Multi-core Approach to Solve Efficiently Big Shortest Path Problems

Manuel Mejia-Lavalle$^{(\boxtimes)}$ ⓘ, Javier Ortiz ⓘ, Alicia Martinez ⓘ,
Jose Paredes ⓘ, and Dante Mujica ⓘ

Tecnologico Nacional de Mexico/CENIDET, 62490 Cuernavaca, MOR, Mexico
{mlavalle, ortiz, amartinez, joseparedes16c,
dantemv}@cenidet.edu.mx

Abstract. A Third Generation Artificial Neural Network plus a Parallel Multi-Core approach is presented. This approach is capable of efficiently tackle the problem of finding the shortest path between two nodes, for big cases with thousands of nodes. The efficient solution of the shortest path problem has applications in such important and current areas as robotics, telecommunications, operation research, game theory, computer networks, internet, industrial design, transport phenomena, design of electronic circuits and others, so it is a subject of great interest in the area of combinatorial optimization. Due to the parallel design of the Pulsed Neuronal Network presented here, it is possible speed up the solution using parallel multi-processors; this solution approach can be highly competitive, as observed from the good results obtained, even in cases with thousands of nodes.

Keywords: Shortest path problems · Pulsed Neural Network · Parallel multi-core

1 Introduction - Motivation

Given a set of multiple nodes connected with a certain cost, the shortest path problem consists to find a route that links a starting node with a final or target node in such a way that the sum of the costs of that trajectory is the minimum possible. A simple way to describe the problem is to make an analogy with a group of cities: each city is a node and the distance between two cities is the cost. However, this problem finds real-world applications in multiple and diverse domains. In graph theory there are formal definitions for this problem [2].

Computationally the route graph is normally represented by an adjacency matrix of size $n \times n$, where n is the number of nodes of the problem: if the element i, j of the adjacency matrix is zero, it indicates that from node i to node j there is no link; on the other hand, if the matrix element has a positive value, it will indicate the cost incurred by transiting from node i to node j. Although in appearance the problem seems simple, in reality it is a problem of high complexity that becomes evident when we try to find optimal solutions for networks with hundreds or thousands of connected nodes. This is

© Springer Nature Switzerland AG 2019
L. Martínez-Villaseñor et al. (Eds.): MICAI 2019, LNAI 11835, pp. 200–211, 2019.
https://doi.org/10.1007/978-3-030-33749-0_17

because the number of possible routes grows exponentially in relation to the number of nodes, so it is not feasible to analyze all possible combinations in a reasonable time, even using the fastest computers.

The problem of finding the path or the shortest route between two nodes has been widely studied in the area of combinatorial optimization [1] due to the importance it has related to such current domains as: robotics, telecommunications, artificial intelligence and machine learning, operation research, game theory, computer networks, internet, industrial design, telematics, transportation phenomena, design of very large integrated electronic circuits VLSI, and has even been applied to risk situations and decision problems [1].

There are several algorithms that seek to solve the problem without having to go through all the possible routes. But, even using an efficient algorithm that does not analyze all possible routes, for a problem with 9,000 nodes it would take around 81 million operations to find an optimal or near optimal solution.

Among the best known efficient algorithms are Dijkstra, Bellman-Ford, Floyd-Warshall, Johnson, Gabow, Thorup, Pettie-Ramachandran or Viterbi [1]. Even from the area of Artificial Intelligence, proposals such as the *Branch & Bound* or the algorithm A^* [2] have emerged. Looking for efficiency, not all algorithms guarantee finding the optimal solution (the lowest cost route), but they offer solutions close to the optimum. Additionally, all these algorithms have been designed to be solved essentially in a sequential manner.

In the present work the application of the connectionist approach of the Artificial Neural Networks (ANN) [3] is proposed and presented, in particular the Pulse-Coupled ANN (PCNN) adapted to solve the shortest path problem. This is due to the fact that ANN has an intrinsically parallel design, which makes them susceptible to being more efficient than traditional sequential methods that do not have this connectionist approach. Additionally, PCNN are considered the third generation of ANN and are closer in concept to biological neural networks, which promises a closer approach to the cognitive processes of humans [4]. Once the PCNN finds the target node at a minimum cost, an extraction or Knowledge Explicitation is performed [5], from the information hidden in the PCNN, to recover the final path.

According to the experimentation carried out using cases with thousands of nodes, the results are encouraging both in efficiency and in the quality of the solution. With the experimented cases, response times were obtained in the order of the seconds and all the cases were solved with the optimal solution of minimum global cost.

2   Pulsed Neural Nets for Big Shortest Path Problems

In this Section we present the PCNN adapted to solve big problems that seek the lowest cost path between two nodes. To do this, PCNN are first introduced, to then describe the proposed Pulsed Neural Network.

2.1 Pulse-Coupled Artificial Neural Networks

Within the Artificial Neural Networks (ANN), the third generation corresponds to the so-called Pulse-Coupled (PCNN) and are the ones that in this work we propose and apply to the problem of finding the shortest path between two nodes. The main difference of the PCNN with respect to the two previous generations is that they are a paradigm whose neurons are activated not only by numerical values, but also by pulses or external signals that depend on time [4]. The PCNN is implemented in a model of one neuron for each processing element and its architecture has three modules: (a) the dendrite module, through which the information surrounding the PCNN is fed; (b) the linking module, which joins the input information with the output and (c) the pulse generator, which has a dynamic threshold that is based on the internal process of the same PCNN. The PCNN has the peculiarity that the activity of each neuron affects to a certain degree the neighboring neurons, obtaining an auto-wave effect [4]. Figure 1 shows an example of auto-wave: from an image of a white square, nine outputs of the PCNN are shown in sequence.

Fig. 1. Example for nine epochs for auto-wave effect [4]

Within the PCNN there are several variants, such as the Intersecting Cortical Model or the Spiking Cortical Model [4]. The PCNN proposed here is a variant designed especially for big shortest path problems.

2.2 Contribution: Proposed Pulsed Neural Network Approach

The description of the proposed paradigm is presented in two parts: (a) the process addressed to, from an initial node, to explore the nodes that optimally lead to the target node; (b) the way in which the set of nodes that determine the shortest path is retrieved through the extraction or Knowledge Explicitation [5] of hidden information in the ANN.

Algorithm to Find the Target Node. The PCNN proposed here is an extension of the one presented in [6] named by its authors as AWNN (Auto-Wave Neural Network). In Fig. 2 a neuron of this model is shown.

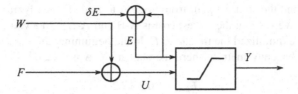

Fig. 2. Pulsed Artificial Neural Network [6]

In Fig. 2 it can be seen that each neuron receives input from the adjacency matrix W (with a complete path between two nodes) and also receives an F value of the additional cost if it continues along a certain route: adding W and F gives the U value that is the total cost incurred by some trajectory until a given moment determined by the dynamic threshold E. In each epoch the parameter E is increased by a constant value δE: if the accumulated cost in U is equal to or exceeds the threshold E, then the neuron is activated taking the output Y the value of "1", otherwise the output of the neuron will be zero. Given a problem with n nodes, the neural network will then have as many neurons as nXn. The auto-wave effect is obtained precisely by making increments in the time of the threshold E. The following equations summarize the behavior of the AWNN neuron that we propose:

$$F_{new} = F_{old} + W_{old,new} \tag{1}$$

$$U_{new,new} = F_{new} + W_{new,new} \tag{2}$$

$$If\ U > E\ then\ Y = 0;\ otherwise\ Y = 1$$

$$E = E + \delta E \tag{3}$$

To make the process more efficient, we define the initial value of E as the lowest cost of the starting node to its next nodes. Similarly, if the costs are positive integers, we recommend using an δE equal to 1 (or normalize all costs of W to be positive integers). Next, we will illustrate with a simple example the way in which the proposed AWNN works. We start with an adjacency matrix W with 5 nodes that define an interconnection graph. The example matrix W is:

W	A	B	C	D	E
A	0	2	3	7	2
B	2	0	3	0	0
C	3	3	0	6	0
D	7	0	6	0	4
E	2	0	0	4	0

$$(4)$$

We want to find the shortest path from node A to node D. Analyzing the costs of A to its next nodes, we see that the lowest cost is A-B and A-E with a value of 2, therefore with that value we initialized the threshold E. In the beginning, the F_{new} will be equal to the row of the adjacency matrix where the start node A is located. Then:

$$F_{new} = 0\,2\,3\,7\,2$$

Then the matrix U is updated as indicated by Eq. 2, leaving U with the following information:

U	A	B	C	D	E
A	**0**	**2**	**3**	**7**	**2**
B	0	0	0	0	0
C	0	0	0	0	0
D	0	0	0	0	0
E	0	0	0	0	0

(5)

Next we verify the elements where $U = E$ and the matrix Y is updated, which results in a first output of the AWNN:

Y	A	B	C	D	E
A	0	**1**	0	0	**1**
B	0	0	0	0	0
C	0	0	0	0	0
D	0	0	0	0	0
E	0	0	0	0	0

(6)

Since the A-B and A-E segments have already been selected, they are assigned a "high cost" so that they are no longer used (for example, we use the value 10 as "high cost") and the costs of the B and E rows are increased according to the costs of the matrix W. The matrix U then is updated as follows:

U	A	B	C	D	E
A	**10**	2	3	7	2
B	**10**	0	**2+3**	0	0
C	0	0	0	0	0
D	0	0	0	0	0
E	**10**	0	0	**2+4**	0

(7)

Then the threshold E is increased by 1 and the process is repeated. In this case it is the path A-C that complies with having a cost equal to or less than the threshold E, so the matrix Y is updated to:

Y	A	B	C	D	E
A	**1**	1	1	0	1
B	0	0	0	0	0
C	0	0	0	0	0
D	0	0	0	0	0
E	0	0	0	0	0

(8)

Consequently the matrix U is updated to:

U	A	B	C	D	E
A	10	2	3	7	2
B	10	0	2+3	0	0
C	**10**	**10**	0	**3+6**	0
D	0	0	0	0	0
E	10	0	0	2+4	0

(9)

Then the threshold is increased and then $E = 4$. At this time no path (not previously traveled) is equal to or less than 4, so the output Y is not modified and therefore the matrix U does not change either. Until $E = 6$ it happens that the path E-D $(2 + 4)$ in the matrix U satisfies the threshold and the output is updated:

Y	A	B	C	D	E
A	1	1	1	0	1
B	0	0	0	0	0
C	0	0	0	0	0
D	0	0	0	0	0
E	0	0	0	1	0

$$(10)$$

Since in this step the target node (D) was reached, then the process ends. The cost of the trajectory found is equal to the value of the threshold E, in this case the cost is 6. It is noted that any other path that reaches D would have higher cost, so the path found is the optimum. Figure 3 shows the graph with the 5 nodes and the costs from one node to another; in addition, the optimal path A-E-D found by the PCNN is highlighted with thicker lines.

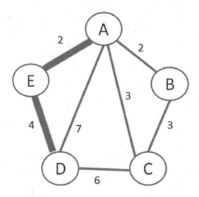

Fig. 3. Solution of the PCNN shown graphically

Obtaining the Shortest Path by Explicitation. The Knowledge Explicitation [5] in the context of ANN consists in extracting the hidden knowledge in the same Neural Network. This sub-topic within the ANN is due to the fact that, in the emergence of this technology, there was a criticism that although neural paradigms gave good results, it was not possible to access the knowledge that the algorithm had automatically generated. It was said then that the ANN were *black box* algorithms.

However, over time, successful proposals have emerged to precisely reveal the hidden knowledge among the neurons, in such a way that the user has access to, for example, production rules that are generated automatically as a result of ANN internal activity. In that sense, we managed to obtain the optimal or lower cost path, extracting the knowledge that remains hidden in the output layer Y of the proposed PCNN. The output layer Y is basically a matrix of size $n \times n$ with values of zeros and ones. The trajectory is retrieved in reverse, jumping from the final node to the initial node. In the output matrix Y, the final node will be found in column i with the same number as the target node. In that column the value "1" will be searched and where it appears, the value of row j will be taken. With this row value you will enter the Y matrix again but now looking in the column with value j, the value "1" and repeating the process until you reach the initial node. In the end, the j values thus recovered will define the minimum cost path. Continuing with the example of the previous section and considering that the final Y output is:

Y	A (i1)	B (i2)	C (i3)	D (i4)	E (i5)
A (j1)	1	1	1	0	1
B (j2)	0	0	0	0	0
C (j3)	0	0	0	0	0
D (j4)	0	0	0	0	0
E (j5)	0	0	0	1	0

$$(11)$$

The final node D is found at $i = 4$ and $j = 5$. Using the value of j as a reference, we go to the column $i = 5$, corresponding to the node E, and where the element marked with "1" is in the row $j = 1$. Using the value of j once more as a reference, we go to the column $i = 1$, corresponding to the node A and where the element marked with "1" is in the row $j = 1$. At this moment the explicitation is finished, since the initial node was reached. In this way, the path of least cost is recovered, which in this case is A-E-D.

3   Parallelization with OpenMP for Speeding up

In Parallel programming based on shared memory among multiple cores is an attractive architecture for scientific computation [7–9], largely due to its high performance, low complexity and of course that is a common and accessible technology at the present time.

Faster execution of complex algorithms is emerging as an important criterion with the technical advancements in multi-core or heterogeneous architectures. OpenMP (Open Multi-Processing) programs are sequential C/C++ or Fortran programs which are augmented by OpenMP compiler directives (pragmas).

In this paper it was considered on the OpenMP program that was written in C++ language, under Xubuntu operating system, TDM-GCC MinGW compiler and a PC with 4 cores and 6 GB of RAM. In order to illustrate the implementation of the proposed parallel multi-core Neural Network, a fragment of the code is shown below.

```
# pragma omp parallel shared (M, F, M_nodes, AWNN_U,
AWNN_Y)
private (i,j)
{
  # pragma omp for
   for ( i=0; i < fil2; i++)
   {
      AWNN_U[i] = new float[col2];
      AWNN_Y[i] = new float[col2];
   }
  # pragma omp for
   for ( i = 0; i < fil2; i++)
   {
      M[i] = 0;
      F[i]  = 0;
      M_nodes[i] = 'n';
      for ( j=0; j < col2; j++)
      {
        AWNN_U[i][j] = 0;
        AWNN_Y[i][j] = 0;
      }
   }
}
```

4 Experiments, Results and Discussion

The test cases were generated randomly. Table 1 shows the results (in milli-seconds) obtained by applying the proposed PCNN, with sequential and OpenMP parallel programming seep up strategy.

Figure 4 shows the same results but in a graphic manner (circles equal OpenMP strategy); observing this figure it can be seen that the behavior of the PCNN is approximately linear in complexity, that is, the processing time depends linearly on the number of nodes. It is important to mention that OpenMP strategy with only 4 cores allows a 35% speed up in average, from 5,500 nodes to 9,000 nodes; if we add more cores, it will be increased this speed up. When we have fully implemented the code in parallel, we expect to obtain much shorter response times. For example, for the case with 9,000 nodes, the expected response time T could drop by about T/81,000,000; in other words, we can reduce 30 millions the execution time with respect to Dijkstra algorithm, for instance. It is noted that in all cases that we experimented, the proposed PCNN find the optimal path.

Table 1. Running time in milli-seconds

Num. nodes	Sequential	OpenMP
5	0.003175	0.007999
30	0.03458	0.04501
50	0.9887	0.4533
100	4.96295	1.0521
200	3.81465	4.999
300	29.552	22.498
400	32.5496	25.000
500	62.1867	39.061
600	75.7672	42.122
700	88.5191	64.020
800	98.7029	66.540
900	216.031	124.165
1,000	288.279	190.501
1,300	301.116	164.425
1,500	562.768	222.167
1,800	591.703	311.682
2,000	717.14	413.162
2,400	1,042.9	614.582
2,600	1,346.87	709.077
3,000	1,807.27	1,504.71
3,500	1,956.36	2,010.29
4,000	2,957.94	2,208.79
4,500	3,980.56	3,280.56
5,000	4,019.82	3,484.29
5,500	7,091.83	4,220.04
6,000	7,380.67	4,222.51
7,000	7,904.95	4,697.08
8,000	9,221.16	6,763.04
9,000	10,962.2	8,574.50

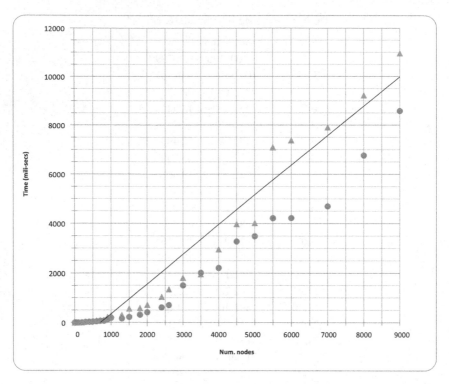

Fig. 4. Running time results for several node quantity (circles equal OpenMP strategy; triangles equal to sequential approach; straight line represent hypothetical linear complexity)

5 Conclusions and Future Work

A Pulse-Coupled Neural Network capable of satisfactorily solving the problem of the shortest path has been proposed and described. According to the results obtained, our proposal competes with other existing methods mentioned in the specialized literature, since it has an approximately linear complexity: this is its principal strenght. The principal limitation is the need of a parallel implementation in order to obtain the maximal reduction time.

Applying shared memory multi-core processor speed up strategy [7–9] we obtain additional 35% reduction in processing time with only 4 cores, when number of nodes is 5,500 and up; if we add more cores the speed up will be increased. When we have fully implemented the code in parallel, we expect to obtain much shorter response times. Additionally we considerer, for future work, experiment with real world cases such as those mentioned in [10] and problems when there is no path between two nodes.

References

1. Moustapha, D., Mark, K.: Advances in Combinatorial Optimization. World Scientific, Singapore (2016)
2. Thulasiraman, K., Arumugam, S., et al.: Handbook of Graph Theory. CRC Press, Boca Raton (2016)
3. Daniel, G.: Principles of Artificial Neural Networks. World Scientific, Singapore (2013)
4. Lindblad, T., Kinser, J.: Image Processing Using Pulse-Coupled Neural Networks. Springer, London (1998). https://doi.org/10.1007/978-1-4471-3617-0
5. Chuanli, Z., Jinzheng, R.: Elicitation of decision maker preference by artificial neural networks. In: IEEE International Conference on Neural Networks and Brain (2005)
6. Ma, Y., Zhan, K., Wang, Z.: Applications of pulse–coupled neural networks. Springer, Heidelberg (2011). https://doi.org/10.1007/978-3-642-13745-7
7. Hijaz, F., Kahne, B., Wilson, P., Khan, O.: Efficient parallel packet processing using a shared memory many-core processor with hardware support to accelerate communication, In: IEEE International Conference on Networking, Architecture and Storage (NAS), pp. 122–129 (2015)
8. Dagum, L., Menon, R.: OpenMP: an industry standard API for shared-memory programming. IEEE Comput. Sci. Eng. 5(1), 46–55 (1998)
9. Chapman, B., Jost, G., Van Der Pas, R.: Using OpenMP: portable shared memory parallel programming, vol. 10. MIT Press, Cambridge (2008)
10. Raphael: Stack Exchange (2012). https://cs.stackexchange.com/questions/1151/where-to-get-graphs-to-test-my-search-algorithms-against. Accessed 10 Aug 2019

Prediction of Student Attrition Using Machine Learning

Sarahi Aguilar-Gonzalez and Leon Palafox[✉]

Universidad Panamericana, Mexico City, Mexico
{0189970,lpalafox}@up.edu.mx

Abstract. Student attrition is one of the most important problems for any school, being it private or public.

In public education, a high attrition rate reflects poorly in the school, as it is wasting public taxes on students that do not finish their majors. In private education, it means the school revenue decreases considerably. Much work has been done on predicting churn rates in the Telecommunication industry, in this work we use similar techniques to predict churn rates in education.

We explore the data extensively and see the possible correlations between attrition and variables like entrance examination, place where the students are from and grades up to the point of abandonment of the major.

Keywords: Attrition · Machine learning · Decision trees

1 Introduction

Mexico's higher education system has experienced a significant growth in the last decades. In 1970–1971, around 270 000 students were enrolled in 385 universities across Mexico [8], and by 2017–2018, these figures increased up to 4.5 million of students enrolled in more than 6 000 universities [9]. Furthermore, remarkable progress has been made in terms of increasing educational attainment in higher education in Mexico; in the last sixteen years, the percentage of young adults who have completed higher education went from 17% to 23% [8].

"Education at a Glance: OECD Indicators" is a study on the state of education systems in OECD and partner countries [7], one of which is Mexico. This yearly publication enables Mexico to be compared in a global context. In Mexico, only 17% of all adults between 25 to 64 years old have a degree, which leaves the country in the last place from the OECD. In fact, this last figure is far from the OECD average (37%) and below other countries from Latin America like Chile (23%), Colombia (23%), Costa Rica (23%) and Argentina (21%) [8].

Higher education holds itself as one of the most determining factors for an ambitious future, both for individuals and for a complete nation [6], yet, it also faces numerous difficulties. One of those issues is attrition. Attrition in higher education can be a consequence of different factors. Studying the factors behind

© Springer Nature Switzerland AG 2019
L. Martínez-Villaseñor et al. (Eds.): MICAI 2019, LNAI 11835, pp. 212–222, 2019.
https://doi.org/10.1007/978-3-030-33749-0_18

attrition rates in higher education is key to develop suitable retention strategies or policies.

Financial factors may have a significant role for explaining college dropouts. Stinebrickner and Stinebrickner in Learning about Academic Ability and the College Dropout Decision (2012) based on data obtained from the Berea Panel Study conclude that financial factors are not determinant of college dropouts [10]. However, Mexico's situation may be different considering its economy. To begin with, in 2014, Mexico was the third least country in annual expenditure by educational institutions per students out of all OECD countries [8]. Also, in 2017–2018, the ratio between total graduated students against enrolled students was lower for public universities than for private universities [11]. The problem, however, can be explained both by economic reasons of the institutions individually, and by the socioeconomic difficulties of the population.

2   Background and Previous Work

In an attempt to understand the factors behind Mexico's attrition in college from a quantitative perspective, we explored data from the Engineering School from the last years from the private university Universidad Panamericana located in Mexico City, and, using Machine Learning algorithms, we built a model to predict the probability of a student dropping out. There is similar work on analyzing university attrition in homogeneous and small populations through Machine Learning. In Predicting Students Drop Out: A Case Study (2009) by Dekker, Pechenizkiy and Vleeshouwers, they explore a case study demonstrating the effectiveness of simple and intuitive classifiers (decision trees) on data from 648 students from the Electrical Engineering department of Eindhoven University of Technology [4]. In Mexico, The University Scholastic Desertion in Mexico. The experience of the Universidad Autónoma Metropolitana Campus Iztapalapa by Lagunas and Vázquez, is a qualitative study on the causes or motives of the dropout student in all programs from the public university Universidad Autónoma Metropolitana Campus Iztapalapa located in Mexico City using data obtained from surveys [5]. Other than that, national efforts of research on this topic are limited to governmental publications such as Visión y acción 2030 Propuesta de la ANUIES para renovar la educación superior en México by the National Association of Universities and Higher Education Studies (ANUIES from its Spanish initials) which explores potential improvements on Mexican public policies on education (2018) [3].

Our work differs from the rest as we will be using features, besides university grades, that have not been yet taken into account in much of the previous research. We worked with students' high school graduation grades, which will allows us to explore to what extent performance in previous educational stages could potentially affect future ones. Also, with the same objective in mind, we worked with the score obtained on university's both admission and diagnostic exam. Another feature we worked with is the average scholarship percentage that each student had throughout their major. Scholarship percentage can say a lot about student's profile as these are granted by Universidad Panamericana in most cases to either those students with great admission applications (considering high school final grade and scores on the admission and diagnostic exams) and/or with a critical socioeconomic status. On top of that, we also took into account the students' municipality of origin since it could give us a broad idea of their socioeconomic background due to the differences between each municipality in Mexico City in those terms.

3   Data Analysis

As mentioned above, the dataset we worked with is from the School of Engineering from the private university Universidad Panamericana located in Mexico City and is composed of 731 records of students enrolled from January of 2009 to August of 2014, and a total of eight features. Taking into account that major programs in this school last four years, all student records in the dataset belong to students whose graduation year was 2018.

The first feature is our dependent variable: a Boolean that tells if the student dropped out or not. In the dataset, 30% of the students (223) are dropouts.

The second and third features are the numerical scores of the two exams taken by the student in their admission process. These two exams integrate the nationally standardized EXANI-II examination, designed by National Center of Evaluation for Higher Education (Ceneval from its Spanish initials) from Mexico. This examination puts into test the theoretical knowledge from higher education aspirants and is used to support admission processes in higher education institutions in Mexico. EXANI-II integrates two exams. The first one is EXANI-II Admission, which works as an instrument that evaluates the academic aptitude, that is to say, the potential that aspirants have to initiate higher education. It considers knowledge and skills on mathematical thinking, analytical thinking, language structure and reading comprehension, which are considered predictive indicators of overall knowledge. The second one is EXANI-II Diagnostic, which evaluates the proficiency in disciplinary areas related to contents that they studied in high school and that are fundamental to initiate a higher education program related to those specific areas. For admission process on the School of Engineering of Universidad Panamericana, the EXANI-II Diagnostic evaluates the field of "Engineering and technology", which tests aspirants' knowledge and skills on mathematics, physics, writing, and English language. The results of EXANI-II are delivered on a scale called the Ceneval index, in which 700 points is the minimum score and 1,300 is the maximum. EXANI-II is designed so that the majority of the population that takes it achieves an expected average performance close to 1,000 [1].

The fourth feature is the student's high school final grade. In Mexico, usually this grade is the average of the final grade from each of the three academic years that compose high school in the country. Figure 3 shows the distribution of this feature in our dataset.

The fifth feature is the student's university final grade. In the School of Engineering of the Universidad Panamericana this final grade is the average of

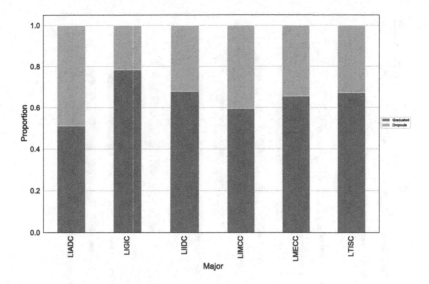

Fig. 1. Proportion of graduated students and dropout students by Major

all final grades from all classes taken in the whole major all weighting equally. In the case of dropouts, this grade is the average of all coursed classes before the student dropped out. Its scale goes from 0 to 10, however an average below 6 is considered a failing grade.

Scholarships as a discount on the monthly tuition, are available in the School of Engineering of Universidad Panamericana. Scholarships can be granted to students due to many reasons, just as by them having a top high school grade and getting a high score on both the EXANI-II admission and diagnostic examinations, being a university's employee or relative to one, being part of one of the university's representative sports teams, or because of their socioeconomic status. In any case, scholarship percentages may vary throughout semesters as the student must meet certain conditions to do so. For instance, a student with a scholarship must have a cumulative average grade above eight and have none failed subjects to keep it for the next semester. The sixth feature is the average scholarship percentage that students had throughout their major, in case they were granted one. Scholarships can range from 10% to 100%.

The sixth feature is categorical, and it is the major in which the student was enrolled. In Fig. 1, we can observe that there is not a significant variation between the proportion of dropouts among the six different majors as they are all around 30%. However, when we compare the program with the highest attrition rate (LIADC) with the program with the lowest attrition rate (LIGIC), there is in fact a great difference, but this could be an effect of the total number of students enrolled in the major. LIGIC is the program with the largest total, and in consequence, the proportion of dropouts is affected to a lesser extent with every dropout.

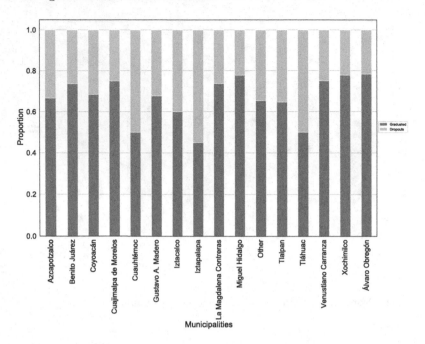

Fig. 2. Proportion of graduated students and dropout students by Municipality

The seventh feature is also categorical and is the municipality from Mexico City in which the student lived when he or she enrolled university. There are 16 municipalities in total in Mexico City, but we dismissed one as there were no record of any student that came from there. Also, we also took into consideration an extra category for those students that lived somewhere outside the city.

According to Mexico's Social Development Information System (SIDESO, from its Spanish initials), and as we can see in Table 1, the five municipalities with the highest percentage of territorial units with a really high degree of marginalization are: Milpa Alta, Tláhuac, Magdalena Contreras, Xochimilco and Iztpalapa. In Fig. 2, we are able to observe that the five municipalities with higher attrition rates are Iztapalapa, Tláhuac, Cuauhtémoc, Iztacalco and Tlalpan, from which two are also in the list of the five municipalities with higher degree of marginalization by territorial unit. Students who come from municipalities with high degree of marginalization, are more likely to be facing financial issues at home, and this could potentially lead them to drop out.

Another thing to notice is that Milpa Alta was the only municipality from which there were no records of students that lived there, and is also the municipality which 100% of its territorial units have a really high degree of marginalization. Accessibility to private universities, as Universidad Panamericana, due to their high tuition fees, are not accessible to everyone.

In Fig. 3, we are able to notice a linear relation between university final grade and high school final grade of students, which means that students' academic

Table 1. Percentage of territorial units with really high degree of marginalization according to SIDESO [2]

Municipality	Percentage of territorial units really high degree of marginalization
Milpa Alta	100%
Tláhuac	46%
Magdalena Contreras	44%
Xochimilco	38%
Iztapalapa	35%
Álvaro Obregón	24%
Gustavo A. Madero	24%
Tlálpan	23%
Cuajimalpa	19%
Azcapotzalco	7%
Iztacalco	5%
Venustiano Carranza	5%
Miguel Hidalgo	4%
Coyoacán	3%
Cuauhtémoc	0%
Benito Juárez	0%

performance in high school does give us an idea of how the student may perform during university. Furthermore, we can observe that although students' university final grade is a great determinant for dropouts, when a student also has a low high school final grade, dropping out becomes more likely. Additionally, we can clearly see that the percentage in scholarship does increase when the student has a great high school final grade and even more when university final grade is also high.

What we can observe in Fig. 4 is that there is a slight linear relation between EXANII-II admission score and university final grade, which means that the student's performance in this test could potentially reveal about the student's performance once in university. With this graph we can see how related a great performance in the test with the percentage of scholarship.

4 Modelling Student Attrition

4.1 Preprocessing

In our dataset, we had a total of 7 independent variables, from which five were numerical and two were categorical. In order to standardize our dataset, we chose to create categorical features out of the five numerical, which resulted in a dataset of a total of 66 features.

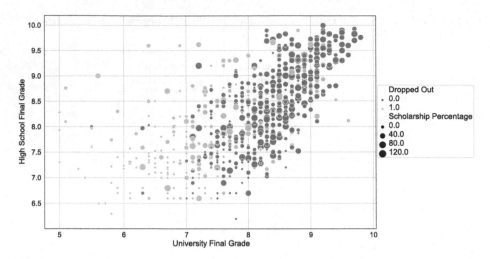

Fig. 3. University final grade against high school final grade

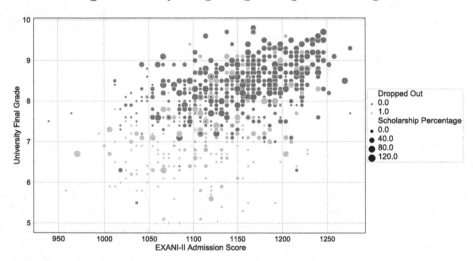

Fig. 4. EXANII-II admission score against university final grade

4.2 Principal Component Analysis

Due to the high number of features, we choose to do a linear dimensionality reduction by value decomposition of the data to project it to a lower dimensional space. In order to determine, how many components we required to do so, Principal Component Analysis was used to learn how explained variance changed by number of components. A 0.68 of the variances of our dataset is explained by 17 features, as we can observe in Fig. 5.

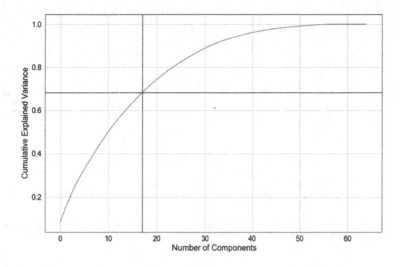

Fig. 5. Cumulative explained variance

4.3 Logistic Regression with Cross Validation

We chose to model dropouts with a logistic regression using cross-validation. We worked with 5 folds, minimized loss as the multinomial loss fit across the entire probability distribution and a maximum number of iterations of 3000.

For each potential number of principal components from 1 to 66, we ran a logistic regression with cross-validation in order to evaluate how precision, F1 and recall scores varied. As we can see in Fig. 6, with 17 principal components we achieved the highest precision and F1 score. In order to achieve the best recall score, we would have to use 34 principal components, however we would be sacrificing a high precision and F1 scores. Therefore, we chose to work with 17 principal components.

Nevertheless, for reference and as a control method, we ran three other models. One using logistic regression with cross-validation, but on all features. Another one using only logistic regression on all features. And a final one, using logistic regression on 17 principal components.

4.4 Gradient Boosting

Furthermore, aside from using logistic regression, we used a Gradient Boosting Machine (GBM) model. The basic idea behind a Gradient Boosting Machine is to combine the results obtained from various methods into an efficient decision-making rule so that in our application dropout behavior can be forecasted with better accuracy.

The gradient boosting model allowed us to get the importance of each of the features. What we can learn from Fig. 7 is that low final university grades are determinant for dropouts. Scholarship percentage also plays an important

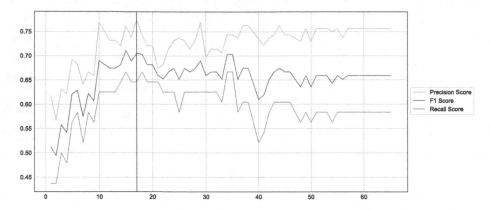

Fig. 6. Precision, F1 and recall scores by number of components using logistic regression with cross-validation

role when it comes to attrition. In the 20 features with highest importance, we can also find three features of municipality, from which two (Benito Juárez and Álvaro Obregón) are the municipalities that most students come from.

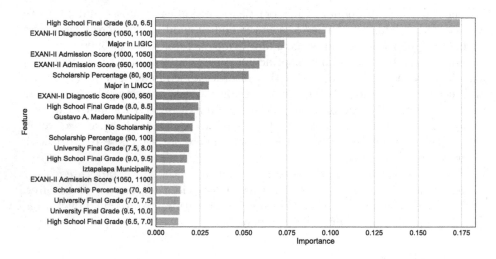

Fig. 7. 20 Features with highest importance based on the gradient boosting model

5 Evaluation

Definitely, all models perform substantially better than a random guess. Performance was comparable across models, yet the logistic regression model using cross-validation and 17 principal components had the best performance over-all in terms of precision, F1 and recall scores, which means that it is not only capable to identify those students who will stay in school, but is able to identify those students who will dropout, which is the outcome of interest of this investigation. When only using either cross-validation or 17 principal components, the latter option gets better scores, and definitely, when not using any technique, the model weakens significantly. When it comes to F1 score, using cross-validation becomes useless in our logistic regression models when not using 17 principal components. In terms of precision and F1 scores, the Gradient Boosting model, performs better than any of the three logistic regression models. In fact, the area under the curve of the gradient boosting model and the logistic regression using only 17 principal components are higher than the rest. These results are shown in Table 2 (Fig. 8).

In general terms, judging from our accuracy and recall scores, our models do work effectively when predicting those students who will drop-out, but not necessarily when predicting those students who won't drop-out.

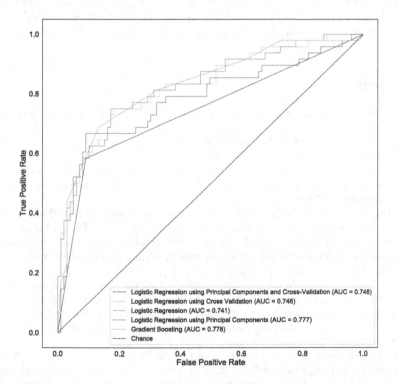

Fig. 8. ROC curves with their respective area under the curve of all five models

Table 2. Precision, F1 and recall scores of all five models

Model	Precision	F1	Recall
Logistic Regression with CV and 17 PC	0.761	0.666	0.711
Logistic Regression with CV	0.756	0.583	0.658
Logistic Regression	0.737	0.583	0.651
Logistic Regression with 17 PC	0.775	0.646	0.705
Gradient Boosting	0.717	0.688	0.702

6   Conclusion and Future Work

The idea behind this investigation is to build an early intervention system to identify those students with high probability of dropping out and taking the correct measures to either prevent it from happening or to even speed up the students' decision to drop out.

In this work we didn't use many other variables like associated income, or neighborhood, or family background. As we can aggregate these variables in the model, we will be able to make more precise and punctual predictions on whether a student will abandon their major.

References

1. Examen nacional de ingreso. http://www.ceneval.edu.mx/exani-ii. Accessed 24 June 2019
2. Sistema de informacion de desarrollo social. http://www.sideso.cdmx.gob.mx/index.php?id=11. Accessed 24 June 2019
3. ANUIES: Visión y acción 2030: Propuesta de la anuies para renovar la educación superior en méxico. Asociación Nacional de Universidades e Instituciones de Educación Superior (2018)
4. Dekker, G.W., Pechenizkiy, M., Vleeshouwers, J.M.: Predicting students drop out: a case study. In: International Working Group on Educational Data Mining (2009)
5. Lagunas, J.R., Vázquez, J.M.H.: La deserción escolar universitaria en méxico. la experiencia de la universidad autónoma metropolitana. Revista Electrónica "Actualidades Investigativas en Educación" 8(1), 1–30 (2008)
6. Ma, J., Pender, M., Welch, M.: Education pays 2016: the benefits of higher education for individuals and society. Trends in higher education series. College Board (2016)
7. OECD: Education at a Glance 2018 (2018). https://doi.org/10.1787/eag-2018-en. https://www.oecd-ilibrary.org/content/publication/eag-2018-en
8. OECD: Higher Education in Mexico (2019)
9. SEP: Principales Cifras 2017–2018. Secretaria de Educacion Publica (2019)
10. Stinebrickner, T.R., Stinebrickner, R.: The effect of credit constraints on the college drop-out decision a direct approach using a new panel study. Working Paper 13340, National Bureau of Economic Research, August 2007. https://doi.org/10.3386/w13340. http://www.nber.org/papers/w13340
11. Anuario Educación Superior: Anuarios estadisticos de educacion superior (2019). http://www.anuies.mx/informacion-y-servicios/informacion-estadistica-de-educacion-superior/anuario-estadistico-de-educacion-superior

Optimization of Modular Neural Networks for Pattern Recognition with Parallel Genetic Algorithms

Fevrier Valdez$^{(\boxtimes)}$, Patricia Melin, and Oscar Castillo

Division of Graduate studies, Tijuana Institute of Technology,
Calzada Tecnologico S/N, 22450 Tijuana, Mexico
{fevrier,pmelin,ocastillo}@tectijuana.mx

Abstract. We describe in this paper the use of Modular Neural Networks (MNN) for pattern recognition with parallel processing using a cluster of computers with a master-slave topology. In this paper, we are proposing the use of MNN for face recognition with large databases to validate the efficiency of the proposed approach. Also, a parallel genetic algorithm for architecture optimization was used to achieve an optimal design of the MNN. The main idea of this paper is the use of parallel genetic algorithms to find the best architecture with large databases of faces, because when the database to be considered is large, the main problem is the processing time to train the MNN. Network parameters are adjusted by a combination of the training pattern set and the corresponding errors between the desired output and the actual network response. To control a learning process, a criterion is needed to decide the time for terminating the process.

Keywords: Neural networks · Genetic algorithms · Optimization methods · Evolutionary computation

1 Introduction

Several approaches using Neural Networks for pattern recognition have been proposed, and some of them can be found in [4,6–8,16–19]. There are some works, like [17], which propose parallel implementations using threads, threads bring with them their own problems of synchronization and management overhead. In the same way [17] proposes a PVM (Parallel Virtual Machine), threads, and MPI for Self Organizing Maps (SOM), but they suffer from their own limitations. However, the main motivation to implement a cluster of computers with modular neural networks is because we can train the neural network faster than using a single processor. We describe in this paper the use of MNNs for pattern recognition using a cluster of computers for parallel processing. In this case, we are using the Face recognition database from Essex University [18] to test the proposed approach. The paper is organized as follows: in Sect. 2, a description about Neural Networks and Genetic Algorithms is presented, in Sect. 3,

© Springer Nature Switzerland AG 2019
L. Martínez-Villaseñor et al. (Eds.): MICAI 2019, LNAI 11835, pp. 223–235, 2019.
https://doi.org/10.1007/978-3-030-33749-0_19

the architecture of used MNN used and the data base images are presented, in Sect. 4, the master-slave topology used in this paper is shown, in Sect. 5, the experimental results are given, in Sect. 6 a comparison results with other similar approaches is shown, and finally in Sect. 7 the conclusions obtained in this paper are presented. The main contribution in this paper is that we can build a hierarchical genetic algorithm in parallel with the aim of optimizing Modular Neural Network Architectures.

2   Modular Neural Networks

A modular neural network is a neural network characterized by a series of independent neural networks moderated by an intermediary. Each independent neural network serves as a module and operates on separate inputs to accomplish some sub task of the complete task the network is expected to perform [4,19]. The intermediary takes the outputs of each module and processes them to produce the output of the network as a whole. The intermediary only accepts the modules outputs and it does not respond to, nor otherwise signal, the modules. Similarly, the modules do not interact with each other. There are many features that make them different from monolithic neural networks, among those features are:

Reduction of Complexity, [2] Robustness, [11] Scalability and Computational Efficiency [1].

2.1   Supervised Learning

In this paper, supervised learning for training the neural network was used. Supervised learning is based on a direct comparison between the actual network output and the desired output. For supervised learning, an error measure, which shows the difference between the network output and the output from the training samples, is used to guide the learning process. Some recent advances in supervised learning have been reviewed in [4,5,12,14,21,22].

2.2   Genetic Algorithms for Optimization

John Holland, from the University of Michigan initiated his research on genetic algorithms at the beginning of the 1960 s. His first achievement was the publication of Adaptation in Natural and Artificial Systems [10,20] in 1975.

The essence of the GA in both the theoretical and practical domains has been well demonstrated [9,13]. The concept of applying a GA to solve engineering problems is feasible and sound. However, despite the distinct advantages of a GA for solving complicated, constrained and multi-objective functions where other techniques may have failed, the full power of the GA in real applications is yet to be exploited [3].

3   Modular Neural Network Architecture

We are using a MNN in this paper for the proposed approach. Figure 1 shows the particular architecture used for this work and is described as follows: we use 3 modules, where each module has one layer of input for the data, which receive each image of the person to recognize. Each module receives one section of the images to train the MNN. Also, 2 hidden layers are used and one layer in the output of the MNN, in the integrator block we are considering different integration methods. Finally, the recognized person is shown in the last block with this architecture.

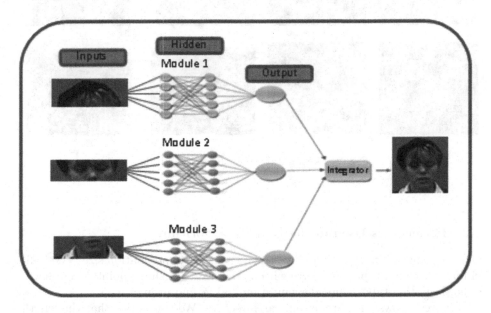

Fig. 1. MNN architecture

3.1   Database of Face Recognition

We used the Face Recognition Data of the University of Essex, UK. This database has the following characteristics: It contains 395 individuals (male and female), 20 images per individual. Contain images of people of various racial origins, mainly of first year undergraduate students, so the majority of individuals are between 18–20 years old but some older individuals are also present. Some individuals are wearing glasses and have beards. Figure 2 shows some of the persons included in this database.

Fig. 2. Essex database for face recognition

3.2   Parameters Used in the Genetic Algorithm

Chromosome = binary with 49 bits, generations = 10, population size = 30 individuals, selection type = roulette wheel, crossover = a single point, % crossover = 90, Mutation type = breader mutation and % mutation = 0.05.

Figure 3 shows the chromosome architecture. We can notice that the length is 49 bits. For this paper, this configuration was necessary because, the first 8 bits were used to save the information of the layer 1 of the module 1, the bit 9 to 16 were used to save the information of the layer 2 of module 1. The following 8 bits were used to save the information of the layer 1 of module 2. Another other 8 bits were necessary to save information of the layer 2 of module 2. For the module 3 the same configuration was used that the other 2 modules. Finally, the last bit was used to save the learning method.

4   Master Slave Topology

The easiest way to implement Genetic Algorithms on parallel computers is to distribute the evaluation of fitness among several slave processors while one master executes the GA operations (selection, crossover, and mutation). This paper is focused on a synchronous master-slave GA. Although more efficient implementations are possible, the objective is to give a simple lower bound on the

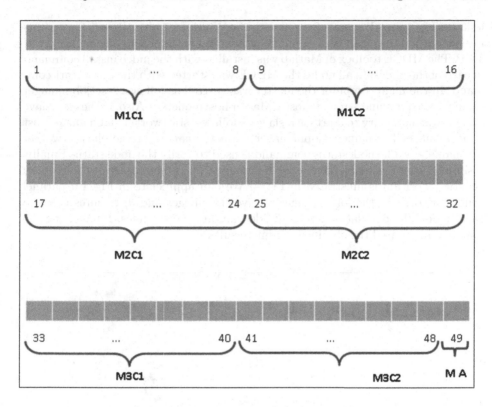

Fig. 3. Chromosome architecture

potential benefits that should be expected of parallel GAs. The execution time of master-slave GAs has two components: the time used in computations and the time used to communicate information among processors. The computation time is largely determined by the size of the population, so one may be tempted to reduce the population to make the GA faster. In this topology, there is a master computer, which assigns tasks to the slaves nodes or workers. The master slave topology works as follows:

Master: The tasks of the master computer are: Distribute and manage the tasks, response integration, send and receive the tasks to the slaves and save the results. Slaves: The tasks of the slave computers are: run the process sent by the master and send the results to the master. To make the cluster of computers perform the tests made in this paper we used the following computer specifications: Computers = Four computers with 2 Quad Core, RAM memory = 6 GB, Storage = 600 GB in Hard disk and Speed processors = 2.4 GHz. The MATLAB Distributed Computing Engine (MDCE) service must be running on all machines being used for the master or slaves. This service manages the job manager and worker processes. One of the major tasks of the MDCE service is to recover the job manager and worker sessions after a system crash, so that jobs and tasks are not lost as a result of such accidents. The cluster configuration was implemented as follows: The network was configured with the Windows 7 ultimate edition operating system and the protocol of communication used in the cluster of computers was TCP. The MDCE toolbox of Matlab was installed with the mdce install command in each of the nodes. In all nodes the MDCE was started with the mdce start command. In the main computer the master was started as follows: startjobmanager -name <Master name>-remotehost <Master hostname> -v Also, in the each slave node it was necessary to start each slave as follows: startworker -jobmanagerhost <job manager hostname> -jobmanager <Master name> -remotehost <worker hostname> -v The nodestatus command is used to verify the node status Finally, a simple test to validate the cluster was made. The architecture of the parallel genetic algorithm is illustrated in Fig. 4. We can appreciate in Fig. 4 a parallel genetic algorithm, the job manager receive the images and distributes them to each node. The population size is divided among the modules. Finally, the job manager integrated the obtained module results.

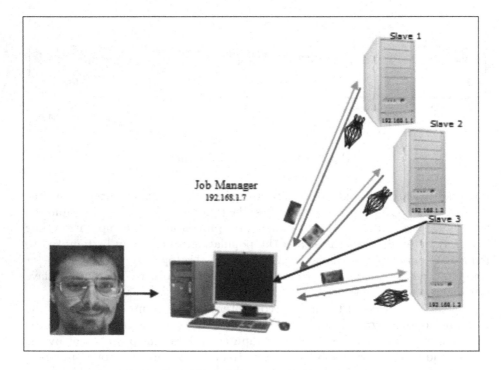

Fig. 4. Architecture of parallel genetic algorithm

5   Simulation Results

We describe in this Section the simulation results of the proposed approach for face recognition with modular neural networks.

The challenge is to find the optimal architecture of this type of MNN, which means finding out the optimal number of layers and nodes of the modules of the neural network. We are using the Essex face database with 3900 grayscale images in JPG format of 195 subjects, 14 images by each subject were used for training the MNN and 6 images were used to recognition. Regarding the genetic algorithm for MNN evolution, we used a hierarchical chromosome for representing all the relevant information of the network.

The fitness function used in this case for the MNN combines the information of the error objective and also the information about the number of total nodes as a second objective. This is shown in the following equation.

$$f(z) = \left(\frac{1}{\alpha \times Ranking(Objv1) + \beta \times Objv2} \right) \times 10 \tag{1}$$

The first objective is basically the average sum of squared of errors as calculated by the predicted outputs of the MNN compared with real values of the function. This is given by the following equation.

$$f_i = \frac{1}{N} \sum_{i=1}^{N} (Y_i - y_i) \tag{2}$$

The second objective is the complexity of the neural network, which is measured by the total number of nodes in the architecture. The final topology of the neural network for the problem of face recognition is obtained by the Genetic Algorithm. The optimal architecture achieved with the Genetic Algorithm is presented in Table 1. The Genetic Algorithm optimized the architecture for the problem of face recognition. We can note that the optimized architecture with the GA in Table 1, how the GA obtained two hidden layers with 3 modules and different number of neurons in each module. The training methods used with the architecture were the Gradient descent with adaptive learning rate backpropagation (traingda), and Gradient descent with momentum and adaptive learning rate backpropagation training (traingdx). Also, we changed the number of epochs to train the MNN between 500 and 1000. With this final architecture the Modular Neural Network was trained and the experimental are shown as follows. Table 2 shows the experimental results with the architecture presented in Table 1 in a sequential form. In Table 2 the MNN was trained with the Gradient descent with adaptive learning rate backpropagation training method. It can be note that how the training time in sequential form is higher. The best percentage

Table 1. Optimized architecture with the genetic algorithm

e2	3 modules		
Hideen layers	Neurons in module 1	Neurons in module 2	Neurons in module 3
1	350	301	340
2	135	143	195

of identification for this experiment was 92.22%, and we are changing the number of epochs and the error goal was 0.00001.

Each module was trained in one processor using the Machine Distributed Engine (MDCE) of Matlab. We are using a cluster of computer because the main problem is that when the database is large, the training time is very large. Therefore, in this paper, we have implemented a cluster of computer to obtain faster results. We are reporting several tests with sequential running and parallel mode. We can note in those experiments how is possible to obtain results quickly. Also, we can see how the optimized architecture obtained with the GA achieves good results.

Table 2. Experimental results in sequential form with the traingda training method

Epoch	Error	Training Time (HMS)	% Ident
500	0.00001	00:59:52	82.89
500	0.00001	00:58:22	82.99
500	0.00001	00:53:18	85.29
700	0.00001	01:13:29	91.28
700	0.00001	01:23:08	91.28
700	0.00001	01:13:16	87.77
1000	0.00001	01:45:08	91.71
1000	0.00001	01:43:30	91.45
1000	0.00001	01:42:10	92.22

In Table 3 the MNN was trained with the gradient descent momentum and an adaptive learning rate (traingdx). The best percentage of identification for this experiment was 93.16%, and the number of epochs was changed and the error goal was 0.00001.

Table 4 shows the experimental results in parallel form with the Gradient descent with adaptive learning rate backpropagation (traingda), with 500 and 700 epochs and a goal error of 0.00001. It can be noted that the training time using a cluster of computers is less than using sequential processing.

In Table 5 experimental results were made in parallel form with the gradient descent momentum and an adaptive learning rate (traingdx), with 500 and 700 epochs and a goal error of 0.00001. Also, it can be seen that the training time using a cluster of computers is less than to make this process in sequential form. With this method we achieved a good result, which is shown in row 4 in this test with a 94.71 % of identification and a training time of 1 hour with 36 min.

Table 6 shows the average of the experimental results in sequential form of 10 runs in the same conditions. The best average obtained is shown in the third row. However, the training time was of 2 hours with 26 min.

Table 3. Experimental results in sequential form with traingdx training method

Epoch	Error	Training Time (HMS)	% Ident
500	0.00001	00:53:33	90.59
500	0.00001	00:56:07	90.85
500	0.00001	00:55:10	90.85
700	0.00001	01:05:33	91.45
700	0.00001	01:22:52	92.22
700	0.00001	01:11:13	92.22
1000	0.00001	01:43:45	93.16
1000	0.00001	01:43:30	93.16
1000	0.00001	01:42:15	92.82

Table 4. Experimental results in parallel form with traingda training method

Epoch	Error	Training Time (HMS)	% Ident
500	0.00001	00:27:47	87.94
500	0.00001	00:22:13	85.72
500	0.00001	00:22:05	85.72
700	0.00001	00:30:22	88.81
700	0.00001	00:34:05	88.79
700	0.00001	00:31:23	88.79

Table 5. Experimental results in parallel form with traingdx training method

Epoch	Error	Training Time (HMS)	% Ident
500	0.00001	00:26:54	91.88
500	0.00001	00:22:22	91.88
500	0.00001	00:23:18	91.88
700	0.00001	01:36:22	94.71
700	0.00001	01:31:04	92.12
700	0.00001	01:27:41	92.91

Table 6. Average of experimental results in sequential form of 10 runs

Training Method	Epoch	Training Time (HMS)	% Ident
Trainscg	500	01:38:02	94.13
Trainscg	700	02:26:22	94.39
Trainscg	1000	03:05:45	94.85
Traingdx	500	00:51:48	90.57
Traingdx	700	01:07:45	91.69
Traingdx	1000	01:42:48	92.91

In Table 7 we show the average of experimental results in parallel form of 10 runs in the same conditions. The best average obtained is shown in the second row. The training time was of 1 hours with 29 min.

Table 7. Average of experimental results in parallel form of 10 runs

Training Method	Epoch	Training Time (HMS)	% Ident
Trainscg	500	00:57:53	94.58
Trainscg	700	01:29:56	94.71
Traingdx	500	00:24:38	91.88
Traingdx	700	00:39:18	93.58
Traingda	500	00:24:02	86.46
Traingda	700	00:30:22	88.80

6   Comparison of Results

In Table 8 the comparison of results with respect to other approaches that have used this face database is presented. The proposed approaches were called PMN-NPGA (Parallel Modular Neural Networks with Parallel Genetic Algorithms) and SMNNSGA (Sequential Modular Neural Networks with Sequential Genetic Algorithms). We can note in Table 8 how this approach can be used when de number of images is increased, because with small databases the difference with other similar methods is very small. However, with large databases a parallel approach is necessary.

Table 8 shows a comparison of results with other approaches that use the same face database. The first, two and three methods use via Non-Negative Matrix Factorization (NMF) to represent human facial image in low frequency sub band, which is able to realize through the wavelet transform. Wavelet transform (WT), is used to reduce the noise and produce a representation in the low frequency domain, and hence making the facial images insensitive to facial expression. After wavelet decomposition, NMF is performed to produce region or part-based representations of the images [18]. The best results obtained with the third approach (SFNMF) was 97.58% using 150 images to train and 350 images to identification. Also, with the same number of images our proposed method PMNNPGA was better than one and two methods but similar with respect to third method. However, we can see than our method was better than Eigen faces method. In other cases other methods were better than our approach but our method was designed to work with large face database, for example, our method was tested with more images than another methods achieving good results.

Table 8. Comparison results with other methods

Method	Database	Persons/Images by persons	Images to train	Images to identify	% of Identification
NMF [15]	Essex(Faces-94)	50/10	150 (30%)	350 (70%)	93.38 %
LNMF [15]	Essex(Faces-94)	50/10	150 (30%)	350 (70%)	94.95 %
SFNMF [15]	Essex(Faces-94)	50/10	150 (30%)	350 (70%)	97.58 %
PMNNPGA	Essex(Faces-94)	50/10	150 (30%)	350 (70%)	97.14 %
SVM [15]	Essex(Grimace)	18/20	216 (66%)	144 (34%)	98.13 %
PMNNPGA	Essex(Grimace)	18/20	216 (66%)	144 (34%)	95.83 %
Eigenface [15]	Essex(Grimace)	18/20	144 (34%)	216 (66%)	69.40 %
W + PCA [15]	Essex(Grimace)	18/20	144 (34%)	216 (66%)	98.50 %
CB PCA [15]	Essex(Grimace)	18/20	144 (34%)	216 (66%)	100 %
PMNNPGA	Essex(Grimace)	18/20	144 (34%)	216 (66%)	95.13 %
SMNNSGA	Essex	195/20	2730 (70%)	1170 (30%)	91.58 %
PMNNPGA	Essex	195/20	2730 (70%)	1170 (30%)	91.90 %
SMNNSGA	Essex(Full)	389/20	4668 (60%)	3112 (40%)	85.49 %
PMNNPGA	Essex(Full)	389/20	4668 (60%)	3112 (40%)	

7   Conclusions

The analysis of experimental results of the parallel genetic algorithms for Optimization of Modular Neural Networks for Pattern Recognition, lead us, to verify clearly the importance of using several processors to solve this type of problems to achieve fast results. Also, using a cluster of computers we can train the neural networks for pattern recognition with large databases, in this case, faces of persons with large databases. The identification rates with the sequential and parallel methods are very similar, however, the difference is in the training time using a cluster of computers is less than using sequential processing.

In this paper, modular neural networks with genetic algorithms were developed for pattern recognition. The genetic algorithm was used to optimize the layers, neurons by layers and the training method. Also, our approach was compared with other similar approaches.

The experimental results obtained in this paper give us good results. However, the parameters used in the MNN can be improved with an optimization method, because, for this research the parameters were randomly changed.

Also, the main difference between running the GA in parallel or sequentially form was the training time, for example an experiment, the training time was 8:15:46 hrs in sequential form, and 4:26:09 hrs in parallel form with similar conditions. As future work we can consider the following: Genetic Algorithms, we can use other genetic algorithms with other parallel architectures for example, GA coarse grained, multi populations and hybrids. With their representations (ring, torus, cube, hypercube). And in addition with asynchronous communications, as in this work we developed a genetic algorithm in parallel with the master-slave architecture and synchronous communication. Also, we can test with a different MNNs and make changes in the integration method. Feature extraction and databases: we can use other faces databases, for example, "Pie database" which has 14.000 images and "Multi Pie" with 700,000 images, which would be useful to perform several tests.

Acknowledgement. We would like to express our gratitude to CONACYT, Tijuana Institute of Technology for the facilities and resources granted for the development of this research, and Dr. Libor Spacek for the facilities of the face recognition database.

References

1. Azam, F.: Biologically inspired modular neural networks. Ph.D. thesis, Citeseer (2000)
2. Azam, F., VanLandingham, H.: A modular neural network method for robust handwritten character recognition. In: Artificial Neural Networks for Intelligent Engineering, vol. 98, pp. 503–508 (1998)
3. Back, T., Fogel, D., Michalewicz, Z.: Handbook of Evolutionary Computation. Oxford University Press, Oxford (1997)
4. Baesens, B., et al.: Neural networks and learning systems come together. IEEE Trans. Neural Netw. Learn. Syst. **23**(1), 1–6 (2012). https://doi.org/10.1109/TNNLS.2011.2180851
5. Castillo, O., Melin, P.: Hybrid intelligent systems for time series prediction using neural networks, fuzzy logic, and fractal theory. IEEE Trans. Neural Netw. **13**(6), 1395–1408 (2002)
6. Gaxiola, F., Melin, P., Valdez, F., Castro, J.R.: Person recognition with modular deep neural network using the iris biometric measure. In: Castillo, O., Melin, P., Kacprzyk, J. (eds.) Fuzzy Logic Augmentation of Neural and Optimization Algorithms: Theoretical Aspects and Real Applications. SCI, vol. 749, pp. 69–80. Springer, Cham (2018). https://doi.org/10.1007/978-3-319-71008-2_6
7. Gaxiola, F., Melin, P., Valdez, F., Castro, J.R., Manzo-Martinez, A.: PSO with dynamic adaptation of parameters for optimization in neural networks with interval type-2 fuzzy numbers weights. Axioms **8**(1), 14 (2019). https://doi.org/10.3390/axioms8010014
8. Gaxiola, F., Melin, P., Valdez, F., Castro, J.R.: Optimization of deep neural network for recognition with human iris biometric measure. In: Melin, P., Castillo, O., Kacprzyk, J., Reformat, M., Melek, W. (eds.) NAFIPS 2017. AISC, vol. 648, pp. 172–180. Springer, Cham (2018). https://doi.org/10.1007/978-3-319-67137-6_19
9. Goldberg, D.: Genetic Algorithms. Addison Wesley, Boston (1988)
10. Holland, J.: Adaptation in Natural and Artificial System. The University of Michigan Press, Ann Arbor (1975)
11. Lee, T.: Structure level adaptation for artificial neural networks. Springer, Boston (1991). https://doi.org/10.1007/978-1-4615-3954-4. Kluwer Academic Publishers
12. Ma, S., Ji, C.: Performance and efficiency: recent advances in supervised learning. Proc. IEEE **87**(9), 1519–1535 (1999)
13. Man, K., Tang, S., Kwong, K.: Genetic Algorithms: Concepts and Designs. Springer, Heidelberg (1999). https://doi.org/10.1007/978-1-4471-0577-0
14. Muller, B., Reinhardt, J., Strickland, M.: Neural networks: An Introduction. Springer, Berlin (1995). https://doi.org/10.1007/978-3-642-57760-4

15. Neo, H., Teoh, B.: a novel spatially confined non-negative matrix factorization for face recognition. Science City, Japan, Tsukuba (2005)
16. Rumelhart, D.E., Hinton, G.E., Williams, R.J., et al.: Learning representations by back-propagating errors. Nature **323**(6088), 533–536 (1986). https://doi.org/10.1038/323533a0
17. Seiffert, U.: Artificial neural networks on massively parallel computer hardware. In: ESANN, pp. 319–330 (2002)
18. Spacek, L.: Face Recognition Data, University of Essex, UK (2010). https://cswww.essex.ac.uk/mv/allfaces/
19. Mandal, T., Majumdar, A., Wu, Q.M.J.: Face recognition by curvelet based feature extraction. In: Kamel, M., Campilho, A. (eds.) ICIAR 2007. LNCS, vol. 4633, pp. 806–817. Springer, Heidelberg (2007). https://doi.org/10.1007/978-3-540-74260-9_72
20. Valdez, F., Melin, P., Castillo, O.: Evolutionary method combining particle swarm optimisation and genetic algorithms using fuzzy logic for parameter adaptation and aggregation: the case neural network optimization for face recognition. Int. J. Artif. Intell. Soft Comput. **2**(1/2), 77–102 (2010)
21. Valdez, F., Vázquez, J., Gaxiola, F.: Fuzzy dynamic parameter adaptation in ACO and PSO for designing fuzzy controllers: the cases of water level and temperature control. Adv. Fuzzy Syst. **2018**, 19 (2018). https://doi.org/10.1155/2018/1274969
22. Valdez, F., Castillo, O., Jain, A., Jana, D.K.: Nature-inspired optimization algorithms for neuro-fuzzy models in real-world control and robotics applications. Comput. Int. Neurosc. **2019**, 2 (2019). https://doi.org/10.1155/2019/9128451

Optimization and Planning

A Scaled Gradient Projection Method for Minimization over the Stiefel Manifold

Harry Oviedo$^{(\boxtimes)}$ and Oscar Dalmau

Centro de Investigación en Matemáticas, CIMAT A.C., Guanajuato, Mexico
{harry.oviedo,dalmau}@cimat.mx

Abstract. In this paper we consider a class of iterative gradient projection methods for solving optimization problems with orthogonality constraints. The proposed method can be seen as a forward-backward gradient projection method which is an extension of a gradient method based on the Cayley transform. The proposal incorporates a self-adaptive scaling matrix and the Barzilai-Borwein step-sizes that accelerate the convergence of the method. In order to preserve feasibility, we adopt a projection operator based on the QR factorization. We demonstrate the efficiency of our procedure in several test problems including eigenvalue computations and sparse principal component analysis. Numerical comparisons show that our proposal is effective for solving these kind of problems and presents competitive results compared with some state-of-art methods.

Keywords: Nonlinear programming · Gradient projection method · Orthogonality constraints · Stiefel manifold

1 Introduction

In this paper we consider the problem of minimizing a continuously differentiable and bounded from below function $\mathcal{F} : \mathbb{R}^{n \times p} \to \mathbb{R}$ on the matrix set $St(n, p)$ of size n-by-p defined as $St(n, p) := \{X \in \mathbb{R}^{n \times p} : X^\top X = I\}$, which is a compact sub-manifold embedded in the Euclidean space $\mathbb{R}^{n \times p}$ [1], and it is known as the Stiefel manifold. This problem can be formulated mathematically as

$$\min_{X \in \mathbb{R}^{n \times p}} \mathcal{F}(X) \quad s.t. \quad X^\top X = I, \tag{1}$$

This kind of problem frequently appears in a wide collection of applications such as eigenvalue problems and subspace tracking [29,30], 1-bit compressive sensing [3,16], sparse principal component analysis [18], quadratic assignment problems [29], Kohn-Sham total energy minimization [31], pattern recognition (dimensionality reduction techniques) [14], linear eigenvalue problem [24], joint diagonalization [13,27], the orthogonal procrustes problem [10,22], color image restoration and conformal mapping construction [15], the maxcut problem and the leakage interference minimization [17].

© Springer Nature Switzerland AG 2019
L. Martínez-Villaseñor et al. (Eds.): MICAI 2019, LNAI 11835, pp. 239–250, 2019.
https://doi.org/10.1007/978-3-030-33749-0_20

Only a few simple cases of problem (1) (for example, finding the extreme eigenvalues, orthogonal procrustes problems) have global solutions with closed expressions. In most cases, we need to use iterative methods for solving theses problems. It is not an easy task to solve problem (1), due to the orthogonality constraints may lead to many different local minimizers. In particular, applications such as the maxcut problem and the leakage interference minimization [17] are NP-hard.

In this paper, we introduce a scaled gradient projection method for optimization problems on the Stiefel manifold. The proposed method can be seen as an extension of the iterative scheme proposed by Wen and Yin in [29]. We provide some theoretical results under backtracking Armijo line-search. Finally, in order to demonstrate the efficiency and effectiveness of the new method, we compare our proposal with different gradient-type methods existing in the literature by using two test problems, including eigenvalue computations and sparse principal component analysis.

Related Works. Due to the wide applicability and fundamental difficulty of minimizing differentiable function over $St(n,p)$, several iterative methods have been proposed to solve problem (1). Most of the proposed methods correspond to first-order methods based on Riemannian gradient methods [1,4,7,9,19,21,29], generalizations of the non-linear conjugate gradient method [9,23,28,33], and also Newton and quasi-Newton methods [11,12,25,26]. Other methods based on generalized power iterations, augmented lagrangean multipliers algorithms and Bregman's iterations have been proposed in [15,18,20].

In this article, we introduce a generalization of the algorithm proposed by Wen and Yin in [29], which at present, remains as one of the most efficient approaches to solve (1). In [29] the authors proposed a method based on the Cayley transform, which updates the iterate X_{k+1} using the following recursive formula

$$X_{k+1} = (I + \frac{\tau}{2}A)^{-1}(I - \frac{\tau}{2}A)X_k, \tag{2}$$

where $A \in \mathbb{R}^{n \times n}$ is a skew-symmetric matrix related to the Riemannian gradient of $\mathcal{F}(\cdot)$ and $\tau > 0$ represents the step-size of the algorithm in each iteration. The main advantage of this scheme is that it guarantees the feasibility of each iterate X_{k+1} without using a reorthogonalization process. In addition, when $n \leq \frac{p}{2}$ the updating scheme (2) can be rewritten in an equivalent way that only needs a matrix inversion of size $2p \times 2p$ which is computationally less expensive than directly inverting in (2). It is well known that the iterate X_{k+1} given by (2) is a point on the curve $Y(\tau)$ defined implicitly as follows

$$Y(\tau) = X_k - \frac{\tau}{2}A(X_k + Y(\tau)). \tag{3}$$

Observe that the iterative scheme (3) gives equal weight to the iterates $Y(\tau)$ and X_k (the formula uses the weight equal to 1/2). In this paper we introduce a new iterative scheme based on (3) which incorporates a convex combination between X_k and $Y(\tau)$ with an adaptive weight. We will show numerically that this adaptive approach can be more effective than Wen-Yin's method to deal with the general problem (1).

Outline. The rest of this paper is organized as follows. In the next paragraph, some preliminaries definitions and notations are reviewed. The necessary optimality conditions associated to problem (1) are presented in Sect. 2. Section 3 is devoted to the development of a new scaled gradient projection method for solving problem (1). In Sect. 4, some numerical experiments with real and synthetic data are presented. In this section we address the linear eigenvalue problem and the sparse principal component analysis problem. Finally, our conclusions are given in Sect. 5.

Notations. Throughout this work, we denote by $Tr[X]$ to the trace of a given matrix X. We also use the Euclidean inner product $\langle A, B \rangle := Tr[A^\top B]$ between two matrices $A, B \in \mathbb{R}^{n \times n}$. The Frobenius norm of $A \in \mathbb{R}^{n \times n}$ is defined as $||A||_F := \sqrt{\langle A, A \rangle}$. A square matrix $W \in \mathbb{R}^{n \times n}$ is called skew-symmetric if $W^\top = -W$. Let $\mathcal{F}(X) : \mathbb{R}^{n \times p} \to \mathbb{R}$ be a real-valued continuously differentiable function, the Euclidean gradient of $\mathcal{F}$ is denoted by $G := \mathcal{D}\mathcal{F}(X) := \left(\frac{\partial \mathcal{F}(X)}{\partial X_{i,j}} \right)$. Furthermore, the directional derivative of $\mathcal{F}$ at X in a direction Z is

$$\mathcal{D}\mathcal{F}(X)[Z] := \lim_{\tau \to 0} \frac{\mathcal{F}(X + \tau Z) - \mathcal{F}(X)}{\tau} = \langle G, Z \rangle. \tag{4}$$

2   First-Order Optimality Conditions

By introducing a Lagrange multiplier $\Lambda \in \mathbb{R}^{p \times p}$, we have the Lagrangian function associated to (1)

$$\mathcal{L}(X, \Lambda) = \mathcal{F}(X) - \frac{1}{2} \langle \Lambda, X^\top X - I_p \rangle. \tag{5}$$

From the general theory of constrained optimization, we know that $X \in \mathbb{R}^{n \times p}$ is a candidate for a local minimizer of (1), if X satisfies the Karush-Kuhn-Tucker conditions,

$$\mathcal{D}\mathcal{L}_X(X, \Lambda) = G - X\Lambda \quad = 0, \tag{6a}$$
$$\mathcal{D}\mathcal{L}_\Lambda(X, \Lambda) = X^\top X - I_p = 0, \tag{6b}$$

for some matrix Λ of Lagrange multipliers. From (6a) and (6b), it is straightforward to prove that

$$\mathcal{D}\mathcal{L}_X(X, \Lambda) = G - XG^\top X = AX, \tag{7}$$

where $A = GX^\top - XG^\top$. Since all methods describe here are feasible the condition (6b) is always satisfied. Thus we only need to find a matrix X satisfying the condition (7). In the rest of this work, we will denote by $\nabla \mathcal{F}$ to the gradient of the Lagrangian function respect to X, that is, $\nabla \mathcal{F}(X) := AX$.

3   Optimization Method

In this section, we propose an optimization method to solve (1). We focus on first-order methods based on gradient projection, which are particularly efficient when we have a closed expression available for the projection operator.

Consider the gradient method applied to the Lagrangian function associated to (1), which generate a new iterate $Y(\bar{\tau})$, from X, as a point on the curve,

$$Y(\tau) = X - \tau \nabla \mathcal{F}(X), \tag{8}$$

where $\tau > 0$ is the step-size. This method is one of the simplest procedures for solving an unconstrained optimization problem, due to it enjoys low memory requirements and arithmetic operations, which makes it attractive to solve optimization problems on the matrix space. By introducing a parameter $\mu \in [0,1]$ and an implicit term, we arrive at the following forward–backward gradient method,

$$Y(\tau) = X - \tau((1-\mu)\nabla \mathcal{F}(X) + \mu \nabla \mathcal{F}(Y(\tau))), \tag{9}$$

which is an adaptation of the gradient method (8), that incorporates future information and it use, as search direction, a convex combination between the current gradient and the gradient evaluated at the future iterate. In order to obtain an explicit scheme related to (9), we approximate $\nabla \mathcal{F}(Y(\tau))$ by $AY(\tau)$, which leads to the following iterative scheme

$$Y(\tau) = X - \tau A((1-\mu)X + \mu Y(\tau)). \tag{10}$$

Observe that if $\mu = 0.5$ then the iterative formula (10) is equivalent to the Wen and Yin's method [29], and actually the new iterate $Y(\bar{\tau})$ belongs to $St(n,p)$. By a simple calculation, we obtain an explicit expression equivalent to (10),

$$Y(\tau) = X - \tau(I - \mu \tau A)^{-1} \nabla \mathcal{F}(X). \tag{11}$$

Now, consider the update scheme (11). Then, it is not difficult to prove that $Y(\tau) \in St(n,p)$ if and only if $\mu = 0.5$. Thus the principal drawback of (11) is that the new iterate $Y(\tau)$ may not be a feasible point. In order to overcome this issue, we consider the following projection operator over the Stiefel manifold

$$\pi(X) = \arg \min_{Q \in St(n,p)} ||X - Q||_F. \tag{12}$$

The following proposition, demonstrated in [19], gives us a close expression to compute the projection of any matrix over $St(n,p)$. In this proposition $U \in \mathbb{R}^{n \times n}$, $V \in \mathbb{R}^{p \times p}$ are orthogonal matrices, $\Sigma \in \mathbb{R}^{n \times p}$ is rectangular diagonal matrix with non-negative real numbers on the diagonal and $I_{n,p} \in \mathbb{R}^{n \times p}$ is rectangular diagonal matrix with diagonal entries equal to 1.

Proposition 1. *Let* $X \in \mathbb{R}^{n \times p}$ *be a rank* p *matrix. Then,* $\pi(X)$ *is well defined. Moreover, if the SVD of* X *is* $X = U \Sigma V^\top$*, then* $\pi(X) = U I_{n,p} V^\top$*.*

Incorporating the projection operator $\pi(\cdot)$, defined in (12), with the iterative scheme (11), we arrive to our scale projection gradient method for solving the general problem (1), which computes the new iterate by a point on the curve

$$Y(\tau) = \pi(X - \tau D(\mu, \tau)\nabla\mathcal{F}(X)), \tag{13}$$

where $D(\mu, \tau) = (I_n + \mu\tau A)^{-1}$ and $\mu \in [0, 1]$ are the scaling matrix and the scaling parameter respectively. The following lemma provides us some interesting properties of our scheme (13).

Lemma 1. *Consider the curve $Y(\tau)$ defined in (13), with $X \in St(n, p)$. Then the following properties are satisfied.*

1. *The scaling matrix $D(\mu, \tau) = (I_n + \mu\tau A)^{-1}$ is positive definite for all (μ, τ) $\in \mathbb{R}^2$.*
2. *For $\mu = 1/2$, $Y(\tau)$ is reduced to the Cayley transform method (2). In addition, the derivative of $Y(\tau)$ with respect to τ at $\tau = 0$ is*

$$\dot{Y}(0) = -\nabla\mathcal{F}(X). \tag{14}$$

3. *$Y(\tau)$ is a descent curve at $\tau = 0$, that is*

$$D\mathcal{F}(X)[\dot{Y}(0)] = -\frac{1}{2}\|A\|_F^2 < 0. \tag{15}$$

4. *If we rewrite the matrix A as $A = UV^\top$ where $U = [G, X]$ and $V = [X, -G]$ then (13) is equivalent to the following scheme*

$$Y(\tau) = \pi(X - \tau U(I_{2p} + \mu\tau V^\top U)^{-1}V^\top X). \tag{16}$$

3.1   Step-Size Selection Rules

In this subsection, we describe how we select the step-size τ in (13). As we know, the Barzilai-Borwein [2] step-sizes (BB-steps) can speed up the performance of the gradient projections methods significantly almost without increasing the computational cost. For this reason, we use the following two BB-steps at the k-th iteration

$$\tau_k^{BB1} = \frac{\|S_{k-1}\|_F^2}{|\langle S_{k-1}, Y_{k-1}\rangle|} \quad \text{and} \quad \tau_k^{BB2} = \frac{|\langle S_{k-1}, Y_{k-1}\rangle|}{\|Y_{k-1}\|_F^2}, \tag{17}$$

where $S_{k-1} = X_k - X_{k-1}$ and $Y_k = \nabla\mathcal{F}(X_k) - \nabla\mathcal{F}(X_{k-1})$. In particular, we adopt the adaptive strategy proposed by Dai and Fletcher in [6],

$$\tau_k^{ABB} = \begin{cases} \tau_k^{BB1} & \text{for odd k;} \\ \tau_k^{BB2} & \text{for even k.} \end{cases} \tag{18}$$

In addition, we combine this step-size (18) with the nonmonotone line search technique proposed by Zhang and Hager in [32], in order to ensure the global convergence of our proposed method.

3.2   The Algorithm

In this subsection, we introduce a heuristic to choose the scaling parameter μ and then, we present the proposed algorithm. From our numerical experience, we know that a fixed weight μ is not good enough for minimizing nonlinear and non-convex functions. For this reason, we propose an adaptive strategy to adjust this parameter along the iterations. In order to measure the progress of each iteration, we introduce the following ratio,

$$\psi(\mu) = \frac{\|\nabla \mathcal{F}(X_{k+1})\|_F}{\|\nabla \mathcal{F}(X_k)\|_F}. \tag{19}$$

Then, if $\psi(\mu) < 1$ the current weight is called "successful"; otherwise, the is "unsuccessful", in the last case we decrease the weight as follow $\mu = \max(\min(0.9\mu, 0), 0.5)$. Observe that a small value of $\psi(\mu)$ indicates that the current μ is working well. Hence, the weight is increased only if the step is successful but the residual ratio $\psi(\mu)$ is too large, that is, if $0.5 \leq \psi(\mu) < 1$ then we increment μ as follow $\mu = \max(\min(1.1\mu, 1), 0)$.

Observe that if $\mu = 0$ in (13) then the proposed method is reduced to the standard gradient projection method, and if $\mu \neq 0$ then our method incorporates implicit information.

Algorithm 1. Scaled Gradient Projection Method for Stiefel Manifold Constrained Optimization (SGPM)

Require: $X_0 \in St(n, p)$, $\tau > 0$, $0 < \tau_m \leq \tau_M$, $\eta \in [0, 1)$, $\mu, \rho_1, \epsilon, \delta \in (0, 1)$, $Q_0 = 1$,
    $C_0 = \mathcal{F}(X_0)$ k=0.
Ensure: X^* an ϵ-KKT point.
 1: **while** $\|\nabla_X \mathcal{L}(X_k)\|_F > \epsilon$ **do**
 2:     **while** $\mathcal{F}(Y(\tau)) > C_k + \rho_1 \tau D\mathcal{F}(X_k)[\dot{Y}(0)]$ **do**
 3:         $\tau = \delta\tau$,
 4:     **end while**
 5:     Update $X_{k+1} = Y(\tau)$, with $Y(\cdot)$ according to (13).
 6:     Compute the ratio $\psi(\mu)$ according to (19).
 7:     **if** $\psi(\mu) \geq 1$ **then** set $\mu = \max(\min(0.9\mu, 0), 0.5)$.
 8:     **if** $0.5 \leq \psi(\mu) < 1$ **then** set $\mu = \max(\min(1.1\mu, 1), 0)$.
 9:     Calculate $Q_{k+1} = \eta Q_k + 1$ and $C_{k+1} = (\eta Q_k C_k + \mathcal{F}(X_{k+1}))/Q_{k+1}$.
10:     Choose $\tau = \tau_{k+1}^{ABB}$ with τ_{k+1}^{ABB} defined as in (18).
11:     $\tau = \max(\min(\tau, \tau_M), \tau_m)$.
12:     Increment k as $k = k + 1$.
13: **end while**
14: $X^* = X_k$.

Now we present two theoretical result available for Algorithm 1.

Theorem 1. *Let $\{X_k\}$ be an infinite sequence generated by Algorithm 1 with $\eta = 0$. Then any accumulation point X_* of $\{X_k\}$ satisfies the Karush-Kuhn-Tucker conditions* (6a)–(6b).

The following result establish the global convergence of the Algorithm 1.

Corollary 1. *Let $\{X_k\}$ be an infinite sequence generated by Algorithm 1 with $\eta = 0$. Then $\lim_{k\to\infty} \|\nabla_X \mathcal{L}(X_k)\|_F = 0$.*

Proof. The proof of this corollary is a direct consequence of Theorem 1 and the compactness of the Stiefel manifold.

4 Numerical Experiments

The experiments of this section aim to show the practical usefulness of SGPM for eigenvalue computations and sparse principal component analysis. All the numerical tests are carried out by using MATLAB running on an intel(R) CORE(TM) i7-4770, CPU 3.40 GHz with 500 GB HD and 16 GB RAM. To illustrate the efficiency of our algorithm, we compare Algorithm 1(SGPM) with the *OptStiefelGBB* proposed in [29], and also with the Riemannian gradient projection method *Grad–retrac* [21].

In our numerical tests, we consider the following stopping rules. Let's denote by $rel_k^x := \frac{\|X_{k+1}-X_k\|_F}{\sqrt{n}}$, $rel_k^f := \frac{|\mathcal{F}(X_{k+1})-\mathcal{F}(X_k)|}{|\mathcal{F}(X_k)|+1}$. Then, we stop the algorithms if one of the following conditions holds: (i) $k \geq M$; (ii) $\|\nabla_X \mathcal{L}(X_k)\|_F \leq \epsilon$; (iii) $rel_k^x \leq \epsilon_x$ and $rel_k^f \leq \epsilon_f$; (iv) $\mathtt{mean}([rel_{k-\min\{k,T\}+1}^x, \ldots, rel_k^x]) \leq 10\epsilon_x$ and $\mathtt{mean}([rel_{k-\min\{k,T\}+1}^f, \ldots, rel_k^f]) \leq 10\epsilon_f$, where $N = 3000$ is the maximum number of iteration. We set $\epsilon = 1e-5$, $\epsilon_x = 1e-15$, $\epsilon_f = 1e-15$ and $T = 5$ for all methods. In addition, in our Algorithm 1, we set $\tau_m = 1e-15$, $\tau_M = 1e+15$, $\eta = 0.85$ and $\delta = 0.2$ and the initial parameter μ is $\mu = 0.85$. For all experiments we randomly generate the starting point X_0 using the following Matlab command $[X_0, \sim] = \mathtt{qr}(\mathtt{randn}(n, p), 0)$.

Additionally, *Time, Nfe, Nitr, NrmG* and *fval* denote the averaged total computing time in seconds, the averaged number of function evaluations, the averaged number of iterations, the averaged residual $\|\nabla \mathcal{F}(X^*)\|_F$ where X^* is the optimum estimated by the method, respectively. In all experiment we solve 30 independent instances for the different values of (n, p) and then we report all these averages.

4.1   Linear Eigenvalue Problem

Given a real symmetric matrix $A \in \mathbb{R}^{n \times n}$, the linear eigenvalue problem is formulated as the following optimization problem on the Stiefel manifold

$$\max_{X \in \mathbb{R}^{n \times p}} \mathcal{F}(X) = Tr[X^{\top}AX] \quad s.t. \quad X^{\top}X = I_p. \tag{20}$$

Note that the global solution of (20) is the matrix $X^* \in \mathbb{R}^{n \times p}$ whose columns are the eigenvectors of A associated with the p-largest eigenvalues of A. This kind of problem arise in fields of data mining, for example in locally linear embedding (LLE) [14], principal component analysis (PCA) [14], Laplacean eigenmaps [14], orthogonal neighborhood preserving projection (ONPP) [14], among other.

Firstly, we compare our proposal with *OptStiefelGBB* computing the two largest eigenvalues using the 25 instances of large sparse matrices with $n \geq 4000$ taken from the UF Sparse Matrix Collection [8]. For this experiment, we set $\epsilon = 1e{-}6$, $\epsilon_x = 10e{-}18$ and $\epsilon_f = 10e{-}18$ for all methods in order to obtain accurate solutions. In addition, we choose $X_0 = I_2$, the matrix formed by the first two columns of the identity matrix. Table 1 reports the numerical results corresponding to this experiment. In this table, we can see that our SGPM is quite competitive on most problems in terms of CPU times and number of iterations, and obtain a performance very similar to *OptStiefelGBB*.

4.2   Sparse Principal Component Analysis

In this section, we compare three algorithms for solving sparse principal component analysis (sparse PCA). The goal of sparse PCA is to find main components with very few nonzero entries. For a given data matrix $A \in \mathbb{R}^{m \times n}$, the sparse PCA that seeks the leading r ($r < \min\{m, n\}$) sparse loading vectors by solving the following optimization problem

$$\min_{X \in \mathbb{R}^{n \times p}} \mathcal{F}(X) = -Tr[X^{\top}A^{\top}AX] + \lambda||X||_1 \quad s.t. \quad X^{\top}X = I, \tag{21}$$

where $||X||_1 = \sum_{i,j} |X_{i,j}|$ and $\lambda > 0$ is the regularization parameter. In order to deal with this kind of problems, we replace the l_1-norm in the objective function by the pseudo–Huber loss approximation $||X||_1 \approx \sum_{i,j}(\sqrt{X_{ij}^2 + \delta^2} - \delta)$ for some fixed small positive δ. Note that the parameter δ determines the trade-off between the smoothness of the objective function and the goodness of the approximation, that is, $\sum_{i,j}(\sqrt{X_{ij}^2 + \delta^2} - \delta) \to ||X||_1$ when δ tends to zero.

The random data matrices $A \in \mathbb{R}^{m \times n}$ considered in this subsection were generated using the Matlab command `randn`(m, n), then we shifted the columns of A such that their mean is equal to 0, and finally the columns were normalized. In addition, we fixed $\delta = 1e{-}5$ in all experiments and the initial matrix X_0 was randomly generated over the Stiefel manifold. The numerical results associated to this experiments are summarized in Table 2. In this table, we report the average number of iterations, average sparsity, the average CPU time (in seconds)

Table 1. Computing the first two largest eigenvalues of 25 instances in the UF Sparse Matrix Collection.

Name	n	OptStiefelGBB				SGPM			
		Nfe	Nrmg	Nitr	Time	Nfe	Nrmg	Nitr	Time
msc04515	4515	547	7.98e−6	329	0.30	1171	1.14e−5	449	0.53
s1rmq4m1	5489	754	8.29e−6	383	0.59	609	6.18e−6	338	0.57
s1rmt3m1	5489	389	9.61e−6	273	0.30	1012	6.16e−6	409	0.70
s2rmq4m1	5489	331	9.19e−6	252	0.29	632	9.81e−6	329	0.55
s2rmt3m1	5489	314	9.63e−6	246	0.25	881	2.92e−6	414	0.64
s3rmq4m1	5489	365	5.81e−6	272	0.35	227	1.93e−6	219	0.26
s3rmt3m1	5489	328	1.93e−6	252	0.27	255	8.15e−6	241	0.24
s3rmt3m3	5489	289	9.04e−6	231	0.22	331	7.81e−6	251	0.28
fv1	9604	3978	3.63e−5	3000	3.24	3091	2.51e−5	3000	3.13
fv2	9801	3976	7.38e−5	3000	3.32	3100	3.01e−5	3000	3.12
fv3	9801	3847	1.00e−4	3000	3.26	3081	3.03e−5	3000	3.12
Kuu	7102	291	9.54e−6	216	0.32	196	9.35e−6	189	0.24
Muu	7102	51	7.57e−6	40	0.04	45	9.27e−6	41	0.04
bcsstk16	4884	638	2.72e−4	565	0.60	145	2.87e−6	136	0.13
bcsstk17	10974	127	4.89e−4	114	0.19	123	5.33e−6	114	0.20
bcsstk18	11948	272	1.28e−4	246	0.33	205	9.22e−6	200	0.31
bcsstk28	4410	77	4.69e−6	67	0.06	75	4.08e−6	70	0.07
bcsstk36	23052	2071	5.51e−6	903	6.49	1134	9.64e−6	873	4.09
ex15	6867	1559	1.2e−3	861	0.80	518	7.36e−5	404	0.34
finan512	74752	289	5.11e−6	217	2.42	235	1.36e−6	218	2.42
msc23052	23052	1222	7.15e−6	775	4.06	1178	9.44e−6	859	4.27
nasa4704	4704	320	5.29e−7	301	0.17	75	3.15e−6	72	0.04
nasasrb	54870	285	2.53e−4	219	2.32	219	7.11e−6	213	2.03
nd3k	9000	272	5.88e−6	209	1.50	218	4.14e−6	204	1.21
sts4098	4098	55	5.96e−6	48	0.05	50	3.97e−6	45	0.03

and the average of the gradiente norm $\|\nabla\mathcal{F}(X)\|_F$ obtained by all algorithms. The experiments of this subsection were taken form [5]. From Table 2 we see that *SGPM* is faster than *OptStiefelGBB* in most of the problems tested, obtaining more accurate solutions in terms of Nrmg. In addition, we observe that our algorithms obtained similar and competitive results to the *Grad–retrac* procedure.

Table 2. Numerical results on sparse principal component analysis random problems.

		OptStiefelGBB				Grad–retrac				SGPM			
r	λ	Nitr	Nrmg	Time	Sp	Nitr	Nrmg	Time	Sp	Nitr	Nrmg	Time	Sp
						$n = 500, m = 10$							
2	0.5	233	7.16e−6	0.06	36.7	203	6.68e−6	0.11	36.7	215	7.95e−6	0.06	36.7
2	1	151	7.22e−6	0.03	36.4	157	6.96e−6	0.08	36.4	145	7.07e−6	0.03	36.4
5	0.5	834	1.86e−5	0.27	89.9	672	8.28e−6	0.39	89.9	609	8.70e−6	0.22	89.9
5	1	640	3.33e−5	0.21	89.4	591	7.63e−6	0.35	89.5	553	7.96e−6	0.20	89.5
10	0.5	2456	2.13e−3	1.12	160.3	1989	6.60e−3	1.38	161.1	2012	3.68e−3	1.01	161.4
10	1	1620	5.46e−5	0.81	161.8	1643	2.31e−4	1.26	160.7	1456	9.07e−6	0.78	161.6
						$n = 2000, m = 10$							
2	0.5	1417	2.50e−3	4.19	73.4	332	7.79e−6	1.12	73.4	379	8.07e−6	1.78	73.4
2	1	413	4.16e−5	1.21	73.1	223	8.24e−6	0.73	73.1	295	7.22e−6	1.22	73.1
5	0.5	3000	2.98e−4	10.45	181.7	1058	8.84e−6	4.22	181.7	916	8.07e−6	4.20	181.7
5	1	2774	2.75e−4	9.78	181.3	864	8.62e−6	3.46	181.3	928	9.17e−6	4.43	181.3
10	0.5	3000	2.63e−1	12.64	327.1	2267	2.55e−2	10.22	326.7	2337	6.62e−1	10.45	326.9
10	1	3000	1.87e−1	12.60	325.7	1786	8.72e−6	8.06	324.8	2017	8.14e−6	9.99	324.9
						$n = 3000, m = 100$							
2	0.3	2210	2.40e−3	15.36	87.3	994	9.31e−6	7.80	87.3	1124	8.93e−6	11.80	87.3
2	0.6	1802	1.20e−3	13.15	87.6	863	8.42e−6	7.38	87.6	897	8.14e−6	8.62	87.6
5	0.3	3000	2.90e−3	22.80	217.6	2584	8.40e−4	21.18	217.5	2522	1.94e−2	21.75	217.6
5	0.6	3000	1.90e−3	22.40	217.3	1836	2.80e−5	14.41	217.3	1749	4.02e−5	13.35	217.3
10	0.3	3000	4.84e−2	25.81	431.4	2994	1.51e−1	25.39	431.4	3000	5.30e−2	26.53	431.4
1	0.6	3000	2.20e−2	25.22	431.1	2961	3.45e−2	24.37	431.2	2883	4.50e−3	22.61	431.1

5 Conclusions

In this work, we have proposed a scaled gradient projection method for solving optimization problems with orthogonality constraints. The proposed method uses an adaptive scaling matrix, which is updated according to the gradient norm. This technique allows the method, in each iteration, to use information from both the current iteration and future information. In order to guarantee the feasibility of each iterate, we use a projection operator. In addition, we incorporated a Barzilai-Borwein-like adaptive step-size to accelerate the convergence. We also establish the global convergence of method. Finally, from the numerical experiments carried out, we conclude that our algorithm performs comparable to other efficient iterative methods and its effectiveness is also confirmed.

Aknowledgement. This work was supported in part by Consejo Nacional de Ciencia y Tecnología (CONACYT) (Mexico), grant 258033.

References

1. Abrudan, T.E., Eriksson, J., Koivunen, V.: Steepest descent algorithms for optimization under unitary matrix constraint. IEEE Trans. Sig. Process. **56**(3), 1134–1147 (2008)

2. Barzilai, J., Borwein, J.M.: Two-point step size gradient methods. IMA J. Numer. Anal. **8**(1), 141–148 (1988)
3. Boufounos, P.T., Baraniuk, R.G.: 1-bit compressive sensing. In: 42nd Annual Conference on Information Sciences and Systems, 2008. CISS 2008, pp. 16–21. IEEE (2008)
4. Cedeño, O.S.D., Leon, H.F.O.: Projected nonmonotone search methods for optimization with orthogonality constraints. Comput. Appl. Math. **37**(3), 1–27 (2017). https://doi.org/10.1007/s40314-017-0501-6
5. Chen, S., Ma, S., So, A.M.C., Zhang, T.: Proximal gradient method for manifold optimization. arXiv preprint arXiv:1811.00980 (2018)
6. Dai, Y.H., Fletcher, R.: Projected Barzilai-Borwein methods for large-scale box-constrained quadratic programming. Numer. Math. **100**(1), 21–47 (2005)
7. Dalmau-Cedeño, O., Oviedo, H.: A projection method for optimization problems on the stiefel manifold. In: Carrasco-Ochoa, J.A., Martínez-Trinidad, J.F., Olvera-López, J.A. (eds.) MCPR 2017. LNCS, vol. 10267, pp. 84–93. Springer, Cham (2017). https://doi.org/10.1007/978-3-319-59226-8_9
8. Davis, T.A., Hu, Y.: The university of Florida sparse matrix collection. ACM Trans. Mathem. Softw. (TOMS) **38**(1), 1 (2011)
9. Edelman, A., Arias, T.A., Smith, S.T.: The geometry of algorithms with orthogonality constraints. SIAM J. Matrix Anal. Appl. **20**(2), 303–353 (1998)
10. Eldén, L., Park, H.: A procrustes problem on the stiefel manifold. Numer. Math. **82**(4), 599–619 (1999)
11. Hu, J., Jiang, B., Lin, L., Wen, Z., Yuan, Y.: Structured quasi-newton methods for optimization with orthogonality constraints. arXiv preprint arXiv:1809.00452 (2018)
12. Hu, J., Milzarek, A., Wen, Z., Yuan, Y.: Adaptive quadratically regularized newton method for riemannian optimization. SIAM J. Matrix Anal. Appl. **39**(3), 1181–1207 (2018)
13. Joho, M., Mathis, H.: Joint diagonalization of correlation matrices by using gradient methods with application to blind signal separation. In: Sensor Array and Multichannel Signal Processing Workshop Proceedings, 2002, pp. 273–277. IEEE (2002)
14. Kokiopoulou, E., Chen, J., Saad, Y.: Trace optimization and eigenproblems in dimension reduction methods. Numer. Linear Algebra Appl. **18**(3), 565–602 (2011)
15. Lai, R., Osher, S.: A splitting method for orthogonality constrained problems. J. Sci. Comput. **58**(2), 431–449 (2014)
16. Laska, J.N., Wen, Z., Yin, W., Baraniuk, R.G.: Trust, but verify: fast and accurate signal recovery from 1-bit compressive measurements. IEEE Trans. Sig. Process. **59**(11), 5289–5301 (2011)
17. Liu, Y.F., Dai, Y.H., Luo, Z.Q.: On the complexity of leakage interference minimization for interference alignment. In: 2011 IEEE 12th international workshop on Signal Processing Advances in Wireless Communications, pp. 471–475. IEEE (2011)
18. Lu, Z., Zhang, Y.: An augmented lagrangian approach for sparse principal component analysis. Math. Program. **135**(1–2), 149–193 (2012)
19. Manton, J.H.: Optimization algorithms exploiting unitary constraints. IEEE Trans. Sig. Process. **50**(3), 635–650 (2002)
20. Nie, F., Zhang, R., Li, X.: A generalized power iteration method for solving quadratic problem on the stiefel manifold. Sci. China Inf. Sci. **60**(11), 112101 (2017)
21. Oviedo, H., Lara, H., Dalmau, O.: A non-monotone linear search algorithm with mixed direction on stiefel manifold. Optim. Methods Softw. **34**(2), 1–21 (2018)

22. Oviedo, H.F.: A spectral gradient projection method for the positive semi-definite procrustes problem. arXiv /abs/1908.06497v1 (2019)
23. Oviedo, H.F., Lara, H.J.: A riemannian conjugate gradient algorithm with implicit vector transport for optimization in the stiefel manifold. Technical report, Technical report. UFSC-Blumenau, CIMAT (2018)
24. Saad, Y.: Numerical Methods for Large Eigenvalue Problems. Manchester University Press, Manchester (1992)
25. Sato, H.: Riemannian newton's method for joint diagonalization on the stiefel manifold with application to ica. arXiv preprint arXiv:1403.8064 (2014)
26. Seibert, M., Kleinsteuber, M., Hüper, K.: Properties of the bfgs method on riemannian manifolds. Mathematical System Theory C Festschrift in Honor of Uwe Helmke on the Occasion of his Sixtieth Birthday, pp. 395–412 (2013)
27. Theis, F.J., Cason, T.P., Absil, P.-A.: Soft dimension reduction for ICA by joint diagonalization on the stiefel manifold. In: Adali, T., Jutten, C., Romano, J.M.T., Barros, A.K. (eds.) ICA 2009. LNCS, vol. 5441, pp. 354–361. Springer, Heidelberg (2009). https://doi.org/10.1007/978-3-642-00599-2_45
28. Urdaneta, H.L., Leon, H.F.O.: Solving joint diagonalization problems via a riemannian conjugate gradient method in stiefel manifold. In: Proceeding Series of the Brazilian Society of Computational and Applied Mathematics, vol. 6, no. 2 (2018)
29. Wen, Z., Yin, W.: A feasible method for optimization with orthogonality constraints. Math. Program. **142**(1–2), 397–434 (2013)
30. Yang, B.: Projection approximation subspace tracking. IEEE Trans. Sig. Process. **43**(1), 95–107 (1995)
31. Yang, C., Meza, J.C., Lee, B., Wang, L.W.: KSSOLV – a matlab toolbox for solving the kohn-sham equations. ACM Trans. Math. Softw. (TOMS) **36**(2), 10 (2009)
32. Zhang, H., Hager, W.W.: A nonmonotone line search technique and its application to unconstrained optimization. SIAM J. Optim. **14**(4), 1043–1056 (2004)
33. Zhu, X.: A riemannian conjugate gradient method for optimization on the stiefel manifold. Comput. Optim. Appl. **67**(1), 73–110 (2017)

Local Sensitive Hashing for Proximity Searching

Karina Figueroa[1,2](✉) ⓘ, Antonio Camarena-Ibarrola[1,3] ⓘ,
and Luis Valero-Elizondo[1,2] ⓘ

[1] Universidad Michoacana de San Nicolás de Hidalgo, Morelia, Michoacán, Mexico
{karina,valero}@fismat.umich.mx
[2] Facultad de Ciencias Físico-matemáticas, San Nicolás de los Garza, Mexico
[3] Facultad de Ing. Eléctrica, Morelia, Mexico
camarena@umich.mx

Abstract. Proximity or similarity searching is one of the most important tasks in artificial intelligence concerning multimedia databases. If there is a distance function to compare any two objects in a collection, then similarity can be modeled as a metric space. One of the most important techniques used for high dimensional data is the permutation-based algorithm, where the problem is mapped into another space (permutations space) where distances are much easier to compute, but solving similarity queries with the least number of distances computed is still a challenge. The approach in this work consists in using Locality-Sensitive Hashing (LSH). The experiments reported in this paper show that the proposed way to adapt LSH to the permutation based algorithm has a competitive tradeoff between recall and distances.

Keywords: Similarity searching · Nearest neighbor ·
Permutation-based algorithm

1 Introduction

Proximity or similarity searching is the core of many problems in artificial intelligence. Most of which are related to multimedia databases, where an exact search is useless. Instead, the elements in these databases must be comparable using a distance function, in order to decide which elements are similar to a given query; usually the distance function is expensive to compute. There are many multimedia databases in which the only way to compare its elements is through the distance function, but even in these collections of unstructured objects, fast searching can be accomplished, Lets explain first some useful concepts.

A metric space is a pair $(\mathbb{X}, d)$, where $\mathbb{X}$ is the universe of objects and d is a distance function which defines how similar the objects are, that is $d : \mathbb{X} \times \mathbb{X} \to \mathbb{R}^+$. The distance function must satisfy the following properties which make d a metric; that is, let $x, y, z \in \mathbb{X}$, d: symmetry $d(x, y) = d(y, x)$, reflexivity $d(x, x) = 0$, strict positiveness $d(x, y) > 0 \leftrightarrow x \neq y$, and triangle inequality

© Springer Nature Switzerland AG 2019
L. Martínez-Villaseñor et al. (Eds.): MICAI 2019, LNAI 11835, pp. 251–261, 2019.
https://doi.org/10.1007/978-3-030-33749-0_21

$d(x, y) \leq d(x, z) + d(z, y)$. The database is a finite subset of valid objects $\mathbb{U} \subseteq \mathbb{X}$, $n = |\mathbb{U}|$.

Considering that our problem is similarity searching, there are basically two kinds of queries:

- *range queries* which consist in retrieving the elements from $\mathbb{U}$ within a radius given to the query q; that is $R(q, r) = \{u \in \mathbb{U} | d(u, q) \leq r, \forall u \in \mathbb{U}\}$.
- *k-nearest neighbors queries* retrieve elements of $\mathbb{U}$ that are closest to q, $|NN_K(q)| = K$, and $\forall v \in NN_K(q), w \in \mathbb{U} - NN_K(q), d(v, q) \leq d(w, q)$. In case of ties any k-element that satisfies the query can be chosen.

The naive approach to solve queries is through sequential scan (i.e. brute force), however for huge databases such approach is not realistic since distances are expensive to compute. Our goal is to answer the queries reducing the number of distances to be computed as much as possible. The solution is normally implemented in two phases, first, an index is built, which is done offline, only then, in the second phase, queries can be solved using the index for that purpose, this is normally done online.

There are several algorithms proposed for metric spaces, however, most of them just work in low intrinsic dimension spaces, as the intrinsic dimension grows the performance falls, this problem is known as *curse of dimensionality* [4]. Fortunately, there are algorithms designed for high intrinsic dimensions [5], some of the bests use the permutation-based approach [1,3].

In this paper, we propose to use the core of the permutation-based algorithm (PBA) in combination with Locality-Sensitive Hashing (LSH) [13]. In Sect. 2 previous work are described, and in Sect. 3 the novel proposal is explain. The results are shown in Sect. 4 with real databases. Finally, conclusions and future work are in Sect. 5.

2   Related Work

The state-of-the-art methods are, basically, divided in three families [3,5,11,12, 14]. *Pivot-based, partition-based, and permutation-based algorithms.*

Pivot-based algorithms [5] select a set of elements and call them *pivots*. Each pivot computes its distances to all the elements in the database, all these distances are stored. When a query is given, these algorithms compute the distances between the query and the pivots, then with the stored distances and thanks to the triangle inequality approximate distances between the query and the rest of the elements çan be inferred and so discard many objects that should not be included in the candidate list. These are effective algorithms for low intrinsic dimensions problems.

Partition-based algorithms [11] make zones using some previous selected objects called *centers*. In a similar way to pivots, partition-based algorithms use the triangle inequality to obtain a list of candidates. This strategy works for medium (not too high) dimensionality.

Since our proposal is based on the Permutation-based algorithm, we will now describe it in detail.

2.1 Permutation-Based Algorithm

In [2,3] PBA was introduced. With this technique, first a subset of elements is chosen, they are called *permutants*, that is $\mathbb{P} = \{p_1, \ldots, p_k\}$, where $\mathbb{P} \subseteq \mathbb{U}$. Each $u \in \mathbb{U}$ defines a permutation by ordering the elements in $\mathbb{P}$ according to the distance to them. That is, for all $1 \leq i < k$, $d(\Pi_u(i), u) \leq d(\Pi_u(i+1), u)$. The position of a permutant i can be represented by $\Pi_u^{-1}(i)$. In order to answer a query, when it is given, the permutation's query is computed and now the problem is to find the most similar permutations in the database. The comparison between permutations was proposed in [2] and recently a new dissimilarity was introduced in [9]. The core idea is to compute how far the position of a permutant is between two permutations. The metric for this purpose is *Spearman Rho* [3,6,7] defined as follows:

$$S_\rho(\Pi_u, \Pi_q) = \sqrt{\sum_{1 \leq i \leq k} (\Pi_u^{-1}(i) - \Pi_q^{-1}(i))^2} \tag{1}$$

2.2 Locality-Sensitive Hashing

Locality-Sensitive Hashing (LSH) was introduced in [10]. The main idea of hashing is storing similar objects in the same bucket with high probability. The core of this technique are the hash functions which maximize collisions between similar elements. LSH uses a set of hash tables ($\mathbb{L}$), each with its own hash function. An instance (λ^i, f^i) is a hash table (λ^i) along with its hash function (f^i). The probability to find similar elements grows as the number of instances increases.

Locality-Sensitive Hashing of Permutantions. In [8], the authors proposed using permutations to define new hash functions. That is, each permutation in the database is mapped to a number (i.e. a bucket in a hash table). For example, one of the hash functions sums the first 3 positions of the permutation, the result determines the bucket in the corresponding hash table.

3 Proposed Algorithm

In this article, a new algorithm for fast searching is proposed. The proposal will be described in two parts: first, the algorithm to build the index will be explained, then, the way to answer queries using the index.

Let $\mathbb{U}$ be the database and $\mathbb{P} = \{p_1, p_2, \ldots, p_k\} \subseteq \mathbb{U}$, $k = |\mathbb{P}|$ be the randomly selected elements of the database called permutants. Each $u \in \mathbb{U}$ computes all distances to the set of permutants $\mathbb{P}$, that is $D_u = \{d(u, p_1), \ldots, d(u, p_k)\}$. PBA stores the permutation of each u. Instead, our proposal consists in building hash functions from the information regarding the order of the permutants with to each object u. The hash function codes in binary whether one permutant is closer than another, or if the opposite is true.

It is important to mention that when u is at the same distance of two different permutants, it breaks the tie by using the classic PBA. That is, if $d(u, p_i) = d(u, p_j)$ the permutation is p_i, p_j when $i < j$, otherwise, the permutation is p_j, p_i.

It may occur that $d(q, p_i) < d(q, p_j)$ but the nearest neighbor of the query q is u and its distances are $d(u, p_i) > d(u, p_j)$, (but what if $d(u, p_i)$ is slightly greater than $d(u, p_j)$), then the order of the permutants for u will be different than the order for q. This problem is depicted in Fig. 1(a). Notice that u_1 (the one closer to q) has permutants p_1 and p_2 in reversed order with respect to q, furthermore, u_2 has the same order for those permutants as q does. The hash would find u_2 as the object closest to q missing the real closest one which is u_1. To avoid that problem a margin of tolerable differences of distances between any object and two given permutants is used so both u_1 and u_2 would be still considered (u_1 is not prematurely discarded), the tolerance zone is a parameter r as depicted in Fig. 1(b).

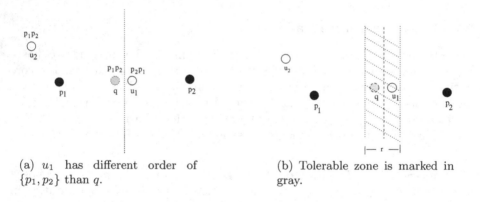

(a) u_1 has different order of $\{p_1, p_2\}$ than q.

(b) Tolerable zone is marked in gray.

Fig. 1. Example of an inversion of permutants when elements are approximately at the same distance close to two different permutants.

In order to keep the core of each permutation, the order of some pair of elements (p_i, p_j) will be represented using two bits with a function $B_u(p_i, p_j)$ defined as follows:

Let $p_i, p_j \in \mathbb{P}$ and let r the parameter defined above, there are 3 cases:

$$B_u(p_i, p_j) = \begin{cases} 11 & \text{if } |d(p_i, u) - d(p_j, u)| \leq r \\ 10 & \text{if } d(p_i, u) < d(p_j, u) \\ 01 & \text{if } d(p_i, u) > d(p_j, u) \end{cases} \qquad (2)$$

The values of B are $\{01, 10, 11\}$, where 11 means u is almost as near (r-near) to p_i as it is to p_j; 01 means that u is closest to p_i than to p_j and 10 is the opposite case.

3.1   Building the Index

For Locallity-Sensitive Hashing a set of hash functions has to be built, in this proposal, the idea is to take pairs of permutants and form a hash value by concatenating the proximity codes explained above. Let $\mathbb{M}$ be the set of pairs of permutants of length k, there are $k \times (k-1)$ different possible pairs, then not all of them can be used since there are too many of them, a subset may be chosen with some rule or $\mathbb{M}$ may be built by randomly selecting the pairs.

Choosing a Subset Using a Proposed Rule. Set $\mathbb{M}$ may simply be built as $\mathbb{M}' = \{(p_1, p_2), (p_2, p_3), \ldots, (p_{k-1}, p_k)\}$, or as $\{(p_1, p_3), (p_2, p_4), \ldots, (p_{k-2}, p_k)\}$. This strategy will be called HB. The concatenation of these bits will called *signature*, and it is built as follow:

$$S_u = B_u(p_1, p_2)| \ldots |B_u(p_{k-1}, p_k)|B_u(p_1, p_3)|B_u(p_2, p_4)| \ldots |B_u(p_{k-2}, p_k).$$

The length of the signature in bytes would be $\gamma = \frac{(2k-3)*2}{8}$.

Random Selection. For this strategy β pairs of permutants are chosen randomly, avoiding any pair of permutants to be chosen twice. This strategy will be called HBR.

3.2   Locality Sensitive Hashing of Permutations Using Bits

Let $\mathbb{L}$ be a set of hash tables, each hash table λ^i has its own function f^i, an instance is then (λ^i, f^i), where $\lambda^i \in \mathbb{L}$, $1 \leq i \leq m$, $m = |\mathbb{L}|$. The size of every hash table is α. Each hash function is defined as follows:

Each instance i has associated function f^i which computes a hash value for each object u using its signature (S_u), that is $v^i = f^i(S_u)$. The hash value v^i will be the bucket for element u at hash table λ^i. Similar elements should have the same hash value with high probability.

In hashing different objects may go to the same bucket (i.e. collisions), which is normal. The functions defined below generate equivalence classes each of them are intended to allocate similar objects in the same bucket.

Since we have two strategies, two different ways of building sets of hash functions will be defined, as follow:

Choosing a Subset (HB). According the proposal: let S_u a signature of u with length γ bytes. Each function j must be computed as follow, where $1 \leq j \leq m$. Let $\&$ is the bitwise-AND-operation, and $\%$ is the modulo-operator.

$$f^i(S_u) = \left(\sum_{j=1}^{\gamma} (S_u[j] \ \& \ \mathtt{mask}^i) \ \% \ \alpha \right) \tag{3}$$

In Table 1, the masks used for hash functions are shown.

Table 1. Hash functions

Hash table	Mask defined in Eq. 3
(λ^1, f^1)	$\texttt{mask}^1 = 0101\ 0101$
(λ^2, f^2)	$\texttt{mask}^2 = 1010\ 1010$
(λ^3, f^3)	$\texttt{mask}^3 = 1000\ 1110$
(λ^4, f^4)	$\texttt{mask}^4 = 1100\ 1100$
(λ^5, f^5)	$\texttt{mask}^5 = 0100\ 1111$
(λ^6, f^6)	$\texttt{mask}^6 = 0110\ 0110$
(λ^7, f^7)	$\texttt{mask}^7 = 1001\ 0110$

Random Selection (HBR). For this strategy, we have β pairs, then there are $2 \times \beta$ bits. For each λ^i, exactly 10 random bits were chosen and concatenated to form a hash value between 0 and 1024, that is $\alpha = 1024$. This idea is depicted in Fig. 2.

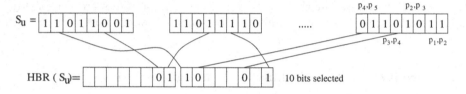

Fig. 2. Example of random bits used to get a hash value. The first row is a signature of an element S_u. The second one is the hash value.

Time Query. For a given query q, let Q_q be the distances between the query and all the permutants, with this information and parameter r, the signature of query S_q is determined.

The list of candidate objects $\mathbb{C}$ is the union of the sets of elements in the buckets $v_q^i = f^i(S_q)$ for all instances i. Let $\lambda^i[v_q^i]$ be the set of objects in bucket v_q^i for hash table λ^i, that is:

$$\mathbb{C} = \cup_{i=1}^m \lambda^i[v_q^i] \tag{4}$$

Details of Implementation. In order to be reproducibility, in Algorithm 1 is presented the building of the different hash tables. In the other hand, the second phase, time query, is shown at Algorithm 2.

4   Results and Discussion

In this section the performance of the proposal in real databases is shown.

Algorithm 1. Building the index

Let $\mathbb{L}$ the set of Hash Tables, $m = |\mathbb{L}|$
for $u \in \mathbb{U}$ do
   for $i = 1$ to m do
      $v_u^i \leftarrow f^i(S_u)$
      $\lambda^i[v_u^i] \leftarrow \text{add}(u)$
   end for
end for

Algorithm 2. Query time

Let q the query, r a range, and S_q its signature
Let $\mathbb{C}$ an empty set
for $i = 1$ to m do
   $v_q^i \leftarrow f^i(S_q)$
   $\mathbb{C} \leftarrow \mathbb{C} \cup \lambda^i[v_q^i])$
end for
for each $u \in \mathbb{C}$ do
   if $d(u, q) \leq r$ then
      u is part of the answer
   end if
end for

4.1 Colors Database

This database consists of 112,682 color histograms of images, represented as 112-dimensional vectors. The Euclidean distance was used to compare elements as the simplest alternative.

The performance of our technique is shown in Figs. 3 and 4 for NN = 1 and NN = 2 respectively.

In Fig. 3(a) the recall is shown for (NN = 1). Notice that using HBR strategy with $r = 0.15$ has an excellent recall, almost perfect. However, in Fig. 3(b) it can be seen that the size of $\mathbb{C}$ (candidate list) is too large. Considering a tradeoff between elements retrieved and number of distances computed, the best performance is for HB with $r = 0.15$ and 32 permutants. Using 8 permutants, the best result is achieved with HBR and $r = 0$.

For NN = 2 (two nearest neighbors), very similar results to NN = 1 were obtained. In Fig. 4(a) the best result corresponds to HB with $r = 0.1$ and 32 permutants. However when using 8 permutants the best result was achieved by HBR with $r = 0$.

4.2 NASA Database

This dataset consists of 40,150 feature vectors in $\mathbb{R}^{20}$ (compared with Euclidean Distance). These 20-dimensional vectors were generated from images downloaded from NASA (available at http://www.dimacs.rutgers.edu/Challenges/Sixth/software.html), there are no duplicate vectors.

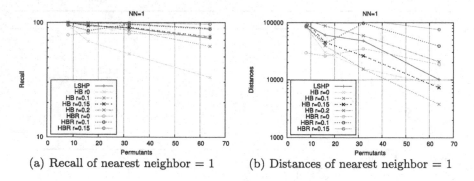

(a) Recall of nearest neighbor = 1   (b) Distances of nearest neighbor = 1

Fig. 3. Performance of the proposal for the colors database. The left side shows the recall, the right side shows the number of distances computed.

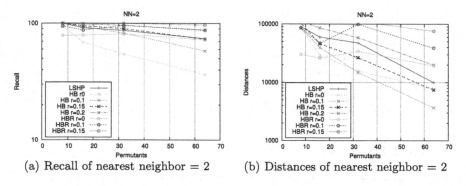

(a) Recall of nearest neighbor = 2   (b) Distances of nearest neighbor = 2

Fig. 4. Performance of the proposal for the colors database. The left side shows the recall, the right side shows the number of distances computed.

In Fig. 5(a) the recall is shown for (NN = 1). Nothing beats LSHP except HBR for $r = 0.15$, but the number of distances computed turned out to be higher than that of LSHP as can be observed in Fig. 5(b). However HB with either $r = 0.1$, $r = 0.15$, and $r = 0.2$ outperforms LSHP in terms of distances computed for any number of permutants and still having a competitive recall of about 80% in the case of HBR with $r = 0.2$.

For NN = 2, as seen in Fig. 6(a), both LSHP and HB with $r = 0.2$ have the best recall for 8 and 16 permutants, also LSP and HBR for $r = 0$ have both the best recall for 32 permutants, although again HBR with $r = 0.15$ outperforms both for 64 permutants. However HB with $r = 0.2$ needs to compute far less distances than LSHP and would definitely be the best method when using 8 or 16 permutants.

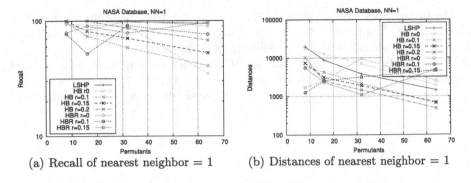

(a) Recall of nearest neighbor = 1   (b) Distances of nearest neighbor = 1

Fig. 5. Performance of the proposal for the nasa database. The left side shows the recall, the right side shows the number of distances computed.

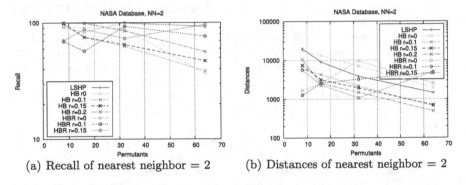

(a) Recall of nearest neighbor = 2   (b) Distances of nearest neighbor = 2

Fig. 6. Performance of the proposal for the nasa database. The left side shows the recall, the right side shows the number of distances computed.

5   Conclusions and Future Work

In this paper, a novel strategy to face the similarity searching problem was proposed. When a query is given, the proposed method requires constant time to answer the proximity queries. The proposal is using the core of permutation based algorithm to represent that information with some bits, after that, some bits are selected which combined are the key in a hash table. Using several bits a locality sensitive hashing can be designed.

The proposed method uses two bits to represent the way a query *sees* two especial objects (i.e. permutants). The main idea is that if the query object sees several pairs in the same order as another object does, then, it is very likely that the other object is near to the query object.

The experimental results show that this proposal is competitive with the state-of-the-art, for some set of hash functions the recall is better than similar proposals. And for other set of hash functions, the proposed technique outperform the state-of-the-art in terms of number of distances computed to solve a query.

As future work, we are considering to represent the same information (the order of a pair) but with just one bit. This modification would allow for using more pairs of permutants, and possibly improving recall.

It might also be worth exploring another set of hash functions, which would keep the permutation (or just one pair of it) for each element, and when the candidate list is computed, it can be sorted by similarity with the permutation of the query.

References

1. Amato, G., Savino, P.: Approximate similarity search in metric spaces using inverted files. In: Lempel, R., Perego, R., Silvestri, F. (eds.) 3rd International ICST Conference on Scalable Information Systems, INFOSCALE 2008, Vico Equense, Italy, 4–6 June 2008, p. 28. ICST/ACM (2008). https://doi.org/10.4108/ICST. INFOSCALE2008.3486
2. Chávez, E., Figueroa, K., Navarro, G.: Proximity searching in high dimensional spaces with a proximity preserving order. In: Gelbukh, A., de Albornoz, Á., Terashima-Marín, H. (eds.) MICAI 2005. LNCS (LNAI), vol. 3789, pp. 405–414. Springer, Heidelberg (2005). https://doi.org/10.1007/11579427_41
3. Chávez, E., Figueroa, K., Navarro, G.: Effective proximity retrieval by ordering permutations. IEEE Trans. Pattern Anal. Mach. Intell. (TPAMI) **30**(9), 1647–1658 (2009)
4. Chávez, E., Navarro, G.: A probabilistic spell for the curse of dimensionality. In: Buchsbaum, A.L., Snoeyink, J. (eds.) ALENEX 2001. LNCS, vol. 2153, pp. 147–160. Springer, Heidelberg (2001). https://doi.org/10.1007/3-540-44808-X_12
5. Chávez, E., Navarro, G., Baeza-Yates, R., Marroquín, J.: Proximity searching in metric spaces. ACM Comput. Surv. **33**(3), 273–321 (2001)
6. Diaconis, P., Graham, R.L.: Spearman's footrule as a measure of disarray. J. R. Stat. Soc. Ser. B (Methodol.) **39**(2), 262–268 (1977)
7. Fagin, R., Kumar, R., Sivakumar, D.: Comparing top k lists. SIAM J. Discrete Math. **17**(1), 134–160 (2003)
8. Figueroa, K., Camarena-Ibarrola, A., Valero-Elizondo, L., Reyes, N.: Locality-sensitive hashing of permutations for proximity searching. J. Intell. Fuzzy Syst. **36**, 4677–4684 (2019)
9. Figueroa, K., Paredes, R., Reyes, N.: New permutation dissimilarity measures for proximity searching. In: Marchand-Maillet, S., Silva, Y.N., Chávez, E. (eds.) SISAP 2018. LNCS, vol. 11223, pp. 122–133. Springer, Cham (2018). https://doi.org/10. 1007/978-3-030-02224-2_10
10. Gionis, A., Indyk, P., Motwani, R.: Similarity search in high dimensions via hashing. In: VLDB 1999 Proceedings of the 25th International Conference on Very Large Data Bases, pp. 518–529 (1999)
11. Hjaltason, G., Samet, H.: Index-driven similarity search in metric spaces. ACM Trans. Database Syst. **28**(4), 517–580 (2003). https://doi.org/10.1145/958942. 958948
12. Samet, H.: Foundations of Multidimensional and Metric Data Structures. The Morgan Kaufmann Series in Computer Graphics and Geometric Modeling. Morgan Kaufmann Publishers Inc., San Francisco (2005)

13. Tellez, E.S., Chavez, E.: On locality sensitive hashing in metric spaces. In: Proceedings of the Third International Conference on Similarity Search and Applications, SISAP 2010, pp. 67–74. ACM, New York (2010). https://doi.org/10.1145/1862344.1862355
14. Zezula, P., Amato, G., Dohnal, V., Batko, M.: Similarity Search: The Metric Space Approach. Advances in Database Systems, vol. 32. Springer, Heidelberg (2006)

Parallel Task Graphs Scheduling Based on the Internal Structure

Apolinar Velarde Martínez$^{(\boxtimes)}$ (iD)

Instituto Tecnológico El Llano Aguascalientes,
Carretera Aguascalientes-San Luis Potos í Km. 18, El Llano, Aguascalientes, Mexico
apolinar.vm@llano.tecnm.mx

Abstract. It is well known that Parallel Task Graphs (PTG) are modeled with Directed Acyclic Graphs (DAG Tasks). DAG tasks are scheduled in Heterogeneous Distributed Computing Systems (HDCS) for execution with different techniques which seek to reduce completion of each PTG. Proposed planning techniques generally only make use of the critical path in planning as an internal characteristic of the DAG Task, helping to optimize scheduling. In this study it is shown that analyzing other internal characteristics, such as layering and graph density aside from the critical path of DAG workflow tasks, before being scheduled in execution locations, can improve computer system performance, as well as optimize the use of their resources. For the above, the internal characteristics considered in this study of each DAG task are: the critical path, layering as well as graph density. The analyzed DAG tasks are synthetic loads produced with a graph generation algorithm as well as real application graphs. The findings obtained with the experiments performed show that the distribution estimation algorithm obtains better response times than the genetic algorithm.

Keywords: Directed Acyclic Graph · Parallel Task Graphs ·
Heterogeneous Distributed Computing Systems

1 Introduction

In recent years, DAG tasks running on Heterogeneous Distributed Computing Systems (HDCS) which represent Parallel Task Graphs (PTG) or parallel programs, have been used to model scientific applications of workflow and real-world applications [1–3]. DAG tasks are a collection of different subtasks that are constituted by a main task and its underlying tasks. In order for DAG tasks to be executed in parallel within the HDCS, they must be scheduled by different planning algorithms based on the time and precedence restrictions of their subtasks [2, 4–7]. To plan DAG tasks in a HDCS, a planning algorithm proceeds in two steps: first it finds an optimal allocation for each task, this being the number of processors where task execution time is minimal considering that minimizing

This proyect is sponsored by Tecnológico Nacional de Mexico TecNM.

L. Martínez-Villaseñor et al. (Eds.): MICAI 2019, LNAI 11835, pp. 262–276, 2019.
https://doi.org/10.1007/978-3-030-33749-0_22

this time does not imply using a greater number of processors and, that cost function is not monotonous; secondly, it determines the placement for the assigned tasks, this is the set of current processors where each task is executed minimizing total application completion time [4,5,7,8].

The planning and execution of DAG tasks in an HDCS has become common due to two situations: first, the problems that current computing equipment presents, such as internal heating and excessive energy consumption, thus, physical limitations present a fundamental obstacle for increasing clock speeds [12]; second, the increase in demand for greater computational power when problem solving due to high processing and storage requirements [9]. Furthermore, there is an issue in parallel task application planning techniques with heterogeneous cases [5], in order to obtain the best performance from multicore computers, an algorithm design with parallelism in mind would be optimal [12].

To verify the functionality and optimality of a planning algorithm in an HDCS, DAG tasks are extracted from real applications or by means of synthetic loads. The real applications used in planning tests are the decomposition of Lu [7], the elimination of Gauss-Jordan [7], molecular dynamic code [9,10], and the Fast Fourier Transform [9]; Synthetic loads are constructed by algorithms that generate random graphs to produce synthetic loads [11] such as Uunifast-Discard [2] or are extracted from the standard task graphs project (STG) [7].

When executing planning algorithms, graphs are submitted to planning processes where each node is distributed to a processing element, that respects precedence constraints and looks for an allocation that decreases the total execution time of parallel tasks: the makespan, by assigning a more appropriate processor for each task [5–8]. The proposed planners seek to balance the use of resources while reducing the execution times of queued tasks.

Due to the fact that the problem of planning DAG tasks is NP-Hard [2,5–8,12,13], different strategies have been developed to address it. It has been shown that planning DAG tasks without taking into account the internal structure, the dependencies between the subtasks in the planning process, nor the start times of each subtask, can lead to pessimistic results when executing the planning algorithms, as show in [2]. One feature that has been well studied is the critical path of the DAG task [2,5–8]: the path that has the most weight from a source node to a receiving node [5–8,12]. Solution strategies based on the critical path include the migration of algorithms produced for homogeneous environments to heterogeneous environments with heuristic and metaheuristic techniques [2,5,6]. These solutions build node assignments to processors based on the critical path, which are represented according to the metaheuristics used; a number of iterations are generated until finding the optimal solution. Other algorithms base their functionality exclusively on the structures of the generated critical paths [8,12].

For DAG task planning in a heterogeneous system as shown in this study, and in [11], the following characteristics are considered: the critical path of DAG tasks, the width of the DAG tasks that produces the degree of parallelism of said task, the levels of DAG tasks (layering) and the density of DAG tasks that determines the dependencies that exist between two levels of said tasks; the characteristics extracted from the DAG are transformed into values and used in the Univariate Marginal Distribution Algorithm (UMDA), a heuristic optimization method that does not need to adjust a large number of parameters, and that identifies interrelationships between the variables that represent the generated planning solutions. For the development of this research we use the concept of an objective system based on clusters.

The contributions in this study are:

- A justification of the analysis of the internal structure of DAG tasks is described.
- An analysis of DAG tasks, which allows the extraction of the internal characteristics of said tasks include: the critical path, the width of the task that produces the degree of parallelism, the levels of the task (layering) and the density of the task that determines the dependencies that exist between the two levels of the task, prior to the allocation of the resources requested by the task.
- A new methodology for the first step of scheduling, integrates a resource matrix of the target system and a characteristics matrix of queued DAG tasks for optimizing the allocation of task completion times, and resources usage.

This work is organized as follows. Section 2 lists the basic concepts used throughout this paper. Section 3, related works explain studies that deal with planning problems and critical paths, and studies that have proposed solutions to the layering problem in DAG tasks. Justification of the analysis of the internal structure of DAG tasks, is described in Sect. 4. Section 5, presents the Univariate Marginal Distribution Algorithm, which is used in this work. Section 6, explains the proposed method. Section 7, explains utilized resources of software in the proposed method. Experiments are explained in Sect. 8. Discussion of results appears in Sect. 9. In Sect. 10, three subsequent future investigations are explained, that can improve this work. Finally in Sect. 11 the conclusions are detailed.

2   Basic Concepts

The following concepts are used in this paper.

Definition 1. The objective system is constituted by heterogeneous processors m with processing cores n and the set of processors is denoted by $\pi = \{\pi_1, ..., \pi_m\}$. Processor cores are denoted as: π_m where π is the number of the processors and m is the number of processing cores contained in the processor.

Definition 2. A DAG task can be modeled by an Directed Acyclic Graph (DAG) $T = (N, E)$ where: $N = \{\eta_i : i = 1, ..., N\}$ is a set of N nodes or subtasks and $E = \{E_{i,j} : i, j = 1, ..., N\}$ is a set of E edges. Parallel Task

Graph T can be characterized by $(\eta_i, \{1 \leq j \leq \eta_i | \tau_{i,j}\}, G_i, M_i, W_i)$ where η_i is the number of subtasks of T_i, the second parameter is the set of subtasks, G_i is the set of relations directed between the subtasks, M_i is the number of levels of τ_i and W_i the width of each level of τ_i (represented by a vector). DAG Tasks consist of a set of nodes and edges (directed relationships). The nodes represent the execution requirements of the task while the directed relationships show the execution flow.

Definition 3. A directed relationship from subtask $\tau_{i,j}$ to $\tau_{i,k}$ means that $\tau_{i,k}$ can start its execution only if $\tau_{i,j}$ completes its own. In this case we call $\tau_{i,j}$ a parent sub-task of $\tau_{i,k}$ and $\tau_{i,k}$ the child of $\tau_{i,j}$. Each sub-task in a given DAG task can have several parents and children. An initial subtask is a subtask without parents, while a final subtask is a subtask without children. A DAG task has a start subtask and a finish subtask.

Definition 4. The set of DAG Tasks that represents a synthetic load is denoted by $\tau = \{\tau_1, ..., \tau_n\}$.

Definition 5. The length of the critical path of a DAG Task [7], is denoted by:

$$M = \lceil \frac{\sum W_{n_i}}{cp \; length} \rceil$$

where M is the minimum number of processors, W_{n_i} the processing time of task i.

Definition 6. The height of a vertex is denoted by [7]:

$$height(n_i) = \begin{cases} 0 \; if \; PRED(n_i) = \emptyset \\ \\ 1 + max(height(n_j)) \forall n_j \in PRED(n_i) otherwise \end{cases} \tag{1}$$

Definition 7. The cost of calculating an Execution Cost (EC) of sub-task represented by a node expressed in flops, is the cost of executing a sub-task once it is assigned to a processor. The cost of executing the total of the subtasks of task i, is expressed as:

$$\sum_{\forall \tau_{i,j} \in \tau_i} EC_{i,j} \tag{2}$$

Definition 8. The cost of communication represented by $CC_{\tau_{i,j} \to \tau_{i,k}}$ between subtasks $\tau_{i,j}$ and $\tau_{i,k}$ is expressed in bytes.

Definition 9. Makespan, the length of the scheduling produced by the algorithm, expressed as:

$$makespan = max(FT(n_i)) \tag{3}$$

With the above definitions, we consider a system with a set π of processors, a synthetic load represented by a set τ of tasks that is constituted by T DAG tasks. Each DAG task is planned in the heterogeneous π group of processors through a process respecting the execution requirements, the directed relationships and the start times of each DAG task.

3   Related Works

In this paper, when dealing with DAG task planning problems in an HDCS, different research plans are described that consider the critical path to be one of the characteristics of the DAG tasks internal structure, considering also the dependencies between the subtasks; It also describes works that have proposed solutions to the problem of DAG task layering, and works that have explored the characteristic of maximum parallelism in DAG tasks using the number of links in each layer. Studies that deal with scheduling problems and critical paths are: [2,5–8,12]. Studies that have proposed solutions to the layering problem in DAG tasks are: [14,15].

4   Justification of the Analysis of the Internal Structure Of DAG Tasks

Although it is clear that a plan based on the critical path always involves a planning for the nodes that remain in it, the dependencies of each node of the critical path with the predecessor and successor nodes cannot be ignored. The preceding nodes must also be assigned before the execution of the nodes of the critical path and must have a view of the subsequent nodes. In this study we also consider the following internal characteristics of DAG tasks, which provide information on the structure of said task, and should be considered in the planning and assignment of the task to the target system:

- The width of the DAG Task that produces the degree of parallelism [5] indicates the maximum number of processors used in a DAG level.
- The density of the DAG Task, which determines the dependencies that exist between two levels of a DAG task [5], and indicates the level of communication between subtasks, indicating to the algorithm that there is a high level of communication between the two-level subtasks. Subtasks should be located within the nearest processors to avoid a potentially complex redistribution of data, that can be generated between the data elements of origin and destination that are distributed among multiple processors.
- DAG task jumps, the execution paths of different lengths [5] presented by the DAG task allowing the determination of relationships between tasks.
- It has been found that, analyzing only the critical path of the DAG task leads to a vertical analysis of the DAG Task and does not consider the previous parameters.

5   UMDA Algorithm

A Univariate Marginal Distribution Algorithm [16], is classified within the estimation of distribution algorithm, whose functionality is based on estimate marginal probabilities of a selected population. It was designed for problems where the components of a solution are independent (linearly separable), and a selection method is needed to identify the subset of good solutions from which to calculate the univariate marginal probabilities.

6 Developed Method

The solution proposed in this study does not modify the Parallel Task Graph, nor subgraphs created for the analysis. The discipline of the queue is FCFS, and it is large enough to accommodate a large number of DAG workflow instances. To exemplify the proposed method we use an HDCS like the one shown [13].

7 Utilized Resources

Utilized resources: the resource matrix, the characteristics matrix of the evaluated DAGs, the allocation matrix and the matrix of the start times of the tasks. These four data structures are used during the planning for each of the analyzed DAGs.

The resource matrix, is a symmetric matrix where the characteristics of the number of resource cores of the target system is stored, as well as, the Hamming Distance (HD) of each resource against all existing resources in the system; in this matrix the search for resources is carried out once the characteristics have been extracted from the DAG task.

This matrix stores the characteristic of the number of processing cores, without considering the processor speeds. Each time a new resource is added, its characteristics are extracted and placed in the resource matrix through characteristic extraction algorithms and ordering of resources. The characteristics of the resources that remain in the matrix are: the identification number of the resource (an incremental number generated according to its integration into the grid), the resource processing cores and the Hamming distance of the resource in question, among others. The objective of this matrix is to alleviate the problem of changes in the availability of resources [6], which occurs during the release and allocation of resources.

Each time a DAG task level has finished its execution, the resources are released and made available for subsequent tasks, allowing reusability of the resources; the release of resources is done with the verification of the dependencies of the tasks. When a task frees the resources from a previous level, they can be taken by the subtasks of the subsequent levels to avoid the task migration.

When a set of tasks remains in the same network and set of processing cores within the same processor, the Hamming distance and the communication time between them is 0. The Hamming distance of the processors is calculated from the cluster where the task queue resides, as this is from where the tasks are sent to the processors once they have been planned.

The characteristics matrix of DAG tasks stores the data obtained by the feature extraction algorithm: the DAG identification number, the number of DAG routes, the number of DAG levels together with the number of vertices for each level and the density of the DAG task. The identification number of the DAG task is assigned according to its arrival to the system queue. DAG task routes are extracted using the Depth First Search algorithm, whose worst case temporal complexity is $O(b^m)$. The number of DAG task levels and the number of vertices of each level are generated with the same algorithm. The feature table is not shown for space. The DAG tasks shown in Figs. 1 and 2 contain the same number of nodes and their characteristics have been extracted;

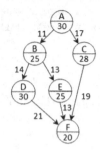

Fig. 1. A six node DAG task.

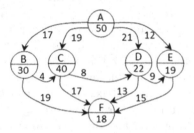

Fig. 2. A six node DAG task.

The allocation matrix is created each time the appropriate DAG task resources are searched for. This matrix's rows contain each system processor along with its number of cores, and in each column the DAG task nodes. Each time a resource search is performed for a DAG task, value of 1 is marked in the column indicating that the processor can contain the node of that task. Only the list of all the processors that were selected in the allocation process appears in the assignment matrix. The algorithm takes care of assigning a node for each processing cores, to avoid the overload of threads or processes in each cores.

Start times task matrix: This data structure stores the calculation of the start time of each DAG task, it contains the identifier of the task, the time of arrival of the task, the start time of the task and the time of completion of the task. Each parameter of this matrix is calculated for each DAG task node. The task arrival time is the time in which the task was queued. The start time of the task is a parameter that is calculated according to the formula 4:

$$S_t(T_n) = EX_t(\sum_{T_1}^{n-1}) + DCT_t(\sum_{T_1}^{n-1}) + ST_{T_n \to \pi_m} \tag{4}$$

Where: $S_t(T_n)$, is start time of the task, $EX_t(\sum_{T_1}^{n-1})$ is execution time of its predecessor nodes, $DCT_t(\sum_{T_1}^{n-1})$, corresponds to data communication time of its predecessor nodes, and $ST_{T_n \to \pi_m}$ is sending time of task to the processor.

The execution time of its predecessor nodes is considered a value of 0 when the task has no parent nodes and, when the task does have predecessor nodes this time is the summation of the execution times of its predecessor nodes. The data communication time from its predecessor nodes to the task is obtained when calculating the communication times for all the parent tasks of the node; from this operation, the time with the highest value is obtained, which means that the task must wait until all its parent nodes have finished executing it. The time of sending the task to the processor is considered a fixed parameter of 5 nanoseconds for each unit of Hamming distance.

Task completion time is the time that is registered in the matrix once the task has finished its execution in the processor; this parameter is calculated by the formula 5:

$$TCT_t = S_t(T_n) + ET_t(T_n) \tag{5}$$

Where: TCT_t is task completion time, $S_t(T_n)$ is task start time, and $ET_(T_n)$ is task execution time.

For start tasks that have no predecessors, the start time is limited by the release of the processor that was assigned to it during the assignment phase of the processors to the tasks, that is, if the processor is free at the time of its assignment, only the time of sending the task to the processor is considered; On the other hand, if the processor is busy, the time the task waits to be sent to the processor will be considered. An unoccupied processor has a higher probability of being assigned, while a busy processor has a lower probability of being assigned. The start time of the task is calculated when all the predecessor nodes have finished their execution.

7.1 Algorithm Steps

This section describes each of the six steps of the proposed algorithm.

Random DAG Task Generation. For the generation of the proposed method test, the synthetic loads are generated with two of the methods described in [17]; method 5 of the Markov Chain Method and method 6 the parallel approach for the random generation of graphs on GPU's. The purpose of these two methods is to experiment with the characteristics of the DAG tasks exposed in [17]. It is possible to change the method of generating the synthetic loads in order to experiment with other methods different from those proposed in this paper.

Extraction of DAG Characteristics. This step of the algorithm extracts all the DAG task execution routes along with their lengths. Each route is evaluated for its cost of execution and communication costs. An ordering of the costs of each task is done by the algorithm. The route with the highest costs is considered the critical DAG task path and has the highest priority of assignment, the rest of the routes are considered subcritical paths and take priority in system resources allocation. Once the characteristics of the DAG task have been extracted, they are placed in the characteristics matrix according to the order of the analyzed DAG tasks.

Searching the Resource Matrix for the Best DAG Task Resource. In order to locate the resource that will be assigned to the task, two search criteria are considered: the generated DAG task routes along with the DAG task levels. In this phase two conditions can occur: the task can be scheduled in a free processor or the task can be planned in a busy processor; either of these two conditions is ideal for the next step of the algorithm.

The first resources search criteria is based on the number of routes generated from the DAG task. This process assigns resources using each of the DAG task routes considering the first route in the characteristics matrix (column 2) to be the critical path with the highest priority of assignment, the rest of the routes are considered subcritical paths by the algorithm. The graph is first relieved of vertices that constitute the critical path and consecutively each one of the subcritical paths, a process similar to the one done in [8]. The algorithm verifies the processing cores in each processor with the number of nodes in each route.

A search is performed according to the number of nodes in the route for a processor with the number of cores equal to or less than the number of nodes in the given route. If the number of nodes in the route is greater than the maximum number of cores that one (or more) of the processors of the system has, the divide and conquer method is therein applied: it divides the number of nodes in the route by two, rounds to the lower number, and returns to look for a processor with that number of nodes. If it is not possible to cover the number of nodes of the route with this division, the two results are divided again by two; this condition ends when a given number of nodes can be covered by the number of system processor cores.

In the DAG of Fig. 1, the critical path has 4 vertices, the algorithm will then look for a first assignment of a 4 core PE (Processing Element), if it is not able to locate the route in a PE with this characteristic, it will seek to assign two PE dual core, for A and B nodes with a minimum Hamming distance of 0 corresponding to a processing element within the same local network (LAN). The next step seeks to assign the following DAG task route without considering the vertices already assigned; the example in question seeks to assign vertex D and a subsequent step seeks to assign vertex F, both with a dual core PE; in case of not getting a PE with these characteristics, it will look for two PE.

In the assignment matrix, the nodes are assigned to the processing cores of each processor in the following way: when a processor's number of cores is equal to or less than the number of route nodes this processor is placed in the allocation matrix indicating which nodes of the DAG task to be assigned to that processor. This assignment of cores to nodes indicates how many DAG task nodes will remain in the same cluster for processing and how many nodes should be placed in other clusters; given the cluster diversity where the nodes are assigned, the Hamming distance is calculated to determine the communication load (overhead) that the task will generate during its processing. It is clear that the minimization function will look to process all the DAG task nodes in the same cluster. The second resource search criteria are the DAG task levels. The information provided by the DAG task levels are: the number of levels and the number of vertices per level. For Fig. 1 DAG task, assignment by routes is the most feasible process to accelerate the execution of the task, this however is not the case for Fig. 3 DAG task due to the large number of generated routes; for this case the algorithm seeks to assign only 3 PE in the following way: for level 1 it looks for a PE with a processing cores, for level 2 the algorithm seeks to assign a PE with 8 processing cores (according to definition 3), and for the last DAG task level, a single or double core PE is desirable. For cases utilizing the three PEs, a minimum Hamming distance should be adhered to. Once the three PEs are assigned, the processing of the DAG is done in a sequential manner so that the processing data flows in the same direction, as shown in Fig. 1(b). For the case that the algorithm does not locate a PE octa core, re-apply the divide and conquer method in order to locate two PE quad cores with a minimum Hamming distance. With this second search criterion, the assignment matrix is created to assign the nodes to the processing cores of each processor in the same way that the assignment was made for the DAG task routes.

Start Time Calculation of Each Task. To calculate the start time of a task the following 4 parameters are used:

1. Processor status. If the processor is free, then the task can start its execution and only the time of the transfer of the task is considered. Second, if the processor is busy, then the waiting time in the queue is considered, plus the time of the transfer of the task.
2. The execution time of parent tasks n. For any task that has one or more parent tasks, the completion time of each parent task is considered; the longest completion time is considered most out of all parent tasks.
3. Data communication time of parent tasks n. This parameter is obtained from the time that the data takes to reach the processor assigned to the task; the longest communication time is considered most.
4. Task sending time to the processor is a parameter that depends on the speed of the network and is calculated by two parameters: if the task is assigned in the same network, the internal speed of the network is considered, if the task is sent to an external network, then the internal speed of the network plus the speed of the external network is considered.

The Best Assignment Determined by the UMDA Algorithm. The UMDA algorithm is executed based on the results presented by the allocation matrix that contains the Hamming distances of the nodes located in the processors, the parameter of the state of the processor and the task location parameter in the cluster. The different node assignments are intended to minimize the Hamming distance, which provides the location of the task in the cluster or in the HDCS clusters. A high value in Hamming's distance indicates that the task was disaggregated into several clusters. The parameter of the state of the processor: occupied or unoccupied. A value of 0 is given to an idle processor at the time of its assignment and, a value of 1 is assigned to an occupied processor. The task location parameter in the cluster, is a value that is obtained from the distance of the cluster, where the task queue resides to the cluster in which the task can be executed. The value assigned to this parameter, is related to the number of clusters that the task has to pass through in order to, reach the cluster where it will be executed. For example, suppose that the DAG task 1 is located in cluster 2 and cluster 3, the location parameter of the task will then take the value of the time needed to locate the task in both clusters. When a task is located in the same cluster where the queue resides, it receives a 0 value in this parameter. For our example case, the queue resides in cluster 1 and the results of the three parameters described are shown in the table.

Algorithm Parameters. Initial population. First, the initial population is created by using information obtained from all the generated assignments (solutions) in the HDCS under the two search criterions. Second, some of the individual of $\hat{p}$ are selected by the standard truncation selection method, in this way we select half of the initial population, denoted by P_0^{Se}; the selection is carried out by a function that minimizes the values of the 3 parameters. The selection is carried out probabilistically in the event that there are ties when evaluating individuals.

The joint probability distribution expresses the characteristics of the selected individuals. Interdependencies between variables are not considered, so they are considered independent from the rest, that is:

$$P_1(x) = P_1(x_1, ...x_3) = \prod_{i=1}^{3} p(x_i | D_0^{Se}) \tag{6}$$

The model is specified by 3 parameters.
$p(x_i | D_0^{Se})$ with $i = 1, 2, 3$

An estimation is made from the individual archive by the corresponding relative frequency.

$$\hat{p} = (X_i = 1 | D_0^{Se}) \tag{7}$$

Table 1, represents the case file consisting of the individuals obtained from the simulation of $P_1(x)$. The values of the parameters are shown in the same table.

Table 1. File of cases for the solutions generated for the DAGs of the Figs. 1 and 2.

$S_1 : 0$	$S_2 : 0.75$	$S_3 : 0.33$	$S_4 : 0.33$	$S_5 : 0.5$	$S_6 : 0$	$S_7 : 0.5$	$S_8 : 0.25$
$S_1 : 0$	$S_2 : 0$	$S_3 : 0.33$	$S_4 : 0.33$	$S_5 : 0.5$	$S_6 : 0$	$S_7 : 0$	$S_8 : 0.25$

The previous steps are repeated until the following stop conditions are verified: the maximum number of populations is indicated in the algorithm, or when the population does not improve individual bests obtained in the previous generations. This phase of the algorithm determines whether the DAG task is assigned to the selected resources or put in the queue to await execution.

8   Experiments

Algorithm design. The project code is developed in standard C language, using dynamic memory for the generation of the DAG task. The manipulation of the resources used by the algorithm explained in Sect. 7, is done through static memory. All the information generated during the executions is sent to data files for further analysis. The project code is stored in a cloud-based computational reproducibility ocean code platform.

Target system. The experiments are carried out in a distributed heterogeneous system, which is constituted by a server farm, each with a quad core processor and a personal computer LAN network.

The DAG task generation parameters remain unchanged in the algorithm. Synthetic loads were generated with 50, 100, 150, 200, 250, 500,1000 y 1500 tasks. Experiments made with real data have included the Fast Fourier Transform. In this study we examine only the parameters: Average wait time for tasks in the queue and the makespan.

Average wait time for tasks, this parameter indicates the time that the tasks waits in the queue to be scheduled in the target system, but it is also a parameter that indicates the speed or slowness of the algorithm for scheduling realization total. Figure 3 shows the times consumed by the algorithm with the different synthetic loads. As the graph shows, the planning times remain constant when the workloads increase, which indicates that the algorithm will schedule at the same speed even with overload in the system. Since the UMDA algorithm does not perform solution representation operations like the genetic algorithm, it shows uniform response times. The Average wait time for tasks in queue is a parameter that has been studied extensively in this work for 3 main reasons: it is fundamental in the response times of the HDCS, it allows to evaluate the convergence times of the heuristic algorithm and allows the comparison between heuristic techniques.

Makespan. The values of the makespan are obtained in the same executions with which the average waiting time is obtained. The results of the experiments with this parameter are shown in Fig. 4. The values produced with the different workloads show an improvement trend for UMDA, although in the central point of the graph both methods produce very close values in the times. Alternative processes have been proposed, to further improve response times.

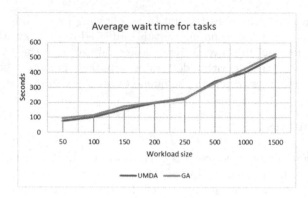

Fig. 3. Average waiting time for tasks with workloads generated.

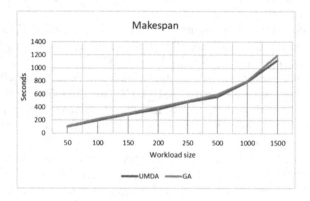

Fig. 4. Produced makespan with workloads generated.

9   Discussion of Results

In this work, three characteristics of the DAG are considered, which allows assigning a task with greater accuracy in the HDCS and comparing two heuristic algorithms. Although there are many observations, emphasis is placed on the agglomeration of tasks. While the UMDA manages to disperse the tasks in the HDCS, genetic algorithm agglomerates the tasks in close clusters with great intensity ("takes care" of the time of sending the tasks to distant nodes); this has an impact on the final execution time of each task, because when a task finishes its execution and it is dispersed in the HDCS, it is necessary to meet its results a long waiting time. Although this represents a disadvantage, the use of resources is optimized.

It is clear to note that UMDA manages to overcome the genetic algorithm in the two parameters in the experiments; the genetic algorithm needs a "tune" of its parameters when the characteristics of the DAG Task are extracted, and in this way to be able to carry out the planning of the populations, while UMDA does not need it; by not making a "tune" necessary the UMDA allows to improve computer system performance.

10   Conclusions

This paper presents a new method based on the internal characteristics of the DAG, to schedule parallel tasks in an HDCS. The characteristics extracted constitute the populations that are evaluated by the UMDA algorithm and the genetic algorithm. UMDA is population-based technique without an inspiration and does not depend on intonation parameters, as does the genetic algorithm. The findings obtained with the experiments performed show that the UMDA produce better response times than the genetic algorithm, by measuring the average waiting time and overcome the results of makespan. Special attention has been placed on these two parameters, because they demonstrate the effectiveness of the method in terms of response times. For the verification of the method described, specific algorithms have been used to generate synthetic loads of DAGs; Additionally, DAG Tasks of real applications have been used.

References

1. Briceno, L., et al.: Robust static resource allocation of DAGs in a heterogeneous multicore system. Parallel Distrib. Comput. **73**, 1705–1717 (2013). https://doi.org/10.1016/j.jpdc.2013.08.007
2. Qamhieh, M., Fauberteau, F., George, L., Midonnet, S.: Global EDF scheduling of directed acyclic graphs on multiprocessor systems. In: Proceedings of the 21st International Conference on Real-Time NET Study and Systems, Sophia Antipolis, France, pp. 287–296 (2013)
3. Xhafa, F., Abraham, A.: Computational models and heuristic methods for grid scheduling problems. Future Gener. Comput. Syst. **26**, 608–621 (2010). https://doi.org/10.1016/j.future.2009.11.005
4. Zheng, W., Sakellariou, R.: Stochastic DAG scheduling using a Monte Carlo approach. J. Parallel Distrib. Comput. **73**, 1673–1689 (2013). https://doi.org/10.1016/j.jpdc.2013.07.019
5. Takpé, T.N., Suter, F.: Critical path and area based scheduling of parallel task graphs on heterogeneous platforms. In: 12th International Conference on Parallel and Distributed Systems ICPADS 2006, Minneapolis, United States, July 2006 (2006). https://doi.org/10.1109/ICPADS.2006.32
6. Rahman, M., Venugopal, S., Buyya, R.: A dynamic critical path algorithm for scheduling scientific workflow applications on global grids. In: Third IEEE International Conference on e-Science and Grid Computing (e-Science 2007), Minneapolis, United States, 10–13 December (2007). https://doi.org/10.1109/E-SCIENCE.2007.3
7. Badawi, A., Shatnawi, A.: Static scheduling of directed acyclic data flow graphs onto multiprocessors using particle swarm optimization. Comput. Oper. Res. **40**, 2322–2328 (2013). https://doi.org/10.1016/j.cor.2013.03.015
8. Khan, M.A.: Scheduling for heterogeneous systems using constrained critical paths. Parallel Comput. **38**, 175–193 (2012). https://doi.org/10.1016/j.parco.2012.01.001

9. Akbari, M., Rashidi, H.: A multi-objectives scheduling algorithm based on cuckoo optimization for task allocation problem at compile time in heterogeneous systems. Expert Syst. Appl. **60**, 234–248 (2016). https://doi.org/10.1016/j.eswa.2016.05.014

10. Yu, S., Li, K., Xu, Y.: A DAG task scheduling scheme on heterogeneous cluster systems using discrete IWO algorithm. J. Comput. Sci. **26**, 307–317 (2018). https://doi.org/10.1016/j.jocs.2016.09.008

11. Velarde, A.: Random generation of directed acyclic graphs for planning and allocation tasks in heterogeneous distributed computing systems. J. Comput. Sci. **1**, 793–802 (2018). https://doi.org/10.1007/978-3-030-01174-1_61

12. Chang, D.H., Son, J.H., Kim, M.H.: Critical path identification in the context of a workflow. Inf. Softw. Technol. **44**, 405–417 (2002). https://doi.org/10.1016/S0950-5849(02)00025-3

13. Xu, Y., Li, K., Hu, J., Li, K.: A genetic algorithm for task scheduling on heterogeneous computing systems using multiple priority queues. Inf. Sci. **270**, 255–287 (2014). https://doi.org/10.1016/j.ins.2014.02.122

14. Nikolov, S., Tarassov, A.: Graph layering by promotion of nodes. Discrete Appl. Math. **154**, 848–860 (2006). https://doi.org/10.1016/j.dam.2005.05.023

15. Healy, P., Nikolov, N.S.: How to layer a directed acyclic graph. In: Mutzel, P., Jünger, M., Leipert, S. (eds.) GD 2001. LNCS, vol. 2265, pp. 16–30. Springer, Heidelberg (2002). https://doi.org/10.1007/3-540-45848-4_2

16. Brownlee, J.: How to Layer a Directed Acyclic Graph (2011)

17. Velarde Martinez, A.: Random generation of directed acyclic graphs for planning and allocation tasks in heterogeneous distributed computing systems. In: Arai, K., Kapoor, S., Bhatia, R. (eds.) SAI 2018. AISC, vol. 858, pp. 793–802. Springer, Cham (2019). https://doi.org/10.1007/978-3-030-01174-1_61

Bounded Region Optimization of PID Gains for Grid Forming Inverters with Genetic Algorithms

Juan Roberto López Gutiérrez[✉][iD], Pedro Ponce Cruz[iD],
and Arturo Molina Gutiérrez[iD]

Instituto Tecnologico de Estudios Superiores Monterrey, Monterrey, Mexico
A01334289@itesm.mx, {pedro.ponce,amolina}@tec.mx

Abstract. Tuning conventional controllers could be a difficult task when experimental methodologies are implemented. Moreover, nowadays, Microgrids (MGs) require specific operation responses that could be achieved if the conventional controllers are correctly tuned. As a result, an optimization methodology that gets the correct parameters of conventional controller can improve the performance of the (MGs). This paper proposes the tuning of the conventional controllers used in a Grid Forming Inverters (GFMI) two voltage PID control loops, two current PID control loops, and the frequency PID controller. In a conventional control architecture of a GFMI. In GFMIs that act as voltage sources within a MG system, an incorrect tuning would harm the regulation of the dispatched voltage and frequency values to the linked electrical loads. Previously, optimization methods have been used for tuning conventional controllers, however, this is usually done in a grid-connected configuration. This work delimits the possible gain values to a desired controlled system response, by then optimizing over the controller requirements using genetic algorithms. In addition, a complete study of the tuning process under different genetic algorithm parameters (population and mutation) is presented.

Keywords: Genetic algorithms · PID control · Grid forming inverter · Microgrid

1 Introduction

The integration of the Renewable Energy Sources (RES) in a MG is mainly done through Power Converters (PCs). According to [8], three configuration

This research is a product of the Project 266632 "Laboratorio Binacional para la Gestión Inteligente de la Sustentabilidad Energética y la Formación Tecnológica" ("Bi-National Laboratory on Smart Sustainable Energy Management and Technology Training"), funded by the CONACYT (Consejo Nacional de Ciencia y Tecnología) SENER (Secretaría de Energía) Fund for Energy Sustainability (Agreement S0019201401).

© Springer Nature Switzerland AG 2019
L. Martínez-Villaseñor et al. (Eds.): MICAI 2019, LNAI 11835, pp. 277–289, 2019.
https://doi.org/10.1007/978-3-030-33749-0_23

types of PCs can be found in a MG, Grid-Feeding, Grid-Forming, and Grid-Supporting PC. Its configuration depends mostly on the operating conditions of the MG [4], that is to say, In a grid-connected operation the PCs in a MG need to function as grid-feeding devices, following the voltage and frequency references dictated by the Conventional Utility Network (CUN), whereas, in stand-alone operation, the voltage and frequency references coming from the CUN are lost, forcing the associated PCs of a MG to work as grid-forming devices [12], particularly, this configuration of PCs pose some challenges regarding the voltage and frequency regulation across the MG's energy bus supplying the local loads. Ergo, the control objective of a grid-forming PC becomes the regulation of the voltage and frequency within nominal values across the MG [2].

The most commonly implemented technique for grid-forming PCs is the voltage and frequency control using a cascade control structure as reviewed in [5], this control architecture presents multiple PID controllers which can be tuned to fit a specific control response depending on the system parameters. Nonetheless, a disadvantage of PID controllers is their high sensitivity to parameter variations, which may result in an unregulated output of a PC.

Genetic algorithms are known for being a natural selection and classic evolutionary optimization method. This optimization method has been applied to different areas to the extent of power electronics control and parameter selection as in [7], one main disadvantage of this method is the computational time required for the algorithm to yield a global minimum value [10]. The work in [9] and [6] employ an optimization technique to tune a PID controller of a given PC. The work in [9] adopts the Ziegler Nichols tuning method to select the search region of a PID controller gains, by then using a genetic algorithm. In [6] Particle Swarm Optimization is used to optimize the parameters of a PI controller without specifying a searching region, this particular approach results in a large number of iterations of the optimization method. Also, genetic algorithms have been used in the subject of optimizing the power generation shared among RES in [1].

This work presents a new approach towards the tuning of the PID controller parameters of the different control layers within the cascade control architecture of a grid-forming inverter, where genetic algorithm is used to tune the gains of the different PID controllers, the proposed method can be differentiated from others reported in the state of the art since this method works by delimiting the possible gain values and then selecting an operating range according to a specific characteristic of the desired closed-loop system step response, by then, optimizing over a desired operating range, this leads to an optimized set of proportional, integral, and derivative controller gains for a specific response characteristic, taking fewer iterations of the optimization process.

Afterwards, the same bounded search region method is applied to test a single controller of the converter against changes in the inverter's parameters, specifically the LC output filter inductance and capacitance values; showing that this method can also be applied to estimate the range of parameter variations in the LC output filter according to the desired gain of a selected controller.

2   Genetic Algorithms Optimization

Genetic algorithm has a wide range of application in engineering areas since its first appearance in 1970 [10]. This algorithm is known for being of a classical evolutionary nature, mimicking the mechanics of natural selection where only the most adapted organism survive [3]. This optimization method works by manipulating an initial population, where it chooses the best-fit individual according to the desired objective function, by then creating children with characteristics contained in the initial individuals.

The basic structure of the genetic algorithm can be sectioned in operations such as selection, crossover, mutation, and evaluation [11]. The selection operation is processed in which some individuals form the population are chosen due to their initial value being a potential solution, the selected individuals are the copied into children generations by the properties of crossover and mutation, where a new evaluation is performed and the process repeats itself until a global optimal solution is found.

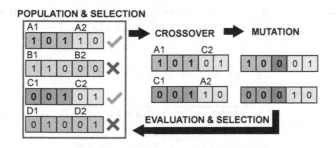

Fig. 1. Genetic algorithm diagram

The crossover operations have the objective of taking the similarities of the best fit values from the parents or previous generations and creates children with common characteristics [10], the mutation operation helps the optimization process to avoid falling in a local minimum or maximum value by changing one factor of a generated children [11]. Figure 1 shows the functioning of these operations.

3   System Description

The system exposed in this work consists of a DC/AC switching converter, also known as an inverter. The output of the PC is of a three-phase AC type voltage signal, which is then connected to an LC filter with the task of refining the output AC signal, the grid-forming control in a rotatory reference frame architecture of an inverter is composed as in Fig. 2, where L_f, R_f, and C_f are the LC output filter parameters [5].

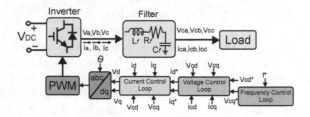

Fig. 2. Grid forming inverter control architecture

The first step towards the right tuning of the PID controllers in Fig. 2 is to obtain the transfer functions which describe the system behavior according to the respective control layer. The resulting transfer functions below are obtained by comparing the output value to the desired one of the reference of the particular control layer, the resulting data was then used in the *Plant Identification Toolbox* of the *MATLAB* software. The obtained transfer function for the frequency control loop is described by (1), the transfer functions representing External Voltage Control Loop (EVCL) and Inner Current Control Loop (ICCL) layers in their corresponding *d*- and *q*-components were obtained as (2), (3), (4) and (5) respectively.

$$\frac{0.99992}{(0.036577\ s + 1)(0.022108\ s + 1)} \tag{1}$$

$$\frac{0.84218}{(0.013257\ s + 1)(0.010599\ s + 1)} \tag{2}$$

$$\frac{2.2809}{(0.0010599\ s + 1)(0.0027875\ s + 1)} \tag{3}$$

$$\frac{3.7109(0.055311\ s + 1)}{(0.097717\ s + 1)(0.1\ s + 1)} \tag{4}$$

$$\frac{0.025879(0.053651\ s + 1)}{(0.013\ s + 1)(0.021\ s + 1)} \tag{5}$$

The obtained transfer functions take part in the objective functions employed for the optimization of the different PID controller gains, for that matter, a quantitative analysis of the performance of the different control systems is done to evaluate the improvement of the optimization genetic algorithm implementation.

Integral of Time Multiplied by Absolute Error (ITAE), Integral Time Squared Error (ITSE), Integral Absolute Error (IAE), and Integral Square Error (ISE) performance indexes were selected as the objective function to measure the stationary and dynamic error, defined by (6), (7), (8), and (9) respectively, where $e(t)$ is the error between the step reference and the closed-loop settling value, the corresponding closed-loop step response is described by (10), where the TF variable is the transfer function describing the system, K_p, K_i, and K_d are the PID controllers gains which are the parameters to be optimized in order to enhance the system response according to each system constrain.

$$ITAE = \int_0^T t\,|e(t)|\,dt \tag{6}$$

$$ITSE = \int_0^T te(t)^2 dt \tag{7}$$

$$IAE = \int_0^T |e(t)|\,dt \tag{8}$$

$$ISE = \int_0^T e(t)^2 dt \tag{9}$$

$$CL = \left(K_p + \frac{K_i}{s} + K_d\,s \right) \times TF \tag{10}$$

4   Tuning Procedure

The tuning procedure consists in evaluating each system to different constraints regarding the settling time, maximum settling point, and minimum settling point of the closed-loop response of each system's objective function, described by (10). Each closed-loop system step response is adapted to the desired system response using the *PID tuner toolbox*, once the desired response is achieved, a given range of controller gain values is proposed, by then evaluating the objective function in the possible gain range and looking for those values that satisfy the aforementioned constraints. The genetic algorithm is then used to evaluate the objective function in the reduced searching area formed by the gain combinations that fit the desired system response.

4.1   Searching Region Delimitation

As a case of study, the searching region for the optimized gains of the five different PID controllers is delimited by a certain characteristic of their corresponding closed-loop step response. For all controllers the delimiting characteristics of choice were the settling time in the closed-loop system response, the settling time depends on which case is being analyzed. Table 1 shows the setting time characteristic for each PID gain region is listed, as the corresponding K_p, K_i, and K_d limits for each controller.

To visualize the searching region within the established K_p, K_i and K_d intervals, the relationship between the controller gains are plotted. In this work, only the External Voltage Loop Control (EVLC) is analyzed, however, all five controllers are tuned following the same procedure. Figure 3 is divided into two regions, the blue region represents the possible combination of controller gains that result in a desired closed-loop step response according to the previously mentioned step characteristics constrains, therefore, the region represented

Table 1. Setting time searching range

GA settlin time constrains and limits								
Characteristic	Settling time		K_p		K_i		K_d	
Controller	*min*	*max*	*min*	*max*	*min*	*max*	*min*	*max*
EVCL d-	1e−2	4e−2	0	100	2000	2500	0	1
EVCL q-	1e−3	4e−3	0	10	500	1000	0	0.01
ICCL d-	1e−2	4e−2	0	50	1000	1500	0	1
ICCL q-	1e−2	4e−2	0	100	15e3	20e3	0	1
Frequency	1e−4	4e−4	0	100	2000	2500	0	1

by the pink color is the gain combinations that have an undesired controller response. Figure 4 shows the area for the EVLC loop that results in peak value of the closed-loop step response between 0.9 and 1.1 and a setting timeless or equal than the one listed in Table 1, this forms a searching optimization area reducing the optimization zone.

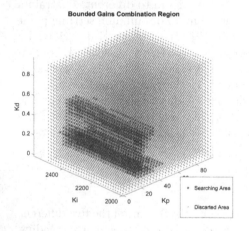

Fig. 3. Gain combination EVLC in d component (Color figure online)

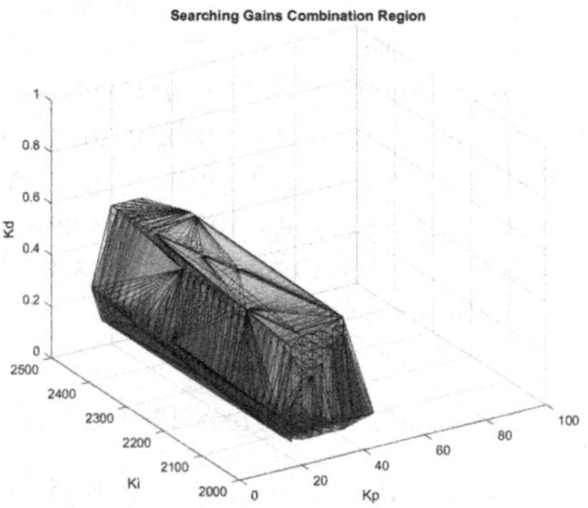

Fig. 4. Searching region EVLC in d component

4.2 PID Gains Genetic Algorithm Based Optimization

Once the searching regions for each system were obtained an optimization process using genetic algorithms is used to search for the optimal gain combination that results in the desired closed-loop characteristics within the searching area. This work uses the *ga function* from the *Matlab* simulation software to compute the optimization process. To assess the effect of the different genetic algorithm parameters such as the mutation ration and population size in the PID tuning procedure a correlation is done to obtain the different gains of the controllers. This work also evaluates the optimization process in different indexes to authenticate the obtained results. Therefore, the objective function being established in Eqs. (6), (7), (8), and (9), the corresponding constrains and the lower and upper bounds for each system are listed in Table 1.

The genetic algorithm optimization is set for 3 variables, resenting the K_p, K_i and K_d gains, the population size vector is set as 25, 50, and 100 with a uniform mutation vector of 0.1, 0.01, and 0.001 the constraint tolerance is set for 1×10^{-8} and the function tolerance as 1×10^{-6}.

In this case of study, the genetic algorithm is executed for an unbound and bound region of each system, the bounds being the searching areas obtained in the previous subsection. That being, both simulations limited by the same upper and lower bounds according to Table 1, however, the second execution of the genetic algorithm is done within the searching area constraint. The obtained gains for each execution of the different evaluating indexes are listed in Table 2 for the ITSE index and Table 3 for the ITAE, these tables shows the correlation between the mutation ration and the population size effect over the three gains of the EVCL, the parameters KP, Ki, and Kd represent the values obtained in an unbounded scenario, while the KPC, Kic, and KdC are the gain values obtained within the bounded region.

Table 2. PID parameters obtained with ITSE index

ITSE									
Mutation	K_p	Population			Mutation	KPC	Population		
		25	50	100			25	50	100
	0.1	45.496	52.410	50.391		0.1	36	55	55
	0.01	48.537	56.574	56.882		0.01	36	55	55
	0.001	48.537	48.537	56.882		0.001	36	55	55
Mutation	K_i	Population			Mutation	KiC	Population		
		25	50	100			25	50	100
	0.1	2015.729	2214.224	2109.29		0.1	2058.7	2329.1	2304.775
	0.01	2158.54	2252.978	2387.455		0.01	2058.7	2329.1	2304.775
	0.001	2158.55	2252.978	2387.455		0.001	2058.7	2329.1	2304.775
Mutation	K_d	Population			Mutation	KdC	Population		
		25	50	100			25	50	100
	0.1	0.255	0.3112	0.296		0.1	0.482	0.135	0.135
	0.01	0.255	0.311	0.334		0.01	0.482	0.135	0.135
	0.001	0.255	0.3112	0.334		0.001	0.482	0.135	0.135

Table 3. PID parameters obtained with ITAE index

ITAE									
Mutation	K_p	Population			Mutation	KPC	Population		
		25	50	100			25	50	100
	0.1	45.497	52.411	50.391		0.1	36	55	55
	0.01	48.538	56.575	56.882		0.01	36	55	55
	0.001	48.538	48.538	56.882		0.001	36	55	55
Mutation	K_i	Population			Mutation	KiC	Population		
		25	50	100			25	50	100
	0.1	2015.7	2214.2	2109.3		0.1	2058.7	2329.1	2304.8
	0.01	2158.5	2253.0	2387.5		0.01	2058.7	2329.1	2304.8
	0.001	2158.5	2253.0	2387.5		0.001	2058.7	2329.1	2304.8
Mutation	K_d	Population			Mutation	KdC	Population		
		25	50	100			25	50	100
	0.1	0.255	0.311	0.297		0.1	0.483	0.136	0.136
	0.01	0.255	0.311	0.334		0.01	0.483	0.136	0.136
	0.001	0.255	0.311	0.334		0.001	0.483	0.136	0.136

5   L-C Output Filter Parameter Variation

When working with Grid Forming Inverters (GFMI) one of the main concerns is frequency regulation and pure sinusoidal voltage and current waveforms at the output side of the power converter. The harmonic distortion of the output voltages of a GFMI is dependent on the parameters of the output side L-C filter. By not having a proper design for the output L-C filter, the quality of the output voltage supplied to the load is severely affected. The proper design of an output L-C filter allows the generation of quasi-pure sinusoidal voltages with low harmonic distortion.

The most present problem regarding the cascade PID controller architecture for GFMIs is that of the parameter variations in the inverter, for instance, the parameters corresponding to the L-C filter at the output of the inverter may change their value over time, affecting the PID controllers performance, since these are tuned for a specific operating point. For this manner, the bounded search area method can also be applied to obtain the maximum variation in the L-C output filter values according to the tuned controllers; in a more complex application this method is used in this work to compute the relationship between the controller gains and the L-C filter parameters, specifically the proportional gain in the EVLC.

This parameters-gain relationship can be appreciated in Fig. 5, where the inductor and capacitor values are tested against the proportional gain of the EVLC.

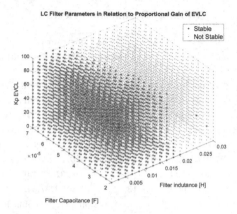

Fig. 5. L-C filter parameters relationship with the proportional gain of the EVLC

6   Results and Discussion

Several simulations were run where different population and mutation ratio values were tested against each other to observe how to take the best advantage of the optimization algorithm in the process of tuning a the controllers of a GFMI, in both scenarios, the constrained and unconstrained searching regions.

In all five cases, the bounded and unbounded tuned controllers are capable of making their respective system reach and track the step reference properly. In all cases it is demonstrated a better behavior of the constrained genetic algorithm gains optimization, the unconstrained tuned gains show a larger overshoot over the gains tuned by the bounded genetic algorithm. Also, the settling time is similar, if not, improved in the constrained gains. A quantitative analysis of the performance of the different control systems is done to evaluate the improvement of the optimization genetic algorithm implementation with four different evaluating indexes, ITAE, ITSE, IAE, and ISE were selected as the objective function to measure the stationary and dynamic error, defined by (6) and listed in Table 4.

Form Tables 2 and 3, the effect of the mutation ratio and the population size can be analyzed, it becomes clear that population size is the factor that affects directly the obtained gain values, however in an unconstrained environment the mutation ratio may affect the obtained gains, while in a constrained simulation it has no effect. It is duly noted that the population size is directly related to the obtained gain values in all four indexes of evaluation. The controlled response of the system is improved with a smaller population size in a constrained environment.

As can be seen, the number of generations is diminished in the bounded genetic algorithm execution, resulting in faster computing time for each set of gains. Figures 6 and 7 show the best fitness plot for the unbounded and bounded generations for the EVCL in the d-component.

Table 4. Evaluation indexes

FVAL					FVAL constrained				
Mutation	ITSE	Population			Mutation	ITSE	Population		
		25	*50*	*100*			*25*	*50*	*100*
	0.1	1.04E−09	7.21E−12	2.13E−13		*0.1*	7.54E−08	1.23E−08	1.20E−08
	0.01	2.34E−09	3.40E−10	8.31E−13		*0.01*	7.54E−08	1.23E−08	1.20E−08
	0.001	2.34E−09	1.18E−09	8.31E−13		*0.001*	7.54E−08	1.23E−08	1.20E−08
Mutation	ITAE	Population			Mutation	ITAE	Population		
		25	*50*	*100*			*25*	*50*	*100*
	0.1	1.04E−09	7.21E−12	2.13E−13		*0.1*	7.54E−08	1.23E−08	1.20E−08
	0.01	2.34E−09	3.40E−10	8.31E−13		*0.01*	7.54E−08	1.23E−08	1.20E−08
	0.001	2.34E−09	1.18E−09	8.31E−13		*0.001*	7.54E−08	1.23E−08	1.20E−08
Mutation	IAE	Population			Mutation	IAE	Population		
		25	*50*	*100*			*25*	*50*	*100*
	0.1	1.00E−02	1.00E−02	1.00E−02		*0.1*	1.00E−02	1.00E−02	1.00E−02
	0.01	1.00E−02	1.00E−02	1.00E−02		*0.01*	1.00E−02	1.00E−02	1.00E−02
	0.001	1.00E−02	1.00E−02	1.00E−02		*0.001*	1.00E−02	1.00E−02	1.00E−02
Mutation	ISE	Population			Mutation	ISE	Population		
		25	*50*	*100*			*25*	*50*	*100*
	0.1	1.00E−02	1.00E−02	1.00E−02		*0.1*	1.00E−02	1.00E−02	1.00E−02
	0.01	1.00E−02	1.00E−02	1.00E−02		*0.01*	1.00E−02	1.00E−02	1.00E−02
	0.001	1.00E−02	1.00E−02	1.00E−02		*0.001*	1.00E−02	1.00E−02	1.00E−02

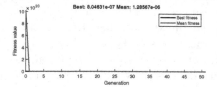

Fig. 6. GA EVLC d-component best fitness plot unbounded

Fig. 7. GA EVLC d-component best fitness plot bounded

From the best fitness plots, it is noticeable that the unbounded tuning needs more generations to get an optimized system response, while the bounded tuning takes one-tenth or less iteration than the unbounded tuning.

The evaluation of the obtained gains is done in a step response of the closed-loop system with the EVLC-d. Figure 9 shows the result of the controlled step response with gains obtained in the unconstrained area, where Fig. 8 illustrates the step response of the gains obtained within the constrained area.

Once optimized and in order to verify the obtained values for the different gains of the PID controllers, a simulation of the system described in Sect. 4 is performed, the obtained gains are incorporated in the grid-forming control architecture, the resulting voltage and frequency responses are obtained and shown in Fig. 10. It can be appreciated that the reference voltage of 240 V is achieved within minimal frequency distortion thanks to the right tuning of different PID controllers. The simulations are performed with the following parameters, the simulation time was limited to 0.1 s with a sample time of $1e^{-6}$, the solver of choice was Ode1 (Euler). The inverter parameters consist of an in inductance of $10e^{-3}$ H, a capacitance of $35e^{-6}$ F, the DC link deeding the inverter is set to deliver 500 V and a reference frequency of 60 Hz for the inverter output; the grid forming inverter feeds a linear load of 90 Kw.

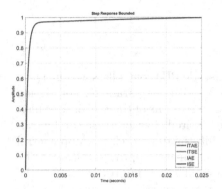

Fig. 8. Step response bounded

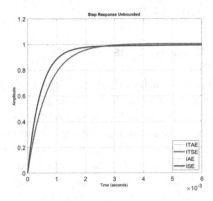

Fig. 9. Step response unbounded

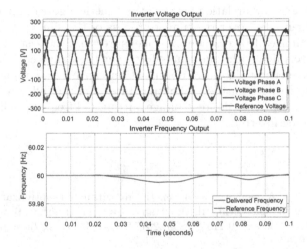

Fig. 10. Regulated grid forming voltage and frequency

Formerly, when the PID controllers are correctly tuned to a desired closed-loop response, the possible variation of the L-C output filters was analyzed and the relationship between the L-C filter values and the variation in the proportional gain of the EVLC is obtained. The results in Fig. 5 show that output voltage and frequency is highly dependent on the inductance filter values rather than in the proportional gain of the controller or the filter capacitance.

7 Future Work

Based on the results exposed in this work, a GFMI can be constructed in hardware in the loop simulation to verify the proposed methodology. Also, this work can be expanded to any gain-based controller sensitive to parameter variations, where the flexibility and the functioning of a controller can be observed for any governing parameter.

8 Conclusions

A new approach towards the right tuning of cascade PID controllers within a grid forming control architecture is performed along with the parameter correlation between the controller gains and the parameter variations of the L-C output filer. The analyzed searching regions show that any desired characteristic can be chosen to have a possible gain combination to fulfill the desired closed-loop control response. The genetic algorithm used for the optimization process turned to be efficient, however slow regarding computation timing, and improvement over the computational time is achieved due to a constraint searching area, making the genetic algorithm optimization process ten times faster with the more suitable result, despite the random mutation nature of the algorithm, in a constrained scenario the proposed method was able to get to the same results regarding the mutation ratio. The cross-relation between the genetic algorithm parameters are analyzed and their effect over the tuning process of the simulated grid-forming inverter. An optimized PID cascade control ensures that the system achieves the voltage reference value with minimum effect over the delivered frequency. In a further test, the genetic algorithm optimization can be also applied to obtain an accurate set of values for the L-C output filter and the different gains in the controllers according to the desired voltage output and frequency characteristics of the gird-forming inverter.

References

1. Askarzadeh, A.: A memory-based genetic algorithm for optimization of power generation in a microgrid. IEEE Trans. Sustain. Energy 9(3), 1081–1089 (2018). https://doi.org/10.1109/TSTE.2017.2765483. https://ieeexplore.ieee.org/document/8078257/
2. Balaguer, I.J., Lei, Q., Yang, S., Supatti, U., Peng, F.Z.: Control for grid-connected and intentional islanding operations of distributed power generation. IEEE Trans. Industr. Electron. 58(1), 147–157 (2011). https://doi.org/10.1109/TIE.2010.2049709
3. Cruz, P.P.: Inteligencia Artificial. Con Aplicaciones a la Ingeniería, p. 378
4. Hooshyar, A., Iravani, R.: Microgrid protection. Proc. IEEE 105(7), 1332–1353 (2017). https://doi.org/10.1109/JPROC.2017.2669342
5. Khamis, A., Ghani, M.R.A., Kim, G.C., Kamarudin, M.N., Shahrieel, M., Aras, M.: Voltage and frequency control of microgrid systems with demand response, p. 7

6. Li, Z.W., Zang, C.Z., Zeng, P., Yu, H.B., Li, H.P.: The controller parameters optimization for droop controlled distributed generators in microgrid. Appl. Mech. Mater. **672–674**, 1329–1335 (2014). https://doi.org/10.4028/www.scientific.net/AMM.672-674.1329. https://www.scientific.net/AMM.672-674.1329
7. Liserre, M., Dell'Aquila, A., Blaabjerg, F.: Genetic algorithm-based design of the active damping for an LCL-filter three-phase active rectifier. IEEE Trans. Power Electron. **19**(1), 76–86 (2004). https://doi.org/10.1109/TPEL.2003.820540. http://ieeexplore.ieee.org/document/1262055/
8. Rocabert, J., Luna, A., Blaabjerg, F., Rodríguez, P.: Control of power converters in AC microgrids. IEEE Trans. Power Electron. **27**(11), 4734–4749 (2012). https://doi.org/10.1109/TPEL.2012.2199334. http://ieeexplore.ieee.org/document/6200347/
9. Sadasivarao, M.V., Chidambaram, M.: PID controller tuning of cascade control systems using genetic algorithm. J. Indian Inst. Sci. **86**, 343–354 (2006)
10. Srinivas, M., Patnaik, L.: Genetic algorithms: a survey. Computer **27**(6), 17–26 (1994). https://doi.org/10.1109/2.294849. http://ieeexplore.ieee.org/document/294849/
11. Tang, K., Man, K., Kwong, S., He, Q.: Genetic algorithms and their applications. IEEE Signal Process. Mag. **13**(6), 22–37 (1996). https://doi.org/10.1109/79.543973. http://ieeexplore.ieee.org/document/543973/
12. Vandoorn, T.L., Meersman, B., De Kooning, J.D., Vandevelde, L.: Transition from islanded to grid-connected mode of microgrids with voltage-based droop control. IEEE Trans. Power Syst. **28**(3), 2545–2553 (2013). https://doi.org/10.1109/TPWRS.2012.2226481. http://ieeexplore.ieee.org/document/6476047/

Differential Evolution Based on Learnable Evolution Model for Function Optimization

Esteban Morales[1]([✉]), Cristina Juárez[1], Edgar García[2], and José Sanchéz[1]

[1] Universidad Autónoma del Estado de Méxio,
Mexico City, Estado de México, Mexico
zayn@live.com.mx
[2] Escuela Militar de Transmisiones, Mexico City, Mexico

Abstract. With the advance of technology, the generation of massive amounts of information grows every day, generating complex problems difficult to manage in an efficient way. Therefore, researchers have studied and modeled the way in which natural biological systems react and behave in certain situations, allowing to developed algorithms that exhibit a capacity to learn and/or adapt to new situations, obtaining better results than traditional approaches. In this article we present a new variant of the Differential Evolution (DE) algorithm inspired by the concept of the Learnable Evolution Model (LEM) to enhance the search capability through a selection mechanism based on machine learning to create a set of rules that allows the inferring of new candidates in the population that emerge not only the random scan. The proposed algorithm is tested and validated on a set of 23 bechmark test functions and its performance is compared with other metaheuristics. Results indicate that the proposed DE+LEM is competitive with other metaheuristic.

Keywords: Learnable Evolution Model (LEM) · Differential Evolution (DE) · Optimization

1 Introduction

Evolutionary algorithms have been used widely for solving optimization problems involving a large number of parameters and/or unknown variables. And although they constitute a valuable tool for solving such problems, the computational challenges generated by modern applications often involve complex solutions with a high-dimensionality, significantly reducing the performance of standard variant of the algorithm. Due to this, in recent years the traditional techniques of measurement and analysis of data have changed. Programs are now able to produce better performances, make better decisions and adapt independently when new data is presented, learning from their previous attempts to process similar things, so their ability to automatically analyze a large amount of data at a much faster rate [24].

© Springer Nature Switzerland AG 2019
L. Martínez-Villaseñor et al. (Eds.): MICAI 2019, LNAI 11835, pp. 290–302, 2019.
https://doi.org/10.1007/978-3-030-33749-0_24

The Evolutionary Computation focuses on the study of computational systems that resemble simplified versions of the processes and mechanisms of biological evolution, in order to achieve them [2]. The term "evolutionary computation" or "evolutionary algorithm", can be defined as a set of techniques inspired by Neo-Darwinism where the processes of reproduction, mutation, competition and selection are essential for natural evolution [22].

The Differential Evolution (DE) algorithm, was firstly proposed by Storn and Price in 1995 [28,29]. DE is one of the most efficient and versatile evolutionary computing algorithms [6], from which many variants have been proposed and analyzed in literature to significantly improve the performance of the algorithm in convergence rate, final accuracy, and robustness [9,38], focused on the setting of control parameters such as scaling factor (F) [32], crossover rate (Cr) [40], population size (NP), as well as on the selection mechanism, and mutation strategies [10,12,17].

As the DE is a parameter-dependence algorithm, the selection of the parameter setting may vary when solving different problems, so that, the performance of DE depends on the ability to adapt these operators, tuning the parameter manually might need expensive computation [12]. This consideration motivated researchers to design a self-adaptive strategy to adapt these parameters, such as: [1,21,30,31,39,40], as well as different schemes of DE. Detailed summary and analysis of the literature and some important development prospects are presented in [6,7].

This paper presents a new design methodology of DE using the Learnable Evolution Model (LEM) to enhance the search capability through a selection mechanism based on machine learning. Work related to LEM includes research on hybrid algorithms to solve-real-world combinatorial or global optimization problems such as LEM for Multi-Objective optimization (LEMMO) [13,14], LEM with k-nearest-neighbour "LEM(KNN)" [26], LEM with Entropy-based Discretization "LEM(ED)" [27], LEM with ID3 decision tree learning "LEM(ID3)" [25], Global-best Harmony Search using LEM (GHS+LEM) [5], and Polynomial Neural Networks Based on LEM3 (PNN-LEM) [11]. This experiments with different implementations of LEM have demonstrated that it significantly and consistently speeds up the evolutionary process in terms of the evolution length, that is, achieving good results in relatively few evaluations, so that, LEM is particularly suitable for optimization problems in which the fitness evaluation is time-expensive.

The remaining parts of the paper are organized as follows. Section 2, describes the basic concepts related to classical DE. Section 3 provides an overview of the LEM methodology. The proposed new algorithm, DE+LEM, is explained in Sect. 4. Simulation results for the comparison of DE+LEM with the classical DE are shown in Sect. 5. Finally, the paper is concluded in Sect. 6.

2   Classical Differential Evolution Algorithm

DE is an evolutionary algorithm (EA) which is inspired by the laws of Darwininsm where stronger and adapted individuals have greater chances to survive and evolve [29]. EA simulate the evolution of individuals through the selection, reproduction, crossover and mutation methods, stochastically producing better solutions at each generation [8]. Similar to other evolutionary algorithms for optimization problems, DE is a population-based algorithm, which uses the evolution of a population of NP individual vectors. Each individual x denotes one potential solution of the problem, which is defined as follows:

$$x_{i,G} = \{x_{1,i,G}, x_{2,i,G}, \ldots, x_{D,i,G}\}, \ i = 1, 2, \ldots, NP \tag{1}$$

where D is the number of decision variables of the optimization target, NP is the population size, and G denotes the generation number, $G = 0, 1, \ldots, G_{max}$.

The evolutionary process of DE algorithm consists of four main procedures: initialization, mutation, crossover and selection [6,9,15].

Initialization. An initial population is generated, usually, with a uniform random distribution within the search space S constrained by the prescribed minimum and maximum parameter bounds for each of the variables involved. Therefore, each individual can be initialized as follow:

$$x_{j,i,0} = x_{j,min} + rand_{i,j}[0,1] \cdot (x_{j,max} - x_{j,min}) \tag{2}$$

where $rand_{i,j}[0,1]$ is a uniformly random value ranging from 0 to 1.

Mutation. After initialization, DE creates a donor/mutant vector $v_{i,G}$, randomly selecting three candidate solutions x_{r1}, x_{r2}, x_{r3} from the current population, with respect to each target vector $x_{i,G}$. There are various mutation schemes, in this paper, we use the basic DE/$rand$/1 strategy that is represented as:

$$v_{i,G} = x_{r1,G} + F \cdot (x_{r2,G} - x_{r3,G}), \ r1 \neq r2 \neq r3 \neq i \tag{3}$$

where F is a user-specified value within the range of $[0, 1]$ representing a mutation control parameter.

Crossover. The mutant vector $v_{i,G}$ is combined with the target vector $x_{i,G}$ to produce the trial vector using different schemes. In DE, two crossover operators are commonly used: exponential (two-point-modulo) and binomial (uniform). Binomial crossover is the most frequently employed, which is defined as follows:

$$u_{j,i,G} = \begin{cases} v_{j,i,G} & \text{if } rand(0,1) \leq CR \text{ or } j = j_{rand} \\ x_{j,i,G} & \text{otherwise} \end{cases} \tag{4}$$

where $i = 1, 2, \ldots, NP$, $j = 1, 2, \ldots, D$, and index $j_{rand} \in [1, 2, \ldots, D]$ is chosen randomly. Cr is a user-defined crossover probability $\in [0,1]$.

Selection. After the crossover process, the trial vector $u_{i,G+1}$ and the target vector $x_{i,G}$ are compared using the objective function value. If vector $u_{i,G+1}$ yields a better cost function value than $x_{i,G}$, then $u_{i,G+1}$ will replace $x_{i,G+1}$; otherwise, the target vector (old value) $x_{i,G}$ will remain in the population for the next generation. The selection operation can be expressed as follows:

$$x_{i,G+1} = \begin{cases} u_{i,G+1} & \text{if } f(u_{i,G+1}) \leq f(x_{i,G}) \\ x_{i,G} & \text{otherwise} \end{cases} \tag{5}$$

Once the population is created, a simple cycle involving mutation, crossover and selection stages is repeated until the optimum is located, or until some specific termination conditions are met, for example, until the number of generations reaches a pres-established maximum.

3 The Learnable Evolution Model

The LEM consists of elements typically found in evolutionary computation, such as generation of initial population, evaluation, and selection of candidate solutions, however, has a different approach to the Darwinian-type model. LEM represents a form of non-Darwinian evolutionary computation [4], which refers to the development of algorithms in which the creation of new individuals in the population is guided partially, by an "intelligent agent", rather than done through mutation and/or recombination operators employed in "Darwinian-type" evolutionary methods [36].

The first version of the LEM methodology was introduced in [18]. Subsequently LEM2 was developed, an improved expansion and implementation of the methodology that differs from the first version in a number of features, of which the most important is the implementation of the uniLEM mode, and of the startover, the dinamically adjusted quantization level, and the fitness-based selection method [3]. Later, the team that developed LEM implemented LEM3, which employs a machine learning program for attributional rule learning called AQ21. In contrast to previous implementation, LEM3 allows different types of attributes, new hypothesis instantiation algorithms, and Action Profiling Function (APF) that allows switching between modes of LEM operation [36], such as Learn and Instantiate, Adjust Representation, Probe, and Randomize.

3.1 The LEM Algorithm

The central engine of evolution in LEM is the use of machine learning to direct the evolutionary process [19,35]. Specifically, in LEM, whose algorithm is presented in the Algorithm 1, creation of new candidate solutions is done by applying hyphotesis learning and instantiation. The overall idea is to combine evolutionary search and learning, where the result of the 'learning' period is then used somehow to inform the next 'evolution' period. LEM may alternate between these two modes of operation. The Darwinian Evolution mode is based on traditional evolutionary computation methods, such as selection, combination and mutation, while Machine Learning mode is used to generate new candidate solutions through a three-step process:

1. *Example preparation*, is the process in which it is determined that individuals in a population (or a group of individuals from previous populations) are better than others in performing certain tasks, dividing the candidate solutions into group of High-performing (H-group) and Low-performing (L-groups). This split is done based on the values of the fitness function. There are two methods of creating these groups [34].

Algorithm 1. Pseudocode of a general LEM algorithm.

Data: The population size (NP), Learning threshold, Objective function.
Result: The best individual.
1 Create an initial population of candidate solutions.
2 Evaluate candidate solutions in the initial population.
3 **while** *Stop criteria are not satisfied* **do**
4 | Create new candidate solutions by machine learning:
5 | Identify groups of high- and low-performing candidate solutions.
6 | Apply machine learning to distinguish between the groups.
7 | Instantiate the learned hypothesis.
8 | Evaluate fitness of the new candidate solutions.
9 |_ Select a new population.

(a) Fitness-based selection. Selects solutions whose fitness values are within given thresholds for H-and L-groups.
(b) Population-based selection. Selects a specified percentage of candidate solutions from the population for each group.
2. *Hypothesis generation*, is the process which applies a learning technique to create a hypotheses that describes the differences between groups of high performing and low performing individuals. Such hypotheses explain why some candidate solutions perform better than others.
3. *Hypothesis instantiation*, is the process during which new individuals are generated through a process of deliberate reasoning that involves the characteristics learned in the form of attribution rules.

The search mechanism conducted in Machine Learning mode can be interpreted as a progressive partitioning of the search space. An H-group description hypothesizes a region or regions that likely contain the optimal solutions [33]. Each subsequent H-group description hypothesizes a new, typically more specialized, partition of the search space. New representations are created by removing attributes irrelevant to the considered problem, by modifying domains of attributes, and by creating new attributes [37]. Due to this effect, the LEM evolution process may converge to the optimum (local or global) much more rapidly than Darwinian-type evolutionary algorithms [11].

4   Proposed DE+LEM Algorithm

Inspired by the concept of the LEM proposed by Michalski [19], this paper proposes a new variation of DE algorithm. LEM can work as a combination of Machine Learning mode and Darwinian Evolution mode (duoLEM), or in Machine Learning mode alone (uniLEM). Machine Learning mode can potentially employ any machine learning method that is able to create discriminant description of individuals in a population. Darwinian Evolution mode can employ any existing method of evolutionary computation that uses some form of mutation, crossover (optionally) and selection operators, for example, DE.

In this article the duoLEM is used. The new proposal is named DE+LEM and the steps of the algorithm are presented in the Algorithm 2. The first step of the algorithm is to generate an initial population randomly. This step determines the value of the fitness function for every individual in the population. New individuals are generated by instantiating these hypotheses, or by evolution, or are randomly generated. If operating mode is learning, then create new candidate solutions by learning, this algorithm identify groups of high- and low-performing, label them as good and bad intervals by observing the relative proportions of gene values from the H-group. After a successfull process, new individuals are evaluated and incorporated into the new population. Selection of individuals into the new population is done using the method known as rank-based selection. The evolution mode begins when DE learning mode is finished, employing Darwinian-type operators such as mutation and crossover.

Algorithm 2. Pseudo-code for DE+LEM algorithm

    Data: $Population_{size}$, $Operating_{mode}$, $Problem_{size}$, Cr, F
    Result: S_{best}
1   Population $\leftarrow$ InitializePopulation($Population_{size}$, $Problem_{size}$);
2   EvaluatePopulation(Population);
3   $S_{best} \leftarrow$ GetBestSolution(Population)
4   **while** $\neg$ $StopCondition()$ **do**
5   **if** $Operating_{mode} == Learning$ **then**
6   Population $\leftarrow$ SortRowsSolution(Population, 1)
7   **for** $P_i \in Population$ **do**
8   L-group $\leftarrow$ CalculateLowGroup(Population)
9   H-group $\leftarrow$ CalculateHighGroup(Population)
10   Bounds $\leftarrow$ ValidationBounds($Problem_{size}$, L-group, H-group)
11   NewPopulation $\leftarrow$ HillClimbing(S_{best}, $Problem_{size}$, Bounds);
12   **if** $Operating_{mode} == Evolution$ **then**
13   **for** $P_i \in Population$ **do**
14             $S_i \leftarrow$ NewSample(P_i, Population, $Problem_{size}$, F, Cr);
15   NewPopulation $\leftarrow$ S_i
16   **if** $Operating_{mode} == StartOver$ **then**
17   NewPopulation $\leftarrow$ Randomizing();
18   EvaluatePopulation(Population, NewPopulation);
19      $S_{best} \leftarrow$ GetBestSolution(Population);

In DE+LEM, the 'learning' corresponds entirely to the process of classification into these groups based entirely on fitness, focusing the population on regions increasingly defined by H-group. As the optimization progresses, the population will lose diversity. To counter this, DE+LEM adds randomly generated individuals to a population in order to introduce diversity, or replacing 10% of the population in a start-over process.

5 Experimental Study

In order to test the efficiency of the proposed algorithm, our experiment's results were compared with other existing popular algorithms. Four optimization algorithms have been chosen namely, standard DE [29], Grey Wolf Optimizer (GWO) [20], Gravitational Search Algorithm (GSA) [23] and LEM(ID3) [25]. These algorithms are widely employed to compare the performance of optimization algorithms. The proposed algorithm is tested and validated on a set of 23 benchmark test functions from IEEE CEC 2005 special session [16]. The benchmark functions used are minimization functions and can be divided into four groups: unimodal, multimodal, fixed-dimension multimodal, and composite functions.

Parameter setting generally used for all conducted experiments adapted from the literature, unless a change is mentioned, is as follow: the number of generations is 1000, problem dimension is 30, population size is 30, the mutation factor is 0.7, crossover rate is 0.9, high and low threshold is 30%, learning gap is 1, and evolution gap is 1. Algorithms were tested with 30 independent runs for each test functions in order to compile comprehensive data and generate statistically significant results. All the algorithms are developed in the Matlab R2016b environment, and executed on a Computer with a Intel(R) Core(TM) i7-5500U CPU @ 2.40 GHz, 7.7 GiB of RAM running Linux Mint 19.1 64 bits.

5.1 Simulation Results Analysis

This section shows the experiments performed to evaluate the performance of the algorithm. Figure 1(a) shows the twenty-first generation of the population, and we see continued reduction in the 'spread' of the population, and for a given threshold (30%) the H-group (circles) and L-group (cross) are formed. The best solution is represented by a blue asterisk and the population generated by LEM with pink asterisks, and (b) convergence graph after generation 100.

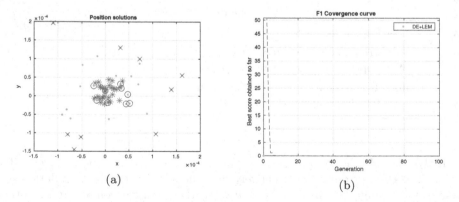

(a)   (b)

Fig. 1. (a) Example illustration and (b) convergence graph on 2-D for $f1$. (Color figure online)

The proposed algorithm solves the problem quickly. However, many basic algorithms can solve $f1$, which is why the algorithm is also analyzed by optimizing the function $(f4)$ and $(f5)$ in a matter of minimization when D = 30 y number of generations is 1000, shown in the Fig. 2. The detailed test results of DE+LEM on benchmark functions are shown in Table 1 in terms of the best fitness values (Best), the worst fitness values (Worst), the mean and the standard deviation (SD).

Table 1. Simulation results of DE+LEM.

Function	Mean	SD	Best	Worst
$f1$	2.1648E−23	3.3031E−23	6.8378E−26	1.3163E−22
$f2$	7.9538E−09	2.4330E−08	2.6261E−10	1.3213E−07
$f3$	1.5437E+03	1.9383E+03	6.3465E+00	8.6133E+03
$f4$	1.6237E−25	7.0440E−26	6.7406E−26	3.2006E−25
$f5$	2.8761E+01	2.2814E+01	2.8674E+01	2.9713E+01
$f6$	9.8816E−24	1.9187E−23	2.2595E−25	1.0039E−22
$f7$	3.6768E−03	1.8019E−03	1.2490E−03	7.6873E−03
$f8$	−3.4682E+03	4.5839E+02	−4.0370E+03	−2.9245E+03
$f9$	1.7253E+02	1.6648E+01	1.3668E+02	2.0408E+02
$f10$	1.5608E−12	1.7921E−12	1.9629E−13	7.7351E−12
$f11$	3.1335E−04	1.6650E−03	0.0000E+00	9.1271E−03
$f12$	1.3571E−07	6.8675E−07	4.3077E−26	3.7593E−06
$f13$	1.9450E−22	2.9687E−22	2.5876E−25	1.2844E−21
$f14$	4.6907E+00	3.8462E+00	9.9800E−01	1.3637E+01
$f15$	1.2249E−03	3.1206E−03	3.2964E−04	1.7362E−02
$f16$	−1.0289E+00	1.4047E−02	1.0316E+00	−9.5457E−01
$f17$	3.9789E−01	2.3834E−05	3.9789E−01	3.9790E−01
$f18$	4.2013E+00	2.8694E−00	3.0000E+00	1.2918E+01
$f19$	−3.8420E+00	2.6170E−02	−3.8628E+00	−3.7652E+00
$f20$	−3.2454E+00	1.0836E−01	−3.3219E+00	−2.9259E+00
$f21$	−6.9844E+00	3.5280E+00	−1.0153E+01	−2.6305E+00
$f22$	−9.1282E+00	2.8991E+00	−1.0402E+01	−2.7519E+00
$f23$	−9.4103E+00	2.6044E+00	−1.0536E+01	−2.8055E+00

It is important to mention that for the results shown in the functions $f2$, $f16 − 18$ were tested with 6 dimensions, $f15$, $f21 − 23$ with D = 4, $f19$ with D = 3 and $f20$ with D = 6. More details are described in [20]. Simulation results for the comparison of DE+LEM with the classical DE and other algorithms on various testbed benchmark functions are listed in Table 3. For the comparative algorithms, we take the mean results directly from the cited publication. Empirical evidence suggests that this general strategy is certainly more often effective than not. Although the results obtained are not better in all cases, DE+LEM shows a competitive performance that can be improved in terms of the number of function evaluations and problem dimensionality.

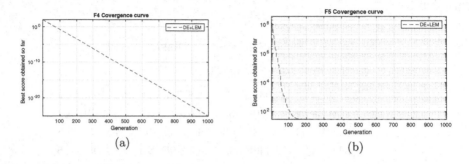

(a)　　　　　　　　　　　　　　　　(b)

Fig. 2. Convergence graph on 30-D of (a) $f4$ and (b) $f5$.

Table 2 show results for the comparison of the mean values for LEM(ID3), and DE+LEM on the 30-D versions of the CEC 2005 test suite.

Table 2. Comparison of DE+LEM with LEM(ID3).

No	DE+LEM	LEMID3
$f1$	2.1648E−23	3.4788E−13
$f3$	1.5437E+03	1.6532E−10
$f5$	2.8761E+01	1.5081E+02
$f8$	−3.4682E+03	3.1318E+03
$f9$	1.7253E+02	7.8419E−07
$f10$	1.5608E−12	2.0151E+01
$f11$	3.1335E−04	2.9580E−02

The results shown here indicate that DE+LEM is competitive with other metaheuristic, and could be used to solve various real life problems. From these results, we can arrive at a conclusion that DE+LEM can find excellent solutions with only 100 iterations which reflect the fast convergence speed of the proposed algorithm.

Table 3. Comparison of DE+LEM with different algorithms

No	DE+LEM	GWO	DE	GSA
$f1$	2.16E−23	6.59E−28	8.2E−14	2.53E−16
$f2$	7.95E−09	7.18E−17	1.5E−09	0.055655
$f3$	1.54E+03	3.29E−06	6.8E−11	896.5347
$f4$	1.62E−25	5.61E−07	0	7.35487
$f5$	28.761E+00	26.81258	0	67.54309
$f6$	9.88E−24	0.816579	0	2.5E−16
$f7$	0.003676	0.002213	0.00463	0.089441
$f8$	−3468.2	−6123.1	−11080.1	−2821.07
$f9$	172.53	0.310521	69.2	25.96841
$f10$	1.5608E−12	1.06E−13	9.7E−08	0.062087
$f11$	0.0003133	0.004485	0	27.70154
$f12$	1.3571E−07	0.053438	7.9E−15	1.799617
$f13$	6.8675E−07	0.654464	5.1E−14	8.899084
$f14$	4.6907	4.042493	0.998004	5.859838
$f15$	1.2249E−03	0.000337	4.5E−14	0.003673
$f16$	−1.0289	−1.03163	−1.03163	−1.03163
$f17$	0.39789	0.397889	0.397887	0.397887
$f18$	4.2013	3.000028	3	3
$f19$	−3.8420	−3.86263	N/A	−3.86278
$f20$	−3.2454	−3.28654	N/A	−3.31778
$f21$	−6.9844	−10.1514	−10.1532	−5.95512
$f22$	−9.1282	−10.4015	−10.4029	−9.68447
$f23$	−9.4103	−10.5343	−10.5364	−10.5364

6   Conclusion Remarks

In this article we present a new variant of DE algorithm inspired by the concept of the LEM to enhance the search capability through a selection mechanism based on machine learning to create a set of rules that allows the inferring of new candidates in the population that emerge not only the random scan. The proposed algorithm is tested and validated on a set of 23 bechmark test functions from IEEE CEC 2005 special session, were used to conduct comprehensive experiments to analyze the performance of DE+LEM. It was compared with classical DE, GWO algorithm and GSA. The experimental results showed that DE+LEM achieve a competitive overall. In future work, the problem dimensionality will be increased and the use of a small population will be studied. In addition this proposed method will be used to solve realworld optimization problems and be extended to handle constrained optimization problems.

References

1. Brest, J., Greiner, S., Boskovic, B., Mernik, M., Zumer, V.: Self-adapting control parameters in differential evolution: a comparative study on numerical benchmark problems. IEEE Trans. Evol. Comput. **10**(6), 646–657 (2006)
2. Brownlee, J.: Clever algorithms: nature-inspired programming recipes (2011)
3. Cervone, G.: LEM2: theory and implementation of the learnable evolution model. Reports of the Machine Learning and Inference Laboratory, MLI, p. 99Y (1999)
4. Cervone, G., Kaufman, K.A., Michalski, R.S.: Recent results from the experimental evaluation of the learnable evolution model (2002)
5. Cobos, C., Estupiñán, D., Pérez, J.: GHS+ LEM: global-best harmony search using learnable evolution models. Appl. Math. Comput. **218**(6), 2558–2578 (2011)
6. Das, S., Mullick, S.S., Suganthan, P.N.: Recent advances in differential evolution-an updated survey. Swarm Evol. Comput. **27**, 1–30 (2016)
7. Das, S., Suganthan, P.N.: Differential evolution: a survey of the state-of-the-art. IEEE Trans. Evol. Comput. **15**(1), 4–31 (2010)
8. De Jong, K.A.: Evolutionary Computation: A Unified Approach. MIT Press, Cambridge (2006)
9. Deng, L.B., Wang, S., Qiao, L.Y., Zhang, B.Q.: DE-RCO: rotating crossover operator with multiangle searching strategy for adaptive differential evolution. IEEE Access **6**, 2970–2983 (2018)
10. Epitropakis, M.G., Tasoulis, D.K., Pavlidis, N.G., Plagianakos, V.P., Vrahatis, M.N.: Enhancing differential evolution utilizing proximity-based mutation operators. IEEE Trans. Evol. Comput. **15**(1), 99–119 (2011)
11. Farzi, S.: The design of self-organizing evolved polynomial neural networks based on learnable evolution model 3. Int. Arab J. Inf. Technol. **9**(2), 124–132 (2012)
12. Fu, Y., Wang, H., Yang, M.Z.: An adaptive population size differential evolution with novel mutation strategy for constrained optimization. arXiv preprint arXiv:1805.04217 (2018)
13. Jourdan, L., Corne, D., Savic, D., Walters, G.: LEMMO: hybridising rule induction and NSGA II for multi-objective water systems design. In: Procceedings of the Eighth International Conference on Computing and Control for the Water Industry, vol. 2, pp. 45–50 (2006)
14. Jourdan, L., Corne, D., Savic, D., Walters, G.: Preliminary investigation of the 'learnable evolution model' for faster/better multiobjective water systems design. In: Coello Coello, C.A., Hernández Aguirre, A., Zitzler, E. (eds.) EMO 2005. LNCS, vol. 3410, pp. 841–855. Springer, Heidelberg (2005). https://doi.org/10.1007/978-3-540-31880-4_58
15. Lei, Y.X., Gou, J., Wang, C., Luo, W., Cai, Y.Q.: Improved differential evolution with a modified orthogonal learning strategy. IEEE Access **5**, 9699–9716 (2017)
16. Liang, J.J., Suganthan, P.N., Deb, K.: Novel composition test functions for numerical global optimization. In: 2005 Proceedings 2005 IEEE Swarm Intelligence Symposium, SIS 2005, pp. 68–75. IEEE (2005)
17. Mallipeddi, R., Suganthan, P.N., Pan, Q.K., Tasgetiren, M.F.: Differential evolution algorithm with ensemble of parameters and mutation strategies. Appl. Soft Comput. **11**(2), 1679–1696 (2011)
18. Michalski, R.S.: Learnable evolution: combining symbolic and evolutionary learning (1998)
19. Michalski, R.S.: Learnable evolution model: evolutionary processes guided by machine learning. Mach. Learn. **38**(1–2), 9–40 (2000)

20. Mirjalili, S., Mirjalili, S.M., Lewis, A.: Grey wolf optimizer. Adv. Eng. Softw. **69**, 46–61 (2014)
21. Qin, A.K., Huang, V.L., Suganthan, P.N.: Differential evolution algorithm with strategy adaptation for global numerical optimization. IEEE Trans. Evol. Comput. **13**(2), 398–417 (2009)
22. Quintero, L.V.S., Coello, C.A.C.: Una introducción a la computación evolutiva y alguna de sus aplicaciones en economía y finanzas//an introduction to evolutionary computation and some of its applications in economics and finance. Rev. de Métodos Cuantitativos para la Economía y la Empresa **2**, 3–26 (2016)
23. Rashedi, E., Nezamabadi-Pour, H., Saryazdi, S.: GSA: a gravitational search algorithm. Inf. Sci. **179**(13), 2232–2248 (2009)
24. Roberts, R.: Machine Learning: The Ultimate Beginner's Guide to Neutral Networks, Algorithms, Random Forests and Decision Trees Made Simple. Springer, Berlin (2017)
25. Sheri, G., Corne, D.: Learning-assisted evolutionary search for scalable function optimization: LEM(ID3). In: 2010 IEEE Congress on Evolutionary Computation (CEC), pp. 1–8. IEEE (2010)
26. Sheri, G., Corne, D.W.: The simplest evolution/learning hybrid: LEM with KNN. In: 2008 IEEE Congress on Evolutionary Computation (IEEE World Congress on Computational Intelligence), CEC 2008, pp. 3244–3251. IEEE (2008)
27. Sheri, G., Corne, D.W.: Evolutionary optimization guided by entropy-based discretization. In: Giacobini, M., et al. (eds.) EvoWorkshops 2009. LNCS, vol. 5484, pp. 695–704. Springer, Heidelberg (2009). https://doi.org/10.1007/978-3-642-01129-0_79
28. Storn, R., Price, K.: Differential evolution-a simple and efficient adaptive scheme for global optimization over continuous spaces. ICSI, Berkeley (1995)
29. Storn, R., Price, K.: Differential evolution-a simple and efficient heuristic for global optimization over continuous spaces. J. Global Optim. **11**(4), 341–359 (1997)
30. Tanabe, R., Fukunaga, A.: Success-history based parameter adaptation for differential evolution. In: 2013 IEEE Congress on Evolutionary Computation (CEC), pp. 71–78. IEEE (2013)
31. Tang, L., Dong, Y., Liu, J.: Differential evolution with an individual-dependent mechanism. IEEE Trans. Evol. Comput. **19**(4), 560–574 (2015)
32. Wang, Y., Cai, Z., Zhang, Q.: Differential evolution with composite trial vector generation strategies and control parameters. IEEE Trans. Evol. Comput. **15**(1), 55–66 (2011)
33. Warden, T., Wojtusiak, J.: Learnable evolutionary optimization in autonomous pickup & delivery planning: a scenario, system architecture and initial results. TZI-Bericht Nr 55 (2010)
34. Wojtusiak, J.: The LEM3 system for multitype evolutionary optimization. Comput. Inform. **28**(2), 225–236 (2009)
35. Wojtusiak, J., Kaufman, K.A.: Ryszard S. Michalski: the vision and evolution of machine learning. In: Koronacki, J., Raś, Z.W., Wierzchoń, S.T., Kacprzyk, J. (eds.) Advances in Machine Learning I. SCI, vol. 262, pp. 3–22. Springer, Heidelberg (2010). https://doi.org/10.1007/978-3-642-05177-7_1
36. Wojtusiak, J., Michalski, R.S.: The LEM3 system for non-Darwinian evolutionary computation and its application to complex function optimization. Technical report (2005)
37. Wojtusiak, J., Warden, T., Herzog, O.: The learnable evolution model in agent-based delivery optimization. Memetic Comput. **4**(3), 165–181 (2012)

38. Yu, W.J., et al.: Differential evolution with two-level parameter adaptation. IEEE Trans. Cybern. **44**(7), 1080–1099 (2014)
39. Zhang, J., Sanderson, A.C.: JADE: adaptive differential evolution with optional external archive. IEEE Trans. Evol. Comput. **13**(5), 945–958 (2009)
40. Zhou, Y.Z., Yi, W.C., Gao, L., Li, X.Y.: Adaptive differential evolution with sorting crossover rate for continuous optimization problems. IEEE Trans. Cybern. **47**(9), 2742–2753 (2017)

Best Paper Award, Second Place

Towards Constant Calculation in Disjunctive Inequalities Using Wound Treatment Optimization

Hiram Ponce[✉], José Antonio Marmolejo-Saucedo,
and Lourdes Martínez-Villaseñor

Facultad de Ingeniería, Universidad Panamericana,
Augusto Rodin 498, 03920 Mexico City, Mexico
{hponce,jmarmolejo,lmartine}@up.edu.mx

Abstract. When using the mixed-integer programming to model situations where the limit of the variables follows a box constraint, we find nonlinear problems. To solve this, linearization techniques of these disjunctive inequality constraints are typically used, including constants associated to the variable bounds called M-constants or big-M. Calculation of these constants is an open problem since their values affect the reliability of the optimal solution and convergence of the optimization algorithm. To solve this problem, this work proposes a new population-based metaheuristic optimization method, namely wound treatment optimization (WTO) for calculating the M-constant in a typical domain known as the fixed-charge transportation problem. WTO is inspired on the social wound treatment present in ants after raids. This method allows population diversity that allows to find near-optimal solutions. Experiments of the WTO method on the fixed-charge transportation problem validated its performance and efficiency to find tighten solutions of the M-constant that minimizes the objective function of the problem.

Keywords: Mixed-integer programming · Big-M · Metaheuristics · Optimization · Fixed-charge transportation

1 Introduction

Usually, when we use mixed-integer programming to model situations where the limit of the variables follows a box constraint, we find nonlinear problems. To solve this, linearization techniques of these constraints are typically used. However, the transformation of these constraints, i.e. disjunctive inequalities, uses constants associated with the upper and lower bounds that the variables must consider. These limits depend on the particular problem in question. We see some examples in supply chain transportation, energy transportation and network-flow problems in general.

Typically, this constant used in the disjunctive constraints are called "big-M". Different values of the big-M in these inequalities can lead to obtain different

© Springer Nature Switzerland AG 2019
L. Martínez-Villaseñor et al. (Eds.): MICAI 2019, LNAI 11835, pp. 305–316, 2019.
https://doi.org/10.1007/978-3-030-33749-0_25

values in the objective function and in the solution variables. That is why several authors have focused their efforts on finding a constant that returns reliable results in their problems.

For instance, Camm et al. [5] state that textbooks advice to use simply large numbers for M in constraints, hence the choice of M can imply serious computational implications. They say that by making M arbitrarily large, the feasible region of linear programming relaxation is unnecessarily expanded. Although techniques to tighten linear programming relaxation such as pegging of variables or fixing binary variables prior to branch and bound have been studied since the 80's, but these practices are not taken into account. Castro et al. [6] also assert that modelers typically do not bother to find the tightest parameters, replacing M with a global value. Recently, Tres Palacios et al. [19] presented a new big-M reformulation for generalized disjunctive programs. The authors, instead of using one M-parameter for each constraint, they presented a new approach in which multiple M-parameters are used for each constraint. They compared their approach against traditional big-M and in their results, in most cases, the new formulation allows multiple M-parameters to be smaller than a single M-parameter and therefore a tighter formulation.

As shown above, the big-M calculation is still an open problem in mixed-integer programming with disjunctive inequality constraints. Finding a tighter M-constant will impact on [5, 6, 19]: reliable optimization results, improvement in the optimal values of the objective function, less computational implications like divergence, as well as positive impact on optimization problems like supply chain transportation, energy transportation, network-flow, among others. In that sense, there is a need to find new ways to calculate M-constants.

To solve that problem, we are considering to use a population-based metaheuristic optimization method for computing the M-constants. Mainly, metaheuristic approaches have been used for dealing with large and complex optimization problems. Easiness of implementation, few tunable parameters and acceptable performance are the most common reasons of their adoption [16,21]. However, these methods suffer to fall in local optima mainly because of rapid losing of the population diversity [3,14]. This premature convergence issue can be associated to poor performance in individuals, which it can be related to some level of injury. Recently, research in biology [9] discovered that during termite raids in the sub-Saharan Africa, some ants from the species *Megaponera analis* get injured (i.e. open wounds and bites) by termite soldiers. But after raids, healthy ants developed social and individual behavior for wound treatment in injured ants. Injured ants after treatment in less than 12 h had a mortality of 10% while injured ants not treated by their ant-mates had a mortality of 80% [9]. In that sense, the observations in social wound treatment can provide inspiration for new mechanisms in population-based metaheuristic optimization methods.

Thus, this paper proposes a new population-based metaheuristic optimization method based on the social wound treatment of ants, for calculating the M-constants. In particular, we implemented this optimization method to calculate the M-constant in the fixed-charge transportation problem. The contributions of this work can be listed as: (i) the proposal of a new population-based metaheuristic optimization method based on the social wound treatment namely wound treatment optimization (WTO), (ii) the application of WTO to calculate the best M-constant in the fixed-charge transportation problem, and (iii) the open opportunity to find a new way to calculate tighten M-constants in mixed-integer programming with disjunctive inequality constraints.

The rest of the paper is organized as follows. Section 2 presents some works related to computing the M-parameter in different scenarios of mixed-integer programming. Section 3 describes the fixed charge cost problem. Later on, Sect. 4 presents the wound treatment optimization algorithm. Section 5 describes the experiments and the results obtained. Finally, we conclude the work.

2   Related Work

In order to limit the value of a set of variables in mixed-integer programming, a big-M is typically used based on the value of a binary variable. Big-M is used in supply chain, production planning, location transportation, and fixed-charge problems in various domains.

Hong et al. [12] proposed an energy-Internet-oriented architecture of micro-grid energy management system for China. The operation of multi-energy micro-grids with the uncertainties of distributed energy resources and loads was formulated as a two-stage robust operation problem and solved by the column and constraints generation algorithm. The authors used big-M method to handle the inequality constraints about variables of the max-min slave problem. With the aim of solving the fixed-charge network flow problem, Kim et al. [13] proposed a hybrid solution method combining constraint programming and linear programming optimization. Their hybrid approach generates search trees slightly larger than mixed integer programming (MILP) trees, hence it solves each relaxation more quickly. The big-M constraint was used to ensure that fixed cost is incurred if an arc carries positive flow.

Deepak et al. [7] implemented big M and revised simplex method in order to optimize the time coordination of over-current relays in a distribution network. They also identify the optimized time multiplier setting of the relay. Wei et al. [20] optimized an electrified transportation network enabled by wireless power transfer technology coupled with a power distribution network. The power flow of the power distribution network is modeled through Dist-Flow equations. They proposed an optimal traffic power flow model in order to find the best generation schedule and charge congestion tolls. The mixed nonlinear program with traffic user equilibrium constraints is reformulated as a mixed-integer second-order cone program (MISOCP), whose global optimal solution requires reasonable computation effort. They used the big-M method when linearizing the Wardrop user equilibrium conditions. They chose M-constant according to the largest possible travel cost of the corresponding O-D pair.

Ding et al. [8] presented a big-M based mixed-integer quadratic programming (MIQP) method to solve economic load dispatch problem with disjoint prohibited zones. They introduced binary variables for each prohibited zone and the constraints on disjoint feasible zones are replaced by complimentary linear constraints using the big-M method. The mixed-integer quadratic programming problem reduced the model complexity and computational effort needed.

3 The Fixed-Charge Transportation Problem

The fixed-charge transportation problem is a particular kind of problems of transportation and assignment in mathematical programming. Originally, the problem was proposed in [11]. This problem consists in the assignment of transport routes of commodities to plants, deposits and customers. Each link between two elements of the transportation network considers the fixed cost for using that route and the variable cost depending on the number of commodities that flow along the route. If we decide to use a specific route in the transportation network, the mathematical structure of the problem presents an unimodular matrix of constants. For this reason, the flow of commodities always ensures to be an integer value, see [4].

It is known that solving the fixed-charge transportation problem is cataloged as NP-hard [1,10], so the solving algorithms focus on a solution in efficient calculation times for instances of limited size. Since then, various methods of solution have been proposed. Among them, we can mention network-flow methods, algorithms based on duality theory [2], heuristics [11] and meta-heuristics [4,18].

3.1 The Mathematical Model

Let $M > 0$ be a constant that allows the flow through the path $i - j$ and note that $y_{ij} = 1$ if and only if $x_{ij} \geq 0$. Then, the fixed-charge transportation can be expressed as the optimization problem [11] shown in (1):

$$\min_{x_{ij}, y_{ij}} z = \sum_i \sum_j (c_{ij} x_{ij} + f_{ij} y_{ij})$$

$$s.t.$$

$$\sum_i x_{ij} = d_j, \forall j \tag{1}$$

$$x_{ij} \leq M y_{ij}, \forall i, j$$
$$x_{ij} \geq 0, \forall i, j$$
$$y_{ij} \in \{0, 1\}, \forall i, j$$

where, i is the source node, j is the destination node, c_{ij} is the variable cost of the route $i - j$, f_{ij} is the fixed cost of the route $i - j$, x_{ij} is the amount of commodities flow from node i to node j, and y_{ij} is a binary variable that equals to 1 if the route $i - j$ is utilized, otherwise is equals to 0.

4   Wound Treatment Optimization

In order to solve the above problem, we propose a population-based metaheuristic optimization method based on social wound treatment between individuals. Following, the biological inspiration as well as the formulation of the algorithm are described.

4.1   Social Wound Treatment of Ants in Termite Raids

In a recent biology study, Frank et al. [9] reported social wound treatment in the ant species namely *Megaponera analis* located in the sub-Saharan Africa. These ants are specialized in hunting termites from the subfamily Macrotermitinae [9,15]. Ants live in large groups in an organized way. When hunting, the ants are divided in those who attack in mass while others kill and carry out the termites. After the raid is over, ants return back to the nest with the hunted termites, but some injured ants remain in the battle ground asking for help through pheromones. These injured ants typically lose limbs or have termites clinging to them [9].

At this stage is when treatment begins. Some healthy ants investigate the state of the injured ants. If ants are fatally injured, these are left behind or carried away from the nest. Few of injured ants are not noticed or ignored by the healthy ants. And most of the ants average-injured are picked up or carried out to the nest. It is considered successful rescue if injured ants are carried out to the nest. Once in the nest, ants that lose limbs adapt to walk with less limbs (those with four and five limbs can almost recover the full performance). In the other ants, termites clinging are got removed from them and rehabilitation is performed. The open wounds are cleaned; and grooming is performed by healthy ants. After investigation, researchers [9] observed that injured ants after received treatment, in less than 12 h, had a mortality of 10% while injured ants, not treated by their nest-mates, had a mortality of 80%.

This social wound treatment is important in this ant species, mainly related to the number of ants in the group. In fact, these groups of ants are large and they have high birth rate, and losing few of injured ants would not be a problem or be easier to replace them. Contrary to this logic, *Megaponera analis* ants perform rescue and treatment to injured ants, increasing the fitness of the nest [9].

4.2   Synthesis of the Biological Inspiration

Social wound treatment can serve as mechanism for improving the performance of population-based metaheuristic optimization methods. In this regard, we propose the wound treatment optimization (WTO) algorithm for continuous problems. The idea behind this method considers a set of individuals as possible solutions that interact among them. Each individual is evaluated in terms of the level of injury. Average-injured individuals accept help from healthy individuals while heavy-injured ones decease and new individuals are born.

The method synthesizes the following rules extracted from observations: (i) individuals are evaluated in levels of injury: *healthy*, *average* and *heavy*; (ii) healthy individuals are good candidates; (iii) average-injured individuals receive treatment from healthy ones; (iv) heavy-injured individuals decease, so new individuals are born; and, (v) treated individuals tend to survive, and non-treated individuals tend to fail.

4.3   Algorithm Formulation

Consider a minimization problem of the objective function f unconstrained. For D-dimensional search space and N individuals, let x_i be an individual in the population such that $x_i \in \mathbb{R}^D$. Then, $x_i = (x_1, \ldots, x_j, \ldots, x_D)$ is a candidate solution. Particularly, x_i is bounded in the range $[L_j^{min}, L_j^{max}]$.

For initialization, individuals are randomly created as in (2) for all $i = 1, \ldots, N$ and $j = 1, \ldots, D$; where r_i is a random value between $[0, 1]$.

$$x_{i,j}(0) = (L_j^{max} - L_j^{min}) \times r_i + L_j^{min} \tag{2}$$

Let also g_{best} be the best individual with fitness function $f(g_{best})$. Initially, g_{best} is assigned as in (3) with $t = 0$.

$$g_{best}(t) = \arg\min\{f(x_i(t))\}, \forall i = 1, \ldots, N \tag{3}$$

WTO is an iterative algorithm. The following procedures are considered at each iteration, until a stop criterion is reached.

Three levels of injury are declared: $S_{healthy}, S_{average}$ and S_{heavy} for healthy, average- and heavy-injured individuals, respectively. Each individual is assigned to one level of injury, as follows. First, the fitness function $f(x_i)$ is calculated for all individuals, and sorted in descending order (for minimization). Then, two parameters are set: $p_{healthy}$ that represents the percentage of healthy individuals and p_{heavy} for the percentage of heavy-injured individuals, both in range $[0, 1]$. An individual $x_i \in S_{healthy}$ if it is one member of the first $\lceil p_{healthy} \times N \rceil$ individuals in the sorted population. An individual $x_i \in S_{heavy}$ if it is one member of the last $\lceil p_{heavy} \times N \rceil$ individuals in the sorted population. Otherwise, $x_i \in S_{average}$.

From the biological inspiration, healthy individuals are considered good candidates and no updating is required. Then, average-injured individuals, $x_i \in S_{average}$, are updated using (4), where $x_{healthy}$ is randomly picked up from the subset of healthy individuals $S_{healthy}$, h_{rate} is called the help rate, and r^1 and r^2 are random values in the range $[0, 1]$.

$$\begin{aligned} x_{i,j}(t+1) = &\, h_{rate} \times x_{i,j}(t) \\ &+ r_{i,j}^1 \times (x_{healthy,j}(t) - x_{i,j}(t)) \\ &+ r_{i,j}^2 \times (g_{best,j}(t) - x_{i,j}(t)) \end{aligned} \tag{4}$$

After (4) is computed, individuals are limited to the boundaries L_j^{min} and L_j^{max} such that the boundary condition of the candidate solutions is fulfilled.

Notice that this heuristic rule considers update the individual using the information of two healthy individuals, i.e. the best candidate solution g_{best} and one random healthy individual $x_{healthy}$, in order to promote exploitation; while, random values r_1 and r_2 promote exploration. The help rate value h_{rate} performs the level of support that the average-injured individual requires at iteration t. Lastly, the subset of heavy-injured individuals, $x_i \in S_{heavy}$, are replaced with probability $1 - p_{alive}$ (previously set) by new random individuals x_i using (2). This rule prevents rapid convergence in local optima.

Algorithm 1 summarizes WTO for implementation purposes.

Algorithm 1. Wound treatment optimization.

Input: population size N, percentage of healthy individuals $p_{healthy}$, percentage of heavy-injured individuals p_{heavy}, help rate h_{rate}, probability of alive p_{alive}, and bounds L^{min} and L^{max}.

Output: best individual g_{best}.

1: Initialize iterator $t = 0$.
2: Initialize the set of individuals $x_i, \forall i = 1, \ldots, N$ using (2).
3: Determine the best individual $g_{best}(t)$ using (3).
4: **while** not reach a stop criterion **do**
5:     Set the level of injury of individuals $S_{healthy}, S_{average}, S_{heavy}$.
6:     **for** $i = 1$ to $|S_{average}|$ **do**
7:         Choose $x_{healthy}$ randomly from $S_{healthy}$.
8:         **for** $j = 1$ to D **do**
9:             Update $x_{i,j}(t+1)$ using (4).
10:         **end for**
11:     **end for**
12:     **for** $i = 1$ to $|S_{heavy}|$ **do**
13:         **if** $random < (1 - p_{alive})$ **then**
14:             Replace x_i randomly with an individual from $S_{healthy}$.
15:         **end if**
16:     **end for**
17:     Evaluate the fitness function f of all individuals.
18:     Update the best solution g_{best} using f.
19:     $t \leftarrow t + 1$.
20: **end while**
21: **return** g_{best}.

4.4   Example

Consider the continuous optimization problem as stated in (5) in which f is the 2D-*Ackley* function.

$$\min_{x_1, x_2} f = -20 \exp[-0.2\sqrt{0.5(x_1^2 + x_2^2)}]$$

$$- \exp[0.5(\cos(2\pi x_1) + \cos(2\pi x_2))] + e + 20 \tag{5}$$

$$s.t. -5 \leq x_1, x_2 \leq 5$$

To solve this problem, we set WTO with the parameters: $N = 20$, $p_{healthy} = 0.2$, $p_{heavy} = 0.5$, $p_{alive} = 0.1$ and $h_{rate} = 0.7$. For this example, we only compute the first 20 iterations. At each iteration t, WTO performed the configuration of the population as shown in Fig. 1.

During the first iteration $t = 1$, individuals are randomly located. In Fig. 1, individuals are marked with colors representing the healthy (red), average-injured (blue) and heavy-injured (green) ones. The best individual g_{best} is marked with a black circle. In this simple example, it is evident that healthy individuals are near the optimal point, heavy-injured individuals are those farest away from the optimal point, and the remaining candidate solutions are the average-injured individuals. After several iterations ($t = 6$), average-injured individuals are closer to the healthy ones and heavy-injured individuals tend to be far away. In addition, healthy individuals are near g_{best}. Almost at iteration $t = 14$, healthy and average-injured individuals are around the optimal point and the fitness evaluation decreases significantly. In this example, a near-optimal solution at $f(g_{best}) = 0.0060082$ is reached in just 20 iterations.

As observed, healthy individuals attract (i.e. treat) average-injured ones promoting exploitation in the search, while heavy-injured individuals add more exploration in the search space.

5   Experimental Results

We conducted an experiment on the fixed-charge cost problem to calculate the best M-constant using WTO. We set an instance of the fixed-charge problem with variable costs $c(i, j)$, fixed costs $f(i, j)$ and demand $d(j)$, from sources $i = 1, 2, 3$ to destinations $j = 1, 2, 3$, as shown in (6), (7) and (8), respectively.

$$c(i, j) = \begin{bmatrix} 3 & 2 & 5 \\ 4 & 4 & 6 \\ 3 & 6 & 7 \end{bmatrix} \tag{6}$$

$$f(i, j) = \begin{bmatrix} 5 & 6 & 7 \\ 5 & 6 & 7 \\ 5 & 6 & 7 \end{bmatrix} \tag{7}$$

$$d(j) = \begin{bmatrix} 20 & 30 & 25 \end{bmatrix} \tag{8}$$

We optimize the problem with WTO using the following parameters: number of individuals $N = 5$, percentage of healthy individuals $p_{healthy} = 0.2$, percentage of heavy-injured individuals $p_{heavy} = 0.5$, percentage of replacement $p_{alive} = 0.1$ and help rate $h_{rate} = 0.7$. We consider as injury function the sum of the objective function of the fixed charge problem z and the M constant, as expressed in (9). At each individual evaluation, the problem in (1) was solved using the branch and bound method [17].

$$f_{injury} = z + M \tag{9}$$

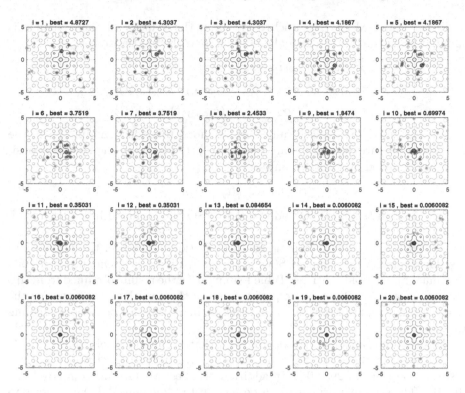

Fig. 1. Example for solving the *Ackley* function. x_1: horizontal-axis and x_2: vertical-axis. Evolution of the individuals during WTO. Marks, *red*: healthy individuals, *blue*: average-injured individuals, *green*: heavy-injured individuals, and *black − circle*: best individual. (Color figure online)

For experimental purposes, we compared WTO with the well-known particle swarm optimization (PSO) method and one modification similar to WTO. As a summary of the algorithms, PSO is a population-based metaheuristic optimization algorithm. It sets a population of N particles that represent candidate solutions. Each particle $p_i = (p_1, \ldots, p_j, \ldots, p_D)$ of D dimensions records the best solution, p_{best}, found at iteration t. In addition, the whole algorithm records the best particle solution, g_{best}, found at iteration t. To move particles, each one has a velocity v_i. In the simple-PSO, at each iteration t, the velocity of each particle is updated following the rule shown in (10), where α_1 and α_2 are the cognitive and social coefficients.

$$
\begin{aligned}
v_{i,j}(t+1) = v_{i,j}(t) \\
+ \alpha_1 \times r_{i,j}^1 \times (p_{best,j}(t) - x_{i,j}(t)) \\
+ \alpha_2 \times r_{i,j}^2 \times (g_{best,j}(t) - x_{i,j}(t))
\end{aligned}
\tag{10}
$$

In the standard-PSO, at each iteration t, the velocity of each particle is updated using the rule of (11), where w refers to the inertia weight.

$$v_{i,j}(t+1) = w \times v_{i,j}(t)$$
$$+ \alpha_1 \times r_{i,j}^1 \times (p_{best,j}(t) - x_{i,j}(t)) \qquad (11)$$
$$+ \alpha_2 \times r_{i,j}^2 \times (g_{best,j}(t) - x_{i,j}(t))$$

In either method, velocity values are bounded to velocity limits. Then, the position of all particles are updated using (12). Once again, the resultant positions are bounded by position limits.

$$x_{i,j}(t+1) = x_{i,j}(t) + v_{i,j}(t+1) \qquad (12)$$

Details of the simple-PSO and standard-PSO can be found in literature [14, 16, 21].

For this case study, we conducted 10 repetitions of each of the population-based methods (WTO, simple-PSO and standard-PSO), independently, with 300 maximum number of iterations. Table 1 summarize the results obtained from this experiment and Fig. 2 shows the performance of these methods representing the mean optimal value (strong line) and the mean ± standard deviation (shading area).

As shown in Table 1, it can be observed that the injury level value in WTO was obtained in the range 259.2570 ± 0.2565 over the 10 repetitions, and the best optimal value of 293.0010. In addition, the best M-constant computed was 30.0010. The same performance can be seen in Fig. 2, where WTO converges to the optimal M-value after 100 iterations. On the other hand, both simple-PSO and standard-PSO reported bigger values of the mean optimal and standard deviation 257x times larger than the one of WTO. This is an issue for simple-PSO and standard-PSO that WTO can overcome easily.

Table 1. Performance of the M-constant optimization using the population-based methods.

Algorithm	Mean optimal	Std. dev. optimal	Min. iteration	Mean runtime	Best optimal	Best min point
WTO	259.2570	0.2565	8	90.2911	293.0010	30.0010
Simple-PSO	384.8604	70.5833	10	87.2557	299.5928	36.5928
Standard-PSO	363.1087	66.0339	4	88.9522	293.5899	30.5899

This experiment was run in a MacBook Pro with i5 processor at 3.1 GHz and 8 GB RAM. On that computer, WTO solved the problem in a mean runtime of 146.66 s.

From the above experiment, we can corroborate that the M-constant influences in the evaluation of the objective function z of the fixed-charge cost problem (1). In this case, we compute an optimal M-constant that is the minimum value that allows it to calculate the minimum z. To this end, it is important to highlight that a good choice of the constant in disjunctive inequalities will impact in the performance of the optimization process of the overall problem.

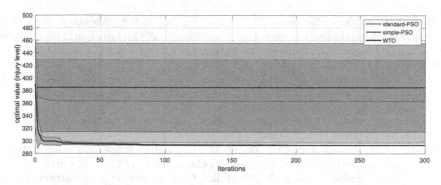

Fig. 2. Performance of the population-based methods showing the mean optimal value (strong line) and the mean ± standard deviation (shading area).

6 Conclusions

This paper presented a population-based metaheuristic optimization algorithm, i.e. WTO, for calculating constants in disjunctive inequalities problems. In particular, we proved our proposed method on the fixed-charge transportation problem.

This work proposed a new biologically inspired optimization algorithm based on the social wound treatment on ants. In this case, we formulated the WTO method and presented a simple example showing the ability to find the near-optimal value in the Ackley function. After that, we applied this algorithm to compute the minimum M constant value on the fixed-charge transportation problem that allows to compute the optimal objective function. From the results, we concluded that WTO successfully solved the problem by measuring the convergence rate in the optimal value (i.e. injury level). In addition, we also computed the mean runtime value.

In this work we also contribute to raise awareness that it is important to bother finding the tightest possible values for big-M parameters.

For future work, we are considering the implement WTO method in parallel computing for improving the computational performance and the quality of the solution. In addition, we are also investigating the extension of the applicability of WTO to other constants calculation in different disjunctive inequalities optimization problems.

References

1. Angulo, G., Van Vyve, M.: Fixed-charge transportation problems on trees. Oper. Res. Lett. **45**(3), 275–281 (2017). https://doi.org/10.1016/j.orl.2017.04.001. http://www.sciencedirect.com/science/article/pii/S0167637717302134
2. Balinski, M.L.: Fixed-cost transportation problems. Nav. Res. Logist. Q. **8**(1), 41–54 (1961). https://doi.org/10.1002/nav.3800080104. https://onlinelibrary.wiley.com/doi/abs/10.1002/nav.3800080104

3. Bansal, J., Singh, P., Saraswat, M., Verma, A., Jadon, S.S., Abraham, A.: Inertia weight strategies in particle swarm optimization. In: 2011 Third World Congress on Nature and Biologically Inspired Computing, pp. 633–640. IEEE, Salamanca (2011)
4. Calvete, H.I., Gale, C., Iranzo, J.A., Toth, P.: A matheuristic for the two-stage fixed-charge transportation problem. Comput. Oper. Res. **95**, 113–122 (2018). https://doi.org/10.1016/j.cor.2018.03.007. http://www.sciencedirect.com/science/article/pii/S0305054818300765
5. Camm, J.D., Raturi, A.S., Tsubakitani, S.: Cutting big M down to size. Interfaces **20**(5), 61–66 (1990)
6. Castro, P.M., Grossmann, I.E., Zhang, Q.: Expanding scope and computational challenges in process scheduling. Comput. Chem. Eng. **114**, 14–42 (2018)
7. Deepak, A., Madhu, S., Raju, M., Swathika, O.G.: Optimum coordination of over-current relays in distribution systems using big-m and revised simplex methods. In: 2017 International Conference on Computing Methodologies and Communication (ICCMC), pp. 613–616. IEEE (2017)
8. Ding, T., Bo, R., Gu, W., Sun, H.: Big-M based MIQP method for economic dispatch with disjoint prohibited zones. IEEE Trans. Power Syst. **29**(2), 976–977 (2014)
9. Frank, E.T., Wehrhahn, M., Linsenmair, K.E.: Wound treatment and selective help in a termite-hunting ant. Proc. R. Soc. B: Biol. Sci. **285**(1872), 1–8 (2018)
10. Guisewite, G.M., Pardalos, P.M.: Minimum concave-cost network flow problems: applications, complexity, and algorithms. Ann. Oper. Res. **25**(1), 75–99 (1990). https://doi.org/10.1007/BF02283688
11. Hirsch, W.M., Dantzig, G.B.: The fixed charge problem. Nav. Res. Logist. Q. **15**(3), 413–424 (1968). https://doi.org/10.1002/nav.3800150306. https://onlinelibrary.wiley.com/doi/abs/10.1002/nav.3800150306
12. Hong, B., Zhang, W., Zhou, Y., Chen, J., Xiang, Y., Mu, Y.: Energy-internet-oriented microgrid energy management system architecture and its application in China. Appl. Energy **228**, 2153–2164 (2018)
13. Kim, H.J., Hooker, J.N.: Solving fixed-charge network flow problems with a hybrid optimization and constraint programming approach. Ann. Oper. Res. **115**(1–4), 95–124 (2002)
14. Kiran, M.S.: Particle swarm optimization with a new update mechanism. Appl. Soft Comput. **60**(11), 670–678 (2017)
15. Longhurst, C., Johnson, R., Wood, T.: Predation by Megaponera foetens (fabr.) (Hymenoptera: Formicidae) on termites in the Nigerian southern Guinea Savanna. Oecologia **32**(1), 101–107 (1978)
16. Marini, F., Walczak, B.: Particle swarm optimization (PSO). A tutorial. Chemometr. Intell. Lab. Syst. **149**(Part B), 153–165 (2015)
17. Przybylski, A., Gandibleux, X.: Multi-objective branch and bound. Eur. J. Oper. Res. **260**(3), 856–872 (2017)
18. Tari, F.G., Hashemi, Z.: Prioritized K-mean clustering hybrid GA for discounted fixed charge transportation problems. Comput. Ind. Eng. **126**, 63–74 (2018). https://doi.org/10.1016/j.cie.2018.09.019. http://www.sciencedirect.com/science/article/pii/S0360835218304352
19. Trespalacios, F., Grossmann, I.E.: Improved big-M reformulation for generalized disjunctive programs. Comput. Chem. Eng. **76**, 98–103 (2015)
20. Wei, W., Mei, S., Wu, L., Shahidehpour, M., Fang, Y.: Optimal traffic-power flow in urban electrified transportation networks. IEEE Trans. Smart Grid **8**(1), 84–95 (2017)
21. Zhang, Y., Wang, S., Ji, G.: A comprehensive survey on particle swarm optimization algorithm and its applications. Math. Problems Eng. **2015**(931256), 1–38 (2015)

Automatic Diet Generation by Particle Swarm Optimization Algorithm

Magda López-López[✉], Axel Zamora[✉], and Roberto A. Vazquez[✉]

Applied Intelligent System Lab, Facultad de Ingeniería, Universidad La Salle México, Benjamin Franklin 45, Col. Condesa, 06140 Mexico City, Mexico
{magda.lopez,jorge.zamora,ravem}@lasallistas.org.mx

Abstract. Deficient nutrition has caused high rates of overweight and obesity in the Mexican population, increasing the cases of people with diabetes and hypertension. In order to solve this, it is necessary to promote a change in the alimentation to reduce the rates of overweight and obesity. To achieve this, we propose a friendly solution to generate a change in the eating habits of the Mexicans by the generation of balance diets. Diet automation has been already created with different algorithms and applications in the past, but with a different purpose and objectives. Particularly, this work is focused on the design of balanced diets applying a Particle Swarm Optimization algorithm. The proposed methodology considers the physical characteristics of the user. To validate the accuracy of the proposed methodology several experiments were performed to asses if the proposal is capable of achieving the calorie goal in terms of the Harris-Benedict equation. The experimental results suggest that it is possible to generate diets using Particle Swarm Optimization algorithms with an error less than 10%.

Keywords: Automatic diet generation · Particle Swarm Optimization · Basal Metabolic Rate

1 Introduction

In recent years, the Mexican population has had an increase in cases of people with alimentation problems. That is because in Mexico is more common to eat in the street instead of prepare healthy food. Due to this, it is necessary to generate an answer to this problem. This work considers using the Particle Swarm Optimization algorithm (PSO) to create balanced diets according to the needs of each individual. It is focus on help people to reduce their consumption of junk food, improve their alimentation habits and reduce the rates of overweight in the population. This problem has already been studied previously, but with other algorithms and for other purposes. Such as the works published by Lv on [9] and [10], where applies the quantum genetic algorithm and the quantum particle swarm optimization algorithm respectively for the multi-objective nutritional diet optimization problem. He also compares the algorithms against

© Springer Nature Switzerland AG 2019
L. Martínez-Villaseñor et al. (Eds.): MICAI 2019, LNAI 11835, pp. 317–329, 2019.
https://doi.org/10.1007/978-3-030-33749-0_26

another algorithms. And [14] that focused their work on create optimized diets for diabetic people. All these works had significant results for the diet generation and optimization problem. The challenge for our research is to improve the results of the previous works by applying a different algorithm and adding the price of the food as a restriction. The methodology proposed applies the Harris-Benedict equation based on the characteristics of the person to generate automatic balanced diets by applying the Particle Swarm Optimization algorithm (PSO). The equation is used to determine the basal metabolic rate and in conjunction with the equivalent portions of food, it is possible to create balanced diets with restrictions of macronutrients and price.

2 Basic Concepts

In this section, it is described the most relevant concepts to understand which is the process of designing a diet. In the same way, it is also described the Particle Swarm Optimization technique use to design the most suitable diet to achieve the calorie goal.

2.1 Diet Calculation

It is known that a balanced diet in conjunction with an exercise routine, can help people to improve their health. But a complete and balanced diet is difficult to create, and can vary from each individual, according with their characteristics. The diets consist in a specific number of calories that are different from one person to another, and they always need to provide the enough daily nutrients as proteins, lipids and more. Also, the kids, the seniors and the overweight people need different kinds of diets that the work is not considering. This makes necessary to stablish a range of age (18–65) and the purpose of this work (take people to a healthier life) to avoid confusions. The diet problem could be represented as a linear optimization problem, as described by Stigler in 1945 [13], with the objective of find a low-cost diet that meet nutrient and caloric requirements. The linear problem formulation is defined by the objective function (Eq. 1), that minimize the cost of the aliment included in a diet, the constraint (Eq. 2) makes sure that all the nutrients in each portion of food is the necessary and the definition of the domain of variable p (Eq. 3).

$$min \sum_i c_i p_i \tag{1}$$

$$\sum_i m_{ij} p_i \geq b_j, \forall j \in \{0, ...N\} \tag{2}$$

$$p_i \geq 0, \forall i \in \{0, ...F\} \tag{3}$$

Where:

c: cost of the food
p: amount of food
m_{ij}: amount of nutrients in each food
b: minimal requirement of nutrients
N: set of nutrients considered in the problem
F: set of available foods

The original solution of this problem only considers a set of 77 foods, which is not a large variety of foods that can provide different tasty meals. For that reason, is necessary to propose a variation of the diet problem solved with an evolutionary computational approach.

The proposal in this research consist on minimizing the number of calories consumed in a day by a healthy person based on equivalent portions of food, that meet requirements of the grams of protein, fat and carbohydrates needed in a nutritive and balance diet.

Let define x_i as the decision variable that represents the amount of $Kcal$ contained in the portion of equivalent food $i \in [1, 24]$, n_{ij} as the grams of macronutrient [4] $j \in \{1, 2, 3\}$ (protein, carbohydrates and fat) contained in the portion of equivalent food $i \in [1, 24]$, c_i as the cost of the portion of equivalent food $i \in [1, 24]$, g_j as the equivalent percentage of macronutrient $j \in \{1, 2, 3\}$ in grams, b as the maximum budget for the entire diet. The linear problem proposed formulations is defined in the following Eqs. (4)–(7) according with [8]:

$$min| \sum_i x_i - Kcal| \tag{4}$$

Subject to

$$\sum_i n_{ij} \leq g_j, \forall j \in \{1, 2, 3\} \tag{5}$$

$$\sum_i c_i \leq b_i, \forall i \in [1, 24] \tag{6}$$

$$0 \leq x_i \leq 5616, \forall i \in [1, 24] \tag{7}$$

Where g_1 corresponds to the grams of protein (Eq. 8), g_2 to the grams of Fat (Eq. 9), g_3 to the grams of carbohydrates (Eq. 10) and $Kcal$ is the number defined by (Eq. 11) or (Eq. 12).

$$g_1 = \frac{Kcal * 0.30}{4} \tag{8}$$

$$g_2 = \frac{Kcal * 0.20}{9} \tag{9}$$

$$g_3 = \frac{Kcal * 0.50}{4} \tag{10}$$

$$Kcal = 6.4 + (13.7 + w) + 5h - 6.76a \tag{11}$$

$$Kcal = 655.1 + (9.6 + w) + 1.8h - 4.7a \tag{12}$$

Where w denotes weight in kilograms, h is related to height in centimeters and a represents the age in years of the subject.

The objective function is stated as Eq. 4, tries to minimize the difference between the calories at the formulated diet and $Kcal$, where $Kcal$ denotes the number of calories that a healthy adult must consume a day in a diet (also called Basal Metabolic Rate [6]) that is calculate based on the weight, height and age. In this paper $Kcal$ is calculated with the Harris-Benedict formula which is different for men (see Eq. 11) and for women (see Eq. 12).

Inequality (5) is the first constraint that maintains the amount in grams of protein, carbohydrates and fat under the requirements, the same happens to inequality (6) that keep into the budget the total cost of the entire diet, Eq. 7 defines the domain of the variable x_i, setting 5616 as the upper limit because the total number of items in the data source used in this work.

Beside the number of calories, the requirement of macronutrients, proteins, fat, and carbohydrates, according with literature [2], must be calculated based on the percentage of the total energy in $Kcal$ corresponding of each macronutrient listed on the Table 1 to convert the percentage of energy in grams. The Table 2 shows the equivalent of grams of each macronutrient in $Kcal$, that has to take in count to make the conversion.

Table 1. Percentage of energy of macronutrients

Macronutrient	Percentage
Proteins	30%
Fat	20%
Carbohydrates	50%

Table 2. Grams of energy of macronutrients

Macronutrient	Energy in Kcal
1 g Proteins	4
1 g Fat	9
1 g Carbohydrates	4

2.2   Particle Swarm Optimization

Particle Swarm Optimization (PSO) algorithm was utilized for the generation and automation of diets. This algorithm proposed by Kennedy and Eberhart in 1995 [7] is based on the behavior of the animals (swarm) and helps to find the best value in a space of search. It is composed by particles that are in charge of finding the best result. The space of search is divided with swarms and represents where the algorithm is going to look for the value. The PSO algorithm has three different parameters that help to reach the goal. The parameters are the inertia, the maximum velocity and the number of particles in the swarm. These values define the characteristics of the swarm and represent the way that the algorithm follows to reach the goal.

The PSO algorithm uses a collection of particles that move around the search space based on the best past location and the best location of the whole swarm. The velocity with the particle moves in each iteration is updated by using Eq. 13, where $v_i(t+1)$ is the new velocity for the particle i, $v_i(t)$ is the actual velocity at time t, c_1 is the weighing coefficient for the personal best position, c_2 is the weighting coefficient for the global best position, $p_i(t)$ is the position of particle i at time t, p_i^{best} represents the best position of particle i, p_{gbest} is the best position of the entire swarm, r is the function $rand()$ that generates a number in the interval $[0, 1]$.

$$v_i(t+i) = v_i(t) + c_1 r(p_i^{best} - p_i(t)) + c_2 r(p_{gbest} - p_i(t)) \tag{13}$$

$$p_i^{best}(t+1) = \begin{cases} p_i^{best} & \text{if } f(p_i(t+1)) > p_{gbest} \\ p_i(t+1) & \text{if } f(p_i(t+1)) \leq p_{gbest} \end{cases} \tag{14}$$

$$p_{gbest} = minp_i^{best}, i\forall\{1, N\} \tag{15}$$

$$p_i(t+1) = p_i(t) + v_i(t) \tag{16}$$

In a minimization problem, the personal best position at time $t+1$ is calculate by Eq. 14. The global best position is calculated with Eq. 15 where N is the number of particles in the swarm. The particle new position $p_i(t+1)$ is updated using Eq. 16.

Algorithm 1 Pseudo-code of PSO

Initialize the particles position in the swarm
Evaluate the initial position in the objective function
while *stopping criteria not met* **do**
    find personal best position for each particle
    find global best position
    find the new velocities of the particles
    Update the new position of the particles
    Evaluate the new position in the objective function

end

The Algorithm 1 describe the general steps of the PSO algorithm.

3 Proposed Methodology

The propose methodology is divided in 4 steps and tries to generate automatic diets by applying a Particle Swarm Optimization algorithm. The first step defines the way on obtaining the nutritional information of the equivalent portions of food. The second step build the fitness function which measure the quality of the designed diet. The third step was is focused on the codification of the solution. Finally, taking into acche solutions generated with PSO, the final result is a balance diet based on a nutritional manual. In this section this steps are described in detail.

3.1   Database Information

The data used to calculate the fitness function in PSO algorithm, was obtained from a .csv (coma separated value) file queried of the data source that contains the index of the equivalent portion of food, quantity of energy in Kcal on the equivalent portion of food, quantity of protein, carbohydrates, fat in grams and the cost in Mexican pesos (MXN). In every iteration of the algorithm, the solution represented as a 24 index array, is evaluated in the fitness function, every index is searched in the data source and pull the information to calculate the fitness. At the end of the iterations, the best solution is codified as the final result by querying to the data base in order to know all the details about each index corresponding to a food, such as food name description, portion and quantity of food to consume.

3.2   Fitness Function

As the Caloric Restricted Diet Problem defined is a restricted optimization, the PSO algorithm just consider restriction for the bounds of the values the restriction variable could take, they do not deal with other type of constraints, but the method of penalty functions [3] provides a way to solve constrained optimization problems using algorithms for unconstrained problems. That is why the fitness function used by the algorithm to solve the optimization problem will be a penalized objective function, would then be the unpenalized objective function plus a penalty defined as Eq. 17, the penalty function will be Static Penalty Function as stated in [3] to handle these constraints.

$$min| \sum_i x_i - Kcal| + \sum_k C_k \delta_k \forall k \in \{1,..K\} \tag{17}$$

C_k represent a constant imposed for violation of constraint k, $\delta_k = 1$ if constraint k is violated, otherwise $\delta_k = 0$ and K is the number of constraints in the problem, in this case are four, three constraints for the macronutrients restriction and one for the cost restriction.

3.3   Particle Representation

The solution will be represented as a list of 24 different integers representing an index of a equivalent portion of foods, classified by food groups as seen in Fig. 1 that must be eaten during a day in the different meals.

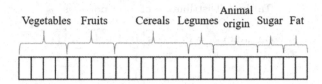

Fig. 1. Structure of the particle in terms of different food groups

3.4 Diet Design

The structure of the diet design was based on a nutrition manual published by Instituto Mexicano del Seguro Social (IMSS) [12]. Table 3 show the distribution of the equivalent portions of food. Table 4 list the distribution of the food groups through the meals that must be consumed during the day.

It is recommended to have certain number of equivalent portions of foods [12]. In Table 3 it is set an approximation of the number of portions.

Table 3. Portions of food

Food group	# of equivalent portions
Vegetables	4–5
Fruits	3–5
Cereals	6–11
Legumes	1–2
Animal origin	2–5
Milk	1–3
Fat	1–2
Sugar	1–2

According with the average of a caloric restricted diet that is between 1200 Kcal and 2000 Kcal [11], 24 portions of food could meet the requirements with the following distribution of meals: Breakfast (B), Snack 1 (S1), Lunch (L), Snack 2 (S2) and Dinner (D) in order to eat in a balanced and healthy way.

In this distribution, Milk group is considered as part of animal origin food group according with the SR database [1].

The result will be a diet plan with 24 equivalent portions of food sorted in 5 different meals according with Table 4.

Table 4. Distribution of food portions

Food group	#Portions	B	S1	L	S2	D
Vegetables	4	1		2		1
Fruits	4	1	1	1		1
Cereals	6	2		2	1	1
Legumes	2	1				1
Animal origin	4	1		2		1
Fat	2	1		1		
Sugar	2	1				1
TOTAL	24					

4 Experimental Results

In other to evaluate the accuracy of this methodology, it was used a dataset from the United States Department of Agriculture Agricultural Research Service USDA National Nutrient Database for Standard Reference (SR) [1] as the information source about nutritional data of foods in its last update of March of 2018. It contains data on 7793 food items and up to 150 food components. The source provides the information food that represents a portion of 100 g of the item, but also provides the information for an equivalent portion of the food, that is the information used for this paper. SR presents a large variety of food and drinks categories including alcoholic beverage, baby food, fast food, restaurant foods (foods from a specific provider). These categories where not considered into the 7 food groups present in this research. The considered categories are listed in Table 5 with the name of the food group that belongs to and the number of foods in the group.

The cost of the food is obtained by the INEGI [5] that is the monthly price average in MXN of the products. The prices used in this work are queried from the last semester of the 2018.

These experiments were performed on a Windows 10 computer with Intel Core i7 7500U CPU with 2.70 GHz clock and 8 GB of Ram memory. PSO was implement and compiled in Java 8.

As already mentioned in this work, the PSO algorithm has three different parameters, the inertia was configured in the set {0.4, 0.6, 0.8, 0.099}, the maximum velocity was varied in the set {0.9, 1.5, 10}, the values for C_1 and C_2 were set as 0.9 by default for all the experiments and the number of particles in the swarm was 20. In order to choose the best and worst value, the average and the standard deviation for each configuration, the program was repeated 20 times. The basal metabolic rate was configured as 1800 Kcal with a restriction of 135 g of protein, 40 g of fat, 225 g of carbohydrates and a budget of $200 MXN.

The parameters definition for each experiments are listed in Table 6 and results of the experiments are shown in Table 7. Each row of the tables corresponds 20 repetitions of an experiments with the same configuration. The third

Table 5. Distribution of food portions

Food category in SR	Food group	Symbol	#
Vegetables and Vegetable Products	Vegetables	V	767
Fruits and Fruit Juices	Fruits	F	345
Breakfast Cereals	Cereals	C	874
Baked Products			
Cereal Grains and Pasta			
Legumes and Legume Products	Legumes	L	425
Nut and Seed Products			
Sausages and Luncheon Meats	Animal origin and Milk	A	2824
Pork Products			
Beef Products			
Finfish and Shellfish Products			
Lamb, Veal, and Game Products			
Poultry Products			
Dairy and Egg Products			
Fats and Oils	Fats	F	214
Sweets	Sugar	S	357

column of the parameters definition table represent the value for inertia and the fourth one is the value for the parameter of velocity. The second column of Table 7 shows the average of the 20 experiments with that configuration of parameters, the third and fourth column represents the best and worst result in the 20 experiments for the configuration. The last column is the standard deviation.

Figure 2 shows the evolution of the fitness through the iterations in two test realized with the parameters of the second configuration that generated the best results that are shown on Table 6. The result 1 started with a fitness of 2074 and finished with the best fitness of 165. And the result 2 started with a fitness of 1628 and finished with the best fitness of 172. For the different configurations the best results were closed to the expected caloric goal. And the worst results did not achieve the caloric goal in 1000 iterations. Although good results were obtained that were very close to the solution, it can also be mentioned that results were found that did not meet the stop criteria. The solution exceeded the acceptable error rate of 10%. This can be due to the configuration of the velocity at which the particle moved in the search space, which was not fast enough in some tests to fill a solution with the error percentage. It is present the final result of a generated diet by the algorithm, Table 8 shows a list of 24 food, divided in the five meals that must be consume per day generated by the algorithm as a solution. Table 9 shows the cost and kcal for each food in the generated solution.

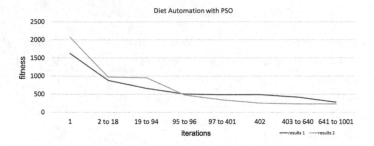

Fig. 2. Experimental results comparison

Table 6. Parameter definition

Parameter			
#	Number of particles	Inertia	Max velocity
1	20	0.4	0.9
2	20	0.4	1.5
3	20	0.4	10
4	20	0.6	0.9
5	20	0.6	1.5
6	20	0.6	10
7	20	0.8	0.9
8	20	0.8	1.5
9	20	0.8	10
10	20	0.99	0.9
11	20	0.99	1.5
12	20	0.99	10

Table 7. Results of the experiments with 12 different parameter configuration

Number of $Kcal$ generated			
#	Average	Best	Worst	Standard deviation
1	1888.1703	1817.817	1978.15	55.2001265
2	1906.02555	1799.9715	2123.639	96.3897121
3	1899.75943	1805.956	2084.005	96.7634151
4	1903.38748	1795.641	2065.5345	77.5908577
5	1917.22255	1805.984	2106.559	73.6772987
6	1876.86038	1801.433	2052.0695	72.9780086
7	1906.4946	1796.8525	2012.086	56.1456722
8	1897.06253	1805.3175	2086.0765	67.8421622
9	1871.70098	1793.4955	1955.4635	51.4958125
10	1891.84368	1794.183	2028.1615	67.2637242
11	1881.62213	1797.112	2033.8975	79.5025364
12	1906.75193	1806.9165	2116.425	101.598672

Table 8. Diet generated example

Meal	#	Food description	Portion	Unit
Breakfast	1	RAMBUTAN, CND, SYRUP, PK	1	cup
	2	COOKIES, VANILLA, WAFERS, LOWER FAT	1	large
	3	WAFFLE, BTTRMLK, FRZ, RTH, TSTD	1	waffle round (4″ dia)
	4	PINE NUTS, PINYON, DRIED	10	nuts
	5	YOGURT, PLN, SKIM MILK	1	container (6 oz)
	6	SYRUPS, TABLE BLENDS, PANCAKE, W/2% MAPLE, W/K	1	tbsp
	7	OIL, CORN, INDUSTRIAL & RTL, ALLPURP, SALAD OR COOKING	1	tsp
	8	COWPEAS, LEAFY TIPS, CKD, BLD, DRND, WO/SALT	1	cup, chopped
Snack 1	9	LEMON JUICE, RAW	1	wedge yields
Lunch	10	MUSHROOMS, SHIITAKE, DRIED	1	mushroom
	11	ARROWHEAD, CKD, BLD, DRND, W/SALT	1	corm, medium
	12	LEMON JUC FROM CONC, CND OR BTLD	1	tbsp
	13	COOKIES, OATMEAL, COMMLY PREP, SOFT-TYPE	1	cookie
	14	BISCUITS, PLN OR BTTRMLK, PREP FROM RECIPE	1	biscuit (2-1/2″ dia)
	15	BEEF, RND, TOP RND, LN & FAT, 0″ FAT, SEL, CKD, BRSD	3	oz
	16	BEEF, TOP SIRLOIN, STEAK, LN & FAT, 1/8″ FAT, CHOIC, CKD, BRLD	3	oz
	17	OIL, INDUSTRIAL, PALM KERNEL, CONFECTION FAT	1	tsp
Snack 2	18	MUFFINS, WHEAT BRAN, TOASTER-TYPE W/RAISINS, TSTD	1	muffin, toaster
Dinner	19	SPINACH, CKD, BLD, DRND, WO/SALT	1	cup
	20	LONGANS, RAW	1	fruit without refuse
	21	BREAD, WHITE, COMMLY PREP (INCL SOFT BREAD CRUMBS)	1	slice, thin
	22	BEANS, KIDNEY, RED, MATURE SEEDS, CKD, BLD, WO/SALT	1	cup
	23	CHICKEN, BROILERS OR FRYERS, DK MEAT, DRUMSTK, MEAT OLY, CKD, BRSD	1	drum- stick with skin
	24	ICE CREAMS, CHOC, LT	1	serving

Table 9. Cost and energy of the generated diet

Meal	#	Price	Kcal	
Breakfast	1	$29.75	175.48	Kcal
	2	$0.50	26.46	Kcal
	3	$20.00	101.97	Kcal
	4	$2.50	6.29	Kcal
	5	$9.30	95.2	Kcal
	6	$3.00	53	Kcal
	7	$0.50	40.5	Kcal
	8	$2.12	11.66	Kcal
Snack 1	9	$3.00	1.298	Kcal
Lunch	10	$2.50	10.656	Kcal
	11	$1.50	9.36	Kcal
	12	$3.00	2.55	Kcal
	13	$3.00	61.35	Kcal
	14	$2.00	211.8	Kcal
	15	$13.43	170	Kcal
	16	$20.00	218.45	Kcal
	17	$3.00	39.78	Kcal
Snack 2	18	$5.00	106.42	Kcal
Dinner	19	$7.95	41.4	Kcal
	20	$5.00	1.92	Kcal
	21	$1.50	53.2	Kcal
	22	$3.00	224.79	Kcal
	23	$5.70	156.45	Kcal
	24	$5.00	127.16	Kcal
	Total	*$152.25*	*1947.144*	*Kcal*

5   Conclusions

The proposed methodology in order to generate automatic diets considering the physical characteristics of the user to obtain the basal metabolic rate in terms of the Harris-Benedict equation for achieve the design of an accurate diet was presented in this paper. The design process is conducted by means of the particle swarm optimization algorithm (PSO) using the equivalent portions of food that allow to optimize the quantity of calories with restrictions of macronutrients and price. The result show that the diet automation based on PSO is capable of generate balanced diets with a low percentage error and a considerable effectiveness. It is important to mention that the PSO algorithm also find an acceptable solution with less than 1000 iterations. Nowadays, we are evaluating different swarm intelligence techniques that allow to find the best diets with few iterations such as the ABC algorithm as presented in [8]. Furthermore, we are also exploring a multi-objective approach to include different goals to design a better diet.

Acknowledgment. The authors would like to thank Universidad La Salle México for the economic support under grant number NEC-10/18.

References

1. U.S.D. of Agriculture Agricultural Research Service (USDA): USDA food composition databases, April 2018. https://ndb.nal.usda.gov/ndb/search/list?home=true
2. del Carmen Iarritu Pérez, M.: Elaboracin de una dieta. http://www.edu.xunta.gal/centros/ieschapela/system/files/ELABORACI%C3%93N%20DIETAS_1.pdf
3. Coit, D.W., Smith, A.E.: Penalty functions. Section C 5.2 of Handbook of Evolutionary Computation (1995)
4. Food and Agriculture Organization of the United Nations (FAO): Macronutrientes y micronutrientes (2015). http://www.fao.org/elearning/Course/NFSLBC/es/story_content/external_files/Macronutrientes%20y%20micronutrientes.pdf
5. Instituto Nacional de Estadstica y Geografía (INEGI): Consulta en línea. consulta de precios promedio, July 2018. http://www3.inegi.org.mx/sistemas/inp/preciospromedio/
6. Harris, J.A., Benedict, F.: A biometric study of human basal metabolism. Proc. Natl. Acad. Sci. USA **4**(12), 370–373 (1918)
7. Eberhart, R., Kennedy, J.: Particle swarm optimization, pp. 1942–1948. IEEE (1995)
8. López-López, M., Zamora, A., Vazquez, R.A.: Automatic diet generation by artificial bee colony algorithm. In: Tan, Y., Shi, Y., Niu, B. (eds.) ICSI 2019. LNCS, vol. 11655, pp. 299–309. Springer, Cham (2019). https://doi.org/10.1007/978-3-030-26369-0_28
9. Lv, Y.: Combined quantum particle swarm optimization algorithm for multiobjective nutritional diet decision making. Harbin University of Commerce, Harbin, China (2009)
10. Lv, Y.: Multi-objective nutritional diet optimization based on quantum algorithm. Harbin University of Commerce, Harbin, China (2009)
11. Pérez Lizaur, A.B., Marván Laborde, L., Palicios, B.: Sistema Mexicano de Alimentos Equivalentes, 4th edn. Fomento de Nutricin y Salud, A.C., Mexico City (2014)
12. Instituto Mexicano del Seguro Social (IMMS): Guía de Alimentos para la Población Mexicana. Secretaria de Salud (2010)
13. Stigler, G.: The cost of subsistence. J. Farm Econ. **27**, 2 (1945)
14. Yanping, W.G.: Applications of MOGA in nutritional diet for diabetic patients. Henan University of Technology, College of Information Science and Technology, Zhengzhou, China (2009)

Solving Dynamic Combinatorial Optimization Problems Using a Probabilistic Distribution as Self-adaptive Mechanism in a Genetic Algorithm

Cesar J. Montiel Moctezuma[1], Jaime Mora[2],
and Miguel Gonzalez-Mendoza[2(✉)]

[1] Instituto Mexicano del Transporte, Querétaro, Mexico
cmontielmoctezuma@gmail.com
[2] Tecnologico de Monterrey, Monterrey, Mexico
{jmora,mgonza}@tec.mx

Abstract. In recent years, the interest to solve dynamic combinatorial optimization problems has increased. Metaheuristic algorithms have been used to find good solutions in a reasonably low time, in addition, the use of self-adaptive strategies has increased considerably because they have proved to be a good option to improve performance in these algorithms. In this research, a self-adaptive mechanism is developed to improve the performance of the genetic algorithm for dynamic combinatorial problems, using the strategy of genotype-phenotype mapping and probabilistic distributions. Results demonstrate the capability of the mechanism to help algorithms to adapt in dynamic environments.

Keywords: Genetic algorithm · Self-adaptive mechanism · Dynamic combinatorial optimization problems

1 Introduction

In the last two decades, the interest for the solution of combinatorial optimization problems in dynamic environments has greatly increased, and to solve them researchers have developed mechanisms that help metaheuristics to adapt to changes that exist during the execution of these algorithms.

This kind of problems can be represented by many production and services problems, including the reduction of the product's cost and the improvement of the company's profit. Furthermore, minimizing the transportation cost is one of the cost reduction methods in which the products are transported from the origin place to the destination(s) place(s) with minimum cost [1].

Even defining Dynamic Combinatorial Optimization Problems (DCOP's or Dynamic COP's) is a challenging task because in real problems as transportation of mercancy there are a lot of variables to consider which cannot be identified until work with real cases. In general, researchers usually define optimization problems that change over time as Dynamic Problems, Time-Dependent Problems, or Dynamic Optimization Problems [2]. In existing metaheuristics studies, the considered problems

© Springer Nature Switzerland AG 2019
L. Martínez-Villaseñor et al. (Eds.): MICAI 2019, LNAI 11835, pp. 330–349, 2019.
https://doi.org/10.1007/978-3-030-33749-0_27

are either defined as a sequence of static problems linked up by some dynamic rules or as a problem that have time-dependent parameters in its mathematical model.

Usually, for stationary Combinatorial Optimization Problems (COP's), the goal of a metaheuristic algorithm is to find the global optimum as fast and precise as possible, and the performance measures used to evaluate an algorithm are the convergence speed and the rate to get the optimum over multiple runs.

However, the goal of metaheuristics to solve Dynamic COP's turns from to find the global optimum as fast as possible [3], to track the optimum as close as possible to real time on dynamic environments; in several cases, the algorithm needs to detect the changes, and then, it needs to track the changing optimum (local optimum or global optimum). In additions, in environments where there exists a correlation between changes, the optimization algorithm needs to learn from its previous experience to improve the search in the solution space. Otherwise, the optimization process after each change will be explained like the process to solve different problems starting from the old population.

Heuristics and metaheuristics are methods that have been used to solve different problems in logistics as cost reduction in supply chain distribution [4, 5] and facility location problems [6], even in manufacturing like optimization of manufacturing systems [7, 8] and cellular manufacturing models [9].

This paper focuses on theoretical dynamic combinatorial problems to demonstrate the ability of the mechanism to adapt in dynamic environments which could describe the behavior of a real problem. In this case, the mechanism was implemented in a travelling salesman problem which can be generalized in several problems such as vehicle routing problem, and it is used in several areas of logistics and manufacturing.

2 Dynamic Problems

Many dynamic test problems have been used in the literature [10] which have features and can be classified into different groups based on the following criteria:

- **Time-Linkage:** Whether the future behavior of the problem depends on the current solution found by an algorithm or not.
- **Predictability:** Whether the generated changes are predictable or not.
- **Visibility:** Whether the changes are visible to the optimization algorithm and whether the changes can be detected by using just a few detectors.
- **Constrained problem:** Whether the problem is constrained or not.
- **Number of objectives:** Whether the problem has single objective or multiple objectives.
- **Types of changes:** Detailed explanation of how changes occur in the search space.
- **Cyclicity:** Whether the changes are cyclic/recurrent in the search space or not.
- **Periodicity:** Whether the changes area periodical or not.
- **Factors that change:** Changes may involve parameters of objective functions, variables domain, variables number, constraints, among others.

2.1   Dynamic Combinatorial Optimization Problems

The problems defined in this research are Travelling Salesman Problem (TSP) and One-Max problem, which have been considered in their static and dynamic form to extend the analysis of several assessments between a set of configurations for genetic algorithm and a self-adaptive mechanism proposed implemented in genetic algorithm to improve the search of solutions in dynamic environments. The algorithm will be explained in next section.

One Max Problem. The One-Max Problem (or Bit Counting) is a simple problem consisting in maximizing the number of ones of a bit-string. Formally, this problem can be described as finding a string $\vec{x} = x_1, x_2, \ldots, x_n$, with $x_i \in 1$, that maximizes the following equation:

$$F(\vec{x}) = \sum x_i^n i = 1 \tag{1}$$

Many authors, studying this problem, define this problem as a simple unimodal function and for a simple hill-climber using a traditional bit-flipping Neighborhood Search (NS) operator. However, a GA does not search over this simple 'Hamming' landscape. It is easy to analyze the landscape induced by a traditional NS operator, but the position is a little more complicated for the operators normally used by a GA, this is the reason of why this problem is important.

   This is the simplest problem that can be selected, to convert this problem of a static environment to a dynamic environment is needed to change the search, it means, if the objective function is to find most of 1's in the solution, the change will be to find the most of 0 s in the solution. This causes that the algorithms start to converge in determined generations, and when the change appears, all the solutions that have a good fitness, they are changing by the worst solution because they have the worst fitness in that moment.

Travelling Salesman Problem. Dynamic traveling salesman problems (DTSP) have a wide range of real applications, especially in the optimization of dynamic networks, like network planning and designing, load-balance routing, and traffic management.

   An example of a DTSP is defined in [11] as a TSP with a dynamic cost (distance) matrix as follow:

$$D(t) = d_{i,j}(t)_{n*n} \tag{2}$$

where: $d_{i,j}(t)$ is the cost from city i to city j, and n is the number of cities. DTSP can be defined as $f(x, t)$, the objective of DTSP is to find a minimum-cost route containing all cities at time t. It can be described as:

$$f(x, t) = Min \sum_{i=1}^{n} d_{ti,ti+1}(t) \tag{3}$$

where: $x_i \in 1, 2, \ldots, n$ denotes the i-th city in the solution such that $x_n + 1 = x1$ and, if i is different of j, and x_i different of x_j.

This problem have been used in different manufacturing problems such as distribution and routing problems [12–14] and in some cases to optimize facilities [15] and machines location [16].

3 Solution Algorithms

3.1 Genetic Algorithm

Genetic Algorithms (GA's) have been developed by J. Holland in the 1970 s (University of Michigan, USA) to understand the adaptive processes of natural systems [17].

GA's are performed in three steps: the first one is focused in the creation of population of candidate solutions generated randomly according with the objective function of the problem. The second step is focused on the evaluation of individuals according with the objective function. Finally, in the last step, parents will be selected of the population, then is applied the crossover operator to these parents to build new solutions called children, then, the mutation operator is applied to these children. The new children population will be the population for the new generation of parents, and this process will be repeated until a stop criterion is met [18]. This process is shown in the Fig. 1.

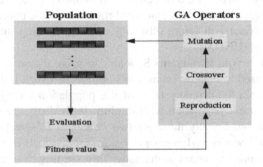

Fig. 1. Generic genetic algorithm process

3.2 Adaptive and Self-adaptive Methods

It is well known that the choice of parameter settings for metaheuristic algorithms has a dramatic impact on their search performance and this has attracted considerable interest in various mechanisms that in some way attempt to automatically adjust the algorithms parameters for a given problem. Adaptive and self-adaptive methods are used to solve problems that have dynamic features.

In [19], there is a classification given according to the levels of adaptation or the mechanics that they used. In the classification about mechanics exist: static, deterministic, adaptive and self-adaptive. In static the users that develop the algorithm define the parameters values manually; in deterministic is used a heuristic function to define the values; in adaptive mechanic, a heuristic function uses feedback while the algorithm is running; and in self-adaptive, the parameters are encoded as part of individuals allowing the algorithm to operate directly on the parameters.

In self-adapt levels exist environment, population, individual and component. On environment level, the changes will be on the fitness function; on population level, the changes will be on the individuals set; on individual level, changes are directly related with each individual; and the last one, component level, changes are made on components of each individual, for example genes in genetic algorithm.

Adaptation and self-adaptation have been explored over the majority of genetic algorithm components, but these mechanisms do not have relevant improvements on all of them. The most considerable improvement is in mutation and crossover operations, where rules or new genetic operators are specified to preserve the population distribution and a degree of diversity in future offspring. Ingo Rechenberg proposed the first deterministic adaptation rule for the mutation parameter, known as the 1/5 rule, that indicates that in each generation must exist 1/5 of total genes mutated. A propose of the use of a crossover operator named simulated binary reproduction (SBX) on real genetic algorithms is presented by Deb and Beyer in [20], where SBX creates children solutions in proportion to the difference in parent solution, their purpose is to obtain similar results as evolutionary strategies, but using genetic algorithms. Another work is [21] which uses a genetic operator known as multiple crosses per couple (MCPC) in which the number of crossovers allowed per individual is encoded in the chromosome. Similar results are obtained via the design of self-adaptive crossover operator, specifying rules such as preservation of the statistical moments in the population distribution and the degree of diversity in future offspring in [22], defining uniformly unimodal distribution crossover (UNDX).

In [23] is used GA with Immigrants Schemes to solve dynamic routing problems, these schemes are based in random immigrants approach, which is a quite natural and simple way to maintain the diversity level of the population through replacing some individuals of the current population with random individuals, called random immigrants, every generation. Usually there are two strategies to select individuals in the population that should be replaced: replacing random individuals or replacing the worst ones. They used Memory Schemes at the same time, in this case it works by storing useful information from the current environment, either implicitly through redundant representations or explicitly by storing good (usually best) solutions of the current population in an extra memory. The stored information can be reused later in new environments. Finally they build a hybrid between immigrants and memory schemes.

4 Mechanism Description

The proposed mechanism is based on the idea of a genotype-phenotype mapping function which generates random values for each parameter in the algorithms according to a Weibull probability distribution. This mechanism belongs to self-adaptive methods in the individual level. Before to explain how the mechanism works is needed to explain genotype-phenotype mapping idea and how the Weibull probability distribution works.

4.1   Genotype-Phenotype Mapping

The genotype and phenotype terms were created by Wilhelm Johannsen in 1911. Genotype is the complete hereditary information of an organism, even if it is not expressed. The phenotype is a property observed in the organism, such as morphology, development or behavior. This distinction is fundamental in the study of trait heredity and its evolution. Map a set of genotypes to a set of phenotypes is sometimes referred to as a genotype-phenotype mapping. Genotype of an organism is an important factor in the development of its phenotype, but it is not the only one. Even two organisms with the same genotypes normally differ in their phenotypes [24].

The first studies about genotype-phenotype mapping in computation are related with genetic programming in the Banzhaf and Keller's work [25], they focused their work in Motoo Kimura's bio molecular research in 1968, where is postulated that changes in molecules genotypes are phenotypically neutral, it means, several genotypes codified the same phenotype. These research is called as neutral theory of molecular evolution of Motoo Kimura. Banzhaf and Keller proposed a genotype-phenotype mapping for genetic programming where they modified the non-viable genotypes to correct them with others nearby. An example of this idea used in genetic algorithms is show in [26], where authors described a strategy to guide the search according with the mutation. The evolutive advantage is given by some synonyms mutate towards more significant phenotypes than others.

4.2   Weibull Distribution Function

Probability distribution functions were used to define the mapping function in which a genotype represents a phenotype, these functions were used indirectly to generate values for each parameter in the algorithms, and this is the reason to explain each section of the proposed mechanism.

A probability distribution is a mathematical function that can be thought of as providing the probabilities of occurrence of different possible outcomes in an experiment, it means, the probability distribution is a description of a random phenomenon in terms of the probabilities of events.

The Weibull distribution is the most commonly used distribution for modeling reliability data or survival data. It has two parameters, which allow it to handle increasing, decreasing or constant failure-rates. It is defined as:

$$f_x(x) = \begin{cases} k \frac{x^{k-1}}{\lambda^k} e^{-(x/\lambda)^k} & \text{if } x \geq 0 \\ 0 & \text{if } x < 0 \end{cases} \tag{4}$$

where $k > 0$ is the shape parameter and $\lambda \geq 0$ is the scale parameter of the distribution. Its complementary cumulative distribution function is a stretched exponential function. If the quantity x is a time-to-failure, the Weibull distribution gives a distribution for which the failure rate is proportional to a power of time. The shape parameter, k, is that power plus one, and so this parameter can be interpreted directly as follows:

- A value of k < 1 indicates that the failure rate decreases over time. This happens if there is significant infant mortality, or defective items failing early and the failure rate decreasing over time as the defective items are weeded out of the population.
- A value of k = 1 indicates that the failure rate is constant over time. This might suggest random external events are causing mortality, or failure.
- A value of k > 1 indicates that the failure rate increases with time. This happens if there is an aging process, or parts that are more likely to fail as time goes on.

Figure 2 shows how this distribution changes according with different values for each parameter.

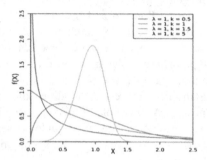

Fig. 2. Weibull distribution graph for different configurations on each parameter

4.3   Proposed Mechanism

The algorithm is based on the idea of a genotype-phenotype mapping (explained above) function which generates random values for each parameter in the algorithms according to a Weibull probability distribution.

To select the best probability distribution, 3 different distributions were tested: normal, exponential and Weibull distributions. The Weibull distribution function got the best results, because it is quite simple to manipulate the values of its parameters to generate many forms of this probability distribution, and this helps the adaptation of the parameters of the algorithms. This is the reason why Weibull distribution is the only one mentioned on this research.

Generating Individuals. First, to generate each individual for algorithms is needed to consider two aspects, the first one is the solution size, it represents the original size for a solution that solves the problem; the second aspect is focused in the considered size for the Weibull distribution parameters, this represents a part of an individual which contains the parameters k and λ to generate a Weibull distribution (see Fig. 3).

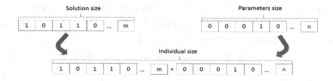

Fig. 3. Representation of individuals

The segment of the individual which consider the parameters of the Weibull distribution needs two main features: (a) The size needs to be even. (b) The size is represented in binary code. The first feature is defined because this segment is divided in two parts the first part represents k and the second part represents λ, and both parameters need the same quantity of binary elements to map the values in decimal integers. The feature (b) is defined because is easier to work with binary values in most of the algorithms, it is recommended that the parameters representation is also binary, for this is needed a mapping function that transforms binary values into integer decimal values for each distribution parameter (see Fig. 4).

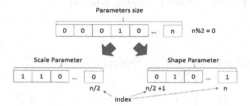

Fig. 4. Representation of parameters segment of an individual into Weibull parameters

To define the table size of the mapping function to transform the parameters, it is necessary to define the lower and upper limits that will be used for the Weibull parameters; the minimum recommended value for the parameters k and λ is 1, to avoid the form that this distribution has between the 0–1 values, because it tends to be a logarithmic distribution, and it does not give good results for mechanism purposes; the upper limit value is recommended to use values according to the number of binary bits to be used, if you want to handle only 3 bits it is recommended to use a limit of 8, if you want to use 4 bits a limit of 16, for 5 bits a limit of 32, and so on, this is to avoid normalizing from decimal to binary values (see Fig. 5).

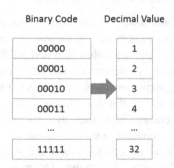

Fig. 5. Mapping function to transform parameters

Generating Random Values with Weibull Distribution. With the parameters k and λ is possible to generate a Weibull distribution just is needed to substitute this values in the Eq. 4, then with the distribution is easy to get the Cumulative Distribution Function (CDF). The CDF is used to generate random numbers in a range defined by the same Weibull distribution through the Inverse Transformation method.

Inverse Transformation method is a method that used the cumulative distribution function F(x) of the Weibull distribution, being that F(x) is defined in the interval (0, 1), it is possible to generate a uniform random number R and try to determine the value of the random variable for which the cumulative distribution is equal to R, it means that, simulated value of the random variable that follows a probability distribution f(x) which is determined by solving the following equation:

$$F(x) = R \rightarrow x = F^{-1}(R) \tag{5}$$

And for the Weibull distribution the inverse function is:

$$F(x) = 1 - e^{-(x/\lambda)^k} \rightarrow x = \lambda[-Ln(1 - u)]^{\frac{1}{k}} \tag{6}$$

where u is a random value $u \in U(0, 1)$.

Generating Random Parameters for Algorithms. Finally, the random values will be defined between a range delimited by the same Weibull distribution, which is usually related to the limits of the values of the parameters k and λ. Now it is necessary to generate a mapping function that transforms the obtained random value to a value that represents a parameter of the algorithms, in GA, the parameters that the algorithm used are commonly probabilities and this is the reason that the parameters need to be mapped between 0 and 1 values.

The mapping function is defined to evaluate and to obtain the parameter values for the algorithm. The value obtained from the CDF is divided by the maximum value that can be obtained in the Weibull distribution, this is to normalize it in the range of 0 and 1, and this value is the new one for each parameter.

Mechanism in Genetic Algorithm. Genetic algorithms have two main operators, crossover and mutation, the parameters can obtain values between 0 and 1. The idea of how the mechanism works on this algorithm is based on the mutation and crossover operators for binary individuals, it means that the parameters segment on each individual will evolve with this genetic operators on each generation, but the operators will focus on evolve this segment such as the algorithm were solving binary problems; if the problem is defined in a non-binary space, such as combinatorial problems as the TSP, the individuals segment which contains a problem solution will be solved with genetic operators focused on this kind of problem, and the segment which represent the parameters will be solved like a binary problem. The pseudo-code that represents this idea is explained as follows, the mechanism is implemented to update parameters on each individual with the code in blue:

```
PROCEDURE GeneticAlgorithm:
  population = GeneratePopulation()
  REPEAT
    FOR population:size/2 DO
      parents = SelectParents(population)
      childs = Crossover(parents)
      Mutation(children)
      UpdateParameters(children)
      Childpopulation <- children
    END FOR
  UNTIL stopCriterion
END PROCEDURE
FUNCTION Crossover(parents)
  crossoverProbabilityParent1 = GetParameter(parent1)
  crossoverProbabilityParent2 = GetParameter(parent2)
  IF   random < crossoverProbabilityParent1 AND
       random<crossoverProbabilityParent2 THEN
    CrossoverParents(parents)
  END IF
END FUNCTION
FUNCTION Mutation(children)
  mutationProbability = GetParameter(children)
  FOR elementInChromosome DO
    IF random < mutationProbability THEN
      Mutates(child.element)
    END IF
  END FOR
END FUNCTION
FUNCTION UpdateParameters(childs)
  crossoverProbabilityChild1 = GetParameter(child1)
  crossoverProbabilityChild2 = GetParameter(child2)
  mutationProbabilityChild1 = GetParameter(child1)
  mutationProbabilityChild2 = GetParameter(child2)
  IF random < crossoverProbabilityChild1 AND
     random < crossoverProbabilityChild2
    BinaryCrossover(children)
  END IF
  BinaryMutation(child1; mutaitonProbabilityChild1)
  BinaryMutation(child2; mutaitonProbabilityChild2)
END FUNCTION
```

5   Results

The implementations were tested and benchmarked in 2 experiments. In the first experiment the One-Max problem was tested, this problem was configured on an instance with 50 bits length. The second experiment was tested on TSP problem with TSPLib where 2 instances were obtained called "a280" and "ulysses22", the first one has 280 cities and the other one has 22 cities, the matrix distance is obtained with Euclidean distance between cities. On each dynamic instance, the changes were realized every 50 generations and every 300 generations. For both experiments, 100 runs were generated for each instance, and the average of the results were used to compare the algorithms. All algorithms were tested in a computer with Intel i7-4800MQ processor with 2.7 GHz and 16 GB RAM. Implementations were coded using Java version 8, jdk 1:8:092 and jre 1:8:0144.

The algorithms used to compare the mechanism proposed were selected by their results in an analysis realized previously through a Design of Experiments (DOE) to consider different configurations and prove which configuration(s) of genetic algorithms are the best to solve this kind of problems. The parameters used to generate these configurations were population, mutation probability and crossover probability. The values considered for each parameter on this DOE were:

- Mutation Probability = .1, .5 y .9
- Crossover Probability = .1, .5 y .9
- Population = 50, 150, 300

With these values were obtained 27 different configurations for the GA. The results obtained in the first experiment for these 27 algorithms are shown in Appendix A, in the Figures A1–A2 for a static environment and in the Figures A3–A4 for a dynamic environment. The results obtained in the second experiment are shown in the Figures A5–A6 for a static environment and Figures A7–A8 for a dynamic environment.

The algorithms were selected according to the best results obtained and the population with a balance between exploration and exploitation strategies, in Figures A9–A10 are shown the results of this analysis for One-Max problem and in Figures A11–A12 for TSP problem. On these graphs, a clustering strategy was used to identify the features of the algorithms with the best results for each problem. In One-Max problem the clusters with best results are orange cluster (static) and red cluster (dynamic). In TSP the clusters with best results are blue cluster (static) and red cluster (dynamic). The algorithms with better results are shown in the Table 1.

Table 1. Algorithms selected with the best best-average results to compete against the mechanism proposed

Algorithm	Problem	Population value	Cross over value	Mutation value
GA9	One-Max	300	.9	.1
GA18	One-Max	300	.9	.5
GA27	One-Max	300	.9	.9
GA1	Dynamic One-Max	50	.1	.1
GA10	Dynamic One-Max	50	.1	.5
GA19	Dynamic One-Max	50	.1	.9
GA19	TSP	50	.1	.9
GA20	TSP	150	.1	.9
GA21	TSP	300	.1	.9
GA11	Dynamic TSP	150	.1	.5
GA20	Dynamic TSP	150	.1	.9
GA21	Dynamic TSP	300	.1	.9

The parameters used to test the mechanism were mutation probability and crossover probability. The mechanism proposed was evaluated in static problems (See Figs. 6 and 7) and in dynamic problems, to ensure that it will have good results in static problems and not only in dynamic problems.

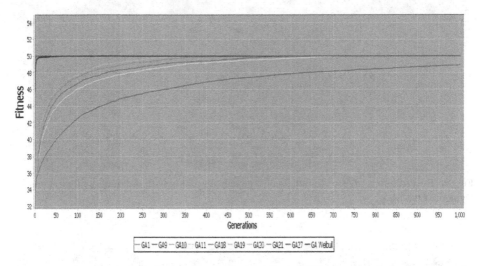

Fig. 6. Results of GA Weibull against genetic algorithm with different configurations for static One-Max

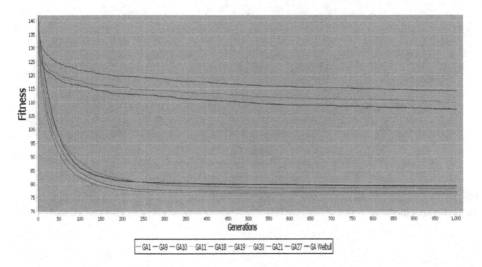

Fig. 7. Results of GA Weibull against genetic algorithm with different configurations for static TSP

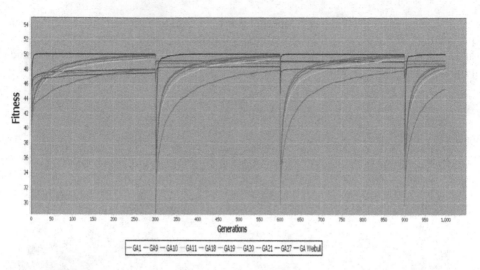

Fig. 8. Best solutions of GA Weibull against genetic algorithm with different configurations for Dynamic One-Max

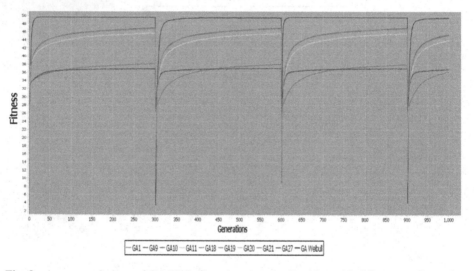

Fig. 9. Average solutions of GA Weibull against genetic algorithm with different configurations for Dynamic One-Max

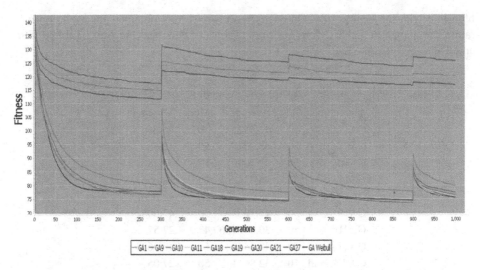

Fig. 10. Best solutions of GA Weibull against genetic algorithm with different configurations for Dynamic TSP

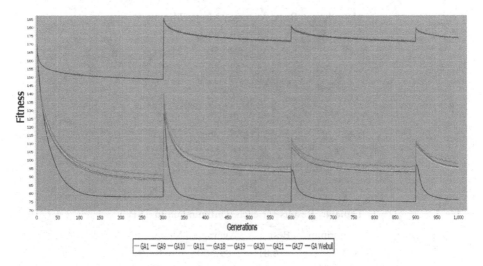

Fig. 11. Average solutions of GA Weibull against genetic algorithm with different configurations for Dynamic TSP

In Figs. 8, 9, 10 and 11 are represented the results about dynamic problems, in both cases the mechanism improves the genetic algorithm and it helps to track the optimal solution when a change occurs, in all graphics the mechanism is represented by the blue line with the best results. On each algorithm, results obtained for each configuration are shown in Table 2 for One Max, Table 3 Dynamic One Max, Table 4 TSP and Table 5 Dynamic TSP.

Table 2. Results for each configuration in One Max problem

Algorithm	Best	Average	Mode	Minimum
GA1	50	47.5922	50	46.64
GA9	50	48.2436	50	47.66
GA10	50	47.7099	50	47.28
GA11	50	45.2242	49	40.6667
GA18	50	48.252	50	48.0067
GA19	50	47.7065	50	47.6082
GA21	50	30.046166	47	27.57
GA27	50	48.2448	50	48.0633
GA Weibull	50	32.8611	50	27.05

Table 3. Results for each configuration in Dynamic One Max problem

Algorithm	Best	Average	Mode	Minimum
GA1	49	45.2046	49	42.1
GA9	50	36.8534	50	24.2
GA10	49	45.3747	49	42.87
GA11	48	44.0205	43	37.5267
GA18	50	36.8391	50	24.7533
GA19	49	45.3738	49	42.83
GA21	50	36.1885	50	22.2767
GA27	50	36.8146	50	24.8033
GA Weibull	50	49.4188	50	45.64

Table 4. Results for each configuration in TSP

Algorithm	Best	Average	Mode
GA1	76.8119	89.5805	76.8119
GA9	114.0008	146.4622	126.7976
GA10	76.1759	88.05	76.1759
GA11	76.3119	88.0503	76.3119
GA18	109.7748	146.1850	163.4686
GA19	75.5088	87.5741	75.5088
GA21	75.5088	87.6917	75.5088
GA27	107.2962	146.1011	125.7882
GA Weibull	75.3097	80.4664	79.1822

Table 5. Results for each configuration in Dynamic TSP

Algorithm	Best	Average	Mode
GA1	63.4885	97.7229	87.438
GA9	106.0332	173.1659	144.1324
GA10	66.1179	95.8859	78.0715
GA11	66.211	94.5666	76.374
GA18	94.6573	173.7578	214.5497
GA19	61.852	95.5419	70.1903
GA21	64.335	95.7753	77.8263
GA27	102.047	173.8176	140.1949
GA Weibull	61.6235	75.8967	79.2923

6 Discussion

The main conclusion is, at least for the proposed experiments, if genetic algorithm uses the mechanism proposed, it improves a lot the strategy to search optimal solutions in dynamic problems. When the problem is different, the mechanism does not have any problem to adapt when changes occur, it has the advantage to find the optimum to fast and it helps the population to converge to this value(s). When a change occur, it does not have any problem to get out of local optimum solution and to find another optimal solution, it indicates that the self-adaptation is responsible to change the diversification strategy by an intensification strategy when the algorithm needs to find solutions in new areas, moreover, it changes diversification by intensification when there not exist changes in the solution space and the algorithm needs to find solutions in the shortest possible time, the mechanism can manage the changes between these strategies because it increased or decreased the mutation and crossover probabilities according with needs of the algorithm. Furthermore, if the solution space has more than one optimal solutions, the mechanism improves the possibility to find them because the individuals in population do not depend on the others, due to each individual has an independent evolutive behavior.

Solutions demonstrates that mechanism improves the performance of the algorithms to solve these problems, and it indicates that it can be implemented in generalized problems as vehicle routing problems in some practical cases, just is needed to adjust the objective function, variables and restrictions according with the real problem.

As future work, this mechanism will be implemented in other algorithms and it will be used to solve more complex problems, besides, it will be used to modify another parameters such as population. Furthermore, it will be compared with other existing self-adaptive mechanism and it will be tested to solve vehicle routing problems in logistic and manufacturing real cases.

Appendix A

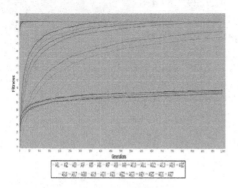

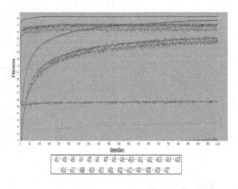

Fig. A1. Best solutions for static One-Max problem (50 bits);

Fig. A2. Average solutions for static One-Max problem (50 bits)

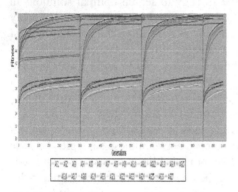

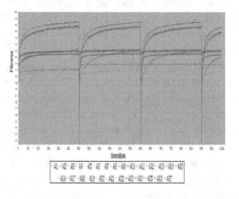

Fig. A3. Best solutions for dynamic One-Max problem (50 bits);

Fig. A4. Average solutions for dynamic One-Max problem (50 bits)

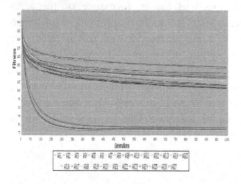

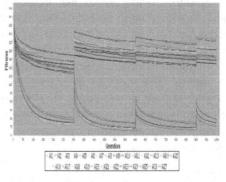

Fig. A5. Best solutions for static TSP problem (ulysses22);

Fig. A6. Average solutions for static TSP problem (ulysses22)

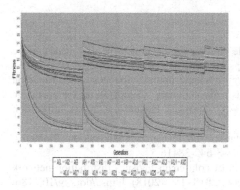

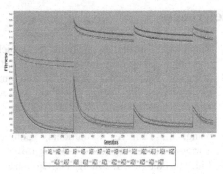

Fig. A7. Average solutions for dynamic TSP problem (ulysses22);

Fig. A8. Average solutions for dynamic TSP problem (ulysses22)

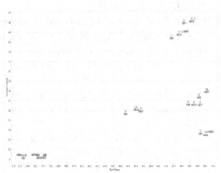

Fig. A9. Best-average results for static One-Max problem (maximization);

Fig. A10. Best-average results for dynamic One-Max problem (maximization)

Fig. A11. Best-average results for static TSP problem (minimization);

Fig. A12. Best-average results for dynamic TSP problem (minimization)

References

1. Majid, Y., Esmaile, K.: Solving the vehicle routing problem by a hybrid metaheuristic algorithm. J. Ind. Eng. Int. **8**, 11 (2012). https://doi.org/10.1186/2251-712X-8-11
2. Yang, S., Nguyen, T.T., Li, C.: Evolutionary dynamic optimization: test and evaluation environments. In: Yang, S., Yao, X. (eds.) Evolutionary Computation for Dynamic Optimization Problems. SCI, vol. 490, pp. 3–37. Springer, Heidelberg (2013). https://doi.org/10.1007/978-3-642-38416-5_1
3. Yang, S., Yao, X.: Evolutionary Computation for Dynamic Optimization Problems. Springer, Heidelberg (2013). eBook ISBN 978-3-642-38416-5
4. Liu, H., Pretorius, L., Jiang, D.: Optimization of cold chain logistics distribution network terminal. EURASOP J. Wirel. Commun. Netw. **2018**, 158 (2018). https://doi.org/10.1186/s13638-018-1168-4
5. Cepolina, E.M., Farina, A.: A new urban freight distribution scheme and an optimization methodology for reducing its overall cost. Eur. Transp. Res. Rev. **7**, 1 (2014). https://doi.org/10.1007/s12544-014-0149-x
6. Razi, F.F.: A hybrid DEA-based K-means and invasive weed optimization for facility location problem. J. Ind. Eng. Int. (2018). https://doi.org/10.1007/s40092-018-0283-5
7. Kumar, V.M., Murthy, A., Chandrashekara, K.: A hybrid algorithm optimization approach for machine loading problem in flexible manufacturing system. J. Ind. Eng. Int. **8**, 3 (2012). https://doi.org/10.1186/2251-712X-8-3
8. Tayyab, M., Sarkar, B., Yahya, B.N.: Imperfect multi-stage lean manufacturing system with rework under fuzzy demand. Mathematics **7**, 13 (2019). https://doi.org/10.3390/math7010013
9. Khorasgani, S.S., Ghaffari, M.: Developing a cellular manufacturing model considering the alternative routes, tool assignment, and machine reliability. J. Ind. Eng. Int. **14**, 627 (2018). https://doi.org/10.1007/s40092-017-0239-1
10. Yang, S., Jiang, Y., Nguyen, T.T.: Metaheuristics for dynamic combinatorial optimization problems. IMA J. Manag. Math. **24**(4) (2012). https://doi.org/10.1093/imaman/dps021
11. Li, C., Yang, M., Kang, L.: A new approach to solving dynamic traveling salesman problems. In: Wang, T.-D., Li, X., Chen, S.-H., Wang, X., Abbass, H., Iba, H., Chen, G.-L., Yao, X. (eds.) SEAL 2006. LNCS, vol. 4247, pp. 236–243. Springer, Heidelberg (2006). https://doi.org/10.1007/11903697_31
12. Volling, T., Grunewald, M., Spengler, T.S.: An integrated inventory-transportation system with periodic pick-ups and leveled replenishment. Bus. Res. **6**, 173 (2013). https://doi.org/10.1007/BF03342748
13. Gilberto Pérez Lechuga: Optimal logistics strategy to distribute medicines in clinics and hospitals. J. Math. Ind. **8**, 2 (2018). https://doi.org/10.1186/s13362-018-0044-5
14. Henn, S., Koch, S., Doerner, K.F., et al.: Metaheuristics for the order batching problem in manual order picking systems. Bus. Res. **3**, 82 (2010). https://doi.org/10.1007/BF03342717
15. Srikakulapu, R., Vinatha, U.: Optimized design of collector topology for offshore wind farm based on ant colony optimization with multiple travelling salesman problem. J. Mod. Power Syst. Clean Energy **6**, 1181 (2018). https://doi.org/10.1007/s40565-018-0386-4
16. Moslemipour, G.: A hybrid CS-SA intelligent approach to solve uncertain dynamic facility layout problems considering dependency of demands. J. Ind. Eng. Int. **14**, 429 (2018). https://doi.org/10.1007/s40092-017-0222-x
17. Holland, J.H.: Adaptation in natural and artificial systems. Master's thesis, University of Michigan Press, Ann Arbor, MI (1975)

18. Liao, Y.-H., Sun, C.-T.: An Educational Genetic Algorithms Learning Tool (2001). http://www.ewh.ieee.org/soc/es/May2001/14/Begin.htm. Accessed 2016
19. Bonilla Vera, J.A., Mora-Vargas, J., González-Mendoza, M., López Sánchez, I.A., Montiel Moctezuma, C.J.: Brief review of techniques used to develop adaptive evolutionary algorithms. Open Cybern. Syst. J. **11**, 1–12 (2017). https://doi.org/10.2174/1874110x 01711010001
20. Deb, K., Beyer, H.-G.: Self-adaptation in real-parameter genetic algorithms with simulated binary crossover. In: GECCO, pp. 172–179 (1999)
21. Esquivel, S.C., Leiva, H.A., Gallard, R.H.: Self adaptation of parameters for MCPC in genetic algorithms. J. Comput. Sci. Technol. **2**, 1–8 (2000)
22. Kita, H.: A comparison study of self-adaptation in evolution strategies and real-coded genetic algorithms. Evol. Comput. **9**, 223–241 (2001)
23. Cheng, H., Yang, S.: Genetic algorithms for dynamic routing problems in mobile ad hoc networks. In: Yang, S., Yao, X. (eds.) Evolutionary Computation for Dynamic Optimization Problems. SCI, vol. 490, pp. 343–375. Springer, Heidelberg (2013). https://doi.org/10.1007/978-3-642-38416-5_14
24. Vera, J.A.B.: Investigación del rol del mapeo genotipo-fenotipo y del operador de mutación en algoritmos genéticos aplicados a problemas dinámicos. Master's thesis, Tecnologico de Monterrey, Mexico (2011)
25. Keller, R.E., Banzhaf, W.: Genetic programming using genotype-phenotype mapping from linear genomes into linear phenotypes. In: Proceedings of the First Annual Conference on Genetic Programming, pp. 116–122 (1996). ISBN 0-262-61127-9
26. Mora, J., Stephens, C., Waelbroeck, H.: Symmetry breaking and adaptation: evidence from a toy model of a virus. Biosystems **51**, 1–14 (1997). https://doi.org/10.1016/S0303-2647(98)00093-8

Fuzzy Systems, Reasoning and Intelligent Applications

Cross-Cultural Image-Based Author Profiling in Twitter

Ivan Feliciano-Avelino[1]($\boxtimes$), Miguel Á. Álvarez-Carmona[2,3],
Hugo Jair Escalante[1], Manuel Montes-y-Gómez[1], and Luis Villaseñor-Pineda[1]

[1] Laboratorio de Tecnologías del Lenguaje,
Instituto Nacional de Astrofísica, Óptica y Electrónica (INAOE), Puebla, Mexico
{ivan.feliciano,hugojair,mmontesg,villasen}@inaoep.mx
[2] Consejo Nacional de Ciencia y Tecnología (CONACYT), Mexico City, Mexico
[3] Unidad de Transferencia Tecnológica,
Centro de Investigación Científica y de Educación Superior de Ensenada
(CICESE-UT3), Ensenada, Mexico
malvarez@cicese.mx

Abstract. Recent works have shown that it is possible to use information extracted from images to address the task of automatic gender identification. These proposals have validated their solutions using monolingual datasets, i.e., collections where images are shared by users having the same mother tongue. This paper aims to test the usefulness of images collected from users who do not share the same language. In principle, these users present cultural differences, which may be reflected in the images they share. However, a cross-cultural image-based approach would be very useful for languages where data is not available or scarce. The experiments presented demonstrate that characteristics obtained from the images, regardless of the users' mother tongue, can be used for gender prediction. They mainly confirm the usefulness of a cross-cultural image-based approach, showing that culturally different individuals with equivalent profiles traits tend to share similar images.

Keywords: Author profiling · Gender identification · Image labels

1 Introduction

The content shared through social networks includes data in different modalities such as text, images, audio, and video. All this data can be used to extract valuable information from users. The author profiling (AP) task focuses on the analysis of shared content in order to predict different attributes of authors such as their gender, age, personality, native language, or political orientation [9]. The identification of such aspects can be applied in a wide variety of fields, for example, gender and age identification have been used in marketing and legal investigations [7]. From the marketing point of view, this information is useful for companies to be able to know if a product is of interest to a particular group

© Springer Nature Switzerland AG 2019
L. Martínez-Villaseñor et al. (Eds.): MICAI 2019, LNAI 11835, pp. 353–363, 2019.
https://doi.org/10.1007/978-3-030-33749-0_28

[8]. From a forensic perspective, in many criminal cases, the culprits hide their real identities to avoid being detected [2].

The most common approach to tackle the AP task is analyzing the texts written by the authors/users. For example, [2,4] and [5] used texts from social networks to classify authors by gender and age. Besides this text-based approach, some other works like [6], as well as the PAN 2018 AP task [9], have accomplished the gender identification from a multimodal perspective, where *images* are included as a complementary source of information in addition to text. These works have openly exposed the potential of using the images' information to profile social media users. Nevertheless, they have validated their solutions using only monolingual datasets, i.e., collections of images belonging to users with the same mother tongue. This motivates the question of whether the images shared by social media users are language dependent or not.

To further investigate this latter point, in this paper we study the usefulness of images collected from users having different languages. Particularly, we consider a cross-cultural image-based approach for gender identification. In our experiments, we use the images shared by Arabic, English and Spanish speaking Twitter users. The obtained results are encouraging, they show that culturally different individuals, with equivalent profiles traits, tend to share similar images. This observation is an important contribution to the field since it opens new possibilities to enhance the profiling of authors/users from languages with scarce resources.

The rest of the paper is organized as follows: Sect. 2 describes previous work in author profiling, focusing on the description of image-based approaches; Sect. 3 presents the used image-based representation; Sect. 4 details the configuration for the cross-cultural AP experiments; Sect. 5 shows the obtained results and presents an analysis of the similarities and differences between Twitter users from different languages; finally, Sect. 6 depicts the main conclusions of this experiment.

2   Related Work

There is a significant amount of author profiling works considering textual features. In this case, the proposed approaches are language-dependent and even domain-dependent [3,10].

Nowadays, images are a very popular kind of content in most social media platforms. This has motivated their use in the gender identification task. Most works consider visual information that is extracted from the images shared by the users [11,14,15], but some have also used information from the profile pictures or regarding the color patterns [6]. Also, some works have employed the image tags specified by the own users [16]. It is important to notice that most of these works have exclusively considered data from English speaking users.

In the previous year, the AP shared task at PAN 2018 [9] focused on the gender identification problem from a multimodal perspective, where texts and images were given for a set of Twitter users. This evaluation exercise considered data from three languages: Arabic, English, and Spanish. The participants used different approaches to solve the problem at hand, where solutions based on deep learning techniques were the most outstanding. For those considering only images, three different approaches were used: based on face recognition, based on pre-trained models for image labeling, and based on basic image processing techniques such as color histograms. The most prominent results were obtained by the second approach. In particular, [1,12] and [13] used as feature extractor the VGG16 deep network [17], considering different levels of abstraction. Then, the generated vector(s) were used as the input to the classification models that predict the gender of the authors.

3   Representing Users Through Their Images

Our proposal follows the same scheme as [1], where each author is represented by a *single* average vector that contains information from all her/his images. Figure 1 shows the process for the construction of an author representation. First, each image is analyzed by a pre-trained convolutional neural network, in particular, a VGG16 network trained over the ImageNet collection. The output of this network is a probability distribution over 1,000 possible labels regarding different objects and scenes presumably contained in the image. Then, in a subsequent step, it is computed the average of the vectors from all the images of the given author. This operation is computed per feature as defined in Formula 1, where N indicates the number of images shared by the author. The resultant vector is the author's representation. Later, the vectors from all users are feed to a classification model that predicts the gender of the authors (for more details refer to Sect. 4)[1].

$$average(X^1, X^2, \ldots, X^{1000}) = \frac{1}{N}(\sum_i^N X_1^i, \ldots, \sum_i^N X_{1000}^i) \tag{1}$$

4   Cross-Cultural AP: Experimental Settings

The objective of our experiments is to show that the images shared by users in social media are independent of their language. In other words, we aim to show that culturally different individuals, but with equivalent profiles traits, tend to share similar images. This will be done through the gender identification task by testing the usefulness of images collected from users who do not share the same language.

---

[1] A different scheme was also tested: each image was treated separately (without computing the average of the representations of the images), so that in order to infer the authors' profile, a vote was made, according to the genre predicted by the classifier for each single image. However, this approach did not show good results, probably due to the small number of images per author.

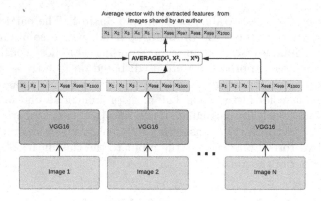

Fig. 1. The construction of the image-based authors' representations.

For the experiments, we consider three languages: Arabic, English, and Spanish, and employ a *cross-cultural* evaluation approach. That is, we train a classifier using the images from each one of the languages, and then we evaluate the built classifiers in the rest of the languages. For example, we train a classifier using the images from male and female English-speaking users and then we use this classifier to determine the gender of Arabic-speaking users.

In the experiments we use a collection of images from Twitter provided by the organizers of the PAN 2018 AP task [9]. This collection gathers data of users from the three languages mentioned above; it includes ten images per user. The image sets are balanced with respect to gender. Table 1 describes the collections with regard to their language and number of users.

Table 1. Number of users for each language for training and test sets. In all collections there is the same number of male and female users.

	Arabic	Spanish	English	Total
Training	1500	3000	3000	7500
Test	1000	2200	1900	5100
Total	2500	5200	4900	12600

As previously described, to generate the descriptors of the images we used the VGG16 convolutional neural network trained on ImageNet. For the classification, we used a support vector machine (SVM) classifier with a linear kernel. We applied a grid search to find the best value of the parameter C of the SVM model; we evaluated the following values $\mathbf{C} = \{0.01, 0.1, 1, 10, 100\}$. For all the trained models, the best value for C was 1, except for the model using the Arab collection, where optimal C was 10. As baseline, we consider the results from the monolingual classification scenarios, where the classifiers are trained and tested using images from users of the same language. The used evaluation measure is accuracy.

All experiments were run on a computer with an Intel Core i5-7300HQ processor running at 3.5 GHz, 8 GB of RAM, an NVIDIA GeForce GTX 1050 GPU, and a 250 GB SSD device.

5 Results and Discussion

Table 2 reports the results from our experiments. It presents two types of results: from monolingual experiments, where training and test data belong to users from the same language, and from *cross-cultural* experiments, where users from training and test have different languages. Besides, this table shows the results obtained by a general model trained with the images from users of the three languages. The accuracies in bold fond indicate the best results per language.

From these results, we can obtain some interesting conclusions. Firstly, in most of the cases, the cross-cultural results are very similar to those from the monolingual experiments, indicating to a certain extend that Twitter users from different cultures (using different languages), but having similar profiling traits, tend to share similar images. The worst results correspond to the cases where images from Arab-speaking users were employed as training data. Although, the cultural differences between Arabic speakers and the users from the other two languages, we presume these results are mainly caused by the small size of the Arabic dataset, which is half of the other languages collections. Secondly, and as a consequence of the first observation, adding information to the training set, regardless of the users' language, help to construct better classifiers for gender identification.

Table 2. Accuracy results for all cross-cultural AP experiments.

Training language	Test language	Acc
Arabic	Arabic	0.68
Spanish	Arabic	0.70
English	Arabic	0.69
ALL	Arabic	**0.71**
English	English	**0.70**
Arabic	English	0.63
Spanish	English	0.67
ALL	English	**0.70**
Spanish	Spanish	0.67
Arabic	Spanish	0.63
English	Spanish	0.67
ALL	Spanish	**0.68**

5.1   Content Extracted from the Images

This section presents an analysis of the kind of features extracted from the users' images. The main goal of this analysis is twofold. On the one hand, to show the similarities among the images shared by users from different languages and, on the other hand, to identify the set of features that are the most discriminative between men and women regardless of their language.

It is important to mention that this analysis is done over the labels extracted by the VGG16 pre-trained model. Due to the diversity of the images and also to the specificity of some labels, the labeling of the images has errors. Nevertheless, these errors are consistent, e.g., pictures of women with long hair were usually marked with the label *wig*, and, therefore, they do not considerably affect the classification task.

Figure 2 shows the image labels that are in the intersection among the 50 most frequent labels of the three languages, for females and males respectively. It is easy to observe that some labels are frequent in both men and women. For example, web site, book jacket, envelope, comic book and menu, which in many cases correspond to cell phone screenshots or images that contain a textual message. This figure also evidences some labels that are only frequent in the images from one single-gender, but that are common across the different languages. For example, women tend to share more images with sunglasses, pajamas, fur coats, miniskirts, brassieres, hair sprayers and stoles than men, whereas men tend to share more images with Windsor ties, soccer balls, ballplayers, rugby balls, scoreboards, shoe shops, and military uniforms than women.

(a) Females most frequent labels.

(b) Males most frequent labels.

Fig. 2. Word clouds showing the intersection of the 50 most frequent labels from each language, for women and men respectively.

To further explore the differences between men and women. We compute the information gain for all the labels in each of the three languages. Then, we selected the top 100 labels for each language and intersect them. The resultant set comprises the more discriminative labels between men and women, independently of their language. This set contains the following labels: hair spray, ballplayer, brassiere, stole, blenheim spaniel, bath towel, persian cat, over skirt, miniskirt, velvet, lipstick, wig, shih tzu, spatula, and suit.

For better visualization of the kind content shared by Twitter users, Figs. 3 and 4 show some of the images associated to two of the highest discriminative labels: *bath towel*, which is highly associated to women, and *ballplayer*, which is associated to men. Analyzing the images with the label bath towel, we can observe that images with this label, whatever the language of the users, tend to contain pictures of pets and babies. On the other hand, images with the label ballplayer are related to sports.

Fig. 3. Examples of images shared by Arabic, Spanish and English speaking female users that contain the label *bath towel*.

5.2 Similar but Not the Same

As noted in the previous section, the images shared by users of social networks, regardless of their mother tongue, have enough information to be used in author profiling tasks, particularly for gender identification. In this way, images can be used as an *interlingua*, and thus they could be used for scenarios/languages with few or no data collections. However, despite the coincidences, it is clear that there are cultural differences which must be reflected in the shared images. According to this, we show a brief analysis identifying cultural differences between users. In particular, we focus the analysis among users whose cultural difference is presumably greater, that is, users whose mother tongue is Arabic versus English and Spanish users.

Arab   **Spanish**   **English**

Fig. 4. Examples of images shared by Arabic, Spanish and English speaking male users that contain the label *ballplayer*.

To carry out this analysis, we compute the difference between the average vector from all Arabic speaking users and the average vector from the English and Spanish users. Figures 5 and 6 show the 20 labels which have the greatest differences, where labels with positive values are mainly identified in images from Arabic speaking users, and labels with negative values are not common among them. From these results, it is clear that the content from the shared images is not completely universal and some cultural elements remain. For example,

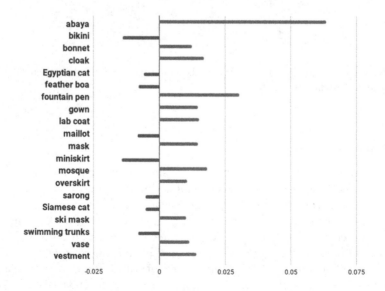

Fig. 5. Arab females comparison with other speaking user languages.

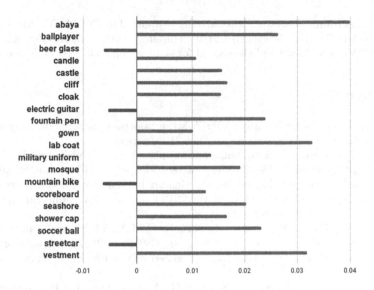

Fig. 6. Arab males comparison with other speaking user languages.

posted images from Arabic speaking users frequently contain entities like abaya and mosque, and also entities like mask and over-skirt, which probably are wrong labels for images containing women wearing a burka. On the contrary, images containing women garments and pets, such as bikini, miniskirt, and cats, are more common in English and Spanish speaking users than in Arabic users.

6   Conclusions

In this paper, we have proposed a cross-cultural image-based approach for gender identification in social media. This approach was evaluated over a collection of Twitter images from users of three different languages: Arabic, English, and Spanish. The results have shown that the content of the images is mostly independent of the users' language, that is, users of different mother tongues, but with equivalent profile traits, tend to share similar images. This is an important finding for AP applications since it opens new possibilities to enhance the profiling of authors/users from languages with scarce resources.

In this work, we have focused on the gender identification task because it is the information provided by the used dataset. However, we plan to extend our study to other attributes of the authors such as age and educational level. Additionally, another possible direction for future work considers the analysis of the level of abstraction of the users' representations. We plan to experiment with other image labeling methods and to consider a different number of labels, particularly a set of more general labels.

Acknowledgement. This work was partially supported by CONACYT-Mexico under grants CB-2015-01-257383, FC-2016-2410. The first author thanks for scholarship CONACyT-Mexico 924024 and the second for scholarship CONACyT-Mexico 401887.

References

1. Aragón, M.E., López-Monroy, A.P.: A straightforward multimodal approach for author profiling. http://ceur-ws.org/Vol-2125/paper_96
2. Cheng, N., Chandramouli, R., Subbalakshmi, K.: Author gender identification from text. Digit. Investig. **1**, 78–88 (2011). https://doi.org/10.1016/j.diin.2011.04.002
3. Ciot, M., Sonderegger, M., Ruths, D.: Gender inference of Twitter users in non-English contexts. In: Proceedings of the 2013 Conference on Empirical Methods in Natural Language Processing, pp. 1136–1145 (2013)
4. Fatima, M., Hasan, K., Anwar, S., Nawab, R.M.A.: Multilingual author profiling on Facebook. Inf. Process. Manag. **4**, 886–904 (2017). https://doi.org/10.1016/j.ipm.2017.03.005. http://www.sciencedirect.com/science/article/pii/S0306457316302424
5. Gómez-Adorno, H., Markov, I., Sidorov, G., Posadas-Durán, J.P., Sanchez-Perez, M.A., Chanona-Hernandez, L.: Improving feature representation based on a neural network for author profiling in social media texts. Comput. Intell. Neurosci. 2 (2016)
6. Merler, M., Cao, L., Smith, J.R.: You are what you tweet... pic! Gender prediction based on semantic analysis of social media images. In: 2015 IEEE International Conference on Multimedia and Expo (ICME), pp. 1–6. IEEE (2015)
7. Miller, Z., Dickinson, B., Hu, W.: Gender prediction on twitter using stream algorithms with n-gram character features. Int. J. Intell. Sci. **04**, 143–148 (2012). https://doi.org/10.4236/ijis.2012.224019
8. Rangel, F., Rosso, P.: Use of language and author profiling: identification of gender and age. In: Natural Language Processing and Cognitive Science (2013)
9. Rangel, F., Rosso, P., Montes-y Gómez, M., Potthast, M., Stein, B.: Overview of the 6th author profiling task at pan 2018: multimodal gender identification in Twitter. http://ceur-ws.org/Vol-2125/
10. Rangel, F., Rosso, P., Potthast, M., Stein, B.: Overview of the 5th author profiling task at pan 2017: gender and language variety identification in Twitter. In: Working Notes Papers of the CLEF (2017)
11. Shigenaka, R., Tsuboshita, Y., Kato, N.: Content-aware multi-task neural networks for user gender inference based on social media images. In: 2016 IEEE International Symposium on Multimedia (ISM), pp. 169–172, December 2016. https://doi.org/10.1109/ISM.2016.0040
12. Sierra, S., Gonzáles, F.: Combining textual and visual representations for multimodal author profiling. In: CLEF 2018 Working Notes (2018). http://ceur-ws.org/Vol-2125/paper_219.pdf
13. Takahashi, T., Tahara, T., Nagatan, K., Miura, Y., Taniguchi, T., Ohkuma, T.: Text and image synergy with feature cross technique for gender identification. In: CLEF 2018 Working Notes (2018). http://ceur-ws.org/Vol-2125/paper_83.pdf
14. Vijayaraghavan, P., Vosoughi, S., Roy, D.: Twitter demographic classification using deep multi-modal multi-task learning. In: Proceedings of the 55th Annual Meeting of the Association for Computational Linguistics (Volume 2: Short Papers), pp. 478–483. Association for Computational Linguistics, Vancouver,

Canada, July 2017. https://doi.org/10.18653/v1/P17-2076. https://www.aclweb.org/anthology/P17-2076

15. Ma, X., Tsuboshita, Y., Kato, N.: Gender estimation for SNS user profiling using automatic image annotation. In: 2014 IEEE International Conference on Multimedia and Expo Workshops (ICMEW), pp. 1–6, July 2014. https://doi.org/10.1109/ICMEW.2014.6890569

16. You, Q., Bhatia, S., Luo, J.: A picture tells a thousand words-about you! user interest profiling from user generated visual content. Sig. Process. **124**, 45–53 (2016)

17. Zisserman, A., Simonyan, K.: Very deep convolutional networks for large-scale image recognition, April 2015. https://arxiv.org/abs/1409.1556

Application of Fuzzy Logic in the Edge Detection of Real Pieces in Controlled Scenarios

José Daniel Vargas-Proa[1], Carlos Fabián García-Martínez[1], Miroslava Cano-Lara[1], and Horacio Rostro-González[2(✉)]

[1] Depto. de Mecatrónica, Instituto Tecnológico Superior de Irapuato, Irapuato, Gto, Mexico
danielvp.msn@gmail.com, carlosgarciafm@gmail.com, miroslava.cano@itesi.edu.mx
[2] Depto. de Electrónica, Universidad de Guanajuato, DICIS, Salamanca, Gto, Mexico
hrostrog@ugto.mx

Abstract. Industrial processes such as manufacturing and machining parts, fault detection and quality control are some of the areas of study that encompass computational vision techniques, image processing and currently fuzzy logic. Particularly, the edge detection of objects in captured images is a technique widely used in industrial automated systems. In this work, we propose a technique for edge detection in digital images obtained from real pieces based on fuzzy logic. The fuzzy inference model works with 18 Mamdani type rules and was built with 8 input variables and one output variable. It is, the processing of the image was performed under the conditions of the lighting scenario, background and the color of the piece. The performance of the algorithm was evaluated on several images captured from different work environments and it was compared with traditional computer vision methods using gradient operators. The use of fuzzy logic in image processing expands the possibilities to solve a problem and provides more answers over the restrictions of classical methods.

Keywords: Fuzzy inference · Computer vision · Edge detection

1 Introduction

Currently, technological and industrial development is growing in such a way that quality requirements in the manufacture process of products increase. Therefore, it is necessary to use automatic systems for the evaluation of the quality of such products, most of them through image processing. In agriculture, image processing and computational vision are used for extracting fruit and vegetable characteristics, classifying them according to their appearance and improving the quality of the product [1]. In medicine, edge detection algorithms are widely used to visualize parts of the brain in a region of interest to help specialists in a medical diagnostic [2, 3].

© Springer Nature Switzerland AG 2019
L. Martínez-Villaseñor et al. (Eds.): MICAI 2019, LNAI 11835, pp. 364–376, 2019.
https://doi.org/10.1007/978-3-030-33749-0_29

In manufacturing, fuzzy logic is applied as inference systems that control the parameters of surface roughness, cutting force, feed force, etc., during the fabrication of a piece. Optimization techniques are applied to machining of materials, increase thus the useful life of the tools commonly used in turning [4] and CNC milling [5], and gives a quality in its final product. One of the applications is found in the extraction of edges, where techniques such as computational vision are used to describe character-istics of shape and size of an object in a digital image. It is well known that, in images taken from the real world (images that are not created artificially), the separation between two segments of the image is not perfectly defined, so it can be said that there is uncertainty about the pixels that are part of the edge. The decision about whether a pixel belongs to the edge or not becomes a task not so easy to perform. In this context, fuzzy logic provides great advantages in the analysis and processing of images, resulting in a system of obtaining edges more robust and with a wide range of pos-sibilities to solve the problem, and that in comparison with traditional edge detection methods our proposal can deal with the uncertainty present in the information [6].

This work designs a method based on fuzzy logic for edge detection in images taken from real pieces in scenarios where the lighting characteristics, camera position, background of the image, etc. are controlled, obtaining simpler images to process. The performance of this method is compared to other edge detection methods using an ideal edge map made with design software like reference.

2 Related Work

There is a variety of computational techniques used to obtain edges in digital images. From evaluating the performance of classical methods for the detection of edges in medical images [7], to analyzing with image processing algorithms such as Canny for the detection of edges in fish when compared with the operators of Sobel, Prewitt and Roberts; the Canny operator showed better performance, but more computational cost [8]. In [9], the authors make a comparison between several methods of edge detection, where declivity edge detector and modified declivity edge detector are presented. Experimental tests show that the modified declivity edge detector has better results, even than the Canny operator, obtaining fine edges in real world images, with a low processing time.

Recent methods have been developed for the detection of edges using fuzzy logic [10, 11], in which, based on a set of inference rules designed by an expert, it is concluded which pixels belong, or not, on the edge of the figure. It was possible to work with uncertainty due to noise, contrast or lighting present in the image. Obtaining better results when compared with the Sobel operator, with the only disadvantage that it requires more processing time in the use of fuzzy logic. In 2017, in [12] the author proposes a method for edge detection in color images using the multidirectional Sobel filter, in the HSV color space. Tests were carried out on digitally designed images and images taken from the real world, obtaining edges that are shown in the distinctive color of the original image and with a good thickness.

Using fuzzy logic, in [13] a method of obtaining edges in color images and in gray scales was developed, comparing results obtained by different defuzzification methods.

The advantage of using fuzzy logic in obtaining edges is to present a greater robustness in the algorithm. In [14], the authors mention the advantages of the method developed for edge detection based on fuzzy logic, among which the production of thin edges, the detection of lines in all directions and the speed of the method by using few functions of membership. In [15], a comparison is made between established edge detectors, evaluating the performance they have when adding a percentage of noise to the image. Fuzzy logic improves edge detection in noise images, with fewer false edges detected. In [16], it is explained that to obtain better results with fuzzy logic it is necessary to apply masks larger than the conventional 3 × 3.

3   Methodology

3.1   Image Acquisition

The process of edge detection in this work starts with an image taken from a real piece, which was performed in a controlled scenario as shown in Fig. 1. In this setup, we set two lamps with cold light at 60° of the object of interest, the camera was placed 0.2 m perpendicular to the object, and different background colors were used for results comparison.

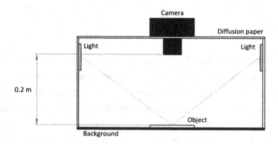

Fig. 1. Scenario for capturing the image.

3.2   Processing Sequence

The algorithm for obtaining edges consists of 4 main stages. In the first, captured images are converted from color to gray scale. Then, we performed the fuzzification of the intensities of the pixels in the image, which are evaluated using a set of inference rules, and finally we obtain an output value for each pixel in the image, after defuzzification. This process is represented in the block diagram of Fig. 2.

The conversion of RGB to gray scale for the input image was performed by the weighted sum of the three components, as described in the following Eq. 1 [17]:

$$C = 0.3R + 0.59G + 0.11B \tag{1}$$

The grayscale image provides a gray intensity level component that goes from 0, which represents the black color, to 255 the white color.

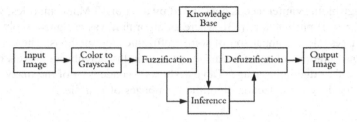

Fig. 2. The grayscale image is evaluated in the fuzzy inference system, going through its different stages until obtaining a result image where the pixels belonging to the edge are shown in white and the pixels in the background are shown in black.

3.3 Fuzzy Inference System

Obtaining the edges of the image, taken from a real piece, it was used a design of a fuzzy inference system to assign to each pixel of the image, a certain degree of membership to the edges of the piece, using fuzzy sets. Using a 3×3 mask, shown in Fig. 3, we obtain the 8 input variables P_1 to P_8, for the fuzzy system, which are the neighbors of the pixel of importance P_0. This is required to calculate its membership to the edge of the object in the image.

P_1	P_2	P_3
P_4	P_0	P_5
P_6	P_7	P_8

Fig. 3. Mask 3×3 for evaluation of membership to the edge of the object in the image.

For the input variables, two fuzzy sets were used, classifying the pixels according to their color intensity. The sets "W" (White) and "B" (Black) are represented by two trapezoidal membership functions throughout the range 0–255. The output variable has only the fuzzy set "Edge", represented by a singleton function at point 255 (Fig. 4).

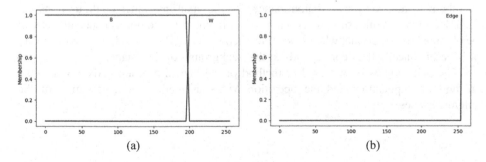

Fig. 4. Membership functions (a) Input variables, (b) Output variable.

The stage of fuzzy inference is constituted by a set of 18 Mamdani rules, which are based on the rules presented in [13], where an algorithm was designed to obtain edges in color images and a comparison of some defuzzification methods. These rules consider 18 configurations of color intensities present in the neighboring pixels of a pixel belonging to the edge in an image. Table 1 shows a condensate of the fuzzy inference rules used for the edge detection algorithm in images of real pieces.

Table 1. Fuzzy inference rules.

Inputs								Output
P1	P2	P3	P4	P5	P6	P7	P8	P0
W	W	W	W	W	B	B	B	Edge
B	B	B	W	W	W	W	W	Edge
B	W	W	B	W	B	W	W	Edge
W	W	B	W	B	W	W	B	Edge
B	B	W	B	W	B	W	W	Edge
W	W	B	W	B	W	B	B	Edge
B	W	W	B	W	B	B	W	Edge
W	B	B	W	B	W	W	B	Edge
B	B	B	B	W	W	W	W	Edge
W	W	W	B	W	B	B	B	Edge
B	B	B	W	B	W	W	W	Edge
W	W	W	W	B	B	B	B	Edge
W	B	B	W	B	W	W	W	Edge
W	W	W	W	B	W	B	B	Edge
B	B	W	B	W	W	W	W	Edge
W	W	W	B	W	B	B	W	Edge
B	B	W	B	W	B	B	W	Edge
W	W	W	B	B	B	B	B	Edge

The SOM (Smallest of Maximum) method [18] was used for defuzzification by converting the result set of inferences to a crisp output value that represents the intensity of a pixel in the output image. This method facilitated the use of a single membership function for the output, since, for the pixel intensities configurations not included in the 18 rules of Table 1 (cases of no membership to border), a result set will be obtained of zeroes, that when it is defuzzified by the SOM method, the zero intensity will be obtained, which corresponds to the background of the image.

The operation MIN was used as method of the logical operation AND and as the method of implication, and the operation MAX as method of aggregation of the inference rules.

3.4 Figure of Merit

The method of evaluation of edge detectors known as "Figure of Merit" proposed by Pratt [19] is a measure of differences that makes a comparison between an ideal edge map and a real edge detector. This method is defined by Eq. 2:

$$R = \frac{1}{N} \sum_{i=1}^{N_R} \frac{1}{1 + kd} \qquad (2)$$

Where $N = MAX(N_I, N_R)$, N_I and N_R are the number of pixels of the ideal edge and the number of pixels of the real edge respectively, d is the distance measured in pixels, between the pixel position of the real edge (x_1, y_1) and its ideal position on the edge map (x_2, y_2), calculated with the expression $d = \sqrt{(x_2 - x_1)^2 + (y_2 - y_1)^2}$. And k is a scaling factor by which poorly placed edge pixels are penalized. In this work, a value of k = 0.02 was used.

Due to the factor $\frac{1}{N}$ the values of R are normalized, so $R = 1$ indicates a perfectly detected edge and $R = 0$ is a totally erroneous edge.

4 Experimental Results

Images of 686 × 686 pixels captured in the scenario are shown in Fig. 1, where yellow RGB(230,188,52), red RGB(251,112,73), green RGB(44,164,126) and black RGB (29,31,43) backgrounds were used. The piece of study is a mechanical piece of a pipe system, of white tonality, circular exterior geometry, and trapezoidal grooves inside the piece. The algorithm based on fuzzy logic was compared with classical methods of image processing, using the operators Roberts, Prewitt and Sobel for edge detection described in [9], which were developed in Matlab software. Table 2 shows the operators used to obtain edges in the piece.

Table 2. Operators for edge detection.

	Convolution mask	
Operator	Mask G_x	Mask G_y
Roberts	$\begin{bmatrix} 1 & 0 \\ 0 & -1 \end{bmatrix}$	$\begin{bmatrix} 0 & 1 \\ -1 & 0 \end{bmatrix}$
Prewitt	$\begin{bmatrix} -1 & 0 & 1 \\ -1 & 0 & 1 \\ -1 & 0 & 1 \end{bmatrix}$	$\begin{bmatrix} 1 & 1 & 1 \\ 0 & 0 & 0 \\ -1 & -1 & -1 \end{bmatrix}$
Sobel	$\begin{bmatrix} -1 & 0 & 1 \\ -2 & 0 & 2 \\ -1 & 0 & 1 \end{bmatrix}$	$\begin{bmatrix} 1 & 2 & 1 \\ 0 & 0 & 0 \\ -1 & -2 & -1 \end{bmatrix}$

Using Eq. 2, a numerical evaluation of the mentioned edge detectors was obtained, using images created manually in the GIMP software, as ideal edge maps. Figures 5, 6,

7 and 8 show the results obtained from obtaining borders using a yellow, red, green and black background, respectively. In the images with lighter backgrounds, such as yellow and red, shadows were obtained in the image caused by the same piece. In the image with green background, in the same way shadows are obtained, but they are less noticeable than it is in the previous cases, due to the tone of the background of the image, and in the case of the image with a black background, the shadows around the figure are almost imperceptible. Edge detection algorithms sometimes show these shadows as false edges, which is sought to eliminate with the use of different background colors.

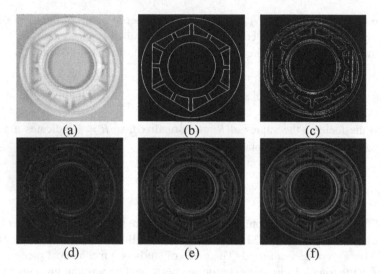

Fig. 5. Obtaining borders with yellow background. (a) Input image, (b) Ideal edges (c) Fuzzy logic, (d) Roberts, (e) Prewitt, (f) Sobel. (Color figure online)

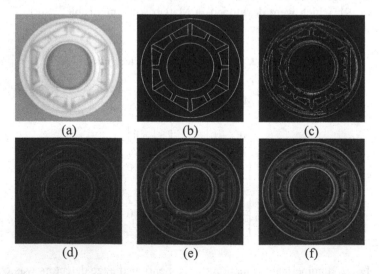

Fig. 6. Obtaining borders with red background. (a) Input image, (b) Ideal edges (c) Fuzzy logic, (d) Roberts, (e) Prewitt, (f) Sobel. (Color figure online)

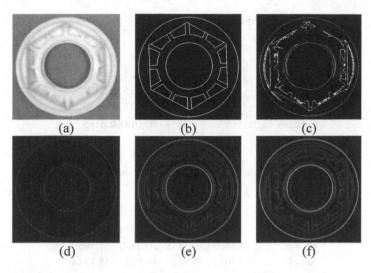

Fig. 7. Obtaining borders with green background. (a) Input image, (b) Ideal edges (c) Fuzzy logic, (d) Roberts, (e) Prewitt, (f) Sobel. (Color figure online)

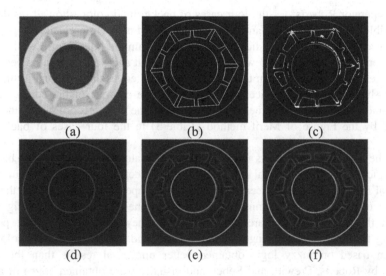

Fig. 8. Obtaining borders with black background. (a) Input image, (b) Ideal edges (c) Fuzzy logic, (d) Roberts, (e) Prewitt, (f) Sobel.

Table 3 shows the values obtained from the evaluation of Eq. 2 on the edges obtained from the image of the real piece for each background color. In a complementary manner, Table 4 shows the processing times, in seconds, of each of the edge detection methods.

Table 3. Comparison of edge detection algorithms.

Method	Background color			
	Yellow	Red	Green	Black
Roberts	0.0045	0.0027	0.0001	0.0927
Prewitt	0.1304	0.4171	0.3315	0.5830
Sobel	0.3474	0.5737	0.5271	0.6630
Fuzzy logic	0.4762	0.4856	0.3011	**0.8168**

Table 4. Comparison of the processing time in seconds.

Method	Background color			
	Yellow	Red	Green	Black
Roberts	11.0313	11.1719	11.6094	10.2813
Prewitt	36.5469	36.3438	36.3750	37.7969
Sobel	36.7031	35.5469	35.8125	35.7344
Fuzzy logic	93.9688	93.7668	93.8906	93.9219

The operator Roberts, for the four cases of background color, showed results with little visible edges and which are not completely defined. Numerically, it presented values lower than 0.1, which indicates that the algorithm did not perform well. Among the three operators, (Roberts, Prewitt and Sobel) Prewitt and Sobel show the best visual results, presenting similarities in terms of the detected edges and the tonality in which they are shown. Small differences were shown in the contrast of the edges with the background, being Sobel the best numerically of the two, according to the value obtained by the Figure of Merit method (Table 3) in the four cases of background color.

For the 4 background colors used, the Sobel operator and the algorithm based on fuzzy logic have the best visual results, in their respective cases, having quite close numerical results. In red and green backgrounds, the operator Sobel exceeds the fuzzy logic, since this operator determines in a better way the inner edges of the figure and although the edges detected are a little blurred, they are in the correct position according to the ideal edge image. For the yellow and black background colors, the algorithm based on fuzzy logic obtained better numerical results than the results obtained by Roberts, Prewitt, and Sobel, and visually were obtained edges of a good thickness, and a white color that easily distinguishes itself from the bottom. The fuzzy logic algorithm applied to the black background obtained a figure of Merit value of 0.8168, as is shown in bold in Table 3, being the one with the best numerical result among all the algorithms with their respective background colors.

Regarding the processing time, Roberts algorithm takes 10 s, being the fastest, while fuzzy logic uses more than 90 s to obtain the edges, but the results obtained are acceptable in comparison with the increased time for the background black color. In the case of the green and red colors, better results are obtained with Sobel with processing times of approximately 30 s.

The edges of the grooves inside the piece, in general, are more difficult to detect for the 5 algorithms evaluated, due to the little difference in tones that exists between each internal region of the piece. The use of different background colors greatly helps the detection of the outer edges of the piece, since there is a better contrast between the background and the piece, it is easier to detect a change in the color intensities of the image. This can be seen more easily in Fig. 9, which shows the comparison of the frequency histogram for each image.

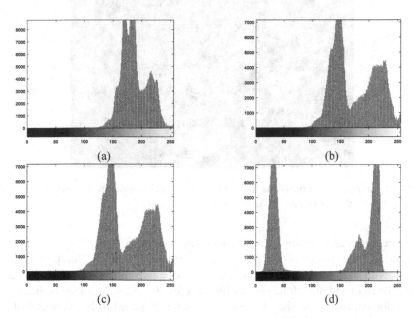

Fig. 9. Comparison of the frequency histogram for each of the background colors used. (a) Yellow background, (b) Red background, (c) Green background, (d) Black background. (Color figure online)

Comparing the frequency histograms of the images taken with different background colors, it can be observed that for the darker backgrounds the separation between the pixel concentration of the piece and the pixel concentration of the background is better appreciated, being the black background where there is a greater contrast and in yellow color a lower contrast.

As an edge detection application, the dimensions of the piece were measured in pixels. The edge image obtained from fuzzy logic with a black background was used, as it was the one that showed the best results. A rectangle was drawn that contains the figure, as well as horizontal and vertical axes that pass through the center of the piece. The intersections of the axes with the inner and outer circumferences of the piece were marked with a white X as is shown in Fig. 10.

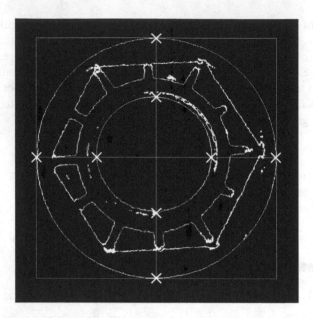

Fig. 10. Measurement of dimensions, in pixels, of the mechanical part of a pipe system, using edges detected by the application of fuzzy logic.

The measurements obtained from the piece are shown in Table 5. It is observed that the width and the height of the piece are different by a pixel. Comparing the top thickness with the bottom one, we notice that there is a difference of 12 pixels, and between the right and the left there is a difference of 10 pixels. This may be because the figure is not symmetric, so that, in case the piece is required to be symmetrical in its dimensions to correctly fulfill its function, it would mean that the piece is defective. Another possibility is that these differences are caused by the position in which the piece was placed at the moment of capturing the image.

Table 5. Measures in pixels obtained from the edges of the real piece.

Section	Measure
Total height	580
Total width	581
Top thickness	144
Bottom thickness	156
Left thickness	147
Right thickness	157

5 Conclusions

Edge detection in digital images is a technique that uses computational vision to obtain and extract image characteristics. The processing in images taken of real-world pieces requires more sophisticated algorithms for obtaining edges, due to many factors that influence the capture of the image as lighting, background color, among others. For this reason, the objective of this work is the application of an algorithm based on fuzzy logic for the detection of edges in images taken from real pieces, in scenarios where the variables that affect the capture of the image are controlled, obtaining simpler images to process. A comparative study of the influence of the background color on edge detection of the piece was made and, at the same time, the performance of the fuzzy logic was evaluated compared with the methods for edge detection of Roberts, Prewitt and Sobel, using the figure of Merit method to obtain a numerical value of the performance of the algorithms, based on an ideal edge map created manually in a design software.

The experimental results showed a better performance of the algorithm based on fuzzy logic, obtaining well defined edges and with good contrast between the background and the edge. It was observed that the use of fuzzy logic implies a higher computational cost compared with the classic methods of obtaining edges, but in relation to the improvement in the quality of the obtained edges, it can be said that the increase of the processing time is acceptable. Comparing the results obtained by the different background colors used in the capture of the image, it was observed that, when there is greater contrast between the color of the background and the color of the object, the quality of the outer edges of the piece increases. And, in the opposite case, the closer the color intensities between the background and the object are, the algorithm's performance will be lower in these areas. In this way, it can be concluded that the best result in the edge detection was obtained by applying fuzzy logic using a contrasting background with the color of the real piece, in this case the black color.

Acknowledgements. CONACYT Project FC2016-1961 "Neurociencia computacional: de la teoría del desarrollo de sistemas neuromórficos".

References

1. Bhargava, A., Bansal, A.A.: Fruits and vegetables quality evaluation using computer vision: a review. J. King Saud Univer. Comput. Inf. Sci. (2018, in press)
2. Senthilkumaran, N., Kirubakaran, C., Tamilmani, N.: Fuzzy edge detection using fuzzy C-means thresholding for MRI brain image. Int. J. Comput. Sci. Eng. **6**(4), 209–213 (2018)
3. Senthilkumaran, N., Kirubakaran, C., Tamilmani, N.: Fuzzy edge detection using minimum cross entropy thresholding for MRI brain image. Int. J. Comput. Sci. Eng. **6**(7), 271–274 (2018)
4. Soepangkat, B.O.P., Soesanti, A., Pramujati, B.: The use of Taguchi-Grey-Fuzzy to optimize performance characteristics in turning of AISI D2. Appl. Mech. Mater. **312**, 211–215 (2013)
5. Das, B., Roy, S., Rai, R.N., Saha, S.C.: Application of grey fuzzy logic for the optimization of CNC milling parameters for Al–4.5% Cu–TiC MMCs with multi-performance characteristics. Eng. Sci. Technol. Int. J. **19**, 857–865 (2015)

6. Chacón, M.M.I.: Fuzzy logic for image processing: definition and applications of a fuzzy image processing scheme. In: Bai, Y., Zhuang, H., Wang, D. (eds.) Advanced Fuzzy Logic Technologies in Industrial Applications. AIC, pp. 101–113. Springer, London (2006). https://doi.org/10.1007/978-1-84628-469-4_7

7. Sarkar, S., Mandal, A.: Comparison of some classical edge detection techniques with their suitability analysis for medical images processing. Int. J. Comput. Sci. Eng. 3(1), 81–87 (2015)

8. Shrivakshan, G.T., Chandrasekar, C.: A comparison of various edge detection techniques used in image processing. Int. J. Comput. Sci. 9(5), 269–276 (2012)

9. Bhardwaj, S., Mittal, A.: A survey on various edge detector techniques. Proc. Technol. 4, 220–226 (2012)

10. Suryakant, N.K.: Edge detection using fuzzy logic in Matlab. Int. J. Adv. Res. Comput. Sci. Softw. Eng. 2(4), 38–40 (2012)

11. Abdallah, A.A., Ayman, A.A.: Edge detection in digital images using fuzzy logic technique. Int. J. Comput. Inf. Eng. 3(3), 540–548 (2009)

12. Bora, D.J.: A novel approach for color image edge detection using multidirectional sobel filter on HSV color space. JCSE Int. J. Comput. Sci. Eng. 5(2), 154–159 (2017)

13. Nikitha, B.S., Myna, A.N.: Fuzzy logic based edge detection in color images. Int. Adv. Res. J. Sci. Eng. Technol. 2(7), 65–69 (2015)

14. Liang, L.R., Looney, C.G.: Competitive fuzzy edge detection. Appl. Soft Comput. 3, 123–137 (2003)

15. Haq, I., Shah, K., Khan, M.T., Azam, K., Anwar, S.: Fuzzy logic based edge detection for noisy images. Tech. J. Univ. Eng. Technol. (UET) Taxila 20(2), 81–86 (2015)

16. Pugin, E.V., Zhiznyakov, A.L.: Edge detection in remote sensing images based on fuzzy image representation. In: 3rd International conference Information Technology and Nanotechnology 2017, pp. 201–206. Vladimir State University, Vladimir (2017)

17. Kanan, C., Cottrell, G.W.: Color-to-Grayscale: Does the Method Matter in Image Recognition? PLoS ONE 7(1), 29740, 1–7 (2012)

18. Tóth-Laufer, E., Takács, M.: The effect of aggregation and defuzzification method selection on the risk level calculation. In: 2012 IEEE 10th International Symposium on Applied Machine Intelligence and Informatics (SAMI), pp. 131–136. Herl'any (2012)

19. Pratt, W.K.: Introduction to Digital Image Processing, 1st edn. CRC Press Taylor & Francis Group, Boca Raton (2013)

Grey-Fuzzy Approach to Support the Optimisation of the Shot Peening Process

José Solis-Cordova[1], Sandra Roblero-Aguilar[2],
Nelva Almanza-Ortega[2], and José Solis-Romero[2(✉)]

[1] Instituto Tecnológico y de Estudios Superiores de Monterrey campus
Edo. de Méx., Carretera Lago de Guadalupe Km. 3.5, 52926 Monterrey,
Estado de México, Mexico
jj.solcor@tec.mx
[2] SEP/TecNM/Instituto Tecnológico de Tlalnepantla,
54070 Tlalnepantla de Baz, Estado de México, Mexico
{sroblero,jsolis}@ittla.edu.mx, avlenylen@hotmail.com

Abstract. Materials for aerospace industry such as aluminium alloys are of prime use in a variety of components. Performance and reliability of these components and structures mostly lie down on the fatigue resistance among other structural characteristics. Shot peening processing is widely employed to improve the fatigue properties. However, proper selection and control of peening factors (parameters) is needed to ensure that peening effects became beneficial rather than detrimental. The present study focuses on finding optimal peening parameters by considering multiple performance characteristics using grey fuzzy methodology. Adaptive neuro-fuzzy inference system (ANFIS) approach was used to investigate the effects of the input parameters, namely, shot type, coverage and incidence angle on the performance parameters, i.e. residual stresses, work hardening and stress concentrations. A confirmation test in terms of fatigue resistance was also carried out to validate the results from which and improvement was obtained.

Keywords: Fuzzy logic · ANFIS · Shot peening · Fatigue

1 Introduction

Engineering surface treatments such as shot peening (SP) have been known to provide a highly effective, versatile and relatively inexpensive method for reducing damage caused by fatigue in metallic materials. It is nowadays used with many different components like aircraft wings, fuselage, etc. In scale and scope the variety of SP applications is remarkable [1]. Evidently, in aerospace industry this process must be accomplished to very stringent specifications to meet safety requirements. This later, demands selection and control of peening parameters. SP is a cold-working process that hardens the surface of a metallic component by bombarding it with a stream of small balls called shots. Generally speaking, SP is viewed as a process involving multiple and progressively repeated impacts. The indentation at each point of impact is the result of

© Springer Nature Switzerland AG 2019
L. Martínez-Villaseñor et al. (Eds.): MICAI 2019, LNAI 11835, pp. 377–390, 2019.
https://doi.org/10.1007/978-3-030-33749-0_30

local plastic deformation. In this sense, the main parameters that control the performance of this process can be identified as media (shot), intensity, incidence angle and coverage. Meanwhile, residual stresses, surface roughness and work hardening are recognized as the main effects induced in the surface layers of the material [2]. Peening parameters and the induced changes observed on the topmost surface and beneath it are depicted in Fig. 1. To obtain optimised and improved conditions for effective strengthening there should be an adequacy for making a decision on the parameters and their levels. Over the last three decades, large amount of research has been accomplished regarding the SP process optimisation [3–6]. Researches have utilised statistical design of experiments (DOE) techniques to evaluate the interaction effect of the process parameters [7, 8], from where the Taguchi approach has become a widespread tool because it utilises a particular design of an orthogonal array to assess the quality characteristics through a reduced number of experiments [9]. Nevertheless, the Taguchi method is limited when dealing with multi-response problems. To address this issue, numerical approaches like finite elements (FE) [10], response surface methodology (RSM) [11], artificial intelligence (AI) methods such as adaptive neural fuzzy inference system (ANFIS) [12, 13], etc. have been successfully performed in order to optimise the desired objectives. As for the SP process, due to its specific nature of the input/output data, there is a need of using one of those numerical techniques that consider non-linear statistical analysis for dealing with ill-defined and uncertain data.

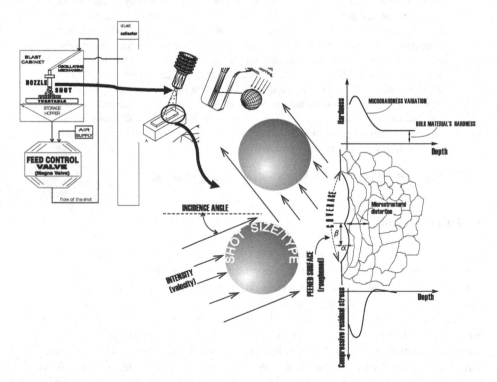

Fig. 1. Schematic illustration of the peening process parameters and the induced surface/subsurface microstructural/mechanical modifications.

Logical, mathematical and statistical approaches provide elimination of inconvenient alternatives and select the most effective parameters letting make multi-criteria decisions. From an extensive list of methods, TOPIS (Technique for Order Performance by Similarity to Ideal Solution), COPRAS (Complex Proportional Assessment), GRA (Grey Relational Analysis) and SAW (Simple Additive Weighting) are widely applied on the engineering field. In this paper, GRA along with ANFIS are combined to manage from process parameters to multi-responses. On one side, GRA effectively performs the conversion of multi response optimisation to the single objective. On the other side, a fuzzy inference system (FIS) utilising fuzzy if-then rules can model the quantitative features of human knowledge and reasoning processes without using conventional mathematical tools [14, 15]. However, FIS has a clear disadvantage in that it lacks successful learning mechanisms. The excellent property of ANFIS is that it compensates for the disadvantage of FIS with the learning mechanism of neural networks. The ANFIS architecture can be obtained by embedding the FIS into the framework of adaptive networks. In this way, the non-linear and complex relationship of the SP process parameters can conveniently be investigated on the mechanical responses through the use of the hybrid GRA-ANFIS approach. The present study proposes a hybrid approach based on GRA-ANFIS to optimise the performance characteristics of an Aluminium Alloy by SP.

2   Materials and Methods

2.1   Specimens and Peening Parameters

This research focuses in obtaining the optimal SP conditions applied on the Aluminium Alloy (AA) 7150-T651. This material is commonly utilised by the aircraft structures [6]. Two different specimen profiles were employed for applying the SP and from where data are extracted. A coupon specimen, for assessing the peening mechanical and microstructural characteristics and a hourglass shape specimen for the constant amplitude fatigue testing, as shown in Fig. 2.

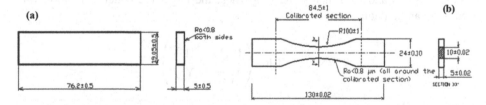

Fig. 2. Specimen profiles: Dimensions for the coupon (a) and the hourglass (b) Dimensions are in mm. The drawings are not to scale.

Chemical composition of the AA is (% wt): 0.5 S, 0.5 Fe, 3.8–4.9 Cu, 0.3–0.9 Mn, 1.2–1.8 Mg, 0.1 Cr, 0.25 Zn, 0.15 Ti, Al Base. Mechanical properties are: Yield strength = 325 MPa, Ultimate strength = 470 MPa, Young Modulus = 72.5 GPa,

Fatigue Limit = 220 MPa and microhardness Vickers = 120–130. In this study, three factors of control and four levels are utilised and listed in Table 1. The assumption is based on the supposition that there is no interaction between each factor.

Table 1. Factors and the control levels.

Factors	Type/Size of shot				Coverage (%)				Incidence angle (°)			
Levels	S230	CCW20	S110	S330	50	100	200	400	30	90	45	90

Where, shot S230, CCW20, S110 and S330 are little balls made of steel with 0.34, 0.72. 0.55 and 0.84 mm in diameter, respectively. The CCW20 shot is a particular rounded steel shot but manufactured from wire. On the other hand, coverage is given in percentage, where 100% represents a surface completely indented. The incidence angle is given in sexagesimal degrees, where 90° is considered an output position of the shot through the nozzle, perpendicular to the surface to be impacted.

2.2 Grey-Fuzzy Taguchi Approach

A $L_{16}(4^3)$ orthogonal array experiment was selected to produce a uniform distribution of multi-responses under experimental control factors (Table 2). Orthogonal arrays exhibit self-balancing properties and make up only a fraction of full factorial experiments. The signal-noise ratio (S/N) was employed for adjusting the quality of output in the Taguchi method. In this piece of research, the smaller the better S/N metric was assigned to the surface roughness factor. It was estimated by the following mathematical expression:

$$S/N = -10 \, \log \left(\frac{1}{n} \sum_{i=1}^{n} Y_i^2 \right) \tag{1}$$

where Y_i is the experimental value of the ith trial, and n is the number of trials. For the residual stresses and work hardening properties, the larger the better estimation was used and can be defined as:

$$S/N = -10 \, \log \left(\frac{1}{n} \sum_{i=1}^{n} \left(\frac{1}{Y_i^2} \right) \right) \tag{2}$$

Based on the orthogonal results, the conversion of multi response optimisation to the single objective method is carried out by GRA effectively. This is performed according to the following parts;

(a) The response should be normalised and S/N ratio is then used. Using (3) provides calculation for normalised values of k_{th} performance of the sequence $x_i^*(k)$, for this particular case, the larger the better metric is used for the residual stresses and work hardening responses;

$$x_i^*(k) = \frac{x_i(k) - \min x_i(k)}{\max x_i(k) - \min x_i(k)} \tag{3}$$

(b) The Eq. (4) is the smaller the better metric used for the stress concentrations response;

$$x_i^*(k) = \frac{\max x_i(k) - x_i(k)}{\max x_i(k) - \min x_i(k)} \tag{4}$$

A normalised matrix is generated with (3) and (4). From this matrix, a reference value is determined as the largest value of normalised value for each criterion:

$$x_0'(k) = \max_{i=1}^n x_i^*(k) \tag{5}$$

The difference matrix by taking the difference between the normalised entity and reference value is determined as:

$$\Delta_{oi}(k) = \left\| x_0'(k) - x_i^*(k) \right\| \tag{6}$$

The relationship between the ideal and actual normalised results are expressed by evaluating the grey relational coefficient.

$$\delta_{oi}(k) = \frac{\min_{i=1}^n \min_i^m \Delta_{oi}(k) + \zeta \times \max_{i=1}^n \max_{j=1}^m \Delta_{oi}(k)}{\Delta_{oi}(k) + \zeta \times \max_{i=1}^n \max_{j=1}^m \Delta_{oi}(k)} \tag{7}$$

where ζ $(0 \leq \zeta \leq 1)$ is known as the distinguish coefficient or the index for distinguishability. If the value of ζ is small there will be higher distinguishability. In most situations, ζ is taken the value of 0.5 because this value provides moderate distinguishing effects and good stability [16]. The grey relational grade is a single numerical value which depicts the optimisation of the multiple performance characteristics, mathematically expressed as:

$$\gamma_{oi} = \frac{1}{m} \sum_{i=1}^m \delta_{oi}(j) \tag{8}$$

The grey relational grade is calculated by using (8) while considering the same weightage for performance characteristics, i.e. 1. In (8) m represents the number of performance characteristics assuming that they are equally important. Hence, the greatest value of grey relational grade represents the level of process parameters for optimal performance characteristics.

Table 2. Orthogonal array and its factors, control levels, with responses. Shaded cells (run 8) provide optimum control parameters.

RUN	ORTHOGONAL ARRAY L₁₆(4³)					FACTORS			RESPONSES (experimental data)		
	A	B	D			A Shot (mm)	B Coverage (%)	D Angle (degrees)	RS (MPa)	Work hardening $Hv_{0.1\,max}$	Stress concentrations K_t
									These are the values of Y en (1) and (2)		
1	1	1	1	1	1	S230 (0.584)	50	30	-117.6	153	1.39
2	1	2	2	2	2		100	90	-321.7	167	1.45
3	1	3	3	3	3		200	45	-233.8	154	1.4
4	1	4	4	4	4		400	90	-284.6	164	1.55
5	2	1	2	3	4	CCW20 (0.5)	50	45	-287.2	168	1.44
6	2	2	1	4	3		100	90	-260.2	152	1.57
7	2	3	4	1	2		200	30	-153.9	155	1.6
8	2	4	3	2	1		400	90	-363.8	155	1.74
9	3	1	3	4	2	S110 (0.279)	50	90	-306.7	151	1.45
10	3	2	4	3	1		100	45	-115.5	155	1.44
11	3	3	1	2	4		200	90	-135.4	163	1.49
12	3	4	2	1	3		400	30	-205.0	160	1.56
13	4	1	4	2	3	S330 (0.838)	50	90	-290.5	162	1.43
14	4	2	3	1	4		100	30	-180.2	158	1.48
15	4	3	2	4	1		200	90	-347.9	163	1.47
16	4	4	1	3	2		400	45	-247.4	157	1.65

ANFIS is an artificial intelligence way used for solving complicated and nonlinear systems [17–19]. It is a data driven procedure which can be used to provide the solution of function approximation problems in a neural network platform. Here at first a FIS comprising of an initial fuzzy model is formed, based on the fuzzy rules extracted from the input- output data set. In the next step the neural network is used to fine tune the rules of the initial fuzzy model that was built. Using ANFIS methodology the network is trained. The structure of the ANFIS model used in this study [20] comprises node segments and five different layers (fuzzy layer, product layer, normalised layer, layer of defuzzification and output layer). Each of the layers contains several nodes described by node functions. The mechanism of fuzzy reasoning for deriving an output f given an input vector [x, y] is shown in Fig. 3. The rule base contains the fuzzy if-then rules of Takagi and Sugeno's type [20] described as follows:

$$\text{If } x \text{ is A and } y \text{ is B then } z \text{ is } f(x, y)$$

where A and B are the fuzzy sets in the antecedents and $z = f(x, y)$ is a crisp function in the consequent. Usually $f(x, y)$ is a polynomial for the input variables x and y. If $f(x, y)$ is taken to be a first order polynomial a first order Sugeno fuzzy model is formed. For a first order two rule Sugeno fuzzy inference system, the two rules may be stated as:

$$\text{Rule 1}: \text{ If } x \text{ is } A_1 \text{ and } y \text{ is } B_1 \text{ then } f_1 = p_1 x + q_1 y + r_1$$
$$\text{Rule 2}: \text{ If } x \text{ is } A_2 \text{ and } y \text{ is } B_2 \text{ then } f_2 = p_2 x + q_2 y + r_2$$

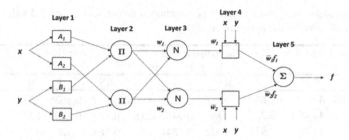

Fig. 3. Type Takagi and Sugeno ANFIS structure.

The individual layers of the above ANFIS structure are described below:

Layer 1. Every node i in this layer is adaptive with a node function $O_i^1 = \mu_{A_i}(x)$. where, x is the input to node i, A_i is the linguistic variable associated with this node function (Low, Medium and High for this study) and μ_{Ai} is the membership function of A_i. Usually $\mu_{Ai}(x)$ is chosen as

$$\mu_{A_i}(x) = \frac{1}{1 + \left[\left(\frac{x - c_i}{a_i}\right)^2\right]^{b_i}} \text{ or } \mu_{A_i}(x) = \exp\left\{-\left(\frac{x - c_i}{a_i}\right)^2\right\}$$

Layer 2. Each node in this layer is a fixed node which calculates the firing strength w_i of a rule. The output of each node is the product of all incoming signals to it and is given by, $O_i^2 = w_i = \mu_{A_i}(x) \times \mu_{B_i}(y), \quad i = 1, 2$

Layer 3. Every node in this layer is a fixed node. Each ith node calculates the ratio of the ith rule's firing strength to the sum of firing strengths of all the rules. The output from the ith node is the normalised firing strength given by, $O_i^3 = \bar{w}_i = \frac{w_i}{w_1 + w_2}, \quad i = 1, 2$

Layer 4. Every node in this layer is an adaptive node with a node function given by $O_i^4 = \bar{w}_i f_i = \bar{w}_i(p_i x + q_i y + r_i), \quad i = 1, 2$ where $\bar{w}_i$ is the output of the layer 3 and is the consequent parameter set.

Layer 5. This layer comprises of only one fixed node that calculates the overall output as the summation of all incoming signals, i.e.

$$O_i^5 = overall\ output = \sum_i \bar{w}_i f_i = \frac{\sum_i w_i f}{\sum_i w_i} \quad i = 1, 2$$

3 Results and Discussion

3.1 Grey-Taguchi

A normalised matrix was constructed for the three experimental responses by (1) and (4). The grey relational coefficients were determined and the grey relational grade of comparability sequence for $k = 1$–16 was obtained as shown in Table 3.

Table 3. Normalised data and GR grade performance characteristics. Shaded value in column GRC is and indicative of the optimum conditions.

	Normalized data S/N Eq. (2)			Normalized data Grey Eq. (3)			GR coefficients Eq. (7)			GRG Eq.(8)
	RS	WH	SC	RS	WH	SC	RS	WH	SC	
1	41.408	43.694	-2.860	0.016	0.123	0.000	0.337	0.363	0.333	0.344
2	50.151	44.454	-3.227	0.893	0.944	0.188	0.824	0.899	0.381	0.701
3	47.377	43.750	-2.923	0.615	0.184	0.032	0.565	0.380	0.341	0.428
4	49.085	44.297	-3.807	0.786	0.774	0.485	0.700	0.689	0.493	0.627
5	49.164	44.506	-3.167	0.794	1.000	0.157	0.708	1.000	0.372	0.693
6	48.306	43.637	-3.918	0.708	0.062	0.542	0.631	0.348	0.522	0.500
7	43.745	43.807	-4.082	0.250	0.245	0.626	0.400	0.398	0.572	0.457
8	51.218	43.807	-4.811	1.000	0.245	1.000	1.000	0.398	1.000	0.799
9	49.734	43.580	-3.227	0.851	0.000	0.188	0.771	0.333	0.381	0.495
10	41.252	43.807	-3.167	0.000	0.245	0.157	0.333	0.398	0.372	0.368
11	42.632	44.244	-3.464	0.139	0.717	0.309	0.367	0.638	0.420	0.475
12	46.235	44.082	-3.862	0.500	0.543	0.514	0.500	0.522	0.507	0.510
13	49.263	44.190	-3.107	0.804	0.659	0.126	0.718	0.595	0.364	0.559
14	45.115	43.973	-3.405	0.388	0.425	0.279	0.449	0.465	0.410	0.441
15	50.829	44.244	-3.346	0.961	0.717	0.249	0.928	0.638	0.400	0.655
16	47.868	43.918	-4.350	0.664	0.365	0.764	0.598	0.441	0.679	0.573

The average of the GRG for each level of the test parameters is compiled in Table 4. This response table contains values obtained when the highest number is withdrawn from each row. The rank is an indicative of the significance in the contribution of the particular parameter under analysis. It can be readily deduced from the response table that incidence angle has the highest contribution, followed by coverage, and then shot parameter. The optimal condition for the tested parameters for maximum residual stresses and work hardening and minimum stress concentrations (surface roughness) is found to be A2 (shot type/size = CCW20), B4 (coverage = 400%) and D2 (incidence angle = 90°). These optimum parameters are in line with the resulted parameters from experiment 8 as can be seen in Table 3 along with Table 2. As previously stated, the largest value for the GRG, i.e. run 8, corresponds to the optimum condition that satisfies the selected criteria of the multi-responses.

Table 4. Response table for GRG at each level of the process parameters.

Parameter	GRG averages				Max	Rank	Optimum parameter and level	Actual value
	Level 1	Level 2	Level 3	Level 4				
Shot (A)	0.525	0.613	0.462	0.557	0.613	3	**A2**	CCW20
Coverage (B)	0.523	0.503	0.504	0.627	0.627	2	**B4**	400
Incidence angle (D)	0.438	0.634	0.516	0.569	0.634	1	**D2**	90

3.2   Grey-ANFIS Model Structure and Parameters

In this study, the Matlab ANFIS toolbox is used for ANFIS applications. The structure of proposed ANFIS networks consisted of three input variables including the GRC of the residual stresses (RS), work hardening (WH) and stress concentrations (SC). The value for output layer was the Grey Relational Fuzzy Grade (GRFG). The input space is decomposed by three fuzzy linguist variables. In this paper, triangular membership functions (MFs) were utilised to construct the suggested models. It was stablished to use twenty-seven fuzzy rules to determine the GRFG. The fuzzy rule viewer for the FIS environment (where the Mamdani inference system prevails) is shown in Fig. 4. As an example, some of the designed rules in the FIS environment are described as follows:

Rule 1: If (RS is Low) and (WH is Low) and (SC is Low) Then (GRFG is VeryVery Low).
Rule 2: If (RS is Low) and (WH is Low) and (SC is Medium) Then (GRFG is Very Low).
Rule 27: If (RS is High) and (WH is High) and (SC is High) Then (GRFG is VeryVery High).

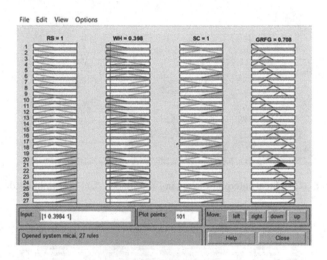

Fig. 4. Rule viewer of fuzzy model in the FIS environment.

The ANFIS-GUI is created on the ANFIS editor and predicts the output. The loaded data and training data are shown in the testing data and predicted data of the interphase of the Fig. 5. These training and checking data sets are collected based on the observation of the target system and are stored in separate files. The ANFIS models were trained, from 78 number of nodes. A number of linear parameters was 108. A number of nonlinear parameters was 27. The total number of parameters was 135. A number of training data pairs was 16. Number of checking data pairs: 0, number of fuzzy rules: 27. Furthermore, up to 50 epochs were specified for training process to assure the gaining of the minimum error tolerance. Backpropagation optimisation method for training the FIS was selected in this study due to the fact that is widely used for engineering applications. In order for obtaining the ANFIS grades, the GRC's must be introduced in the fuzzy rule viewer of ANFIS. The fuzzy rule viewer for the ANFIS environment (once the Mamdani inference system is converted into Sugeno inference system through a few particular commands of Matlab) is shown in Fig. 6.

The grey relational grade, grey relational fuzzy grade and ANFIS grade are shown in Fig. 7. The higher of GRG, GFRG and ANFIS grade means the better corresponding to multiple responses. The highest grade in Fig. 7 can be considered to be closed to the optimal. However, as can be appreciated in Fig. 7 (circled in dash), all the grades from the different approaches are very close each other in experiment 8, with the maximum grade value. It seems to be that ANFIS is in-between the GRG and GRFG, thus, ANFIS would be the technique to be chosen for SP optimisation of the process parameters. Experiments 2 and 5 also provide high grade values for all approaches. According to Table 2, factors and levels resemble to experiment 8, all in terms of the larger RS and WH.

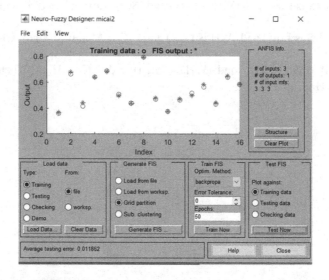

Fig. 5. Graphical interphase showing the loaded data and training data.

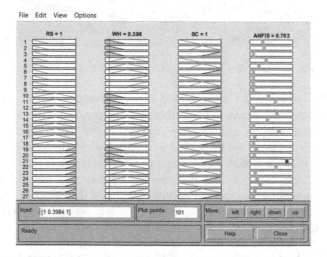

Fig. 6. Rule viewer of fuzzy model in the ANFIS environment.

The average of the ANFIS grades for each level of the test parameters is compiled in Table 5 and plotted in the graph of Fig. 8. It can be observed from the graph and the response table that incidence angle has slightly the highest contribution compared to those of coverage and shot. Optimum conditions for the tested parameters remain alike the parameters shown in Table 4. Such conditions are indicated by arrows in Fig. 8. These optimum parameters are also in line with the resulted parameters from experiment 8 as shown in Fig. 7 along with Table 2 (shadowed row). As previously stated, the largest value for the ANFIS, i.e. run 8, corresponds to the optimum condition which satisfies the selected criteria of the multi-responses.

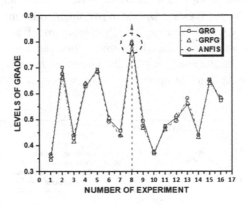

Fig. 7. Behaviour of the resulted grades by each approach.

Table 5. Response table for ANFIS at each level of the process parameters.

Parameter	ANFIS Averages				Max	Rank	Optimum parameter and level	Actual value
	Level 1	Level 2	Level 3	Level 4				
Shot (A)	0.530	0.602	0.454	0.564	0.602	3	**A2**	CCW20
Coverage (B)	0.527	0.497	0.499	0.627	0.627	2	**B4**	400
Incidence angle (D)	0.436	0.630	0.521	0.564	0.630	1	**D2**	90

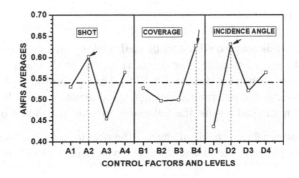

Fig. 8. ANFIS averages.

3.3   Fatigue Resistance with Optimum Conditions

Conventional uniaxial tension-tension fatigue tests were carried out using hourglass specimens as described in Sect. 2.1. SP of the specimens was undertaken according to optimum conditions, i.e. A2(shot type/size = CCW20), B4(coverage = 400%) and D2 (incidence angle = 90°). The results of fatigue tests are graphically presented in the form of Wöhler stress versus cycles to failure (S-N) curves over a wide range of applied stresses as depicted in Fig. 9. The fatigue endurance is defined as the endurance stress at or below which a specimen can sustain cycling for up to 7×10^6 cycles without failing.

Trends observed in the fatigue life curves revealed that shot peened specimens have a marginally superior life compared to those unpeened, specifically at an intermediate zone of the low cycle fatigue regions. Optimum peening conditions, on the whole, were found to be better as expected from the ANFIS estimations. Furthermore, there was a discernible improvement in endurance by peened specimens when tested at stresses around 300 MPa. The fatigue endurance for the unpeened material was approximately 230 MPa, whilst for the peened at optimum condition was 225 MPa.

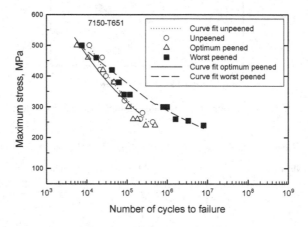

Fig. 9. Axial loading, constant amplitude S-N curves for peened at resulted conditions and unpeened specimens of AA 7150-T651.

4   Conclusions

Grey relational analysis coupled with ANFIS methodology was successfully applied in this experimental piece of research. The objective of this study was to obtain the best fatigue performance of the shot peened AA 7150-T651 given the application of optimised peening conditions, determined through a systematic study. Based upon the experimental and numerical results, the following conclusions can be drawn:

1. The plethora of variables capable of altering the peening process, and hence fatigue life, is a strict process control and therefore a systematic study using ANFIS is pertinent.
2. Coverage and incidence angle were identified as largely the peening responses.

3. The AA 7150-T651 peened to optimum conditions (CCW20, 400%, 90°) exhibited superior fatigue performance than initial peened conditions, and also to unpenned surfaces.
4. The result of the confirmation experiment and fatigue testing implies that the Grey-fuzzy logic methodology is very effective for optimising the multi-response characteristics in SP within the ranges of the control factors studied.
5. The advantages of the Grey-fuzzy logic approach compared to classical methods lay on speed, simplicity, and low cost. Therefore, this approach could be considered to be applied in engineering situations, such as shot peening, laser peening, burnishing, water peening, and other deposition processes like thin films, etc.
6. From the results obtained, it is shown that the Sugeno system performs quite well for approximating reasoning that can provide logical implications in the form of a set of rules useful for optimisation of multiple responses in the case of the shot peened metallic materials. Although in some cases is not appropriate to explore the logical deductive consequences of a set of if-then implications, these have been quite successful on practical applications, mainly in the field of control systems. One reason for employing this kind of systems is the fact that they are universal approximators that allow knowledge to be included in the form of linguistic rules that can be used for local fine-tuning.

Acknowledgements. The authors would like to thank the Secretary of Public Education of Mexico/TecNM for the financial support. The University of Sheffield, U.K., for offering facilities to implement the project is also gratefully acknowledged.

References

1. Wagner, L.: Response of light alloys to shot peening: comparison of magnesium and aluminium alloy. Met. Finish. News **3**, 12–13 (2002)
2. Mylonas, G.I., Labeas, G.: Numerical modelling of shot peening process and corresponding products: residual stress, surface roughness and cold work prediction. Surf. Coat. Technol. **205**(19), 4480–4494 (2011)
3. George, P.M., Pillai, N., Shah, N.: Optimization of shot peening parameters using Taguchi technique. J. Mater. Process. Technol. **153–154**, 925–930 (2004)
4. Evans, R.W.: Shot peening process: modelling, verification, and optimisation. Mater. Sci. Technol. **18**(8), 831–839 (2002)
5. Khany, S.E., et al.: An experimental study of the effect of shot peening on the low carbon steel and identification of optimal process parameters. Mater. Today Proc. **2**(4), 3363–3370 (2015)
6. Nam, Y.-S., et al.: Use of response surface methodology for shot peening process optimization of an aircraft structural part. Int. J. Adv. Manuf. Technol. **87**(9), 2967–2981 (2016)
7. Mahagaonkar, S.B., Brahmankar, P.K., Seemikeri, C.Y.: Effect on fatigue performance of shot peened components: an analysis using DOE technique. Int. J. Fatigue **31**(4), 693–702 (2009)
8. Rodopoulos, C.A., et al.: Optimisation of the fatigue resistance of 2024-T351 aluminium alloys by controlled shot peening—methodology, results and analysis. Int. J. Fatigue **26**(8), 849–856 (2004)

9. Fowlkes, W., Creveling, M.: Clyde, Engineering Methods for Robust Product Design: Using Taguchi Methods in Technology and Product Development. Addison Wesley Longman, Inc., Boston (1995)

10. Bagherifard, S., Ghelichi, R., Guagliano, M.: Numerical and experimental analysis of surface roughness generated by shot peening. Appl. Surf. Sci. **258**(18), 6831–6840 (2012)

11. Unal, O.: Optimization of shot peening parameters by response surface methodology. Surf. Coat. Technol. **305**, 99–109 (2016)

12. Sun, L.-X., Li, M.-Q., Li, H.-M.: Prediction model for surface layer microhardness of processed TC17 via high energy shot peening. Trans. Nonferrous Metals Soc. China **27**(9), 1956–1963 (2017)

13. Karataş, C., Sozen, A., Dulek, E.: Modelling of residual stresses in the shot peened material C-1020 by artificial neural network. Expert Syst. Appl. **36**(2), 3514–3521 (2009)

14. Zadeh, L.A.: Fuzzy sets. Inf. Control **8**(3), 338–353 (1965)

15. Sugeno, M., Kang, G.T.: Structure identification of fuzzy model. Fuzzy Sets Syst. **28**(1), 15–33 (1988)

16. Chang, T.C., Lin, S.J.: Grey relation analysis of carbon dioxide emissions from industrial production and energy uses in Taiwan. J. Environ. Manag. **56**(4), 247–257 (1999)

17. Jang, J.-S.R.: ANFIS: adaptive-network-based fuzzy inference system. IEEE Trans. Syst. Man Cybern. **23**(3), 665–685 (1993)

18. Jang, J.-S.R., Sun, C.-T., Mizutani, E.: Neuro-Fuzzy and Soft Computing: A Computational Approach to Learning and Machine Intelligence. Prentice-Hall Inc., USA (1997)

19. Jang, J.R., Chuen-Tsai, S.: Neuro-fuzzy modeling and control. Proc. IEEE **83**(3), 378–406 (1995)

20. Sugeno, T.T.A.M.: Derivation of fuzzy control rules from human operator's control action. In: Proceedings of IFAC Symposium Fuzzy Information, Knowledge Representation and Decision Analysis (1983)

An Approach to Knowledge Discovery for Fault Detection by Using Compensatory Fuzzy Logic

Francisco G. Salas$^{(\boxtimes)}$ (iD), Raymundo Juarez del Toro, Rafael Espin, and Juan Manuel Jimenez

Facultad de Contaduria y Administracion, Universidad Autonoma de Coahuila, Blvd. Revolucion 151 Oriente, Col. Centro, 27000 Torreon, Coahuila, Mexico
francisco.salas@uadec.edu.mx

Abstract. Failure diagnosis and prevention are crucial areas of interest for the proposal of innovative methods and techniques that can help to increase the availability of industrial machinery and other complex systems. In this work we propose a Knowledge Discovery scheme, based on a Compensatory Fuzzy Logic (CFL), for failure detection and prevention. With an exploratory approach, the proposed methodology includes obtaining a characterization of operating conditions of a system, which can be useful for detecting harmful conditions. As a case of study we obtain data of operating conditions of a direct current (DC) motor. A set of fuzzy predicates are formulated and evaluated using the degrees of membership of the variables of the motor to adequate fuzzy membership functions. The truth values resulting of such evaluations are analyzed in view of the empiric knowledge of failures occurrence of DC motors. The main contribution of this work is to explore the possible advantages of using the compensatory fuzzy logic approach for fuzzy predicate evaluation for fault detection and prevention, which could be applied later to more complex systems.

Keywords: Knowledge Discovery · Fuzzy logic · Failure detection · Interpretability

1 Introduction

Fault diagnosis and prevention techniques in industrial machinery are important study areas from the economic point of view since early diagnosis and prevention of failures can avoid unexpected breakdowns in industrial processes, along with the consequence of economic losses. The need for improved methods for failure detection and prevention has led to the application of a variety of techniques, ranging from Signal Processing - based condition monitoring to Artificial Intelligence - based techniques, such as Genetic Algorithms, Neural Networks, Clustering Analysis, Particle Swarm Optimization, Fuzzy Logic and others for the development of new methods [1].

© Springer Nature Switzerland AG 2019
L. Martínez-Villaseñor et al. (Eds.): MICAI 2019, LNAI 11835, pp. 391–402, 2019.
https://doi.org/10.1007/978-3-030-33749-0_31

Relevant previous related works include a fault detection method based on an incremental learning algorithm for Support Vector Machines, which was proposed in [1] for fault recognition in High Voltage Circuit Breakers (HVCB). The method was verified on its application to detecting four common faults of the HVCB. In [2] an intelligent machine fault diagnosis scheme is proposed, which is based on wavelet decomposition of signals and extraction of statistical features at different decomposition depths to characterize the machine health status. The proposed scheme is applied to the fault diagnosis of bearings and gears of a rotating machine. In [3] a methodology of Knowledge Discovery is proposed for the data driven-based fault diagnostics in building energy systems, in which the key algorithm is the classification based on associations. This approach integrates both supervised fault diagnostics and unsupervised association rule mining. A signal model-based fault coding to monitor circuit response after being stimulated to perform fault diagnostics and prediction in analog circuits is proposed in [4]. Fault coding is treated as an optimization problem and the optimized solution forms a fault code representing fault class, suitable for realizing fault detection for different components.

On the other hand, Knowledge Discovery can be described as an approach for developing reliable and effective computational tools for analyzing large datasets with the purpose of extracting new knowledge from data [5]. Knowledge Discovery from Data often is identified as Data Mining, although in a strict sense, Data Mining can be rather considered as a tool or methodology for the purpose of Knowledge Discovery [5]. The fields of application of Knowledge Discovery from Data are very diverse, from marketing, banking, bioinformatics, scientific analysis in medicine, to a diversity of other applications in decision support systems [6].

Fuzzy Logic has been a very useful approach to represent expert knowledge of the operation of systems or processes from experimental sources or mathematical models. Fuzzy logic can be roughly defined as a variety of methodologies proposing logical consideration of imperfect and vague knowledge [7]. From an elemental perspective, the focus of Fuzzy logic is on linguistic variables in natural language and aims to provide foundations for approximate reasoning with imprecise propositions. It reflects both the rightness and vagueness of natural language in common-sense reasoning. It can be pointed out that a particularly interesting attribute of Fuzzy logic is its interpretability, which is the property fulfilled by a logical theory such that there is a two sided relationship between the results of the calculus upon the field of such theory over its objects by using its operators and, on the other side, the meanings of the objects represented in the natural or professional language [8]. In this sense, interpretability is a desired property for a fault detection system based on fuzzy logic, as it could help to build more intuitive and concrete relationships between the results of knowledge discovery processes and real objects of study. A recently proposed fuzzy logic system that exhibits the interpretability property is the Compensatory Fuzzy Logic (CFL) [9]. According to [8], such an approach satisfies the characteristics of descriptive and normative approaches to decision making.

In this work we are focused in developing a method for failure detection based on a fuzzy logic system that exhibits the property of interpretability. Due to this, in this work we propose, with an exploratory approach, a methodology for failure detection based on obtaining a characterization of operating conditions of a system by applying CFL. The CFL is applied in a scheme of proposition and evaluation of fuzzy predicates. As case of study, we obtain data of operating conditions of a direct current (DC) motor by conducting numerical simulations of a mathematical model of the DC motor. From this simulation the variables or states of the motor are obtained. A number of appropriate fuzzy membership functions are formulated for evaluating the membership of the variables of the motor to them. A set of fuzzy predicates are formulated, from which the truth values are evaluated. The results of such evaluations are analyzed in view of expert knowledge on the operating of the DC motor. The main contribution of this work is to explore the possible advantages of using the CFL approach for fuzzy predicate evaluation for fault detection and prevention, which could be further applied to more complex systems.

The remains of this work is structured as follows. In next section CFL is described. In Sect. 3 the methodology for this work is outlined. Next, in Sect. 4 the procedure of evaluation of fuzzy predicates is described. Then, in Sect. 5 the results of numerical simulations and evaluation of fuzzy predicates are shown and discussed. Finally, some concluding remarks are given.

2   Compensatory Fuzzy Logic

A fuzzy predicate or conditional fuzzy proposition can be formed by using the conjunction and implication operators on fuzzy propositions, i.e., x_1 is K_1, x_2 is K_2, x_n is K_n, and z is M, where K_1, K_2, K_n, and M, are linguistic labels representing fuzzy sets associated with the base variables x_1, x_2, x_n and z. Then, a fuzzy predicate has the form:

$$x_1 \text{ is } K_1 \text{ and } x_2 \text{ is } K_2 \text{ and } \ldots \text{ and } x_n \text{ is } K_n \text{ implies } z \text{ is } M.$$

where x_1 is K_1, x_2 is K_2, x_n is K_n are the premises and z is M is the conclusion.

CFL is a multivalued logic axiomatic approach that must satisfy characteristics of a descriptive and a normative approaches to decision making. CFL is different to traditional Fuzzy Logic (FL) by the set of axioms on which is based [8]. For FL the truth value of a conjunction is always smaller or equal than the truth values of its components. According to [10], in CFL, the decrease of the truth value in a component variable is compensated by the increase in another variable to allow for higher values on the conjunction. An analogous behaviour can be seen in disjunctions. This behaviour makes CFL an interesting approach to model decision-making realized by humans [11]. CFL is based on the four following continuous operators: a conjunction $C : [0,1]^n \rightarrow [0,1]$, a disjunction $D : [0,1]^n \rightarrow [0,1]$, an order $O : [0,1]^n \rightarrow [0,1]$ and a negation $N : [0,1] \rightarrow [0,1]$ that a satisfies a certain set of axioms [10].

A particular system of CFL [12] in the family of Quasi Arithmetic Mean based Compensatory Logic (QAMBCL) is the Geometric Mean based Compensatory Logic (GMBCL). In this logic system, the implication operator is

$$i(y, \mu_M(z)) = 1 - \sqrt{y - y\mu_M(z)} \tag{1}$$

where $y = c(\mu_{K_1}(x_1), \mu_{K_2}(x_2), \ldots, \mu_{K_n}(x_n))$ is the conjunction of the fuzzy membership degrees $\mu_{K_1}(x_1), \mu_{K_2}(x_2), \ldots, \mu_{K_n}(x_n)$ and is computed as

$$y = c(\mu_{K_1}(x_1), \mu_{K_2}(x_2), \ldots, \mu_{K_n}(x_n)) = \sqrt[n]{\Pi_{i=1}^n \mu_{K_i}(x_i)} \tag{2}$$

and $\mu_M(z)$ is the fuzzy membership degree of variable z to the fuzzy set M. Some examples of application of CFL are in business decision making, such as knowledge discovery in Mexican Economy [9], decision making illustrating competitive positioning model [8]. Moreover, medical applications for identifying resonance images are reported in [13] and [14].

3   Methodology

The methodology of the proposed approach is outlined below.

1. Identifying the variables of interest for characterization of abnormal operation conditions of the system under study.
2. Proposing fuzzy membership functions for fuzzy characterization of the system, which includes formulation of linguistic labels and fuzzy propositions.
3. Formulation of fuzzy predicates.
4. Evaluation of fuzzy predicates by using GMBCL, which includes:
   - Simulation of the model (or data recollection) of the system under study.
   - Evaluation of the fuzzy functions.
   - Evaluation of the fuzzy predicates.
5. Analysis of the truth values obtained from the fuzzy predicates.

3.1   Mathematical Model of a DC Motor

The equations of the model of a DC motor are [15]

$$L\frac{di}{dt} + Ri + k_e\frac{d\theta}{dt} = V, \tag{3}$$

$$J\frac{d^2\theta}{dt^2} + b\frac{d\theta}{dt} = T_a \tag{4}$$

where variables i and θ are the armature current and the angular position of the shaft of the motor, respectively. $\frac{d\theta}{dt}$ is the velocity of the shaft of the motor. Parameters L, R, b, V, J and k_e are the armature inductance, armature resistance, viscous friction coefficient, magnitude of the applied voltage, rotor inertia and motor constant, respectively. T_a is defined as the acceleration torque. By considering a load torque T_L applied to the motor, we can rewrite Eq. (4) as

$$J\frac{d^2\theta}{dt^2} + b\frac{d\theta}{dt} = T_e - T_L \tag{5}$$

where T_e is the electric torque defined as

$$T_e = k_t i \tag{6}$$

with k_t as the torque constant of the motor. The variables of interest or state variables for studying the fault occurrence in this work are i and $\dot{\theta} = \frac{d\theta}{dt}$. Moreover, parameters b and T_L are important from the viewpoint of detection of safe or unsafe operating conditions. Thus, based on an empirical understanding of the operation of DC motors, in this work we make the following assumptions:

A1: Increment of b corresponds to abnormal operating conditions of the motor, which can lead to motor failure.

A2: Increment of b can be detected by measuring changes in state variables i and/or $\dot{\theta}$.

A3: Increment of T_L corresponds to abnormal operating conditions of the motor, which can be lead to motor failure.

A4: Increment of T_L can be detected by measuring changes in state variables i and/or $\dot{\theta}$.

Therefore, a scheme of variation of parameters b and T_L as functions of time is proposed in order to simulate changes in motor operating conditions. For this purpose, we propose two simulation cases:

Case I: b is not constant but is time variable. T_L is constant.
Case II: T_L is not constant but is time variable. b is constant.

3.2   Fuzzy Membership Functions

Evaluation of fuzzy predicates requires to evaluate the fuzzy membership degrees of state variables to fuzzy membership functions. Selection of the membership functions was based on the linguistic labels chosen to characterize the state

Table 1. Full names and abbreviated names of the linguistic labels for variables and parameters

Variables	Linguistic labels
Armature current (AC)	Normal (N), High (H)
Rotor velocity (RV)	Low (L), Normal (N)
Load torque (TL)	Normal (N), High (H)
Friction coefficient (FC)	Normal (N), High (H)

variables i and $\dot{\theta}$ and variable parameters b and T_L. The linguistic labels were selected based on a dualistic classification of each of the variables. This selection of linguistic terms was done for the sake of simplicity. However, by choosing more linguistic terms for each variable, the characterization could be done in a more precise way. Nevertheless, more linguistic terms would increase the quantity of fuzzy predicates to be evaluated, with the consequent rise in complexity and computing time. The linguistic labels are shown in Table 1. In this table, the full names and the abbreviated names of the variables and labels are shown. The label Normal represents an operating condition close to the rated values of armature current and rotor velocity of the motor, and the estimated values of load torque and friction coefficient in a particular application. The labels High and Low represent operating conditions that are significantly above or below, respectively, to the rated values. The selected fuzzy membership functions are sigmoid and complementary sigmoid functions. Sigmoid function parameters are c (inflexion point) and a (slope at c). In Fig. 1 a sigmoid function and a complementary sigmoid functions are shown. These functions were plotted in Matlab with parameters $c = 5$ for both functions, $a = 1$ for sigmoid and $a = -1$ for complementary sigmoid.

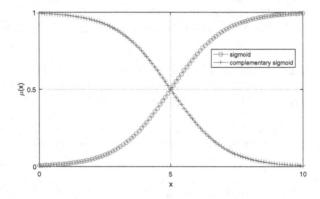

Fig. 1. Sigmoid function and complementary sigmoid functions for fuzzification of variables of interest. Parameters used for plotting are: $c = 5$ (inflexion point) for both functions, $a = 1$ (slope at c) for sigmoid function and $a = -1$ for complementary sigmoid function

3.3   Fuzzy Predicates

According to the linguistic labels that can be assigned (see Table 1), two fuzzy propositions were created for each variable. For example, by assigning linguistic labels to variable armature current AC, the fuzzy propositions **Armature Current is High** and **Armature Current is Normal**, were created. In our study, in simulation case I the independent variables are armature current and rotor velocity, with friction coefficient as the dependent variable and constant load torque. In simulation case II the independent variables are armature current and rotor velocity, with load torque as the dependent variable and constant friction coefficient. This selection of independent and dependent variables was done with the purpose of identify risk situations in variables subject to external disturbances due to changing environmental or working conditions. In simulation case I, the premise of the first fuzzy predicate is the conjunction of the two fuzzy propositions created by assigning one linguistic label to each of the independent variables, this is, armature current and rotor velocity. The conclusion of the first fuzzy predicate is the first fuzzy proposition created by assigning one linguistic label to the dependent variable, this is, the friction coefficient. According to this procedure, the first fuzzy predicate is:

Normal Armature Current *and* **Low Rotor Velocity** *imply* **Normal Friction Coefficient**. By combining in this way the two fuzzy propositions for each of the three variables and parameters, a set of eight fuzzy predicates is obtained.

In simulation case II, the premise of the first fuzzy predicate is the conjunction of the two fuzzy propositions created by assigning one linguistic label to each of the independent variables, this is, armature current and rotor velocity. The conclusion of the first fuzzy predicate is the first fuzzy proposition created by assigning one linguistic label to the dependent variable, this is, the load torque. In a similar way to simulation case I, according to this procedure, the first fuzzy predicate is:

Normal Armature Current *and* **Low Rotor Velocity** *imply* **Normal Load Torque**. Similarly to Case I, by combining in this way the two fuzzy propositions for each of the three variables and parameters, a set of eight fuzzy predicates is obtained. The full set of fuzzy predicates obtained in both cases is shown in abbreviated form in Table 2.

Table 2. Fuzzy predicates for Cases I and II

Number	Fuzzy predicates for Case I	Fuzzy predicates for Case II
1	N AC and L RV imply N FC	N AC and L RV imply N TL
2	N AC and N RV imply N FC	N AC and N RV imply N TL
3	H AC and L RV imply N FC	H AC and L RV imply N TL
4	H AC and N RV imply N FC	H AC and N RV imply N TL
5	N AC and L RV imply H FC	N AC and L RV imply H TL
6	N AC and N RV imply H FC	N AC and N RV imply H TL
7	H AC and L RV imply H FC	H AC and L RV imply H TL
8	H AC and N RV imply H FC	H AC and N RV imply H TL

Table 3. DC motor parameters for numerical simulations

Parameter	Value	Units
J	0.0167	kgm^2/s^2
k_e, k_t	0.8	N m/s
R	0.5	Ω
L	0.003	H
V	220	Volt

4   Evaluation of Fuzzy Predicates

4.1   Numerical Simulations

The state variables and parameters of the system were obtained by means of numerical simulations of the model in Eqs. (3), (5) and (6). The DC motor parameters used for numerical simulations are shown in Table 3. Note that in simulation case I parameter b is variable and parameter T_L is constant: $T_L = 150$ [Nm], while in simulation case II parameter T_L is variable and parameter b is constant: $b = 0.01$ [Nm/s]. For both simulation cases, numerical simulations were conducted for a time period of 5 s. Initial conditions for all the state variables were zero.

As a result of the numerical simulations of the model of the DC motor, a set of 501 values of each state variable and parameter was obtained for both simulation cases. These vectors represent the temporal evolution of the variables in a time period of 5 s.

Table 4. Partitions of fuzzy membership functions, cases I and II. Parameter c is the inflexion point and parameter a is the slope at the inflexion point. There are not fuzzy functions for TL in Case I, and there are not fuzzy functions for FC in case II. Letters N/A mean "not applicable"

Cases	Variables			
	AC	RV	FC	TL
I	MF Normal	MF Low	MF Normal	N/A
	$c = 229$, $a = -0.2$	$c = 132$, $a = -0.2$	$c = 0.25$, $a = -25$	
	MF High	MF Normal	MF High	
	$c = 229$, $a = 0.2$	$c = 132$, $a = 0.2$	$c = 0.25$, $a = 25$	
II	MF Normal	MF Low	N/A	MF Normal
	$c = 189$, $a = -0.1$	$c = 157$, $a = -0.1$		$c = 150$, $a = -0.1$
	MF High	MF Normal		MF High
	$c = 189$, $a = 0.1$	$c = 157$, $a = 0.1$		$c = 150$, $a = 0.1$

4.2   Fuzzy Membership Degrees

The partitions or parameters of the sigmoid and complementary sigmoid Fuzzy Membership Functions are shown in Table 4, for both simulation cases. The full names of the Fuzzy Membership Functions (MF), such as Normal, Low and High, are shown. Parameter c is the inflexion point and parameter a is the slope at the inflexion point. There are not fuzzy functions for TL in Case I, and there are not fuzzy functions for FC in case II. Letters N/A mean "not applicable".

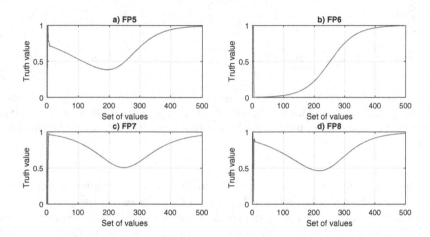

Fig. 2. Truth values of fuzzy predicates in simulation case I: (a) Fuzzy predicate 5, (b) Fuzzy predicate 6, (c) Fuzzy predicate 7, (d) Fuzzy predicate 8. Values at vertical axis are truth values of the predicates. Horizontal axis is the set of simulation values, from 1 to 501

4.3   Evaluation of Fuzzy Predicates

The fuzzy membership degrees of each of the state variables and parameters were used to evaluate the fuzzy predicates in Table 2. Such evaluation was carried out by using the operators Conjunction and Implication (Eqs. (2) and (1), respectively) of GMBCL.

5   Results and Discussion

From the viewpoint of prevention of harmful conditions that could lead to failures of the device, the fuzzy predicates of interest are those in which the conclusion express a harmful situation or consequence in the device or process. It can be noticed that in Case I the fuzzy predicates that represent harmful conditions are the predicates in which the conclusion is High Friction Coefficient (HFC). These are the predicates 5–8 shown in Table 2 for Case I. In a similar way, in Case

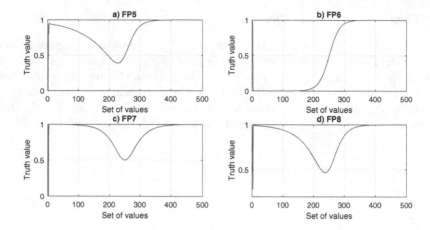

Fig. 3. Truth values of fuzzy predicates in simulation case II: (a) Fuzzy predicate 5, (b) Fuzzy predicate 6, (c) Fuzzy predicate 7, (d) Fuzzy predicate 8. Values at vertical axis are truth values of the predicates. Horizontal axis is the set of simulation values, from 1 to 501

II the fuzzy predicates that represent harmful conditions are the predicates in which the conclusion is High Load Torque (HTL). These are the predicates 5–8 in Table 2 for Case II. In consequence, in order to analyze the obtained truth values of these predicates, we consider only predicates 5–8 in Table 2 for both cases.

The obtained truth values of the fuzzy predicates of interest, i.e., predicates 5–8, are plotted in Figs. 2 and 3, for simulation cases I and II, respectively. Note in these figures that the initial values oscillate from zero to one in amplitude, due to the transient response of the DC motor. After the transient response, the truth values obtained in both simulation cases have a very similar evolution. In particular in Fuzzy predicates 5, 7 and 8, the initial and final values are near to the unity, with a tendency to diminish and increase in the middle part of the evolution time. However, Fuzzy predicate 6 in both cases exhibits a different evolution, with very small initial values and a tendency to rise up in the middle part of the evolution time and get a final value of 1.

From a global point of view of the experiments, the truth values of the predicate 6, in both cases, do not confirm its validity over the full range of values of the state variables. Therefore, in this work we can reject predicate 6, in both cases, as a fuzzy predicate that describes the behaviour of the system in a way useful for prevention of failures. On the other hand, the truth values of the fuzzy predicates 5, 7 and 8 hold values above 0.5 over the full range of values of the state variables. Moreover, these values are close to 1 in the extremes of the range. Therefore, in this work we consider that these fuzzy predicates describes consistently the behaviour of the system in a useful way for prevention of failures.

From the empirical knowledge on the operation of DC motors it is known that high armature current can be an indicator of an abnormal condition. The same can be said of low rotor velocity, when it is operating below the rated velocity for a certain configuration. One of both conditions, high armature current or low rotor velocity can be viewed as an alerting signal of malfunctioning. Moreover, if both conditions are present at the same time, the alerting signal would be more convincing. Thus, in this sense, the obtained truth values of the fuzzy predicates are consistent with the empirical knowledge on DC motors operation.

6   Conclusions

In this work we have proposed an original approach to knowledge discovery for failure detection and prevention, by applying CFL. This approach allows us to obtain a characterization of the system by identifying a set of variables of interest. The degrees of membership of such variables to fuzzy membership functions are obtained and used to calculate the truth values of a set of fuzzy predicates, which have been previously formulated to extract useful knowledge for prevention of failures. The validity and applicability of the truth values of predicates are analyzed for failure prevention purposes. This approach is applied to the characterization of four variables of interest in a DC motor. The obtained fuzzy predicates prove to be useful after being analyzed under the point of view of the empiric knowledge of failures occurrence of DC motors.

The approach of this work was an exploratory one, with the purpose of verify the feasibility of CFL in a failure detection and prevention scheme, applied to a case of study of a physical device as an elementary application. However, by considering the obtained results in this work, the proposed approach can be extended to more complex systems. Proposed future work includes to consider larger sets of state variables and linguistic terms for characterization of a system in order to obtain more complete and useful information for failure prevention and detection.

References

1. Geng, P., Song, J., Xu, C., Zhao, Y.: Fault pattern recognition method for the high voltage circuit breaker based on the incremental learning algorithms for SVM. In: 2016 International Conference on Condition Monitoring and Diagnosis (CMD), Xi'an, China, pp. 693–696 (2016). https://doi.org/10.1109/CMD.2016.7757917
2. Shen, C., Wang, D., Kong, F., Tse, P.W.: Fault diagnosis of rotating machinery based on the statistical parameters of wavelet packet paving and a generic support vector regressive classifier. Measurement **46**, 1551–1564 (2013). https://doi.org/10.1016/j.measurement.2012.12.011
3. Liu, J., Li, G., Liu, B., Li, K., Chen, H.: Knowledge discovery of data-driven-based fault diagnostics for building energy systems: a case study of the building variable refrigerant flow system. Energy **174**, 873–885 (2019). https://doi.org/10.1016/j.energy.2019.02.161
4. Liu, Z., Liu, T., Han, J., Bu, S., Tang, X., Pecht, M.: Signal model-based fault coding for diagnostics and prognostics of analog electronic circuits. IEEE Trans. Ind. Electron. **64**, 605–614 (2017). https://doi.org/10.1109/TIE.2016.2599142

5. Pham, H.N.A., Triantaphyllou, E.: The impact of overfitting and overgeneralization on the classification accuracy in data mining. In: Maimon, O., Rokach, L. (eds.) Soft Computing for Knowledge Discovery and Data Mining, pp. 391–431. Springer, Boston (2008). https://doi.org/10.1007/978-0-387-69935-6_16

6. Morik, K.: Applications of knowledge discovery. In: Ali, M., Esposito, F. (eds.) IEA/AIE 2005. LNCS (LNAI), vol. 3533, pp. 1–5. Springer, Heidelberg (2005). https://doi.org/10.1007/11504894_1

7. Bojadziev, G., Bojadziev, M.: Fuzzy Logic for Business, Finance and Management, 2nd edn, p. 43. World Scientific, Singapore (2007)

8. Espin-Andrade, R.A., Gonzalez, E., Pedrycz, W., Fernandez, E.: An interpretable logical theory: the case of compensatory fuzzy logic. Int. J. Comput. Intell. Syst. **9**, 612–626 (2016). https://doi.org/10.1080/18756891.2016.1204111

9. Rosete, A., Ceruto, T., Espin, R.A., Marx-Gomez, J.: A general method for knowledge discovery approach using compensatory fuzzy logic and metaheuristics. In: Espin, R.A., Marx-Gomez, J., Racet-Valdes, A. (eds.) Towards a Trans-Disciplinary Technology for Business Intelligence Gathering Knowledge Discovery, Knowledge Management and Decision Making, Shaker, Aachen, pp. 240–270 (2011)

10. Bouchet, A., Pastore, J.I., Espin-Andrade, R., Brun, M., Ballarin, V.: Arithmetic mean based compensatory fuzzy logic. Int. J. Comput. Intell. Appl. **10**(2), 213–243 (2011). https://doi.org/10.1142/S1469026811003070

11. Andrade, R.A.E., Fernández, E., González, E.: Compensatory fuzzy logic: a frame for reasoning and modeling preference knowledge in intelligent systems. In: Espin, R., Pérez, R.B., Cobo, A., Marx, J., Valdés, A.R. (eds.) Soft Computing for Business Intelligence. SCI, vol. 537, pp. 3–23. Springer, Heidelberg (2014). https://doi.org/10.1007/978-3-642-53737-0_1

12. Espin-Andrade, R.A., González Caballero, E., Pedrycz, W., Fernález, E.R.: Archimedean-compensatory fuzzy logic systems. Int. J. Comput. Intell. Syst. **8**, 54–62 (2015). https://doi.org/10.1080/18756891.2015.1129591

13. Meschino, G.J., Espin, R.A., Ballarin, V.L.: A framework for tissue discrimination in magnetic resonance brain images based on predicates analysis and compensatory fuzzy logic. Int. J. Intell. Comput. Med. Sci. Image Process. **2**, 207–222 (2008). https://doi.org/10.1080/1931308X.2008.10644165

14. Meschino, G.J., Ballarin, V.L., Espin, R.A.: Image segmentation with predicate analysis and compensatory fuzzy logic. In: Espin, R.A., Marx-Gomez, J., Racet-Valdes, A. (eds.) Towards a Trans-Disciplinary Technology for Business Intelligence Gathering Knowledge Discovery, Knowledge Management and Decision Making, Shaker, Aachen, pp. 210–225 (2011)

15. Krishnan, R.: Electric Motor Drives: Modeling Analysis and Control. Prentice Hall, Upper Saddle River (2001)

A Resilient Behavior Approach Based on Non-monotonic Logic

José Luis Vilchis Medina[1][✉], Pierre Siegel[1][✉], Vincent Risch[1][✉], and Andrei Doncescu[2][✉]

[1] Aix-Marseille Univ, Université de Toulon, CNRS, LIS, Marseille, France
{joseluis.vilchismedina,pierre.siegel,vincent.risch}@lis-lab.fr
[2] LAAS, CNRS, Toulouse, France
andrei.doncescu@laas.fr

Abstract. In this article we present an approach for representing a resilient system which has the capability of absorb perturbations and overcome a disaster. A framework called KOSA is depicted, which is a world that contains a set of knowledge describing objectives, states and actions, linked by a set of rules. This link is expressed by a default theory. First, we define resilience as a relation among states and objectives. Secondly, from a given state, extensions are calculated, which provides information where to go to the future state. The connection, among two or more states creates different configurations that we call trajectories. These connections represent an evolution of the knowledge. Consequently, this reveals the existence of a resilient trajectory. Examples of piloting an airplane are concerned through this paper. Eventually, we present a discrete theoretical behavior of the complete model. Finally the notion of distance among extensions is introduced.

Keywords: Resilience · Non-monotonic logic · Default logic · Minsky model · Decision-making under uncertainty

1 Introduction

In every approaches, resilience always concerns the capability for a system to absorb disruptions and overcome a disaster[1],[2]. For example, nature exhibits many resilient behaviors: flock of birds, school of fish, ecological disasters... This behavior allows flocks of birds and schools of fishes to survive in an uncertainty environment, looking for food in order to preserve the species despite of predators. Ecological disasters such as seaquakes, tornados and earthquakes involve a resilient behavior since in all the cases after disasters occurred, elements of the nature will find an equilibrium point. These examples can be translated in an abstract way. For instance, consider two systems, s_1 and s_2, which both are connected in some manner there exists two types of connections with a view to

---

[1] https://en.wikipedia.org/wiki/Resilience.
[2] https://dictionary.cambridge.org/search/english/direct/?q=resilience.

© Springer Nature Switzerland AG 2019
L. Martínez-Villaseñor et al. (Eds.): MICAI 2019, LNAI 11835, pp. 403–413, 2019.
https://doi.org/10.1007/978-3-030-33749-0_32

keep a balance among both systems. First, a positive feedback is a process in which the effects of small perturbations in s_1 affects s_2, producing disturbances in s_2 which in turn will also affect s_1. This can lead to collapse of both s_1 and s_2. A positive feedback causes instability, the output of a system is generally an exponential growing, chaotic behavior or diverge from an equilibrium point. On the other hand, a negative feedback produces a reduction at its output, leading to stability or equilibrium point, reducing the effects of disturbances [1,10].

1.1 Resilience: State of the Art

Here, we consider Holling's definition about resilience. He defined it regarding four properties: *reorganization, exploration, release* and *conservation* [5,6]. Resilience was recently studied from a logical point of view: non-monotonic logic [11] was used to describe, mainly, two of the four properties defined by Holling: *exploration* and *conservation* (mostly, to *explore* solutions and *conserve* consistency when facing of disruptions).

From this view, we discuss some questions that motivated this study: *What is the relation among states and objectives? Is there a resilient behavior? Are there resilient trajectories?*

In this article, we introduce a model which allows to understand the property of resilience and the interactions among the elements of a system. Regarding the first question about the relation among states and objectives, this is a non-monotonic relation. Thanks to non-monotonic logic, we can formalize contradictories states, when perturbations occurred, and conserve the consistency of the knowledge according to the objectives. Regarding the resilient behavior and resilient trajectories, we need define some concepts. In general physics, a trajectory is defined as the successions of the positions of a body in a framework [2,3]. In this context, a trajectory will be defined as successions of jumps among fixed points. A fixed-point [4] is a solution of an equation or a system of equations. These fixed points are obtained using defaults from a default theory. This default theory is the core of default logic [16] that is a type of non-monotonic logic [17]. To get a resilient behavior, we redefine Minsky model which, according to Minsky [12,13], refers to three fundamental parts: a *current state* in which a situation develops, a *second state* on which we want to stay, and finally, the *difference* among both states. Through this study, examples of piloting an airplane are going to be explained. There are many cases that involve contradictories situations, e.g. emergency landing, bad human decisions, system failures... [9,14,15]. Recently, fatal accidents have occurred with 737 MAX airplanes operated by Boeing[3]. On the one hand, software in MCAS[4] was not resilient to adapt the physical modifications of the engines in order to optimize fuel consummation. On the other hand, pilots on board also were not resilient to overcome the situation since they were not trained to solve the bad measures displayed on the cockpit. In summary, these problems were the result of two non-resilient systems, because of a system failure and incomplete information.

---

[3] https://www.boeing.com/commercial/737max/737-max-software-updates.page.
[4] Maneuvering Characteristics Augmentation System.

1.2 Classical Logic

Logic is a particular way of thinking, it studies the formal principles of inference. This is logical consequences from given axioms. Formal systems, e.g., propositional, predicate, modal... are symbolic constructions in a particular language which allows to study inference [17]. Propositional logic is defined as least set of expressions satisfying: $\top$ (true) and $\bot$ (false) are formulas, and if A and B are formulas: $\neg A$ (not A), $A \wedge B$ (A and B), $A \vee B$ (A or B) and $A \rightarrow B$ (A implies B). A *proposition* can be any sentences, e.g., "It's a sunny day", "Robert can pilot his airplane". Propositional variables are denoted by a, b, c... The sentence "It's a sunny day" could be represented by a, and the other sentence "Robert can pilot his airplane" by b. It can be composed to create complex sentences, e.g., "It's a sunny day and Robert can pilot his airplane", resulting: $a \wedge b$. First-Order Logic (FOL) or predicate logic is an extension of propositional logic that includes universal and existential quantifiers, $\forall$ and $\exists$, respectively. Predicates are denoted by P, Q, R... FOL is very expressive, so it is very natural to formalize sentences. For instance, We can formalize the next sentence: "all airplanes land on wheels", with the following rule:

$$\forall y, Airplane(y) \rightarrow Land\_on\_wheels(y) \tag{1}$$

But we also know that some floatplanes are airplanes that do not land on wheels and some airplanes use skis to land on ice or snow. So, we have the following rules:

$$\forall y, Ski\_airplane(y) \rightarrow Airplane(y) \tag{2}$$

$$\forall y, Ski\_airplane(y) \rightarrow \neg Land\_on\_wheels(y) \tag{3}$$

We can see that formalizations (1) and (3) are contradictory. This is because classical logic, such as FOL, is monotonic. This property is very important in the world of mathematics, because it allows to describe lemmas previously demonstrated. But this property cannot be applied to uncertain, incomplete information or exceptions. In such situations, we would expect adding new information or set of formulas to a model, the set of consequences of this model to be reduced. Formally the property of monotony is: $A \vdash w$ then $A \cup B \vdash w$. The problem leads directly to the general representation of common sense knowledge. By moving to non-monotonic framework, we can carry out the principle of explosion and nevertheless reach a conclusion.

1.3 Default Logic

It is one of the best known formalization for default reasoning, founded by Raymond Reiter. This kind of formalization allows to infer arguments based on partial and/or contradictory information as premises [16]. A default theory is a pair $\Delta = (D, W)$, where D is a set of defaults and W is a set of formulas in FOL. A default d is: $\frac{A(X):B(X)}{C(X)}$, where $A(X), B(X), C(X)$ are well-formed formulas. $A(X)$ are the *prerequisites*, $B(X)$ are the *justifications* and $C(X)$ are the *consequences*. Where $X = (x_1, x_2, x_3, \ldots, x_n)$ is a vector of free variables (non-quantified). Intuitively a default means, "if $A(X)$ is true, and there is no evidence that $B(X)$ might be false, then $C(X)$ can be true". The use of defaults implies the generation of sets containing the consequences of these defaults, called extensions. An extension can be seen as a set of beliefs of acceptable alternatives. Formally, an extension of a default theory Δ is the smallest set E of logical formulas for which the following property holds: If d is a default of D, whose the prerequisite is in E, and the negation of its justification is not in E, then the consequent of d is in E [16].

Definition 1. *Let $\Delta = (D, W)$, an extension E of Δ is define:*

- $E = \bigcup_{i=0}^{\infty} E_i$ with:
- $E_0 = W$ and,
- for $i > 0$: $E_{i+1} = Th(E_i) \cup \{C(X) \mid \frac{A(X):B(X)}{C(X)} \in D, A(X) \in E_i, \neg B(X) \notin E\}$

Where as $Th(E_i)$ is the set of formulas have derived from E_i. A default is said to be normal when defaults have the form: $\frac{A(X):C(X)}{C(X)}$. The main result regarding normal defaults theories is that at least one extension is always guaranteed. The original version of the definition of an extension is difficult to compute in practice. Since it involves checking that $\neg B \notin E$ while E is not yet calculated. In the case of normal defaults, E is an extension of Δ if and only if: we replace $\neg B(X) \notin E$ by $\neg C(X) \notin E_i$. Regarding the rules (1) and (3), we can refine the sentence *"all airplanes land on wheels"* by *"generally, airplanes land on wheels"*. Having a default theory that is composed of $D = \{\frac{Airplanes(y):Land\_on\_wheels(y)}{Land\_on\_wheels(y)}\}$, and a knowledge about airplanes:

$$W = \{Floatplane(y) \rightarrow Airplane(y), Floatplane(y) \rightarrow \neg Land\_on\_wheels(y)\}.$$

Using D, we can note that the prerequisite $Airplane(y)$ is true and the justification $Land\_on\_wheels(y)$ is inconsistent with W, because of:

$$Floatplane(y) \rightarrow \neg Land\_on\_wheels(y),$$

then we cannot conclude that floatplanes land on wheels. But we know that some floatplanes have wheels, formally, $W \cup \{Floatplane\_wheels(y) \rightarrow Airplane(y)\}$. With this a new information, the prerequisite of D is true and the justification is consistent, hence we can conclude that there are floatplanes that have wheels and land on wheels.

2   KOSA

KOSA is an acronym for Knowledge-Objectives-States-Actions framework. It is a formalization in default logic which allows to study the property of resilience. KOSA is a theory which use non-temporal logic to describe its evolution. This theory is used to describe a resilience system.

Definition 2. *A KOSA theory is a default theory* $\Delta = (D, W)$, *where* $W = (R \cup I)$:

- *D is a set of defaults which represents uncertain rules. It contains actions:* $\frac{A(x):B(x)}{C(x)}$, *and perturbations:* $\frac{:C(x)}{C(x)}$,
- *R is a set of formulas in FOL which represents certain rules,*
- *I is a set of grounded literals which represents the state of a system, thereafter we will say that I is a state.*

$$D = \{d_1, d_2, d_3, \cdots\}, \ R = \{r_1, r_2, r_3, \cdots\}, \ I = \{i_1, i_2, i_3, \cdots\}$$

Therefore a *KOSA theory*, $\Delta = (D, (R \cup I))$, has two types of knowledge: *static* and *dynamic*. D and R are *static*, when KOSA evolves these rules do not change. On the other hand, I is the dynamic system.

Definition 3. *A transition is a change of state,* $\Delta = (D, (R \cup I)) \rightsquigarrow \Delta' = (D, (R \cup I'))$. *Considering that D and R are static, the evolution occurs when I changes. Hence a transition amounts to* $I \rightsquigarrow I'$.

Example 1. In the context of piloting an airplane, a transition $I \rightsquigarrow I'$ can be as follows:

$$D = \{\frac{emergency : Land()}{Land()}, \frac{\neg obstacle : Land()}{Land()}, \frac{: Yoke()}{Yoke()}, \frac{: \neg Motor()}{\neg Motor()} \cdots\}$$

$$R = \{Aircraft() \rightarrow Flight(), \cdots\}$$

We have D and R that are fixed rules, and I will change, for instance:

$$I = \{Altitude(50), Compass(north), AirSpeed(80), \cdots\}$$

$$I' = \{Altitude(80), Compass(west), AirSpeed(70), \cdots\}$$

Definition 4. *A* perturbation *is a modification of some values of I.*

Figure 1 represents a perturbation that can trigger a transition. In practice, perturbations can have many causes, e.g. when the pilot pulls the yoke (yoke's position changes), the wind changes (airspeed changes), instructions are given by the control tower (state of flight changes) ... In a real system, disruptions occur very often, e.g., airplane's position changes even if all parameters are stables[5].

Definition 5. *A* trajectory $T = \{I = i_0, i_1, i_2, \cdots, i_{n-1}, i_n = I'\}$ *is a sequence of states with* $W = (R \cup I)$ *consistent. A long-term objective* I' *is the last element of a sequence T, and intermediates objectives are* i_k *with* $0 \leq k < n$.

Figure 2 is a trajectory T with some perturbations. For the moment we can consider that *short-terms objectives* are *intermediates objectives* with a reduced number of states. Further on, we will detail the formal definition of *short-term objectives*.

---

[5] In fact, there are two types of disturbances, internal (pilot pulls the yoke) and external (changes in the environment). We just mention them but we are not going to detail them because of place unavailable.

$$\wr$$
$$I \rightsquigarrow I'$$

Fig. 1. A vertical arrow represents a perturbation that can trigger a transition.

$$\wr \wr \qquad \wr$$
$$T = \{I = i_0, i_1, i_2, \cdots, i_{n-1}, i_n = I'\}$$

Fig. 2. A trajectory T with some perturbations.

Example 2. During a take-off, an airplane should have above stall speed as a *short-term objective*. Once take-off is done, he should climb to increase in altitude, which is another *short-term objective*. He will maintain this objective until he reaches a specific altitude and keep on, a *long-term objective*. To summarize, piloting an airplane is following different objectives and changing them depending of the disruptions.

Definition 6. *Let Δ a KOSA theory, T is a trajectory of Δ and I' an objective of T (that means I' is the last element of T).*

- *$K = (\Delta, T)$ is resilient, if for all perturbations on T there exists $K' = (\Delta, T')$, such that I' is the objective of T'.*
- *Δ is resilient, if for all trajectories T, $K = (\Delta, T)$ is resilient.*

Considering that all the parameters of the states can be modified. We have that Δ is resilient if $K = (\Delta, T)$ can reach an objective I' of T from a perturbed state I_p, passing from I_p to I' with $W = (R \cup I)$ consistent. We give a method to find a trajectory T using default logic. Consider both $K = (\Delta, T)$ and an objective I' of T. Given a perturbation in the current state I (perturbed state I_p), this will trigger a calculation of extension E. Selecting the best extension E it will be possible to reach I'. For that, we consider that each default has a ponderation with different criteria (these could be importance, security, legislation, ...), e.g. $d_x = [C_1, C_2, \ldots, C_m]$ with $C_m \in [0, 1, 2, \ldots, 100]$. Then, $E = \{d_1, d_2 \ldots\} = \{[d_{1C_1}, d_{1C_2}, \ldots], [d_{2C_1}, d_{2C_2}, \ldots] \ldots\}$, that means a default d_1 has more than two ponderations criteria d_{1C_1} and d_{1C_2}, a default d_2 has more than two ponderations criteria d_{2C_1} and d_{2C_2}, and so on. We can see that each extension has multiple criteria, we need to separate each criterion for each extension. For this we are inspired by previous research [11,18]. For a given E with two default d_1, d_2 and two criteria C_1, C_2, a normalization can be as follows:

$$|d_{1C_1}| = \frac{d_{1C_1}}{d_{1C_1}} + \frac{d_{1C_2}}{d_{1C_1}} + \cdots + \frac{d_{1C_m}}{d_{1C_1}}$$

$$|d_{2C_2}| = \frac{d_{2C_1}}{d_{1C_2}} + \frac{d_{2C_2}}{d_{1C_2}} + \cdots + \frac{d_{2C_m}}{d_{1C_2}}$$

$$\vdots \qquad \vdots \qquad \vdots \qquad \vdots$$

$$|d_{xC_m}| = \frac{d_{xC_1}}{d_{1C_m}} + \frac{d_{xC_2}}{d_{1C_m}} + \cdots + \frac{d_{xC_m}}{d_{1C_m}}$$

If we continue the normalization for all E calculated, we will have an array of extensions E and normalization criteria. Applying an opportunistic principle [7,8] which in decision theory is a minimax function, we obtain a solution E_n. This E_n is the best solution to reach I'. In this way we have the transition from I_p to I'. However, if there are more perturbations there will be *intermediate objectives*, resulting a trajectory $T = \{I_p = i_0, i_1, i_2, \cdots, i_{n-1}, i_n = I'\}$. To be more realistic, we can considerate a system with an *long-term objective* I' interacting through an uncertainty environment, a perturbed state I_p triggers a computation of extensions E at moment S_p, $E = \{I_0, I_1, I_3, I_5\}$, then an extension I_1 is chosen using the same principle as before in this section. At some moment, perturbation ζ_1 occurs and extensions are computed one more time: $E = \{I_1, I_4, I_5, I_6\}$, and I_6 is selected. This process occurs every moment a perturbation ζ occurs. In this sense, an objective I' is the concatenation among states I_k and perturbations ζ, a trajectory can be as follows: $T_\star = \{I_1 \cdot \zeta_0 \cdot I_6 \cdot \zeta_1 \cdot I_3 \cdot \zeta_2 \cdot I_6 \cdot \zeta_3 \cdot I_5 \cdot \zeta_4 \cdot I_4 \cdot \zeta_5 \cdot I_1 \cdots\}$. Depending on the force of ζ different trajectories can be generate, for instance: $T_\Delta = \{I_5 \cdot \zeta_0 \cdot I_4 \cdot \zeta_1 \cdot I_3 \cdot \zeta_2 \cdot I_6, \zeta_3 \cdot I_5 \cdot \zeta_4 \cdot I_4 \cdot \zeta_5 \cdot I_6 \cdots\}$ (Fig. 3 represents the evolution of trajectories).

The different between $T_\star$ and T_Δ is the magnitudes of the forces ζ, that's means if a trajectory is longer then ζ has a great impact and vice-versa. In practice, grounded states I are made at each interval of time. This depends of sampling time of the system.

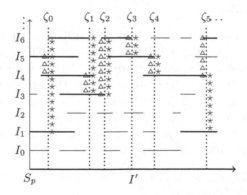

Fig. 3. Evolution of trajectories $T_\star$ and T_Δ.

Definition 7. *Let $K = (\Delta, T)$ resilient where Δ is a KOSA theory and T is a trajectory of Δ. There is a* strong *or* safe *resilience on T.*

- strong *resilience is the ability of $K = (\Delta, T)$ to reach an objective I' (an objective I' is the last element of T) regardless of the perturbations it suffers,*
- safe *resilience is the ability of $K = (\Delta, T)$ to transform a final objective I' to an intermediate objective I'', in order to maintain in good conditions the elements of a physical system.*

Example 3. In aviation, pilots in a twin-engine aircraft can land with a single one because the other suffered damage in mid-flight[6], this can be considerate as a *strong* resilience.

Example 4. When an electric motor rotates certain revolutions per minute and at some point it has a fault. The motor could demand more current to maintain the revolutions. Thanks to new technology this kind of electrical systems include protection systems. In case of a fault, it should enter a *safe* resilience so as not to damage resistors and transistors due to this excess current (Fig. 4).

$$T = \{I = i_0, i_1, i_2, \cdots, i_{n-1}, i_n = I'\}$$

$$\{i_2', \cdots, i_{n-1}', i_n' = I'' = I'\}$$

Fig. 4. A trajectory T with a perturbation on i_1 and the transformation of it with the same objective $I' = I''$.

2.1   Minsky's Model

This is a model that was created by Minsky [12,13]. The principle of this model lies on the fact of having three fundamental parts. First, a current state in which a situation develops, second at state on which we want to be. Finally, the difference between both states. The difference are the necessary stages to reach the desired state (Fig. 5 represents Minsky model). The principle of Minsky model is introduced in $K = (\Delta, T, I')$. This will allow to have a measure of distance among *intermediates objectives*. That is, for a given state I and a *long-term objective* I', this gives a distance to another nearby objective I_k.

Definition 8. *For a given state I, a short-term objective is the closest state I_k where there are fewer disturbances.*

---

[6] https://www.cbsnews.com/news/small-plane-makes-emergency-landing-on-new-jersey-beach-today-2019-06-01/.

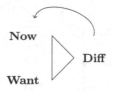

Fig. 5. Minsky model.

The purpose of a distance is to know about the shape of the trajectory T in Δ. To carry out this hypothesis, we include an axis that represents the current states I and another axis for the *long-term objectives, I'*.

Definition 9. *Vertical axis (want-axis) contains the objectives I'. Horizontal axis (now-axis) is composed of the states I.*

Remark 1. A point on want-axis is an objective that is accessible through a trajectory T (Axis are represented in Fig. 6).

Proposition 1. *The radius $\bar{p}$ of an extension E is the sum of its ponderations, considering the intersection of now–want axis as the origin.*

Proof.. From a given $K = (\Delta, T, I')$ where Δ is a KOSA theory $\Delta = (D, W = (R \cup I))$ each default d_x in D has criteria defined by $d_x = [C_1, C_2, \ldots, C_m]$ with $C_m \in [0, 1, 2, \ldots, 100]$.

Then, defaults $E = \{d_1, d_2 \ldots\} = \{[d_{1C_1}, d_{1C_2}, \ldots], [d_{2C_1}, d_{2C_2}, \ldots] \ldots\}$ [16]. To obtain the radius $\bar{p}$ of a E we sum the values of each poderation. For $n > 0$, we have the radius for all defaults E_n computed:

$$E_0 = \sum \{d_1, d_2 \ldots d_x\} = \bar{p}$$

$$E_1 = \sum \{d'_1, d'_2 \ldots d'_x\} = \bar{p'}$$

$$\vdots \qquad \vdots \qquad \vdots \qquad \vdots$$

$$E_n = \sum \{d^n_1, d^n_2 \ldots d^n_x\} = \bar{p^n}$$

The representation of the radius $\bar{p^n}$ can be seen in Fig. 6, the radius of $E_{0,1,2}$ and a fixed objective I'. □

3 Discussion and Conclusion

The importance of using a non-monotonic logic, particulary default logic, is to be able to find consistent solutions. We presented an approach for representing a resilient system which has the capability of absorb *perturbations* and overcome a disaster. A *KOSA theory* $\Delta = (D, W = (R \cup I))$ is defined with the purpose of study a resilient behavior. It is a default theory which use not temporal logic to

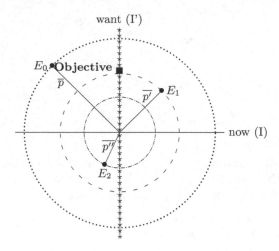

Fig. 6. Radius $\overline{p}, \overline{p'}, \overline{p''}$ of defaults $E_{0,1,2}$, respectively, and a fixed objective I' (black rectangle).

describe its evolution. We proved that it exists a resilient trajectory T, for any perturbation (incomplete, partial and contradictory informations). Considering that a perturbed state I_p can be inconsistent. This *trajectory* is a sequence of states, $T = \{I = i_0, i_1, i_2, \cdots, i_{n-1}, i_n = I'\}$ with $W = (R \cup I)$ consistent. A *long-term objective* I' is the last element of a sequence T, and *intermediates objectives* are i_k with $0 \leq k < n$. The introduction of Minsky model to our *KOSA theory* is presented, thanks to this we could have a first step to study the shape of the *trajectories* T. Also the notion of distance among *extensions* is introduced.

To answer the questions that motivated this investigation: *What is the relation among states and objectives?* We can say that the relation among states and objectives is non-monotonic. *Are there resilient trajectories?* We demonstrated that all Δ is resilient, if $K = (\Delta, T)$ can reach an objective I' of T from a perturbed state I_p, passing from I_p to I' with $W = (R \cup I)$ consistent. *Is there a resilient behavior?* We demonstrated that exists a resilient behavior, if all trajectories of Δ are resilient. We presented a discrete theoretical behavior of the trajectories. The main objective of this research was to conduct a purely logical study. *KOSA theory* does not use learning techniques to infer conclusions which will be interesting for the future, e.g. it could be the use of this type of method to learn the necessary rules to achieve an objective. This study provides the basis for generalizing Definition 6. In which one could consider finding the universe of resilient *trajectories* for any *perturbation*. That is, no matter what the *perturbation* is, we could find the universe of *trajectories* to achieve the desired objective.

Finally, a practical application [11] without resilience was performed on an embedded computer which calculates the extensions for stabilization of a motorized glider.

Acknowledgments. We would like to extend my thanks to the people who contributed their criticisms and comments in the development of this article, either directly or indirectly.

References

1. Bellman, R.: Stability Theory of Differential Equations. Courier Corporation, North Chelmsford (2008)
2. Benenson, W., Harris, J.W., Stöcker, H., Lutz, H.: Handbook of Physics. Springer, New York (2006)
3. Chepyzhov, V.V., Vishik, M.I.: Attractors for Equations of Mathematical Physics, vol. 49. American Mathematical Society, Providence (2002)
4. Granas, A., Dugundji, J.: Fixed Point Theory. Springer, New York (2013)
5. Holling, C.S.: Resilience and stability of ecological systems. Annu. Rev. Ecol. Syst. **4**(1), 1–23 (1973)
6. Holling, C.S.: Understanding the complexity of economic, ecological, and social systems. Ecosystems **4**(5), 390–405 (2001)
7. Janis, I.L., Mann, L.: Decision Making: A Psychological Analysis of Conflict, Choice, and Commitment. Free Press, New York (1977)
8. Kahneman, D., Tversky, A.: Prospect theory: an analysis of decision under risk. In: Handbook of the Fundamentals of Financial Decision Making: Part I, pp. 99–127. World Scientific (2013)
9. Li, G., Baker, S.P., Grabowski, J.G., Rebok, G.W.: Factors associated with pilot error in aviation crashes. Aviat. Space Environ. Med. **72**(1), 52–58 (2001)
10. Lyapunov, A.M.: The general problem of the stability of motion. Int. J. Control **55**(3), 531–534 (1992)
11. Medina, J.L.V., Siegel, P., Risch, V., Doncescu, A.: Intelligent and adaptive system based on a non-monotonic logic for an autonomous motor-glider. In: 2018 15th International Conference on Control, Automation, Robotics and Vision (ICARCV), pp. 442–447. IEEE (2018)
12. Minsky, M.: A framework for representing knowledge (1974)
13. Minsky, M.: The Emotion Machine, vol. 56. Pantheon, New York (2006)
14. Oster, C.V., Strong, J.S., Zorn, C.K.: Why Airplanes Crash: Aviation Safety in a Changing World. Oxford University Press, Oxford (1992)
15. Oster, C.V., Strong, J.S., Zorn, K.: Why airplanes crash: causes of accidents worldwide. Technical report (2010)
16. Reiter, R.: A logic for default reasoning. Artif. Intell. **13**(1–2), 81–132 (1980)
17. Russell, S.J., Norvig, P.: Artificial Intelligence: A Modern Approach. Pearson Education Limited, Malaysia (2016)
18. Toulgoat, I., Siegel, P., Doncescu, A.: Modelling of submarine navigation by non-monotonic logic. In: 2011 International Conference on Broadband and Wireless Computing, Communication and Applications, pp. 447–454. IEEE (2011)

A Playground for the Value
Alignment Problem

Antoni Perello-Moragues[1,2,3(✉)] and Pablo Noriega[1]

[1] IIIA-CSIC, Barcelona, Spain
{tperello,pablo}@iiia.csic.es
[2] Aqualia, Barcelona, Spain
antonio.perello@fcc.es
[3] Universitat Autònoma de Barcelona, Barcelona, Spain

Abstract. The popularity of some recent applications of AI has given rise to some concerns in society about the risks of AI. One response to these concerns has been the orientation of scientific and technological efforts towards a responsible development of AI. This stance has been articulated from different perspectives. One is to focus on the risks associated with the autonomy of artificial entities, and one way of making this focus operational is the "value-alignment problem" (VAP); namely, to study how this autonomy may become provably aligned with certain moral values. With this purpose in mind, we advocate the characterisation of a problem archetype to study how values may be imbued in autonomous artificially intelligent entities. The motivation is twofold, on one hand to decompose a complex problem to study simpler elements and, on the other, the successful precedents of this artifice in analogous contexts (e.g. chess for cognitive AI, RoboCup for intelligent robotics). We propose to use agent-based modelling of policy-making for this purpose because policy-making (i) constitutes a problem domain that is rich, accessible and evocative, (ii) one may claim that it is an essentially value-drive process and, (iii) it allows for a crisp differentiation of two complementary views of VAP: imbuing values in agents and imbuing values in the social system in order to foster value-aligned behaviour of the agents that act within the system. In this paper we elaborate the former argument, propose a characterisation of the archetype and identify research lines that may be systematically studied with this archetype.

Keywords: Ethics in AI · Agent-based simulation · Policy-making · Policy values

1 Introduction

There is concern in society about the dangers of AI [6,44]. Although concerns may be founded, we propose to see beyond the Frankenstein/Terminator image and focus on dangers that are specific to AI and how to address them. This more

© Springer Nature Switzerland AG 2019
L. Martínez-Villaseñor et al. (Eds.): MICAI 2019, LNAI 11835, pp. 414–429, 2019.
https://doi.org/10.1007/978-3-030-33749-0_33

focused view has been adopted by a large part of the AI community and one may recognise three main strategies to address these concerns:

Strategy 1. It consists in taking a classical moral approach that does, in the field of AI, what is usually done in other fields: emphasis in a proper ethical education and developing a sense of responsibility that is specific to the field. This strategy is reflected in several manifestos and put into practice through institutions, programs and projects that promote an AI that has been qualified as "human-centred", "responsible" or "ethical". For instance, [12,17,34].

Strategy 2. With a crisp understanding of AI potential, it directs efforts towards the formulation, promotion and adoption of legislation, guidelines, principles, standards, certification mechanisms and similar ways of identifying specific risks that may be better characterised, allocated prevented and eventually minimised or repaired. For instance [22].

Strategy 3. It adopts the stance of taking advantage of the power of AI to solve the problems caused by AI. This strategy is following several paths; one is to "teach computers to do the right thing" [3,6]. A second articulation is to find ways to "guarantee" that machines behave morally or to build autonomous systems that are "provably aligned" with a set of values [36]. This last formulation is what is called the *value alignment problem* (VAP). Although it is unlikely that the value alignment problem may be solved for every autonomous system, it is plausible to characterise a class of autonomous systems that may be imbued with values and to develop formal and methodological means to eventually support their provability.

With this aim in mind, we advocate a restricted version of VAP that facilitates addressing several of these underlying issues. The point is to establish an objective frame of reference where ethical questions may be worked out and eventually produce insights that may apply to value aligned behaviour within some well defined conditions. We propose to use the problem of policy-making and to explore this problem through agent-based simulation. The choice of subject matter is based on the understanding that policy-making is a value-driven activity, that involves two complementary perspective of values: first, the social values that a policy-maker seeks to imbue in a social system and, second, the values imbued in the behaviour of individual policy-subjects. The choice of agent-based modelling, as we argue in Sect. 2, is a methodological decision that fosters a bare-bones description of the problem that may be appropriate for a crisp formulation of some questions and an objective assessment of possible answers.

The approach of characterising a "landmark" model for complex scientific problems has proven effective before in several cases. In the case of AI, chess-playing for symbolic cognitive AI and *Robocup* for intelligent robotics come immediately to mind. Our proposal is more modest in scope, but the underlying questions are no less significant. Thus, the questions that may be addressed with this landmark model should promote several research and development lines and that the impact of the research and development spawned by it should have a beneficial impact on the development of an ethically responsible AI.

This paper is essentially an elaboration of these matters and hence it is structured as follows. In Sect. 2 we advocate the suitability of agent-based modelling (ABM) for value-driven policy-making. In Sect. 3 we outline a conceptual framework for value-driven policy-making. In fact, we propose a "metamodel" that establishes the components needed to characterise the archetype problem, we then propose a refinement of that metamodel to characterise a more concrete form of the archetype that we call a *landmark class* and, in order to end up with restricted enough versions of the archetype we choose a particular landmark subclass to define a *challenge*. Finally, in Sects. 4 and 5 we outline a research programme around the type of questions for which the archetype, or more specifically its challenge subclass, provide motivation and the grounds to develop theory and technology to imbue values in autonomous intelligent systems. A summary of the background of our proposal is in Appendix.

2   Why ABM of Value-Driven Policy-Making?

Policy-making is, intrinsically, a value-driven process: policy-makers design policies in order to achieve a "better—with respect to some value system—state of the world". In order to achieve that goal, policy-makers make use of means of different sorts that foster behaviour of other stakeholders towards those ends. Policy stakeholders decide what are the "right" actions to take and assess the "goodness" of the state of the world but with respect to their own values.

The design of a public policy separates value alignment in two complementary perspectives: the problem of imbuing values in the global emergent behaviour of systems involving autonomous entities, on one hand; and the problem of imbuing values in the behaviour of individual autonomous agents. In the first case, policy instruments foster value aligned behaviour and policy objectives make explicit those values that intend to be achieved. In the second case, one may study how values are involved in the decision making of individuals and how their behaviour is aligned to their own individual values and to the values fostered by the social policy. Each perspective allows for exploration of different questions. By choosing a particular policy domain many conceptual and methodological concerns become easier to handle and one may get an empirical grounding and validation for some assumptions.

Agent-based modelling is a convenient way to explore these matters because it provides a refutational framing of value-related modelling. In fact, it motivates identifying and objectifying value-related assumptions, it provides a test-bed for operationalisation of core value notions (value assessment, representation, commensurability, etc.); it constitutes a shared platform to explore several aspects of value-driven behaviour (argumentation, negotiation, value adoption, etc.), and it provides experimental support for insights. Moreover, it also provides running examples of value-imbued systems as a side effect.

As will become clear with the next sections, expected outcomes follow three paths that we claim will be fruitful and significant: (i) formal results: on a cognitive theory of values, on institutional design, on value alignment assessment,

Table 1. Abstraction process for building simulators of public policies

	Reality	Formal abstraction	Simulation
World	W	D	$W' \leftarrow \Sigma(I(p))$
Policy	$\mathcal{P}$	$P = \langle D, V, \Pi, S \rangle$	$p \leftarrow i(P)$

on value-imbued agreement technologies; (ii) methodological guidelines for value representation, value-driven decision-making architectures, value-enhancing governance, uses of the simulations, etc.; and (iii) collateral uses like: methodology and workbenches for value-driven policy-models, frameworks for development and deployment of policy-support systems, experimental platforms for the study of social psychology and collective social phenomena.

3 A Conceptual Framework for ABM of Value-Driven Policy-Making

In loose terms, a public policy is a proposal to improve reality. In essence, *reality* (W) refers to a "fragment of the real world that is relevant" for the policy. This fragment is abstracted into a "model" (D) whose "implementation" (I) and running (Σ) produces a "simulated world" (W') that corresponds with the relevant fragment of reality (Table 1).

A policy *proposal* consists of two types of elements: the "ends" that will be used to assess the *improvement*, and the "means" that will be used to achieve those ends. In other words, we define a (model of) public policy through four main elements: (i) a policy domain (D), which is that part of reality that the policy is intended to improve; (ii) the set of values (V) with respect one intends to assess the improvement; (iii) a policy-schema (Π), which is the core of the *proposal* (what to improve and how); and (iv) the population of stakeholders (S) that are involved in the policy *proposal*.

We are interested in building agent-based simulators of such policies. We shall call them Agent-Based *Value-Driven Policy*-making *Simulators* (VDPS, for short) (see [29]). These simulators are nothing more than the instantiation of a model of a public policy ($p \leftarrow i(P)$), its implementation ($I(p)$), and the computational environment where we run the simulations ($\Sigma(I(p))$) (Table 1). Theoretically, these systems could inform and support actual policy-making in the real world ($\mathcal{P}$).

All this may be expressed in more precise terms through the following working definitions:

Working Definition 1. *A **policy** is a tuple* $P = \langle D, V, \Pi, S \rangle$, *where*

- D *is a policy-domain;*
- V *is a set of values;*
- Π *is a policy-schema;*

– *A is a set of stakeholders.*

Working Definition 2. *A **value-driven policy simulator** is a tuple* $VDPS = \langle M_{vdps}, I, \Sigma \rangle$, *where*

– M_{vdps} *is the metamodel for such systems;*
– *I is the implementation platform (e.g. NetLogo, Repast, etc.);*
– Σ *is the simulation environment.*

The idea of a metamodel (see Appendix) is to provide *affordances* that enable the modeller to express those features and functionalities which facilitate the construction of the model.[1]

In our case, we want an abstract description of any policy, being this detailed enough to capture everything that is common to policies (and distinguishes them from other socio-cognitive technical systems (see Appendix)). The purpose is to instantiate a description, which then will be implemented in a platform and used for simulation. For that reason we explain the four elements we said constitute a policy: the *policy domain*, a *policy-schema*, the *values* in the policy, and the *stakeholders* involved.

First, the *policy domain* needs to be concrete enough (whatever is involved in, say, policies for the urban water management). Thus, we need an ontology (i.e., entities that constitute the world: water, households, tariffs, utility companies, etc.), and the semantics and pragmatics that describe their functioning (e.g., household water supply is measured in cubic meters, and the tariff is proportional to their actual water use). In other words:

Working Definition 3. *A **policy domain** D includes:*

1. *A **domain model**, given by*
   1.1. *The **ontology**, **semantics** and **pragmatics**.*
   1.2. *The **state of the world**, which is a finite set of variables that stand for crude facts.*
2. *An **institutional framework**, that contains*
   2.1. ***Policy instruments**: actions, norms, and activities (i.e., organised collections of actions performed by agents with specific roles)*
   2.2. *"**Shells**" for policy instruments (means to specify new actions, norms and activities).*
   2.3. ***Governance framework** to regulate those entities.*
3. ***Stakeholder roles**, defined in terms of capabilities, norms that govern their role-specific behaviour, and relationships among roles.*

Next, we need to model *values*. For that purpose, we start assuming we have a set of values, a set of agents, and the *policy-domain*:

---

[1] The model, its implementation and the resulting simulated world constitute a socio-cognitive technical system (see Appendix). The metamodel of Working Definition 7 characterises the sub-class of value drive policy-making simulators.

Working Definition 4. *Given a set of **domain values** V, a set of **domain actions** A, a set of **domain norms** N, a set of **domain activities** C and a set of **domain roles** R. We distinguish between*

1. **Social values,** *which are those values that are involved in the definition of the policy (i.e., chosen by the policy-makers) and in the evaluation of the social outcomes. We assume that actions, norms, and activities are associated with these values:* $V_{social} = \{\langle a_i, v_a \rangle, \langle n_j, v_n \rangle, \langle c_k, v_c \rangle\}$, *where*
   - $v_a \subset V$ *are all the values involved in the **action** a_i (inputs, outputs).*
   - $v_n \subset V$ *are all the values involved in the **norm** n_j (preconditions, actions and postconditions).*
   - $v_c \subset V$ *are all the values involved in the **activity** c_k (values in all actions and norms that define the protocols).*
2. **Stakeholders' values,** *which are those values that are held by individual agents and may be specific to some roles:* $v_r \subset V$
3. **Value assessment conventions**
   3.1. *Define how to assess the degree of satisfaction of a set of values in a given state of the world.*
   3.2. *Define how to compare two states of the world (i.e., order states with respect to a set of values).*
   3.3. *Define how to assess the contribution of an action towards a set of values.*

A *policy-schema* is the way a policy is meant to be implemented: its *means* and *ends*. In more precise terms:

Working Definition 5. *A **policy-schema** is a tuple* $\Pi = \langle means, ends \rangle$, *where*

1. **Means** *are the ways to improve the state of the world, and include a set of **instruments** to influence and foster behaviour and make those means effective;*
2. **Ends** *are the description of the expected improvements, and include the set of **indicators** to measure the performance of the policy.*

For example, an *end* for urban water policy may be to guarantee a safe supply of water, which may be represented by a combination of *indicators* like water use (e.g. litres per person and day), water quality parameters (e.g. nitrates in milligrams per litre), etc. The *means* of the policy are interventions like controlling water supply and demand, which are implemented through corresponding *instruments* as higher tariffs for large consumers, smart water-meters that block supply when water use is abnormally high, etc.

The stakeholders are those agents—who may be individuals, groups of individuals, or organisations—who are capable of performing some actions in the policy domain and are subject to the means and ends instituted by the policy. Thus, a stakeholder is characterised by the capabilities that allow it to act in the policy domain (e.g., use water, influence and be influenced by neighbours, advocate for a change of tariffs, etc.) and by its decision model. We claim that this model involves values and other cognitive constructs like beliefs, motivations, personality, abstract reasoning, etc., which we lump into a "mindframe".

Working Definition 6. *A population of **stakeholders** is constituted by agents who are provided with:*

1. ***Capabilities**, i.e., actions that are able to be performed.*
2. ***Values** and **value assessment conventions**.*
3. ***Mindframes**, i.e., the decision model and inputs used (e.g., beliefs, resources, personality, etc.).*

When we put all these components together we can define a metamodel for VDPS as:

Working Definition 7. *A **metamodel** for value-driven policy simulators M_{vdps} provides affordances to specify:*

1. *A **policy-domain**;*
2. ***Policy-schemas**;*
3. *A set of **domain values**;*
4. *A population of **stakeholders**.*

While the metamodel M_{vdps} should aid modelling of any value-driven simulator, one may narrow the scope to a particular policy domain and be more explicit about the requirements of some metamodel components and define, with the more restrictive metamodel a "landmark class" of value-driven simulators that is still rich enough for theory and technological development. For example, if the class is restricted to urban water use policies, one does not have to deal with "all" possible values, but only to the ones that apply to the urban water domain; and therefore one does not need to model any possible action or event that affects the physical-socio-economic but only those means and ends linked with urban water use that have an impact in decision-making and assessments of the state of the world that are value-based.

While the aforementioned limitations do not entail any qualification of value theory, we propose to adopt two non-essential assumptions: consequentalism and commensurability of values. We claim that these assumptions still leave a rich enough class and also facilitate a systematic exploration of policy-simulations with other value-theory assumptions with the archetype defined through.

Working Definition 8. *A **landmark** class for value-driven policy simulators in a particular policy domain D^* is the class of models that may be specified with the refinement of metamodel M_{vdps} as a metamodel $M_{vdps}^{D^*}$ with the following components:*

1. *The domain submodel is restricted to the physical, economic and social environment of a particular D^*.*
2. *The list of relevant values involved in simulation are specific to D^* and thus their operationalisation has to be D^*-specific.*
3. *Agent models need only be concerned with reasoning about D^*-relevant values.*
4. *Roles, actions, norms and activities are also D^*-specific.*
5. *The state of the world is represented by a **finite set of indicators** (domain variables and constants).*

6. *All values may be defined as a combination of indicators.*
7. *Value assessment for decision-making and for moral judgement is based in the* **indicator-based definition of values** *and value aggregation models that use those indicators.*

Note that both consequentalism and commensurability are rather natural for agent-based simulation. In the generic metamodel for VDPS M_{vdps} we do not commit to a specific operationalisation of these assumptions but only that any model may involve that type of operationalisation. We propose to narrow further the scope of the archetype through a refinement of $M_{vdps}^{D^*}$ where the domain variables of each value (i.e. contextualised values are translated into indicators) and the value aggregation models are made explicit in the specification of a simulator.

Working Definition 9. *A* **challenge** *is a subclass of a landmark class through the refinement of $M_{vdps}^{D^*}$, where*

1. *For each value in $M_{vdps}^{D^*}$, the set of state indicators that are involved in its definition are chosen from the larger set of indicators of the contextualised values of the specific domain.*
2. *A set of value aggregation models are defined (for instance, an utility function).*

The idea is to work, for example, in an ideal city with an explicit definition of a state of the world, a ground ontology, social model and institutional framework (that may be expanded through policy instruments), a list of values that need to be operationalised (i.e. contextualised and translated into indicators), but this operationalisation is made explicit so it can be compared. Modest applications in the water domain have been used to study innovation-focused policies in farmer communities [30] (namely, innovation policy value is translated into adoption rate, promoted by means of subsidies, for farmers who are profit-driven), and modelling stakeholders' advocacy for policy shifts in the urban water domain [31] (stakeholders have different values and perceive them differently, and may propose policy instruments according to their evaluation of the state of the world).

4   Some Lines of Research and Development

One may organise a research programme around the policy-making archetype. One may start with the definition of a "challenge" test case whose domain submodel is properly implemented and publicly available. It may then be used to explore in a systematic way several questions that underlie the general value alignment problem.

The guiding light of this exploration is the dual aim of imbuing values in the system and imbuing values in autonomous agents. With that in mind one may split research and development along interleaving paths. The following list is but a rough one.

What Is a Value in Policy-Making. Find a useful definition of value. What are the differences between the use of the notion of value in policy-making and other contexts. What classes of values are involved in policy-making. Are value classes different for different stakeholders?

What Values to Use? What value sets have been proposed? What is the theoretical foundation? What is the backing? What methodology? What is the relationship between values and disvalues? What is the relationship among values? How are values ranked? Scope of applicability? Values for specific domains? Values for specific populations? How are values contextualised? How context alters the ranking? What contexts alter the rankings more?

Value Operationalisation. What is the meaning of a value? Methodologies? How is the value assessed? What are the conditions for assessment? What needs to be observable in the world to assess a given value? What actions affect or are affected by those observable entities? How are alternative definitions justified? Empirical backing?

Values and Policy Ends. What are the principal values in a policy? How are they captured in the ends of the policy? Indicators vs indexes? Value aggregation for ends? Can ends evolve? How ends relate with different values and disvalues? End commensurability?

Values and Policy Means. How are values linked to actions? How are values linked to norms? How are values linked to sanctions? How can one measure the significance of values, norms, rhetorical messages with respect to a value? What types of instruments are available for imbuing values? Are there some that are specific to classes of values? How to observe value effects with successions of actions? What are the costs of complying with a value? How to evaluate the quality of a means? How are alternative definitions justified? Empirical backing?

Value Aggregation. Alternative models? Advantages? Preferred contexts for application? Reliability? Testability? Robustness?

Reasoning with Values? What are the characteristics of value as a mental construct? What are the connections between values and goals, motivation, personality, beliefs, social environment, mind frames? Argue with values in mind?

Policy Assessment. When is a policy "good"? When is it effective? What features need to be assessed in a public policy? What means and ends are better for a policy? Existing policy assessment guidelines and practices? What values are meant to be imbued?

The Archetype in the Wider Context of Policy-Making. How are simulations part of the policy-making cycle? Where can simulation be used, how, and to what advantage? How policy simulation may be used as a support tool for policy making? How can a policy-making simulator be extended into a policy-support system?

Ethical Aspects Involved in the Use of Value-Driven Agent-Based Simulators. What to put into the model? How "good" is the model? What are the responsibilities of the designer? What are the responsibilities of the user of the simulator? What is different in agent-based simulation and other type of models?

5   Closing Remarks

Problem Definition. We propose to frame the problem as follows: (i) study the process of policy-making as an instance of two aspects of value-alignment: instituting value-based governance, and programming value-driven behaviour; (ii) build an agent based simulator as an experimental environment; (iii) use socio-cognitive artificial agents as experimental subjects; (iv) make the problem operational by designing an archetype version of the simulator; (v) design a test-bed platform for challenges.

Practical Matters. One may proceed as follows: (i) use environmental policies as the archetype policy domain and water use policies for a landmark class; (ii) build the test-bed platform on top of existing domain models and agent-based modelling tools.; (iii) specify a challenge instance; (iv) provide a test bed platform with a precise (challenge) instance of the archetype where policy designers may test policy means and ends as well as agent architectures. Such instance would contain a working policy domain simulator, a data set to feed simulations and a core set of tools and shells; (v) define "game rules" that establish standard experimental scenarios.

Significance. As suggested in the Online Manifesto [16], being human in an hyper-connected era entails interacting in an augmented nature with autonomous intelligent entities that are artificial. We are witnessing the power of AI and fear we will loose control before we fully understand it [11]. That is why research and development that guarantees that artificial entities behave ethically is transcendental and urgent. We are convinced that a wise and timely way to approach this colossal task is to design a problem archetype that captures some key features of the value alignment problem, and simplify the archetype into challenges that facilitate and motivate the systematic exploration of fundamental questions.

Acknowledgements. This research has been supported by the CIMBVAL project (Spanish government, project # TIN2017-89758-R). The first author is supported with the industrial doctoral 2016DI043 grant of the Catalan Secretariat for Universities and Research (AGAUR), sponsored by FCC AQUALIA, IIIA-CSIC, and UAB.

Appendix: Background

Values

Values are constructs that are grounded on universal human needs [40]. Presumably, they are cognitive socio-cognitive constructions that articulate these human needs as principles or standards of preference. Indeed, values are involved in motivation and goal-setting [28], and it has been suggested that they are also involved in political cognition [8,41], as they serve as moral intuitions for individuals [20]. For more practical terms, values play a role in the behaviour of agents [25,28].

Schwartz and Bilsky [40] provided an exhaustive definition of values: values are (a) concepts or beliefs, (b) about desirable end states or behaviours, (c) that transcend specific situations, (d) guide selection or evaluation of behaviour and events, and (e) are ordered by relative importance. They derived such cognitive notion of values from universal human needs (i.e. individual biological organism, social agent and interaction, and welfare of the community).

There is no consensus on the categories of values. Rokeach [35] developed the Rokeach Value Survey—on which Schwartz and Bilsky draw their primary work—to determine the value priorities of individuals and distinguished between *instrumental values* (i.e., related to modes of behaviour) and *terminal values* (i.e., desirable end-states of existence); and also between *individual values* (i.e., related to satisfying individual needs and self-esteem) and *societal values* (i.e, related to societal demands, since *supra-individual entities* (e.g., society, organisations, etc.) "socialise the individual for the common good to internalise shared conceptions of the desirable").

One of the most notable works on values, the Schwartz Theory of Basic Values, defines 10 sets of values that pursue a particular objective or goal [39]: Power; Achievement; Hedonism; Stimulation; Self-direction; Universalism; Benevolence; Conformity; Tradition; and Security. This theory has been used to study in political domains (e.g., voting behaviour [41]), and even has been subject of study to enhance their usability in public administration and policy studies (see, for instance, [45]).

Cognitive Function of Values. Values are largely stable social and internal cognitive constructs that represent individuals' moral intuitions and which guide social evaluation and action [20]. Accordingly, values play a role in perceiving the relevant fragment of the world, in evaluating the state of such, and in motivating responding action. It has been suggested that values are essential for the socio-political cognition of individuals (regarding social outcomes and public affairs) [8].

Generally speaking, decision-making within a particular context pose ethical dilemmas that present trade-offs between multiple values, revealing desirable but opposing outcomes. Noteworthy, any decision is value-laden because it reflects the hierarchy of values of the decision-maker.

When multiple values are involved in decision-situations, we say that values are made *commensurable* by means of *value aggregation models*. These decision-making components afford individuals to consider multiple values and solve value trade-offs, eventually making a decision. With this in mind, there are at least two relevant components in *value aggregation models*: (i) the value system, that defines the type of values considered (e.g., Schwartz, Rokeach, etc.); and (ii) the aggregation model (e.g., satisficing combinations, aggregation functions, etc.).

Usually, such models are implemented as aggregation functions that reflect a multi-criteria decision analysis (MCDA) [33]. Sophisticated mathematical protocols have been developed to generate *value functions* (see [1]) and *value hierarchies* (see [37]).

Working Assumptions on Values. We adopt the following assumptions about values to ground a working framework:

- **Cognitive understanding of values.** Values are constructs that serve as cognitive heuristics and moral intuitions of individuals, and therefore they guide perception, evaluation and decision-making in any context [20,40].
- **Commensurability of values.** Although one can say that values are incommensurable and cannot be measured on a common scale [33], we stick to the fact that individuals *act* and *make decisions*, which requires to solve ethical dilemmas and value trade-offs (e.g. for which we presume *bounded rationality* is crucial). Thus, values are, at least, *cognitively commensurable*.
- **A consequentialist view of values.** The focus of value-driven decisions is placed on their consequences, rather they nature and definition. In other words, the discussion is not about what a particular value is, but rather, given a definition of that particular value, whether actions promote or not that value.

Values in Norms and in Actions Values are related to norms. Values serve as guiding and evaluative principles that capture what is right and wrong, while norms are rules that prescribe behaviours and particular courses of action. Accordingly, norms are an "implementation" of what values express (either as a personal norm in the cognition of the individual or as a institutional norm in the social space).

According to our working framework, an action A may promote a value α and demote a value β depending on their consequences and how value α and value β are understood. Alternatively, an action A is aligned with a value α if the outcome improves the state of the world with respect to how that value α is understood. Following this approach, a norm N is aligned to a value α when it prescribes actions that promote value α and prohibits actions that demote value α.

Policy-Making

Public policies are plans of action that address what has been defined as a collective problem [13] in order to produce a desirable society-level outcome. Values play a role in policy decisions, as they are involved when defining public issues, desirable states of the world, and courses of action worth to be considered [8,43].

Ideally, policy-making cycle is often described as a linear cycle that includes agenda-setting, design, implementation, application, evaluation and revision (i.e., maintain, redesign, or terminate the policy). The truth is that policy-making is far more complex and uncertain than a linear process [8,9,38]. Noteworthy, policy decisions are usually made without enough information—which is not only based on scientific evidence, but also on habits and intuitions [9]—in a space where multiple stakeholders are involved—who have competing values and interests, and mobilise diverse resources [13]—but they still may have substantial impact—whose consequences are often not totally foreseen [42].

Policy Domains. A policy domain is an abstraction of the reality that serve to draw the boundaries of the relevant fragment of the world to be considered when addressing public issues. In simple terms, it consists of going from a messy problematic situation to a structured well-defined problem, which affords to conceive policies to tackle it [21].

Paradigms are taken-for-granted descriptions and theoretical analyses that constrain the range of alternative policy options [23]. Paraphrasing Campbell [10], paradigms act as "cognitive background assumptions that constrain action by limiting the range of alternatives that policy-making elites are likely to perceive as useful and worth considering" when addressing public issues. These paradigms are supported by language and discourse, contributing to form "mental structures that shape the way we see the world" [24].

Policy Ends and Indicators, and Policy Means and Instruments. In simple terms, public policies are a set of values (i.e., what is valued by the society at large), ends (i.e., what state of the world reflects them), and means (i.e., how that state is going to be achieved).

Following this view, ends must be described clearly as objectives that are meant to be achieved by the intervention. The assessment of the degree of success may rely on indexes and indicators—either quantitative or qualitative—that stand for those end states and are computed from variables of the relevant world.

In the same vein, means aim to produce a change on the relevant world (typically, a behavioural change on target groups) so as to drive the system towards a desirable state of the world. They may be implemented with diverse instruments (e.g., financial, economic, regulatory, etc.).

Policy Assessment Practices. It is common to assess policies prior to their enactment (*ex ante* assessment). For instance, the European Commission refers to this process as Impact Assessment (IA), and considers it necessary when the expected economic, environmental or social impacts of interventions are likely to be *significant* (see [15]). The main steps of the process consists of analysing (i) the definition of the problem and boundaries and scales of the system; (ii) the policy ends and how are they going to be measured; (iii) the policy means and how are they going to be implemented; and finally (iv) the policy evaluation on which base the enactment, redesign, or termination decisions.

We distinguish between *effective* policies and *good* policies [32]. The former are those policies whose social outcome is consistent with the policy declared objectives. In contrast, the latter are those policies whose social outcome is "good" according to the values held by stakeholders.

Agent-Based Simulation (ABS) for Policy-Making

Simulation is the imitation of a real-world process or system over time, and can contribute to policy assessment without disturbing the real social system and committing resources [7], as well as identifying counter-intuitive situations. ABS use a type of computational models that are able to explicitly simulate the actions and social interactions of groups of individuals within an artificial environment, thus generating "artificial societies" [18].

With this in mind, agent-based simulation (ABS) has been acknowledged as a useful tool to support policy-making and *ex ante* policy assessment [19]. ABS contributes to reliably anticipate data that is not currently known [14], and can be combined with other ICTs to enhance their potential (e.g., data analysis and statistics, output visualisation, etc.). Although ABS is promising, several concerns have been posed, as it can backfire if used without proper precaution [5].

Socio-cognitive Technical Systems

Socio-cognitive technical systems (SCTS) are social coordination systems [2] that articulate on-line interactions of autonomous agents that are socially rational [26]. They are composed of two first class entities: a social space where all interactions take place, and agents that interact within that environment. One presumes that the social space has a fixed ontology (the *domain ontology*), that at any given time it is in a *state*—that is an instance of the Cartesian product of a finite number of domains, whose union is a subset of the domain ontology. The state of the system changes only as a result of an action that complies with the system regulations the moment it is attempted, or because an event that is compatible with those regulations takes place.

SCTS can be decomposed in three "views": W that is the fragment of the world that is relevant for the system, I an institutional representation of the conventions that define the system, and T the implementation of I that creates the on-line version of W. The views are interrelated in such a way that an attempted action modifies the state of the system if and only if that action is admitted by the system interface, which in turn should happen if and only if the attempted action complies with the conventions established in I (and those conventions are properly implemented in T). An admitted action changes the state of the world according to the conventions in I that specify the way the input is processed in T. In the case of value-driven policy simulators, these three views correspond to the simulated world, the (abstract) model of the world and the implementation of the model.

In practice, the institutional specification (I) is achieved by instantiating a *metamodel* that includes *ad-hoc* languages and data structures to represent key distinctive features (*affordances*) of a family of SCTS (e.g., crowd-based systems, electronic institutions [2], normative multiagent systems [4], second-order simulation [27]).

References

1. Alarcon, B., Aguado, A., Manga, R., Josa, A.: A value function for assessing sustainability: application to industrial buildings. Sustainability 3(1), 35–50 (2011)

2. Aldewereld, H., Boissier, O., Dignum, V., Noriega, P., Padget, J.: Social Coordination Frameworks for Social Technical Systems. Law, Governance and Technology Series, vol. 30. Springer, Cham (2016). https://doi.org/10.1007/978-3-319-33570-4
3. Allen, C., Varner, G., Zinser, J.: Prolegomena to any future artificial moral agent. J. Exp. Theor. Artif. Intell. **12**, 251–261 (2000)
4. Andrighetto, G., Governatori, G., Noriega, P., van der Torre, L.W.N. (eds.): Normative Multi-Agent Systems, vol. 4. Dagstuhl Publishing, Saarbrücken (2013)
5. Aodha, L., Edmonds, B.: Some pitfalls to beware when applying models to issues of policy relevance. In: Edmonds, B., Meyer, R. (eds.) Simulating Social Complexity. UCS, pp. 801–822. Springer, Cham (2017). https://doi.org/10.1007/978-3-319-66948-9_29
6. Awad, E., et al.: The moral machine experiment. Nature **563**, 59 (2018)
7. Banks, J.: Handbook of Simulation. Wiley, Hoboken (1998)
8. Botterill, L.C., Fenna, A.: Interrogating Public Policy Theory. Edward Elgar Publishing, Cheltenham (2019)
9. Cairney, P.: The Politics of Evidence-Based Policy Making. Palgrave Macmillan, Basingstoke (2016)
10. Campbell, J.L.: Institutional analysis and the role of ideas in political economy. Theory Soc. **27**(3), 377–409 (1998)
11. Collingridge, D.: The Social Control of Technology. Palgrave Macmillan, Basingstoke (1981)
12. Asilomar Conference: Asilomar AI principles (2017). https://futureoflife.org/ai-principles/. Accessed 13 2019
13. Dente, B.: Understanding Policy Decisions. SpringerBriefs in Applied Sciences and Technology. Springer, Cham (2013)
14. Edmonds, B.: Different modelling purposes. In: Edmonds, B., Meyer, R. (eds.) Simulating Social Complexity. UCS, pp. 39–58. Springer, Cham (2017). https://doi.org/10.1007/978-3-319-66948-9_4
15. European Commission: Better Regulation Toolbox. https://ec.europa.eu/info/better-regulation-toolbox_en. Accessed 20 Mar 2019
16. Floridi, L. (ed.): The Onlife Manifesto, pp. 7–13. Springer, Cham (2015). https://doi.org/10.1007/978-3-319-04093-6_2
17. Floridi, L., et al.: AI4People - an ethical framework for a good AI society: opportunities, risks, principles, and recommendations. Minds Mach. **28**(4), 689–707 (2018). https://doi.org/10.1007/s11023-018-9482-5
18. Gilbert, G.N., Conte, R.: Artificial Societies: The Computer Simulation of Social Life. UCL Press, London (1995)
19. Gilbert, N., Ahrweiler, P., Barbrook-Johnson, P., Narasimhan, K.P., Wilkinson, H.: Computational modelling of public policy: reflections on practice. J. Artif. Soc. Soc. Simul. **21**(1), 14 (2018)
20. Hitlin, S., Pinkston, K.: Values, attitudes, and ideologies: explicit and implicit constructs shaping perception and action. In: DeLamater, J., Ward, A. (eds.) Handbook of Social Psychology. Handbooks of Sociology and Social Research, pp. 319–339. Springer, Netherlands (2013). https://doi.org/10.1007/978-94-007-6772-0_11
21. Hoppe, R.: Heuristics for practitioners of policy design: rules-of-thumb for structuring unstructured problems. Public Policy Adm. **33**(4), 384–408 (2018)
22. IEEE: Ethically aligned design, version 2 (2017). https://ethicsinaction.ieee.org/. Accessed 13 2019
23. Jasanoff, S., Wynne, B.: Science and decision making. In: Rayner, S., Malone, E.L. (eds.) Human Choice and Climate Change, pp. 1–87. Battelle Press, Columbus (1998)

24. Lakoff, G.: Don't Think of an Elephant! Chelsea Green Publishing, Hartford (2004)
25. Miceli, M., Castelfranchi, C.: A cognitive approach to values. J. Theory Soc. Behav. **19**(2), 169–193 (1989)
26. Noriega, P., Padget, J., Verhagen, H., d'Inverno, M.: Towards a framework for socio-cognitive technical systems. In: Ghose, A., Oren, N., Telang, P., Thangarajah, J. (eds.) COIN 2014. LNCS (LNAI), vol. 9372, pp. 164–181. Springer, Cham (2015). https://doi.org/10.1007/978-3-319-25420-3_11
27. Noriega, P., Sabater-Mir, J., Verhagen, H., Padget, J., d'Inverno, M.: Identifying affordances for modelling second-order emergent phenomena with the WIT framework. In: Sukthankar, G., Rodriguez-Aguilar, J.A. (eds.) AAMAS 2017. LNCS (LNAI), vol. 10643, pp. 208–227. Springer, Cham (2017). https://doi.org/10.1007/978-3-319-71679-4_14
28. Parks, L., Guay, R.P.: Personality, values, and motivation. Pers. Individ. Differ. **47**(7), 675–684 (2009)
29. Perello-Moragues, A., Noriega, P.: Using agent-based simulation to understand the role of values in policy-making. In: Advances in Social Simulation – Looking in the Mirror (in Press)
30. Perello-Moragues, A., Noriega, P., Poch, M.: Modelling contingent technology adoption in farming irrigation communities. J. Artif. Soc. Soc. Simul. (in Press)
31. Perello-Moragues, A., Noriega, P., Popartan, A., Poch, M.: Modelling policy shift advocacy. In: Proceedings of the Multi-Agent-Based Simulation Workshop in AAMAS 2019 (in Press)
32. Perry, C.: ABCDE+F: a framework for thinking about water resources management. Water Int. **38**(1), 95–107 (2013)
33. Van de Poel, I.: Values in engineering design. In: Meijers, A.W.M. (ed.) Handbook of the Philosophy of Science, pp. 973–1006. Elsevier (2009)
34. Poel, I.: Translating values into design requirements. In: Michelfelder, D.P., McCarthy, N., Goldberg, D.E. (eds.) Philosophy and Engineering: Reflections on Practice, Principles and Process. PET, vol. 15, pp. 253–266. Springer, Dordrecht (2013). https://doi.org/10.1007/978-94-007-7762-0_20
35. Rokeach, M.: The Nature of Human Values. Free Press, New York (1973)
36. Russell, S.: Provably beneficial artificial intelligence. Exponential Life, BBVA-Open Mind, The Next Step (2017)
37. Saaty, T.: The Analytic Hierarchy Process. McGraw-Hill, New York (1980)
38. Sabatier, P.A.: Theories of the Policy Process. Westview Press, Boulder (1999)
39. Schwartz, S.H.: Universals in the content and structure of values: theoretical advances and empirical tests in 20 countries. In: Zanna, M.P. (ed.) Advances in Experimental Social Psychology, vol. 25, pp. 1–65. Academic Press (1992)
40. Schwartz, S.H., Bilsky, W.: Toward a universal psychological structure of human values. J. Pers. Soc. Psychol. **53**(3), 550–562 (1987)
41. Schwartz, S.H., Caprara, G.V., Vecchione, M.: Basic personal values, core political values, and voting: a longitudinal analysis. Polit. Psychol. **31**(3), 421–452 (2010)
42. Simon, H.A.: Administrative Behavior: A Study of Decision-Making Processes in Administrative Organization. Macmillan, Oxford (1957)
43. Stewart, J.: Value conflict and policy change. In: Stewart, J. (ed.) Public Policy Values, pp. 33–46. Palgrave Macmillan, London (2009)
44. Susskind, J.: Future Politics: Living Together in a World Transformed by Tech. Oxford University Press, Oxford (2018)
45. Witesman, E., Walters, L.: Public service values: a new approach to the study of motivation in the public sphere. Public Adm. **92**(2), 375–405 (2014)

A Model Using Artificial Neural Networks and Fuzzy Logic for Knowing the Consumer on Smart Thermostats as a S³ Product

Omar Mata[1](✉) ⓘ, Pedro Ponce[1] ⓘ, Isabel Méndez[1] ⓘ,
Arturo Molina[1] ⓘ, Alan Meier[2] ⓘ, and Therese Peffer[3] ⓘ

[1] Tecnologico de Monterrey, 14380 Mexico City, Mexico
{omar.mata, pedro.ponce, A01165549, armolina}@tec.mx
[2] University of California Davis, Davis, CA 95616, USA
akmeier@ucdavis.edu
[3] University of California Berkeley, Berkeley, CA 94720, USA
tpeffer@berkeley.edu

Abstract. The correct and continuous use of s³ products at home can be beneficial for the environment and at the same time could generate cost savings on bills. An automated home where the user has no interaction may be the most efficient and eco-friendly option, but it is not always the most comfortable option for the user. On the other hand, if the user interacts with the system as he pleases, the system may be wasting energy, so a middle point must be found. If the system learns about the user's behavior and tries to shape it in order to make it eco-friendlier with the correct motivation, an engagement to this kind of behavior can be achieve. A first approach of the framework is presented, where a classification of the type of consumer is proposed depending on its personality to find his engagement on ecological behavior (EB). First, an artificial neural network is used to get the personality of the consumer. Then a Mamdani inference system is used with the result of the ANN to get an initial level of ecological behavior engagement.

Keywords: Ecological behavior engagement · Personality · Fuzzy systems · Artificial neural network

1 Introduction

It is very common that product designers spend too many time creating high-quality products for the market to embrace but is not that common that the product adapts itself to the customer needs. The whole process of making a new product is very sophisticated and on top adding the sophistication of the human behavior the problem may be seem impossible to address.

Nowadays artificial intelligence has become a powerful tool that helps us to tackle problems in an easiest way. Making systems that can better classify or even understand how people interact with the product. This is part of the new idea for making sensing, smart and sustainable products. This paper shows a first approach for understanding

L. Martínez-Villaseñor et al. (Eds.): MICAI 2019, LNAI 11835, pp. 430–439, 2019.
https://doi.org/10.1007/978-3-030-33749-0_34

costumers for their personalities to create a framework in which the product itself can adapt to the type of user and engage him into a more ecological behavior.

1.1 Personality

In psychology, a proposed descriptive theory of five broad and replicable personality traits [1] have been vastly supported and often referred to as the "Big Five" [2]:

1. Openness to experience relates to the fact of appreciating divergent thinking, new social, ethical and political ideas, behaviors and values. Individuals Open to Experience are curious, imaginative and unconventional. Openness to experience is linked to success in adaption to change [3].
2. Conscientiousness is associated with self-discipline, competence, dutifulness and responsibility. Conscientious individuals are rational, purposeful, strong-willed, like to follow rules and have clear objectives. Conscientiousness is significantly linked to performance [4].
3. Extraversion refers to the tendency to be energized by social interactions, excitement and diverse activities. Extraverted individuals are talkative, assertive and optimist [4].
4. Agreeableness is characterized by altruism, modesty, straightforwardness and a cooperative nature. Agreeable individuals are sympathetic to others and tolerant [5].
5. Neuroticism relates to the tendency to experience negative emotions such as fear and sadness. Individuals with high neuroticism levels are impulsive, stressful and bad-tempered [5].

These personality traits have shown a close relation between the personality of a person and their behavior in different domains [6]. Furthermore, research linking personality and environmental behaviors showed somewhat mixed results yet the capability to predict environmental concern with the personality seems to be possible.

Recent studies explore different methodologies to predict, link or engage into a pro-environmental behavior as an effect of the Big Five. The results are consistent, where at higher level of agreeableness and openness a greater environmental engagement is present. Whereas conscientiousness shown a little positive influence on environmental engagement, it is more likely to be related with environmental concern. However, extraversion seemed not to have major impact on the behavior. Finally, neuroticism showed an unexpected finding, because of this kind of people tends to be more worried about negative outcomes they resulted to be more environmental concern [7–9].

As the Big Five have been proven to relate with pro-environmental behaviors, there is still missing a way to classify this kind of behaviors. According to the Organization Citizenship Behavior for the Environment (OCBE) a tri-dimensional model is proposed [10].

1. Eco-initiatives relate to personal actions such as making suggestions for energy conservation, voluntary initiatives to reduce energy consumption, etc.
2. Eco-civic engagement provides support for eco-initiatives as a result of participating in environmental programs.

3. Eco-helping involves promoting or encouraging ecological behaviors to consider environmental concerns.

   Lohyd et al. presented a study of the effects of the Big Five on the OCBE model. They showed that openness is linked to eco-helping, conscientiousness relates with eco-initiatives and extraversion predicted eco-civic engagement [11]. While the OCBE model indeed refers to an organizational scenario, is a good first approach to comprehend the relation that could exist between personality and environmental behavior.

   On the other hand [13] showed a segmentation of five types of costumers related to energy use based on expressed attitudes and behaviors.

1. Green advocate. Show the most positive overall energy-saving behaviors, have the strongest positive environmental sentiments and has interest in new technologies.
2. Traditionalist cost-focused energy savers. Their energy-saving behavior is more motivated by the cost savings than the environmental impact and has limited interest in new technologies.
3. Home-focused selective energy savers. Are concerned about saving energy, are more interested in home-improvement efforts.
4. Nongreen selective energy savers. Show selective energy saving behaviors, focused on "set and forget" type of interventions, are not concerned about environmental considerations.
5. Disengaged energy waters. Less motivated to save money through energy savings, are not concerned about environmental and are not particularly interested in new technologies.

   As no one has provided a way to segment the type of costumers related to energy, this paper proposes a model using the big five traits of personality to predict the costumer's EB engagement.

2 Framework on Smart Thermostats

A framework is proposed in Fig. 1 to improve the engagement on environmental behaviors in people regarding power consumption using s^3 products. We focus firstly on thermostats as a device that depending of its correct use can improve power consumption on households. The thermostat interface uses this framework where the user is first classified depending on its personality with a level of EB engagement, then a gamification method is applied to improve the user's environmental behavior hence reducing power consumption while the framework keeps learning and self-adapting to keep the user's engagement.

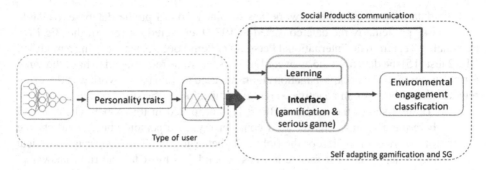

Fig. 1. Proposed framework

What this article focuses on is the first part of the process, the classification of the user depending of its personality. The Fig. 2 shows in detail how the level of EB is obtaind.

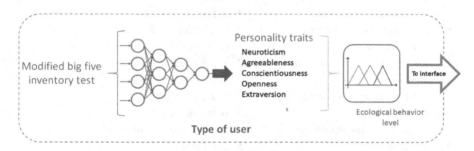

Fig. 2. Type of user classification

First a modified BFI-2 survey of 15 question is applied to the costumer, the answers are evaluated with an ANN and gives the percentage of each personality trait. Then the personality traits are evaluated in a Mamdani inference system to finally obtain the level of ecological behavior expected of the consumer.

2.1 Artificial Neural Network

The main structure of the artificial neural network is shown in Fig. 3. This type of ANN is a multilayer network and uses feedforward connected neurons, meaning that the input signals only flow "forward" to the output signals. A sigmoid activation function for the neurons in the hidden layers was used and for the output, linear function neurons.

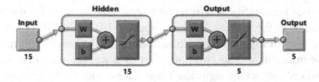

Fig. 3. ANN topology

The data used to train the network was obtained from a public database available online [14], particularly the data consisted in 19719 answered surveys of the Big Five Personality Test from the International Personality Item Pool. As we are using a modified BFI-2 test [15] the data from the answered surveys had to be re-arranged to have the same format as our test. The backpropagation algorithm used to train the network was Bayesian regularization that uses an adaptive weight minimization as the stop condition.

The Table 1 shows the modified BFI-2 [12] proposed in this paper. There are 15 items where the user must answer as "I consider myself a person who..." and choose whether the answer of the left or the right suits better to him. The answer is numerical from 1 to 5 where 1 is most for the left answer and 5 is most for the right answer.

Table 1. Example of modified BFI-2 test

1.	is quiet	2	is sociable
2.	is cold/uncaring	5	is compassionate
3.	is disoganized	4	keeps thins tidy
4.	is relaxed	1	worries a lot
5.	has few artistic interests	3	is fascinated by art, music or literature
6.	prefers others to take charge	3	is a leader
7.	is rude to others	5	is respectful
8.	has difficulty getting started on tasks	2	is persistent
9.	feels secure	1	tends to feel depressed
10.	has little interest in abstract ideas	3	is a deep thinker
11.	is low active	3	is full of energy
12.	tends to find faults with others	4	assumes the best of people
13.	is careless	5	is reliable
14.	is emotionally stable	3	is temperamental
15.	has little creativity	3	is original

2.2   Mamdani Type Inference for Level of Ecological Behavior

It has been observed in several studies that particular personality traits are associated with an environmental concern and also with pro-environmental behaviors.

Using the results of Brick [7] and Taciano [8] where they collect several studies to correlate the personality traits with environmental attitudes, we are proposing a model to get a level of EB expected on a person based on its personality traits to make a classification of the type of user, to finally adapt the interface of the product to better suit him.

According to the segmentation proposed [13]: Green advocate (GA), Traditionalist cost-focused (TC), Home-focused selective (HF), Nongreen selective (NG) and Disengaged energy waster (DE), for each of them a radar map was generated according to the correlation of personality to later use it to generate the rules for the fuzzy system. GA was considered as the highest level of expected EB while DE is the lowest level.

As it can be seen in Fig. 4 the openness trait is almost linearly correlated with the level of EB. Neuroticism is also correlated but in a weaker way than openness. The extraversion trait only showed a significant correlation with the home-focused selective level of behavior while agreeableness only was found with the highest levels of ecological behavior. Finally, conscientiousness trait showed no significant difference between all the levels of EB.

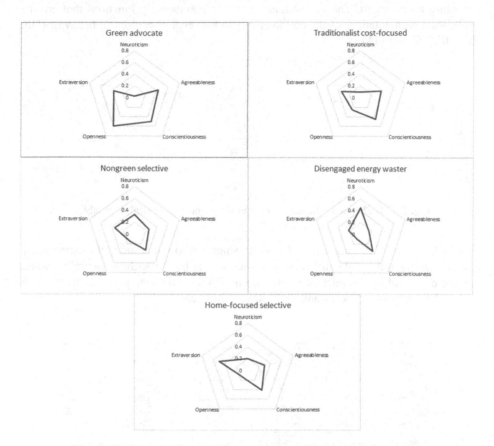

Fig. 4. Radar map of personality correlation with the type of costumer

With this information a fuzzy logic system is proposed with 5 input variables, one for each trait and one output variable indicating the level of ecological behavior (Fig. 5).

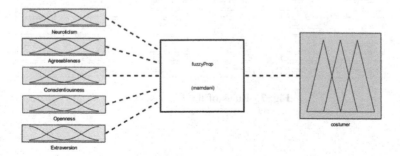

Fig. 5. Fuzzy system

Each input variable has 2 membership functions as shown in Fig. 6 that depend on the correlation found in the previous maps, note that these functions can be modified according to an expert. The output function has 5 membership functions that are the established segmentations of the costumer due to the level of ecological behavior (DE, NG, HF, TC and GA).

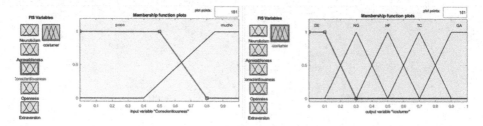

Fig. 6. Membership functions for input (left) and output (right) variables.

Finally, a set of 32 linguistic rules were generated to relate the input membership functions to the output. When the input values are set by the artificial neural network, this are evaluated by the inference system, Fig. 7 shows the activation of the 32 rules during the evaluation process and the output value generated.

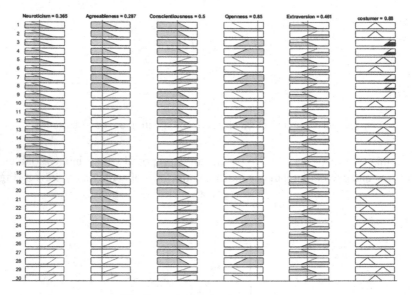

Fig. 7. Rules of the fuzzy system

3 Model Test

The presented model corresponds to the very first part of the framework. To verify if the output somehow describes correctly the person in terms of his level of ecological behavior by its personality traits, some tests were taken in which a person had to respond the 15-question survey and then identify himself with a type o consumer related with his energy use. The answers were compared with the output of the fuzzy system to validate the model.

Taking the responses shown in Table 1, a function in Matlab was made to evaluate them with the trained net. Figure 8 shows the function with the values of the table as the inputs. The output of the function corresponds to the percentage of each of the personality traits that describes that person. The order of the values is: extraversion, agreeableness, conscientiousness, neuroticism, and openness.

```
>> y = BFI_N({[2;5;4;1;3;3;5;2;1;3;3;4;5;3;3]});
>> y{1}

ans =

    0.7333
    0.4666
    0.5333
    0.6667
    0.7334
```

Fig. 8. ANN results

The result found that this person is highly open and extraverted while not so much agreeable and somewhat conscious and with temper. Looking back to Fig. 4, the openness and neuroticism traits are the more influent on the level of EB while extraversion somewhat affects positively the level of EB. Inspecting the results, it can be expected a level of EB between TC and GA because the high openness (.73) and extraversion (.73) traits while the neuroticism trait may reduce a little the level of EB.

This individual previously identified himself as a traditionalist cost-focused (TC) energy saving type of person. Figure 9 shows the evaluation of the fuzzy system with the personality traits. The level of EB obtained is .7547 suggesting a TC inclined to GA type of person. The results matched with what the person previously reported.

```
>> o1 = evalfis([.66 .46 .53 .73 .73],fuzzyProp)

o1 =

    0.7547
```

Fig. 9. Fuzzy system evaluation

4 Conclusions

While it is too difficult to understand a costumer on what is what motivates him to continue using a product and moreover to change his behavior on a particular subject, this paper presented a first approach for classifying the type of costumer with a 15-question quick survey for tailoring a product to try to engage him into a more ecological behavior. This is the first part of a whole system in which depending of the proposed classification, the product can change its interface and keep learning from the user to adapt to his likes or needs.

The proposed model seems to classify and assign a level of BE accordingly to the personality of the costumer. It uses the knowledge of experts with artificial intelligence tools, giving the opportunity to change the model somehow easily to increase the accuracy of it.

Working with human behavior is a difficult task because there is no universal truth. This model was design with 19 thousand responses from a test where no differences in demographic information were made. The next step is to add demographic information to see if the model still can predict the level of BE with some accuracy to make it more reliable.

Acknowledgement. The authors would like to thank the CITRIS & ITESM funding for the project "A strategy to Increase Energy Savings from Smart Thermostats Based on Gamification and Deep Learning".

References

1. McCrae, R., Costa, P.: Personality trait structure as a human universal. Am. Psychol. **52**, 509–516 (1997)
2. John, O., Srivastava, S.: The Big Five trait taxonomy: History, measurement, and theoretical perspectives. In: Pervin, L., John, O. (eds.) Handbook of Personality: Theory and Research, pp. 102–138. Guilford Press, New York (1999)
3. Rothmann, S., Coetzer, E.: The big five personality dimensions and job performance. SA J. Ind. Psychol. **29**, 68–74 (2003)
4. Barrick, M., Mount, M.: The big five personality dimensions and job performance: a meta-analysis. Pers. Psychol. **44**, 1–26 (1991)
5. Judge, T., Higgins, C., Thoresen, C., Barrick, M.: The big five personality traits, general mental ability, and career success across the life span. Pers. Psychol. **52**, 621–652 (1999)
6. Paunonen, S.: Big Five factors of personality and replicated predictions of behavior. J. Pers. Soc. Psychol. **84**, 411–422 (2003)
7. Brick, C., Lewis, G.: Unearthing the "green" personality: core traits predict environmentally friendly behavior. Environ. Behav. **5**, 635–658 (2016)
8. Taciano, L., Chris, G.: The big five personality traits and environmental engagement: associations at the individual and societal level. J. Environ. Psychol. **32**, 187–195 (2012)
9. Jacob, B.: Personality and environmental concern. J. Environ. Psychol. **30**, 245–248 (2010)
10. Boiral, O., Paillé, P.: Organizational citizenship behaviour for the environment: measurement and validation. J. Bus. Ethics **109**, 431 (2012)

11. Lohyd, T., Sowon, K., Sébastien, F.: Who are the good organizational citizens for the environment? An examination of the predictive validity of personality traits. J. Environ. Psychol. **48**, 185–190 (2016)
12. Rammstedt, B., John, O.: Measuring personality in one minute or less: a 10-item short version of the Big Five Inventory in English and German. J. Res. Pers. **41**, 203–212 (2007)
13. Frankel, D., Heck, S., Tai, H.: Using a consumer-segmentation approach to make energy-efficiency gains in the residential market. McKinsey & Company (2013)
14. N.A.: Open psychology data: Raw data form online personality tests (2019). https://openpsychometrics.org/_rawdata/. Accessed 20 June 2019
15. Soto, C., John, O.: The next Big Five Inventory (BFI-2): developing and assessing a hierarchical model with 15 facets to enhance bandwidth, fidelity, and predictive power. J. Pers. Soc. Psychol. **113**, 117–143 (2017)

Methodology for the Implementation of Virtual Assistants for Education Using Google Dialogflow

Roberto Reyes[✉], David Garza, Leonardo Garrido, Víctor De la Cueva,
and Jorge Ramirez

Writing Lab, TecLabs, Vicerrectoría de Investigación y Transferencia de Tecnología,
Tecnológico de Monterrey, 64849 Monterrey, NL, Mexico
{a00344331,a00820764}@itesm.mx, {leonardo.garrido,vcueva,juresti}@tec.mx

Abstract. We developed a virtual assistant that enables students to access interactive content adapted for an introductory undergraduate course on artificial intelligence. This chatbot is able to show answers to frequently asked questions in a hierarchical structured manner, leading students by either voice, text or tactile input to the content that better solves their questions and doubts. It was developed using Google Dialogflow as a simple way to generate and train a natural language model. Another convenience of this platform is its ability to collect usage data that is potentially useful for lecturers as learning indicators. The main purpose of this paper is to outline the methodology that guided our implementation so that it can be reproduced in different educational contexts and study chatbots as tools for learning. At the moment, several articles, news and blogs are writing about the potential, implementation and impact chatbots have in general contexts, however there is little to no literature proposing a methodology to reproduce them for educational purposes. In that respect, we developed four main categories as a generic structure of course content and focused on quick implementation, easy updating and generalization. The final product received a general approbation of the students due to its accessibility and well structured data.

Keywords: Virtual assistants · Education · Dialogflow · Chatbots · Intelligent tutoring · Educational innovation · Tec-21 · Higher education

1 Introduction

Conversational bots have many applications throughout the industry and in recent years they have been developed for educational purposes. The ability to serve with questions and answers to thousands of students at the same time is perfect to counter the scarcity of teachers and lecturers in schools and universities around the globe. It also creates a better tool for online courses to improve their students performance.

© Springer Nature Switzerland AG 2019
L. Martínez-Villaseñor et al. (Eds.): MICAI 2019, LNAI 11835, pp. 440–451, 2019.
https://doi.org/10.1007/978-3-030-33749-0_35

The content of each course is unique and varies depending on the subject and the lecturer's approach. One of our main objectives from this paper is to adapt any educational content into a well structured chatbot using Dialogflow. Dialogflow is a Google service that runs on Google Cloud Platform which basically allows any user to build engaging voice and text-based conversational interfaces [8]. Ideally, we could gather information that is relevant to the student. This can be accomplished through questions and answers between the students in a discussion forum, mail or any message application. In this way, the chatbot will know what is the most common subject that is being consulted and could hierarchically order the information that is provided by the lecturer in books, documents and slideshows into sections and subsections to ease the student with this tool. As useful as a chatbot can be, it is not intended to replace the lecturer. The educational tool we developed and tested throughout this paper offers menus and suggestions to provide the student with visual and auditory content making it more attractive.

Dialogflow presented a big constraint for our development, which is the difficulty to work in this platform, as it sometimes froze or even closed while using it. It is essential that the lecturer, without having prior knowledge to chatbots or AI, can be capable of creating, modifying and implementing changes to this educational tool in a simple and efficient manner. We took advantage of the API provided by Dialogflow to implement a Google sheets capable of modifying and creating a chatbot with Dialogflow, without working directly on that platform. As it is still robust, is more stable and friendly. Another advantage of google sheets is the possibility to incorporate certain techniques of data augmentation to generate training examples to improve the accuracy of the machine learning model. Data augmentation using deep neural networks for Acoustic Modelling have proven effective dealing with data sparsity [2]. These results are important for chatbots because they lead to a better understanding of the user's input through NLP with a smaller training set. We could also take advantage of grammatical patterns and synonyms to create questions similar to the ones provided by the students.

2   Background

Throughout the years, the educational system has progressed along with new technologies and theories. The modern student has the ability to take notes in a tablet, where he can take pictures or add screenshots of the teacher's presentation to his own notes, send an e-mail to the lecturer any time and check for any homework at a learning management platform. Although these technologies enhance the students with the lecturer's response at a specific question, interacting with the educator outside the classroom becomes inefficient as the number of pupils grow.

Chatbots are computer programs designed to hold conversations with users using natural language [1]. One of their main advantages is to have the ability of possessing a friendly database which can be accessed by anyone, as long as the user speaks the same language of the chatbot. There is no need for a background on computer science or to even know how to use a computer, the only thing that is needed is to ask the questions and a well structured chatbot shall answer and direct to the correct response. For this to happen, we found ourselves in the need to translate our natural language for the system to understand, thus, we recurred to NLP (Natural Language Processing). The majority of these state-of-the-art NLP systems address their single problem by applying linear statistical models [5] and deep learning.

Chatbots have become increasingly common in recent years [1] thus, different types have developed for distinct tasks. Deterministic chatbots are created to exhibit exactly the same behaviour each time they encounter the same situation while non deterministic or evolving (dynamic) chatbots include a learning component that allows them to take past interactions and outcomes and adjust their behaviour accordingly [3].

3 Related Work

The development of conversational agents has been one of the main areas of focus in the field of artificial intelligence. These ideas were given birth half a century ago, when Turing in *The Imitation Game* [15] proposed a test of a machine's ability to behave as a human in a conversation. Many attempts, such as Weizenbaum's *ELIZA* [16] at MIT, have been made ever since to pass this test. Even though the objective of designing a general intelligence has not been accomplished, these efforts have drawn a path for the development of better agents. Recent efforts to calculate sentence similarity uses bigrams [9].

Chatbots have shown success in educational environments. A state-of-the-art review from 1405 papers dedicated to this manner showed that it was becoming obvious that chatbots have great potential in education but are just starting to enter this field [10]. Jill Watson was developed to improve the student's retention of material with success in a course on Artificial Intelligence at Georgia Tech, they came to the conclusion that although their primary motivation was to cover a large ratio of students per lecturer, in order to make a more specific chatbot it would gradually move from an episodic memory of previous question-answer pairs to use semantic processing [4].

Education being a global problem, in the Universidad Nacional de Córdoba, Argentina [6], researchers compared the use of Alice and a chatbot for high school programs and came to the conclusion that although the chatbot had a better response coming from the students, the response also depended whether they were male or female. The reason they found was that girls had a better experience in verbal oriented activities, while boys preferred a more structured mechanism such as ALICE [17].

At Georgia Institute [7] a similar problem was approached to help high school students contrasting four different platforms. Within the list, they evaluated Dialogflow and it came to be the lowest false intent-id match of all four, which is a desirable feature in this rubric. In the end, they discuss the implementation of

Node.js to process the server side and client side request, because it can handle a large scale of simultaneous connections with high output.

At the moment, several articles, news and blogs are writing about the potential the chatbots have, for example having a response immediately 24/7, taking education to the next level with up-to-date technologies [11], spaced interval learning in order to review the lesson before forgetting it [12]; others are discussing the important role they can play in education and how they are changing it, for example, learning being personalized at any student vs lecturer ratio and have automated grading [13]. There are also companies surging from the need of making these chatbots, one example is Botsify.com which enables teachers to create chatbots from templates already established [14]. Although there is a lot of material related to chatbots in education, there is no concrete methodology for anyone to develop its own assistant.

Recent implementations of virtual assistants for education. For example, Sánchez-Díaz et al. [1] introduced the concept of function-parameter modeling, in which intents are treated as functions that receive parameters (entities). This model was specially useful for trying to implement a chatbot using one of the popular commercial platforms.

4   Methodology

We divide methodology in two parts: knowledge abstraction and response generation. Knowledge abstraction has to do with the analysis of course content (which we will call data). On the other hand, response generation depends on the characteristics of the data generated in the process of knowledge abstraction, and also, it depends on the features of the tools available for Dialogflow and its various integrations.

4.1   Knowledge Abstraction

Knowledge abstraction involves three phases: gathering, manipulation and augmentation. These phases are mostly independent from the content of the chatbot.

Data Gathering. The first step is to generate a knowledge base. This step involves finding key concepts of the course and gathering information about them. Developers might want to focus on the syllabus of the course to get a general idea of the main ideas and topics. Ideally, the lecturer hands in a list of topics with its main concepts ordered in a hierarchical structure. Then, one generates a bunch of questions. These questions might come from online records (such as discussion forums, social media interaction with students or messaging applications), homework assignments, and frequently asked questions the teacher is aware of. After this process, developers can then classify this questions in categories according to the topic they relate to. These categories structure the content of the chatbot.

Data Manipulation. The second step is to store this information in a database. This will enable developers to manipulate data. For instance, developers can create two spreadsheets, one with the syllabus of the course ordered by topics and accompanied by the most relevant concepts of each topic, and another spreadsheet with the set of questions found in a discussion forum together with their answers. Then, they can classify each question with its corresponding topic by looking for the keywords (aka the concepts contained in the first spreadsheet) within the question or the answer strings. This consists technically in the implementation of a classification algorithm that labels each question-answer pair. These labels must be given a degree of confidence and then checked by a human to confirm its validity.

The database might contain questions with similar answers, this should mean that these questions have the same goal or purpose, so one can group them in categories, which will later evolve into Dialogflow intents. Therefore, developers should associate to each question-answer pair a label indicating the name of the intent to which they belong. This will later ease the process of taking information from the database to Dialogflow. Here human intervention is crucial in the sense that the degree of "similarity" between answers to different questions is not well defined, it is left to the criteria of the teacher and developer. This is the step that allows generalization, because this criteria is not the same for all subjects or courses.

Data Augmentation. Data manipulation can be taken to another level by introducing data augmentation. This can increase the number of training examples available for the natural language processing model within Dialogflow. Using the intents, one can lookup for correlations between questions and answers that belong to the same intent.

These correlations can be pictured as keywords (also called entities) in common, and they can be extracted to be later used to produce more training examples. In other words, sometimes answers themselves can be used to produce questions, and these questions should belong to the same intent. Developers can generate another spreadsheet with intents with their corresponding entities. This is very useful since Dialogflow notices entities and the model learns better when certain entities appear only within a single entity.

4.2   Response Generation

There is a thorough description of how entities and intents work within Dialogflow, but it is precise to elaborate about how the way things are already implemented in this platform can benefit the proposed methodology. Intents are built upon three basic components: contexts, training examples and responses. Contexts serve the purpose of layering the conversation in such a way that, when they are present, they allow only certain intents to be activated. Training examples are sentences, and they are found in two categories: templates and examples. Both of them label these sentences using entities or just the plain intent in which they are contained. Responses are the outputs of intents, so each time a user entry corresponds to an intent, its response is triggered. They appear in several ways, the most common is simple text, but Dialogflow allows direct integration with apps that fit content into cards, carousels, tables, lists and other structures of content.

Entities, as previously said, are keywords that may or may not be classified according to its function. There are entities that correspond to geographical locations, numbers, or dates. These are popular in the context of customer service, for example taking the order of a client. But for educational purposes not so much, so an option is to make an intent for each concept, this way we can group data resulting from students interaction with the bot not only using specific questions, but also using this broader constructs. Besides the advantage in the analytics, there is also a benefit for intent recognition, since every time an entity is detected the number of possible intents that match the query is reduced.

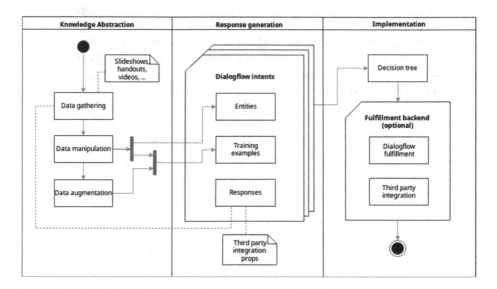

Fig. 1. Graphical representation for the sections in which we divide the methodology and how they are related to each other

It is important to comment on the issues of writing a response. We know the way students watch slide shows is different from how they are supposed to interact with a virtual assistant. This difference introduces the need of content adaptation, the process of finding a media which best transmits the desired message. For instance, when outlining a procedure, we want to show a list of steps instead of a paragraph, or if it is rather a concept best described with a picture or a video, we want to be able to show this content as well as a description. We propose using Actions On Google cards or similar for short factual answers, lists or carousels for procedures, and simple responses with more specific questions. Also, comes the question of whether the agent is going to say every written word, or is it just going to expect the user to read it. We found it was better to use a mixture of both: let the agent tell the user what it is showing, but not the actual content, because it is otherwise annoying to hear the agent speak for a long time. As an example, if the user asks for the algorithm of BFS, then the agent would say: "Here is the algorithm of BFS", and then it show the algorithm as a list of steps.

4.3   Flow of Conversation and Decision Trees

In the next two subsections, we talk about flow of conversation and how to face some problems regarding the machine learning model. These topics attempt to provide useful advice for how to implement the methodology more efficiently.

Decision trees are also called conversation trees and are used to implement the structure of a virtual assistant. They are made up from nodes, where each of these contain an answer to a particular query. The task of the developer is then to give each node a conditional that is activated when the user's query matches the response contained in the node (with some degree of accuracy). This last step is done with the aid of keywords and natural language recognition. In Dialogflow, nodes are equivalent to intents, Fig. 2 shows the structure of the decision tree we utilized in further detail.

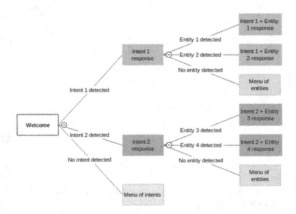

Fig. 2. Basic structure of a proposed decision tree with two intents and four different entities that work with those intents. The purpose of this structure is to respond to fallback cases with intent or entity menus from which the user can pick one interactively. Another part of the proposed tree that is not observed here, but has to do with the non-linear flow of conversation, is the presence of jumps between related nodes, such that one can directly visit father and sibling nodes. Finally, it is important to say that the user can also go directly to the third layer nodes by asking with both entities and intents recognized by the chatbot

The first step towards implementing a decision tree is defining a flow of conversation. The flow of conversation defines the interaction with the user. It refers to the way the agent handles bifurcations in the middle of a conversation, and how it travels through the content. We have found that flows of conversation can be categorized in linear and non-linear.

Linear Flow. It is a flow of conversation that consists in two steps, question and answer. These are what we call FAQ bots and are relatively easy to implement, because the decision tree has only one branch of nodes. However, they are helpful only if an instruction manual is provided. This manual must tell what content the assistant can provide and how is the user expected to interact with it.

Non-linear Flow. This flow of conversation relies heavily on suggestions and allows for exploring the decision tree much more structure deeply. The decision tree is not different at all from the implementation of the linear flow, but the key difference is that it features jumps between nodes. These jumps enable suggestions to directly link to any other node within our decision tree.

The steps outlined so far have to do directly with the methodology and are presented in Fig. 1.

4.4   Underfitting vs. Overfitting

Every machine learning application has to deal with the bias vs. variance problem. Here we present some general types of problem we have faced at the stage of implementation and testing.

Underfitting Due to the Lack of Entities. The lack of entities can generate an underfitting problem because the agent looses the chance of identifying every parameter it needs to give a relevant answer. This problem can rise from the process of design, and is particularly problematic when intents are not specific enough. The bot will not understand the particular needs of the user, just grasp a general context that is not useful enough.

Underfitting Due to the Excess of Entities. Here there are so many entities declared that different intents may contain several entities in common, and thus have a strong correlation. This may lower the degree of confidence of the agent with respect to the right response.

Overfitting Due to Unsimplified Intent. This problem has a similar nature to last one, the difference is that now it does not have to do with entities at all, but with the words used in the training examples. Also, the result is completely different because since we use overly complicated or worded sentences as training examples the result is that the agent is trained to recognize very specific patterns of words. The consequence is that the agent is not able to identify this intent unless the sentences have a very specific structure.

Overfitting Due to Separable Entities. Some entities with multiple words can be separated to avoid this problem, it depends on what kind of entities we are dealing with, because there are cases in which this change is rather harmful. For example, if we want the agent to answer questions like: "what is the difference between Fast Fourier Transform and Fourier Transform?", then we have to specify that FFT is one entity and FT is another.

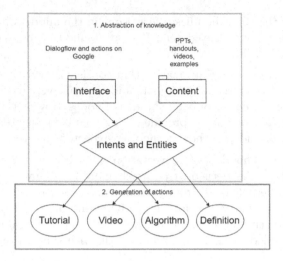

Fig. 3. Abstraction of knowledge and generation of actions applied to the case study

5   Case of Study

Dialogflow gave us the tool to create a chatbot and provide it to any user around the world with access to internet. The only two requisites to "enter" the chatbot is to have the Google Assistant App and to know the name of the conversational system in order to request it. Dialogflow is built in layers as a decision tree. An important feature in Dialogflow is the ability to save contexts during the conversation. For example, if a user is talking about dogs, and he proceeds to say "show me a picture" the chatbot should show him a picture of a dog, but if there is no context in the conversation of anything and the user asks for a picture, the response shall be "a picture of a dog or a cat".

Complementary to Dialogflow's interface we integrated the chatbot to Actions On Google interface using Node.js, which is an asynchronous event driven in JavaScript run time. Node is designed to build network scalable applications, contrary to the most common used currency model where OS threads are employed.

In this case study we applied our methodology for an undergraduate program in four classes in a Mexican university. The first thing was to obtain the data for the chatbot and classify it. Since this is an AI introductory class, the topics covered were six basic search algorithms. The lecturer handed slide shows and with the information which, as this project is pioneer, was subtracted by a human. In this case it is obvious to section the data in this 6 categories and the abstraction of knowledge is shown in Fig. 3. To make it user friendly, we made an effort to design the flux of the conversation as natural as it could be, by adding suggestions at some nodes. This way, the user is able to explore the whole chatbot and can be more confident on what he will be answered. However, suggestions are truly just that: suggestions. The user can navigate freely through the chatbot

Fig. 4. For the case study, the chatbot is in Spanish because the classes were imparted in this language. The first thing the chatbot shows is a short greetings and the instructions of what it can do. Above the microphone are the buttons added with Node.Js

without having to take any specific route, an example of these suggestions is shown on Fig. 4 just above the microphone icon. After the data was categorized and structured, we adapted our structure to be: each algorithm on the top layer, and on the next layer each task. As we discussed earlier, Dialogflow manages intents and entities, each task will be an entity and each single node will be an intent.

6   Discussion

It is possible to generalize the methodology since it is content independent. The methodology predicates on the need of a database of questions which are then grouped using labels called intents. These categories are the ones that depend on the course, so even if every course is structured different the fact that it has a structure allows this kind of abstraction. There might more intents for certain use cases, or intents with fewer user examples, but this is a minor concern for implementation purposes.

The use case outlined in the last section is an adaptation to a small set of concepts related to the field of computer science (they are algorithms), hence the possibility to replicate a very similar implementation with success in any other course that deals with algorithms.

Through the experience designing chatbots and flows of conversation in particular, we have observed that there are two main categories of answers: conceptual and procedural. Conceptual answers are solved giving facts about the asked concept, these are: the definition, explanation, characteristics, etc. In contrast, procedural answers involve sometimes not just one fact, but often a series of steps towards a solving a particular problem. One good example of these is the tutorials intent.

A very important part on implementation is the automation of each methodological step. Developers can automate the process of manipulating data from spreadsheets by writing scripts using Python or JavaScript. They can proceed with data augmentation in the same manner. Also, it is possible to upload and update data from the servers of Dialogflow using its API. The idea is to start building intents from the API instead of manually copying the information that is already contained in a database.

7   Conclusions

The proposed methodology consists of two main phases: knowledge abstraction and response generation. The former is subdivided into: data gathering, which is providing the raw data; data manipulation, which manages and classifies data for design purposes; and data augmentation, which is an extra step for increasing the number of examples available for the training process of the machine learning model. The later involved response generation, which manages how entities and intents are treated to show useful content depending on the type of interaction between the user and the chatbot. It is also important to highlight the relevance of capturing this information as nodes of a decision tree and choosing a convenient flow of conversation.

Future work is going to outline the influence of virtual assistants in the performance of students. Collaboration with other institutions and replication within similar and different educational contexts is needed in order to make further studies and obtain conclusive results about the impact of virtual assistants in education. For instance, the case of study was one particular implementation (for a very specific set of needs, in a narrow context), what we need is a broader set of contexts from which to capture the data generated by users and analyze it.

Acknowledgements. Authors would like to acknowledge the financial support of Writing Lab, TecLabs and NOVUS Grant of Tecnológico de Monterrey, México, for the production of this work.

Authors thank Diego Solís Valles for presenting the classification of the underfitting and overfitting problem. We also thank Diego Adolfo José Villa, Uriel Ávila, and Moisés Benavides for their aid in the implementation of this chatbot.

References

1. Sánchez-Díaz, X., Ayala-Bastidas, G., Fonseca-Ortiz, P., Garrido, L.: A knowledge-based methodology for building a conversational chatbot as an intelligent tutor. In: Batyrshin, I., Martínez-Villaseñor, M.L., Ponce Espinosa, H.E. (eds.) MICAI 2018. LNCS (LNAI), vol. 11289, pp. 165–175. Springer, Cham (2018). https://doi.org/10.1007/978-3-030-04497-8_14

2. Cui, X., Goel, V., Kingsbury, B.: Data augmentation for deep neural network acoustic modeling. IEEE/ACM Trans. Audio Speech Lang. Process. (TASLP) **23**, 1469–1477 (2015)
3. Paikari, E., van der Hoek, A.: A framework for understanding chatbots and their future. In: 11th International Workshop Proceedings on Cooperative and Human Aspects of Software Engineering. ACM (2018)
4. Goel, A., Polepeddi, L.: Jill Watson: a virtual teaching assistant for online education. Georgia Institute of Technology (2016)
5. Collobert, R., et al.: Natural language processing (almost) from scratch. J. Mach. Learn. Res. **12**, 2493–2537 (2011)
6. Benotti, L., Martínez, M., Schapachnik, F.: Engaging high school students using chatbots. In: 2014 Conference Proceedings on Innovation Technology in Computer Science Education. ACM (2014)
7. Dutta, D.: Developing an intelligent chat-bot tool to assist high school students for learning general knowledge subjects. Georgia Institute of Technology (2017)
8. Google: Dialogflow (2019). https://dialogflow.com. Accessed 05 June 2019
9. Setiaji, B., Wahyu, F.: Chatbot using a knowledge in database: human-to-machine conversation modeling. In: 2016 7th International Conference on Intelligent Systems, Modelling and Simulation (ISMS). IEEE (2016)
10. Winkler, R., Söllner, M.: Unleashing the potential of chatbots in education: a state-of-the-art analysis (2018)
11. Kayla, M.: Chatbotslife (2018). https://chatbotslife.com/how-can-we-use-chatbots-in-education-3ddae688160f. Accessed 07 June 2019
12. Branislav, S.: eLearning industry (2017). https://elearningindustry.com/chatbots-in-education-applications-chatbot-technologies. Accessed 07 June 2019
13. Monica, G.: Towards data science (2019). https://towardsdatascience.com/5-ways-artificial-intelligence-and-chatbots-are-changing-education-9e7d9425421d. Accessed 07 June 2019
14. Botsify: Botsify (2019). https://botsify.com/education-chatbot. Accessed 07 June 2019
15. Turing, A.M.: Computing machinery and intelligence. In: Epstein, R., Roberts, G., Beber, G. (eds.) Parsing the Turing Test, pp. 23–65. Springer, Dordrecht (2009). https://doi.org/10.1007/978-1-4020-6710-5_3
16. Weizenbaum, J.: ELIZA–a computer program for the study of natural language communication between man and machine. Commun. ACM **9**(1), 36–45 (1966)
17. Erwin, V.: Chatbots (2019). https://www.chatbots.org/chatbot/a.l.i.c.e/. Accessed 07 June 2019

Audio-Visual Database for Spanish-Based Speech Recognition Systems

Diana-Margarita Córdova-Esparza[1]([✉]), Juan Terven[2], Alejandro Romero[1],
and Ana Marcela Herrera-Navarro[1]

[1] Facultad de Informática, UAQ, Universidad Autónoma de Querétaro,
Av. de las Ciencias S/N, Campus Juriquilla, 76230 Querétaro, Mexico
diana_mce@hotmail.com, jarg.romero25@gmail.com, anaherreranavarro@gmail.com
[2] AiFi Inc., 2388 Walsh Av., Santa Clara, CA 95051, USA
j.r.terven@ieee.org

Abstract. Automatic speech recognition involves an understanding of
what is being said. It can be audio-based, visual-based, or audio/visual-
based according to the type of inputs. Modern speech recognition systems
are based on machine learning techniques, such as deep learning. Deep
learning systems improve their performance when more data are used to
train them. Therefore, data has become one of the most valuable assets
in the field of Artificial Intelligence. In this work, we present a methodology to create a database for audio/visual speech recognition. Due to
the lack of Spanish datasets, we created a comprehensive Spanish-based
speech recognition dataset. For this, we selected hundreds of YouTube
videos, found the facial features, and aligned the voice beside text with
millisecond accuracy using IBM speech-to-text technology. We split the
data into three speaker face angles, where the frontal angle represents
the simple case, and right-left angles represent harder cases. As a result,
we obtained a dataset of more than 100 thousand samples consisting
of a small video with its respective annotation. Our approach can be
used to generate datasets on any language by merely selecting videos in
the desired language. The database and the source code to create it are
open-source.

Keywords: Database · Speech recognition · Machine learning

1 Introduction

Visual speech recognition is the ability to recognize speech from visual information only [3]. Audio-visual speech recognition combines acoustic and visual
information to recognize what is being said. Applications of this technology
include dictation systems, transcription of silent films, assistive technologies for
people with hearing disabilities, and solving multi-speaker simultaneous speech
[3, 4].

In this work, we propose a methodology to semi-automatically create
databases for training speech recognition systems based on either visual or audio-
only inputs or audio-visual inputs. The database can be created on any language

L. Martínez-Villaseñor et al. (Eds.): MICAI 2019, LNAI 11835, pp. 452–460, 2019.
https://doi.org/10.1007/978-3-030-33749-0_36

by changing the input data and the language of the text-to-speech engine. To test the system usability and contribute to the field, we created an extensive Audio-visual Spanish-based dataset with more than 100,000 samples containing the video with annotated spoken text and 3D mouth features. We also split the data into three face views: frontal view, angle view, and side view.

The source of the videos is YouTube, from where we select videoblogs, TED talks, news, and others. Each sample lasts from one to six seconds and has one to five spoken words with their respective annotation. For storage and copyright issues, we only provide the annotation of the videos with their respective timestamp (start and end of the sample) and the corresponding video link.

1.1 Previous Work

In the literature, we can find several databases that contain annotated images, which are useful for training and testing machine learning algorithms for Computer Vision. The main objective of Computer Vision is the analysis and understanding of a real-world scene captured in an image using a camera. Typical tasks include detection and recognition of objects present in an image, determine what attributes these objects have, and provide a semantic description of the scene. With the advent of public standardize datasets, researchers were able to compare their results on a common benchmark. In the following, we will describe commonly used datasets for computer vision tasks, and we will end with audiovisual speech recognition datasets.

Object recognition is one of the most common tasks in Computer Vision, and it was the one that started the deep learning paradigm -now known as *modern computer vision*- with the requirements of large datasets. Caltech 101 is based on Google images from 101 categories. With approximately 50 images per category [7]. Caltech 256, contains 256 object categories with a total of 30607 images [8], this database represented an improvement for Caltech 101, due to the increase in the number of categories and images for each of them. ImageNet was the stepping stone in large scale benchmark databases used by academia and industry. ImageNet in its current state consists of 12 subtrees with 5247 sets of synonyms (synsets) and 14 million images in total, its main applications are recognition, classification and automatic grouping of objects [5]. Another database focused on recognition is PASCAL visual object classes (VOC), used as a reference in the recognition and detection of categories of visual objects. It provides the user with a set of standard image and annotation data used for machine learning [6].

The Scene Understanding (SUN) database is also used for the recognition of real-world scenes. It contains 899 categories and 130,519 images that show different human activities such as: eating in a restaurant, reading in a library, sleeping, etc. The scenes and their associated functions are closely related to the visual characteristics that structure the space [10].

Microsoft Common Objects in COntext (MS COCO) is a popular database used for detection, recognition, segmentation and human pose estimation, contains 91 categories of everyday objects, 82 of which have more than 5,000 instances labeled. Unlike ImageNet, COCO has fewer categories but more instances in each category, which helps in learning detailed object models [9].

Regarding speech recognition, the work in [4] describes a method to generate a large-scale database from television transmissions automatically. With this approach, they generated the Lip Reading in the Wild (LRW) database with more than one million instances of words, spoken by more than a thousand different people. Lip Reading Sentences in the Wild (LRS2) [3] and Lip Reading in Profile (LRS3) [1] are audiovisual databases also used for speech recognition. LRS2 consists of thousands of sentences obtained from the British Broadcasting Corporation (BCC) and each sentence is up to 100 characters long. LRS3 is a multimodal database for the recognition of audiovisual speech. It includes facial tracks of more than 400 h of TED and TEDx videos, along with their corresponding subtitles.

Inspired by their work, we developed a method to create audiovisual speech recognition datasets for any language automatically. Given the lack of these type of datasets for the Spanish language, we created the first large scale audio-visual speech recognition dataset for Spanish-speaking applications.

The contributions of this work are the following:

1. An extensive database that can be used to train automatic speech recognition systems.
2. The methodology and the free access source code that can be used to generate databases in any other language.

2   Method

This section describes our audio-vision speech recognition dataset generation system. Using this method, we collected thousands of samples covering a vocabulary of more than 10,000 different Spanish words. The procedure is shown in Fig. 1 and consists of the following steps: (1) Select videos, download them, and extract audio; (2) for each audio extract the speech along with timestamps of start and end for each word; (3) crop the speech in samples of no more than five words; (4) determine the video frames involved on each sample and detect the 3D mouth features and face orientation; (5) save the results in file.

In the following subsections, we describe each of these steps with more detail.

2.1   Select Videos and Extract Audio

In this step, we selected Spanish spoken videos from YouTube covering several categories such as TED talks, video blogs, and news. We downloaded the videos an extracted the audio using the following *ffmpeg* command:

$$ffmpeg - ividous.mp4 - acodecpcm_s16le - ac1 - araudio.wav \tag{1}$$

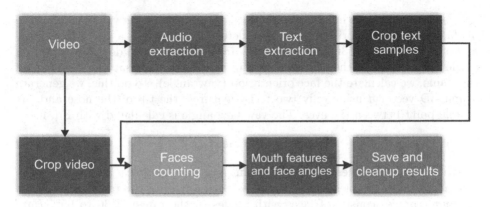

Fig. 1. Procedure to generate the audio-visual speech recognition dataset.

2.2   Timestamped Speech-to-Text

Using IBM's speech-to-text engine, we extracted each word from the audio files including its recognition confidence level and start-end timestamps with millisecond accuracy. To accomplish this, we use *SpeechToTextV1* class from *watson developer cloud* Python library.

2.3   Crop Samples

From the speech-to-text results, we cropped the data in samples containing sentences of one to five words to provide context for homophones words in the training data. Homophones words are identical visually, but its meaning is different, for example, the Spanish words *as, has, haz*. By providing sentences of multiple words, the machine learning models can learn to disambiguate between these words. We omit samples with single words whose length is less than four letters due to ambiguous recognition.

2.4   Selecting Video Frames and Detecting 3D Mouth Features with Face Orientation

Using the speech-to-text timestamps, we calculate the starting video frame and the ending video frame for each data sample using Eqs. (2) and (3):

$$frame1 = s_{min} \times fps \times 60 + (s_{sec} \times fps) \tag{2}$$

$$frame2 = e_{min} \times fps \times 60 + (e_{sec} \times fps), \tag{3}$$

where s_{min}, s_{sec}, e_{min}, and e_{sec} represent the initial minute, initial second, final minute and final second respectively.

Using these frames numbers, we select that portion of the video and run the 3D face alignment algorithm from [2] to determine if there is a face in the frame and obtain the mouth 3D landmarks. If a frame in the video does not contain a single face, we skip to the next sample. Once we determine that there is a face in the frame, we calculate the face orientation (yaw angle). To do this, we generate a unit 3D vector d using only two facial features: the tip of the nose and the middle point between the eyes. The yaw face angle is calculated with Eq. 4.

$$yaw = atan2(d.x, d.z) \tag{4}$$

We split the samples in easy, medium, and hard samples, according to the face angle. *Easy* samples consists of faces with angles in the range of 0 to 35°. *Medium* samples consist of faces with angles in the range of 36 to 65°. *Hard* samples include faces with angles higher than 65°. Figure 2 shows an image with the mouth landmarks and face angle.

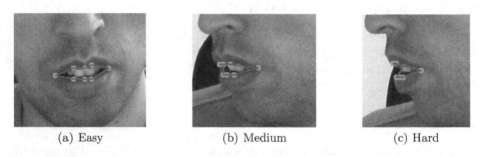

(a) Easy   (b) Medium   (c) Hard

Fig. 2. Face angles. (a) Shows an example of an *Easy* sample with frontal face. (b) Shows an example of a *Medium* sample with face angle in the range of 36 to 65°. (c) Shows a *Hard* sample with a side view (faces with angles greater than 65°).

After filtering the samples without faces, we save the results in a CSV file with the fields *Link, Text, Confidence, Start, End, Mouth features,* and *Difficulty*. Table 1 describes the content of each of these fields.

2.5   Cleanup Results

The generation of the dataset is automatic, however, the results are not perfect. We performed a manual cleanup step where we check each sample and determine if we leave it or remove it from the final results.

3   Results

In total, we annotated hundreds of YouTube videos, creating a corpus of more than 100,000 samples with 32342 different words. Our dataset contains the video link, the text, starting and ending timestamp in seconds with respect to the start

Table 1. Data annotations.

Annotation	Description
Link	YouTube video link without www.youtube.com/
Text	Spoken text in the video sample
Confidence	Average speech recognition score in the range $[0, 1]$
Start, end	Sample start and end timestamp in seconds
Mouth features	Eight 3D mouth features covering the inner lips
Difficulty	Easy, medium or hard, according to the faces angles

of the video, the 3D mouth features with eight features surrounding the inner lip and the sample difficulty. The current version of the dataset contains 34061 easy samples, 20574 medium samples, and 12896 hard samples.

Figure 3 shows the visual sequences for the words *ahora*, *muchas*, and *parece*.

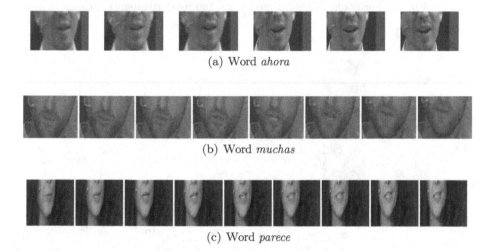

(a) Word *ahora*

(b) Word *muchas*

(c) Word *parece*

Fig. 3. Sample sequences. (a) Shows the visual sequence for the word *ahora*. (b) Shows the visual sequence for the word *muchas*, (c) Shows the visual sequence for the word *parece*

Figure 4 shows the ten most frequent words in the dataset. As described in Sect. 2.3, each sample contains from one to five words. Figure 5 shows the number of samples for each of these cases.

The dataset can be downloaded from the following address http://www.lipreadingdata.com. To ensure reproducible results, we open source the code and it is available at https://github.com/jrterven/audio-visual-dataset.

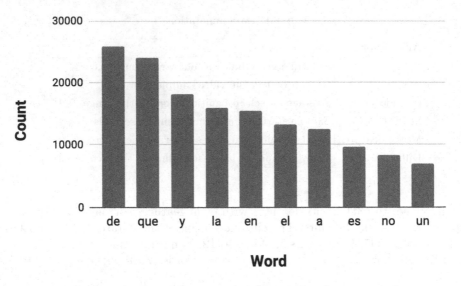

Fig. 4. Word count distribution for the ten most frequent words.

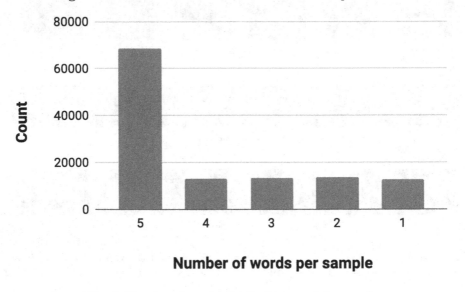

Fig. 5. Number of words distribution per data sample.

4   Discussion

Deep learning systems demand large amounts of data to satisfy their learning capabilities and be able to generalize without over-fitting. In this work, we collected more than 100 thousand training samples where each sample consists of a video with its respective annotation. Each video contains a person quoting from one to five words. The set of video and annotated text can be used to train speech recognition systems based on vision (lip reading), synthetic generation of talking faces for animation purposes or video games. However, this is not new, and there are multiple databases of this type solely for the English language. In this work, we generated an audio-visual speech recognition dataset in Spanish to support the Spanish-speaking scientific community. Furthermore, the proposed methodology can be used to automatically generate databases to train models of audio-visual speech recognition in any language by merely providing the videos in the desired language. One shortcoming of this method is that it makes use of the IBM Audio-to-text engine that runs in the cloud and has a cost per minute. The advantage is that it allows the alignment between video and text with milliseconds accuracy, which is not offered by other free services such as Google Cloud. Another constraint of the proposed methodology is that it only extracts data from videos that contain a single person speaking to ensure that the voice corresponds to the face in the video. This limitation excludes videos that can provide a high diversity of words, such as those available in discussions, interviews, etc. To address this limitation, as future work, we are working on a mouth movement detection system used to extract information from multi-person videos and extend the capabilities of the automatic systems.

5   Conclusions

This paper describes the method of semi-automatic database creation for audio-visual speech recognition systems. To test the technique, we created an extensive database for training computer vision based automatic lip reading systems in the Spanish language. The created database contains more than 100 thousand samples annotated with accurate timestamps and confidence level. The source code used to generate the database is freely available and can be used to create similar databases for other languages.

Acknowledgements. The authors wish to acknowledge the support for this work to Universidad Autónoma de Querétaro (UAQ) through project FIF-2018-06.

References

1. Afouras, T., Chung, J.S., Zisserman, A.: LRS3-TED: a large-scale dataset for visual speech recognition. arXiv preprint arXiv:1809.00496 (2018)
2. Bulat, A., Tzimiropoulos, G.: How far are we from solving the 2D & 3D face alignment problem? (and a dataset of 230,000 3D facial landmarks). In: Proceedings of the IEEE International Conference on Computer Vision, pp. 1021–1030 (2017)
3. Chung, J.S., Senior, A., Vinyals, O., Zisserman, A.: Lip reading sentences in the wild. In: 2017 IEEE Conference on Computer Vision and Pattern Recognition (CVPR), pp. 3444–3453. IEEE (2017)
4. Chung, J.S., Zisserman, A.: Lip reading in the wild. In: Lai, S.-H., Lepetit, V., Nishino, K., Sato, Y. (eds.) ACCV 2016. LNCS, vol. 10112, pp. 87–103. Springer, Cham (2017). https://doi.org/10.1007/978-3-319-54184-6_6

5. Deng, J., Dong, W., Socher, R., Li, L.J., Li, K., Fei-Fei, L.: ImageNet: a large-scale hierarchical image database. In: 2009 IEEE Conference on Computer Vision and Pattern Recognition, pp. 248–255. IEEE (2009)
6. Everingham, M., Van Gool, L., Williams, C.K., Winn, J., Zisserman, A.: The Pascal visual object classes (VOC) challenge. Int. J. Comput. Vis. **88**(2), 303–338 (2010)
7. Fei-Fei, L., Fergus, R., Perona, P.: Learning generative visual models from few training examples: an incremental bayesian approach tested on 101 object categories. Comput. Vis. Image Underst. **106**(1), 59–70 (2007)
8. Griffin, G., Holub, A., Perona, P.: Caltech-256 object category dataset (2007)
9. Lin, T.-Y., et al.: Microsoft COCO: common objects in context. In: Fleet, D., Pajdla, T., Schiele, B., Tuytelaars, T. (eds.) ECCV 2014. LNCS, vol. 8693, pp. 740–755. Springer, Cham (2014). https://doi.org/10.1007/978-3-319-10602-1_48
10. Xiao, J., Hays, J., Ehinger, K.A., Oliva, A., Torralba, A.: SUN database: large-scale scene recognition from abbey to zoo. In: 2010 IEEE Computer Society Conference on Computer Vision and Pattern Recognition, pp. 3485–3492. IEEE (2010)

Best Paper Award, Third Place

A Corpus-Based Study of the Rate of Changes in Frequency of Syntactic Bigrams in English and Russian

Vladimir Bochkarev$^{(\boxtimes)}$ ⓘ, Valery Solovyev ⓘ,
and Anna Shevlyakova ⓘ

Kazan Federal University, Kremlyovskaya Street 18, Kazan 420008, Russia
vbochkarev@mail.ru, maki.solovyev@mail.ru,
anna_ling@mail.ru

Abstract. The article describes general regularities of frequency dynamics of syntactic bigrams and the method used to analyse them. The work objective is to quantitatively estimate the typical rate of change in frequency of syntactic bigrams in English and Russian. Both changes in frequency of words contained in syntactic bigrams and changes in the co-occurrence of these words influence the total rate of changes in frequency of syntactic bigrams. Their contribution to the total rate of frequency changes was estimated using decomposition of the Kullback-Leibler symmetrized divergence. It was also determined to what extent frequencies of the syntactic bigrams respond to major social events. Data on frequencies of syntactic bigrams from the English and Russian sub-corpora of Google Books Ngram were used as a study material. It was found that the regularities of the syntactic bigram usage are similar in English and Russian. The proposed approach can be used in other fields of science.

Keywords: Language changes · Syntactic bigrams · Google Books Ngram · Kullback-Leibler divergence

1 Introduction

Interdisciplinary corpus-based studies of natural languages have become a highly productive subfield of research in the last two decades. There are different approaches to computer processing of linguistic data. For example, linguistic units can be extracted from text corpora [1] and analysed from quantitative and sociolinguistic point of view [2, 3].

Corpus-based studies of words, which are the basic units of a language, are conducted most frequently. For example, Hilpert and Gries [4] use Google Books library data to perform diachronic analysis of frequency of words and study regularities of their use in different years. The issues of birth and death of words were studied in [5].

Besides words, studies of word combinations and collocations are conducted using extra-large text corpora. Juola [6] performs a diachronic study of word combinations and makes an attempt to assess the complexity of the culture and its evolution.

© Springer Nature Switzerland AG 2019
L. Martínez-Villaseñor et al. (Eds.): MICAI 2019, LNAI 11835, pp. 463–474, 2019.
https://doi.org/10.1007/978-3-030-33749-0_37

The quantitative analysis was performed in [7] to study dynamics of syntactic dependencies, the rate of emerging of new dependencies and factors that influence this process.

This work studies the frequency dynamics of syntactic bigrams in Russian and English. The objective is to study factors that influence the rate of changes in frequency of syntactic bigrams. The particular task is to analyse how changes in frequency of words contained in the bigrams and changes of the co-occurrence of these words contribute to the total rate of frequency changes. Besides, the task of the work is to compare the obtained data for these languages and decide whether the inner processes of the development of the languages are similar or have significant differences.

By syntactic bigrams we understand primary units of a syntactic structure denoting a binary relation between a pair of words in a sentence [8, 9]. One of them is the head, another one is its dependent. It is of greater interest to study syntactic bigrams than simple bigrams because sometimes two functional words form a simple bigram and it is difficult to interpret changes in their frequency in terms of semantics or culture. In contrast to previous works, we study not only the number of syntactic bigrams, but also quantitatively analyse the rate of changes in their frequency. The information metrics was used in [10] to perform corpus-based (Google Books Ngram) studies of the rate of changes in frequency of words in different European languages. The same method can be used to estimate the rate of changes in frequency of words and syntactic bigrams.

2   Data

The Google Books Ngram electronic library was used as a study material. This library is criticized by some scientists. They believe that it cannot be regarded as a corpus because it contains texts of different genres and the number of these texts differs greatly. However, the corpus contains a large number of books. The English (common) sub-corpus includes 470 billion words for the period 1505–2008, the Russian sub-corpus includes 67 billion words for the period 1607–2009. The corpus texts reflect the language behaviour almost in all spheres of human life. The large amount of data allows one to obtain more reliable results. Moreover, the Google Books Ngram texts were POS-tagged and syntactic dependencies (we call them syntactic bigrams) were determined [11].

There are 175 million of different syntactic bigrams in the English (common) and 65 million in the Russian sub-corpora of Google Books Ngram. A preliminary selection of bigrams was performed for the analysis, since it is impossible to obtain statistically reliable results for rare bigrams. Besides, a significant number of bigrams contains mis-printed words. Syntactic bigrams, which have been used systematically for a long time, were selected (by analogy with the method of the lexicon core selection proposed in [12]).

Raw data on the frequencies of syntactic bigrams from the Google Books Ngram corpus have been preprocessed. Frequencies of only those bigrams that consist of vocabulary 1-grams (including only letters of the corresponding alphabet and possibly one apostrophe) were used for the analysis. Bigrams or 1-grams, which differ only by case are regarded as one and the same 1-gram or bigram. For example, *History* and *history* is the same 1-gram.

3   Method

The Kullback-Leibler divergence $D_{A,B}$ characterizes deviation of the probability distribution p_i^A from the distribution p_i^B [13]:

$$D_{A,B} = \sum_i p_i^A \log_2 p_i^A - \sum_i p_i^A \log_2 p_i^B \tag{1}$$

Unlike other metrics, the Kullback-Leibler divergence shows the degree of difference between one frequency distribution and the other. It considers the information content of words (the information content of a word occurrence in the text is proportional to the logarithm of its probability taken with the opposite sign). Thus, the same change in the frequency of a rare word and a widely used word has different consequences in terms of the amount of information transmitted. Due to this fact, this measure is widely used in computational linguistics. In many cases, it is preferable to use the symmetrized Kullback-Leibler divergence

$$\rho(A, B) = D_{A,B} + D_{B,A} = -\sum_i \left[p_i^A - p_i^B \right] \log_2 \frac{p_i^B}{p_i^A} \tag{2}$$

It is a good measure for distinguishing two probability distributions (or empirical frequency distributions). The Kullback-Leibler divergence is a dimensional value (measured in bits). To make the interpretation less complicated, it should be normalized by the entropy of the distribution.

The symmetrized Kullback-Leibler divergence was used in [10] to study the rate of change in frequencies of words. In this work, the notion "lexical rate of change" was introduced. It is determined by the following formula:

$$V(t) = \frac{1}{T} \frac{\rho(p(t), p(t - T))}{[H(t) + H(t - T)]/2} \tag{3}$$

Thus, the lexical rate of change is defined as the average normalized Kullback-Leibler divergence per year between two points in time (t and $t - T$). By implication, this value shows the relative rate of change in frequency of lexicon from year to year, taking into account differences in the information content of words.

The rate of change in frequency of English words is shown in Fig. 1. The method is different from one described in [10]. The series of frequencies were smoothed by a median filter to avoid the influence of short-term frequency spikes associated with various historical events. A filter with a window length of 9 years was used for graphs shown in Fig. 1. This allows one to avoid the influence of such frequency spikes with a duration of up to 4 years, after which the frequencies return to their previous values. For example, abrupt changes in frequency of many words are observed in the corpus during wars. However, the frequencies of most words return to their previous values after the end of the wars. Also, the use of the filter reduces the effect of random frequency fluctuations. If we choose the given window length, the values of the filtered frequency series separated by 10 years or more remain uncorrelated. Therefore, the value of the parameter $T = 10$ years is chosen in formula (3).

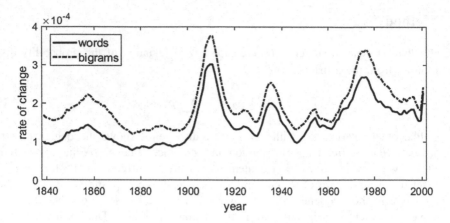

Fig. 1. The rate of change in frequency of words and syntactic bigrams in English

The rate of change was determined in [10] using a sample of 100 thousand most frequent words. The objective of this paper is to study the rate of change in frequencies of syntactic bigrams. For this reason, the sample was formed according to a different principle. We selected syntactic bigrams which occur in the corpus every year for a sufficiently long period of time. The number of the selected English bigrams occurring in the period 1800–2008 was 1,026,098. These syntactic bigrams contain 37,846 unique words, which can be found in the corpus every year (in the given interval) and were used for constructing a curve in Fig. 1. These words can be regarded as words belonging to the core vocabulary. There are various approaches to the definition of the core vocabulary. This issue is discussed, for example, in [12, 14]. The words, which occur in the diachronic corpus every year during the 200-year period, are selected in [12]. These words are called "core lexicon" in this paper. The procedure used in this article is similar to one proposed in [12]. However, there is some difference. Syntactic bigrams found in the corpus every year are selected. Then, a list of words contained in these bigrams is made. Thus, the selection criterion of these words is stricter compared to [12]. The relative frequencies of the selected words were determined in accordance with the base of 1-grams of the common English sub-corpus of Google Books Ngram.

The proposed approach [10] for determining the rate of change in frequency of words can also be used to study changes in frequency of word combinations and collocations. To do this, one needs to replace the numerator in formula (3) by the expression for the Kullback-Leibler symmetrized divergence for the frequency distributions of word combinations in years t and $t - T$. To perform calculations, the frequency series of the syntactic bigrams are preprocessed the way the word frequency series were preprocessed.

The results are also shown in Fig. 1 (the dash-dotted curve). As it was stated above, the curve is built using a sample of 1,026,098 bigrams. As can be seen in the figure, the curves showing rate of change in frequencies of words and syntactic bi-grams are very similar. More precisely, the Spearman correlation coefficient is 0.8846 (p-value is $2.61 \cdot 10^{-4}$). As it was said above, frequencies of bigrams can change due to changes in frequency of words they contain and changes in the word co-occurrence. To determine the contribution of each of these factors, let us consider the structure of the expression for the symmetrized Kullback-Leibler divergence for the frequencies of syntactic bigrams:

$$D_{t,t-T}^{(12)} = \sum_{i,j} \left\{ f_{ij}^{(12,t)} \log_2 \frac{f_{ij}^{(12,t)}}{f_{ij}^{(12,t-T)}} + f_{ij}^{(12,t-T)} \log_2 \frac{f_{ij}^{(12,t-T)}}{f_{ij}^{(12,t)}} \right\} \tag{4}$$

Here $f_{ij}^{(12,t)}$ is the relative frequency of the word combination with the i-th word in the first place and the j-th in the second place for the year t. In contrast to the lexical level, one comes across with a new phenomenon: the divergence determined by formula (4) depends both on the change in frequencies of individual words, and on the changes in relations between them. The next task is to rearrange the terms in (4) and divide the expression into components that are associated mainly with the first or the second of the indicated processes.

To perform the transformations, the expression for the divergence of the distributions of words in the word combination is needed:

$$D_{t,t-T}^{(q)} = \sum_{i,j} \left\{ f_i^{(q,t)} \log_2 \frac{f_i^{(q,t)}}{f_i^{(q,t-T)}} + f_i^{(q,t-T)} \log_2 \frac{f_i^{(q,t-T)}}{f_i^{(q,t)}} \right\} \tag{5}$$

where q, which is equal to 1 or 2, is the place of the word in the word combination, and $f_i^{(q,t)}$ is the relative frequency of the i-th word. To simplify the expression (4), we introduce the normalized frequency of the word combination M_{ij}^t and define it by the expression:

$$M_{ij}^t = \frac{f_{ij}^{(12,t)}}{f_i^{(1,t)} f_j^{(2,t)}} \tag{6}$$

The value in the denominator (6) is the frequency of the phrase that would be used in a random text with an independent and random choice of words. The normalized frequency is related to pointwise mutual information MI (pointwise mutual information, which was initially introduced in theory of information, is used in linguistics to estimate associative connection between words and determining collocations [15]) in a simple relation

$$M = 2^{MI} \tag{7}$$

Thus, one can expect that this value will depend on the degree of associative connection of words in the phrase, but not on their frequencies. Having substituted (6) into (4) and performed some transformations, the quantity $D_{t,t-\Delta}^{(12)}$ can be reduced to the following form:

$$D_{t,t-\Delta}^{(12)} = \left\{D_{t,t-\Delta}^{(1)} + D_{t,t-\Delta}^{(2)}\right\} + \sum_{i,j} \frac{f_i^{(1,t)} f_j^{(2,t)} + f_i^{(1,t-\Delta)} f_j^{(2,t-\Delta)}}{2}\left(M_{ij}^t - M_{ij}^{t-\Delta}\right)\log_2 \frac{M_{ij}^t}{M_{ij}^{t-\Delta}} + \dots$$
$$\dots + \sum_{i,j}\left(f_i^{(1,t)} f_j^{(2,t)} - f_i^{(1,t-\Delta)} f_j^{(2,t-\Delta)}\right)\frac{M_{ij}^t + M_{ij}^{t-\Delta}}{2}\log_2\frac{M_{ij}^t}{M_{ij}^{t-\Delta}} \tag{8}$$

The first term in this expression, enclosed in braces, is the sum of one-dimensional divergences, and thus depends only on changes in frequency of the words themselves. To clarify the meaning of the second and third terms, they are expanded in a Taylor series. On the assumption that the frequency changes are small, we confine ourselves to the first approximation. For the second term, the approximate expression is obtained

$$\approx \frac{1}{\ln 2}\sum_{i,j}\frac{f_i^{(1,t)} f_j^{(2,t)} + f_i^{(1,t-\Delta)} f_j^{(2,t-\Delta)}}{M_{ij}^t + M_{ij}^{t-\Delta}}\left(M_{ij}^t - M_{ij}^{t-\Delta}\right)^2 \tag{9}$$

Hence, it is clear that if the changes are small, this term is always positive and primarily depends on the change of M_{ij}^t (on the change in the co-occurrence of words). Similarly, the following expression is obtained for the third term

$$\approx \frac{1}{\ln 2}\sum_{i,j}\left(f_i^{(1,t)} f_j^{(2,t)} - f_i^{(1,t-\Delta)} f_j^{(2,t-\Delta)}\right)\left(M_{ij}^t - M_{ij}^{t-\Delta}\right) \tag{10}$$

Thus, this term depends both on the increments M_{ij}^t and on the increments of the word frequencies. It is similar to the covariance of these quantities. It was found that in the proposed expressions:

1. the first term shows the contribution of the rate of change in the frequencies of words to the observed values of the rate of change in the frequencies of word combinations;
2. the second term shows the contribution from the change in the co-occurrence of these words (if their frequencies are invariable);
3. the third term is determined both by the change in the co-occurrence of the words and their frequencies.

This allows us to determine what percentage of the changes is caused by the change in the frequency of words themselves and change in their co-occurrence.

4   Results

Figure 2 shows the values of these three components that contribute to the rate of change in frequencies of the syntactic bigrams in different years. The values of the Kullback-Leibler divergence components calculated in accordance with expressions (5, 8, 9 and 10) are normalized to the values of the time interval T and the entropy of the frequency distribution of syntactic bigrams in accordance with expression (3). Figure 2 shows the components mentioned above in the expression for Kullback-Leibler divergence for the frequencies of the syntactic bigrams. It should be noted that the value of the 3rd component (see formulas (8 and 10)) is negative for all years. Therefore, the values of this component are shown with the opposite sign in Fig. 2. The fact that these values are less than zero indicates that the correlation between the increments of the frequencies of words and the increments of the value M_{ij}^{t} is usually negative, although it is small.

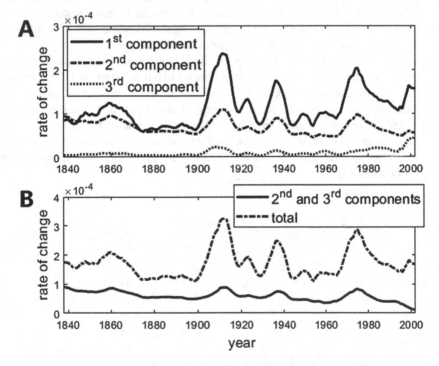

Fig. 2. The rate of change in frequency of syntactic bigrams in English. (A) The contribution of each component. The 3rd component is shown with a minus sign; (B) Total rate of change. The contribution of changes in the co-occurrence of words (the sum of the 2nd and 3rd components)

Therefore, this curve shows the total contribution to the rate of changes in frequency of syntactic bigrams caused by frequency changes in the word co-occurrence. The curve showing the total rate of change in frequencies of syntactic bigrams is shown for comparison (see the curve 'total'). When comparing Figs. 1 and 2, it should be borne in mind that the word frequencies in Fig. 1 are calculated using the 1-gram base and the word frequencies in Fig. 2 are calculated using the selected list of syntactic bigrams. These frequencies are slightly different for two main reasons. Firstly, there are not many rare syntactic bigrams in the list. Secondly, one word can be found in several syntactic bigrams in a sentence.

The curves in Fig. 2 are similar. Strong spikes indicate a response to significant historical events (primarily two world wars) and social changes in society. The spikes are interspersed with relatively smooth sections which are characterized by lower values of rate change and minor fluctuations near the smooth trend line. The curves, except the 2nd component, have some common features. It should be noted that the components associated with the change in co-occurrence of words respond to the historical events less significantly than the components associated with the change in frequencies of words belonging to syntactic bigrams. For example, the peak value of the spike associated with the First World War for the 'total' curve is 2.93 times higher than the values in the previous period (for the 1st component – by 3.8 times and for the sum of the 2nd and 3rd components by 1.8 times). It can be seen that the level of fluctuations of the curves associated with changes in the co-occurrence is significantly low during the periods when no major historical events occur.

One can select two areas without rapid spikes in the figure and estimate how the rate changes over large time intervals. Let us choose two time intervals 1875–1900 and 1945–1965. Historical events happened within these intervals, apparently, did not have a significant impact on changes in frequencies of the words and bigrams. Figure 3 shows boxplots for the rate of change in frequency of syntactic bigrams at specified time intervals (left), the components associated with changes in the frequency of words in the syntactic bigrams (middle) and the components associated with changes in the word co-occurrence (right).

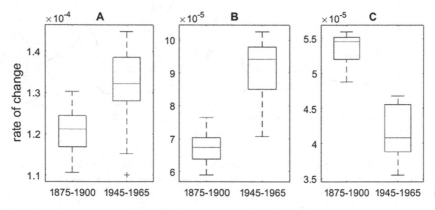

Fig. 3. The rate of change in frequencies of syntactic bigrams in 1875–1900 and 1945–1965 (window A), the values of the component associated with changes in frequencies of words in the syntactic bigrams (window B), and the values of the component associated with changes in the word co-occurrence (window C)

In general, the rate of change in the frequencies of syntactic bigrams tends to increase over 70 years. However, this change is relatively small (taking into account the correlation between the samples, the change in the rate cannot be considered statistically significant). On the contrary, the component associated with the change in the frequency of words in syntactic bigrams during this time significantly increases, and the component associated with the change in co-occurrence has decreased to an even greater degree. Thus, the tendency of the English words (presented in the corpus) to decrease the proportion of components associated with the change in the co-occurrence of words (see in Fig. 2) is also confirmed when considering only "quite" areas.

A similar analysis was also carried out for the Russian language. We selected 539,940 syntactic bigrams which occur in the Google Books Ngram Russian sub-corpus every year in the period 1920–2009. This interval was chosen to avoid difficulties associated with the Russian spelling reform of 1918. The selected syntactic bigrams contain 81,991 unique words. Lemmatization was not used because, when calculating the average frequencies of the lemmas, distortions may occur due to homonymy. We performed calculations for the obtained samples the same way as for the samples of the English syntactic bigrams. The obtained results are shown in Fig. 4 (the curves are marked analogous to the curves in Fig. 2).

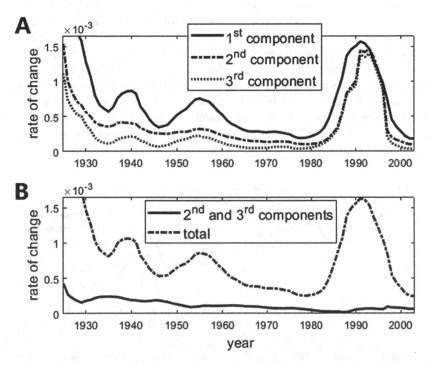

Fig. 4. The rate of change in frequency of syntactic bigrams in Russian. (A) The contribution of each component. The 3rd component is shown with a minus sign; (B) Total rate of change. The contribution of changes in the co-occurrence of words (the sum of the 2nd and 3rd components)

The large values of the rate of change at the beginning of the target time interval are due a relatively small size of the corpus in that time and significant social changes occurring during this period. A significant spike can be observed starting from the end of the 80 s, which is due to the collapse of the Soviet Union and related historical events. It can be seen that the component associated with the change in the frequency of words in the syntactic bigrams (the 1st component) strongly responds to these events. However, the component associated with the change in the word co-occurrence (the sum of the 2nd and 3rd components) has practically no response, its values even slightly decrease during this period.

If not taking into account the spike at the end of 80s–90s years, all the curves tend to decrease in values. It is natural to assume that this can be due to increase of the corpus size with time. The more the corpus size is, the less the random fluctuations of the selected frequencies are. Thus, the estimates of the rate of frequency changes can decrease. This effect explains the behaviour of the curves in the initial section of Fig. 4.

The corpus size has a greater impact on bigram frequencies than on frequencies of words because frequencies of bigrams are significantly lower, and their relative fluctuations are more significant. Therefore, special attention should be paid to the interval 1960–991. The number of books represented in the Google Books Ngram Russian sub-corpus varies greatly in different years. There is the largest number of books in 1960–1991. In this period, 65–85 thousand of books were published in the USSR every year. The corpus contains approximately 10 thousand of volumes (about 1–1.25 billion words) for each year, i.e. not less than 12% of all published books. Thus, there is a 31-year time period during which the corpus size varied within small limits.

The curves in Fig. 4 have a small downward trend in 1960–1985. Thus, the observed tendency to decrease the average rate of change of frequencies of syntactic bigrams cannot be explained only by the increase of the corpus size. Let us consider further how the ratio between the components of the rate of change in frequency changes over time. Figure 5 shows the percentage of the components associated with

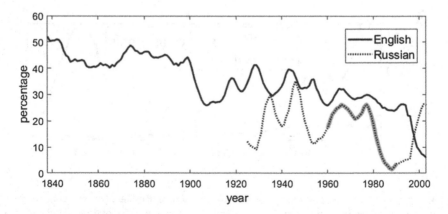

Fig. 5. Percentage of the components associated with the change in the word co-occurrence in the total value of the rate of change for English and Russian sub-corpora of Google Books Ngram. The 1960–1991 interval is marked by the dotted line. The corpus size changed insignificantly at that time

the change in the word co-occurrence in the total value of the rate of change for English and Russian sub-corpora of Google Books Ngram.

As can be seen, the share of the components associated with the change in the word co-occurrence has fallen from 40–50% in the middle of the 19th century to 25% in the 1990s and even lower in the early 2000s. As mentioned above, one of the reasons of this tendency is increase of the corpus size. There are no certain directions of change observed in the most interesting Russian time interval. The range of fluctuations is 21–26%. In the second half of the 1980s and 1990s, a decrease in the proportion of the components associated with the change in the word co-occurrence can be observed, which is due to the increase in the rate of change. By the beginning of the 21st century, the proportion values had returned to its previous level. The obtained data on the Russian language do not contradict the assumption that in "quiet" historical periods, when there are, for example, no wars or revolutions, the share of the components related to the change in the word co-occurrence is approximately constant.

The curves obtained for English and Russian were compared. The share of the components associated with the change in frequency of the word co-occurrence is higher for English than for Russian. However, there is a small area at the end of the graph, where it is lower in English than for Russian. This can be explained by the short-term impact of historical events. However, the values for these languages has converged by the present time.

5   Conclusion

The rate of changes in frequency of syntactic bigrams in Russian and English was calculated in this work. It is smooth in both languages, except for the periods when major events happened in the history of these countries, for example, wars.

When calculating the rate of change, the contribution of changes in the frequency of words in the syntactic bigrams and changes in the word co-occurrence were estimated. The changes in the frequency of words contained in the syntactic bigrams contribute to the rate of change more than changes in frequency of the word co-occurrence. The obtained results correlate with the findings in [7], where increase in the unique bigrams in the corpus was considered. Both processes respond to important historical events but differently. Response of the changes in frequency of the word co-occurrence is significantly lower than the response of frequency changes of words.

The rate of change associated with the changes in the word co-occurrence in English is lower than that in Russian. In conclusion it should be said that regularities associated with the use of syntactic bigrams are similar in both languages.

Acknowledgements. This research was financially supported by the Russian Government Program of Competitive Growth of Kazan Federal University, state assignment of Ministry of Education and Science, grant agreement № 34.5517.2017/6.7, and by RFBR, grant № 17-29-09163.

References

1. Ng, V., Cardie, C.: Automatic keyphrase extraction: a survey of the state of the art. In: Proceedings of the 52nd Annual Meeting of the Association for Computational Linguistics, pp. 104–111 (2014)
2. Michel, J.-B., Shen, Y., Aiden, A., Veres, A., Gray, M., et al.: Quantitative analysis of culture using millions of digitized books. Science **331**(6014), 176–182 (2011)
3. Gerlach, M., Altmann, E.: Stochastic model for the vocabulary growth in natural languages. Phys. Rev. X **10**(3), 021006 (2013)
4. Hilpert, M., Gries, S.: Assessing frequency changes in multistage diachronic corpora: applications for historical corpus linguistics and the study of language acquisition. Lit. Linguist. Comput. **24**(4), 385–401 (2009)
5. Petersen, A.M., Tenenbaum, J.N., Havlin, S., Stanley, H.E., Perc, M.: Languages cool as they expand: allometric scaling and the decreasing need for new words. Sci. Rep. **2**, 943 (2012). PMID 23230508
6. Juola, P.: Using the Google N-Gram corpus to measure cultural complexity. Lit. Linguist. Comput. **28**(4), 668–675 (2013)
7. Bochkarev, V., Solovyev, V., Shevlyakova, A.: Analysis of dynamics of the number of syntactic dependencies in Russian and English using Google Books Ngram. In: CEUR Workshop Proceedings, vol. 2303, pp. 14–25 (2018)
8. Padó, S., Lapata, M.: Dependency-based construction of semantic space models. Comput. Linguistics. **33**(2), 161–199 (2007)
9. Sidorov, G., Velasquez, F., Stamatatos, E., Gelbukh, A., Chanona-Hernández, L.: Syntactic dependency-based N-grams as classification features. In: Batyrshin, I., Mendoza, M.G. (eds.) MICAI 2012. LNCS (LNAI), vol. 7630, pp. 1–11. Springer, Heidelberg (2013). https://doi.org/10.1007/978-3-642-37798-3_1
10. Bochkarev, V., Solovyev, V., Wichmann, S.: Universals versus historical contingencies in lexical evolution. J. R. Soc. Interface **11**, 20140841 (2014)
11. Lin, Y., Michel, J.-B., Aiden, E.L., Orwant, J., Brockman, W., Petrov, S.: Syntactic annotations for the Google Books Ngram corpus. In: Li, H., Lin, C.-Y., Osborne, M., Lee, G.G., Park, J.C. (eds.) 2012 Proceedings of the Conference on 50th Annual Meeting of the Association for Computational Linguistics, vol. 2, pp. 238–242. Association for Computational Linguistics, Jeju Island (2012)
12. Buntinx, V., Bornet, C., Kaplan, F.: Studying linguistic changes over 200 years of newspapers through resilient words analysis. Front. Digit. Hum. **4**, 1–10 (2017)
13. Kullback, S., Leibler, R.A.: On information and sufficiency. Ann. Math. Stat. **22**, 79–86 (1951)
14. Solovyev, V., Bochkarev, V., Shevlyakova, A.: Dynamics of core of language vocabulary. In: CEUR Workshop Proceedings, vol. 1886, pp. 122–129 (2016)
15. Church, K., Hanks, P.: Word association norms, mutual information, and lexicography. Comput. Linguist. **16**(1), 22–29 (1990)

SPI: A Software Tool for Planning Under Uncertainty Based on Learning Factored MDPs

Alberto Reyes[1]([✉]), Pablo H. Ibargüengoytia[1], and Guillermo Santamaría[1,2]

[1] Instituto Nacional de Electricidad y Energías Limpias,
Cuernavaca, Morelos, Mexico
{areyes,pibar,guillermo.santamaria}@ineel.mx
[2] Conacyt, Mexico City, Mexico

Abstract. In this paper the SPI system is presented. SPI is a software tool for planning under uncertainty based on learning Markov Decision Processes. A brief review of some similar tools as well as the scientific basis of factored representations and some of its variants are included. Among these variants are qualitative representations and hybrid qualitative-discrete representations that are the core of the software tool. The functional structure of SPI, which is composed of four main modules, is also described. These modules are: the compiler, the policy server, a format translator and a didactic simulator. The experimental results obtained when testing SPI in a robot navigation domain using different types of representations and different state partitions demonstrated its capability to reduce state spaces.

Keywords: Planning under uncertainty · Factored MDPS · Software tools

1 Introduction

The importance of Markov Decision Processes (MDP) in various scientific and industrial fields is due that the ability that they have to predict the behavior of a system over time and perform decisions based on probability [13]. So that, the applications of MDPs in real-life problems are growing everyday in various domains. In the literature, several approaches from industrial processes management to agro-ecosystems can be found, even in robotics and hospital operations management. Considering that MDPs are very important in several fields of science, digital tools have been developed to help solve this type of problems. Among the tools that we can find in the literature, are: Symbolic Perseus, MDP Toolbox, JMDP and PDM-RC.

Symbolic Perseus (SP) [7] is a point-based value iteration algorithm [6] that uses Algebraic Decision Diagrams (ADD's) [4] as data structure to tackle and solve large factored partially observable MDPs (POMDP's). SP implement ADD's in the Perseus algorithm, as a method to solve the dimensionality issue

© Springer Nature Switzerland AG 2019
L. Martínez-Villaseñor et al. (Eds.): MICAI 2019, LNAI 11835, pp. 475–485, 2019.
https://doi.org/10.1007/978-3-030-33749-0_38

present in this kind of algorithms, preventing the algorithm from being limited to solve problems that only have approximately 1000 states. SP uses ADD's to represent vectors and matrices compactly and to perform symbolically matrices operations for Dynamic Programming (DP) ends. The ADD's aggregate together the entries of vectors that are identical. In this way, matrix operations can be done efficiently by performing the arithmetic operations applied to identical entries only once.

MDP Toolbox [2] contains a set of functions for the resolution of Markov decision processes in discrete time such as: value iteration, policy iteration, linear programming algorithms with some variants, and also proposes some functions related to reinforcement learning. MDP Toolbox use Markov decision processes to model the state dynamics of a stochastic system when this system can be controlled by a decision maker. The toolbox solves MDP's by finding the optimal policy given an optimization criterion. This criterion characterizes the policies which will provide the highest sequence of cumulated rewards, and represents the objective decision makers try to achieve.

[14] developed a Java package for Markov Decision Process (JMDP) which is an object-oriented framework designed to model dynamic programming problems (DP) and Markov Decision Processes. [13] designed the software prototype MDP-RC (Markov decision processes implementing simulated annealing) which can solve several academic problems described in research literature. The software works well for the proposed experimental exercises.

In this paper we describe the SPI software(Planning under Uncertainty System in Spanish) that was developed with the purpose of modelling and solving factored, qualitative and hybrid MDPs. In order to approximate factored MDP, this software uses machine learning techniques. SPI can solve several problems, either described in research books, real-life cases or proposed experimentally. Additionally, considering the relevance and the usability of some of the tools previously presented, SPI software is capable to complement Symbolic Perseus and MDP toolbox through the automatic generation of input files compatibles to each tool.

This paper is organized as follows: In Sect. 2 a brief description of factored, qualitative and hybrid MDP is provided in the context of machine learning. In Sect. 3 the SPI software is presented. Section 4 shows some of the results obtained using SPI software under different state space partitions of the same problem. Finally, in Sect. 5, some conclusions are stated.

2   Factored Markov Decision Processes

A Markov Decision Process (MDP) models a sequential decision problem, in which system evolves over time and controlled by an agent. Moreover, the system is directed by a probabilistic transition function, that maps states and actions to new state, established through the rewards received by the agent depending on the current state and the performed action. In general terms, a MDP is the specification of a sequential decision problem for a fully observable environment, with a Markov transition model and additive rewards [8].

Formally, an MDP is a tuple $M = <S, A_s, \Phi, R>$, where S is a finite set of states $\{s_1, \ldots, s_n\}$. A_s is a finite set of actions for each state. $\Phi : A \times S \to \Pi(S)$ is the state transition function specified as a probability distribution. The probability of reaching state s' by performing action a in state s is written as $\Phi(a, s, s')$. $R : S \times A \to \Re$ is the reward function. $R(s, a)$ is the reward that the agent receives if it takes action a in state s. A policy for an MDP is mapping $\pi : S \to A$ that selects an action for each state. A solution to an MDP is a policy that maximizes its expected case with any given discount factor $\gamma \in [0, 1)$, there is a policy V^* that is optimal regardless of the starting state that satisfies the *Bellman* equation [1].

$$V^*(s) = max_a\{R(s, a) + \gamma \sum_{s' \in S} \Phi(a, s, s')V^*(s')\} \tag{1}$$

Two popular methods for solving this equation and finding an optimal policy for an MDP are: (a) value iteration and (b) policy iteration [8].

Factored Markov Decision Processes (FMDP) are an extension of MDPs that makes it possible to represent the transition and the reward functions of some problems compactly. In FMDP, the state s can be described as a multivariate random variable $\mathbf{X} = (X_1, \ldots, X_n)$ where each variable X_i can take a value in its domain $Dom(X_i)$. Then, a state becomes an instantiation of each random variable X_i and can be written as a vector $\mathbf{x} = (x_1, \ldots, x_n)$ such that $\forall i, xi \in Dom(X_i)$. We denote by $Dom(\mathbf{X})$ the set of possible instantiations for the multivariate variable $\mathbf{X}$. So, the state space S of the MDP is defined by $S = Dom(\mathbf{X})$ [15]. In FMDPs the transition model can be exponentially large if it is represented as matrices, however, the frameworks of dynamic Bayesian networks (DBN) and decision trees give us the tools to describe the transition model and the reward function concisely [11].

2.1   Qualitative MDPs

A qualitative state space Q is defined as a set of states $q_1, q_2, \ldots, q_n$ that have different utility properties, which map the state space into a set of partitions, such that each partition corresponds to a group of continuous states with a similar reward value. In a qualitative MDP, a state partition q_i is a region bounded by a set of constraints over the continuous dimensions in the state space. Evidently, a qualitative state can cover a large number of states with similar properties, taking into a count a fine discretization. Similarly to the reward function in a FMDP, the state space Q is represented by a decision tree (Q-tree), in which each leaf in the decision tree is labeled with a new qualitative state, even for leaves whit the same reward value (Fig. 1). This generates more states but at the same time creates more guidance that helps produce more adequate policies. States with similar reward are partitioned so each q-state is a continuous region [12].

In a Q-tree, branches are constraints for each partition q_i and leaves represent the qualitative states. A graphical representation of the Q-tree in a 2-dimensional space is shows (Fig. 2).

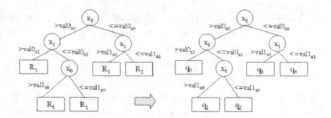

Fig. 1. Transformation of the reward decision tree into a Q-tree.

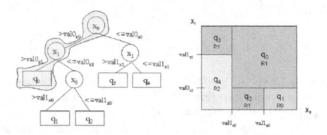

Fig. 2. Graphic representation of Q-tree in a 2-dimensional space.

2.2 Hybrid MDPs

We can define a hybrid MDP as a factored MDP with a set of hybrid qualitative-discrete factors. The qualitative state space Q, is an additional factor that concentrates all the continuous variables. The idea is to substitute all these variables by this abstraction to reduce the dimensionality of the state space. Thus, a hybrid qualitative-discrete state is described in a factored form as $\mathbf{sh} = \{X_1, \ldots, X_n, Q\}$, where $X_1, \ldots, X_n$ are the discrete factors, and Q is a factor that represents the relevant continuous dimensions in the reward function.

2.3 Learning Factored Models

A factored MDP model might be learned from data based on a random exploration in a simulated environment. We assume that the agent can explore the state space, and that for each state–action cycle it can receive some immediate reward. Based on this random exploration, the reward and transition functions are induced.

Given a set of N non-ordered and rough (discrete and/or continuous) random variables $S^j = X_1, \ldots, X_n$ defining a deterministic state, an action a^j executed by an agent from a finite set of actions $A = \{a_0, a_1, \ldots\}$, and a reward (or cost) R^j associated to each state in an instant $j = 1, 2, \ldots, M$, we can learn a factored MDP model as follows:

1. Discretize the continuous attributes from the original sample $D = \{S, R, a\}$. This transformed data set is called the discrete data set $D_d = \{S_d, R_d, a_d\}$.

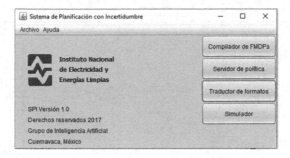

Fig. 3. SPI software main screen

For small state spaces, use conventional statistical discretization techniques. However, in complex state spaces, abstraction techniques are more efficient. For further details see [5,10].

2. From the subset $\{S_d, R_d\}$ induce a decision tree, RDT, using the algorithm C4.5 [9]. This predicts the reward function R_d in terms of the discrete state variables, $X_1, \ldots, X_n$.

3. Format the discrete data set in such a way that the attributes follow a temporal causal ordering. For example variable $X_{0,t}$ before $X_{0,t+1}$, $X_{1,t}$ before $X_{1,t+1}$, and so on. The whole set of attributes should have the form X_t, X_{t+1}, a_t.

4. Prepare a data set for the induction of a set of 2-stage dynamic Bayesian nets. According to the action space dimension, split the discrete data set into $|A|$ subsets of samples for each action. Remove the attribute a_t from all of them.

5. Induce a transition model for each subset using the K2 algorithm [3]. The result is a 2-stage dynamic Bayesian net for each action $a \in A$.

This approximate model can be solved using value iteration to obtain the optimal policy.

3 The SPI Software

The SPI software was developed particularly to model, learn and solve factored MDPs through the use of dynamic programming. As it is observed in its main screen (Fig. 3), SPI has four principal functions: (i) the FMDPs compiler (compilador de FMDPs), (ii) the policy server (servidor de política), (iii) the format translator (traductor de formatos) and (iv) the simulator (simulador). These four options will allow to create decision models from data, query models from other applications, set MDPs problem specifications to be solved with other MDP tools, and generate own data using a 2-D path planning robot simulator. With the idea of showing the inputs and outputs for each function in Fig. 4a functional diagram of SPI is presented.

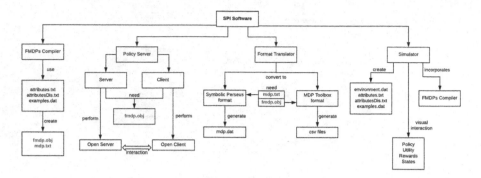

Fig. 4. SPI software functional diagram

The FMDPs compiler (Fig. 5) allows us to generate factored, qualitative and hybrid models based on training data, query the transition model, and query the policy and the utility of an FMDP in particular. With the FMDPs compiler is possible to generate factored models using continuous data, discrete data or both. To compile a problem in SPI, the files: attributes.txt, attributesDis.txt and examples.dat are required, because these contain the basic data to perform the compilation. Once the problem has been compiled, the SPI software generates other files that contains the problem specification and the decision model itself such as *mdp.txt* and *fmdp.obj* respectively.

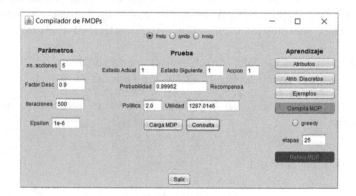

Fig. 5. Compilator

The policy server (Fig. 6a) initializes a TCP/IP socket to interconnect with the policy function of a previously compiled and staged decision model. Once the client is connected to the server, the client can send a valid state number; which will depend on the problem, and the server will respond with the optimal action for that state.

The format translator (Fig. 6b) is a tool that allows to transform the problem specification and FMDP model (contained in the files *mdp.txt* and *fmdp.obj*) into information that can be used by *SP* and *MDP Toolbox* as input files, either for comparison, complement or validation of the results obtained with SPI. The translator converts the *mdp.txt* file into an *mdp.dat* file that is compatible with Symbolic Perseus, and manipulates the *fmdp.obj* file to create several *.csv* files compatible with the MDP Toolbox.

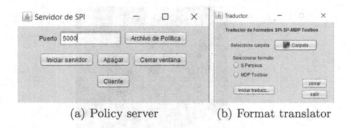

(a) Policy server   (b) Format translator

Fig. 6. Translator

The simulator (Fig. 7) is a didactic tool that allows to generate planning problems and test their solutions in the context of a 2-D robot navigation problem.

The simulator has two panels on the left side: the environment data panel (Datos ambientales) and the robot data panel (Datos robot). The aim of these panels is both the problem specification, and the definition of attributes (attributes.txt) and partition files (atributesDis.txt) for the FMDP compiler. On the right side is the exploration panel, which is more focused to data acquisition, and the SPI planner panel, which is oriented to model retrieving and simulation. With the exploration panel it is possible to create the examples.dat file, which records the training data set. The SPI planner panel loads the fmdp model allocated in the fmdp.obj file and allows to define the type of partition desired, as discrete, qualitative, simple or refined. A central panel displays graphically the planning problem showing a virtual free-flying robot, rewards and penalties, the navigation area and a discrete partition.

From the simulator toolbar it is possible to: (i) load and save navigation environments in the form of the environment.dat file, (Ambiente toolbar item), (ii) call the FMDP compiler, (iii) visualize states, rewards, utility function and optimal policy (Planificador toolbar item).

4 Experimental Results

With the idea of contrast different type of factored representations SPI was tested under different state space partitions in the robot navigation domain. In this setting goals are represented as light-colored square regions with positive immediate reward, while non-desirable regions are represented by dark-colored squares with negative reward. The remaining regions in the navigation area

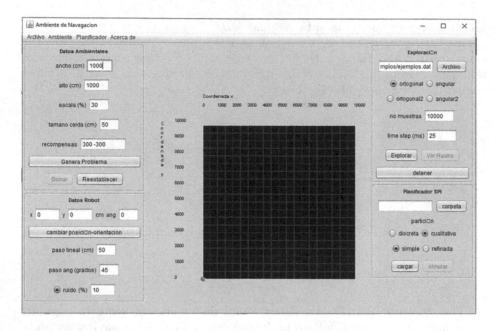

Fig. 7. Path planning simulator

receive 0 reward (white). Experimentally, we express the size of a rewarded (non zero reward) as a function of the navigation area. Rewarded regions are multivalued and can be distributed randomly over the navigation area. The number of rewarded squares is also variable. Since obstacles are not considered robot states, they are not included.

The robot sensor system included the x-y position, angular orientation, and navigation bounds detection. In a set of experiments the possible actions are discrete orthogonal movements to the right, left, up, and down. Figure 8 upper left shows an example of a navigation problem with 26 rewarded regions. The reward function can have six possible values. In this example, goals are represented as different-scale light colors. Similarly, negative rewards are represented with different-scale dark colors. The planning problem is to automatically obtain an optimal policy for the robot to achieve its goals avoiding negative rewarded regions. Figure 8 shows the reward regions, the exploration trace and partition with its corresponding policy for this problem.

Table 1 presents a comparison between the behavior of seven problems solved with a simple discretization approach and a qualitative approach. Problems are identified with a number as shown in the first column. The first five columns describe the characteristics of each problem. For example, problem 1 (first row) has 2 reward cells with values different from zero that occupy 20% of the number of cells, the different number of reward values is 3 (e.g., −10, 0 and 10) and we generated 40,000 samples to build the FMDP model.

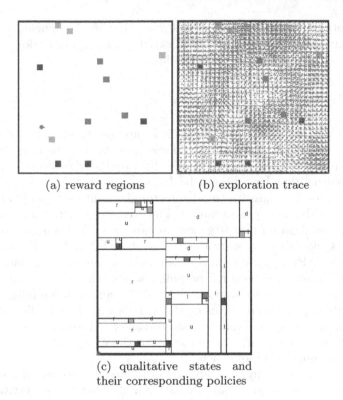

(a) reward regions   (b) exploration trace

(c) qualitative states and
their corresponding policies

Fig. 8. Abstraction process for a motion planning problem using SPI. A color inversion and gray scale format is used for clarification.

As can be seen from Table 1, there is a significant reduction in the complexity of the problems using the qualitative approach. This can be clearly appreciated from the number of states and processing time required to solve the problems.

Table 1. Description of problems and comparison between a "normal" discretization and our qualitative discretization.

Problem				Discrete				Qualitative			
				Learning		Inference		Learning		Inference	
id	No. reward cells	Reward size (% dim)	No. reward values	No. samples	No. states	Time (ms)	No. iterations	Time (ms)	No. states	Time (ms)	No. iterations	Time (ms)
1	2	20	3	40,000	25	7,671	120	20	8	2,634	120	20
2	4	20	5	40,000	25	1,763	123	20	13	2,423	122	20
3	10	10	3	40,000	100	4,026	120	80	26	2,503	120	20
4	6	5	3	40,000	400	5,418	120	1,602	24	4,527	120	40
5	10	5	5	28,868	400	3,595	128	2,774	29	2,203	127	60
6	12	5	4	29,250	400	7,351	124	7,921	46	2,163	124	30
7	14	3.3	9	50,000	900	9,223	117	16,784	60	4,296	117	241

This is important since in complex domains where it can be difficult to define an adequate partition or solve the resulting FMDP problem, one option is to create abstractions and hope for suboptimal policies.

5   Conclusions

The SPI software tool demonstrated that it is capable of solving real-world problems that can be modelled as sequential decision problems. The idea was to show the tools that SPI has for the resolution of Factored Markov decision processes, and the problems that have been solved using this tool. Thanks to the tools that SPI includes, it is possible to solve factored, qualitative and hybrid MDPs optimally using dynamic programming. The advantage of the software is that the problem specification that it generates can be easily transformed to other formats, thus allowing other software tools such as SP and MDP Toolbox, can complement the SPI capabilities in terms of inference algorithms, dimensionality or model validation. Additionally, the policy server which allows queries about the optimal policy of a problem remotely, is an advantage when integrating SPI models to other applications. By using the SPI software under different types of factored representations and different state space partitions it was also demonstrated that there is a significant reduction in the complexity of the problems when using the qualitative approach.

SPI has also successfully been applied in interesting real-world applications such as: dams management, robot navigation and power plant operations, thus generating a positive impact in the academic field.

References

1. Bellman, R.E.: Dynamic Programming. Princeton University Press, Princeton (1957)
2. Chadès, I., Chapron, G., Cros, M.J., Garcia, F., Sabbadin, R.: MDPtoolbox: a multi-platform toolbox to solve stochastic dynamic programming problems. Ecography **37**, 916–920 (2014)
3. Cooper, G.F., Herskovits, E.: A Bayesian method for the induction of probabilistic networks from data. Mach. Learn. **9**(4), 309–347 (1992)
4. Hoey, J., St-Aubin, R., Hu, A., Boutilier, C.: SPUDD: stochastic planning using decision diagrams. In: Proceedings of the 15th Conference on Uncertainty in AI, UAI 1999, pp. 279–288 (1999)
5. Munos, R., Moore, A.: Variable resolution discretization for high-accuracy solutions of optimal control problems. In: Dean, T. (ed.) Proceedings of the 16th International Joint Conference on Artificial Intelligence (IJCAI 1999), pp. 1348–1355. Morgan Kaufmann Publishers, San Francisco (1999)
6. Porta, J.M., Vlassis, N., Spaan, M.T.J., Poupart, P.: Point-based value iteration for continuous POMDPs. J. Mach. Learn. Res. **7**, 2329–2367 (2006)
7. Poupart, P.: Exploiting structure to efficiently solve large scale partially observable Markov decision processes. Ph.D. thesis, University of Toronto (2005)
8. Puterman, M.L.: Markov Decision Processes. Wiley, New York (1994)

9. Quinlan, J.: C4.5: Programs for Machine Learning. Morgan Kaufmann, San Francisco (1993)
10. Reyes, A., Sucar, L.E., Morales, E., Ibarguengoytia, P.H.: Abstraction and refinement for solving Markov decision processes. In: Workshop on Probabilistic Graphical Models, PGM 2006, Chezch Republic, pp. 263–270 (2006)
11. Reyes, A., Sucar, L.E., Morales, E.F.: AsistO: a qualitative MDP-based recommender system for power plant operation. Computacion y Sistemas 13(1), 5–220 (2009)
12. Reyes, A., Sucar, L.E., Morales, E.F., Ibargüengoytia, P.H.: Solving hybrid Markov decision processes. In: Gelbukh, A., Reyes-Garcia, C.A. (eds.) MICAI 2006. LNCS (LNAI), vol. 4293, pp. 227–236. Springer, Heidelberg (2006). https://doi.org/10.1007/11925231_22
13. Sandoval, C., Galindo, X., Salas, R.: Herramienta software para resolver procesos de decisiÃn de Markov utilizando recocido simulado. In: Memorias de la Décima Quinta Conferencia Iberoamericana en Sistemas, Cibernética e Informática (CISCI 2016) (2016)
14. Sarmiento, A., Riaño, G.: JMDP: an object oriented framework for modeling MDPs. In: Informatics Annual Meeting (2006)
15. Sigaud, O., Buffet, O.: Markov Decision Processes in Artificial Intelligence. ISTE Ltd./Wiley, London/Hoboken (2010)

The Blade Runner Scene.
How Human-Machine Contact Incarnates
Social Interaction

Gabriel Alejandro Medina-Aguilar$^{(\boxtimes)}$ (iD)

Universidad Anáhuac Querétaro, Circuito Universidades I, Fracción 2,
76246 Querétaro, Mexico
medinaguilar@hotmail.com

Abstract. The pace of daily life causes new perspectives on the idea of new
and old, human and technical. Within an era of doubts, hope and fear about
technological progress, it's necessary to understand how human condition has
always been related and dependent of technique. It is precisely our relationship
to technology that this text focuses on, but also on the many ways IA has
influenced, or could transform, our idea of humanity. Through an abductive
strategy, several arguments are presented to engage and disengage with both
utopias and dystopias.

Keywords: Artificial intelligence · Human-machine contact · Imaginary of the
technological future

1 Introduction

Bernard Stiegler takes from Socrate the notion of *pharmakon* to think about the digital
and its possible "nature" as a poison or as a remedy. The impact of the intangible digital
environment leads me to think that the technological progress known within the
nineteen preceding years conforms itself a period similar to a century in its own right.
As a result, our relationship to time has changed, and the speed of daily life in mod-
ernized societies is creating a new perspective on the idea of new and old, human and
technical. It is precisely our relationship to technology that this text focuses on, but also
on the many ways IA has influenced, or could transform, our idea of humanity.

According to Griziotti [1], technical mediation is attached to the History of civi-
lizations because it means a mediation between people and society. I try to take this
principle and extend it, so that apart from being a mediation between human and
societies, technique is a mediation between nature (human biological capabilities) and
the individual and social needs for humanity.

Let's take for example the picture of one of the first human beings; he walks for a
few hours and at one point he feels tired, then he looks for something to rest on and
finds a big branch of a tree lying on the ground. For the first time someone *sits*, after
discovering that his body is not "designed" to keep it stand up permanently. The chair,
therefore, means a material mediation between the need to rest and a physical
incompetence. In the case of language, on the contrary, it is the result of the

© Springer Nature Switzerland AG 2019
L. Martínez-Villaseñor et al. (Eds.): MICAI 2019, LNAI 11835, pp. 486–492, 2019.
https://doi.org/10.1007/978-3-030-33749-0_39

relationship between a biological ability to emit sounds and the need to establish social connections. For the example of the chair it is an individual need related to a biological inadequacy and, for the language, a social need related to a physiological aptitude.

Let's take Stiegler and his idea of *pharmakon*, for him the emergence of a technology supposes a political posture, either voluntary or unconscious. In the same way, Feenberg [2] takes part on the idea of non-neutrality of technology. The social groups that result more competent to develop and use technology will be in political advantage compared to individuals that are not capable of leading technological development. During the implementation of a technological object, from its conception to its distribution, there are societal and ideological issues that will be involved. For both authors, the technique carries the principles, values and political perspectives of those who developed it.

In the case of our example, the chair will be designed and improved by the one who has discovered its features, and this design will bear the features of its creator. For the rest of the group, it will be only the recreation of the first model that will allow them to re-appropriate the object in order to have a design allowing to convey the new features.

This issue invites to think in two possible modes to adopt digital technology. The first, already labeled by the researchers of the commons, is mostly commercial, where digital practices of individuals are based either on private platforms that monetize uses while offering free services, as seen by Casilli and Cardon [3], either on services and products sold through a variety of business models that similarly exploit unpaid data. The second approach to digital technology, less visible because its nonprofit nature, is the open culture: free software, open circulation of knowledge, etc. For these communities -most collaborative and based on transparency of usage and operating data- the digital environment is a habitable environment where the commercial profit is only one possibility.

One question is how the principles conveyed by these two technical approaches can shape the way we imagine the future of our *savoir-vivre* and our know-how in society. However, in order to avoid a dichotomous notion of approaches, it will be necessary to consider that both have always coexisted, and that this cohabitation incites imaginaries that are related to contradictions within the symbolic and material dimensions of our relationship to technology.

So, between these two modes of adoption of digital technology, which one appears to be dominant on our relationship with the *machines to communicate* and the *machines that communicate*? The idea of progress is a form of colonizing the future [4], and it should be known how the picturing of the technological future includes a political dimension; in the case it doesn't and we see only isolated photographs, far removed from all historicity, we should speak of illusions of the future, rather than imaginaries, since these should come always with a narrative-historical dimension which supposes a posture taken by individuals.

1.1 Abduction # 1

The interaction we experience with machines (Artificial Intelligence and algorithms) is a human relationship. By taking Feenberg [2] and his contribution to the impossibility of technology to be neutral, I can say on one side that individuals interact with moral values and ideological principles provided by developers through the code of the machine, but on the other hand, even further, we are staging real human relationships at the time we interact with devices like Siri or Alexa, whose performance will be even more complex within a few years on the path to human-like connections. Obviously, it is not an exchange with the machine, because it *does not know*, despite an apparent sense of humor and a fairly cool usability, which can cause in us an emotion as real as the joke of a very close friend.

The female voice is only the chair of a social link hidden behind the algorithm, since we communicate indirectly with the social individuals who programmed the code and provided the behavioral values to this digital assistant, we experience human contact *through* the machine. To get a clearer picture, you must imagine the type of humor Siri would have if *she* were Latin American at the base. It is transmitted to the machine specific code behaviors, adjusted to specific cultural spaces and times.

Moreover, this same principle can be validated when we speak of actual human exchanges, since behind our interlocutor there is always those individuals and institutions that provided him with a *socio-cultural coding,* his cultural software. In this situation, the person has the opportunity to *know*, although this is not always the case and, even in the case where the person knows, is not able to get rid of the code: this cultural software will serve as a toolbox and as a cage simultaneously, in the terms of Wittgenstein. Accordingly, the machine as an interface (and the same for people) will transfer in its way a sort of social and moral principles, so ideological.

These ideas lead me to think whether the notion of humanity, as it is conceived today, is in crisis because of our taming through technology. Schmidt and Cohen [5] - both Google's decision makers-, say that one should not worry about a future where machines control everything, just because it's not possible. However, even if we know that the code cannot control itself or the coder, it is not necessary to wait until algorithmic computing regulates every dimension of social life to imagine how the human condition could change.

From a romanticist point of view, it seems that indeed, humanity is in crisis, because technological objects take spaces previously exclusive to human corporality, but as soon as we try to give examples, we see that the technique has always been there, since it means a complementarity relation between human and things. We reproach the distance and interference in the middle of our telephone exchanges, video callings or the misunderstanding caused by emoji and instant messaging. We do this in a sort of *cult of face to face contact*; like it could represent a pure state where communication work perfectly, without any mediation, as if the epistolary exchanges were not mediated by technological objects such as paper, ink and land or sea transport, being themselves part of a medium in its own right.

However, for certain, modern anthropocentrism is in ultimate agony, according to Sadin [6]. This contemporary French philosopher makes a revision of the principles of *Renaissance*, centered on the human freedom of election around a social and technical know-how. Today, once humanity has been able to automate much of the productive and non-productive life, the machine no longer needs humans to set and enhance his functions, and the human has suffered the loss of an essential part of his inheritance, to resume Marx. We now return to an *anthrobological* condition [6], where the romantic idea of the free and pure human gives way to a human who share more and more his autonomy with machines, every time more capable to master social behaviors. The autonomy of the present human rests more on the algorithmic computation than on an idea of free will, either on the individual level of a woman following the road proposed by Wize, either on the social level of bankers who cannot manage anymore the automatic calculation for global finance.

1.2   Abduction # 2

The human is inseparable from the technique. What makes us human is the development of technique through technological objects, accompanied with a symbolic condition. We can say other animals have *technique*, like the bird making a nest, but never accompanied with symbols, because that object could never be provided of meanings like *home* and *shelter*.

It is then necessary to avoid a romantic and nostalgic view of the human as natural purity. In any case, it could be said that otherness and recognition of the other may be transformed on the context of communications more and more mediated by machines, but at the same time it gives an impression of immediacy, instantaneous communicative situations that spontaneously put us in front of each other, despite the distance and the technical complexity. The human does not disappear, it is dislocated [6]. We have never had the possibility, as today, of eliminating distances with so little effort and resources, with so much fidelity and certainty, the certainty of knowing that a message has arrived at the end of the line, and that it has been read by our interlocutor. All in a context where individuals do not understand the technological object that seems so foreign, like magic, and yet so familiar. Humanity has reached a historical moment when she is no longer able to decipher the technique. The magic object abandons us because its complexity exceeds us, and at the same time allows us to be dislocated; we are everywhere and all without knowing how it was possible. It is in this sense that humanity is no longer the same, if it had always maintained a pedagogical relationship to technology, current technological objects are consumed without questions and become a natural extension of ourselves, unavoidable and frightening at the same time.

1.3   Abduction # 3

Taking over Benjamin, the mechanization and automation of our social ties does not endanger a certain *aura* of direct human encounter. On the contrary, the machine makes emerge the *aura* thanks to the interference of the medium and the distance that separates the encounter. The technical object does not suppress the experience of human contact; on the contrary, it is able to deploy it as soon as one begins to feel regret. One receives a projection in the form of sound and image, almost faithful in totality, and it is precisely this difference resulting from *almost* that returns us to the almost invisible feeling of regret, which seems to remain of major importance during our links with others, since the loss of this regret would mean the abandonment of any political perspective in our relationship to the world. Machines do not make politics [6] because all people will be for them any person and any injustice would be consequently invisible. In a way, we exercise (or we try to exercise) power because there are people who affect us more than others.

A pretty illustrative case of the *almost* is the one of uncanny valley, with which Mori [7] tries to explain how people's emotions towards automatons take the form of empathy when the machine only looks a bit in essence to the human physiognomy, and how this emotion turns uncomfortable as androids or robots become almost identical to humans in facial features, gestures and body movements. That is to say that one can feel empathy towards robots like those in *Stars Wars* because they are far enough from us in terms of corporality and body language, but on the other hand almost perfect automata will make us trouble. The mythical final passage of *Blade Runner* is thus reminiscent of an unknown stage of automatons not distinct from humans, capable of not provoking uncanny valleys and, more important, capable of suppressing *regret*.

I try to stay out of the threshold of romanticism and yet the *almost*, this moment when the machine does not arrive at the identical with the human, seems to become the only possibility for us to take a political stand facing an automated future. The machine is not neutral, indeed, but it is not able to take the power nor to make politics.

That said, we should not neglect the role of technical objects on the political ways of doing things in a society where the developers are no longer concerned by Estate borders that can limit the impact on the social know-how, every time more disturbed by the calculation of behaviors result of a quantization of the self, as for the example of all services of digitization and rational systematization of daily activities such as sport, cooking, urban mobility and domestic purchases.

It is a progressive tendency to abandon calculation by humans, delegating this responsibility to the algorithm; in the same way that the Greeks, according to Socrates, have delegated memory to the technical object which is writing.

This abandonment of rational computing currently represents not only the modeling of social behaviors by the machine, but also the modeling of social life by the automatic modeling already calculated. We are offered profiles of cultural consumption, for example, from an algorithm that systematize our purchases of music and the consumption of genres and songs to draw suggestions that could possibly match our tastes and, in the second degree, they end up making-up our future consumption, in a kind of pyramidal procedure where the discovery and the chance of the base are reduced in each higher state. Finally, we fall into a false serendipity. The *benjaminienne* ability to get lost in the city disappears.

The algorithmic intelligence, according to Benbouzid and Cardon [8], does not make predictions but rather readings of the present and, by finding profiles and regularities, is able to establish the modeling already discussed, since previously, when calculating machines did not exist yet, social life was already full of repetition. The principle of any statistical effort, representativeness, is based on the fact that people collectively follow a regular daily life. If only for diets or the project of life, it is possible to see how difficult it is to live in a real serendipity.

Computer deductive then means a very effective and progressive abandonment of chance and daily discomfort [6], which means eventually a reduction of risk and a decreasing ability to being lost and to be wrong. Our link to the *machines that communicate* is established in environments where human error is easily invisible. The grammatical corrections of search engines and word processing software give an impression of perfection, the living word crystallizes and settles on the stage of the immaculate language, the legitimate linguistic know-how. We will never hear an automaton deceive in conjugation since the machine does not make mistakes, the machine is never wrong despite the bugs, gaps or offsets in the code. The error will always be the only responsibility and strictly human competence.

The impact of a device that forces us to erase the error is reflected in the immediate daily life by human bonds in which the other has no right to be wrong. The principle that drives human bonds in an automated society is the one of productivity. If consumerism consists in conceiving each social relation as the synonym of a commercial exchange, algorithmic automatism, as the principle of all social life, supposes the staging of a calculation mode preceding communication, and the error within such a society is not a loss, but a luxury.

At this point, disobedience, by the moment exclusive to the human, reveals itself as another luxury in the idea of algorithmic automatism. The step that precedes disobedience is that of taking away the technical-magical object presented before.

Such a basic technological object as the car could illustrate this affirmation, by the hand of the Sociology of Use [9–11]: the degree of knowledge and mastery that a person can have regarding the mechanical functioning of a car affects the qualities of the actual use. The more we are aware of the functions of every part inside the engine, the critical distance between them, the temperature and potential friction, the less likely is the fact that the driver causes an early failure in the machine.

This first moment of distance from the object therefore means the removal of its magic veil; is there where we are aware of the technological nature, of the *artificiality* of the machine, and this will be at the origin of a human-machine relationship which, finally, does not neglect the hidden social and technical construction behind the interface of the object.

As for the algorithmic and artificial intelligence, besides a technical failure on the road, it is a question of putting in perspective the development models, the modes of production and the economic models, always present and at the same time transparent to the eyes of consumers and users.

For the moment, some communities in European countries have realized the importance of training in computer languages and have put on the table a controversy that concerns younger people, closer to the world of digital coding, under the notion of an individual less vulnerable to technological tools in the digital development era. Who are Siri and Alexa; who are the first robo-journalists in India, writing on the distance those articles for newspapers in North America and Europe; who are the newborns from algorithmic engineering in China; who is the smart car crashing on a road in Los Angeles?

1.4   Abduction # 4

In the historical moment of the *quasi-human,* algorithmic technology allows us to see how much mechanical there is in us, and how difficult for us humans is to disobey our own social and cultural code. In *benjaminien* terms, the technique is the mastery of the link between humanity and nature to bring us closer to the future, and for this approach is essential a position for the future, because the future is a territory to explore and progress means the search and the desire for its conquest.

2   Conclusion

The machines that communicate by calculation are now on the core of human links because of the *anthrobological* condition [6], a *continuum* from the analogue to the digital world and from the digital to the analogue. In this sense, the digital traditionally understood vanishes, resumes its roots and now is more alike than ever to the analogue dimension and to the resemblance and identity between the machine and the human; just in a moment when that *almost* gives us some time to think about the fact that there is an idea of progress and that there must be lots of it.

References

1. Griziotti, G.: Neurocapitalisme. Pouvoirs numériques et multitudes. C&F Éditions, Paris (2018)
2. Feenberg, A.: Between Reason and Experience: Essays in Technology and Modernity. MIT Press, London (2010)
3. Casilli, A., Cardon, D.: Qu'est-ce que le digital labour? INA Éditions, Paris (2015)
4. Jameson, F.: Arqueologías del futuro. El deseo llamado utopía y otras aproximaciones de ciencia ficción. Akal, Madrid (2009)
5. Schmidt, E., Cohen, J.: El futuro digital. Grupo Anaya, Madrid (2014)
6. Sadin, E.: La humanidad aumentada. La administración digital del mundo. Caja Negra Editores, Buenos Aires (2017)
7. Mori, M.: The uncanny valley. Energy 7(4), 33–35 (1970)
8. Benbouzid, B., Cardon, D.: Machines à prédire. Réseaux 211(5), 9–33 (2018)
9. Flichy, P.: L'innovation technique. La Découverte, Paris (2007)
10. Jouët, J.: Retour critique sur la sociologie des usages. Réseaux Commun. Technol. Société 18(100), 487–521 (2000)
11. Perriault, J.: La logique de l'usage: essai sur les machines à communiquer. Editions L'Harmattan, Paris (2008)

Assessment of Small-Scale Wind Turbines to Meet High-Energy Demand in Mexico with Bayesian Decision Networks

Monica Borunda[1(✉)], Raul Garduno[2], Ann E. Nicholson[3], and Javier de la Cruz[1]

[1] Conacyt - Instituto Nacional de Electricidad y Energías Limpias, Cuernavaca, Mexico
{monica.borunda, javier.delacruz}@ineel.mx
[2] Instituto Nacional de Electricidad y Energías Limpias, Cuernavaca, Mexico
rgarduno@ineel.mx
[3] School of Information Technology, Monash University, Melbourne, Australia
Ann.Nicholson@monash.edu

Abstract. Nowadays, an eco-friendly way to satisfy the high-energy demand is by the exploitation of renewable sources. Wind energy is one of the viable sustainable sources. In particular, small-scale wind turbines are an attractive option for meeting the high demand for domestic energy consumption since exclude the installation problems of large-scale wind farms. However, appropriate wind resource, installation costs, and other factors must be taken into consideration as well. Therefore, a feasibility study for the setting up of this technology is required beforehand. This requires a decision-making problem involving complex conditions and a degree of uncertainty. It turns out that Bayesian Decision Networks are a suitable paradigm to deal with this task. In this work, we present the development of a decision-making method, built with Decision Bayesian Networks, to assess the use of small-scale wind turbines to meet the high-energy demand considering the available wind resource, installation costs, reduction in CO_2 emissions and the achieved savings.

Keywords: Decision-making · Bayesian Networks · Wind energy · Small-scale wind turbine technology · Energy demand

1 Introduction

Nowadays, the utilization of renewable energy has acquired primordial importance due to the critical environmental conditions of our planet, the growing energy demand and the imminent energy limitation from fossil fuels in the future. Therefore, the inclusion of renewable power generation in power systems has become mandatory worldwide.

In particular, Mexico is a privileged country regarding solar and wind energy resources. So far, wind energy projects have been deployed in several places with highly available wind resources. However, such projects consist of wind farms with multi-MW wind turbines. Currently, the development of the wind power sector of medium, mini and micro scale are seen as an alternative to develop regions by the new

© Springer Nature Switzerland AG 2019
L. Martínez-Villaseñor et al. (Eds.): MICAI 2019, LNAI 11835, pp. 493–506, 2019.
https://doi.org/10.1007/978-3-030-33749-0_40

federal administration [1], where the deployment of these technologies is intended to be carried out through programs to have sustainable communities. Therefore the interest to use these resources to generate energy in a distributed and decentralized manner.

Small-scale wind (SSW) power is receiving increasing interest as one potential microgeneration technology with low carbon emissions [2]. A SSW turbine (SSWT) is rated less than 100 kW and requires a smaller area to be profitable. Considering the state-of-the-art technologies, a mini-eolic device requires 10% of the area that a photovoltaic generate the same energy. They are generally used to supply electricity for residential applications and, in the last years new turbine products have appeared on the market at attractive prices and more technology is been developed to boost their implementation [3]. However, the overall potential of SSW turbines to reduce CO_2 emissions and meet the energy demand is not yet entirely clear [4]. There are many cities in Mexico with good wind resources that present an excess in energy consumption in the residential sector. Therefore, the assessment of the implementation of SSW turbines in different cities in Mexico to meet the high-energy demand becomes an important issue to address. However, this is a complex task since there are many factors, with a degree of uncertainty, involved in this problem, and different criteria to be considered in order to provide an appropriate assessment. This problem is suitable to be solved with the paradigm of Bayesian Decision Networks (BDNs) as is done in this work.

In this paper, we develop a support decision system to assess the implementation of SSW turbines to satisfy the high-energy demand of the residential sector in different sites in Mexico. We model the problem into a BDN and consider the reduction on the CO_2 emissions, the installation cost and the savings in the price of the high-energy demand as criteria for the decision-making system. Therefore, our system provides an assessment of the implementation of SSW turbines in different sites in Mexico based on the site's characteristics such as wind potential, type of users of the residential sector and their energy consumption, environmental and economic benefits, and installation cost. In the following section, related work reported in the literature is described. In Sect. 2, the basics of Bayesian Networks (BNs) and BDNs are briefly summarized. The use of SSW power in Mexico and its potential application to the residential electric sector is addressed in Sect. 3. Section 4 presents the construction of the Bayesian Decision model for the system. A case study showing the assessment of SSW power is shown in Sect. 5 and conclusions are presented in Sect. 6.

1.1 Related Work

The assessment of wind power installation is an important topic that has attracted lots of interest in the last decade. Different approaches have been used to develop decision-making methods to allocate wind turbine technologies considering different criteria. Gagliano and colleagues [5] develop a methodology to exploit wind fields using computational fluid dynamics, and considering the geographical information system, in urban environments and present a pilot study in a Sicilian city. Lee et al. [6] present a multi-criteria decision-making model, based on the analytic hierarchy process associated with benefits, opportunities, costs, and risk, to select suitable wind farm projects and a case study in China is considered. Goh and coworkers [7] propose analytic and fuzzy hierarchy process methods to evaluate the priority of criteria in selecting a location for a wind farm and a case study in Malaysia is presented. Likewise, a fuzzy multi-criteria decision-making method is created for onshore wind farm site selection and the Southeast of Spain has been chosen as the study area to carry out its evaluation [8]. On the other hand, a spatial multi-criteria analysis method wind farm site selection, using geographic information systems (GIS), and a case study for New York State is presented in [9]. Likewise, the same method is applied to analyze the suitability for the location of wind farms in Ecuador [10]. An integrated framework to evaluate land suitability for wind farm siting combining multi-criteria analysis with GIS is proposed by Tegou and colleagues [11]. A variety of criteria, such as wind power potential, land cover type, electricity demand, land value and distance from the electricity grid are used to identify potential sites for wind power installations in Greece.

In particular, studies in the assessment and viability of SSW power installation have also been carried out in many countries in the last years. For instance, Carbon Trust [12] elaborated a report on policy insight and practical guidance for SSW energy in the UK back in 2008. This report considers carbon savings and the potential of wind turbines at different sites in the UK, as well as the policies and suitability for the sites under consideration. In 2011, Reuther et al. [13] carried out a feasibility study of small-scale wind turbines for residential use in New Zealand. It considers the residential electricity demand, its policies, and regulations, as well as the wind resource of the site. Ugur and colleagues [14] performed a financial payback analysis of small wind turbines for Istanbul. In 2014, Bortolini and coworkers [15] studied the performance and viability analysis of small wind turbines in the European Union. In 2015, NREL [16] published guidelines for small wind site assessment. It presents a guide for site evaluation considering its wind resource, topography, land-use considerations, safety, and environmental conditions and utility policies, and provides case studies in the USA. Abdelhady et al. [17] performed an economic feasibility analysis of small wind turbines for domestic consumers in Egypt.

2   Bayesian Decision-Making

2.1   Bayesian Networks

A Bayesian Network (BN) is a probabilistic graphical model that allows to reason under uncertainties. This is very useful since many real systems contain different kinds of uncertainty such as (a) ignorance – our knowledge about the system is limited; (b) physical randomness or indeterminism – there are non-deterministic factors in real systems and; (c) vagueness – many systems cannot be modeled with 100% precision. A BN is formed by nodes, which represent a set of random variables, $X = X_1, \ldots X_i, \ldots X_n$, and a set of directed arcs connecting pairs of nodes, $X_i \rightarrow X_j$, representing the direct dependencies between variables. The structure of the network captures the qualitative relationships between variables, such that only nodes affected or caused by each other are connected, with the arc indicating the direction of the effect.

Therefore, each node is specified by a conditional probability distribution, which in the case of discrete variables simplifies to a conditional probability table (CPT). Root nodes have an associated CPT given by its prior probabilities, and nodes with parent nodes need to take into account all possible combinations of values of their parent nodes in their CPT [18].

A BN computes the posterior probability distribution for a set of query nodes, given values for some evidence nodes. Therefore, for a BN containing n nodes, X_1 to X_n, a particular value of the joint distribution of each variable at a specific state $P(X_1 = x_1, X_2 = x_2, \ldots, X_n = x_n) \equiv P(x_1, x_2, \ldots, x_n)$ is given by

$$P(x_1, x_2, \ldots, x_n) = \prod_i P(x_i | Parents(X_i)), \tag{1}$$

where $P(x_i | Parents(X_i))$ is the conditional probability that $X_i = x_i$ given the states of the node parents, $Parents(X_i)$.

Consider the basic example of BN shown in Fig. 1. The CPT is constructed such that (a) each row contains the conditional probability of each node value for each possible combination of values of its parent nodes; (b) each row must sum to 1; (c) a node with no parents has one row (the prior probabilities). Figure 1 shows two nodes X_1 and X_2 with two states each, $X_1 = \{x_{1,1}, x_{1,2}\}$ and $X_2 = \{x_{2,1}, x_{2,2}\}$. The a priori probabilities of node X_1 are defined in Table 1.

Fig. 1. Basic example of BN.

Table 1. A Priori probabilities of the node X_1.

X_1	
$x_{1,1}$	$P(X_1 = x_{1,1})$
$x_{1,2}$	$P(X_1 = x_{1,2})$

The CPT associated with the node X_2 is given by the conditional probabilities $P(X_2|X_1)$ and corresponds to the probability distributions over the states of X_2 given the states of X_1 as shown in Table 2. Therefore, a BN computes the probabilities attached to a node state given the state of one or several variables, becoming a powerful modeling tool for complex systems [19, 20].

Table 2. CPT of the node X_2, given the node X_1.

X_1	$x_{1,1}$	$x_{1,2}$
X_2 $x_{2,1}$	$P(X_2 = x_{2,1}\|X_1 = x_{1,1})$	$P(X_2 = x_{2,1}\|X_1 = x_{1,2})$
$x_{2,2}$	$P(X_2 = x_{2,2}\|X_1 = x_{1,1})$	$P(X_2 = x_{2,2}\|X_1 = x_{1,2})$

2.2 Bayesian Decision Networks

BNs can be extended to support decision-making. A Bayesian Decision Network (BDN) combines data, evidence and probabilistic reasoning with utilities to make decisions that maximize the expected utility [21]. The utility function ranks alternatives according to the usefulness of the outcomes. Therefore, BDNs are suitable to model a system with many variables that require a decision-making process. A BDN contains chance nodes representing random variables, decision nodes representing the decision to be made and, utility nodes representing the utility functions, as shown in Fig. 2.

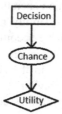

Fig. 2. Generic decision network.

The expected utility is computed depending on the nature of the node. If the node X is a chance node, each outgoing link has a probability and each child has an associated utility. Then, the expected utility is calculated as follows

$$EU(X) = \sum_{C=Children(X)} U(C) \times P(C). \tag{2}$$

Therefore, the decision affects the expected utility, either directly or indirectly, such that the decision influences the real world.

The construction of a BDN involves the modeling of as many aspects as possible of the real world involving the definition of the variables and their values or states, the graph structure, the parameters, the available actions/decisions, and their impact, the utility nodes, and their dependencies, among others. The first step in the process consists of understanding the problem, therefore, in the following section, we describe the problem to be modeled.

3 SSW Energy for Residential Use

3.1 Small-Scale Wind Energy in Mexico

In the last decades, the harnessing of wind energy in Mexico has increased, and currently, it is the second-largest source of renewable energy. The wind energy potential of Mexico is estimated to be around 50 GW. As of 2016, the installed capacity in the country has reached 3,942 MW and it could reach 12 GW by 2020 [22], being able to provide 15% of electric energy in Mexico. Top regions with onshore wind potential are the Isthmus of Tehuantepec and the states of Tamaulipas and Baja California. However, there are more than 40 wind farms in states such as Oaxaca, Baja California, Chiapas, Jalisco, Tamaulipas, San Luis Potosí and Nuevo León.

Mexico's interest in increasing its reliance on renewable energy for power generation has mainly been in the direction of large-scale power projects. In order to harness the exploitation of wind energy, it is necessary to increase the capacity of transport of electric energy from the place of production to the places of consumption. On the other hand, the investment in equipment and permits for this scheme, although it is profitable, is also substantial, so that the large-scale generation business has been restricted to the main players. However, a potential possibility now relies on small-scale distributed energy projects. SSW power projects have become more viable in Mexico, in addition to having abundant wind, currently, there are legal conditions that facilitate self-generation at small and medium scales. In the last years, Mexico has witnessed significant growth in small-scale self-supply or decentralized solar energy systems. In 2014, it was reported that small wind turbines deployment has been limited to about 323 kW installed capacity interconnected to the grid [23]. Therefore, it becomes important to address the assessment of SSW turbines in Mexico and boost distributed energy.

3.2 Domestic Energy Consumption in Mexico

Mexican electric market contemplates five different customer segments according to the final use of energy: residential, commercial, agricultural, industrial and public services. The energy demand in the residential sector strongly depends on the population of each site and its climate. There are four major climates within the Mexican territory: arid, dry tropic, temperate and humid tropic, as shown in Fig. 3, and around half of the Mexicans live in regions with temperate conditions and the other half lives in regions with the other climates.

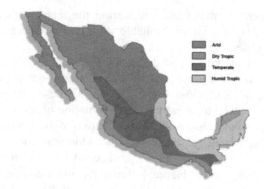

Fig. 3. Main climate regions in Mexico taken from [24].

The residential, or domestic sector, presents the highest number of registered users. Taking into account the above considerations, the Federal Electricity Commission (CFE by its Spanish acronym) has assigned several consumption rates to the residential sector considering the summer minimal average temperature at the consumption zone as shown in Table 1. The eighth rate corresponds to the High Consumption Rate, known as DAC. Every user can reach the DAC rate if the consumed energy exceeds the threshold shown in Table 1.

Although low-priced natural gas has helped to cut electricity rates for industrial users, residential users do not receive heavily subsidized rates. In 2016, the average price of electricity for all types of users, but DAC, was about 0.05 USD/kWh. In contrast, DAC users were paying 0.18 USD/kWh. Therefore, a domestic user exceeding its consumption limit and becoming a DAC user ended up paying 3 times more than a normal tariff since the user is consuming *expensive* energy. To prevent this, domestic users could use micro renewable power in order not to exceed the limit energy consumption and avoid becoming DAC users. Although solar photovoltaic energy could be installed in almost any site in the country, there are regions where DAC users could get profitability installing small wind turbines, since the required area to produce the same power is about 8 times smaller.

The implementation of small wind turbines to produce the energy surplus in order to prevent users from becoming DAC is a way to benefit from SSW power.

4   Bayesian Decision Network Model for SSW Turbine Deployment

The construction of the DBN model consists of defining the problem to be solved and map it into a probabilistic graphical model. In this case, we are interested in developing a decision-maker algorithm to assess the implementation of SSW turbines in different sites in Mexico to meet the high-energy demand in the domestic sector. The question to address is whether SSW power and how many should be installed in populations depending on cost-benefit criteria and considering the relevant factors such as geographic location, weather conditions, available wind energy, energy consumption and type of consumption users.

In order to look for the viability of the implementation of SSW power to meet the high-energy demand in the domestic sector we must consider populations with two characteristics: available wind resource and DAC users. These are the main elements to affect the benefit-cost criteria to assess the implementation of SSW technology and are represented by chance modes. Moreover, the evaluation of the viability of installing the SSW power technology is the problematic to be addressed and is represented by a decision node. Finally, cost-benefit criteria are needed to perform the evaluation and are represented by utility nodes. Figure 4 shows the main architecture of the BDN. However, in order to make a more accurate description of the real-life system, we must include factors that produce a direct effect on the main elements of the network.

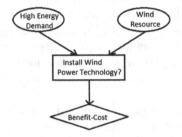

Fig. 4. Main architecture of BDN for the assessment of small-scale wind turbine deployment.

The DBN for the assessment of SSW turbine technology is shown in Fig. 5. Towns in Mexico are located in different geographic zones, each of them with its own weather conditions, such as radiation, ambient temperature, wind, and so on. As we saw before, the user type for domestic energy consumption depends on the minimal average summer temperature; therefore, each zone is characterized by a wind resource and a user type. Moreover, domestic energy consumption also depends on weather conditions, therefore, in this sense; we can include the energy consumption in the characterization of the zone. This is depicted at the top of the network: given a geographic zone, there is a population with its domestic energy consumption, its user type, its DAC users and a corresponding wind resource. The consumed energy exceeding the DAC threshold shown in Table 3 is the *expensive* energy. Therefore, the decision on question is whether is worth producing some, or all, expensive energy with SSW turbines, as shown in the decision node in Fig. 5. Finally, in order to make the decision we must consider the SSW turbine technology to be installed and the produced energy given by the wind resource as well as cost-benefit criteria, represented by the utility nodes and correspond to the reductions in CO_2 emissions, the savings for not producing expensive energy and the installation cost of the SSW turbines. In the next section, we exemplify the use of the network with a case study.

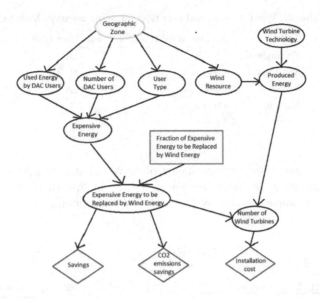

Fig. 5. BDN for the assessment of small-scale wind turbine deployment.

Table 3. Domestic tariffs in Mexico.

Tariff	Average temperature (°C)	Threshold DAC (kWh/month)
1	–	250
1A	25	300
1B	28	400
1C	30	850
1D	31	1000
1E	32	2000
1F	33	2500

5 Assessment of the Implementation of SSW Turbines in Towns in Mexico

As a case study, we consider five towns in Mexico with different wind potentials and high-energy consumption in the residential sector. The wind resource in each town and the main consumer domestic type of user are shown in Table 4. Let us notice that in some sites, for example Parras, there is a spread in the average wind resource, whereas, in other sites, such as San Luis Río, there is a narrow interval of wind velocity. Therefore, there is an uncertainty associated with the system since we cannot assign an exact wind speed at each site and BDN becomes a suitable tool for this condition.

Table 4. Wind resource and user type for some towns in Mexico.

Town	Average wind resource (m/s)	User type
Chihuahua	3.5–4.5	1B
San Luis Río	4.0–4.5	1F
Parras	4.0–5.5	1A
Cancún	4.0–4.5	1C
Tampico	3.5–4.5	1C

The BDN to assess the implementation of SSW turbines in these sites was built with the Netica Software and is shown in Fig. 6. In this BDN, we consider the assessment of the implementation of 5 and 10 kW wind turbines.

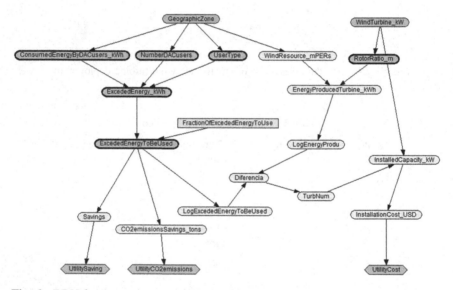

Fig. 6. BDN for the assessment of SSW turbine deployment in some towns in Mexico.

The architecture and operation of the network are described as follows:

- The available wind potential, as well as the consumed energy, the domestic user type and the number of DAC users, depend on the location as it is shown by the parent node *Geographic zone* and its child nodes. The states of the *Geographic zone* node correspond to different towns. Given these variables, one can calculate the excess energy by which normal users became DAC in that area represented by the *ExcededEnergy_kWh* node.
- The *WindTurbine_kW* node represents the SSW technology to be used, corresponding to 5 and 10 kW.
- Given the available wind potential, the energy produced by the SSW turbine is calculated in the *EnergyProducedTurbine_kWh* node.

- The *FractionOfExcededEnergyToUse* node is a decision node. This describes how much energy of the excess energy by which normal users became DAC, is convenient to be produced with the SSW technology. The states of this variable go from 0.1 to 1, indicating 10 to 100%.
- Given the fraction of excess energy to be produced by the SSW technology, the savings in money and in tons of CO_2 emissions are calculated on the nodes *Savings* and *CO2emissionsSavings_tons*.
- Likewise, given the fraction of excess energy to be produced by SSW turbines, the number of turbines required and the installed capacity are given by the *TurbNum* and *InstalledCapacity_kW* nodes.
- Finally, in order to assess every decision, it should be ranked according to the cost-benefit criteria. In this case, the criteria are given by the savings in money and CO_2 emissions and the installation cost of the SSW turbines. The utility nodes provide a gradually ranking, from 0.1 to the less desirable state, till 1, to the most desirable state associated with each criterion. Therefore, the *Utility_Saving* node provides the best ranking of the state where more savings are achieved. On the other hand, the *UtilityCO2emissions* node provides the best ranking to the state that produced fewer tons of CO_2 emissions. Finally, the *UtilityCost* node gives the best ranking to the state where the installation cost is the cheapest.
- The states for all chance nodes are discretized into intervals of values that these variables can take. States are built based on data from 2016.

Therefore, the BDN is able to construct different scenarios corresponding to the amount of excess energy, generated by wind energy, by which normal consumers are prevented to become DAC users. Then, the BDN provides a resultant expected utility for each scenario to rank its viability amongst all different scenarios. Tables 5 and 6

Table 5. Expected utilities for the assessment of 5 kW wind turbine deployment in some towns in Mexico.

% DAC replaced by SSW	Town				
	Chihuahua	San Luis Río	Parras	Cancún	Tampico
10	1.20	0.89	0.87	1.02	0.76
20	1.72	0.89	0.87	1.52	1.06
30	1.70	0.80	0.80	1.70	1.02
40	1.80	0.80	0.85	1.80	1.32
50	1.80	0.80	0.85	1.80	1.42
60	1.90	0.90	0.80	1.90	1.62
70	1.97	0.74	0.90	1.90	1.72
80	1.97	0.74	1.00	1.97	1.70
90	2.07	1.84	1.00	1.97	1.70
100	2.07	1.84	1.00	2.07	1.70

Table 6. Expected utilities for the assessment of 10 kW wind turbine deployment in some towns in Mexico.

% DAC replaced by SSW	Town				
	Chihuahua	San Luis Río	Parras	Cancún	Tampico
10	1.20	0.85	0.97	1.16	0.81
20	1.80	0.85	0.97	1.66	1.11
30	1.69	0.85	0.82	1.70	1.12
40	1.79	0.85	0.87	1.80	1.30
50	1.79	0.85	0.87	1.80	1.52
60	1.89	0.95	0.84	1.90	1.72
70	1.95	0.86	0.94	1.90	1.82
80	1.95	0.86	1.04	1.95	1.69
90	2.05	0.96	1.04	1.95	1.69
100	2.05	0.96	1.04	2.05	1.69

provide the resultant expected utilities, based on the cost-benefit criteria for different scenarios, in the towns under study. The first column refers to the percentage of energy, generated by SSW turbines, by which DAC users can become normal users. The considered towns are at the top of the table and below them resultant expected utility. These results provide us with valuable information for the assessment of the implementation of SWW technology in the country:

- The fact that a town counts with better wind potential does not imply that it is most viable to install SSW technology. Comparing the results from Chihuahua and Parras, it turns out that it is more viable to install the technology in the former town even though its wind potential is smaller than in Parras. This is due to the fact that the population, consumed energy and user type are also relevant to make the decision.
- It is not obvious that 5 kW turbines are more viable to install than 10 kW turbines. In some towns, such as Chihuahua, it is more viable to install 5 kW turbines. On the other hand, there are towns, such as Parras, where it is more viable to install 10 kW turbines.
- It is better to use wind energy to replace the exceed energy produced by DAC consumers.
- Note also that for a given town the viability for SSW turbines installation does not always increase with the percentage of produced wind energy. For example, Tampico with 20% produced wind energy is a more viable scenario compared to the 30% produced wind energy scenario.

These results should be taken with some reserve since the utility functions are simplified and their combination to obtain the resultant utility may be weighted in a different way to assign more importance to any of the criteria.

6   Conclusions

In this work, we design a BN for decision-making to determine the convenience of use SSW turbine generator technology to support residential consumers to get out of DAC tariffs. For the sake of simplicity, we have only considered a few towns with the best wind energy potential and a single type of domestic consumers. However, many towns present more than one type of consumers and this fact should be taken into consideration to build a more realistic decision-making system.

At least three different users can use this decision-making system: domestic consumers, CFE and SSW turbine suppliers. Domestic consumers can use the BDN to know if the use of SSW turbine technology is a viable option to get out of the DAC tariff. CFE may use the BDN to improve the distribution of the electric energy being generated. For instance, CFE can provide the excess energy to industrial consumers, instead of domestic consumers in some regions in Mexico. Lastly, SSW turbine suppliers can use the BDN to identify the best target zones and clients to sell their products. The scope of this work is being extended to include photovoltaic generation. It is believed that small-scale hybrid renewable distributed generation can provide the best solutions to help consumers to avoid DAC tariffs with some other valuable benefits.

Acknowledgments. Monica Borunda wishes to thank CONACYT for her Catedra Research Position with ID 71557, and to INEEL for its hospitality.

References

1. López Obrador, A.M.: Presidencia de la República: Plan Nacional de Desarrollo 2019–2024. Diario Oficial de la Federación. México (2019)
2. Tummalaa, A., Velamati, R.K., Sinha, D.K., Indraja, V., Krishna, V.H.: A review on small-scale wind turbines. Renew. Sustain. Energy Rev. **56**, 1351–1371 (2016)
3. Garduno, R., Borunda, M., Hernandez, M.A., Zubeldia, G.: Speed control of a wind turbine using fuzzy logic. In: Martínez-Villaseñor, L., et al. (eds.) MICAI 2019. LNAI, vol. 11835 pp. 522–536 (2019)
4. Predescu, M.: Economic evaluation of small wind turbines and hybrid systems for residential use. Renew. Energy Environ. Sustain. **1**, 33 (2016)
5. Gagliano, A., Nocera, F., Patania, F., Capizzi, A.: Assessment of micro-wind turbines performance in the urban environments: an aided methodology through geographical information systems. Int. J. Energy Environ. Eng. **4**, 43 (2013)
6. Lee, A.H.I., Chen, H.H., Kang, H.Y.: Multi-criteria decision-making on strategic selection of wind farms. Renew. Energy **34**, 120–126 (2009)
7. Goh, H.H., Lee, S.W., Kok, B.C., Ng, S.L.: Wind farm allocation in Malaysia based on multi-criteria decision-making method. In: 2011 National Postgraduate Conference. IEEE, Kuala Lumpur (2011)
8. Sánchez-Lozano, J.M., García-Cascales, M.S., Lamata, M.T.: GIS-based onshore wind farm site selection using fuzzy multi-criteria decision-making methods. Evaluating the case of southeastern Spain. Appl. Energy **171**, 86–102 (2016)

9. Haaren, R.H., Fthenakis, V.: GIS-based wind farm site selection using spatial multi-criteria analysis (SMCA): evaluating the case for New York State. Renew. Sustain. Energy Rev. **15** (7), 3332–3340 (2011)
10. Villacreses, G., Gaona, G., Martínez, J., Jijón, D.J.: Wind farms suitability location using geographical information system (GIS), based on multi-criteria decisión making (MCDM) methods: The case of continental Ecuador. Renew. Energy **109**, 275–286 (2017)
11. Tegou, L.I., Polatidis, H., Haralambopoulos, D.A.: Environmental management framework for wind farm siting: methodology and case study. J. Environ. Manage. **91**, 2134–2147 (2010)
12. Carbon Trust: Small-scale wind energy. Policy insights and practical guidance. London, UK (2008)
13. Reuther, N., Thull, J.P.: Feasibility study of small and micro wind turbines for residential use in New Zealand. LEaP Research Report No. 30, Canterbury, New Zealand (2011)
14. Ugur, E., Elma, O., Selamogullari, U.S., Tanrioven, M., Uzunoglu, M.: Financial payback analysis of small wind turbines for a smart home application in Istanbul/Turkey. In: International Conference on Renewable Energy Research and Applications (ICRERA), Madrid, Spain (2013)
15. Bortolini, M., Gamberi, M., Graziani, A., Manzini, R., Pilati, F.: Performance and viability analysis of small wind turbines in the European Union. Renew. Energy **62**, 629–639 (2014)
16. Olsen, T., Preus, R.: Small wind site assessment guidelines. Technical Report NREL/TP-5000–63696, Denver, USA (2015)
17. Abdelhady, S., Borello, D., Santori, S.: Economic feasibility of small wind turbines for domestic consumers in Egypt based on the new Feed-in Tariff. Energy Procedia **75**, 664–670 (2015)
18. Pearl, J.: Probabilistic Reasoning in Intelligent Systems: Networks of Plausible Inference. Morgan Kaufmann Publishers, San Francisco (1988)
19. Korb, K.B., Nicholson, A.E.: Bayesian Artificial Intelligence, 2nd edn. CRC Press, Boca Raton (2011)
20. Sucar, L.E.: Probabilistic Graphical Models: Principles and Applications. Springer, London (2015). https://doi.org/10.1007/978-1-4471-6699-3
21. Howard, R.A., Matheson, J.E.: Influence diagrams. Decis. Anal. **3**(2), 127–143 (2005)
22. International Energy Agency: IEA Wind Technology Collaboration Programme 2017 Annual Report. Olympia, USA (2018)
23. Comisión Reguladora de Energía: Reporte Mensual de Estadísticas del Sector Eléctrico, pp. 1–5 (2014)
24. Oropeza-Perez, I., Petzold-Rodriguez, A.: Analysis of the energy use in the Mexican residential sector by using two approaches regarding the behavior of the occupants. Appl. Sci. **8**(11), 2136 (2018)

Ontology-Based Legal System in Multi-agents Systems

Fábio Aiub Sperotto[1,2]([✉]), Mairon Belchior[2],
and Marilton Sanchotene de Aguiar[2]

[1] Sul-rio-grandense Federal Institute of Education, Science and Technology,
Camaquã, RS, Brazil
fabio.sperotto@camaqua.ifsul.edu.br
[2] Federal University of Pelotas, Pelotas, RS, Brazil
{mairon.belchior,marilton}@inf.ufpel.edu.br

Abstract. The development of ontologies associated with multi-agent systems provides mechanisms to model and correlate knowledge about the world to agent applications in various domains where simulations involve agents perform social exchanges or resource consumption. Norms that restrict and guide behavior often regulate the actions of agents, and therefore research on normative systems is necessary. Questions about the definition and construction of legal ontologies have been discussed in this research context. Legal ontologies have been proposed to formulate how laws can be modeled to formalize and manage law information in legal systems about regulation like traffic, taxes and other administrative rules. These ontologies have in their modeling formal laws with the purpose of providing information about permission, prohibition, obligation, rewards and punishments for these agents. Firstly, this article presents and discusses researches on ontologies applied in multi-agent systems, more specifically on legal ontologies. Next, we propose a model of legislative ontology related to the Brazilian domain of laws. The ontology of this model is provided by a web service and applied in multi-agent systems through a middleware. We used as a case study the Brazilian legislation that regulates fishing activity in an example scenario where the components simulate the restrictions for fishermen and government agents. Finally, we present how agent actions can be verified on our model and their applicability to the multi-agent systems.

Keywords: Multi-agent systems · Legal ontology · Brasilian Legislation

1 Introduction

Ontologies are used to capture knowledge about some domain of interest. There's a lot of researchers about ontologies with the purpose of defining the structures about juridic aspects that can be related or not to multi-agent systems (MAS). Norm models and their typification can be found in [12,13,16]. The ontologies,

© Springer Nature Switzerland AG 2019
L. Martínez-Villaseñor et al. (Eds.): MICAI 2019, LNAI 11835, pp. 507–521, 2019.
https://doi.org/10.1007/978-3-030-33749-0_41

meta-ontologies, foundational ontologies and other deep analysis about representativeness of social concepts occurs in [1,7,15,17,25]. There are still others studies to provide a model that understands juridic rules from society to be used computationally [11,22].

Norms are specific points that define a rule or an order that can determine the basis for a normative system, regulating the behavior of agents [4]. The types of these norms may be those of command, authorization, permission and revocation [7]. Commands' norms define the prohibition or obligation of a certain behaviour. The authorization norms (or empowerment) are related to roles that have the power to postulate and apply norms under certain restrictions. The permission norms are associated with behaviours that are not prohibited nor commanded, but actively allowed. There is a lot of works like in [10,12], which specify norms categories, but postulate the same similarity: categorize sets of constraints, punishments and rewards for agent's behavior.

Regarding legal systems, studies pointed how governments has been used semantic tools to management, publish public administrative data [8] and how they make political models available for computational simulation to support decision-making [14]. The web semantic technologies reinforce the openness and interoperability about government data in local, regional and international regulatory workspaces. Foundational and core ontologies has been provided to resolve how this legal information can be accessed, manipulated and interoperated.

The aim of this work is to elaborate an ontology model which provides the basis where Brazilian laws can be modelled and used in MAS. In addition to this model, a software middleware is provided to support the communication to both sides, ontological and simulation MAS platform, in order to have a legal knowledge base modeled and applied to MAS. A local Brazilian law about the legality of fishing during their reproduction period will be used as a case study to illustrate an application scenario of using the proposed model.

2   Legal Ontologies and Multi-agent Systems

Ontologies have been used in multi-agent systems as a model of knowledge domain representation and as a support for agent communication and reasoning [18]. The ontology arises from the necessity of the representation and reuse of knowledge and its relations between concepts and meanings. Thus, proposed ontologies are provided so that it is possible to model the definitions of legal systems in a format where individuals (in the human sense) and agents (software entities) can operate referencing legal and illegal behaviors [4].

Behavioral constraints are usually related to regulation among agents or access to resources or to possible activities that agents assume under certain roles. Compared to society, legislative systems tend to be designed to regulate people and institutions, determining the coexistence between individuals in the same society or between different societies.

The actions of individuals are characterized by their imputations. Imputations are produced by the action of the individual where his behavior is recognized as a condition and the sanction as a consequence, prescribed in some norm [10]. In your work describe a norms hierarchy which defines a superior norm (basic rule) that defines a constitution and the lower norms with instances of those that define the concrete behaviors about prohibition, obligation, permission, among others. This hierarchy may also include relations with national and international legislation.

The norms in agents have been frequently related in researches that apply this concept in the modeling of ontologies. In this sense, normative ontologies model rules that express the restrictions to be applied within a MAS [12]. In this study, the authors present a basic ontology to be used as in future domain ontologies that must define the desired norms. This ontology describes the concepts of norms (with their subclasses), roles, penalty, place, and action.

To each norm, is defined if is active or not (property of validity), indicating one penalty and one action regulation. The subclasses of norms are an obligation, prohibition, and permission. The concept of the role relates to norms instances and a place (role validity with the norm). In penalty, there are subclasses to categorize actions violations: *PermissionPenalty*, *ProhibitionPenalty*, *ObligationPenalty*.

In some surveys of legal area are based on definitions about law and morality, some legal models are based on the Pure Theory of Law [20] and the General Theory of Norms [19]. Research in this area [7,9,10] reports that Kelsen provides a legal methodology, typifying norms (the legal actions of individuals within a society).

Furthermore in [16] is described more studies on legal ontologies, but in this case, use other legal primitives than Kelsen. In contraposition Kelsen, the researcher's approach is to start to think with Alexy's Theory of Fundamental Rights [2]. In this theory, it is defined as norms, rules, and principles. Norms are divided between rules and principles. Rules are norms and cannot be accomplished. Principles are components that have some degree of satisfaction or fulfillment, depending on some legal aspects or facts. Moreover, they are discussed about legal position in that theory that provides the concept about situations in which object has a right against another object, in a legal relation [2].

In [13], the authors proposed an approach that allows the use of ontologies within MAS, by enabling agents to reason about and query elements encoded in ontologies. An infrastructure layer (artifact) coded in CArtAgO was developed to enable ontology reasoning and querying features in different agent-oriented platforms, by using the OWL API[1]. This one allows to create, manipulate and serialize OWL ontologies.

In [7] report an experience of development and test of diverse methodologies to modeling and rationalized about legal knowledge. The researchers developed a framework related to system architectures that reutilized this knowledge. The objective of studies is retrieving abstract legal denominators between those domains in a search of a unified vision in these same domains. The authors propose the central ontologies (they are not domain ontology and is not totally generic ontologies) FOLaw and LRI-Core.

---

[1] http://owlcs.github.io/owlapi.

The FOLaw [25] supply structures which discern the many types of knowledge in legal rationalization. Furthermore, helps in organization and indexation of domain ontologies libraries supporting the acquisition of new knowledge to build new ontologies. The FOLaw is developed upon a semantic sociological of roles take on the legal system. This is, the approach is not purely in law but in one social-legal vision, the start point to modeling is the society itself. In your rationalizer system exists process that follows the flow of knowledge normative categories like meta-legal knowledge, world knowledge and among others. These categories are implemented like functions where receive the actions and return their legality. However, this approach is not used like a concrete ontology (the purpose is to enable a place to extend future domain ontologies).

Analyzing others works and parallel to this one, the authors verify that the legal domain does not seem to have a specific vocabulary, as in other domains. The analyzes report that it is difficult to separate totally legal vocabulary from social activities. The notions of roles, social position, actions, and social relations determine important terms in the field of positive law (in accordance with Kelsen's theory). Therewith they determine the invariability legal concepts are founded upon common sense. This makes it necessary to model and to understand some legal domain, including terms like agents, actions, processes, time, space, among others.

In this way the LRI-Core is proposed, where by design, contains two layers. The base (top) layer defines legal abstract concepts, that which comes from common sense: mental concepts about intention and content, role, social concepts, and physical conceptions of object and processes.

The lower layer expresses the legal ontology by means of the previous concepts, respectively, defining: action and document, norm and organization, judicial organization and, legal action and legal code. From these layers, leaf concepts are generated, where they express base concepts for future domains.

DOLCE and DOLCE-CORE are other options in foundational ontologies scenario where the vision is the universal ontologies to represent knowledge cannot be feasible [5,15]. Both don't be specific ontologies to law modeling, but they are referenced as a base ontology for logical definitions and concept construction to any areas. They are not giving the taxonomy ready for use but gives the logical construction to applied in a domain to generate the final ontology.

The categories in DOLCE [15] are conceived from linguistic analysis and of common sense. The ontology set a series of abstract entities and abstract qualities, providing concepts in ontology as physical, mental and social objects. These concepts should not have individuals in ontology because the purpose of this model is giving a base do extend future concepts. The DOLCE-CORE use as a base the DOLCE but focus only on formal logic of entities that exist in time called temporal particulars.

Related to foundational ontologies there's an LKIF-Core that can be used as a central knowledge component for legal knowledge systems [1]. The LKIF enables the translation between legal knowledge bases and is to be a knowledge representation formalism. Inspired by LRI-Core about a group of "worlds" denoted by concepts modeled like objects, process, mental objects, mental process, and others, LKIF is built on LRI-Core but construct a more rigorous definition of concepts and relations.

The aim of LKIF is group basic concepts of law, depending on what groups of users is related (citizens, legal professionals). It's organized in ten ontology modules: expression, norm, process, action, role, place, time, mereology, legal_action, and legal_role. The ontology used two frameworks: time_modification and rules. Each module has your independent cluster of concepts and all modules and frameworks are organized in layers representing top, intentional and legal levels. If the discourse is about rational agents, your beliefs and your intentions so the intentional layer should be used to organize the related concepts. In that layer, agents, roles and communication (intelligent behavior) are related. The top layer is related to the physical world and time (time interval and moments) and there are concepts like a process similar to LRI-Core about event and time process.

In the legal level is found the concepts about norms, legal actions, and legal roles. The actions can be executed by a person or a legislative group, and this manner provides rights, power, legal roles and other concepts to express normative statements. In this ontology, norms can be about rights or permissions and qualify a certain situation. In permission concept, for example, can be expressed obligation situations and prohibition situations.

Based on all that legal conceptions explained previously about Alexy's Theory [16], the authors show their ontology approach using categories from UFO (Unified Foundational Ontology) [17]. They use UFO as basis ontology and use Alexy's Theory to extend the model. The UFO modeling concepts about a social agent, social reality and physical events. In the social agent, is possible to formalize an a government agent, president agent or any legislative representatives. The norms are considered a set of directives on perform some actions in an organization and are determined by at least one agent which are responsible to define rules in that domain. Others concepts like roles, relators and normative description are reused too.

In the extended model [16], the authors apply and specialization on relators: legal relation and legal relators. Those concepts are provided to represents relations between holder and rights, duties, no-rights and permissions. It's the notion of applied "rights of something" from Alexy's theory. In that ontology, the main idea is to formalize only this part of legal relations, legal acts between agents.

Other legal ontologies like PrOnto can be constructed to model specific regulations and what duties has been applied in some domains [22]. The PrOnto is applied in digital data protection framework called GDPR (General Data Protection Regulation). This regulation is upon obligations involved in processing personal data and all risk belonging to safeguard of that data. The ontology that formalizes this data protection norms has the following concepts: data types and documents, agents and roles, processing purposes, legal bases, processing operations, deontic operations for modeling rights and duties. They use the FOCA methodology [3] that applies SPARQL^2 as one of its evaluation mechanism.

The called "privacy" ontology implements concepts about rights in data subject and the duties about controller and processor (obligation to notify the data breach to the data subject). PrOnto also formalized the concepts of right, obligation, prohibition, and permission but customize obligations and rights acquired from GDPR legislation. To elaborate this the authors analyze the articles on GDPR and proposes an ontology that can register the legal articles of manipulating personal data and who is responsible for the process.

Build legal ontologies in many moments demands not only provide the final ontology but discuss the process to build these ontologies. In [11] is presented a middle-out approach to building legal domain reference ontology for a Legal Knowledge Base system (LKBS). In this research, the authors do not show an operational ontology but discuss strategies to build this type of ontology and start your own model based on Lebanese legal-penal domain. They discuss two construct strategies: bottom-up and top-down. The bottom-up starts analyzing the most specific concept and builds the other parts by generalization. The linguistic study, documents analysis, and other social studies are usually used to extract data structures. In top-down strategy is the opposite, starting to the most generic concept and build the other specialization structures. In this case, experts in the domain area analyze relevant information and refine while understanding the specifications of a structure. In this sense, discuss the existence of advantages and disadvantages to use the split strategies, so the authors bring together both ways to build and middle-out approach.

They approach an ontology with modularization concepts that can be split into small reusable fragments or sub-ontologies. Initially, they used the process of modeling concepts applying previous studies of foundational ontologies, reusing other ontologies that capture similar or complementary knowledge (top-down strategy). After, in bottom-up strategy, uses the process of ontology learning with semi-automatic natural process language (NPL) techniques to extract legal knowledge from legal documents. Using these techniques in your regional criminal legal articles, they extract the main terms used by legislation: infraction, crime, offense, and violation. This study discussed good points about the use of foundational ontologies and NPL techniques to conceive concepts in ontology based on legal documents.

The DOLCE [15] and LKIF-CORE [1] are classified in foundational ontologies and your specifications are a basis to newer ontologies. The similarities between them are how can express the common sense and the linguistics terms. The strong social study made in both approaches can be used to understand time, process and other physical and non-physical concepts in human being to model foundational ontologies. The example is the concepts like process, roles, actions, time and mental objects defined in LKIF-CORE and can be reused in other models (directly or indirectly).

---

^{2} https://www.w3.org/TR/rdf-sparql-query.

In [16] the main focus is on the existence of a legal fact, typifying the notion of social relation in legal norms. For this, the concept of legal relator is applied to describe two or more pairs of associated social moments, like social commitments. This model expresses the rights and the duties of persons (right of education, the right to express an opinion, permission to smoke in open places among others). In the PrOnto ontology [22], concepts are based on specific laws about personal data. It's similar to [16] in the sense of a right and duties model, but the purpose is to use in the regulation process of what to do with data and its violations. The PrOnto aims an implementation of an article about the safeguard of data subjects and provides structures to be used with SPARQL and other mechanisms in the semantic web. The [16] model doesn't aim a specific law article but foments a model to deal about the basics of social commitments.

In [11] the study provides a complete explanation about the process to collect data and build an ontology. The authors approach is to build a model based on the extraction of legal terms in Lebanese penal code and the paper focus on this. After applying automatization techniques of text extraction and provide some statistics of term uses, they define the basic terms, concepts, and the relation between layers of their structure. This is not a complete ontology to be used but a whole middle-out approach process to develop a legal ontology (details of using a final ontology is not provided).

These models provided many different mechanisms to operate a process to build a legal ontology or a complete model to be used. Some models are modeling a good point of view about social commitments and duties, but not about translate law infrastructure in an ontology model. Others models provide a law structure but show how invariably the approaches lead in a legal ontology for a specific domain (government).

3   Legal Ontology for Brazilian Laws

The models described previously provide many mechanisms to model legal ontologies. There are models referenced as central or foundational ontologies while others focused on the process to build ontologies. Regardless of the employed mechanism, in the final steps of model construction, many concepts implemented are related to domain knowledge. Detailed about how ontologies can be integrated within Multi-Agent Systems can be found in [13]. There are a few legal ontologies with a focus in country legislation. The main idea of our work is how ontologies can express the juridic concepts of Brazilian laws and provide this knowledge to MAS.

On the other hand, agents in MAS have few native capabilities to understanding semantic documents, such as ontologies, and to perform direct communication to conceptual specifications in the same documents. They have API's can provide more functionality to access databases different than belief bases while others frameworks[3] can place more mechanisms or artefacts to run with the multi-agent simulation systems.

---

[3] https://jena.apache.org.

Our approach provides a middleware to give a solution to both sides, ontological and MAS platform, in order to have a legal knowledge base modeled
and applied to MAS. The proposed middleware flow is illustrated in Fig. 1. The
agents' behaviors are evaluated for the purpose of obtaining existing violations
based on current legislation. Also in Fig. 1, agents' actions (data about their
behavior) are sent to a software component (middleware). This component will
perform queries to a legal ontology searching for actions' consequences while
applying the law and it answers back to MAS if any rule was violated and what
is the related sanctions or if any reward is available. Thus, any knowledge about
SPARQL queries from MAS developers will be necessary because that component will provide the appropriate communication to the legal ontology model.

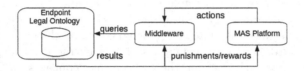

Fig. 1. The proposed middleware flow.

More details about the middleware will be discussed in future work. The
purpose of this study is to provide a legislation ontology structure based on
Brazilian laws. First, a structural analysis of Brazilian laws should be carried
out. After that, the necessary query to explore this ontology will be presented.

In Brazilian laws, there is a normative part which describes the text about the
law that is specified in terms of norms [23]. These norms are divided into articles
that are divided into paragraphs and after that into *caput*, subsections (*incisos*
in portuguese), lines and items. Articles can be grouped into sections, chapters
and books according to their purpose. The purpose of books, for example, can
be to group all information about the same context such as criminal laws, civil
laws or traffic laws.

In *caput* of each article (first article information), the general rule description
should be described, and the details about restrictions and exceptions are left to
paragraphs. Each paragraph must be numbered according to the norms applied
in the article [23]. If there is a paragraph unfolding, a list of detailed information
is placed in subsections. If an item still needs unfolding on that subsections, they
are listed in lines (where norms' conditions are detailed).

The empirical analysis used here is similar to other processes that analyze
manually or automatically articles of law [11,22]. The (automatized) natural language process was not implemented, instead of this, we analysis relevant information of the laws to turn into concepts and their relations. In this case, based
on Brazilian structure law, we have the following succession: law, articles, paragraphs, lines. Paragraphs usually have the law specification and lines describes
the conditions of their applicability.

According to the mentioned Brazilian legal structure, the following main concepts were extracted and they are described as follows. Example of an applicable law scenario is discussed in the next subsection.

Legislation: describes the concept of a law which is specified by norms.

Norm: describes a rule about a resource, event or person. A norm can be an obligation, permission or prohibition. It also can be classified as a punishment when a norm was violated and as a reward when a norm was fulfilled by an agent.

Action: describes the behavior or activity that is accomplished by the agents such as legislators, police officers, citizens or other entities of the society.

Place: is a physical region where norms should apply.

Punishments: describes new regulations when there is a violation of a rule. It is extracted from paragraphs and subsections of a law. Punishments can be classified into Detention, *PayAFine*, and Seizure. Detention should contain minimum and maximum duration (in months or years). *PayAFine* must inform the values and conditions of the fine. A Seizure means gathering resources from violators. These resources are taken for evidence of the infraction.

Environment: refers to knowledge about internal items belonging to the habitat. They can be places (regions) and existing resources. These resources may be the materials from the violators or physical geographically resources such as rivers. The resources can also be non-materials, which refers to mental or monetary resources (currency).

Role: represents a particular position or function being played by a given agent.

The sub-concepts of the norm are similar to [12] except the concepts of reward and punishment. Inspired by [10] about superior and inferior norms and legal base [22], in this work we propose the concept of Norm as sub-concept of Legislation. The legislation represents the description of a law while norms will express details of a law (punishments, rewards, roles, actions and period of validation).

Although the ontologies of foundations provide the basis for any other ontologies of domains to be applied, the concepts of the social object of DOLCE employed in [15] and definitions of roles of LRI-CORE provided in [7] were used in this paper. The concept of a social performs the differentiation between legislators agents and other types of agents. Figure 2 illustrates the concept hierarchy of the proposed legal ontology about Brazilian legislation. This ontology should be considered as the basis and may receive more concepts depending on the domain to which it is applied. For editing tool, the Protégé [21] was used.

The knowledge about the society of agents must follow the ramification initiated by the *Social* concept. Initially, the roles of agents in this society are modeled as sub-concept of *SocialAgent* concept and can be related to other entities in the ontology. Figure 3 shows the relationships between the aforementioned concepts.

The law is expressed by the Legislation concept, and it brings together the concepts of the article and the paragraphs of Brazilian legislation. Articles are

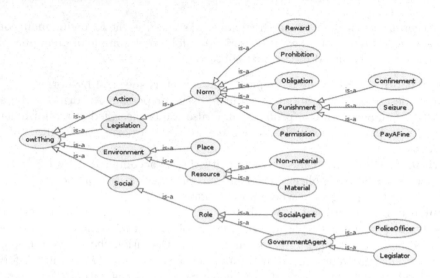

Fig. 2. The concepts hierarchy of ontology.

specified by a Norm describing conditions of law enforcement. Each norm represents the applicability condition of the law related to one or more sub-concepts (apply object property). The roles are associated with norms by the relates object property because one norm may be addressed to specific types of agents.

A norm regulates an Environment of a society. The Reward may have a Resource because the rewards may provide material or non-material to the agents. In domain ontologies, these relationships should express the legislative basis for any Brasilian law where the instances of these concepts provide information from domain.

In addition, Norm instances may have a time configuration, which defines a time interval where the norm is valid. In [12], the norms are active or not and the model in [1] shows a full framework to deal with time (temporal occurrences). We set a solution between both of them. Two data properties of *datetime* (*starts_at* and *ends_at*) were defined in norms instances in order to represent the initial and final date of validity. The Brazilian laws have an initial date of validity and sometimes have a final date where regulation exists only in a time interval. If a norm does not have a final date so it is always active.

4   Case Study

In order to illustrate an application scenario about an example of law, it is used the same case study as in [24], where it is implemented a framework of public policies. In their work, the authors used the legislation about the legality of fishing during their reproduction period (called *piracema* event in Brazil). The work in [24] provides a framework that integrates norms to the JaCaMo MAS platform by relying on concepts about norms and laws [20]. Their work does not address the use of ontologies and uses CArtAgO artifacts to enable the law knowledge inside the social simulation. The legislation used is the Law number 7653 about the protection of fauna and other social security [6].

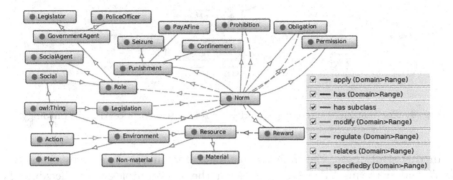

Fig. 3. The relations between concepts.

Article 27 of this law defines punishable crime with imprisonment from 2 (two) to (5) (five) years when occurring violation of the prescribed articles 2, 3, 17 and 18 of this law. In this example, it will be used the paragraph 4 (four) of this law: the prohibition of fishing during their reproduction period. Its lines describe:

a. if a professional fisherman, a fine of 5 (five) to 20 (twenty) National Treasury Obligations (OTN) and suspension of professional activity for a period of 30 (thirty) to 90 (ninety) days;
b. if it is a company that exploits fishing, a fine of 100 (one hundred) to 500 (five hundred) OTN and suspension of its activities for a period of 30 (thirty) to 60 (sixty) days; and,
c. if an amateur fisherman, a fine of 20 (twenty) to 80 (eighty) OTN and loss of all instruments and equipment used in fishing.

Paragraph 4 of article 27 provides a restriction of behavior to fishermen in the consumption of resources in their environment. Through this legal specification, the instances that reflect the current legislation can be seen in Fig. 4.

As shown in Fig. 4, the instance of legislation is *law-7653_article-27_4* (the last number is the number of the paragraph) and the lines of the law are instances of norms. The line c describes if an amateur fisherman fishes when this regulation is active, this person will pay a fine and lose all his/her equipment. As visualized in Fig. 4, the instance of norm *article-27_4_line-c* is associated with other instances through the application and relates object properties. When an amateur fisherman performs the action fish, the norm *article-27_4_line-c* is violated and the punishments instances of *PayAFine* and Seizure are created to this agent that must accomplish it.

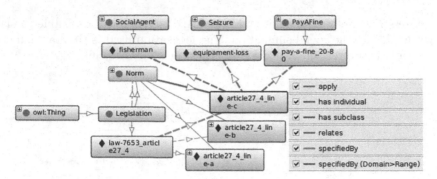

Fig. 4. The instances of concepts and your relation in proposed legal ontology.

In this study case, the middleware illustrated in Fig. 1 receives the action "fish" and performs SPARQL queries on the legal ontology by checking the existing norms definitions to determine if there is a violation of the behavior. In order to be able to perform these queries, a SPARQL server is required. In this case, it was used the Apache Jena Fuseki[4], which provides it through an endpoint this ontology. Inside the middleware, a SPARQL query (see Fig. 5) is set to verify the ontology to search for violations from agent' behaviors.

```
SELECT ?consequences ?type WHERE {      {
    ?law  rdf:type law:legislation  .
    ?law  rdfs:comment ?c  .
    ?law  law:starts_at ?starts_at.
    OPTIONAL { ?law law:ends_at ?ends_at } .
    FILTER(''2019-11-18T16:50:00''^^xsd:dateTime >= ?starts_at  )  .
    ?law ?p ?condition  .
    ?condition law:apply ?consequences  .
    ?condition law:relates ?roles  .
    ?consequences rdf:type ?type  .
}
UNION {
    ?law law:ends_at ?ends_at  .
    FILTER(''2019-11-18T16:50:00''^^xsd:dateTime >= ?starts_at &&
        ''2019-11-18T16:50:00''^^xsd:dateTime < ?ends_at  ).
}
FILTER regex(?c, ''fish'', ''i'')  .
FILTER(?roles = law:fisherman)  .
FILTER(?p = law:specifiedBy)  .
FILTER(?type != owl:NamedIndividual)  . }
```

Fig. 5. The query used in this study case.

The query (Fig. 5) searches the ontology to find a law description which has the action of the agent (regex FILTER). Another information checked is if norms are applied to the same type of agent (roles FILTER). The data queried in SELECT clause uses the relations in the legal ontology and returns what consequences (punishments or rewards) is related to that agent behavior. The same

---

[4] https://jena.apache.org/documentation/fuseki2.

query returns what type of each consequence (fine's payment, seizure of equipment, rewards, obligations or prohibitions, among others). As it has explained previously about the data properties *starts_at* and *ends_at*, it is necessary to tell to query the current *datetime* of the agent's action. The UNION part is applied to a group in the same results the records of laws always active and valid in an interval period. So the MAS will receive back what can happen as consequences of agents' actions based on current legislation.

5 Conclusion and Further Work

The application of ontologies has been considered for decades as an important mechanism, not only for the computational modeling of human knowledge, but also as the provision of this knowledge to the agents. In MAS, ontologies provide a means where agents can recognize and conduct rules that meet domains of particular knowledge.

In this work, the ontology is used as a fundamental piece in a middleware so that agents, implemented in different technologies, can take advantage of these knowledge bases. Discussions on norms and constraints of agent behavior suggest the use of ontological bases as a reinforcement in the understanding of legal systems. These legal systems could be provided based on others bases of rules rather than an ontological basis. However, the legal ontologies providing legal knowledge favor to these computational agents to make future relations and inferences about their behavior restrictions.

The main idea is that, in the future, different legal ontologies could be provided through this Fuseki server and that a web service can be made available to be enjoyed by several MAS. MAS will be able to consume the necessary legislation for their domains of action. Currently, we are developing as part of this research others components for the future model to become a middleware. The proposed middleware integrated with the ontology described in this article will be provided as a component that makes links to that web service.

In relation to the proposed ontology model, some components were not treated in this paper. Authority aspects of legislation such as senators, police forces, judges and who can change instances in the ontology are not addressed here and are for further development. Actions needed to be performed from those government agents can be triggered from ontology in order to these agents knows what to do on agents violators. In addition to future work, aspects of inference are planned. Determining relations with functional, inverse, transitive properties, among others, is important so mechanisms of rationalizers can infer new information based on the modeled facts.

Although the items to be developed in the future, the current use of SPARQL queries provide us with a fast and efficient use of the application ontology proposal. With the query made in the class hierarchy and in the instances (including the properties of existing relations), we can bring existing systems to recognize these proposed models like our ontology.

Acknowledgments. This study was financed in part by the Coordenação de Aperfeiçoamento de Pessoal de Nível Superior - Brasil (CAPES)-Finance Code 001.

References

1. Alexander, B.O.E.R.: LKIF core: principled ontology development for the legal domain. Law Ontol. Semant. Web: Channelling Legal Inf. Flood **188**, 21 (2009)
2. Alexy, R.: Discourse theory and fundamental rights. In: Menéndez, A., Eriksen, E. (eds.) Arguing Fundamental Rights. Law and Philosophy Library, vol. 77, pp. 15–30. Springer, Dordrecht (2006). https://doi.org/10.1007/1-4020-4919-4_1
3. Bandeira, J., Bittencourt, I.I., Espinheira, P., Isotani, S.: FOCA: a methodology for ontology evaluation. arXiv preprint arXiv:1612.03353 (2016)
4. Boella, G., Van Der Torre, L., Verhagen, H.: Introduction to normative multiagent systems. Comput. Math. Organ. Theory **12**(2–3), 71–79 (2006)
5. Borgo, S., Masolo, C.: Foundational choices in DOLCE. In: Staab, S., Studer, R. (eds.) Handbook on Ontologies. IHIS, pp. 361–381. Springer, Heidelberg (2009). https://doi.org/10.1007/978-3-540-92673-3_16
6. Brasil. Lei N. 7.653 de 12 de Fevereiro de 1988. Congresso Nacional, Casa Civil, [S.l.] (1988)
7. Breuker, J., Valente, A., Winkels, R.: Use and reuse of legal ontologies in knowledge engineering and information management. In: Benjamins, V.R., Casanovas, P., Breuker, J., Gangemi, A. (eds.) Law and the Semantic Web. LNCS (LNAI), vol. 3369, pp. 36–64. Springer, Heidelberg (2005). https://doi.org/10.1007/978-3-540-32253-5_4
8. Casanovas, P., et al.: Semantic web for the legal domain: the next step. Semant. web **7**(3), 213–227 (2016)
9. Costa, A.C.R.: Toward a formal reconstruction of Kelsen's theory of legal systems. In: 2nd Workshop-School on Theoretical Computer Science, pp. 165–171 (2013)
10. Čyras, V., Lachmayer, F., Tsuno, G.: Visualization of Hans Kelsen's pure theory of law. In: Proceedings of the Fundamental Concepts and the Systematization of Law, FCASL, pp. 112–122 (2011)
11. El Ghosh, M., Naja, H., Abdulrab, H., Khalil, M.: Towards a middle-out approach for building legal domain reference ontology. Int. J. Knowl. Eng. **2**(3), 109–114 (2016)
12. Felicíssimo, C., Lucena, C., Carvalho, G., Paes, R.: Normative ontologies to define regulations over roles in open multi-agent systems. [S.l.]: AAAI Fall Symposium Roles, an Interdisciplinary Perspective: Ontologies, Programming Languages, and Multiagent Systems (2005)
13. Freitas, A., Panisson, A.R., Hilgert, L., Meneguzzi, F., Vieira, R., Bordini, R.H.: Applying ontologies to the development and execution of multi-agent systems. Web Intell. **15**(4), 291–302 (2017)
14. Furdík, K., Sabol, T., Dulinová, V.: Policy modelling supported by e-participation ICT tools. In: Proceedings of the 4th International Conference on Methodologies, Technologies and Tools Enabling e-Government. University of Applied Sciences, Northwestern Switzerland, Olten, pp. 135–146 (2010)
15. Gangemi, A., Guarino, N., Masolo, C., Oltramari, A., Schneider, L.: Sweetening ontologies with DOLCE. In: Gómez-Pérez, A., Benjamins, V.R. (eds.) EKAW 2002. LNCS (LNAI), vol. 2473, pp. 166–181. Springer, Heidelberg (2002). https://doi.org/10.1007/3-540-45810-7_18

16. Griffo, C., Almeida, J.P.A., Guizzardi, G.: Towards a legal core ontology based on Alexy's theory of fundamental rights. In: Multilingual Workshop on Artificial Intelligence and Law, ICAIL (2015)
17. Guizzardi, G., De Almeida Falbo, R., Guizzardi, R.S.: Grounding software domain ontologies in the unified foundational ontology (UFO): the case of the ODE software process ontology. In: CIbSE, pp. 127–140 (2008)
18. Hadzic, M., et al.: Ontology-Based Multi-agent Systems. Springer, Heidelberg (2009). https://doi.org/10.1007/978-3-642-01904-3
19. Kelsen, H.: General Theory of Norms. Oxford University Press, Oxford (1990)
20. Kelsen, H.: Pure Theory of Law. Lawbook Exchange (2009)
21. Musen, M.A: The Protégé project: a look back and a look forward. AI Matters. Association of Computing Machinery Specific Interest Group in Artificial Intelligence, 1(4) (2015)
22. Palmirani, M., et al.: Legal ontology for modelling GDPR concepts and norms. In: Legal Knowledge and Information Systems: JURIX 2018: The Thirty-first Annual Conference, p. 91. IOS Press (2018)
23. Penna, S.F.P.D.O., Maciel, E.C.B.D.A: Técnica Legislativa - Orientação para a Padronização de Trabalhos. [S.l.]: Senado Federal (2002)
24. dos Santos, I.A.D.S., da Rocha Costa, A.C.: Toward a framework for simulating agent-based models of public policy processes on the Jason-Cartago platform. In: Proceedings of the Second International Workshop on Agent-based Modeling for Policy Engineering (AMPLE 2012), pp. 45–59 (2012)
25. Valente, A., Breuker, J., Brouwer, B.: Legal modeling and automated reasoning with ON-LINE. Int. J. Hum.-Comput. Stud. 51(6), 1079–1125 (1999)

Speed Control of a Wind Turbine Using Fuzzy Logic

Raul Garduno[1]([⊠]), Monica Borunda[2], Miguel A. Hernandez[3], and Gorka Zubeldia[1]

[1] Instituto Nacional de Electricidad y Energías Limpias, Cuernavaca, Mexico
rgarduno@ineel.mx, gorka.z.e@gmail.com
[2] Conacyt - Instituto Nacional de Electricidad y Energías Limpias, Cuernavaca, Mexico
monica.borunda@ineel.mx
[3] Instituto de Estudios de la Energía, Universidad del Istmo, Tehuantepec, Mexico
mahluni2000@yahoo.com.mx

Abstract. Wind turbine generators are highly desirable to operate autonomously throughout the wind speed range below hurricane conditions. A key requirement to achieve this goal is to be able to control the wind turbine speed using a full-scope feedback control scheme. Currently, wind turbine speed is controlled by modulating the angular position of the rotor blades to catch the required amount of kinetic energy of the wind to produce the desired rotational speed. Typically, conventional PI controllers modulate the blades angular position only for wind speeds in the range from 12 m/s through 25 m/s. This paper introduces a fuzzy speed controller to control autonomously the turbine rotational speed in the whole wind speed range from 0 m/s throughout 30 m/s. After presenting several key concepts about small-scale wind turbines, the design of the fuzzy speed controller based on a TSK fuzzy system is introduced. In this regard, the proposed fuzzy speed controller intelligently extends the scope of control below nominal speed and above trip conditions.

Keywords: Intelligent control · Fuzzy controller · Wind turbines · Pitch modulation · Rotor speed

1 Introduction

Wind energy conversion systems based on wind turbines are a very convenient way to harness energy from the renewable wind resource that is widely abundant on planet earth. Production of electric power and reduction of mechanical stress due to variations of wind speed are two of the most important factors in the design of control systems for wind turbine generators. One of the most popular methods used with this purpose is to modify the angular position of the rotor blades, and PID (Proportional Integral Derivative) controllers are the most widely used controllers with this aim.

Regarding control of wind turbine generators by modulation of the angular position of the rotor blades, Uehara and colleagues [1] propose a PID control to limit the

© Springer Nature Switzerland AG 2019
L. Martínez-Villaseñor et al. (Eds.): MICAI 2019, LNAI 11835, pp. 522–536, 2019.
https://doi.org/10.1007/978-3-030-33749-0_42

aerodynamic power captured by the rotor at high wind speeds. This approach has the disadvantage of a low performance at other regions of operation because the design is based on linearization.

There are several other approaches about PID control and fuzzy control. Civelek et al. [2] present the development and simulation of a fuzzy PID and compares it to fuzzy control and PID control, concluding that the fuzzy PID controller has softer and better tracking. Qi and Meng [3] present simulation results of a fuzzy PID controller for power output regulation with pitch variation. Results show an increase on the response speed of the system. Van et al. [4] introduce a fuzzy logic controller with rotor speed and output power as input, and pitch angle reference as output. Results show that the aerodynamic power is softly maintained within nominal values without fluctuations on the output power. This controller was tested in simulations and with a motor-generator testbed.

In this paper, an intelligent fuzzy controller is designed to control the wind turbine rotating speed in the whole wind speed window from 0 m/s throughout 30 m/s. In this regard, the proposed fuzzy speed controller extends the control action below nominal speed (12 m/s) and above trip speed (25 m/s) using fuzzy inference rules. The proposed approach allows the wind turbine to achieve autonomous operation throughout its whole range of operation, as required for an intelligent machine. In Sect. 2, horizontal-axis three blade small-scale (low power) wind turbine generators are introduced as the machines that are required to behave intelligently (to demonstrate intelligent behavior). In Sect. 3, the mathematical model of a wind turbine generator seen as an energy conversion system is introduced by means of the major equations that describe its dynamic behavior, which is to be used for simulation experiments. In Sect. 4, the operation fundamentals of wind turbine generators are presented, as well as the conventional approach to control the wind turbine rotating speed via modulation of the angular position of the rotor blades or pitch control for short. In addition, the basics of fuzzy pitch control are presented. Section 5 introduces the design of the full-scope fuzzy speed controller for low-power small-scale wind turbine generators to operate autonomously using a feedback control scheme. Then, Sect. 6 presents some meaningful simulation experiments to demonstrate the clever performance of the full-scope fuzzy speed controller. Finally, Sect. 7 draws some pertinent conclusions and points out future work that may be worth to be undertaken.

2 Small-Scale Wind Turbine Generators

A modern wind turbine generator is a machine that transforms wind kinetic energy into electrical energy. Various wind turbines have been designed to maximize the turbine energy output, minimize manufacturing, operation and maintenance costs, and to increase efficiency, reliability and availability of the energy conversion process. Wind turbines can be classified according to different characteristics, including type of electrical generator, turbine capacity, flow trajectory of wind regarding turbine rotor, wind turbine type of rotor, etc. [5]. Nowadays, most commercial wind turbine generators belong to the horizontal axis type, in which the axis of rotation of the rotor blades is parallel to the wind flow. This kind of wind turbine generator has the following advantages over vertical axis type: High turbine efficiency, high power density, low cost per unit of output power.

2.1 Horizontal-Axis Wind Turbine Generators

Figure 1 shows a schematic of a horizontal-axis wind turbine. The major components include the rotor blades (1), the blade pitch positioning system (2), the hub to hung up the rotor blades (4), the nacelle positioning system (18) to face the coming wind, the electric subsystem cabinet (13), including protections and switchgear, and the power transformer to connect to the network (14).

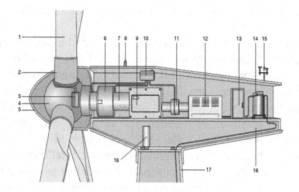

Fig. 1. Major components of a horizontal-axis wind turbine generator.

A major component, not show in the previous figure, is the control system. Mainly, the control system is responsible to modify the orientation of the nacelle to face the incoming wind, and to modify the pitch of the blades to capture the right amount of kinetic energy in the wind. Other responsibilities include governing the electric generator and the power electronic converters.

2.2 Small-Scale Wind Turbine Generators

The scope of the work in this paper is focused in small-scale wind turbine generators. Specifically, a three-blade 1 kW wind turbine generator like that by Tumo-Int in [6] is used to illustrate the concepts. Besides the low power of a small-scale wind turbine generator, the other characteristic that defines such machines is the relatively high nominal rotating speed of the turbine axis, which in this case is about 400 rpm [7]. Under these conditions the ratio from the rotating blade speed to the wind speed or tip speed ratio (TSR) is about 4, compared to 7-8 for large-scale wind turbine generators [8].

The dominant dynamic response of a small-scale wind turbine generator is given by the following equation of motion:

$$J_r \dot{\omega}_r + K_r \omega_r = T_a \tag{1}$$

where: wr is the rotor speed, Kr is the friction coefficient of the support bearings. Jr is the rotor inertia, and Ta is the aerodynamic torque produced by the blades on the rotor. Hence, applying the Laplace transform, the rotor open-loop transfer function is:

$$G(s) = \frac{\omega(s)}{T_a(s)} = \frac{1}{J_r s + K_r} \tag{2}$$

This transfer function is the core of the mathematical model of the wind turbine generator.

3 Model of Wind Energy Conversion System

3.1 Wind Energy Conversion Process

The energy conversion process performed by a wind turbine generator includes conversion from kinetic wind energy to rotational mechanical energy, and conversion from mechanical energy to electrical energy by the generator. Wide-range operation of the wind turbine generator focuses on the conversion from wind kinetic energy to rotor mechanical energy performed by the wind turbine. In this stage major impact on the production of power by the turbine is due to sustained wind speed, the area covered by the rotor blades, and the transformation efficiency determined by the angular position of the blades.

It is necessary to get into the details of the wind turbine generator to understand the details of the wind turbine behavior, dynamic response, operation requirements, automation philosophy, and control actions.

3.2 Power Available in the Wind

Since the rotor dynamics provides the rotating speed after the aerodynamic power provided by the wind it is necessary to find out the kinetic energy available in the wind. The kinetic energy of a mass of air (m) moving at a definite speed (v) is given by the following equation:

$$E = \frac{1}{2} m v^2 \tag{3}$$

Then, the power available in the wind is obtained by derivation of the previous equation with respect to time:

$$P_v = \frac{dE}{dt} = \frac{1}{2} \dot{m} v^2 \tag{4}$$

where the mass flow (mdot) can be expressed as the product of air density times the area going through by the wind, times the speed of the air flow. Hence the power available in the wind is:

$$P_{viento} = \frac{1}{2}\rho A v^3 \tag{5}$$

Furthermore, considering that the blades sweep a circular area, the power available in the wind going through that circular area is given by:

$$P_{viento} = \frac{1}{2}\rho \pi r^2 v^3 \tag{6}$$

3.3   Useful Power from the Wind

Nevertheless, the power transferred from the wind to the wind generator is limited by the speed change in the conversion stage. The highest conversion by an ideal wind turbine is 59% according to Betz theory. Efficiency losses are caused by the viscosity in the blades, the turmoil caused by wind flow in the rotor, etc. In this way, the useful power extracted by the wind turbine from the wind is calculated considering the losses when the wind goes through the blades.

$$P_{util} = \frac{1}{2}\rho \pi r^2 v (v_1^2 - v_2^2) \tag{7}$$

The losses through the blades are accounted by the power coefficient, Cp, which depends on the angular position of the blades, β, and the tip speed ratio, λ [9].

$$C_p(\lambda, \beta) = c_1 \left(\frac{c_2}{\lambda_i} - c_3\beta - c_4\right) e^{\left(-\frac{c_5}{\lambda_i}\right)} + c_6 \tag{8}$$

This relationship has been parameterized to provide the expected optimal TSR, $\lambda = 4$, for small-scale low power wind turbines. Figure 2 shows a family of Cp curves for values from $\beta = 0°$ through $\beta = 32°$. It can be seen that increasing the pitch angle β decreases the coefficient power Cp, and that there is an optimal value of TSR, λopt, for which Cp is the highest, Cpmax, for any given value of the pitch angle, β.

To regulate the power produced by a wind turbine it is necessary to deploy a control system to limit the production of energy to the nominal value avoiding overshoots that will damage the components of the machine.

4   Speed Regulation via Pitch Control

Essential to the operation of a wind turbine generator is the control system, which in a broad sense is composed by multiple sensors, one or more control computers and several actuators. Sensors measure all required mechanical, electrical and

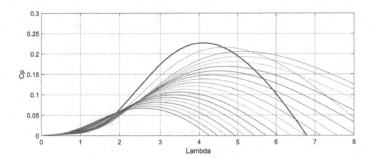

Fig. 2. C_p curves in terms of λ and β.

environmental variables, such as voltages, currents, vibration, temperatures, wind speed, wind direction, blade angular position and nacelle orientation. The control computers receive these measurements and calculate the control signals. Feedback control loops are programmed for the blade positioning system (SPA), nacelle orientation system (SOG), generator excitation system (SESE), machine side converter (CLM) and network side converter (CLR) as shown in Fig. 3. The algorithms in the feedback control loops calculate the corresponding control commands or control signals. Finally, the actuators deliver the power to manipulate the physical mechanisms to achieve the desired rotor and generator rotating speed, the generator output voltage, and the active and reactive power provided by the generator, all in accordance to the desired set-point values [10].

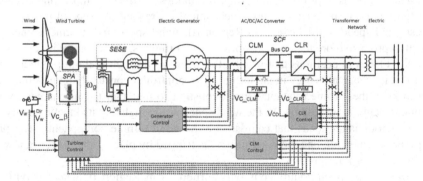

Fig. 3. Schematic diagram of the control system.

4.1 Operation Strategy

The global control objective for the operation of a wind turbine generator is to regulate the electrical power output, which is equivalent to regulate the mechanical power output of the wind turbine. In both cases, power regulation consists on achieving a predefined power curve such as the one in Fig. 4. This power curve is specific for each wind turbine generator and is obtained at laboratories by the manufacturers in accordance to standard IEC-61400 [11].

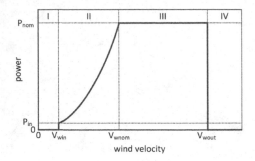

Fig. 4. Typical power curve for a wind turbine/wind turbine generator.

Mechanical power regulation in the wind turbine is performed as rotating speed regulation, because measuring rotating speed is much easier than mechanical power. Later on, power regulation of the whole wind turbine generator is implemented with electric power measurement, which is easy to obtain. So, power/speed regulation of the wind turbine is achieved manipulating the blades angular position or blade pitch with the blade positioning system and the blade pitch feedback control scheme or pitch control for short.

The objectives for pitch control are different at the various regions of the power curve. In Region I, wind speed is too low that the wind turbine is not rotating and the pitch control is off. In Region II, the wind turbine rotates, produces power and accelerates as the wind speed increases. Nowadays, blades are fixed at position cero and pitch control is kept off. In this way, the blades capture the most kinetic energy from the wind and produce the most mechanical energy up to nominal power at the highest wind speed in this region. In Region III, wind speed and its kinetic energy is enough to produce more than nominal power. Nevertheless, pitch control is activated to move the blades at positions that will let the wind go through without producing any additional mechanical energy in the turbine. The controller constantly adjusts the blade pitch to keep the turbine rotational speed constant to maintain the mechanical power output constant too. In Region IV, the wind speed is too high that its kinetic energy can produce aerodynamic loads that can damage the wind turbine components. The pitch controller is turned off, and the wind turbine is tripped by placing the blades in a wide-open position or flag position.

Currently, the pitch controller is only turned-on in Region II, where it typically deals with wind speeds in the range from 12 m/s through 25 m/s using a Proportional + Integral (PI) control algorithm. This paper introduces a PI-like fuzzy controller that can be used all the way from 3 m/s through 30 m/s.

4.2   PI Control

PI control is widely used in industry due to its simple structure, easy realization and robust performance. In fact, PI control accounts for about 90% of the feedback control loops that look as shown in Fig. 5 [12]:

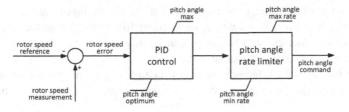

Fig. 5. Feedback control loop with PI control algorithm.

The system refers to the wind turbine and the actuators can be step motors that rotate the blades to the desired position. The angular positions of the blades are measured by encoders that feedback these signals to the pitch controller. The PI algorithm calculates the control signal in terms of the difference between the desired positon and the measured position of the blades using the following algorithm:

$$sc = K_p e + K_i \int_0^t e \tag{9}$$

In the PI control algorithm, the proportional term is related to the rapidity to change the position of the blades, and the integral term is related to the steady state error and can be used to eliminate regulation errors.

The PI controller is not well suited to deal with transition of operating points, such as those at the borders of wind speed regions of the power curve. In addition, since the wind turbine is a non-linear system that behaves differently across the wind speed range of operation, it is known that the PI controller will not perform the same throughout this operating range. A promising solution to this problem is to change the values of parameters Kp and Ki as the wind speed changes.

4.3   Fuzzy Control

Fuzzy controllers offer a promising solution to implement a controller that behaves as a PI controller for each zone of a partition of the operating range or power curve. With this aim, control rules can be defined for the control zones and their transitions. The basic structure of a fuzzy controller is given in Fig. 6.

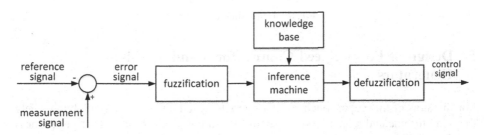

Fig. 6. Block diagram of a fuzzy controller.

At the stage of fuzzyfication, all numerical values of inputs are associated to a linguistic value and are given a degree of membership to the corresponding fuzzy set. The fuzzy sets or membership functions can be any of several shapes, such as triangular, gaussian, sigmoid, trapezoidal, etc.

At each iteration, the inference mechanism can activate one, various or none of the rules. In general, the knowledge base of the fuzzy controller is a set of rules of the form:

$$IF \ \langle antecedent \rangle, \ THEN \ \langle consequent \rangle. \tag{10}$$

The two most common fuzzy inference systems are Mamdani and Takagi-Sugeno-Kan (TSK) [13], with rules of the form:

$$IF \ \langle u_1 \ is \ LU_i \ and\dots and \ u_n \ is \ LU_n \rangle, \ THEN \ \langle z = f_i(u_1, \dots, u_1) \rangle \tag{11}$$

Main difference between TSK and Mamdani is that there is no need to perform the stage of desfuzzification stage because the TSK consequents are lineal functions of the inputs. The output of a TSK fuzzy system is calculated with the following expression:

$$Z_0 = \frac{\sum_{i=1}^{n} \omega_i f_i(x_i, y_i)}{\sum_{i=1}^{n} \omega_i} \tag{12}$$

where the value of ω_i is obtained selecting the smaller input value for each rule R_i [13], as shown in Fig. 7.

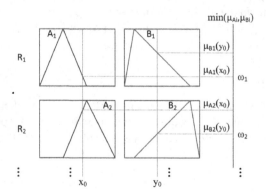

Fig. 7. Determination of ω_i.

5 Design of Fuzzy Speed Control for Wind Turbine Generators

For the aims of this paper, pitch control refers to speed control when involving solely the wind turbine and refers to power control when the whole wind turbine generator is considered. Therefore, the term speed control will be used hereafter to avoid mistakes.

The fuzzy speed controller has three input variables and one output variable. Inputs are the rotating speed error (E), the integral of the speed error (IE), and the wind velocity (WV). The output variable is the control signal (SC). Each input variable is fuzzyfied using various linguistic values defined by fuzzy sets or membership functions. The speed error, E, has three linguistic values: negative error (EN), zero error (EC) and positive error (EP). The corresponding membership functions are shown in Fig. 8. Similarly, the integral of error, IE, also has three linguistic values: integral negative (IN), integral zero (IC) and integral positive (IP). The corresponding membership functions are shown in Fig. 9. For wind velocity, WV, there were defined six linguistic values: low (B), transition (T), high small (AP), high medium (AM), high high (AA) and very high (MA). The membership functions are depicted in Fig. 10.

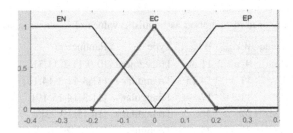

Fig. 8. Membership functions of input variable E.

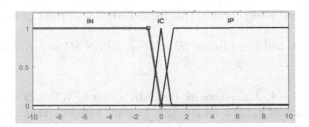

Fig. 9. Membership functions of input variable IE.

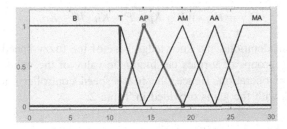

Fig. 10. Membership functions of input variable WV.

The relevance of considering the wind speed as an input variable is that the point of operation of the wind turbine can be referred to it and the zones of the wind speed operating range can be defined as intervals of this input variable. Hence, through fuzzyfication of the wind speed variable it can be implemented a mechanism to detect the point where the wind turbine is operating and to select the PI algorithm that better suits the zone of operation. Another benefit of this approach is that specific PI algorithms can be designed for points of transition. Finally, the action of the fuzzy controller can be extended to those zones not currently covered by conventional controllers, that is, below nominal wind speed and above trip wind speed. Table 1 contains the parameters of the fuzzy sets that define the wind turbine zones of operation.

Table 1. Zones of operation as linguistic values of input variable WV.

Value	WV_{min}	WV_{max}	Type	Parameters
B	0	11.3	Trapezoidal	[0 0 11.3 11.3]
T	11.3	14.15	Triangular	[11.3 11.3 14.15]
AP	11.3	17	Triangular	[11.3 14.15 19]
AM	17	21	Triangular	[14.15 19 23]
AA	21	25	Triangular	[19 23 26.5]
MA	25	28	Trapezoidal	[23 26.5 30 30]

The fuzzy speed controller is a TSK fuzzy system with rules of the form:

$$IF \ \left(WV \ is \ LWV_i \ and \ E \ is \ LE_j \ and \ IE \ is \ LIE_k\right), \ THEN \ SC_i = f_i(Kv_i, Kp_i, Ki_i, Ko_i) \tag{13}$$

where LWV_i for i = 1, 2, ..., 6 are the linguistic values of WV, LE_j for j = 1, 2, 3 are the linguistic values of E, LIE_k for k = 1, 2, 3 are the linguistic values of IE, and $f_i()$ is a control algorithm in terms of the wind speed gain Kv_i, proportional gain Kp_i, integral gain Ki_i, and independent gain Ko_i. Therefore, to implement a PI controller for the i-th zone of operation defined by a linguistic value of the wind speed, LWV_i, the consequents of the rules that are activated in that zone can be defined as:

$$SC_i = Kv_i \cdot WV + Kp_i \cdot E + Ki_i \cdot IE + Ko_i \tag{14}$$

With these considerations, the knowledge base of the fuzzy speed controller consists of 54 rules in groups of 9 rules per linguistic value of the wind speed or equivalently per zone of operation. Hence, the fuzzy speed controller encompasses 6 PI control algorithms with the gains provided in Table 2.

Table 2. Gains of PI control algorithms for each operating zone.

Zone i	LWV_i	Kv_i	Kp_i	Ki_i	Ko_i
1	B	0	0	0	0
2	T	0	0.05	0.17	0
3	AP	0	0.05	0.17	0
4	AM	0	0.03	0.13	0
5	AA	0	0.02	0.09	0
6	MA	0	0.015	0.06	0

6 Full-Scope Speed Control Simulation Experiments

The fuzzy controller is compared to the PI controller when controlling the rotating speed of the model of a 1 kW wind turbine across a large wind speed range. The wind turbine model and both controllers were programmed in Matlab/Simulink. The Fuzzy Logic Toolbox was used to build the fuzzy speed controller.

Wide-range simulations were carried out for wind speeds from 4 m/s through 20 m/s, although the fuzzy speed controller is designed to deal with wind speeds from 0 m/s up to 30 m/s. The rotating speed reference of the fuzzy PI speed controller is set to 400 rpm, which is the nominal rotating speed to obtain 1 kW nominal power. Meanwhile, for the conventional PI controller the reference is set to 400 rpm only in Region III (Fig. 4), in Region II the pitch control signal is set directly to fully closed, 0°, and in Region IV it is set to fully open position, 90°. The fuzzy speed controller nicely deals with all these requirements with specific rules in the knowledge base.

In the PI speed controller, the PI algorithm was tuned at Kp = 0.6 and Ki = 0.5 to be able to deal with most of the wind speed range of operation. On the other hand, in the fuzzy speed controller, the controller gains in the rule consequents of the TSK fuzzy system are those reported in Table 2.

Figure 11 shows results obtained with the fuzzy speed controller for rotating speed (Wr), mechanical power (Pm) and mechanical torque (Tm) for wind speeds from 4 m/s throughout 20 m/s. Figure 12 shows results with the same controller for power coefficient (Cp), pitch angle (B) and tip speed ratio (H) in the same range of wind speeds. As expected, the fuzzy speed controller keeps pitch at zero until wind speed = 11.33 m/s where the speed reference is reached. Thereafter, the pitch angle increases according to the control signal to keep rotating speed and mechanical power at nominal values.

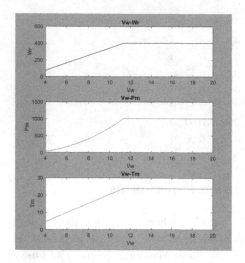

Fig. 11. Wind turbine Wr, Pm and Tm with fuzzy speed controller.

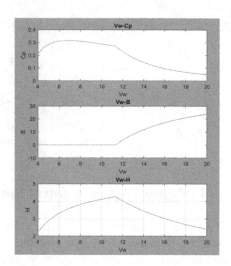

Fig. 12. Wind turbine Cp, B and H with fuzzy speed controller.

Figure 13 shows results obtained with the conventional PI speed controller for rotating speed (Wr), mechanical power (Pm) and mechanical torque (Tm) for wind speeds from 4 m/s throughout 20 m/s. Figure 14 shows results with the same controller for power coefficient (Cp), pitch angle (B) and tip speed ratio (H) in the same range of wind speeds.

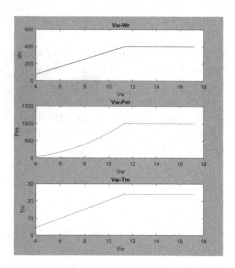

Fig. 13. Wind turbine Wr, Pm and Tm with conventional PI speed controller.

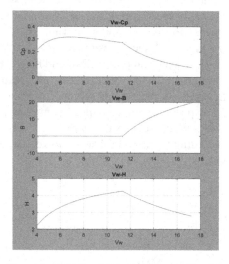

Fig. 14. Wind turbine Cp, B and H with conventional PI speed controller.

Results with both controllers are similar and show the correct behavior. Nevertheless, the simulations with the conventional PI speed controller stop for winds above 18 m/s compared to simulations with winds up to 20 m/s with the fuzzy controller. Therefore, the fuzzy speed controller was able to control in a wider range of wind speeds. Additionally, at the inflexion point at wind speed = 11.33 m/s, the response with the conventional PI controller has a peak which is almost imperceptible due to the large range in the graph vertical axis. The behavior of the controllers at points like that can be seen very easily with the response of the control signal to a step in wind speed. Figure 15 shows the control signal generated by the PI algorithm, and Fig. 16 the control signal provided by the fuzzy system. As shown, fuzzy speed controller deals much better than the conventional PI speed control with points of transition.

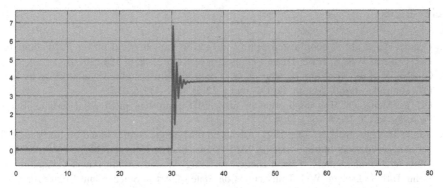

Fig. 15. Control signal issued by PI controller to a step in wind speed.

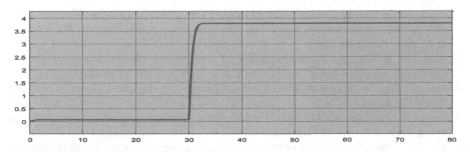

Fig. 16. Control signal issued by fuzzy controller to a step in wind speed.

7 Conclusions

Based on the results of the simulation experiments, it can be said that the fuzzy speed controller has some advantages over the conventional PI speed controller.

The fuzzy speed controller has a much better response in the points of transition. The conventional PI controller presents sudden changes and large oscillations that produce undesired peaks and overshoots in the rotating speed and power. The response of the fuzzy speed control is fast and accurate.

The fuzzy speed controller is able to embrace the zones of wind speed not covered by the conventional PI controller. This has the advantage of not requiring switching between controlled and uncontrolled zones. Thus, requiring only one control strategy for all wind speed range.

Acknowledgements. Mónica Borunda thanks Consejo Nacional de Ciencia y Tecnología (CONACYT) support for her Catedra Research Position with ID 71557, and to Instituto Nacional de Electricidad y Energías Limpias (INEEL) for its hospitality. Gorka Zubeldia thanks Fundación Novia Salcedo and (INEEL) for funding and hosting his stay.

References

1. Uehara, A., et al.: A coordinated control method to smooth wind power fluctuations of a PMSG-based WECS. IEEE Trans. Energy Convers. **26**(2), 550–558 (2016)
2. Civelek, Z., Lüy, M., Cam, E., Barisci, N.: Control of pitch angle of wind turbine by fuzzy PID controller. Intell. Autom. Soft Comput. **22**(3), 463–471 (2015)
3. Qi, Y., Meng, Q.: The application of fuzzy PID control in pitch wind turbine. Energy Procedia **16**(C), 1635–1641 (2012)
4. Van, T.L., Nguyen, T.H., Lee, D.C.: Advanced pitch angle control based on fuzzy logic for variable-speed wind turbine systems. IEEE Trans. Energy Convers. **30**(2), 1–10 (2015)
5. Tong, W.: Fundamentals of wind energy. In: Tong, W. (ed.) Wind Power Generation and Wind Turbine Design. WIT Transactions on State of Art in Science and Engineering, vol. 44, pp. 3–48. WIT Press, Southampton (2010)
6. Tumo-Int: TumoInt 1000 W 3Blades Small Wind Turbine User Manual. Tumo-Int Corporation Limited, Guangzhou (2016)
7. Esparza, U.B.: Diseño y optimización de un sistema de generación aislada de energía eólica orientado a las necesidades de poblaciones sin acceso a la red eléctrica. Universidad Pública de Navarra, Plampona (2011)
8. Ashgar, A.B., Liu, X.: Online estimation of wind turbine tip speed ratio by adaptive neuro-fuzzy algorithm. Int. J. Adv. Comput. Sci. Appl. **9**(3), 28–33 (2018)
9. Heir, S.: Grid Integration of Wind Energy: Onshore and Offshore Conversion Systems. Wiley, Chichester (2014)
10. Garcia, R., Garduno, R.: Modeling a wind turbine synchronous generator. Int. J. Energy Power (IJEP) **2**(3), 64–70 (2013)
11. IEC. Wind energy generation systems - Part 12-1: Power performance measurements of electricity producing wind turbines. Standard: IEC 61400-12-1:2017. Edition 2.0. International Electrotechnical Commission, Switzerland (2017)
12. Qi, J., Liu, Y.: PID control in adjustable-pitch wind turbine system based on fuzzy control. In: 2nd International Conference on Industrial Mechatronics and Automation. IEEE, Wuhan (2010)
13. Yager, R.R., Filev, D.P.: Essentials of Fuzzy Modeling and Control. Wiley, Hoboken (1994)

Hardware Implementation of Karnik-Mendel Algorithm for Interval Type-2 Fuzzy Sets and Systems

Omar Hernández Yáñez$^{(\boxtimes)}$ (ID), Herón Molina Lozano (ID), and Ildar Batyrshin (ID)

Centro de Investigación en Computación, Instituto Politécnico Nacional,
07738 Mexico City, MX, Mexico
omardezlaz@gmail.com, heronmolinalozano@gmail.com, batyr1@gmail.com

Abstract. The trend to accelerate the learning process in neural and fuzzy systems has led to the design of hardware implementations of different types of algorithms. In this paper we explore type-2 fuzzy logic systems acceleration, which can be applied to fuzzy logic control methods, signal processing, etc. Due to the three dimensional membership functions in the input of the system, different algorithms for the output processing stage have been developed. In order to have a fast response in type-2 fuzzy logic systems, in this paper we explore the Karnik-Mendel algorithms (KM), which are used to calculate the centroid at the output processing stage of the interval type-2 fuzzy system, through the application of iterative procedures. Because of the computation complexity of the iterative process, we propose a Hardware implementation of the KM algorithm using a High Level Synthesis tool, making possible to explore different types of implementation in order to obtain a significant reduction in computation time, and a reduction in hardware resources.

Keywords: Karnik-Mendel · Interval type-2 fuzzy systems · High Level Synthesis · FPGA

1 Introduction

Type-2 fuzzy sets are characterized by a three dimensional fuzzy membership functions, unlike a type-1 system where the membership grade is a crisp number in [0, 1]. Such sets can be used in situations where there is uncertainty about the membership grades themselves. When such situation is so undetermined that trouble exists to assign the membership grade even as a crisp number in [0,1], the use of interval fuzzy sets type-2 is proposed. A Fuzzy Logic Systems (FLS) described using at least one type-2 fuzzy set is called a type-2 FLS. Type-1 FLS are unable to handle rule uncertainties, because they use type-1 fuzzy sets that are certain. Type-2 FLS's, are very useful in circumstances where it is difficult to determine an exact membership function, and there are measurement uncertainties. Type-2 FLS are characterized by IF-THEN rules [5], but its antecedent or consequent sets are now of type-2. Interval type-2 FLS, can be

© Springer Nature Switzerland AG 2019
L. Martínez-Villaseñor et al. (Eds.): MICAI 2019, LNAI 11835, pp. 537–545, 2019.
https://doi.org/10.1007/978-3-030-33749-0_43

used when the circumstances are too uncertain to determine exact membership grades such as when the training data is corrupted by, for instance, noise. Similar to a type-1 FLS, a interval type-2 FLS includes a type-2 fuzzyfier, a rule-base, a inference engine and substitutes the defuzzifier by the output processor. The output processor includes a type-reducer and a type-2 defuzzyfier; it generates a type-1 fuzzy set output (from the type reducer) or a crisp number (from the defuzzyfier). Some related work proposes a complete architecture in order to improve efficiency of the complete FLS [8,10]. The Generalized Centroid of an Interval Type-2 Fuzzy Logic System, can be obtained by using KM algorithms (type reduction) which is used for defuzzification [9]. The Karnik Mendel (KM) algorithm lead to approximations of the c_l and c_r values that are defined by [4]:

$$c_l(L) = \frac{\sum_{i=1}^{L} x_i \overline{\mu}_{\tilde{A}}(x_i) + \sum_{i=L+1}^{N} x_i \underline{\mu}_{\tilde{A}}(x_i)}{\sum_{i=1}^{L} \overline{\mu}_{\tilde{A}}(x_i) + \sum_{i=L+1}^{N} \underline{\mu}_{\tilde{A}}(x_i)} \approx c_l \tag{1}$$

$$c_r(R) = \frac{\sum_{i=1}^{R} x_i \underline{\mu}_{\tilde{A}}(x_i) + \sum_{i=R+1}^{N} x_i \overline{\mu}_{\tilde{A}}(x_i)}{\sum_{i=1}^{R} \underline{\mu}_{\tilde{A}}(x_i) + \sum_{i=R+1}^{N} \overline{\mu}_{\tilde{A}}(x_i)} \approx c_r \tag{2}$$

The KM Algorithms 1 and 2 are in charge of locating the switch points [4], the switch point for $c_r(R)$, R, is different from the switch point for $c_l(L)$, L; hence, there are two parts involved in the KM algorithm, one for L and one for R. L and R are the *switch points* that are determined by the KM algorithm. Regardless of what part of the algorithm are used in order to compute the switch points, the final expression for $c_l(L)$ and $c_r(R)$ are Eqs. (1) and (2), respectively.

Algorithm 1. KM Algorithm for $C_r(R)$

$$c_r(R) = \max_{\forall \theta_i \in [\underline{\mu}_i(x_i) \pi_\lambda(x_i)]} \left(\sum_{i=1}^{N} x_i \theta_i / \sum_{i=1}^{N} \theta_i \right)$$

1. Initialize θ_i by setting $\boldsymbol{\theta}_i = \left[\underline{\mu}_{\overline{A}}(x_i) + \overline{\mu}_{\overline{A}}(x_i) \right] / 2$, $i = 1, ..., N$, and then compute

$$c' = c(\theta_1, \ldots, \theta_N) = \sum_{i=1}^{N} x_i \theta_i / \sum_{i=1}^{N} \theta_i$$

2. Find $k(1 \leq k \leq N - 1)$ such that $x_k \leq c' \leq x_{k+1}$
3. Set $\theta_i = \underline{\mu}_{\tilde{i}}(x_i)$ when $i \leq k$, and $\theta_i = \overline{\mu}_{\overline{A}}(x_i)$ when $i \geq k + 1$ and then compute

$$c_r(k) = \frac{\sum_{i=1}^{k} x_i \underline{\mu}_{\overline{A}}(x_i) + \sum_{i=k+1}^{N} x_i \overline{\mu}_{\overline{A}}(x_i)}{\sum_{i=1}^{k} \underline{\mu}_{\overline{A}}(x_i) + \sum_{i=k+1}^{N} \overline{\mu}_{\overline{A}}(x_i)}$$

4. Check if $C_r(k) = C'$. If yes, stop and set $c_r(k) = c_r(R)$ and call k R. If no, go to step
5. Set $C' = C_r(k)$ and go to step 2.

Algorithm 2. KM Algorithm for $C_l(L)$

$$c_l(L) = \min_{\forall \theta_i \in \left[\underline{\mu_{\widetilde{A}}}(x_i) \overline{\mu_{\widetilde{A}}}(x_i) \right]} \left(\sum_{i=1}^{N} x_i \theta_i / \sum_{i=1}^{N} \theta_i \right)$$

1. Initialize θ_i by setting $\boldsymbol{\theta}_i = \left[\underline{\mu_{\widetilde{A}}}(x_i) + \overline{\mu_{\widetilde{A}}}(x_i) \right] / 2$, $i = 1, ..., N$, and then compute

$$c' = c(\theta_1, ..., \theta_N) = \sum_{i=1}^{N} x_i \theta_i / \sum_{i=1}^{N} \theta_i$$

2. Find $k(1 \leq k \leq N - 1)$ such that $x_k \leq c' \leq x_{k+1}$
3. Set $\theta_i = \mu_{\widetilde{i}}(x_i)$ when $i \leq k$, and $\theta_i = \overline{\mu_{\widetilde{A}}}(x_i)$ when $i \geq k + 1$ and then compute

$$c_r(k) = \frac{\sum_{i=1}^{k} x_i \underline{\mu_{\widetilde{A}}}(x_i) + \sum_{i=k+1}^{N} x_i \overline{\mu_{\widetilde{A}}}(x_i)}{\sum_{i=1}^{k} \underline{\mu_{\widetilde{A}}}(x_i) + \sum_{i=k+1}^{N} \overline{\mu_{\widetilde{A}}}(x_i)}$$

4. Check if $C_r(k) = C'$. If yes, stop and set $c_r(k) = c_r(R)$ and call k R. If no, go to step
5. Set $C' = C_r(k)$ and go to step 2.

The growing applications of the FLS have led to the development of hardware implementations [8, 11–13]. To improve the computation cost of this intensive task of iterative procedures we propose the implementation of specialized hardware in order to compute the algorithm. The necessary conditions of hardware to compute the KM algorithm was developed using a high level language description [1], specifically we used Vivado HLS. This tool enables implementing the hardware with C language and exporting the RTL as a Vivado's IP core. The Xilinx Vivado High Level Synthesis (HLS) transforms C++ language code functions into a register transfer level (RTL) implementation IP core that can be synthesized into a Xilinx FPGA [3].

2 Methodology

Sigmoid Interval Membership Functions type-2 were used in order to implement the antecedent functions. Given the interval sigmoid Membership Functions (MF) shown in Fig. 1 the KM algorithm is applied to the membership functions to calculate the centroid of a non-linear surface as a result. Using a Octave script to do the computation the non-linear surface for the type-2 fuzzy system which is shown in Fig. 2. We can see the desired execution of the KM algorithm, hence the function that computes the KM algorithm is the one that will be synthesized by the Vivado HLS tool.

High level synthesis has acquired interest of the scientific community, because it allows to work on a higher level of abstraction making possible to explore different types of digital solutions and implementation methods for hardware architectures [6]. For instance, using HLS, an exploration of all possibilities of design, analysis and performance characteristics of the area can be done, but

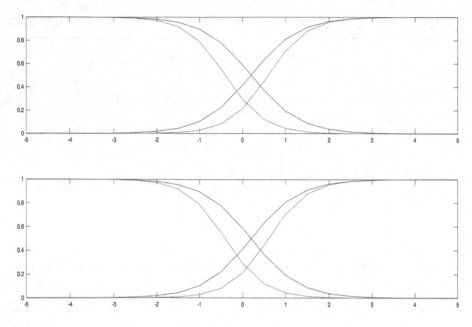

Fig. 1. Sigmoid MF's

most important to implement algorithms on FPGA chips [7]. There were several steps taken in account in order to implement the KM algorithm, first the Octave code must be implemented in C++, some adjustments must be done to the C++ code to meet the requirements of the HLS tool, a test-bench was created for the code is to be tested with a C simulator, after checking that the results are equal to the obtained Octave results, then the code must be synthesized, a high-level synthesis creates the optimal implementation based on default behavior, constraints, and any optimization directives specified.

Optimization directives can be used to modify and control the default behavior of the internal logic and I/O ports [2]. This allowed us to generate variations of the hardware implementation from the same C code finally an RTL Co-Simulation is executed to test the synthesized RTL design. To determine if the design meets the project requirements, it be can reviewed the performance metrics in the synthesis report generated by high-level synthesis. In the HLS tool a variety of parameters must be set for the targeted FPGA, after the process of the Vivado HLS project creation [2], a RTL design is exported as an IP Core, to the Vivado Suite. The final step is to program the FPGA board and check the memory locations that contain the values of the non-linear surface centroid. Also the simulation on the Vivado IDE contains important information for the desired functionality of the algorithm circuitry.

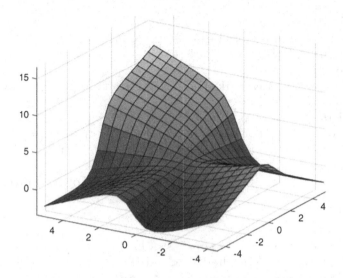

Fig. 2. Non-linear surface results

3 Implementation

Using the Eqs. (1) and (2) a function is created which receives values from the
sigmoid data to compute the KM centroid, this function is the one to be synthesized, to test the algorithm is working as expected, the main function of the
Ocatve script is used as the main test-bench. All of these Octave's script code
must be translated to C++, various directives and adjustments done to the C++
code are the memory allocation on the 1 Port RAM, and the instances limit to
1 function to save area and FPGA resources, to implement the floating point
operations and save area the float point operations are reduced to half point
using 16 bit data length. Vivado HLS provides a half-precision floating-point
data type [3]. This data type provides many of the advantages of standard C
float types but uses fewer hardware resources when synthesized.

Listing 1.1. Test-Bench

```
/*Proof Function (TestBench)*/
int main(void) {
float2 x[n];
float2 y[n];
float2 F[n][n];
linspace(-5, 5, n, x); //Function
linspace(-5, 5, n, y);
cout << endl;
cout << "x=\t";
for (int i = 0; i < n; i++)
        cout << x[i] << "\t";
```

```
cout << endl << "y=\t";
for (int i = 0; i < n; i++)
        cout << y[i] << "\t";
cout << endl << endl;
cout << "Starting_Karnik_Mendel_Algorithm\n" << endl;
for(int r = 0 ; r < n ; r++){
    for(int p = 0 ; p < n ; p++){
        cout << "Iteraction["<<r<<"]["<<p<<"]_=\t";
        F[r][p] = karnik_mendel_T2(x[r], y[p]);
        cout << F[r][p] << endl;
        cout <<"x=\t"<<x[r]<<"\ty=\t"<<y[p]<< endl;
        }
    }
cout << endl;
cout << "*****************" << endl;
cout << "_Program_Finished" << endl;
cout << "*****************" << endl;
return 0;
}
```

In order to check if the code is working a simulation with the updated C code is recommended, to verify the quality of the output using C simulation prior to synthesis. After that the C simulation shows the expected values, the synthesis is executed to obtain the RTL circuit and the Synthesis Report, Vivado HLS automatically creates synthesis reports to help the designer understand the performance of the implementation, it displays the amount of hardware resources required to implement the design on the resources available in the FPGA.

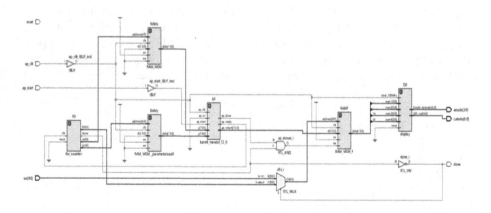

Fig. 3. RTL diagram

If a C test bench was added to the project, we can use it to verify that the RTL is functionally identical to the original C. The C test bench verifies the output from the top-level function for synthesis and returns zero to the top-level function *main()* if the RTL is functionally identical [2]. After the RTL Co-Simulation is launched and passed, the final step in the Vivado HLS flow is to export the RTL design as a block of Intellectual Property (IP) which can be used by other tools in the Xilinx design flow. The RTL design can be packaged into the following output formats: IP Catalog formatted IP for use with the Vivado Design Suite. The RTL diagram is shown in Fig. 3, the Ip core with the KM circuitry is shown as a black box, with the inputs and outputs that were defined in the C++ code. To sweep throw the values of the memory (X and Y axis values), the implementation of a counter is added to the main module, the HLS synthesized RTL design computes the sigmoid MF's that will be the input of the KM circuitry, some Finite State Machines are inferred by the HLS tool because of the use of for loops.

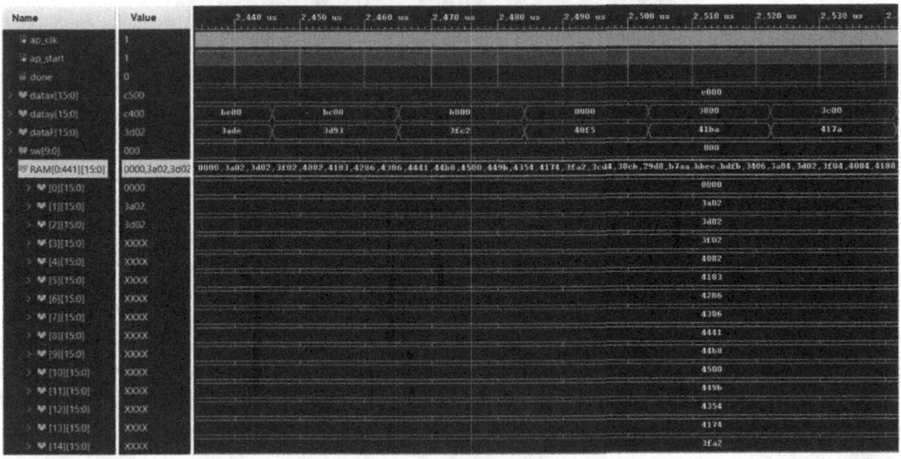

Fig. 4. FPGA's Simulation of the KM algorithm

Finally the pin assignment is done, the memory location containing the Non-linear surface point result is displayed by the 7 segment displays and the clock pin is assigned to the single 100 MHz oscillator included in the board. Once the circuit is completed, to identify possible errors and the circuitry behavior a test-bench file is created in order to run a simulation. Figure 4 shows the RAM memory where the non-linear surface data is stored as half-point (16 bits) data values, once the simulation is done the comparison between the matlab results and the RAM of the simulation is done showing that the values computed by the described hardware are as they were expected, the next step is to program the FPGA in order to see the final test.

Table 1. Time comparison Table

Process	FPGA	Octave
KM_T2	7.465 mS	492.4 mS
KM	17.73 μS	1.14 mS

Fig. 5. FPGA Circuit Board where the KM algorithm was implemented

4   Conclusions

The final results show the algorithm working in the FPGA platform as seen in Fig. 5, also a comparative time Table 1 shows the improvements on the KM algorithm in Octave vs. the FPGA board. As it can be seen the implementation of the KM algorithm shows an improvement in computation of the values of Eqs. (1) and (2). The use of the HLS allows to explore different types of implementation of the KM algorithm, improving the computation time of the algorithm, decreasing the computation cost, and with the proper configuration of the HLS directives a reduction of the FPGA resources. It also allows architecture exploration in the context of hardware design for explainable or interpretable hardware fuzzy systems, where specialized hardware processing units can improve efficiently the computation time, resources, and energy consumption of the applications. Any area where a demanding application of fuzzy systems is involved, dedicated hardware architectures represents an opportunity to get results faster and with fewer computation resources due to the specialized hardware.

Acknowledgments. The research partially supported by project SIP 20196374, Instituto Politécnico Nacional, México.

References

1. Lakshminarayana, A., Ahuja, S., Shukla, S.: Coprocessor design space exploration using high level synthesis. In: 11th International Symposium on Quality Electronic Design (ISQED), pp. 879–884. IEEE, San Jose (2010)

2. XILINX, Vivado Design Suite Tutorial, High-Level Synthesis, UG871 (v 2014.1) (2014)
3. XILINX, Vivado Design Suite User Guide High-Level Synthesis, UG902 (v2017.4) (2018)
4. Mendel, J., Hagras, H., Tan, W.W., Melek, W.W., Ying, H.: Introduction to Type-2 Fuzzy Logic Control: Theory and Applications, 1st edn. Wiley, Piscataway (2014)
5. Castillo, O., Melin, P., Kacprzyk, J., Pedrycz, W.: Type-2 Fuzzy Logic: Theory and Applications. SFSC, vol. 223. Springer, Heidelberg (2008). https://doi.org/10.1007/978-3-540-76284-3
6. Zhang, C., Li, P., Sun, G., Guan, Y., Xiao, B., Cong, J.: Optimizing FPGA-based accelerator design for deep convolutional neural networks. In: The 2015 ACM/SIGDA International Symposium on Field-Programmable Gate Arrays, FPGA 2015, pp. 161–170. ACM, New York (2015)
7. Li, H., Ye, W.: Efficient implementation of FPGA based on Vivado high level synthesis. In: 2016 2nd IEEE International Conference on Computer and Communications (ICCC), pp. 2810–2813. IEEE (2016)
8. Melgarejo, R.M.A., Peña-Reyes, C.A.: Hardware architecture and FPGA implementation of a type-2 fuzzy system. In: Proceedings of the 14th ACM Great Lakes symposium on VLSI, GLSVLSI 2004, pp. 458–461. ACM, New York (2004)
9. Mendel, J.M.: Advances in Type-2 Fuzzy Sets and Systems, Theory and Applications. SFSC, vol. 301. Springer, Heidelberg (2013). https://doi.org/10.1007/978-1-4614-6666-6
10. Juang, C.F., Jang, W.S.: A type-2 neural fuzzy system learned through type-1 fuzzy rules and its FPGA-based hardware implementation. Appl. Soft Comput. 18, 302–313 (2014)
11. Kandel, A., Langholz, G. (eds.): Fuzzy Hardware: Architectures and Applications, 1st edn. Springer, New York (1998). https://doi.org/10.1007/978-1-4615-4090-8
12. Tellez-Velazquez, A., et al.: A feasible genetic optimization strategy for parametric interval type-2 fuzzy logic systems. Int. J. Fuzzy Syst. 20(1), 318–338 (2018)
13. Batyrshin, I.Z., Rudas, I.J., Villa, L.A., Cortés, A.P.: On the monotone sum of basic t-norms in the construction of parametric families of digital conjunctors for fuzzy systems with reconfigurable logic. Knowl. Based Syst. 38, 27–36 (2013)

Designing Fuzzy Artificial Organic Networks Using Sliding-Mode Control

Pedro Ponce[1]([⊠]) [iD], Antonio Rosales[1], Arturo Molina[1],
and Raja Ayyanar[2]

[1] Tecnologico de Monterrey, Escuela de Ingenieria y Ciencias,
Mexico City, Mexico
{pedro.ponce,antonio.rosales,armolina}@tec.mx
[2] Arizona State University, Tempe, AZ, USA
rayyanar@asu.edu

Abstract. Since direct-current (DC) drives are commonly used electric drives, it is imperative to improve their operation under sudden torque-load disturbances. Several industrial applications work under torque-load changes that strongly affect the speed response of the motor, thus deteriorating the performance of the DC drive. On the other hand, discontinuous sliding-mode control (SMC) ensures robustness against disturbances and changes in parameters but has certain drawbacks, such as chattering. In this paper, a fuzzy-logic controller (FLC) based on artificial organic networks is proposed to adjust the control signal of the SMC. This control provides a smooth signal that reduces chatter. The Lyapunov stability of the DC motor driven by the proposed SMC with a fuzzy organic controller is tested and stability margins are computed. The proposed controller is validated via simulation results showing an excellent DC-drive performance. In fact, the fuzzy artificial organic controller can adjust the command signal to improve the transitory response of the DC drive. The proposed controller achieves a good performance for speed controllers using brushless DC motors.

Keywords: Artificial organic networks · Artificial hydrocarbon networks · Intelligent control · Sliding mode control · DC motor

1 Introduction

1.1 Electric Drives

Electric drives based on brushed motors have been used in various industrial applications such as manufacturing systems. The general classification of direct-current (DC) drives is shown below:

- DC drives with brushed motors;
- DC drives without brushless motors.

Both structures require a speed controller to send the command signal to the power-electronics stage that provides modulated voltage to the DC motor to reach the reference speed. Electric-DC drives that include PID controllers can achieve a good speed

© Springer Nature Switzerland AG 2019
L. Martínez-Villaseñor et al. (Eds.): MICAI 2019, LNAI 11835, pp. 546–556, 2019.
https://doi.org/10.1007/978-3-030-33749-0_44

response when they operate under bounded load-torque disturbances. However, if unbounded load-torque disturbances suddenly appear, the PID controller will not be able to maintain a reference speed. Thus, the speed reference suffers considerable degradation. As a result, it is crucial to design new control strategies that improve the speed response under perturbed load disturbances. The block diagram of a DC drive has three main parts, the controller, the power-electronics stage, and the DC brushed motor (see Fig. 1). Typically, the structure of the power-electronics stage in a brushed DC-drive motor is based on a DC-DC converter (H-Bridge). Several techniques have been implemented on speed-control systems for DC drives.

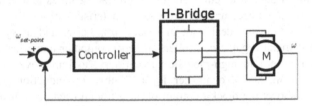

Fig. 1. Block diagram of a DC drive.

Implementation of sliding-mode control (SMC) provides insensitivity against matched/bounded disturbance/uncertainties while ensuring finite-time convergence of the sliding variable to zero. SMC's advantages come with a drawback, namely chattering (high-frequency oscillations with finite amplitude), which is an undesirable phenomenon that causes fatigue or damage to actuators [1]. There exist proposals to attenuate chattering while preserving the benefits of SMC; one approach is designing variable-SMC gains to replace the uninterrupted-control gain (high gain most of the time) by fluctuating gains to decrease the control effort. Commonly, the gain decreases when there are no disturbances/uncertainties or state variations, and increases otherwise. Fuzzy control is a noteworthy technique used to attenuate chattering in SMC systems. In particular, a smooth gain for SMC is computed via fuzzy logic following some membership functions that soften the discontinuity of the SMC. On the other hand, implementation of artificial organic networks (ONs) as a set of fuzzy-inference systems is useful when uncertainties and imprecise and noisy data are presented to the physical system [2]. In this paper, a novel robust controller for a DC motor, composed of a conventional sliding-mode controller and a fuzzy artificial organic network, is presented. The proposed controller ensures regulation of the velocity, despite the presence of load disturbances. Furthermore, the control signal is smooth, since the gains of the SMC are computed via an artificial ONs. Using an extension of the Nyquist stability criteria, the stability and stability margins of the DC motor controlled by SMC-ON are computed.

2   Intelligent Control Systems

2.1   Artificial Organic Networks

Artificial organic controllers (AOCs) are ensembles of type-1 fuzzy-inference systems with artificial hydrocarbon networks. In particular, the artificial-hydrocarbon-network (AHN) technique is a supervised-machine-learning method aimed at extracting information and modeling based on data; it is inspired by the nature of chemical carbon networks [2]. This method simulates artificial carbon nets in which data are packaged into units of information, namely molecules, so as to preserve similar characteristics among encapsulated data. Molecules enclose both data features and behaviors. Thus, stability, robustness, and accuracy are present characteristics in AHNs. Thus, artificial organic controllers typically deal with uncertain, imprecise, and noisy data. Several applications of artificial organic controllers include computer-numerical position control for a two-axis tool in high-precision machinery, a liquid-level controller in a coupled-tanks system, and a controller for a doubly-fed induction-generator wind turbine. Figure 2 shows the block diagram of an artificial organic controller. Roughly speaking, input data are treated as fuzzy implications, and consequent values are represented as packages or molecules of information. The latter units concentrate on the vagueness of information that allows an expert opinion to be combined with real data. In particular, artificial organic controllers use the so-called fuzzy-molecular inference system (FMI), which consists of three steps: fuzzification, fuzzy-inference engine, and molecular-defuzzification.

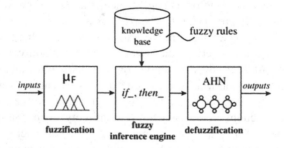

Fig. 2. Block diagram of an artificial organic controller.

The fuzzification step receives an input x known as the linguistic variable, which is mapped to a set of fuzzy sets, F_i, using its membership-function representation, $\mu_{F_i}(x)$, with range [0, 1], as shown in (1):

$$\mu_{F_i} : x \rightarrow [0, 1] \tag{1}$$

Specifically, the membership function represents the degree of belonging of x to the fuzzy set F_i.

Then, the fuzzy-inference-engine step receives the membership value of the inputs. A fuzzy-implication operation is performed to obtain a fuzzy consequent value, y_p. This implication can be written as a fuzzy rule, R_p, as expressed in (2):

$$R_p : if\ x_1 \in A_1 \wedge \ldots \wedge x_m \in A_m,\ then\ y_p = \varphi_j(\mu_\Delta(x_1, \ldots, x_m)) \tag{2}$$

Here, T-norm (Ponce et al. 2013) is used as the min function and the consequent value, y_p, is represented as the associated behavior, φ_j, of a molecular unit (see below). Then, the molecular behavior, φ_j, is evaluated using the result of the T-norm, $\mu_\Delta(x_1, \ldots, x_m)$, as suggested in [2]:

In artificial hydrocarbon networks, a set of interlinked molecules is called a compound. A molecule, M_j, simulates a chemical molecule made of one carbon atom and a set of up to four hydrogen atoms. This configuration is related to the behavior (functional) of the molecule, φ_j, as described by (3)

$$\varphi_j(s) = \sigma \prod_{i=1}^{k \leq 4} (s - h_i), \tag{3}$$

where $\sigma \in \Re$ and $h_i \in C$ are parameters in the functional, simulating the carbon atom and the hydrogen atoms attached, respectively. k represents the number of hydrogen atoms in the molecule and s is the input value to that molecule.

Moreover, if the arrangement of molecules in the compound is serial, then it is called a linear compound. If all the molecules in the compound considered the maximum number of hydrogen values attached – as in chemistry – then it is called a "saturated compound". To this end, artificial organic controllers use a linear and saturated compound to compute consequent values, as suggested in [2]. Figure 3 shows a compound associated with the AOC.

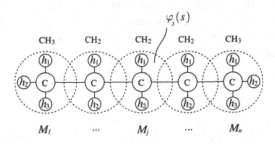

Fig. 3. Representation of a linear and saturated compound used in artificial organic controllers.

Lastly, the defuzzification step uses the center-of-gravity approach to compute the crisp output value y as denoted by (4):

$$y = \frac{\sum_p \mu_\Delta(x_1, \ldots, x_m) y_p}{\sum_p \mu_\Delta(x_1, \ldots, x_m)}. \tag{4}$$

As shown in Fig. 2, a knowledge base is required for the fuzzy-inference-engine step. In particular, the knowledge base represents the set of fuzzy rules, R. It should be remarked that the output variables have to be partitioned in n linguistic units that correspond to a linear and saturated compound made of n molecules. The full description of this intelligent-controller scheme can be found in [2]. The dynamics of the DC brushed motor are represented by the equations [3] and [4]:

$$\begin{bmatrix} \dot{x}_1 \\ \dot{x}_2 \end{bmatrix} = \begin{bmatrix} 0 & 1 \\ -\left(\frac{K^2 + Rb}{LJ}\right) & -\left(\frac{Lb + RJ}{LJ}\right) \end{bmatrix} \begin{bmatrix} x_1 \\ x_2 \end{bmatrix} + \begin{bmatrix} 0 \\ \frac{K}{LJ} \end{bmatrix} u,$$
$$y = \begin{bmatrix} 1 & 0 \end{bmatrix} \begin{bmatrix} x_1 \\ x_2 \end{bmatrix},$$

(5)

where x_1 is the angular velocity and x_2 is the acceleration. The output of the system is y, the control input is u, and the parameters of the motor are damping ratio b, shaft inertia J, speed constant K, armature inductance L, and armature resistance R.

The control objective is to regulate the velocity x_1 to a desired velocity x_{1d}. Choose the sliding surface

$$\sigma = \dot{e} + \alpha e$$

(6)

where $e = x_{1d} - x_1$ and $\alpha > 0$ is a constant. The sliding-mode dynamics are

$$\dot{\sigma} = -\left[-\left(\frac{K^2 + Rb}{LJ}\right) x_1 - \left(\frac{Lb + RJ}{LJ}\right) x_2 + \frac{K}{LJ} u \right]$$

(7)

The relative degree of the DC-motor dynamics in Eq. (5) with respect to σ in Eq. (6) is 1, as can be verified from Eq. (7). Therefore, the implementation of a conventional sliding-mode control (SMC) drives $\sigma \to 0$ in finite time, despite the presence of bounded disturbance/uncertainties [1]. Once the dynamics of a DC motor are on the sliding surface $\sigma = 0$, they are reduced to $\dot{e} = -\alpha e$, where the parameters of the system do not take part. Then, the performance of the controller is insensible to any uncertainty or parameter variation.

Proposition 1. The conventional SMC law

$$u = \frac{LJ}{K} \left[\left(\frac{K^2 + Rb}{LJ}\right) x_1 + \left(\frac{Lb + RJ}{LJ} + \alpha\right) x_2 + M \text{sign}(\sigma) \right]$$

(8)

with $M > 0$ provides the Lyapunov stability of the sliding dynamics in Eq. (7) while ensuring finite-time convergence of $\sigma \to 0$, guaranteeing that the regulation error $= x_{1d} - x_1$ goes to zero asymptotically. Furthermore, when the parameters of the DC motor are unknown, the control objective is to ensure choosing $M > \xi/b$, with $\xi = \left|\left(\frac{K^2 + Rb}{LJ}\right)x_1 + \left(\frac{Lb + RJ}{LJ} + \alpha\right)x_2\right|$ and b being a known constant.

Proof,

Consider the well-known Lyapunov function [1]

$$V = \frac{1}{2}\sigma^2 \qquad (9)$$

The derivative of V throughout the trajectories of the system in Eq. (5) is

$$\dot{V} = \sigma\dot{\sigma} = -\sigma\left[-\left(\frac{K^2 + Rb}{LJ}\right)x_1 - \left(\frac{Lb + RJ}{LJ} + \alpha\right)x_2 + \frac{K}{LJ}u\right] \qquad (10)$$

To provide Lyapunov stability, the condition $\dot{V} < 0$ must be satisfied. Rewriting Eq. (10) as

$$-|\sigma|\left[-\left(\frac{K^2 + Rb}{LJ}\right)x_1 - \left(\frac{Lb + RJ}{LJ} + \alpha\right)x_2 + \frac{K}{LJ}u\right] < 0 \qquad (11)$$

and replacing the control law,

$$u = \frac{LJ}{K}\left[\left(\frac{K^2 + Rb}{LJ}\right)x_1 + \left(\frac{Lb + RJ}{LJ} + \alpha\right)x_2 + M\mathrm{sign}(\sigma)\right],$$

in Eq. (11), we obtain $-|\sigma|M < 0$. Then, the control u in Eq. (8) provides Lyapunov stability of the dynamics in Eq. (7) for any $M > 0$.

The finite-time-convergence property is verified when the inequality

$$\dot{V} \leq -\mu V^{\frac{1}{2}} = -\frac{\mu}{\sqrt{2}}|\sigma|; \quad \mu > 0 \qquad (12)$$

is satisfied. Considering inequality $-|\sigma|M < 0$ and Eq. (12), one obtains that $M = \frac{\mu}{\sqrt{2}}$. Therefore, any $M > 0$ also ensures finite-time convergence of the sliding variable to zero.

If the parameters of the DC motor are unknown and the SMC law is $u = M\mathrm{sign}(\sigma)$, the inequality (11) is rewritten as

$$-|\sigma|\left[-\left(\frac{K^2 + Rb}{LJ}\right)x_1 - \left(\frac{Lb + RJ}{LJ} + \alpha\right)x_2 + \frac{K}{LJ}u\right] < -|\sigma|[-\xi + bM],$$

where $\xi = \left|\left(\frac{K^2 + Rb}{LJ}\right)x_1 + \left(\frac{Lb + RJ}{LJ} + \alpha\right)x_2\right|$ and b is a known constant. Then, choosing $M > \xi/b$ ensures Lyapunov stability. $\qquad \square$

Note that Proposition 1 establishes Lyapunov stability, as well as the existence of sliding motion. In Sect. 4, frequency-domain analysis of a DC motor driven by SMC

Table 1. Relationship between the desired speed and the SMC gain.

ω_d (P.U)	0.05	0.25	0.5	0.75	1
M	−1399	−1423	−2567	−2989	−3890

with FLC is applied to compute stability margins. To attenuate chattering, which is proportional to the value of gain M, a fuzzy artificial organic network (AON) is implemented to calculate M as a function of the desired speed. Table 1 shows the values of gain M for different angular-speed references.

The structure of the fuzzy artificial organic networks was designed according to [2]. This network has three main parts, as explained below.

Step 1. Fuzzification. Five triangular membership functions were defined to map the crisp input (shaft speed) to a fuzzy value; those membership functions are described in Table 2. The parameters of each function were determined experimentally. Since the membership functions have triangular shapes, only three parameters are needed to describe each one.

Step 2. Evaluation of linguistic rules. To evaluate the linguistic rules, the min operator was implemented and the knowledge base is presented in Table 2 The output

Table 2. Description of the membership functions for the input (shaft speed).

Linguistic label	Parameters of triangular membership functions
'NG1'	[−0.4, 0.0537, 0.141]
'NG2'	[0.1, 0.25421, 0.405]
'C'	[0.3651, 0.5085, 0.6436]
'PG2'	[0.5233,0.75849,1.01]
'PG1'	[0.7221,0.99841,1.009]

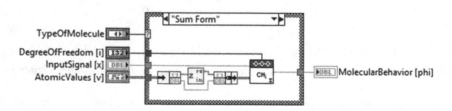

Fig. 4. Molecular behavior programmed in LabView

Table 3. Knowledge-based linguistic rules

Linguistic rules based on antecedents and consequences
Rule 1: if shaft speed is NG1 then the output is N1
Rule 2: if shaft speed is NG2 then the output is N2
Rule 3: if shaft speed is C then the output is CC
Rule 4: if shaft speed is PG2 then the output is P2
Rule 5: if shaft speed is PG1 then the output is P1

Table 4. Knowledge-based linguistic labels and segments rules

Linguistic label	Segment [0, 4]
N1	From 0 to 1.3
N2	From 1.3 to 1.4
CC	From 1.4 to 2.5
P2	From 2.5 to 2.9
P1	From 2.9 to 3.9

 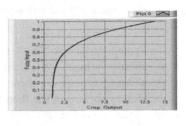

Fig. 5. General primitive-molecule parameters (a) and the relationship between the input and output of the primitive molecule.

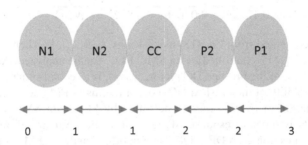

Fig. 6. Artificial organic molecules.

is described using artificial organic networks, which provide a unique characteristic for finding the crisp value. In addition, the sliding-mode controller is delimited according with the description of the molecules. Five linguistic labels for each primitive molecule were implemented (N1, N2, CC, P2, and P1) (Figs. 5, 6 and Tables 3, 4).

Step 3. Defuzzification. to generate crisp values, five similar CH-primitive molecules were used (N1, N2, CC, P2, and P1). Since the relationship between the input and the output required an increment of the value M when the shaft speed rotor increment (see Table 1), it is adequate to use the primitive CH molecule, which promotes an increment in the crisp output. Moreover, this primitive molecule can be very simply deployed in the speed loop shown in Fig. 4.

3   Stability Analysis of Fuzzy Sliding-Mode Controllers

3.1   Stability Analysis of a DC Motor

From the dynamics of the DC brushed motor in Eq. (1) and the parameters this motor, as given in Table 5, the next transfer function can be obtained as

$$W_m(s) = \frac{1.95}{0.1875s^2 + 0.07696s + 3.802} \tag{13}$$

To regulate the speed of the DC motor in the desired set point $x_{1d} = 1 [\text{sec.}^{-1}]$, a fuzzy-SMC is implemented with a sliding surface $\sigma = e + 0.1\dot{e}$, and the following rules:

- Rule A: if the sliding surface is N2, then the output is U_{P2};
- Rule B: if the sliding surface is N1, then the output is U_{P1};
- Rule C: if the sliding surface is Z, then the output is U_z;
- Rule D: if the sliding surface is P1, then the output is U_{N1};
- Rule E: if the sliding surface is P2, then the output is U_{N2}.

Here, $N_1 = -P_1 = -0.01$, $N_2 = -P_2 = -10$, $Z = 0$, $U_{N1} = -U_{P1} = -6$, $U_{N2} = -U_{P2} = -12$, and $U_Z = 0$.

Figure 9 is the graphical interpretation of the HB equation,

$$\frac{1.95}{0.1875s^2 + 0.07696s + 3.802} = -\frac{1}{N(A)},$$

where $N(A)$ is computed from Eq. (13) using Rules A, B, ..., E. Then, the stability of the DC motor in Eq. (1), controlled by an SMC-FLC, can be analyzed. As can be seen, the transfer function of the brushed DC motor, $W_m(s)$, is a second-order system. Hence, measuring the stability of the brushed DC motor in terms of PM and GM, we conclude that the gain margin of the DC motor controlled by FLC with SMC is theoretically infinite, since its frequency response, $W_m(j\omega)$, is in the third and fourth quadrants, avoiding any intersection with DF $-1/N(A)$. On other hand, the PM for the DC motor controlled by SMC-FLC can be computed following the graphical interpretation of Fig. 9, where it is observed that PM = 88.9°.

An equivalent delay to the PM can be computed as $T = PM/\omega_{PM}$, where $\omega_{PM} = 1.49 \times 10^3$ is the frequency associated with the point where the PM is measured, see Fig. 9. Then, the DC motor described by the transfer function in Eq. (13) is stable for any delay of $T < 0.001$ s.

A simulation in Matlab-Simulink was implemented to verify the stability of the PM (see the block diagram in Fig. 8). The results are presented in Figs. 10 and 11. Figure 10 shows the simulation results for the DC motor driven by SMC-FLC, adding a delay of $T = 0.0005$ s. It is apparent that the performance of the controller remains stable, since $T = 0.0005 < 0.001$ s (Fig. 7).

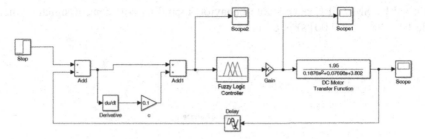

Fig. 7. Block diagram of the Simulink-Matlab simulation

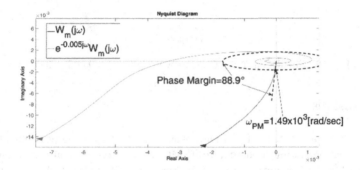

Fig. 8. Graphical interpretation of the solution of the harmonic-balance equation

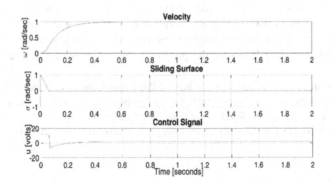

Fig. 9. Simulation of the DC motor with delay $T = 0.0005 < 0.001$ s

Increasing the delay to $T = 0.005 > 0.001$ s, the DC motor's behavior is affected by emerging oscillations in the system, as presented in the simulation results in Fig. 10, as well as in the graphical interpretation presented in Fig. 9. From the perspective of linear-systems theory, the behavior in Fig. 11 is unstable, since sustained oscillations appear, even if the control input becomes discontinuous. Stability-margin analysis, supported by the simulation results in Figs. 10 and 11, shows that DC motors controlled by SMC-FLC have stable behavior, including soft control signals, when a stable PM (88.9° ≈ 0.001 s) is ensured.

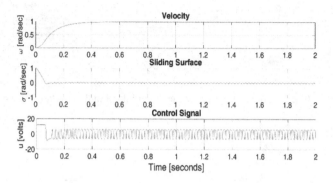

Fig. 10. Simulation of a DC motor with delay $T = 0.005 > 0.001$ s

4 Conclusions

The operation of a brushless DC motor was improved by the implementation of a controller based on sliding-mode control (SMC) and fuzzy artificial organic networks. The proposed controller improved the robustness against load disturbances, as well as speed regulation, compared with conventional PID controllers. Furthermore, the proposed control law smoothly attenuated chattering in SMC systems. The Lyapunov stability of the DC motor with the proposed control was tested. A method for obtaining the robustness metrics (phase and gain margins) of a system controlled by SMC with fuzzy control was presented, and then the phase and gain margins of the DC motor were computed. The advantages of the proposed controller were validated.

Acknowledgment. This research is a product of the Project 266632 "Laboratorio Binacional para la Gestión Inteligente de la Sustentabilidad Energética y la Formación Tecnológica" ["Bi-National Laboratory on Smart Sustainable Energy Management and Technology Training"], funded by the CONACYT SENER Fund for Energy Sustainability (Agreement: S0019201401).

References

1. Utkin, V., Guldner, J., Shi, J.: Sliding Mode Control in Electro-Mechanical Systems. Taylor and Francis Group, Florida (2009)
2. Ponce-Espinosa, H., Ponce-Cruz, P., Molina, A.: Artificial organic networks. In: Ponce-Espinosa, H., Ponce-Cruz, P., Molina, A. (eds.) Artificial Organic Networks. SCI, vol. 521, pp. 53–72. Springer, Cham (2014). https://doi.org/10.1007/978-3-319-02472-1_3
3. Hsu, C.F., Lee, B.K.: FPGA-based adaptive PID control of a DC motor driver via sliding-mode approach. Expert Syst. Appl. **38**, 11866–11872 (2011)
4. Shtessel, Y., Edwards, C., Fridman, L., Levant, A.: Sliding Mode Control and Observation. Birkhäuser, New York (2014)

Performance of Human Proposed Equations, Genetic Programming Equations, and Artificial Neural Networks in a Real-Time Color Labeling Assistant for the Colorblind

Martín Montes Rivera[1]([✉]) [iD], Alejandro Padilla[2],
Julio César Ponce Gallegos[2], Juana Canul-Reich[3],
Alberto Ochoa Zezzatti[3], and Miguel A. Meza de Luna[2]

[1] Universidad Politécnica de Aguascalientes, Aguascalientes, Mexico
martin.montes@upa.edu.mx
[2] Universidad Autónoma de Aguascalientes, Aguascalientes, Mexico
apadilla2004@hotmail.com, julk_cpg@hotmail.com,
meza_capacitacion@hotmail.com
[3] Universidad Juárez Autónoma de Tabasco, Tabasco, Mexico
{juana.canul, alberto.ochoa}@uacj.mx

Abstract. Sight is the most critical sense because of its worth in human life; humans use it to guarantee their safeness, to move around, to identify persons, objects, among other activities. The eyes use two kinds of cells in visual perception, rods for luminosity and cones for color. Colorblindness is a mild disability that affects color perception in close to 10% of the world population. Partial solutions for the colorblind include glasses that increase the distance between colors, avoiding confusing regions when suffering mild colorblindness. Other alternatives include special symbols for labeling objects and text descriptions, but there is not a definitive solution. Alternatively, computer vision has developed some assistants for the colorblind based on color classification, including applications that highlight confusing regions or identify colors selected by the user. Recently, artificial intelligence, together with parallel computing, has become a good alternative in vision assistance, but there are several alternatives with different schemes for performing color classification, those include heuristically tuned human proposed equations, computer-generated equations, and Artificial Neural Networks (ANN's), among others. In this paper, a labeling color assistant for the colorblind is developed using color classification with heuristically (GA and PSO algorithms) tuned proposed equations, genetic programming equations, and ANN's. As a result of this research, is determined the best structure for color classification, based on the accuracy and processing time in a CUDA kernel, so that be possible a real-time labeling system for the colorblind with full high definition images.

Keywords: Colorblindness · Color classification · Genetic programming · Artificial Neural Networks · Particle Swarm Optimization · Genetic Algorithm · Parallel computing

© Springer Nature Switzerland AG 2019
L. Martínez-Villaseñor et al. (Eds.): MICAI 2019, LNAI 11835, pp. 557–575, 2019.
https://doi.org/10.1007/978-3-030-33749-0_45

1   Introduction

The most important sense for humans is the sight because of the several activities that involve it; humans use it to guarantee its safeness, identify healthy food, recognize objects, move around, interpreting signals (safety signals or traffic signals), reading, writing, driving, among others [1–3].

There are several elements involved in the sense of sight, but basically, it starts with the perception of signals in the eyes, then, those signals go to the brain through nerves for being interpreted as images [4, 5].

The eyes perceive light signals with two kinds of cells: rods that perceive the length of the wave light or the quantity of light and the cones that identify the frequency in the wave light or the color; perceived with three possible variations of cones (red, green, and blue cones), that produce the entire visible spectrum of colors [6].

Unfortunately, close to 10% of the world population suffers from a mild disability called Colorblindness, that causes a diminished or absent perception of color. Color-blindness is classified depending on its severity in Anomalous Trichromacy, Dichromacy, and Monochromacy; all of them are subdivided into categories depending on the cone with difficulties [6].

On the one hand, there are some partial solutions for the colorblind with tangible elements, including glasses like those distributed by Encrhoma^{TM} that increase the distance between colors, avoiding confusing regions, but this kind of solution only works for persons with mild Anomalous Trichromacy [6].

Other tangible alternatives used in severe Colorblindness, include special symbols for labeling objects like those proposed by ColorAdd^{TM} (Table 1), these codes are capable of identifying different colors and its luminosity, but despite these possible solutions, there is not a definitive recognized [7].

Table 1. Symbols of ColorADD^{TM} in [7] for the real-time labeling assistant here proposed

Symbol						
Color	Red	Orange	Yellow	Green	Blue	Purple

On the other hand, computer vision has coined other partial solutions using digital cameras for obtaining input data as the eyes do. These solutions include color transformations that change scenes for the colorblind [8–10], assistants that highlight confusing regions [11–13], applications that identify the color of a selected pixel [14], and simulators for increase consciousness about colorblindness [15].

In recent years, Artificial Intelligence (AI) has produced significant advances related to computer vision that could help the colorblind; these include object recognition, image segmentation, image improvement, among others. However, the success of this approach has occasioned that sometimes, people use overparameterized structures instead of more straightforward tasks, consuming unrequired computer power, when classical techniques have enough efficiency for the required application [2, 16, 17].

Examples of techniques that waste extra computing are the AI color classification applications that initially perform a color transformation from native spaces obtained directly from the digital cameras (RGB and Y'UV) to simpler spaces for color classification (HSV, YCbCr, CIELab, among others), which are not required with the AI today techniques [18, 19].

In addition, structure variations in the obtained solutions could make more efficient an AI technique instead of another, for example, human-generated equations are commonly the shortest structures and its numerical parameters are tuned with numerical optimization algorithms like Genetic Algorithms (GA's), Memetic Algorithms (MA), Particle Swarm Optimization (PSO), Ant Colony Optimization (ACO), among others [20]. In general, the use of human proposed equations tuned with a metaheuristic algorithm reaches up to 92% efficiency in color classification, as described in [21–23] and its shortness could help to develop a real-time labeling system for the colorblind.

Alternatively, is possible to use general representations adapted with numerical optimization for modeling the required behavior or application, examples of these are linear regression, quadratic regression, polynomial regression, fuzzy inference systems, or ANN's, among others. Despite its capabilities, these general representations commonly have specific restrictions that could make inefficient its behavior, for example, ANN's with multiple hidden layers must wait for all its previous signals to get its final output [24]. The classification and identification of colors in different applications with ANN's reaches up to 92.18% efficiency in test evaluation and 99.18% in training stage as described in [25–27].

A more complicated situation appears when there is not a human expression for solving a specific problem, instead is possible that AI techniques generate them automatically with automatic programming algorithms, like Genetic Programming (GP) or Particle Swarm Programming (PSP) [28, 29]. The use of GP in color classification reaches up to 99.5%, but this measure comes from the training stage, and there is no data about test results [30, 31]. To the best knowledge of the authors, there are no other reported works tackling color segmentation using GP.

Despite that an AI structure could has a better accuracy compared with others, it is possible that it be so complicated for real-time implementation because there is a limitation in computer power or the input data is enormous, for example in Full High Definition (FHD) images. Then will be required another alternative maybe with lower accuracy but being high parallelizable.

AI capabilities are better exploited today with powerful computers and the use of Graphic Processor Units (GPUs) for parallel computing. These elements have positioned in the first place the fastest computed since 2010 upper other computers that only use CPU computing [32].

GPU computing increases the processing speed in images due to the possibility of dividing images into several sub-sections or threads; allowing parallel processing with an algorithm adapted to parallelism. The programming of this algorithm uses a kernel or section of code that its executed one time per thread concurrently, with each thread assigned to a GPU [33]. In this paper is designed a real-time labeling application for the colorblind that uses the symbols in the ColorADD^{TM} in Table 1.

The implementation of this application is in a CUDA^{TM} kernel that performs classification of colors with GA, PSO, GP, and feedforward ANN's. All of these techniques are compared by efficiency and execution time for determining the best to use in the labeling assistant.

The GA's are used in this research in the optimizing of proposed equations since they have been proved to be useful for testing and fitting quantitative models since the 1950s [34].

PSO algorithm is another technique tested in this work. It belongs to swarm intelligence family, which today is proliferating in applications. Moreover, PSO has shown to be less computationally demanding than GA's, and it obtains good results in low dimensional search spaces with few local optimums [35–38].

ANN's with architecture Feedforward Neural Networks (FNN's) are the AI techniques used in this work as a representative of general tuned structures for solving the color classification problem. This technique was selected because it has been tested in color classification in several works and has shown that it can approximate any function with a finite number of discontinuities [39]. There are other more complicated architectures than FNN's such as the most profound deep neural networks used in current commercial implementations of ANN's that include architectures like Convolutional Neural Networks (CNN's) specialized in object recognition and working with images. Nevertheless, this kind of neurons are computationally demanding and require large data sets for its training, which is not sustainable in this work for processing FHD images in real-time [40].

GP as the most representative element of automatic programming algorithm was the alternative tested for automatic generation of equations to perform color classification. Moreover, GP has obtained effective results in generating equations and programs that better fit to specific problems, with structures related to those found in nature.

For each technique, efficiency and processing time is measured, allowing to identify the best structure for the classification of color in a CUDA^{TM} kernel, required in the colorblind labeling assistant.

2 Theoretical Framework

This section describes the AI algorithms used for generating the different structures tested in the color classification for the colorblind labeling assistant.

2.1 Genetic Algorithms

GA's belong to the family of evolutive algorithms inspired by the selection principles proposed by Darwin. GA's have been used for numerical optimization in several areas since were proposed in the 1950s. They have as main operators population initializing, fitness value calculation, fitness-based selection, crossover, and mutation [41].

The population generation is according to GA's search space ($\mathbb{X}$) using binary string elements ($\mathbb{X} = \mathbb{B}^*$) or genotypes $b^* \in \mathbb{B}^*$ required in the crossover and the mutation operations; while phenotype $x \in \mathbb{X}$ or numerical representation allows getting fitness value calculation. The population (P) depends on the size of the population (S_P), the maximum reachable value ($\max_V$), the minimum reachable value ($\min_V$), and the number of bits for resolution (n_b) [41].

Fitness evaluation maps a numerical value with the objective function $f(x)$ that measures how well adapted is a chromosome in the population [41].

After fitness evaluation, there are different methods for selection for mating pool (M_P), but in this research, tournament selection is used. The tournament selection still being considered a good alternative against noisy data, which is good because of the possibility of having wrong labeled pixels in the training data; tournament selection controls the selection pressure with its size (S_T) [41].

Crossover is used with a random crossover point for obtaining the offspring (O), which is susceptible to mutation operation with the probability of mutation (P_M) considering all the alleles produced in the entire run. The mutation is type uniform.

After that, the population includes all the new chromosomes generated in crossover and mutation.

Finally, the population is sorted based on its fitness, and worst adapted elements are deleted to maintain S_P, for ecological stability [41].

Stop condition of GA in this work is only the number of generations (N_G).

2.2   Particle Swarm Optimization

PSO algorithm belongs to the family of swarm intelligence. Its inspiration came from fish schooling and flocks of birds, it was proposed by Eberhart and Kennedy in 1995, but was modified in 1998 adding an extra inertial coefficient that regulates exploration and exploitation of the search space across iterations, which is used in this work.

Particles are the essential elements of PSO equivalents to the birds that search around the search space $\mathbb{X}^d$ with d dimensions limited by its boundaries according to their upper and lower limits $[L_U, L_L]$. The entire swarm initializes its position randomly uniform across $\mathbb{X}^d$, making that each i particle of the n particles has a position $\vec{X}_i = [x_1, x_2, \ldots, x_d]$ and an initial velocity $\vec{V}_i = 0$ with d elements with limits $[Ls_U, Ls_L]$.

The objective function $f(\vec{X}_i)$ must measure the quality of the position of each particle, to determine the best-known position of the entire swarm $(\vec{P}_G)$ and the best-visited position of each particle $(\vec{P}_i)$.

After initialization, the position of each particle is updated with Eq. (1), until reaching the desired maximum number of iterations N_I, substituting $\vec{V}_i$ calculated per iteration with Eq. (2).

$$\vec{X_i} = \vec{X_i} + \vec{V_i} \tag{1}$$

$$\vec{V_i} = w \cdot \vec{V_i} + c_1 \cdot \vec{R_1} \circ (\vec{P_G} - \vec{X_i}) + c_2 \cdot \vec{R_2} \circ (\vec{P_i} - \vec{X_i}) \tag{2}$$

Where w is the inertial coefficient and is updated depending on the actual iteration (it) and its boundaries $[w_{max}, w_{min}]$ using $w = (w_{max} - w_{min}) \frac{N_I - 1}{N_I} + w_{min}$.

c_1 and c_2 are the personal and social components, both used for regulating exploration and exploitation of the search space, depending on the distance to the best-known positions. The $\overrightarrow{R_1}$ and $\overrightarrow{R_2}$ arrays are random elements that modify the speed array making that PSO be a stochastic algorithm.

During the entire process, particle positions and speeds are under the desired boundaries $[L_U, L_L]$ and $[Ls_U, Ls_L]$. After obtaining the cost value of the new positions of each particle, then, best-known positions are updated.

Finally, when N_I iterations are reached, the best global known position is updated as the best solution.

2.3 Genetic Programming

GP is a technique proposed by John Koza that belongs to the family of evolutionary algorithms and allows automatic generation of unknown structures [31, 42]. This technique used tree-based representations with Lisp language when it was created. Nevertheless, linear representations have shown an improvement over these tree-based elements because they require fewer pointers for its representation, and this structure is a natural representation for computer programs [28, 31].

The GP as an evolutive algorithm uses the operators: randomly initialized population, fitness evaluation, fitness-based selection, crossover operation, and mutation, as the GA's do, but instead of having a binary search space it has a search space of computer instructions [43].

Linear GP controls complexity with the number of operators (N_O), instead of depth in tree-based individuals. Typically linear GP elements are executable instructions in the language used for programming, so its search space is $x \in \mathbb{X}$ with $\mathbb{X}$ as a space of programming instructions.

In this work is required to generate an equation for classification of a specific color, so each element has an equation form.

After generating every element in the population of size (S_P), the objective function $(f(x))$ determines the fitness value of each element. Then, tournament selection with size (S_T) allows generation of the mating pool (M_P) for crossover operation.

The crossover uses two randomly determined crossover points that cut the parents for mixing genetical material in the offspring, like described in [31].

After crossover operation, the mutation with probability (P_M) is applied by using mutation type in-order or with two crossover points for interchanging all the genetical materials between them as described in [44], so that more material can change for maintaining diversity in more complex elements like those in GP [31].

The algorithm runs for a desired number of generations (N_G).

2.4 Feedforward Artificial Neural Networks

ANN's are mathematical models proposed in the 1950s for representing biological neurons. ANN's learn by determining the parameters in their synapsis. Today ANN's have spread in several areas like in classification and regression tasks [40]. The FNN's are ANN's that receives its name because signals travel through them from its input to the output without feedback elements. The structure used in this work is the shown in Fig. 1 [39].

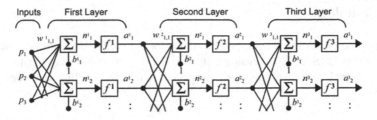

Fig. 1. Fully connected FNN and notation for its elements [39].

With p_R as the R input element of the neuron, $w_{s,i}^m$ as the weight i for the neuron s in the layer m, b_s^m as the bias for the neuron s in the layer m, f^m as the activation function of the neurons in the layer m and a_s^m as the output of the neuron s in the layer m [39], given with Eq. (3) in its matrix form.

$$\mathbf{a}^{m+1} = f^{m+1}\left(\mathbf{W}^{m+1}\mathbf{a}^m + \mathbf{b}^{m+1}\right) \tag{3}$$

The f^{m+1} activation function is hyperbolic tangent sigmoid for hidden layers as in Eq. (4) and linear activation function for output layer as in Eq. (5), because they are together an excellent approximator for functions with finite discontinuities [39].

$$\text{tansig}(n_i^m) = \frac{2}{1 + e^{-2n_i^m}} - 1 \tag{4}$$

$$\text{linear}(n_i^m) = n_i^m \tag{5}$$

With the parameter $n_i^m = \sum_{j=1}^{s^{m-1}} w_{i,j}^m a_j^{m-1} + b_i^m$

Training of FNN's is possible with different algorithms, but the most popular and used is Backpropagation (BP) with gradient descent, that will continue improving the synapsis, while there exists a derivative of the performance function. Moreover, backpropagation has trained FNN's for different proposes, and it improves its training performance when adding momentum and adaptative learning rate, which is used in this work like in [39].

Weights and biases are updated each k iteration with Eqs. (6) and (7), depending on the gradient $\nabla F(\mathbf{x})$, including momentum and the required conditions for adapting learning, like in [39].

$$\Delta\mathbf{W}^m(k) = \gamma\Delta\mathbf{W}^m(k+1) - (1-\gamma)\alpha\mathbf{s}^m\left(\mathbf{a}^{m-1}\right)^T \tag{6}$$

$$\Delta\mathbf{b}^m(k) = \gamma\Delta\mathbf{b}^m(k-1) - (1-\gamma)\alpha\mathbf{s}^m \tag{7}$$

3 Methodology

This section describes the generation of samples for training and the implementation of the algorithms in Sect. 2 to evaluate its capabilities in color classification with a CUDA^{TM} kernel for developing the proposed real-time labeling assistant for the colorblind.

3.1 Samples Generation

GA, PSO, GP, and ANN's are supervised learning algorithms that require sample pairs of inputs and target outputs for its training, as described in Sects. 2.1 to 2.4.

Samples generation in this work implies that a person with a regular sight takes pictures of objects that correspond with the colors for labeling.

The obtained pictures are the input images decomposed into three rows per pixel corresponding with the (r, g, b) tern, which are all put together in (**Im**) a matrix with size $3 \times Q$ containing all the Q samples or pixels in those images.

For obtaining the target image $\mathbf{Tm} = [T_1, T_2, T_i, \ldots, T_Q]$ with size $1 \times Q$, all the obtained pictures reduce its bright by multiplying them per 0.9 for suppressing the full white colors in the image ($\mathbf{Mi} = 0.9 \cdot \mathbf{Im}$), or pixels with the tern $(1, 1, 1)$ in normalized RGB space.

This elimination of full white color allows using it as a mark. **Mi** is edited putting $(1, 1, 1)$ instead of the color in the image to identifying it as a positive sample so that each element of **Tm** could be obtained with the Eq. (8) from the modified images **Mi**.

$$T_i(M_i) = \begin{cases} 1 & \text{if } M_i = (1, 1, 1) \\ 0 & \text{if } M_i = else \end{cases} \tag{8}$$

3.2 GA and PSO Implementation with Proposed Color Equations

In general, all color space representations for digital images, coming from digital cameras has representation in a $\mathbb{R}^3$ space, where each color represents a tern (c_1, c_2, c_3), the tern is (r, g, b) in the RGB native space [45, 46]. Image processing and sometimes AI, perform transformations because could it be challenging to separate a specific color in the RGB space (Fig. 2) [18].

Alternatively, in [18], all the colors for classification are projected into three sub-spaces RG, GB, and BR so that planes become lines reducing the number of parameters for optimization to six coefficients in the in Eqs. (9), (10) and (11), that still related to the native RGB space [18, 19].

If all inequations are satisfied with that pixel value, then, the input color is accepted into its category, and the corresponding output pixel is set to one instead of zero in an output matrix (**Om**) with the same size of input the image. The human proposed equations are tuned with GA and PSO in this work.

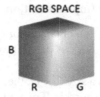

Fig. 2. RGB color space of digital images [18].

$$r \leq \alpha_1 \cdot g + \beta_1 \qquad (9)$$

$$g \leq \alpha_2 \cdot b + \beta_2 \qquad (10)$$

$$\gamma_1 \leq r \leq \gamma_2 \qquad (11)$$

3.3 GP Implementation

GP is adapted for automatic generation of six equations with variable complexity since there are required three inequations for color classification according to [18]. These equations are used one per side of inequation so that GP generates automatically three inequations for color classification, but now they are not limited to be linear like in Eqs. (9), (10) and (11). The general representation of the inequations generated with GP is in Eq. (12). If all inequations are satisfied, then, the input pixel is accepted in its class.

Finally, as in GA and PSO, the input color is accepted into its category, and the corresponding output pixel is set to one in an output matrix (**Om**).

$$f_1(r,g,b) \leq f_2(r,g,b) \qquad (12)$$

There are three different elements used for generating the equations in the GP algorithm, numbers or coefficients, operators, and variables.

Numbers or coefficients are natural numerals from 0 to 10, and if there is required a fraction or a decimal value, it will be generated with the operators, for example $0.1 = 1/10$.

Operators included are all necessary mathematical operations for a polynomial equation: sum $(+)$, rest $(-)$, multiplication $(\times)$, division $(/)$, and power $(\wedge)$. The root can be computed with the power operator.

Variables include the values of the pixels r, g, b, and the elements with the sine function and cosine function of those pixel values since any function can be approximated with a polynomial of sine and cosine functions [28, 42].

3.4   Artificial Neural Networks Implementation

The paired input and output images are obtained for each of the six colors for labeling, as described in Sect. 3.1. These six sets of pairs allow training of six neurons one per each color.

Since the input matrix (**Im**) has a size $3 \times Q$, then the input elements to the neurons are three. The target elements are those in **Tm** with the size $1 \times Q$. Therefore, each neuron has always a single output that indicates in ranges $[0, 1]$ the security of the neuron for recognizing that the pixel corresponds with the color that the neuron detects.

Cross-validation with ten folds allows determining the architecture of hidden layers, as recommended in [39, 40].

After processing all the pixels in the image, then an output image (**Om**) with the same size of the input image is generated, like in the GA, PSO, and GP implementations.

3.5   Objective Function and Performance Function

All the algorithms require a performance function or objective function depending on the algorithm. The selected objective function for GA, PSO and GP was the Mean Absolute Error (MAE) (Eq. (13)), which is a better metric for measure performance instead of MSE when the error is not expected to be Gaussian [47].

$$F(x) = \frac{1}{Q} \sum_{i=1}^{Q} |T_i - O_i| \tag{13}$$

With O_i as the binary i element of the output image matrix (**Om**). Generated as the result of classifying the input image with the structure obtained after training.

MAE in Eq. (13) has an extra term in GP this element is necessary because there is so much more diversity in a population for generating equations than only numbers as in GA and PSO. This term punishes the objective value when there is no pixel activated in the output data, allowing eliminate inequations that cannot be satisfied together (Eq. (14)) where ε is small for suppressing effects when low term is zero.

$$F(x) = \frac{1}{Q} \sum_{i=1}^{Q} |T_i - O_i| + \frac{\varepsilon}{\sum\limits_{i=1}^{Q} O_i} \tag{14}$$

The training of the ANN was done using the performance function MSE as in the algorithm in Sect. 2.4, but after obtaining a trained ANN, the MAE evaluation function was used in the test evaluation of the ANN for allowing comparison with the other algorithms.

Since the other algorithms express classification in a relative measure, the comparison must use a relative expression, which is determined from MAE by multiplying per 100% because if every O_i is different from T_i, then $\frac{1}{Q} \sum_{i=1}^{Q} |T_i - O_i| = 1$.

The objective functions and efficiency measurements in this section are related with separate color identification by comparing the desired labeled image with the output image that has pixels in white for positive samples as the labeled input image. But these are not the output images with the colorADD^{TM} code, the final labelling process for the output image that is retransmitted to the user is described in Sect. 3.6.

3.6   Labeling System

The real-time system generated in this work for labeling colors uses six colors related to the symbols commonly used in the colorADD^{TM} code, the Table 1 shows the images of those codes and its corresponding color in the proposed labeling system.

Labeling system uses six grid images, each one containing several symbols of the corresponding color to label, and with the same size of the images from the digital camera, those images are saved in tensors L_c with size $H \times W \times 3$.

Where $c = 1, 2, \ldots, 6$ for the six colors, H is the height, W is the width of the images and the three is for parameters in the RGB space (r, g, b).

The process of labeling starts by acquiring the camera images in the RGB space, with every input image saved in a tensor I_T with size $H \times W \times 3$.

After that, I_T is processed with one of the AI structures previously trained with the algorithms in Sect. 2.

The resulting processed image is saved in an output tensor O_T with size $H \times W \times 3$, which is a binary element containing three copies of the same output matrix (Om) obtained with one of the trained structures.

The output image presented to the user is the tensor $\mathbf{Lo}$ with size $H \times W \times 3$ computed with Eq. (15).

$$\mathbf{Lo} = \mathbf{I_T} \circ \mathbf{L}_c \circ (\lambda \cdot \mathbf{O_T}) \tag{15}$$

Where $\circ$ is the Hadamard product, and λ is a factor that allows regulating the intensity of the grid image for labeling in the input image.

3.7   CUDA^{TM} Kernel Implementation

Code implementation for GPU parallel computing uses two functions; the first is the main function, which, creates all variables, and second calls one of the three CUDA^{TM} kernels (tuned human proposed equations, generated equations, or ANN's).

The main function starts by reading 12 grid images as color images for the six labeling colors. two per color, one with the text word of the color and the other with colorAdd^{TM} symbol and save them in memory as CV::Mat variables. Then, Another two CV::Mat variables serve as the location for saving the input image acquired with the camera and the output processed image.

CUDA^{TM} uses blocks and the number of threads per block in the kernel allow maximizing of processing speeds when are correctly configured so that blocks share as many information as possible (up to the size of 1024 in one dimension or 32×32 in two dimensions as in digital images, which is the maximum allowed).

Threads per block calculation depend on the image size and the number of blocks. For determining the threads number per dimension t_v is obtained with $t_v = \frac{H + b_v - 1}{b_v}$, where b_v, is the number of blocks in each dimension (two dimensions in images).

After that, a kernel with tuned human proposed equations, generated equations, or ANN's is launched. In the kernel, each pixel is evaluated for determining the output image with Eq. (15) and then, output image its copied from GPU to CPU memory for showing it in the screen.

4 Results

The design of the experiment, the results of color classification, and the results of each kernel are in this section. The general aspects of the experiment are in Sect. 4.1, the description of the results are in Sects. 4.2 to 4.5.

4.1 Design of Experiment

The training process was in Matlab^{TM} where all algorithms were programmed and executed according to Sect. 2, and the kernel programming was in C++ with CUDA tool kit 8.0. The computer used is a Windows 10 desktop with processor Intel(R) Core^{TM} i7-6700 CPU 3.40 GHz, 16.0 GB RAM, video card NVIDIA GeForce GTX 970 and the image acquisition system was a Samsung Note 8 camera configured for HD images with 960×720 pixels resolution for wireless transmitting using DroidCam^{TM}.

Dataset for training is obtained as described in Sect. 3.1, it has 1,593,600 pixels obtained from 83 images with size 120×160. All these images are photographs of objects of each color to classify, in this experiment there were used the basic colors in ColorADD^{TM} (red, orange, yellow, green, blue and purple) with symbols as in Sect. 3.6, the labeling of the dataset was perform by a single person with trichromat vision, all photographs were taken in different scenes with mild light variations.

In all the algorithms data was split into 80% for training and 20% for testing.

During the training stage, the 80% is divided into 10 folds to perform k-fold cross-validation, for finding the best numerical parameters associated with the input parameters for the GA and PSO algorithms, and the parameters that control the structure complexity with ANN and GP, in order to avoid overfitting and underfitting.

After obtaining the best parameters per algorithm, they are used for training again with the entire training samples (80% of the data) and then the trained structure is tested against the remaining 20% that was never used before.

Since all algorithms have several numerical parameters, it would be computationally expensive to use the ten-fold cross-validation for determine them all, with that in mind, some parameters that are not related with the complexity or the size of the search space are fixed parameters heuristically determined.

4.2 Human Proposed Equations

Table 2 shows the GA results for each color, including Heuristically Determined Fixed Parameters (HFP), ten-fold Cross-Validation Parameters (CVP), Cross-Validation Cost with that parameters (CVC), Training Cost with 80% of samples (TRC), Test Validation Cost with the remaining 20% (TEC), relative test error (RT), the relative efficiency (RE), and the solution obtained (SOL). The SOL parameters for human proposed equations are the coefficients of Eqs. (9), (10), and (11), per each color.

Table 2. GA results in color classification.

Color	Red	Orange	Yellow	Green	Blue	Purple
HFP	S_T: 15, S_P: 300, N_G: 300, P_M: 0.04					
CVP	7,200	6,200	7,200	6,80	5,40	6,80
CVC	0.004303	0.015394	0.008196	0.006376	0.008230	0.009341
TRC	0.005573	0.015375	0.008456	0.006816	0.008394	0.009573
TEC	0.005836	0.015519	0.008726	0.006730	0.008496	0.009300
RT	0.584%	1.552%	0.873%	0.673%	0.850%	0.930%
RE	99.416%	98.448%	99.127%	99.327%	99.150%	99.070%
SOL	0.3700	0.2400	0.6050	0.3000	0.2750	0.0500
	0.4750	0.2000	0.3950	0.7875	0.7250	0.7375
	0.2700	0.3000	0.4350	0.7125	0.5250	0.6500
	0.0600	0.0000	0.1250	0.1000	0.0000	0.0125
	0.3200	0.1750	0.1350	0.7500	0.7750	0.6625
	0.0550	0.1600	0.1900	0.0125	0.0250	0.0000

The Table 3 shows the PSO results in color classification for each color. The table includes HFP, CVP, CVC, TRC, TEC, RT, RE, and SOL. The CVP first element is the value for (c_1, c_2) components and the PCV second element is the w value. The RE in Table 3 is bold because it has the best results in the experiment.

Table 3. PSO results in color classification.

Color	Red	Orange	Yellow	Green	Blue	Purple
HFP	d: 6, n: 300, N_I: 50, $[L_U, L_L]$ $[-1, 1]$, $[Ls_U, Ls_L]$: $[0.4, -0.4]$					
CVP	2.4,0.5,1	2.2,0.7,1	1.4,1.1,1		2.0,0.9,1	2.4,0.3,1
			2.2,0.9,1			
CVC	0.003351	0.010952	0.007498	0.004073	0.007482	0.004680
TRC	0.003331	0.010984	0.007480	0.004038	0.007471	0.004676
TEC	0.003530	0.011034	0.007439	0.004044	0.007693	0.005061
RT	0.353%	1.011%	0.744%	0.404%	0.769%	0.506%
RE	**99.647%**	**98.989%**	**99.256%**	**99.596%**	**99.231%**	**99.494%**
SOL	0.3200	0.1763	0.6059	0.2503	0.2683	0.0331
	0.5767	0.2670	0.4062	1.0000	1.0000	1.0000
	0.4276	0.9998	1.0000	1.0000	0.5376	1.0000
	−0.0548	−0.4562	−0.2410	−0.0738	0.0005	−0.0689
	0.5697	0.6567	0.9669	0.4893	1.0000	0.7980
	−0.1063	0.0090	−0.3706	0.1890	−0.0698	−0.0326

The Human proposed equations obtain the best test efficiency result in the relative error, and its structure is the simplest of all the used in this work. However, the variations of luminosity are mild in the training data, and greater variations could not be well supported by this simple structure.

4.3   GP Generated Equations

Table 4 shows the GP results in color classification for each color. The table includes the HFP, CVP, CVC, TRC, TEC, RT, RE, and SOL. Numerical parameters for GP are the number of operators per operation and the number of equations per side of the inequations. The SOL elements in GP are the generated inequations.

Table 4. GP results in color classification.

Color	Red	Orange	Yellow	Green	Blue	Purple
HFP	S_P: 400, S_T: 20, N_G: 1000, P_M: 0.275,					
CVP	5,1	10,1	4,1	3,1	5,1	2,1
CVC	0.006784	0.023042	0.010185	0.008677	0.009464	0.011758
TRC	0.005426	0.029425	0.007955	0.005920	0.008625	0.010889
TEC	0.006733	0.026201	0.009881	0.007304	0.010894	0.013645
RT	0.673%	2.620%	0.988%	0.730%	1.089%	1.365%
RE	99.327%	97.380%	99.012%	99.270%	98.911%	98.635%
SOL	Equation (16) Equation (17) Equation (18)	Similar structure to Red	Similar structure to Red	Similar structure to Red	Similar structure to Red	Similar structure to Red

Equations (16) to (18) are the GP generated inequations for the red color, others colors produce their own equation with similar structure following this methodology.

$$\left[\frac{16}{sin(g)} - 6\right] \leq \left[sin^2(g) + \frac{6}{b \cdot sin(b)}\right] \tag{16}$$

$$\left[\frac{cos(g)}{g \cdot r} - \frac{3}{sin(g)}\right] \leq \left[sin(g) - sin(b) - cos(g) + r^2 - 6\right] \tag{17}$$

$$[b - 9 \cdot g \cdot sin(g) - 5] \leq \left[7 \cdot sin(r) - \frac{9 \cdot g}{2 \cdot b}\right] \tag{18}$$

The generated equations obtain similar efficiency results compared with human proposed equations, but the variations of luminosity can be supported by the algorithm, with the generation of new equations adapted to support light variation, and all these generated structures are highly parallelizable because r, g, and b are arrays with all the pixels of the image, obtaining one thread per pixel.

4.4 Artificial Neural Network Structure

The ANN results are shown in Table 5 including HFP, CVP, CVC, TRC, TEC, RT, RE. Numerical parameters for ANN are the number of layers and neurons per layer. The SOL in this case are the weights and biases.

Table 5. ANN results in color classification.

Color	Red	Orange	Yellow	Green	Blue	Purple
HFP	γ: 0.9, ρ: 0.7, η: 1.05, k_{max}: 3000					
CVP	3,4	3,5	3,5	3,5	3,3	3,4
CVC	0.007445	0.015296	0.009819	0.007524	0.014201	0.007756
TRC	0.003058	0.002876	0.002948	0.003031	0.003028	0.002968
TEC	0.006013	0.023288	0.012165	0.012056	0.014530	0.008064
RT	0.601%	2.329%	1.217%	1.206%	1.453%	0.806%
RE	99.399%	97.671%	98.783%	98.794%	98.547%	99.194%

The ANN's obtain similar efficiency results compared with human proposed equations, and the variations of luminosity can be supported by the algorithm, generating deeper architectures, but the structures are more complex than GP generated equations and have parameters must be trained and adapted to GPU computing.

4.5 CUDA^{TM} Kernel with Structures

The implemented kernels obtain 59.8491 FPS for tuned proposed equations (Fig. 3), 57.6248 FPS for GP equations (Fig. 4) and 32.0034 FPS for ANN's (Fig. 5). The algorithm uses the colorblind simulator model in [15] for showing how a colorblind perceives the symbols. The FPS average decreases in Fig. 6 because of the processing the colorblind model. As shown in Fig. 5 ANN's have difficulties for color labeling because they have several weights trained in Matlab^{TM} that produces precision lost when passing them to the CUDA^{TM} kernel.

Fig. 3. Labeling system, proposed equations.

Fig. 4. Labeling system, generated GP equations.

Fig. 5. Labeling system, ANN's.   **Fig. 6.** Labeling system, generated GP equations and colorblind simulation.

5 Conclusions

In this paper is compared the performance in color classification and the processing time of different structures programmed in a CUDA^{TM} kernel. The color classification here proposed allows implementing a real-time labeling assistant for the colorblind, which adds to camera-acquired images the colorADD^{TM} codes designed for color-blindness assistance. The structures trained include human proposed equations tuned with GA and PSO, automatically generated equations with GP, and ANN's.

The color classification for the labeling assistant obtains different results depending on the used structure.

ANN's are very popular today, but in the color classification system presented in this work, its processing time is lower in comparison with the other techniques. Moreover, ANN's have the lower values in the test evaluation, and for improving its behavior, more hidden layers, training data, and regularization would help, but if the structure increases in complexity processing speed will decrease.

The ANN's also decrease its capabilities, when training in a different language from the CUDA^{TM} kernel C++, it is better to program the entire training algorithm in the same kernel or use a regulation technique for avoiding too small weights because imprecision in their weights affects them enormously.

Human proposed equations obtained the best results in test evaluation and processing speed, but compared with GP generated equations in the labeling system, the generalization is better in GP since that obtained equations recognize better the colors of the objects in the surroundings and with variabilities of light.

In the proposed labeling system, the GP got the best results because the obtained equations generalize better than human proposed equations and the processing speed its just 2.224 FPS lower that tuned proposed equations. GP generated equations can also improve by fine-tuning the numerical parameters in them with the PSO algorithm, which is a common alternative for improving the results of these structures.

6 Future Work

It is required to increase the size of the training data with light variations for improving the capabilities and obtain light robustness generalized equations with GP which has the best results in the labeling system.

Different algorithms of automatic programming should be tested against GP in color classification for comparing their results and find if another technique could improve the accuracy of color classification.

References

1. García-Porrero, J.A., Hurlé, J.M., García-Porrero Alonso, J.: Anatomía humana. McGraw-Hill/Interamericana de España (2005)
2. Rivera, M.M., Díaz, A.P., Reich, J.C., et al.: Augmented reality labels for security signs based on color segmentation with PSO for assisting colorblind people. Int. J. Comb. Optim. Probl. Inform. **10**, 7–20 (2019)
3. Kato, C.: Comprehending color images for color barrier-free via factor analysis technique. In: 2013 14th ACIS International Conference on Software Engineering, Artificial Intelligence, Networking and Parallel/Distributed Computing, pp. 478–483. IEEE (2013)
4. Tanaka, K.D.: A colour to birds and to humans: why is it so different? J. Ornithol. **156**, 433–440 (2015). https://doi.org/10.1007/s10336-015-1234-1
5. Bailey, J.D.: Color Vision Deficiency: A Concise Tutorial for Optometry and Ophthalmology, 1st edn. Richmond Products (2012)
6. Montes Rivera, M., Padilla Díaz, A., Ponce Gallegos, J.C., et al.: Recoloring Ishihara Plates with PSO algorithm and Proposed Equations. In: Robótica y Computación. Investigación y Desarrollo., 1st edn. Tecnológico Nacional de México, La Paz Baja California Sur, México, pp. 174–180 (2019)
7. Neiva, M.: ColorADD, color identification system (2018). http://www.coloradd.net/imgs/ColorADDAboutUs_2015V1.pdf
8. Liu, B., Wang, M., Yang, L., et al.: Efficient image and video re-coloring for colorblindness. In: 2009 IEEE International Conference on Multimedia and Expo, pp. 906–909. IEEE (2009)
9. Huang, J.-B., Chen, C.-S., Jen, T.-C., Wang, S.-J.: Image recolorization for the colorblind. In: 2009 IEEE International Conference on Acoustics, Speech and Signal Processing, pp. 1161–1164. IEEE (2009)
10. Huang, C.-R., Chiu, K.-C., Chen, C.-S.: Temporal color consistency-based video reproduction for dichromats. IEEE Trans. Multimed. **13**, 950–960 (2011). https://doi.org/10.1109/TMM.2011.2135844
11. Lai, C.-L., Chang, S.-W., Sheen, J.: An integrated portable vision assistant agency for the visual impaired people. In: 2009 IEEE International Conference on Control and Automation, pp. 2311–2316. IEEE (2009)
12. Ohkubo, T., Kobayashi, K., Watanabe, K., Kurihara, Y.: Development of a time-sharing-based color-assisted vision system for persons with color-vision deficiency. In: Proceedings of SICE Annual Conference 2010, pp. 2499–2503 (2010)
13. Tanuwidjaja, E., Huynh, D., Koa, K., et al.: Chroma. In: Proceedings of the 2014 ACM International Joint Conference on Pervasive and Ubiquitous Computing - UbiComp 2014 Adjunct, pp. 799–810. ACM Press, New York (2014)
14. Chung, M., Choo, H.: A real-time color-matching method based on smartphones for color-blind people. In: Eighth International Conference on Mob Mobile Ubiquitous Computing, Systems, Services Technologies, UBICOMM 2014, pp. 184–188 (2014)
15. Brettel, H., Viénot, F., Mollon, J.D.: Computerized simulation of color appearance for dichromats. J. Opt. Soc. Am. A **14**, 2647 (1997). https://doi.org/10.1364/JOSAA.14.002647

16. Goswami, T.: Impact of deep learning in image processing and computer vision. In: Anguera, J., Satapathy, S.C., Bhateja, V., Sunitha, K.V.N. (eds.) Microelectronics, Electromagnetics and Telecommunications. LNEE, vol. 471, pp. 475–485. Springer, Singapore (2018). https://doi.org/10.1007/978-981-10-7329-8_48

17. Ku, J., Harakeh, A., Waslander, S.L.: In Defense of Classical Image Processing: Fast Depth Completion on the CPU (2018)

18. Rivera Montes, M., Padilla Díaz, A., Ponce Gallegos, J.C.: Comparative between RGB and HSV color representations for color segmentation when it is applied with artificial neural networks. In: en C. Ma. de Lourdes Sánchez Guerrero Dra. Alma Rosa García Gaona DFJÁR (eds.) Avances en las Tecnologías de la Información. ALFA-OMEGA, pp. 620–638 (2016)

19. Montes, M., Padilla, A., Canul, J., Ponce, J., Ochoa, A.: Comparative of effectiveness when classifying colors using RGB image representation with PSO with time decreasing inertial coefficient and GA algorithms as classifiers. In: Castillo, O., Melin, P., Kacprzyk, J. (eds.) Fuzzy Logic Augmentation of Neural and Optimization Algorithms: Theoretical Aspects and Real Applications. SCI, vol. 749, pp. 527–546. Springer, Cham (2018). https://doi.org/10.1007/978-3-319-71008-2_38

20. Maučec, M.S., Brest, J.: A review of the recent use of Differential Evolution for Large-Scale Global Optimization: An analysis of selected algorithms on the CEC 2013 LSGO benchmark suite. Swarm Evol. Comput. (2018). https://doi.org/10.1016/j.swevo.2018.08.005

21. Nasiri, J.A., Yazdi, H.S., Moulavi, M.A., et al.: A PSO tuning approach for lip detection on color images. In: Proceedings - EMS 2008, European Modelling Symposium, 2nd UKSim European Symposium on Computer Modelling and Simulation, pp. 278–282. IEEE (2008)

22. Vijayanandh, R., Balakrishnan, G.: Performance measure of human skin region detection based on hybrid particle swarm optimization. Int. J. Comput. Theory Eng. 4, 857 (2012)

23. Amelio, A., Pizzuti, C.: A genetic algorithm for color image segmentation. In: Esparcia-Alcázar, A.I. (ed.) EvoApplications 2013. LNCS, vol. 7835, pp. 314–323. Springer, Heidelberg (2013). https://doi.org/10.1007/978-3-642-37192-9_32

24. Bejarbaneh, B.Y., Bejarbaneh, E.Y., Amin, M.F.M., et al.: Intelligent modelling of sandstone deformation behaviour using fuzzy logic and neural network systems. Bull. Eng. Geol. Environ. 77, 345–361 (2018). https://doi.org/10.1007/s10064-016-0983-2

25. Baykan, N.A., Yılmaz, N., et al.: Case study in effects of color spaces for mineral identification. Sci. Res. Essays 5, 1243–1253 (2010)

26. Cengiz, C., Köse, E.: Modelling of color perception of different eye colors using artificial neural networks. Neural Comput. Appl. 23, 2323–2332 (2013). https://doi.org/10.1007/s00521-012-1185-x

27. Al-Mohair, H.K., Mohamad-Saleh, J., Suandi, S.A.: Color space selection for human skin detection using color-texture features and neural networks. In: 2014 International Conference on Computer and Information Sciences (ICCOINS), pp. 1–6. IEEE (2014)

28. Rivera, M.M., Justo, M.O.A., Zezzatti, A.O.: Equations for describing behavior tables in thermodynamics using genetic programming: synthesizing the saturated water and steam table. Res. Comput. Sci. 1, 9–23 (2016)

29. Olmo, J.L., Romero, J.R., Ventura, S.: Swarm-based metaheuristics in automatic programming: a survey. Wiley Interdiscip. Rev. Data Min. Knowl. Discov. 4, 445–469 (2014). https://doi.org/10.1002/widm.1138

30. Ogawa, T., Oshiro, N., Kinjo, H.: Generating function of color information detection using genetic programming. Artif. Life Robot. 14, 480–484 (2009). https://doi.org/10.1007/s10015-009-0704-z

31. Poli, R., Langdon, W.B., William, B., McPhee, N.F., Koza, J.R.: A field guide to genetic programming. [Lulu Press], lulu.com (2008)

32. Karimi, K., Dickson, N.G., Hamze, F.: A Performance Comparison of CUDA and OpenCL (2010)
33. Allusse, Y., Horain, P., Agarwal, A., Saipriyadarshan, C.: GpuCV: a GPU-accelerated framework for image processing and computer vision. In: Bebis, G., et al. (eds.) ISVC 2008. LNCS, vol. 5359, pp. 430–439. Springer, Heidelberg (2008). https://doi.org/10.1007/978-3-540-89646-3_42
34. Davis, L.: Handbook of genetic algorithms. Van Nostrand Reinhold (1991)
35. Evers, G.I., Ghalia, M.B.: Regrouping particle swarm optimization: a new global optimization algorithm with improved performance consistency across benchmarks. In: 2009 IEEE International Conference on System, Man and Cybernetics, pp. 3901–3908 (2009). https://doi.org/10.1109/ICSMC.2009.5346625
36. Jamian, J.J., Abdullah, M.N., Mokhlis, H., et al.: Global particle swarm optimization for high dimension numerical functions analysis. J. Appl. Math. **2014**, e329193 (2014). https://doi.org/10.1155/2014/329193
37. Clerc, M.: Particle Swarm Optimization. ISTE, London (2006)
38. Palupi Rini, D., Mariyam Shamsuddin, S., Sophiyati Yuhaniz, S.: Particle swarm optimization: technique, system and challenges. Int. J. Comput. Appl. **14**, 19–27 (2011). https://doi.org/10.5120/1810-2331
39. Hagan, M.T., Demuth, H.B., Beale, M.H., De Jesús, O.: Neural network design (1996)
40. Goodfellow, I., Bengio, Y., Courville, A.: Deep Learning. The MIT Press (2016)
41. Weise, T.: Global optimization algorithms-theory and application. Self-published 2 (2009)
42. Rivera, M.M., Ramos, M.P., Mora, J.L.O.: Automatic generator of decoupling blocks using genetic programming. In: Elleithy, K., Sobh, T. (eds.) New Trends in Networking, Computing, E-learning, Systems Sciences, and Engineering. LNEE, vol. 312, pp. 281–290. Springer, Cham (2015). https://doi.org/10.1007/978-3-319-06764-3_35
43. Brameier, M., Banzhaf, W.: A comparison of linear genetic programming and neural networks in medical data mining. IEEE Trans. Evol. Comput. **5**, 17–26 (2001). https://doi.org/10.1109/4235.910462
44. Martín Montes Rivera, M.O.A.J.: Path follower algorithm for a Nao humanoid robot. In: Iliana Castro Liera, M.C.L. (eds.) Investigación y Desarrollo en Robótica y Computación. Instituto Tecnológico de la Paz, pp. 168–174 (2016)
45. Gonzalez, R.C., Woods, R.E., Richard, E.: Digital Image Processing. Prentice Hall (2008)
46. Bovik, A.C., Alan, C.: Handbook of Image and Video Processing. Elsevier Academic Press (2005)
47. Chai, T., Draxler, R.R.: Root mean square error (RMSE) or mean absolute error (MAE)? - arguments against avoiding RMSE in the literature. Geosci. Model. Dev. **7**, 1247–1250 (2014). https://doi.org/10.5194/gmd-7-1247-2014

Vision and Robotics

3-D Human Body Posture Reconstruction by Computer Vision

Jacobo E. Cruz-Silva$^{(\boxtimes)}$, Jesús Y. Montiel-Pérez$^{(\boxtimes)}$, and Humberto Sossa-Azuela$^{(\boxtimes)}$

Instituto Politécnico Nacional, Centro de Investigación en Computación,
Av. Juan de Dios Bátiz Esq. Miguel Othón de Mendizábal S/N,
Nueva Industrial Vallejo, 07738 Gustavo A. Madero, Mexico City, Mexico
jacobo8806@hotmail.com, yalja@ipn.mx,
hsossa@cic.ipn.mx

Abstract. Human limb movement sensing is crucial in different areas of science. In this paper, a method for sensing human limb movement and the subsequent reconstruction in a 3-D plane is described. The sensors used in this task are four Microsoft Kinect, which has depth and RGB cameras. Depth images are processed by artificial vision algorithms to delimit an area where the movements will be performed. In the other hand, RGB images are processed by a Convolutional Neural Network to acquire a series of specific points which correspond to the human body's joints. A comparison of the proposed algorithm performance is also described. The equations that relate the information in two dimensions are obtained by processing the four sensors are used to generate a skeleton in 3-D.

Keywords: Artificial intelligence · Computer vision · Convolutional Neural Network · Image processing · Microsoft Kinect

1 Introduction

The movement analysis of the human limbs is a recurrent necessity in different areas of science, such as medicine and robotics. These analysis help improving several rehabilitation therapies for people with disabilities or with a muscular atrophy. In Robotics, the information of those analysis gives the possibility to create autonomous robots with humanized movements, another contribution is the creation of teleoperation methods for robots [26, 27, 29].

The most common methods for sensing the human limbs movements are: through haptic devices [1–4, 30] exoskeletons equipped with motion sensors [5–10] and artificial vision [13, 14, 16–20]. This last method is the basis of this paper.

Artificial vision is a computing tool that can be used to analyze the movements of human limbs in 2-D [25], precisely to determine the joints positions. Unfortunately, the measure in 2-D, is a limitation, given that the humans bodies have several degrees of freedom in order to perform movements in 3-D. This entails a significant information loss of the movements performed by human.

L. Martínez-Villaseñor et al. (Eds.): MICAI 2019, LNAI 11835, pp. 579–588, 2019.
https://doi.org/10.1007/978-3-030-33749-0_46

In recent years, the artificial vision has had a great development due the increase of computing capacity. The number of developed algorithms to be executed in parallel in Graphics Processing Units (GPU) have been increased. The processing time to analyze videos or images has been reduced with the used of these algorithms. Simultaneously, The Artificial Neural Networks (ANN) architectures developed to perform artificial vision have had a greater impetus in order to obtain better and faster results. The ANN architecture which is specially designed to analyze and process video and images is the Convolutional Neural Network (CNN).

2   Method

The proposed model for the sensing human body movements in 3-D is shaped of the following parts and depicted in Fig. 1:

1. Acquisition and processing Kinect sensor images [12].
2. Processing the images with a CNN in order to obtain coordinates in 2-D.
3. Processing the four sets of coordinates to obtain a model in 3-D.

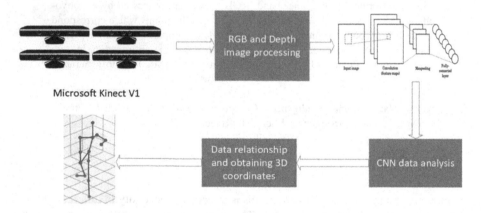

Fig. 1. Schematic diagram of the method for human movements measuring.

2.1   Images Acquisition and Processing

The images are acquired by four Microsoft Kinect Version 1 sensors [12] connected to a single computer. The Kinect sensors are communicated with the computer through the driver OpenKinect [11], this driver allows the connection of multiple sensors in a single computer using USB 3.0 ports that have a direct interaction with the CPU.

The sensors have a video camera VGA 640 × 480 pixels and 30fps RGB, depth sensor with infrared emitter of 830 nm and 60 mW laser diodes and a CMOS infrared camera of 640 × 480 pixels and 30 fps, with operating range of 0.8 m–3.5 m.

The Kinect sensors are placed at a distance of 2.5 m from where the person will be, and at an average height of 0.8 m. This allows the complete detection of a person with a height of 1.80 m. The alignment and positioning of the sensors are done with laser technology levelers, forming a virtual square of 5 m × 5 m (Fig. 2).

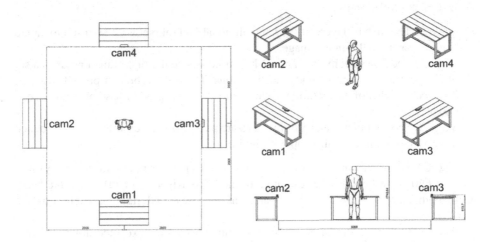

Fig. 2. Kinect sensors positions.

The depth images of the cam1 and cam2 sensors shown in Fig. 3 create a small virtual area, which will delimit the area where the person performs the movements. Preventing the person leaves the effective vision range of the Kinect sensors. There is not an interference between the IR cameras due the cam1 and cam2 are located on a perpendicular position and the distance is enough to avoid the IR beam reach the sensor of another camera. Additionally, the IR camera of cam3 and cam4 are not used.

The depth image is converted to an 8-bit grayscale image, where the different shades of gray correspond to a depth distance. After that, a threshold is applied to certain part of the histogram of the image to eliminate the elements that are not at the desired distance and through a conversion process a binary image is obtained. The result is the location of the test subject in the small virtual area (Fig. 3).

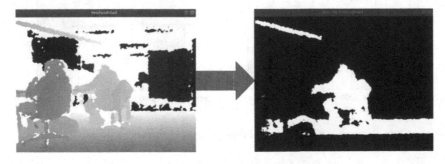

Fig. 3. Acquisition and processing of depth image.

The usage of 4 identical Kinects warranty that images will be the same due the opening of the RGB lens camera are the same. The RGB image are processed by the CNN [15] trained with 24,000 images of MPII Human Pose [32] dataset which is formed of the following stages:

- Stage 0. The first 10 layers of the Convolutional Neural Network are used to create feature maps for the input image.
- Stage 1. The 2-branch multi-stage CNN is used where the first branch predicts a set of 2D confidence maps of body part locations. The second branch predicts a set of 2-D vector fields of part affinities, which encode the degree of association between parts.
- Stage 2. The confidence and affinity maps are parsed by greedy inference to produce the 2-D key points for all people in the image.

The CNN delivers an array for each Kinect sensor of 15 points in 2-D (x, y) in a scale of 640 × 480 pixels (the resolution of the RGB Kinect camera) where the head, neck, both elbows, shoulders, knees and ankles, chest and right and left hips are located.

The CNN is programmed on Caffe [31] framework and is executed in parallel in a GPU with the Compute Unified Device Architecture (CUDA), the execution time is reduced 10 times on this parallel scheme compared to the traditional scheme (execution in CPU), as can be seen in Fig. 4.

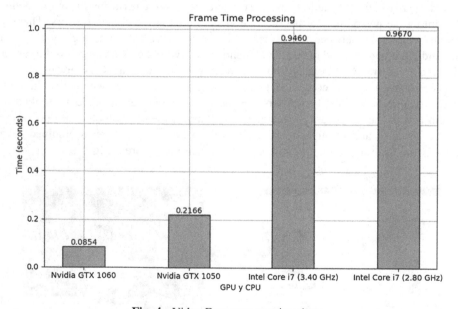

Fig. 4. Video Frames processing times.

2.2   3-D Posture Reconstruction

The main points of human body are identified from 0 to 14 as is shown in Fig. 5.

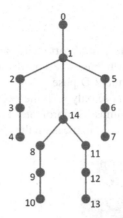

Fig. 5. Human body key points.

The 3-D coordinates are calculated with the relation between the coordinates $(X\_cam(n)[m],\ Y\_cam(n)[m])$ measured by the four sensors. Where the coordinates measured by cam1 and cam4 (Fig. 2) correspond to the coordinates $(X,\ Y)$ and the coordinates of cam2 and cam3 correspond to $(Y,\ Z)$ on a 3D plane.

$$Error\_X = |X\_cam1[n] - X\_cam4[n]| \tag{1}$$

$$X = \frac{(X\_cam1[n] + X\_cam4[n])}{2} \tag{2}$$

$$Y = \frac{(Y\_cam1[n] + Y\_cam4[n])}{2} \tag{3}$$

The error in X axis for the 15 points is measured with (1), where X_cam1 is the X coordinate from cam1 and X_cam4 the X coordinate from cam4. If $Error\_X$ is lower than 50 pixels then X value of the point is estimated by (2), the Y coordinate is estimated by (3), where Y_cam1 is the Y coordinate from cam1 and Y_cam4 the Y coordinate from cam4, this procedure is performed for all the points. Given that the cam2 only can measure correctly the right side (points 2, 3, 4, 8, 9, 10) thus the Z coordinates for those points are equal to X_cam2. At the same time cam3 only can measure correctly the left side (points 5, 6, 7, 11, 12, 13) thus the Z coordinates for those points are equal to X_cam3.

On the other hand, if $Error\_X$ is higher than 50 pixels, the X value of the point is equal to X_cam1 and Y value is equal to Y_cam1. The Z coordinate is assigned with the same procedure described above.

The time required to obtain the 15 points is approximately 1.5 s with the faster GPU shown in the Fig. 4 and the frames required are just 1 per camera, that means, 4 frames are required to obtain 15 point with 3-D coordinate.

3 Results

The test subject was placed in the central part of the sensors' arrangement and he was asked to performed several movements. The coordinates obtained were plotted on a 3-D plot in order to reconstruct the 3-D pose.

The test subject performed a pose only with the extended arms and the straight legs and torso. In this pose, the body limbs' Z coordinates had regular values, as is shown in the Fig. 6. The propose of this pose is to measure the accuracy just in the X and Y axis.

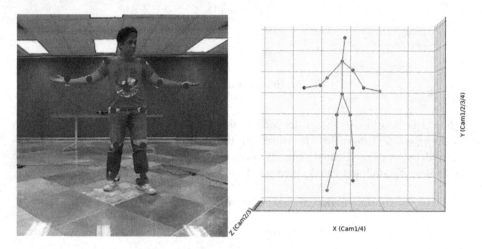

Fig. 6. Initial pose with Z regular values.

The next pose performed is a pose where the subject needed to move the legs and arms in order to not have regular values in the Z axis, this pose helped to measure the accuracy in the Z axis, the Fig. 7 is shown the X and Y axis. The Fig. 8 shown the Z axis.

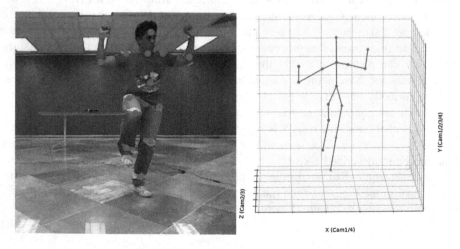

Fig. 7. Pose without Z regular values.

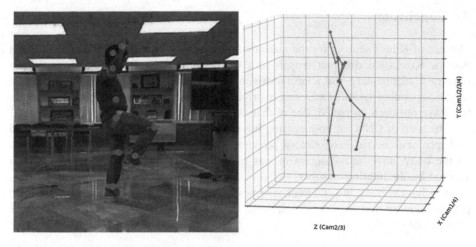

Fig. 8. Pose without Z regular values depth view.

The real joints' positions are manually approaching with an image editing software in which the coordinates are obtained drawing small point on the image, the middle point (X, Y) of the small point is the real joint position. This process is made on several frames in order to collect a point's dataset to measure the error.

$$E_{RM(n)} = \left| \frac{P_{m(n)} - P_{r(n)}}{P_{r(n)}} \right| \tag{4}$$

$$E_{RMF} = \frac{E_{RM(0)} + \cdots + E_{RM(14)}}{15} \tag{5}$$

The measure of error is calculated with (4), where E_{RM} is the Relative Error of the measure, P_m is the measured point's norm and P_r is the real point's norm. The whole Relative Error of a Frame (E_{RMF}) is the mean of the error of the 15 points measured on that frame as is shown in (5) and the mean error of a frame dataset is the mean of the E_{RMF} of every frame of that dataset. The main Relative Error in a dataset is *1.3743%*.

This result is evaluated with the result of previous methods [21, 22, 24, 28], in which the error is between 10% and 2%, which is greater than what was obtained in this method, also in this method only one computer is required, the other methods require one computer per Kinect. Nowadays the Kinect sensors are discontinued by the manufacturer, so that, the Kinect can be easily replaced by other devices [33] with the same technology due the Microsoft Kinect SDK is not used in this method as in the previous ones [21–24, 28].

4 Conclusions

The use of Kinect sensors for the measurement of joints' position is convenient given that the Kinect has different sensors in a single equipment (RGB camera and depth sensor). Unfortunately, the Kinect's drivers are licenses for a singles platform and a specific operating system. Open source drivers have several incompatibilities and errors that have not been corrected, due of that, the use of Kinect becomes more complex.

The used of CNN for pose sensing has greater advantages over the methods based on haptic sensors and exoskeletons because is not necessary to use special equipment on the body, also the measurement was robust due the measurement have not been affected by the lighting changes.

The human body has different volumes on its limbs and the clothes worn by the person increase that volume, despite this, the joints' positions measurement error is considerably small.

Acknowledgements. The authors would like to thank the Instituto Politécnico Nacional for the support to carry out this research. H. Sossa appreciates the economic support received from the SIP-IPN and CONACYT under grants 20190007 and 65 (Frontiers of Science), respectively, to conduct this investigation. J. Cruz appreciates the economic support received from the SIP-IPN under grants 20195940 to conduct this investigation.

References

1. Tsai, A.-C., Luh, J.-J., Lin, T.-T.: A novel STFT-ranking feature of multi-channel EMG for motion pattern recognition. Expert Syst. Appl. **42**, 3327–3341 (2015)
2. Brahmi, B., Saad, M., Ochoa-Luna, C., Rahman, M.H., Brahmi, A.: Adaptive tracking control of an exoskeleton robot with uncertain dynamics based on estimated time-delay control. IEEE/ASME Trans. Mechatron. **23**, 575–585 (2018)
3. Yang, C., Chang, S., Liang, P., Li, Z., Su, C.Y.: Teleoperated robot writing using EMG signals. In: 2015 IEEE International Conference on Information and Automation, pp. 2264–2269 (2015)
4. Liu, L., Zhang, Y., Liu, G., Xu, W.: Variable motion mapping to enhance stiffness discrimination and identification in robot hand teleoperation. Robot. Comput.-Integr. Manuf. **51**, 202–208 (2018)
5. Toyama, G., Hashida, T.: A detachable exoskeleton interface that duplicates the user's hand posture and motions. In: Proceedings of the 9th Augmented Human International Conference, pp. 1–5. ACM, Seoul (2018)
6. Won, J.H., Yang, G.H., Jeon, J.W.: A novel wireless vibrotactile display device for representing 3DOF force feedback in teleoperation. In: 2015 IEEE International Conference on Advanced Intelligent Mechatronics (AIM), pp. 1749–1753 (2015)
7. Du, Y.-C., Shih, C.-B., Fan, S.-C., Lin, H.-T., Chen, P.-J.: An IMU-compensated skeletal tracking system using Kinect for the upper limb. Microsystem Technologies (2018)
8. Brüggemann, B., Röhling, T., Welle, J.: Coupled human-machine tele-manipulation. Procedia Manuf. **3**, 998–1005 (2015)

9. Kim, M.K., Ryu, K., Oh, Y., Oh, S.R., Kim, K.: Implementation of real-time motion and force capturing system for tele-manipulation based on sEMG signals and IMU motion data. In: 2014 IEEE International Conference on Robotics and Automation (ICRA), pp. 5658–5664 (2014)
10. Lu, Z., Cheng, D., Dong, H., Yu, Y.: Study of human motion capture and robot motion replay for lower limb exoskeleton. In: 2017 IEEE International Conference on Cyborg and Bionic Systems (CBS), pp. 206–210 (2017)
11. OpenKinect. https://openkinect.org/wiki/Main_Page. Accessed 14 Aug 2019
12. Microsoft Kinect Xbox 360. https://support.xbox.com/es-MX/xbox-360/accessories/kinect-sensor-components. Accessed 14 Aug 2019
13. Hafiane, S., Salih, Y., Malik, A.S.: 3D hand recognition for telerobotics. In: 2013 IEEE Symposium on Computers & Informatics (ISCI), pp. 132–137 (2013)
14. Zhao, W.: A concise tutorial on human motion tracking and recognition with Microsoft Kinect. Sci. China Inf. Sci. **59**, 93101 (2016)
15. Wei, S., Ramakrishna, V., Kanade, T., Sheikh, Y.: Convolutional pose machines. In: 2016 IEEE Conference on Computer Vision and Pattern Recognition (CVPR), pp. 4724–4732 (2016)
16. Bogo, F., Black, M.J., Loper, M., Romero, J.: Detailed full-body reconstructions of moving people from monocular RGB-D sequences. In: Proceedings of the 2015 IEEE International Conference on Computer Vision (ICCV), pp. 2300–2308. IEEE Computer Society (2015)
17. Ajili, I., Mallem, M., Didier, J.Y.: Gesture recognition for humanoid robot teleoperation. In: 2017 26th IEEE International Symposium on Robot and Human Interactive Communication (RO-MAN), pp. 1115–1120 (2017)
18. Guanglong, D.U., Zhang, P.: Human–manipulator interface using hybrid sensors with Kalman filters and adaptive multi-space transformation. Measurement **55**, 413–422 (2014)
19. Munoz, J.M., Avalos, J., Ramos, O.E.: Image-driven drawing system by a NAO robot. In: 2017 Electronic Congress (E-CON UNI), pp. 1–4 (2017)
20. Saini, S., Zakaria, N., Rambli, D.R.A., Sulaiman, S.: Markerless human motion tracking using hierarchical multi-swarm cooperative particle swarm optimization. PLoS ONE **10**, e0127833 (2015)
21. Kim, Y., Baek, S., Bae, B.-C.: Motion capture of the human body using multiple depth sensors. ETRI J. **39**, 181–190 (2017)
22. Moon, S., Park, Y., Ko, D.W., Suh, I.H.: Multiple Kinect sensor fusion for human skeleton tracking using Kalman filtering. Int. J. Adv. Rob. Syst. **13**, 65 (2016)
23. Córdova-Esparza, D.-M., Terven, J.R., Jiménez-Hernández, H., Vázquez-Cervantes, A., Herrera-Navarro, A.-M., Ramírez-Pedraza, A.: Multiple Kinect V2 calibration. Automatika **57**, 810–821 (2016)
24. Núñez, J.C., Cabido, R., Montemayor, A.S., Pantrigo, J.J.: Real-time human body tracking based on data fusion from multiple RGB-D sensors. Multimed. Tools Appl. **76**, 4249–4271 (2017)
25. Cao, Z., Simon, T., Wei, S., Sheikh, Y.: Realtime multi-person 2D pose estimation using part affinity fields. In: 2017 IEEE Conference on Computer Vision and Pattern Recognition (CVPR), pp. 1302–1310 (2017)
26. Zuher, F., Romero, R.: Recognition of human motions for imitation and control of a humanoid robot. In: 2012 Brazilian Robotics Symposium and Latin American Robotics Symposium, pp. 190–195 (2012)
27. Xu, Y., Yang, C., Zhong, J., Wang, N., Zhao, L.: Robot teaching by teleoperation based on visual interaction and extreme learning machine. Neurocomputing **275**, 2093–2103 (2018)
28. Ajili, I., Mallem, M., Didier, J.-Y.: Robust human action recognition system using Laban Movement Analysis. Procedia Comput. Sci. **112**, 554–563 (2017)

29. Cerulo, I., Ficuciello, F., Lippiello, V., Siciliano, B.: Teleoperation of the SCHUNK S5FH under-actuated anthropomorphic hand using human hand motion tracking. Robot. Auton. Syst. **89**, 75–84 (2017)
30. Ali, S.K., Firdaus, A.R., Tokhi, M.O., Al-Rezage, G.: Tracking human upper-limb movements with sliding mode control type-II fuzzy logic. In: 2016 21st International Conference on Methods and Models in Automation and Robotics (MMAR), pp. 426–431 (2016)
31. Caffe. https://caffe.berkeleyvision.org/. Accessed 14 Aug 2019
32. MPII Human Pose Dataset. http://human-pose.mpi-inf.mpg.de/. Accessed 14 Aug 2019
33. Orbbec. https://orbbec3d.com/. Accessed 14 Aug 2019

Brazilian Traffic Signs Detection and Recognition in Videos Using CLAHE, HOG Feature Extraction and SVM Cascade Classifier with Temporal Coherence

Renata Zottis Junges[1]([⊠]) [iD], Mauricio Braga de Paula[2],
and Marilton Sanchotene de Aguiar[1] [iD]

[1] Federal University of Pelotas,
Pelotas, RS, Brazil
{rzjunges,marilton}@inf.ufpel.edu.br
[2] Mathematics and Statistics Department, Federal University of Pelotas,
Pelotas, RS, Brazil
maubrapa@ufpel.edu.br

Abstract. Worldwide, traffic safety is a strong concern as traffic accidents are one of the leading causes of death. In this context, advanced driver assistance systems (ADAS) and autonomous vehicles are traffic management measures aimed at improving road safety and flow. Automatic detection and recognition of traffic signs are important for intelligent vehicles and ADAS systems. This work proposes a pipeline of digital image processing (DIP) techniques, machine learning (ML), and temporal coherence to perform the detection and recognition of Brazilian traffic signs in videos aiming an application for real-time systems to help in traffic safety and to reduce the number of fatal accidents. We are mainly interested in recognizing signs of speed limit group, no overtaking and obligatory passage, thus our detection considers the traffic sign with a circular shape and red border. For detection, the red color segmentation and the Hough transform are used to find circular regions that will be classified through the SVM algorithm in sign and not sign. For recognition of these signs, the support vector machines (SVM) are used. For speed limit signs the thresholding and contours are used to segment the digits for later classification. Our proposed method achieved an accuracy of 0.82 in detection, an increase of 18% in the number of recognized frames and 0.96 in the recognition stage using temporal coherence.

Keywords: Traffic signs · Detection · Recognition · Temporal coherence · Traffic safety

1 Introduction

Traffic safety has been a strong concern in the last years, mostly in low-income countries where the death rates are three times higher than in high-income coun-

© Springer Nature Switzerland AG 2019
L. Martínez-Villaseñor et al. (Eds.): MICAI 2019, LNAI 11835, pp. 589–600, 2019.
https://doi.org/10.1007/978-3-030-33749-0_47

tries [14]. In 2013, Brazil was the third country that recorded the most deaths in traffic, overpassing 46 thousand deaths [14]. According to World Health Organization (WHO) [14], road traffic injuries are the eighth leading cause of death worldwide – 1.35 million in 2016 – and the leading killer of children and young adults aged between 5 to 29 years old.

According to the Federal Council of Medicine [4], in Brazil, every 60 min, on average, at least five people are killed by traffic accidents. Besides, in the last ten years (2009–2018), there was a increase of 33% in the number of hospitalizations throughout the country, the injuries caused by road disasters cost approximately 3 billion Brazilian Reais from Sistema Único de Saúde (SUS, Single Health System). The SUS is one of the most complex and complete systems of health care in the world and guarantees free access for Brazil's entire population [9].

In this context, there are traffic management measures aimed at improving road safety, advanced driver assistance systems (ADAS) and autonomous vehicles are examples of it. The ADAS intended to help the driver in his driving activities and increase car safety and comfort [2]. Traffic management can be performed by Traffic Sign Detection and Recognition (TSDR) which plays an important role in computer vision field and consists of two steps: Traffic Sign Detection (TSD) following by Traffic Sign Recognition (TSR). The goal of TSD is identifying the region of interests (ROIs) and boundaries of the traffic sign in a given image or frame (in case of video) and TSR deals with the classification of the ROIs.

In this paper, we propose a pipeline of digital image processing (DIP) techniques for TSD and machine learning (ML) for TSR in videos, aiming a real-time application to improve traffic safety. As the traffic signs differ among countries, in this work we focus on the Brazilian signs. Also, we are mainly interested in recognizing signs of speed limit group, no overtaking and obligatory passage, thus our detection considers the traffic sign with a circular shape and red border.

The detection stage has the following steps: (i) based on color information (red color), traffic signs are segmented from the image using HSV (hue, saturation, value) space; (ii) the binary mask generated in the previous step is used to find circular shapes through Circle Hough Transform; (iii) around the obtained circles is calculated a bounding box and the ROI is extracted; (iv) the features are extracted by Histogram of Oriented Gradients (HOG) descriptor; and, (v) these features are the input of Support Vector Machine (SVM) algorithm used to determine if the ROI is or is not a sign.

In the recognition stage, we firstly use HOG following by SVM to classify between no overtaking and obligatory passage or others. If the classification was positive, then a segmentation procedure is applied to separate no overtaking from the obligatory passage; otherwise, the sign is classified as speed limit group. In the speed limit group, we are interested in the limit of the sign, then we apply DIP techniques to make digit segmentation to extract the digits from the sign and then we apply HOG plus multiclass SVM in the digits to decide the value of the speed limit sign. After this process, a bounding box around the sign detected is drawn on the frame together with information about the recognition and a new frame is recorded in an output video.

This paper is organized as follows. Section 2 reviews related work on TSD or TSR. Section 3 details the proposed approach to TSDR and present the datasets used and training step. Section 4 illustrates results and a discussion is performed. Section 5 concludes the paper and discuss future work.

2   Related Work

There are many different methods for TSD and TSR. They are usually divided into three stages: (i) pre-processing and segmentation (ii) feature extraction, and (iii) classification. Commonly a color or shape segmentation is adopted; we use color segmentation followed by shape segmentation as [1,13]. In [1] work, the HSI color space is used in color segmentation and geometric invariant Hu moments is used in shape segmentation; our method uses HSV and circle Hough Transformation. In [5,10] works, they only use color segmentation.

Many features extraction proposals are used for the TSR task, HOGv is used in [8] work; HSI-HOG in [1,5]; LBP in [3,5,10]; area and ratio in [13]; and HOG in [3] and ours. For classification, [1,3,5] and ours use SVM. Other approaches are used too, in [13] ELM algorithm is used, fuzzy integral in [10], AdaBoost and neural network in [10], and random forests in [5].

In the work [6], authors identify and recognize the speed limit traffic signs from Brazil using their own image dataset (not video). Their work uses a window to check if the region is the speed limit sign or not, for recognition, they segment the digits and standardize to 35×35 pixels, so they performed a comparison .among different ML techniques, the SVM showed the best performance.

It is not possible to compare directly the metrics of our algorithm with others because we do not perform the tests on image dataset. Our test set is ROIs coming from the test video. The works [1,3,5,8,10] at least use German Traffic Sign Detection Benchmark (GTSDB) [7] or German Traffic Sign Recognition Benchmark (GTSRB) [11] datasets to train and perform the tests; these datasets contain the German traffic signs and most of them are different in Brazil. The [6] work presents a dataset with Brazilian speed limit signs, but since this dataset is not public, we could not make real comparisons.

In our work, partial GTSRB is used for training traffic sign model and we create the Artificial Digits Dataset (ADD) to recognize the digits from speed limits. To recognize digits in speed limit traffic sign, our algorithm performs this task in the average of 0.094 s per frame while Miyata [10] performs in 1.1 s. With our execution time, we can adapt our approach to the real-time system. Although our algorithm does not classify in big groups of the sign as prohibitory, mandatory and danger, we classify sign to sign indicating their specific values.

3   Proposed Method

In this paper, we propose an algorithm pipeline (shown in Fig. 1) to detect circular traffic signs with a red border in videos and recognize the following signs: no overtaking, obligatory passage, and speed limit group with the speed value. This algorithm is divided into two main stages: detection and recognition. In addition, a temporal coherence step can be applied considering the result of the last N-1 frames, where N is a previously defined number.

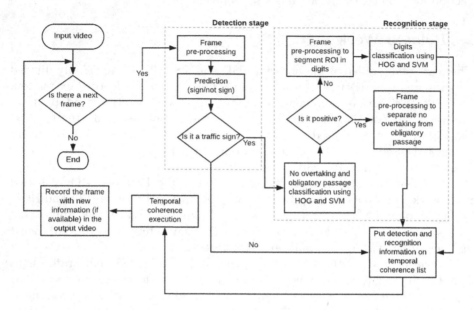

Fig. 1. Flowchart for proposed TSDR algorithm.

The first step of the detection stage is the frame pre-processing where several operations are done in the original frame (Fig. 2) in order to find regions of interest (ROIs) to follow for the prediction step.

In frame pre-processing, we applied Contrast Limited Adaptive Histogram Equalization (CLAHE) [15] on the original frame to improve contrast and achieve a better result in the segmentation. After, we segment the image based on the red color, through HSV color space; in this way, we create a binary image (mask) where the white region corresponds to the pixels in red color and the black region to the background pixels.

Next, we applied a Gaussian filter with 3 × 3-kernel and circle Hough transform algorithm to find circular shapes in the mask; more than one circular shape can be detected, and a bounding box is calculated to covers each circle found, in Fig. 3 is shown the mask with green circle from circle Hough and red rectangles from bounding boxes. After, we use the coordinates of the bounding box to cut out that ROI from CLAHE frame. Then, we resized the ROI to 48 × 48 pixels to classify the ROI into traffic sign or not traffic sign – new ROIs are shown in Fig. 4.

Then, in prediction (sign/not sign) step, we use HOG for feature extraction and insert it into SVM to classify whether the ROI is a traffic sign (positive class) or not (negative class). The ROI follows to the recognition stage if occurs

Fig. 2. Original frame. (Color figure online)

Fig. 3. Mask from frame pre-processing. (Color figure online)

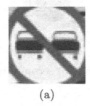

(a)

(b)

Fig. 4. ROIs from circle Hough transform: (a) biggest and (b) smallest circles.

a positive classification, otherwise, this information is recorded in the temporal coherence list.

In the recognition stage, we first classify the ROI – through HOG and SVM algorithm – in no overtaking and obligatory passage (positive class) or other (negative class). If the classification is positive, then we need to distinguish between no overtaking and obligatory passage category. On the no overtaking sign, the internal region has a white diagonal trace from segmentation while the obligatory passage sign does not have any color in it.

Then, we cut off 30% of the ROI bounding box sides, removing the traffic sign outer circle and keeping only the internal region. Thus, we separate these two categories based on whether or not they have white pixels. Nevertheless, if the classification is negative, the ROI follows to frame pre-processing to segment ROI in digits and classify the speed limit traffic sign.

In frame pre-processing to segment ROI in digits we convert the RGB ROI to grayscale and applied inverted thresholding technique to obtain a binary image (Fig. 5(a)). Further, we find the contours through the algorithm presented by Suzuki [12] (Fig. 5(b)), for each contour a bounding box around is created (Fig. 5(c)) if it is located where the digits probably are.

These bounding boxes are cut off the ROI and resized to 48 × 48 pixels, generating new ROIs (shown in Fig. 6). Then, the next step is the digits classification using HOG and SVM to predict the speed value from the speed limit sign.

After the digits classification, information about the ROIs (referring to detection and recognition) from each frame is recorded in the temporal coherence list. The temporal coherence can be seen as a strategy to eliminate or reduce errors

(a)   (b)   (c)

Fig. 5. Frame pre-processing to segment ROI in digits: (a) thresholding, (b) contours, and (c) bounding box.

(a)   (b)

Fig. 6. ROIs from digits segmentation: (a) first and (b) second digits.

in the predictions considering the results of the last N-1 frames of the video. The temporal coherence execution only begins when it has information from N frames, that is, the first N-1 frames do not make use of temporal coherence.

For each ROI of each frame, we store the information of frame number and, if detection occurred, which traffic sign was recognized, the coordinates of the center point of the circle that is around the detected sign, the circle radius, and if the temporal coherence modified this ROI.

We used the Jaccard similarity coefficient to reduce the errors when a traffic sign is detected but does not really exist (false positive). This coefficient calculates the overlap of two sets, in this case, two images. The value of this coefficient varies from 0 to 1, indicating, none to total overlap. In frame N, it is verified if there is any overlap with the ROIs of the last N-1 frames. If there was at least one overlap case it was understood that ROI was actually a sign and not a false positive; otherwise, this ROI was modified in coherence list and now the field about detection has the value False. Thus, many false positives are eliminated.

We used the approach of counting how many traffic signs should exist in the frame under evaluation to verify the true positive case (detected and recognized correctly) or to fix errors as (i) did not detect but the sign exists or (ii) detected but did not recognize. For this, we use a dictionary where the key is the number of ROIs of each frame and the item is the number of times (how many frames) this number appears. However, to account for the dictionary values, we only consider the ROIs which was not modified due to temporal coherence.

The dictionary is organized in descending order based on the values of the items. In this way, it is known which is the most frequent number of signs per frame and in how many frames this count appeared. If the sign has appeared in more than N/2 frames, by the majority, it is considered that the frame under evaluation also has or must have this number of ROIs. If the frame under review

Fig. 7. Final frame.

(frame N) has fewer ROIs than it should, then the temporal coherence determines which are the likely sign through the last frames. This approach, correct errors when the sign was not detected but the sign exists.

On the other hand, if the frame N has the same number of ROIs that it should, means that: (i) detected and recognized correctly or (ii) detected and did not recognize. If all ROIs of the frame N has been recognized, detection and recognition are considered correct; otherwise, it is used the same approach where the frame N has fewer ROIs. Thus, it is possible to discover which is the probable sign that was detected and modify the temporal coherence list to contain this new information; this corrects the problem of detected but did not recognize.

The temporal coherence proposed here does not guarantee the correction of all types of errors but tries to minimize them. Not always the changes made are correct, however, these errors are not propagated by more than N/2 frames.

Finally, a new image (from each frame) is created with the detected traffic sign (circle and rectangle around the sign), recognition information, and recorded at the end of the new video (output video). In Fig. 7 is the final frame corresponding to the original frame shown previously.

We have done these process with other videos with other traffic signs to confirm if our algorithm handles well signs with 3 digits or other speed limits. Using a frame (Fig. 8) from a video with the presence of 4 traffic sign's speed limit, we were able to detect and recognize all of them. The ROIs extracted from the frame are exposed in Fig. 9. The final frame is shown in Fig. 10.

3.1 Datasets

We used the GTSRB dataset presented in Stallkamp [11] as the basis for the creation of the traffic sign dataset. GTSRB contains the German traffic signs, arranged in 43 classes of signs, totalizing 39,209 images. However, several classes have signs that do not exist in Brazil and several traffic signs with the triangular shape, outside the scope of this work.

Fig. 8. Frame with 4 speed limit traffic signs.

Fig. 9. ROIs with bounding boxes around the digits.

Were excluded all image classes with another shape since the interest signs are circular. Also, all signs with the size under than 35×35 pixels and signs considered unsuitable for training due to excessive brightness or low contrast were also removed.

After selecting the best images, the dataset reduced to 406 images, they were resized to 48×48 and grouped in a single folder corresponding to the dataset positive samples. Another 164 signs were removed of traffic videos (not used in test video) and added to the positive sample class. For the creation of negative samples, a script was developed to cut out random regions (with a resolution of 48×48) of a traffic video (also, not used in test video). The result was a total of 570 negative samples.

For no overtaking and obligatory passage dataset, the positive class was created by the manually cut out of a traffic video. In the testing phase, this video was not considered. For the negative class, other pieces of the video were used. In the end, all images were resized to 48×48. In all, there are 159 positive samples and 373 negative samples.

We create a Artificial Digits Dataset containing 17,850 images of digits, each class contains 1,785 binary images with the size of 48×48 pixels. The ADD was created using fonts from library OpenCV and from fonts installed in a personal computer. In order to make the dataset more robust, we used the data augmentation technique, that is used to apply small modifications in each image and generate a new image from this. The transformation applied was: distortion (left and right), random distortion and rotation. The last step to create this

Fig. 10. Output frame with 4 speed limit traffic signs detected and recognized.

dataset was cut off each image around the digit (without background) and then scale to 48×48. In Fig. 11 are shown examples of the artificial digits.

Fig. 11. Samples of digits (concatenated) in ADD

3.2 Training

Three models were trained to constitute the pipeline proposed in this work. The first one was to identify traffic signs, the second one to recognize no overtaking and obligatory passage signs, and the last one was to classify the digits from the speed limit signs. The images used in each training were from datasets discussed previously.

To create all the models, it was used the images with a resolution of 48×48 pixels and for feature extraction, using the HOG algorithm. The HOG algorithm was configured with orientation bins set to 9, 8×8 pixels per cell, 2×2 cells per block, and L1-Hys normalization block. The SVM with a linear kernel was used for the training of model to identify traffic signs and for the training of no overtaking and obligatory passage signs. Nevertheless, to train the model for digits recognition, the non-linear SVM was used with a polynomial kernel, degree 4 and coefficient 8.

Table 1. TSD classification

	N = 1				N = 10				N = 30			
	Prec.	Rec.	F1	Acc.	Prec.	Rec.	F1	Acc.	Prec.	Rec.	F1	Acc.
Detected	0.86	0.50	0.63	–	0.85	0.53	0.65	–	0.82	0.53	0.64	–
Not detected	0.81	0.96	0.88	–	0.82	0.96	0.88	–	0.81	0.95	0.88	–
Average	**0.83**	**0.82**	**0.80**	**0.82**	**0.83**	**0.82**	**0.81**	**0.82**	**0.82**	**0.82**	**0.80**	**0.82**

4   Results and Discussion

To evaluate the proposed approach, we used 14 videos totalizing 4 min and 42 s (approx. 30fps), the image size was 1920×1080 and it was recorded at Pelotas, RS, Brazil. In these videos, the following traffic signs are present: no overtaking, obligatory passage, 40 km/h, 60 km/h, 90 km/h and 100 km/h. The total execution time was 742 s – including the recorded of the output video – each frame was executed in an average of 0.094 s; the temporal coherence execution did not have significant execution time. For the tests, a computer running Ubuntu 18.04.2 LTS with Intel (R) Core (TM) i5-8250 CPU 1.60 GHz x 8 and 7.4 GB of RAM was used. The algorithm was developed in the Python language using OpenCV library for computer vision algorithms and scikit-learn for machine learning methods.

In order to present the results, we tested different temporal coherence size configurations with $N = \{1, 10, 30\}$. When $N = 1$, we did not use temporal coherence. Ground truth and predictions files are needed to compute the following metrics: precision (Prec.), recall (Rec.), F1 score, and accuracy (Acc.). For the detection stage, only the samples that obtained the Jaccard higher than 0.5 were considered as true positive, that is, the predicted ROI should have at least 50% overlap with the corresponding sign of the ground truth file. For recognition, only the analysis of the samples that in the detection resulted in true positive was performed.

Tables 1 and 2 present results for detection and recognition with different values for N. In Table 1, the last line presents the average considering the number of samples for each class. In TSD classification, although the values of these metrics do not seem different, it is perceptible (watching the output video) that the temporal coherence improves the cases of false positive in the detection stage. However, as the false positives were few it was not perceived an improvement in the metrics, but in Table 2 we can note that the total number of frames detected increases with N. In TSR classification, the temporal coherence was efficient because increased the number of recognized signs (from 896 to 1220, representing an increase of 67.98% to 85.98% of positive recognitions) and maintained substantially the same accuracy.

We ran the tests on other videos which did not have the ground truth in the present scenario, then we could not evaluate the metrics in these cases. However, through these videos we were able to test the algorithm under other weather

Table 2. TSR classification

	N = 1	N = 10	N = 30
Total detected frames	1318	1418	1419
Total recognized frames	896	1201	1220
Percentage of recognized frames	67.98%	84.7%	85.98%
Accuracy	0.96	0.94	0.94

conditions, our propose was able to detect and recognize in rainy, cloudy and sunny days. Due to the quality of the camera's mobile phone, the algorithm did not perform well in videos recorded at night. We make available on the internet[1] the generated datasets, all tests performed with and without ground truth and the resulting videos.

5 Conclusions

The present work proposes a pipeline of a system that can be used in the development of ADAS, helping in traffic safety and reducing the number of fatal accidents. In this work, in TSD we achieved good results without temporal coherence but not impressive results with it. However, in TSR stage we got better results with temporal coherence, we increased the number of recognized signs in 18% and maintained substantially the same accuracy (approx. 0.95).

In the related work, TSR is commonly divided into big groups as a danger, mandatory, and prohibitory signs. In this work, the TSR was properly specified, recognizing sign to sign, not only informing the what big group it belongs to. This is useful because with this recognition the car speed can change depending on the maximum speed limit detected, or, a warning can be emitted if the driver is above the maximum speed. With more signs being recognized other measures can be performed with our proposed system aiming more safety in traffic.

A remarkable difficulty for the accomplishment of this work was to find a dataset with Brazilian traffic sign because traffic signs change from country to country. With the use of a robust dataset of traffic signs used in Brazil, the proposed method could have achieved better results.

Another benefit of this work is that the signs can be detected anywhere on the road (left, right and on the road) and not just on the right side and on a two-lane road. Still, it is not necessary to do any type of calibration on the camera for video recording. For future work, we intend to expand the number of traffic sign recognized and evaluate this proposal in real-time situations by analyzing for example only a fraction of the total frames.

Acknowledgments. This study was financed in part by the Coordenação de Aperfeiçoamento de Pessoal de Nível Superior (CAPES/Brasil) and Agência Nacional de Águas (ANA/Brasil) – Edital No. 16/2017.

---

[1] https://bit.ly/2ZeowQP.

References

1. Agrawal, S., Chaurasiya, R.K.: Automatic traffic sign detection and recognition using moment invariants and support vector machine. In: 2017 International Conference on Recent Innovations in Signal processing and Embedded Systems (RISE), pp. 289–295. IEEE (2017)
2. Barthès, J.P.A., Bonnifait, P.: Multi-agent active collaboration between drivers and assistance systems. In: Rossetti, R.J., Liu, R. (eds.) Advances in Artificial Transportation Systems and Simulation, chap. 9, pp. 163–180. Academic Press (2014)
3. Berkaya, S.K., Gunduz, H., Ozsen, O., Akinlar, C., Gunal, S.: On circular traffic sign detection and recognition. Expert Syst. Appl. **48**, 67–75 (2016)
4. Conselho Federal de Medicina: Em dez anos, acidentes de trânsito consomem quase R$ 3 bilhões do SUS, May 2019. http://bit.ly/2EUcB3a. (in Portuguese)
5. Ellahyani, A., El Ansari, M., El Jaafari, I.: Traffic sign detection and recognition based on random forests. Appl. Soft Comput. **46**, 805–815 (2016)
6. Gomes, S.L., et al.: Embedded real-time speed limit sign recognition using image processing and machine learning techniques. Neural Comput. Appl. **28**(1), 573–584 (2017)
7. Houben, S., Stallkamp, J., Salmen, J., Schlipsing, M., Igel, C.: Detection of traffic signs in real-world images: the German traffic sign detection benchmark. In: The 2013 International Joint Conference on Neural Networks (IJCNN), pp. 1–8. IEEE (2013)
8. Huang, Z., Yu, Y., Gu, J., Liu, H.: An efficient method for traffic sign recognition based on extreme learning machine. IEEE Trans. Cybern. **47**(4), 920–933 (2016)
9. Ministério da Saúde: Sistema Único de saúde (SUS): estrutura, princípios e como funciona, June 2019. http://portalms.saude.gov.br/sistema-unico-de-saude. (in Portuguese)
10. Miyata, S.: Recognition of speed limits on speed-limit signs by using machine learning. In: 2017 24th International Conference on Mechatronics and Machine Vision in Practice (M2VIP), pp. 1–9. IEEE (2017)
11. Stallkamp, J., Schlipsing, M., Salmen, J., Igel, C.: Man vs. computer: benchmarking machine learning algorithms for traffic sign recognition. Neural Netw. **32**, 323–332 (2012)
12. Suzuki, S., et al.: Topological structural analysis of digitized binary images by border following. Comput. Vis. Graph. Image Process. **30**(1), 32–46 (1985)
13. Taştimur, C., Karaköse, M., Çelik, Y., Akın, E.: Image processing based traffic sign detection and recognition with fuzzy integral. In: 2016 International Conference on Systems, Signals and Image Processing (IWSSIP), pp. 1–4. IEEE (2016)
14. World Health Organization: Gho – by category – road traffic deaths - data by country, February 2019. http://apps.who.int/gho/data/node.main.A997?lang=en
15. Zuiderveld, K.: Contrast limited adaptive histogram equalization. In: Graphics Gems IV, pp. 474–485. Academic Press Professional, Inc., Cambridge (1994)

A Fast and Robust Deep Learning Approach for Hand Object Grasping Confirmation

Sebastián Salazar-Colores[1] , Arquímides Méndez-Molina[2(✉)] ,
David Carrillo-López[2], Esaú Escobar-Juárez[2] , Eduardo F. Morales[2] ,
and L. Enrique Sucar[2]

[1] Universidad Autónoma de Querétaro, Cerro de las Campanas s/n,
76010 Querétaro, Querétaro, Mexico
s.salazarcolores@gmail.com
[2] Coordinación de Ciencias Computacionales, Instituto Nacional de Astrofísica,
Óptica y Electrónica (INAOE), Luis Enrique Erro # 1,
72840 Tonantzintla, Puebla, Mexico
arquimides.mendez@gmail.com

Abstract. One of the most important skills for service robots is object manipulation, which is still a challenging task. Since object manipulation is a hard task, it is relevant to know if an object was successfully grasped, avoiding future wrong decisions. Object grasp confirmation is commonly solved by using robotic sensors (infrared, pressure, etc.), but, in many cases, these sensors are not available for all robots. In contrast, depth and RGB sensor are present in almost all service robots. In this work a novel computer vision based method oriented to hand object grasp confirmation is proposed, which uses a deep learning network trained with depth maps. In order to measure the performance of the proposed method, experiments were performed using a single-arm manipulator service robot for both known and unknown objects. Experimental results show that the proposed approach correctly identifies 99% of both classes (object grasped or not grasped) with known objects and 92% with unknown objects. The grasping confirmation method was added to the Storing Groceries task, for RoboCup@Home competition, improving its time performance.

Keywords: Service robot · Object manipulation · Object grasp confirmation · Deep learning · Convolutional neural network

1 Introduction

Robotics in its evolution has been leaving aside the repetitive tasks of controlled industrial environments, increasingly moving towards dynamic environ-

---

Sebastián Salazar-Colores (CVU 477758) would like to thank CONACYT (Consejo Nacional de Ciencia y Tecnología) for the financial support of his Ph.D. studies under Scholarship 285651.

L. Martínez-Villaseñor et al. (Eds.): MICAI 2019, LNAI 11835, pp. 601–612, 2019.
https://doi.org/10.1007/978-3-030-33749-0_48

ments with human interaction through what is known as service robots. When introducing service robots into society, they are expected to interact and change the physical world. One of the most important skills for this kind of robots, present in most tasks, is object manipulation.

Object manipulation is a challenging task which involves building novel hardware, designing flexible software and creating fully integrated systems. Different researchers have focused on particular aspects of object manipulation such as object detection [14], grasp pose estimation [6], completion of occluded or partially observed objects [11], manipulation planning [1], and execution [3], among others.

Despite the existing advances, most of the works do not take into account the grasp confirmation, that is, to automatically verify if a robot actually is grasping an object or not after a grasp attempt. Commonly, the percentage of success in the manipulation task is reported and the possibility of retrying the grip for the failed cases is not considered. The automatic confirmation of the grip of objects is very useful (especially for service robots) because it allows the robot to recover from failures, in addition, to avoid future errors such as the attempt to place an object that it is not holding in hand. The automatic grasp confirmation can be done using sensors (infrared, pressure, etc.) in the robotic arm, but also through vision (RGB cameras, Depth maps, etc). The last approach is more practical and generalizable, because no customized hardware is needed, instead it is only necessary that the robot has a RGBD camera. In this way the grasping confirmation problem can be reduced to a problem of image classification.

In the present investigation, a method is proposed to automatically identify success or not of a given grasp attempt. Our method uses Convolutional neural networks (CNNs) [12], a class of deep learning neural networks. CNNs represent a huge breakthrough in image recognition. The neural network is trained using depth images of the manipulator grasping objects (positive class) and also depth maps from the manipulator without grasping any objects (negative class).

The method has been tested for both, known and unknown objects, using a real manipulator robot. Experimental results show that the proposed approach correctly identifies both classes (object grasped or not grasped).

The grasping confirmation method was added to the Storing Groceries task, for RoboCup@Home competition. In this way, a real robot can perform most grasp attempts given the time constraints, which provides better performance in this kind of competitions.

The remainder of this paper is organized as follows. Section 2 reviews some closely related works. Section 3 describes the proposed method. In Sect. 4 the experimental set-up is described and the main results presented. Finally, in Sect. 5, conclusions and future research directions are given.

2   Related Work

With the increasing number of proposed research on grasp assessment, grasp planning, and tactile processing [4], very few of these take into consideration any form of grasp verification [15], understanding this as a way of knowing if the object grasped is indeed in the robot's end effector, using visual information.

Some of them use deep networks as the main processing block [5,6] combined with tactile and visual information as well, while others take a more traditional approach [1,9] or discuss system integration subjects [3]. In [1], it is presented the problem of tracking and grasping a moving object, but not any grasp confirmation at all.

A lot of research focus their efforts on tactile processing [2,6], and adding other external instrumentation [7,10,13], involving more hardware requirements for the robot. Visual (including color and depth) information must be sufficient to appropriately solve the grasping problem.

Although visual sensors are mentioned in [8] (and consequently a form of grasp verification is performed), its information is used to determine the object's position once in the robot's end effector, and the experimental results involve grasping small objects in a controlled environment. Neural networks are also mentioned as a form of a classifier block.

In-hand 3D object reconstruction [11] is also considered. To accomplish this, the object has to be in the robot's end effector, besides the previous generation of arm's trajectories in order to sample the specimen. It is worth saying that this is useful for learning new object geometries from a closer look, where details start to be visible, whenever possible. However, no form of grasp verification is included as part of this work.

Most previous work related to object manipulation focuses on object detection and 3-D modelling; and those that deal with grasp verification use additional sensors. In contrast, in this work we perform grasp verification using only an RGB-D camera, transforming the problem to a binary image classification task.

3   Background

3.1   Convolutional Neural Networks

Convolutional Neural Network (CNN) is a well-known deep learning architecture inspired by the natural visual perception mechanism of the living creatures. In 1990, LeCun et al. [12] published the seminal paper establishing the framework of CNN. They developed a multi-layer artificial neural network which could classify handwritten digits. A CNN can obtain effective representations of the original image, which makes it possible to recognize visual patterns directly from raw pixels with little-to-none preprocessing.

Convolutional Layer. The convolutional layer aims to learn feature representations of the inputs. Convolutional layer is composed of several convolution kernels which are used to compute different feature maps. Specifically, each neuron of a feature map is connected to a region of neighbouring neurons in the previous layer. Such a neighbourhood is referred to as the neuron's receptive field in the previous layer. The new feature map can be obtained by first convolving the input with a learned kernel and then applying an element-wise nonlinear activation function on the convolved results.

Note that, to generate each feature map, the kernel is shared by all spatial locations of the input. The complete feature maps are obtained by using several different kernels. Mathematically, the feature value at location (i, j) in the k-th feature map of l-th layer, $z_{i,j,k}^l$, is calculated by:

$$z_{i,j,k}^l = \mathbf{w}_k^{l\ T} \mathbf{x}_{i,j}^l + b_k^l \tag{1}$$

where $\mathbf{w}_k^l$ and b_k^l are the weight vector and bias term of the k-th filter of the l-th layer respectively, and $\mathbf{x}_{i,j}^l$ is the input patch centered at location (i, j) of the l-th layer. Note that the kernel $\mathbf{w}_k^l$ that generates the feature map $z_{:,:,k}^l$ is shared. Such a weight sharing mechanism has several advantages such as it can reduce the model complexity and make the network easier to train.

Maxpooling Layer. Pooling is an important concept of CNN. It lowers the computational burden by reducing the number of connections between convolutional layers.

A pooling function replaces the output of the net at a certain location with a summary statistic of the nearby outputs. The most commonly used operation is max pooling which reports the maximum output within a rectangular neighborhood.

In all cases, pooling helps to make the representation become approximately invariant to small translations of the input. Invariance to translation means that if we translate the input by a small amount, the values of most of the pooled outputs do not change. Invariance to local translation can be a very useful property if we care more about whether some feature is present than exactly where it is. For example, when determining whether an image contains a face, we do not need to know the location of the eyes with pixel-perfect accuracy, we just need to know that there is an eye on the left side of the face and an eye on the right side of the face. In other contexts, it is more important to preserve the location of a feature.

The use of pooling can be viewed as adding an infinitely strong prior that the function the layer learns must be invariant to small translations. When this assumption is correct, it can greatly improve the statistical efficiency of the network.

Because pooling summarizes the responses over a whole neighborhood, it is possible to use fewer pooling units than detector units, by reporting summary statistics for pooling regions spaced k pixels apart rather than 1 pixel apart.

Relu. Rectified linear unit (ReLU) is one of the most notable non-saturated activation functions. The ReLU activation function is defined as:

$$a_{i,j,k} = max(z_{i,j,k}, 0) \tag{2}$$

where $z_{i,j,k}$ is the input of the activation function at location (i,j) on the k-th channel. ReLU is a piecewise linear function which prunes the negative part to zero and retains the positive part. The simple $max(\Delta)$ operation of ReLU allows it to compute much faster than sigmoid or tanh activation functions, and it also induces the sparsity in the hidden units and allows the network to easily obtain sparse representations. It has been shown that deep networks can be trained efficiently using ReLU even without pre-training. Even though the discontinuity of ReLU at 0 may hurt the performance of backpropagation, many works have shown that ReLU works better than sigmoid and tanh activation functions empirically.

4   Method

4.1   Hardware Setup

The experimentation platform in this work was a mobile manipulator, cataloged as *RB-1*, with some modifications. Important parts are shown in Fig. 1. As relevant characteristics, could be mentioned the following: a ten hours autonomy, an Intel NUC as an embedded computer (i7, four cores at 3.1 GHz, 8 GB RAM), the 6 *DOF* Kinova Mico arm attached to a periscopic torso, a pan-tilt *RGB-D* camera and an auxiliary computer (DELL LapTop i7, four cores at 2.7 GHz and 16 GB RAM); differential traction wheels move around the base and the arm as a whole.

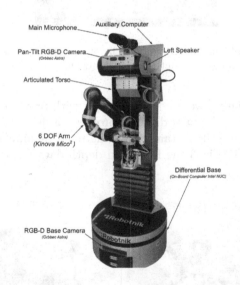

Fig. 1. Mobile Manipulator RB-1 (modified).

A note on the *RGB-D* camera: the minimum (and obtainable) depth distance (according to the manufacturer for *Orbbec Astra 3D* cameras) is *0.6* m. This is an important limitation to mention, because it restricts the grasping detail that could be visualized. RGB and depth resolutions are both 640 × 480 pixels.

As a software interface, the platform uses ROS (*Robotic Operative System*) [16] for interprocess communication purposes. ROS master runs on board (on the Intel NUC), while the auxiliary computer and its associated nodes, run as clients. We use an ethernet local area network and cable for physical communication.

4.2   Selection of Data Source

The robot platform robot has two available source data: RGB and depth data. Both options were considered.

However, and although RGB images does not have the distance limitation that depth maps does (minimum observable depth distance is 0.6 m), the RGB images present a subjacent ambiguity due to the lack of distance information. This fact can be observed in Fig. 2.

Fig. 2. Ambiguity problem in RGB data. The soda can appears to be taken by the manipulating arm, although it is actually on the table.

Due to this ambiguity we used depth maps, with provides robustness to our method. To avoid the minimum distance problem, a default inspection position pose was defined where the distance from the hand manipulator to the camera is more than 0.6 m. In Fig. 3 the RGB and depth data from the proposed pose are shown.

(a)   (b)

Fig. 3. *RGB* and depth image comparison. (a) *RGB* image, (b) *depth* image.

4.3 Depth Maps Analysis

In order to analyze the differences between depth images with and without grasped objects, one thousand depth images of each class were acquired. In Fig. 4 five examples of each class are shown. It can be observed that the difference between the two classes (with and without the object) are not easy to detect, therefore a classical approach to classify the classes is not enough (e.g., k-means, counting the pixels).

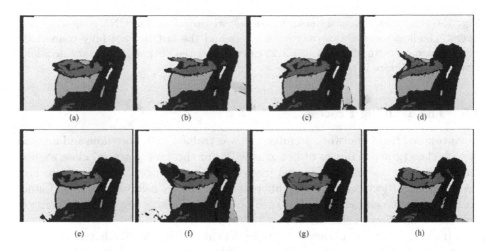

Fig. 4. Depth images with (e-h) and without (a-d) grasped objects.

4.4 Deep Learning Network Design

Due to the outstanding results performed in computer vision problems, a deep learning approach, more specific, a Convolution Neural Network was implemented. To design, train and evaluate the Neural Network, Keras and Tensor-Flow frameworks were used. To train the neural network, an i7@2.80 GHz PC with 16 GB RAM and an Nvidia GTX 950m graphics card was used. Experimentally, different architectures were tested. The best in terms of size and performance, is presented in Fig. 5.

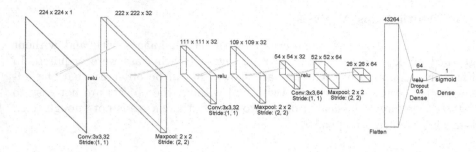

Fig. 5. Convolutional Neural Network architecture proposed. The CNN consists of five layers. The first three are convolutional layers and the last two are fully connected. The input data is an image of 224 × 224 pixels and the output is a binary decision. One is grasped, zero is not.

4.5 The Training Process

The proposed neural network architecture was trained with one thousand images of each class (grasped object or not grasped). For the "not grasped" class we use images with an end effector empty, just changing the fingers configuration. For the "grasped object" class, seven different objects were selected, see Fig. 6, and positioned in the end effector. For each object, the images are obtained using a predefined position as showed in Fig. 3.

The training hyperparameters were: learning rate: 0.001, batch size: 32, epochs: 25, optimizer: Adam. The trainable parameters of the network are 2,797,089. Figure 7 shows the accuracy and loss values of the training process through epochs. Note that high accuracy values are obtained in just four epochs, which indicates that the simple network architecture design is sufficient to correctly discriminate between the classes of this problem.

Fig. 6. Objects used in training process.

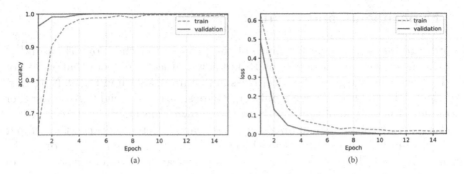

Fig. 7. The training process performance. (a) accuracy, (b) loss. The neural network reaches an stable value in the epoch four.

4.6 Neural Network Integration

Once the model was trained, it was integrated to the decision cycled for grasp confirmation, as it is shown in Fig. 8. First the home service robot through ROS [16] is set to the default inspection position and a depth image is obtained. The Region of Interest of the depth map is passed to the trained model. Based on the depth input image, the model decides the class (grasped or not). Finally, the decision is communicated to the home service robot through ROS [1].

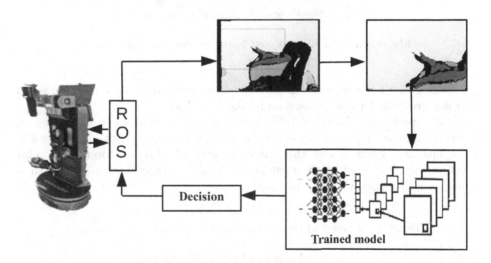

Fig. 8. Proposed method flowchart. Which consists of five steps: image acquisition, ROI detection, classification (CNN), decision, communication to the robot.

---

[1] A video demonstration is accessible through https://youtu.be/yA5_kS3FlUo.

5   Experiments and Results

In order to measure the performance of the proposed method, one thousand of additional images were acquired of 13 unknown objects (objects that were not used to represent the grasped-object class in training), shown in Fig. 9. Note that we select daily use objects, with different shapes, size and weight. Also, another thousand of images were acquired from the known objects.

To generate this, a human operator places each selected object in the gripper while closing the fingers until the object stay firmly grasped. Then, open the fingers to release the object and the process is repeated for different positions of the object in the gripper. In this way we just simulate an automatic grasping, and focus in the grasp confirmation which is the goal of our method.

Fig. 9. Unknown objects used in the experiments for testing.

Table 1 shows the accuracy in percent of the method for each class (grasped and not grasped) for both known and unknown objects.

From the results shown in Table 1, it can be seen that when the proposed method confronts unknown objects the network performance drops by about 6%. In this particular experiment, this is due to the shape of some objects (spoon for example) which can not be observed by the sensor. In general terms, the method achieves high accuracy for all combinations.

Table 1. Accuracy of the experimental evaluation in percentage.

	Known objects	Unknown objects
Grasped	98	92
Not grasped	99	99

Due to the excellent results obtained, the grasping confirmation method was integrated to the Storing Groceries task, for RoboCup@Home[2] competition. Storing Groceries is a Test of Stage I of this competition with focus on object manipulation but also, image classification. The robot helps by storing newly bought groceries in a cupboard next to the objects of the same kind that are already there; for instance by placing fresh apples near other apples. The task must be complete in a given time. In this test grasp confirmation becomes crucial because there are a high probability to miss a grasp attempt. So, if grasp verification is not performed, the robot just go to the cupboard with no object in hand which is a waste of time. A video[3] of our robotic platform performing grasp verification can be consulted in Youtube^{TM}.

6   Conclusions

This work proposed a novel grasp confirmation method based on deep learning applied on depth maps. The findings from the quantitative evaluation show that the proposed method is very accurate (more than 97% average in both known and unknown objects). The main contributions of this work are the Convolutional Neural Network simple architecture design, which permits to train the neural network with low computer requirements; the fast time response when it is applied; and the robustness obtained to use depth maps which are invariant to illumination conditions. These advantages make it possible to integrate the proposed method in a more complex task such as Storing Groceries. Future work will focus, on a multiple grasp verification with different hand positions to improve the robustness of the task for cases where the sensor can not fully observe the grasped object.

References

1. Allen, P.K., Timcenko, A., Yoshimi, B., Michelman, P.: Automated tracking and grasping of a moving object with a robotic hand-eye system. IEEE Trans. Robot. Autom. **9**(2), 152–165 (1993). https://doi.org/10.1109/70.238279
2. Allen, P., Miller, A., Oh, P., Leibowitz, B.: Using tactile and visual sensing with a robotic hand. In: Proceedings of International Conference on Robotics and Automation, vol. 1, pp. 676–681. IEEE (1997). https://doi.org/10.1109/robot.1997.620114
3. Allen, P., Miller, A., Oh, P., Leibowitz, B.: Integration of vision, force and tactile sensing for grasping. Int. J. Intell. Mach. **4**, 129–149 (1999)
4. Bicchi, A., Kumar, V.: Robotic grasping and contact: a review. In: Proceedings 2000 ICRA. Millennium Conference. IEEE International Conference on Robotics and Automation. Symposia Proceedings (Cat. No. 00CH37065), vol. 1, pp. 348–353. IEEE, April 2000. https://doi.org/10.1109/ROBOT.2000.844081

---

[2] www.robocupathome.org.

[3] Service robot performing grasp confirmation in Storing Groceries partial task https://youtu.be/giTvoMBa1Yo.

5. Dang, H., Allen, P.K.: Learning grasp stability. In: 2012 IEEE International Conference on Robotics and Automation, pp. 2392–2397. IEEE (2012)
6. Guo, D., Sun, F., Fang, B., Yang, C., Xi, N.: Robotic grasping using visual and tactile sensing. Inf. Sci. **417**, 274–286 (2017). https://doi.org/10.1016/j.ins.2017.07.017. http://www.sciencedirect.com/science/article/pii/S002002551730837X
7. Hebert, P., Hudson, N., Ma, J., Burdick, J.: Fusion of stereo vision, force-torque, and joint sensors for estimation of in-hand object location. In: Proceedings - IEEE International Conference on Robotics and Automation, pp. 5935–5941. IEEE (2011). https://doi.org/10.1109/ICRA.2011.5980185
8. Heidemann, G., Ritter, H.: Visual checking of grasping positions of a three-fingered robot hand. In: Dorffner, G., Bischof, H., Hornik, K. (eds.) ICANN 2001. LNCS, vol. 2130, pp. 891–898. Springer, Heidelberg (2001). https://doi.org/10.1007/3-540-44668-0_123
9. Jara, C.A., Pomares, J., Candelas, F.A., Torres, F.: Control framework for dexterous manipulation using dynamic visual servoing and tactile sensors' feedback. Sensors **14**(1), 1787–1804 (2014)
10. Konstantinova, J., Stilli, A., Faragasso, A., Althoefer, K.: Fingertip proximity sensor with realtime visual-based calibration. In: 2016 IEEE/RSJ International Conference on Intelligent Robots and Systems (IROS), pp. 170–175, October 2016. https://doi.org/10.1109/IROS.2016.7759051
11. Krainin, M., Henry, P., Ren, X., Fox, D.: Manipulator and object tracking for in-hand 3D object modeling. Int. J. Robot. Res. **30**(11), 1311–1327 (2011). https://doi.org/10.1177/0278364911403178
12. LeCun, Y., et al.: Handwritten digit recognition with a back-propagation network. In: Advances in Neural Information Processing Systems, pp. 396–404 (1990)
13. Patel, R., Curtis, R., Romero, B., Correll, N.: Improving grasp performance using in-hand proximity and contact sensing. In: Sun, Y., Falco, J. (eds.) RGMC 2016. CCIS, vol. 816, pp. 146–160. Springer, Cham (2018). https://doi.org/10.1007/978-3-319-94568-2_9
14. Redmon, J., Angelova, A.: Real-time grasp detection using convolutional neural networks. In: Proceedings - IEEE International Conference on Robotics and Automation, pp. 1316–1322. IEEE (2015). https://doi.org/10.1109/ICRA.2015.7139361
15. Roa, M.A., Suárez, R.: Grasp quality measures: review and performance. Auton. Robot. **38**(1), 65–88 (2015). https://doi.org/10.1007/s10514-014-9402-3
16. System, R.O., June 2019. www.ros.org

Real-Time Monocular Vision-Based UAV Obstacle Detection and Collision Avoidance in GPS-Denied Outdoor Environments Using CNN MobileNet-SSD

Daniel S. Levkovits-Scherer[1], Israel Cruz-Vega[2(✉)] [iD],
and José Martinez-Carranza[3,4] [iD]

[1] Electronics and Circuits Department, Universidad Simon Bolivar,
Caracas, Venezuela
daniellevkovits@gmail.com
[2] Electronics Department, Instituto Nacional de Astrofisica, Optica y Electronica,
San Andrés Cholula, Puebla, Mexico
icruzv@inaoep.mx
[3] Computer Science Department, Instituto Nacional de Astrofisica,
Optica y Electronica, San Andrés Cholula, Puebla, Mexico
carranza@inaoep.mx
[4] University of Bristol, Bristol BS8 1UB, UK

Abstract. In this paper, we propose a monocular vision-based system that uses a MobileNet-SSD CNN for obstacle detection and collision avoidance in GPS-denied outdoor environments. This framework consists of two processes carried out simultaneously in a frame-to-frame basis: (1) an obstacle detector and classifier using a lightweight convolutional neural network with a UAV monocular onboard camera for real-time mobile systems; (2) a collision avoidance algorithm with a proportional controller responsible for the autonomous flight in GPS-denied outdoor environments. However, because object detection and classification are computationally intensive tasks, the processing is carried out off-board on a ground control station that receives online imagery and data of the UAV during the autonomous flight. The novel aspects in this work are related to the capacity of the system to detect and avoid obstacles in real-time with computationally low range hardware without GPU. We exploit public datasets meant for other purposes and carefully selected images to build a new lightweight dataset to train the CNN. Further, the output imagery data is used by a proportional controller that communicates back to the vehicle to evaluate a possible obstacle avoidance trajectory and execute it if necessary. We carried out evaluations and flights in real scenarios with multiple obstacles such as vehicles, people, bicycles, and trees for autonomous flights in GPS-denied outdoor environments with promising results.

© Springer Nature Switzerland AG 2019
L. Martínez-Villaseñor et al. (Eds.): MICAI 2019, LNAI 11835, pp. 613–621, 2019.
https://doi.org/10.1007/978-3-030-33749-0_49

Keywords: Autonomous flight · CNN · Collision avoidance · GPS-denied outdoor environments · MobileNet-SSD · Obstacle detection.

1   Introduction

Unmanned Aerial Vehicles (UAVs), have had a peak since last decade for commercial and scientific use, driving the reduction of costs and miniaturization, thus achieving to increase the number of applications for which they are currently used. Some of the applications range from recreational use, manipulation of objects, transport of lightweight loads to deployment in outdoor areas of difficult access for exploration missions and rescues and victims identification in natural disasters.

The effort to create and improve drone trajectory planning and control strategies has become a scientific and research trend. As well as using drones integrated onboard cameras for applications beyond photography, such as real-time image processing and object detection. As a result of the integration of these, the UAVs began to be used to carry out different tasks autonomously.

Nowadays, drones used for autonomous navigation make use of programmed trajectories, relying entirely on sensors such as GPS and ultrasound to avoid collisions, which have a high consumption of current and memory, reducing flight time and processing speed and thus resulting in low performance for assigned tasks. Another main issue to be addressed is that of drone localization given the partial or total loss of GPS signal.

Motivated by the above, in this work, we address the problem of autonomous flight in outdoor environments with limited or denied GPS signal by using a low-end development UAV and base control station in an efficient way. As well as a monocular onboard camera to process the environment to classify, detect and locate objects such as trees, people, bicycles and vehicles in real-time and process the information for a posterior collision avoidance without any other positioning technique or technology. Besides, we are motivated by the idea of achieving autonomous flight outdoors by using the least set of sensors, this is, a monocular camera and an altimeter, which is attractive in terms of energy consumption efficiency, an incentive for the development of micro aerial unmanned vehicles.

The above calls for a method that enables the drone to autonomously decide whether a detected object is far or close depending on the class and the obstacle-image relation is shown in Fig. 1. Thus we propose a two-step methodology for the autonomous flight where only a monocular onboard camera is used to carry out the detection. The process involves two steps carried out on a frame-to-frame basis. First, the image captured is processed by a Convolutional Neural Network (MobileNet-SSD CNN) [7], whose output will be one of the four classes: People, Bicycle, Tree, Vehicle; and coordinates of each object in the image. A second step will determine whether the object is considered as a proximate collision and avoid it using a reactive control algorithm.

To achieve the above, the CNN architecture [11] has been trained with a modified PASCAL VOC 2007 dataset and a hand made dataset, using only pertinent classes for training the CNN. All the images came from real environments, yet the network is capable of generalizing the characteristics for classification and detection for simulated obstacles resulting in promising results in simulated outdoor environments as well.

Fig. 1. We present a methodology to achieve autonomous flight outdoors with a drone equipped with a monocular camera. We use a deep learning approach [6] to obtain the class and coordinates of the image and thus the proximity and location on a frame-to-frame basis. All this by passing the UAV camera image through a MobileNet-SSD Convolutional Neural Network.

The rest of this paper is organized as follows: Sect. 2 describes relevant related work; Sect. 3 describes our proposed methodology; Sect. 4 describes our experimental framework; finally, our conclusions are discussed in Sect. 5.

2   Related Work

Currently, most of the work in the area is related to autonomous flights using GPS for greater accuracy, which results in higher battery consumption. For this reason, more efficient alternatives are sought that do not involve the use of GPS. When looking for other options in the literature, we found work focused on the use of LSD-SLAM for autonomous navigation [12], as well as Visual SLAM [1], without using GPS in uncontrolled environments [8]. One of the disadvantages presented in [12] is that the mapping cannot be done in real-time, since the need to pause to map the environment and the visual field, being limited by the number of points the system can map, and repeating this process periodically as you go along the environment being mapped. This method is useful for indoor environments with large objects density, as shown in Fig. 2.

Another precise method, but more useful in controlled environments is the VICON system [9], which locates the vehicle with millimetric precision in a 3D space, making use of markers avoiding GPS usage. This system is efficient and robust for evaluating control algorithms and drone specific behaviors, by investigating its effect when moving close to surfaces, as well as to check the stability of air vehicles in general. By being able to map with great precision, this system has an elevated cost in comparison to the vehicle used for the work. This technique requires several infrared cameras for 3D movement detection, and for the measurement to be precise, it is necessary to place markers on the UAV.

Fig. 2. Semidense reconstruction and 3D map of indoor environment mapped with LSD-SLAM [12]

Finally, all of the methods above explained need high processing capacity to function correctly in a real-time autonomous flight [10]. Because of these, we proposed a technique handled with low-cost equipment and processing units, without the need for dedicated GPUs or stereo cameras. We are using only an integrated monocular camera with a low-resolution image processing and without GPS sensor usage, all of the above with a deep learning approach [6]. We employ a MobileNet-SSD Convolutional Neural Network to classify [3], detect and locate possible collision targets and avoid them if necessary using a simple linear feedback reactive control [5].

3   Methodology

Our approach is based on three main components: (1) MobileNet-SSD CNN architecture as an object detector for a monocular onboard camera system; (2) proximity estimation in a single image using bounding box coordinates and aspect ratio; (3) and a Proportional controller.

In this work, we use a quadrotor vehicle with a monocular camera onboard. However, the RGB image acquired with the onboard camera is passed to the Convolutional Neural Network escalade to 320×180 pixels, thus generating an output of the object class and bounding box coordinates of the above, thus obtaining a proximity estimate and an object-image ratio, information that is used by the controller to generate a frame-to-frame basis flight plan. We implemented a P controller to control roll, pitch, yaw, and altitude velocity and thus to achieve drones motion control for an efficient autonomous flight with collision avoidance capabilities without using GPS or other techniques.

The controller error depends exclusively on each speed coordinate. Pitch error depends on the proximity of an object to the UAV, roll velocity error depends on the desired time to avoid the obstacle; yaw error depends on drone deviation angle from taking off position, and altitude velocity error depends on the difference between a desired fixed Z coordinate and actual altitude.

3.1 Simulated and Real Outdoor Environments

The classification and detection of a determined object in images are addressed using a methodology that exploits visual information by processing image pixels from publicly available datasets imagery. For our purpose, we processed images from the Pascal VOC 2007 dataset and a handmade dataset to extract these characteristics maps from both RGB images and bounding box ground truth. The idea behind this approach is to take advantage of the ground truth data available in the dataset imagery, extracting enough characteristics to train the CNN.

The simulated environment aims to establish the MobileNet-SSD capacity of generalization when training with a purely realistic images dataset of people, trees, bicycles, and vehicles, see Fig. 3.

Fig. 3. Simulated outdoor environment for evaluation of our approach in Gazebo 7.

Motivated on the success of the approach above, we modified the algorithms and the communication system to make autonomous flight trials with real UAV and outdoor scenarios. For this, we modified all experimental parameters used for proximity sensing and obstacle avoidance since image- object ratios change drastically compared to simulated scenarios.

3.2 MobileNet-SSD

The MobileNet-SSD network aims to classify, detect and locate objects in an image for a moving robot without the necessity to stop moving to process the environment, hence his lightweight architecture is capable of extracting the necessary data with only one pass through the network. To reduce training time we use Transfer Learning technique [2], this CNN has a pre-trained base net [4] (MobileNet) which characteristics map is used by the SSD (Single Shot Multibox Detector) to improve learning and generalization and determine best adjustable bounding boxes for each object detected.

4   Experiments and Results

In this section, we describe the evaluation results, as well as the experiments realized in the Gazebo simulation world and the tests, accomplished in outdoor environments with one and multiple obstacles. Finally, we compare both tests to demonstrate the effectiveness of the system. To evaluate the performance of our detection capability, we used a dataset containing 6600 images of the four above mentioned classes with a 1-1 proportion for each one. The training dataset contains all the information about ground truth boxes and classes of the objects in each image. We compared the evaluation results of our simulated outdoor environment detector with the real outdoor environment results, carrying out several dozens of flights for each class in both simulation and real environments.

4.1   Simulation Outdoor Environment

For the first one with only an obstacle, the autonomous flight detector achieved 75% for people detection and avoidance, 80% for trees and 100% effectiveness for vehicles. These results reaffirm the capability of the MobileNet-SSD CNN of characteristics generalization due to the network only trained with real environment imagery, see Figs. 4 and 5.

Fig. 4. Tree detection, and collision avoidance during autonomous flight.

Fig. 5. People detection, and collision avoidance during autonomous flight.

4.2   Real Outdoor Environment

The second experiment was developed in a real outdoor rural environment where flights were done in various scenarios with different obstacles. Tree class was used for multiple obstacle autonomous flight tests to ensure the system capability to avoid obstacles in a continuous way, see Figs. 6 and 7.

Fig. 6. Tree and people detection and collision avoidance in a real environment with one obstacle during autonomous flight

Fig. 7. Vehicle detection and collision avoidance in a real environment with one obstacle during autonomous flight

Fig. 8. Multiple tree detection and collision avoidance in a real environment with one obstacle during autonomous flight

The results when carrying out real environment autonomous flights had an improvement of 15% for people and tree classes and a decretion of 5% for vehicles. This improvement is due to the CNN training with real imagery datasets. And the decretion in detection for vehicle class is due to wind and illumination condition in real environments causing the system to collide with the obstacles.

Finally, to demonstrate the capability of the system to carry out autonomous flights with more than one obstacle to evade, as shown in Fig. 8, we made several flights with 2, 3 and 5 objects and the percentage of success went down to 90% for two obstacles and 85% for five obstacles.

5   Conclusions

This paper presents an autonomous flight system for a UAV in environments in GPS-denied areas, using only a monocular RGB camera, an integrated ultrasound sensor, and low-end equipment. A deep learning approach was used, explicitly applying convolutional neural networks for classification and detection of the environment in real time. Not only was it possible to evaluate the feasibility of a reactive autonomous flight policy as initially proposed, but also carry it out in a real system by obtaining optimal results.

The system approach is to use the MobileNet-SSD CNN, which processes the input image, i.e., the classification, detection, and location of the object in the image. For this the network is trained with four classes: vehicles, people, trees and bicycles, which are common in areas with limited or no access to GPS, such as rural areas.

The results presented demonstrate that the proposed method of autonomous navigation provides optimal results; the UAV can effectively execute its flight plan through the different objects offered with rates rounding 90% success of flights performed.

Acknowledgments. We thank the Instituto Nacional de Astrofisica, Optica y Electronica of Mexico (INAOE) for the laboratories and equipment borrowed and Eng.

Roberto Munguia-Silva for the continuous support and collaboration with time and knowledge throughout this project development.

References

1. Blösch, M., Weiss, S., Scaramuzza, D., Siegwart, R.: Vision based MAV navigation in unknown and unstructured environments. In: 2010 IEEE International Conference on Robotics and Automation, pp. 21–28. IEEE (2010)
2. Brownlee, J.: A gentle introduction to transfer learning for deep learning (2017). https://machinelearningmastery.com/transfer-learning-for-deep-learning/
3. Forson, E.: Understanding SSD multibox-real-time object detection in deep learning (2017). https://towardsdatascience.com/understanding-ssd-multibox-real-time-object-detection-in-deep-learning-495ef744fab
4. Howard, A.G., et al.: Mobilenets: efficient convolutional neural networks for mobile vision applications. arXiv preprint arXiv:1704.04861 (2017)
5. Kada, B., Ghazzawi, Y.: Robust PID controller design for an UAV flight control system. In: Proceedings of the World Congress on Engineering and Computer Science, vol. 2 (2011)
6. LeCun, Y., Bengio, Y., Hinton, G.: Deep learning. Nature **521**(7553), 436 (2015)
7. Li, Y., Huang, H., Xie, Q., Yao, L., Chen, Q.: Research on a surface defect detection algorithm based on mobilenet-SSD. Appl. Sci. **8**(9), 1678 (2018)
8. Mancini, M., Costante, G., Valigi, P., Ciarfuglia, T.A.: J-mod 2: joint monocular obstacle detection and depth estimation. IEEE Robot. Autom. Lett. **3**(3), 1490–1497 (2018)
9. Mashood, A., Mohammed, M., Abdulwahab, M., Abdulwahab, S., Noura, H.: A hardware setup for formation flight of UAVs using motion tracking system. In: 2015 10th International Symposium on Mechatronics and its Applications (ISMA), pp. 1–6. IEEE (2015)
10. Nemati, A., et al.: Autonomous navigation of UAV through GPS-denied indoor environment with obstacles. In: AIAA SciTech, pp. 5–9 (2015)
11. Saha, S.: A comprehensive guide to convolutional neural networks - the eli5 way (2018). https://towardsdatascience.com/a-comprehensive-guide-to-convolutional-neural-networks-the-eli5-way-3bd2b1164a53
12. von Stumberg, L., Usenko, V., Engel, J., Stückler, J., Cremers, D.: Autonomous exploration with a low-cost quadrocopter using semi-dense monocular slam. arXiv preprint arXiv:1609.07835 (2016)

Clusterized KNN for EEG Channel Selection and Prototyping of Lower Limb Joint Torques

Lucero Alvarado[✉], Griselda Quiroz, Angel Rodriguez-Liñan,
and Luis Torres-Treviño

FIME, Universidad Autónoma de Nuevo León, Av. Universidad S/N,
Ciudad Universitaria, 66455 San Nicolás de los Garza, Nuevo León, Mexico
{lucero.alvaradorz,griselda.quirozcm,
angel.rodriguezln,luis.torrestv}@uanl.edu.mx

Abstract. In this paper, a method for automatic channel selection of EEG signals acquired during the execution of lower limb movements is presented; for this method the hip and knee joint torques are measured. The method is based on maximizing both the percentage of prototypes extracted and the relative dispersion of its respective torques using a genetic algorithm. The prototyping is made with clusterized KNN, a proposed modification of the K-nearest neighbors algorithm, and the dispersion is computed as the ratio of interquartile ranges (IQR) between original and resulting torques. Results show that frequent channels are consistent with those known to be activated during motor tasks and that additional channels, needed for extracting relevant information from the data, vary from subject to subject. Extracted data can be used as new inputs for later regression tasks and for further analysis in order to characterize neural processes.

Keywords: EEG channel selection · Prototyping · Similarity search · Genetic algorithm

1 Introduction

Mobility impairment is the most common type of disability in North America, according to the Mexican Department of Social Development (SEDESOL) [4] and to the Centers for Disease Control and Prevention (CDC) of the United States [3]. This leads to an increasing interest in developing assistive technology for people with motor impairments; such as prostheses, ortheses and exoeskeletons. Moreover, the control of assistive devices by means of brain-computers interfaces (BCIs) involves many challenges in neuroengineering, one of them the decoding of intention and execution of motor activity from non-invasive measures of the neural activity. With the aim of solving this challenging problem, it is necessary to extract useful neural information, one of the approaches for this

© Springer Nature Switzerland AG 2019
L. Martínez-Villaseñor et al. (Eds.): MICAI 2019, LNAI 11835, pp. 622–632, 2019.
https://doi.org/10.1007/978-3-030-33749-0_50

extraction is to select a subset of channels from electroencephalographic (EEG) recordings.

Current approaches are often based on resulting metrics of regression and classification tasks [7, 9]. The drawbacks of these approaches lie in the assumption that all data points are relevant to the EEG-output relationship, as the noise acquired by the current EEG acquisition methods [2, 8, 14], the noisy nature of the brain signal even at resting state [11, 22], and the neural activity suspected to be time variant [5, 6, 18] may lead to overfitted and misleading models.

Another kind of methods for channel selection are based on extracted features of the acquired EEG signals, in which low frequencies are the most studied ones [17, 19, 21] even if it is known that motor activity is reflected in higher frequencies [23]; these methods pay little or no attention to the studied output variable in the selection of relevant EEG information.

A scheme for EEG channel selection is presented in this paper with the aim of overcoming the previous limitations. The main idea is to extract similar points from the dataset by paying special attention to the contribution of the output variable, the joint torques, to the overall relationship of the dataset in order to find subsets of EEG channels that represent the process and that can be used for further analysis of neural activity in motor tasks of the lower limb.

2   Methods

In this section the methods for prototyping and channel selection are described. The proposed method for prototyping the dataset is the Clusterized KNN algorithm, which is described first in this section. The prototype dataset is optimized to find subsets of EEG channels that increase both the amount of prototypes extracted and their dispersion. This optimization is carried out with a genetic algorithm, which is described later in this section.

2.1   Prototyping Algorithm

The prototyping algorithm used in this study combines time series mapping, similarity search and clustering techniques in order to extract useful information from the dataset. With the aim of selecting prototypes that are similar in the shape of output and feature similarly in inputs, a time mapping is made for each output pattern to a template curve, then the selection of the prototypes is made using a modified version of K nearest neighbors algorithm.

Clusterized KNN. The Clusterized KNN algorithm is a slight modification to the K-Nearest Neighbor regression algorithm [16], it is used to discern between potential outliers and potential prototypes of the dataset. The main stages are explained as follows.

Similarity Measure. The search of the K nearest neighbors of a query vector $\mathbf{x}$ is done with a similarity measure between the query and the remaining points in the dataset, being the Euclidean distance the most commonly used. The drawback of this measure is that it tends to give the same importance to all the dimensions [1].

Therefore, in the Clusterized KNN algorithm, the search of the K nearest neighbors is done with the cosine similarity; this similarity is useful in cases where the direction is more important than the magnitude of the vectors, so that vectors are compared in terms of the relationship across its dimensions [15]. The cosine similarity S between two vectors v_1 and v_2 is computed as follows:

$$S(v_1, v_2) = \frac{v_1 v_2^T}{\|v_1\| \|v_2\|} \tag{1}$$

Estimated Output. The original KNN algorithm for regression estimates the output y of a query vector $\mathbf{x}$ as the mean of the outputs o of each one of its K nearest neighbors, as in the following equation:

$$y = \frac{1}{K} \sum_{k=1}^{K} o_k(x). \tag{2}$$

This means that all of the K nearest neighbors of $\mathbf{x}$ contribute to the estimation of its output. Another approach used for the output estimation is to weight the output o of each one of the K nearest neighbors [10], this weighting is done as follows:

$$y = \frac{1}{K} \sum_{k=1}^{K} \frac{1}{d_k} o_k(x), \tag{3}$$

where d_k is the euclidean distance of $\mathbf{x}$ to each one of its K nearest neighbor.

In order to avoid the contribution of noisy points or outliers in the estimation of the output, a one-dimensional clustering of the outputs of the K nearest neighbors of a query vector $\mathbf{x}$ is done with the assumption that the densest cluster contains the most similar points to that query. The clustering is made using the BIRCH algorithm and the density estimation of each cluster is done with a Gaussian Kernel; both implementations provided by the scikit-learn package for Python [20]. The clustering method was selected because it does not need pre-specification of the number of clusters in the set.

Then the output y of a query vector $\mathbf{x}$ is computed as the mean of the outputs c of each one of the L points in the densest cluster of the K nearest neighbors:

$$y = \frac{1}{L} \sum_{l=1}^{L} c_l(x). \tag{4}$$

Dynamic Time Warping. The Dynamic Time Warping (DTW) is an algorithm used to align time series with shape similarity by creating a warping path with the smallest possible distance. The main advantages of this algorithm are that time series can be aligned even if they are temporally dephased one from another, and that time series are not required to be within the same range of magnitude. The version of DTW used in this work is a band-constrained DTW [24]. Such an algorithm is explained as follows:

Band-Constrained DTW. Two time series, a sequence **A** of length I and a sequence **B** of length J, are expressed as:

$$A = \{a_1, a_2, a_3, ..., a_I\}$$
$$B = \{b_1, b_2, b_3, ..., b_J\}. \tag{5}$$

Then a distance matrix $\mathbf{D}_{I \times J}$ between both time series is computed using the absolute distance among pair of elements $di, dj \in \mathbf{D}$. For creating the warping path, an auxiliary matrix $\mathbf{U}_{K \times L}$ is initialized with representations of positive infinity values, where $K = I + 1$ and $L = J + 1$. The value of $u_{1,1}$ is initialized at 0 and a bound constraint for the warp search is defined as:

$$W_c = \frac{b_p \times J}{100}, \tag{6}$$

where b_p is the percentage of the length of the largest sequence series where the warp path can be created. Then, for each $\{u_{k,l} \in \mathbf{U} \mid k > 1, max(1, k - W_c) < l < min(L, k + W_c)\}$, the cost of the current alignment is computed as in the following equation:

$$u_{k,l} = d_{k-1,l-1} + min\left[u_{k-1,l-1}, u_{k,l-1}, u_{k-1,l}\right], \tag{7}$$

The warping matrix **W** is the submatrix created by taking the last I rows and the last J columns of **U**. Then the best alignment, the warp path, between sequences **A** and **B** is obtained as the path in **W** that goes from $i = 1, j = 1$ to $i = I, j = J$ and minimizes the cost of the alignment.

2.2   Input Selection by Genetic Algorithms

The selection of channels from the EEG signal is done optimizing the number of prototypes extracted with the previously described methods. This optimization is done using a genetic algorithm [12] with the following fitness function.

Fitness Function. In order to avoid the extraction of prototypes with outputs around the mean, the fitness function considers both the quantity of prototypes extracted and the dispersion of the resulting output data. The relative dispersion $RIQR$ is computed as the ratio of the interquartile range of the prototyped outputs IQR_p to the interquartile range of the original outputs IQR_o:

$$RIQR = \frac{IQR_p}{IQR_o}, \tag{8}$$

where the interquartile ranges (IQR) are computed based on first Q_1 and third Q_3 quartiles of the output data [27]:

$$IQR = Q_3 - Q_1. \tag{9}$$

The quantification of the extracted prototypes P_{ext} is done as follows:

$$P_{ext} = \frac{N_p}{N_o}, \tag{10}$$

where N_p and N_o are the lengths of the prototyped and original outputs. Then the fitness function F to be maximized is defined as follows:

$$F = RIQR + P_{ext}. \tag{11}$$

3   EEG Channel Selection

3.1   Data Acquisition

Five healthy volunteer young adults were asked and gave permission to execute three motor tasks, for whom nineteen scalp EEG electrodes (Fp1, Fp2, F7, F8, F3, F4, T3, T4, C3, C4, T5, T6, P3, P4, O1, O2, Fz, Cz, and Pz) were recorded at a rate of 200 Hz using the UPM-PLUS Grass® system by Natus Neurology®. A notch filter was applied to the EEG signals to remove the 60 Hz power line interference. Then the blind source separation (BSS) method [25] was applied with the aim of extracting independent source signals and removing artifacts. The motor tasks consisted of lower limb movements for which the angular positions of the hip joint were estimated from video recordings, captured at 30 fps, of markers attached to the subject's hip and knee joints. Then the joint torques were computed by solving the Euler-Lagrange dynamic model of the hip. Each subject was asked to perform ten series, each one of 10 repetitions, of three different motor tasks. The first trial of each series was retained to create the dataset used in this study, as seen in Fig. 1.

3.2   Implementation of Methods

Genetic Algorithm. Each chromosome in the genetic algorithm represents a selection of channels to be used for the prototyping of the dataset. When evaluating the fitness function, a number of E_{lags} previous values spaced by E_{gap} data points of the selected channels are used to create additional inputs for the prototyping algorithm in order to retain previous information, as several studies show that the pre-motor potential fluctuates between a value of -400 ms to -200 ms prior the execution of movements [13]. A total of -350 ms of previous data is retained in this study. Being 200 Hz the sampling rate of the EEG signals, the data parameters are the following ones:

- Number of EEG lags: $E_{lags} = 10$.
- Gap between consecutive lags: $E_{gap} = 7$.

The genetic algorithm was executed 30 times for each combination of subject and movement in order to optimize the selection of channels of EEG. The number of channels that can be selected by the genetic algorithm ranges from 1 to 19,

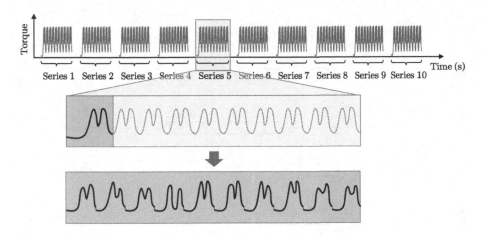

Fig. 1. Selection of the dataset. The top figure shows the 10 series of trials for the same task; the middle figure shows the extraction of the first trial for each series; and the bottom figure shows the final dataset to be used in the analysis, composed of only first trials.

where the latter is the total number of channels available or the dimension of the optimization problem. A high crossover probability was chosen for this study in order to exploit the solutions resulting from early generations of the genetic algorithm, hence the selection of a low mutation probability. The parameters chosen for the implementation of the genetic algorithm are summarized as next:

- Chromosome length: $T_D = 19$.
- Population size: $T_P = 20$.
- Number of generations: $T_G = 20$.
- Crossover probability: $c_p = 0.98$.
- Mutation probability: $m_p = 0.02$.

Prototyping Algorithm. The number of K neighbors of the Clusterized KNN algorithm is chosen based on preliminary experiments, where higher values of relative dispersion $RIQR$ between original and prototyped torques were preferred. The bound constraint b_p is selected as a percentage of the size of the largest sequence in order to avoid paths too far from the linear one. The following parameters for the prototyping algorithm are chosen:

- Number of neighbors in Clusterized KNN: $K = 10$.
- Bound constraint for DTW: $b_p = 25\%$.

The proposed scheme for EEG channel selection is implemented in Python 3.7.3 using the Scientific Python Development Environment (Spyder) included in the Anaconda distribution of Python.

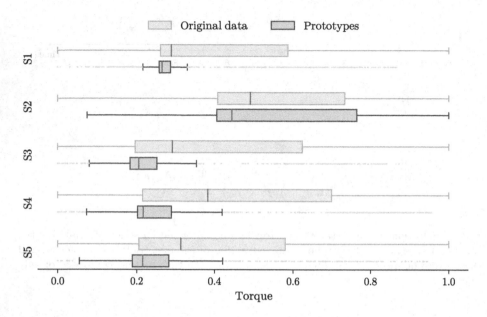

Fig. 2. Comparison of the prototype and original torques of all subjects performing movement 1, in terms of interquartile ranges.

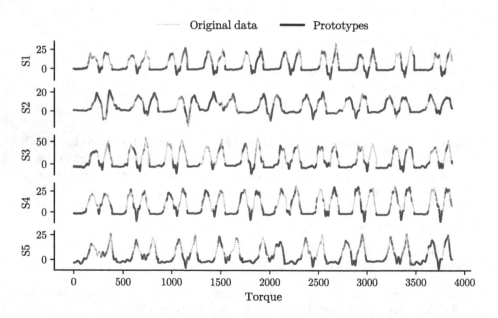

Fig. 3. Overlapped prototyping results for each subject performing movement 1.

4   Results

In order to evaluate the prototyping phase, a comparison is made between the original and the prototyped set of torques. The results for the best prototype extraction (the ones with higher fitness value) of all subjects executing the movement 1 are shown in Fig. 2, from where it is seen that most of the datasets have similar medians and distribution of points. The overlapping of the prototypes extracted by each execution of the genetic algorithm, for all the subjects of movement 1, are shown in Fig. 3, from which we notice that the extracted set is consistent along the executions.

The qualitative results of the channel selection are shown in Fig. 4, and the results of the prototyping and channel selection are summarized in Table 1.

Table 1. Summary statistics of the prototyping extraction and channel selection.

Movement 1									
Subjects	Prototypes in %				RIQR in %				N_{ch}
	Avg.	Worst	Best	Std. Dev.	Avg.	Worst	Best	Std. Dev.	Avg.
Subject 1	51.64	50.51	52.81	0.56	7.69	6.78	8.96	0.55	8
Subject 2	41.31	38.89	44.78	1.45	101.42	85.67	110.36	5.94	8
Subject 3	41.91	39.51	43.44	0.90	14.42	12.39	16.32	0.99	8
Subject 4	40.25	38.86	41.63	0.85	13.42	10.26	18.07	1.85	9
Subject 5	40.54	37.00	44.68	1.79	22.95	21.36	25.27	0.94	5
Movement 2									
Subjects	Prototypes in %				RIQR in %				N_{ch}
	Avg.	Min	Max	Std. Dev.	Avg.	Min	Max	Std. Dev.	Avg.
Subject 1	57.47	55.30	58.77	0.79	6.80	6.54	7.36	0.20	7
Subject 2	44.04	42.02	45.87	1.26	18.05	16.12	19.82	0.92	7
Subject 3	50.68	48.72	51.84	0.70	8.86	8.62	9.20	0.12	7
Subject 4	41.98	40.28	44.49	1.11	29.32	21.74	39.80	5.15	7
Subject 5	41.02	38.88	42.56	0.83	13.80	12.78	14.98	0.51	7
Movement 3									
Subjects	Prototypes in %				RIQR in %				N_{ch}
	Avg.	Min	Max	Std. Dev.	Avg.	Min	Max	Std. Dev.	Avg.
Subject 1	53.02	50.47	54.58	0.91	21.65	19.49	22.98	0.79	7
Subject 2	37.21	35.02	39.28	1.25	97.37	90.74	102.72	3.23	10
Subject 3	46.72	43.59	50.41	1.64	23.70	21.85	26.54	1.10	5
Subject 4	44.14	42.44	46.05	1.03	29.04	28.17	30.36	0.55	7
Subject 5	51.42	50.16	52.58	0.70	16.43	16.03	16.81	0.22	5

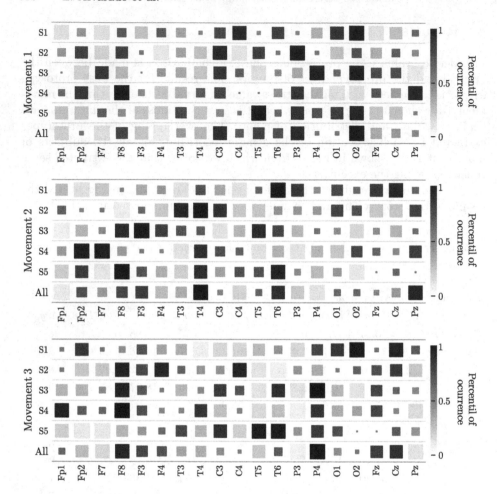

Fig. 4. Results of channel selection for each combination of subject and movement. The stronger the square color of a channel, the more frequently it was selected. The size of each square is associated with whether the channel is one of the most frequent or one of the least frequent.

5   Conclusions

In this work, an approach for EEG channel selection based on the optimization of characteristics of extracted torque data was implemented. As mentioned before, this implementation contrasts with current approaches of channel selection for the field of brain-computer interfaces [7, 9], where the selection is carried out either arbitrarily, by cortex areas, or according to metrics resulting from regression and classification tasks of a desired output variable.

As can be seen from the preliminary results of the implementation, the extracted torques have similar characteristics to the original ones, even if the percentage of extracted prototypes is relatively low. By optimizing the extraction of these prototypes, a subset of EEG channels is proposed by the genetic algorithm, from where it is seen that the most frequent channels coincide with those reported in the literature to be activated during the execution of lower limb movements [26].

As the selection of channels and prototypes is done over torques of each trial mapped to a normalized template, the extracted prototypes can be used for later regression tasks in order to avoid overfitted models.

Further optimization methods must be considered in order to compare the results of the channel selection and to address the optimization problem as a multi-objective one. More studies with a wider range of movements and more subjects must be done with the aim of search generalized patters of channels that better represents the EEG-torque relationship.

References

1. Aggarwal, C.C., Hinneburg, A., Keim, D.A.: On the surprising behavior of distance metrics in high dimensional space. In: Van den Bussche, J., Vianu, V. (eds.) ICDT 2001. LNCS, vol. 1973, pp. 420–434. Springer, Heidelberg (2001). https://doi.org/10.1007/3-540-44503-X_27
2. Ball, T., Kern, M., Mutschler, I., Aertsen, A., Schulze-Bonhage, A.: Signal quality of simultaneously recorded invasive and non-invasive EEG. NeuroImage **46**(3), 708–716 (2009). https://doi.org/10.1016/j.neuroimage.2009.02.028
3. Centers for Disease Control and Prevention (CDC): Disability and functioning (noninstitutionalized adults aged 18 and over) (2016). Accessed May 2019
4. Department of Social Development (SEDESOL): Diagnosis on the situation of people with disabilities in Mexico (2016), Accessed May 2019
5. Ditterich, J.: Evidence for time-variant decision making. Eur. J. Neurosci. **24**(12), 3628–3641 (2006). https://doi.org/10.1111/j.1460-9568.2006.05221.x
6. Druckmann, S., Chklovskii, D.B.: Neuronal circuits underlying persistent representations despite time varying activity. Current Biol. **22**(22), 2095–2103 (2012). https://doi.org/10.1016/j.cub.2012.08.058
7. Duun-Henriksen, J., Kjaer, T.W., Madsen, R.E., Remvig, L.S., Thomsen, C.E., Sorensen, H.B.D.: Channel selection for automatic seizure detection. Clin. Neurophysiol. **123**(1), 84–92 (2012). https://doi.org/10.1016/j.clinph.2011.06.001
8. Ferree, T.C., Luu, P., Russell, G.S., Tucker, D.M.: Scalp electrode impedance, infection risk, and EEG data quality. Clin. Neurophysiol. **112**(3), 536–544 (2001). https://doi.org/10.1016/s1388-2457(00)00533-2
9. Gonzalez, A., Nambu, I., Hokari, H., Wada, Y.: EEG channel selection using particle swarm optimization for the classification of auditory event-related potentials. Sci. World J. **2014**, 1–11 (2014). https://doi.org/10.1155/2014/350270
10. Hechenbichler, K., Schliep, K.: Weighted k-nearest-neighbor techniques and ordinal classification (2004). https://doi.org/10.5282/ubm/epub.1769
11. van den Heuvel, M.P., Pol, H.E.H.: Exploring the brain network: a review on resting-state fMRI functional connectivity. Eur. Neuropsychopharmacol. **20**(8), 519–534 (2010). https://doi.org/10.1016/j.euroneuro.2010.03.008
12. Holland, J.: An Introductory Analysis with Applications to Biology, Control, and Artificial Intelligence. Adaptation in Natural and Artificial Systems, 1st edn. The University of Michigan, Ann Arbor (1975)

13. Jahanshahi, M., Hallett, M.: The Bereitschaftspotential: Movement-Related Cortical Potentials. Springer, New York (2003). https://doi.org/10.1007/978-1-4615-0189-3
14. Jorge, J., Grouiller, F., Gruetter, R., van der Zwaag, W., Figueiredo, P.: Towards high-quality simultaneous EEG-fMRI at 7T: detection and reduction of EEG artifacts due to head motion. NeuroImage **120**, 143–153 (2015). https://doi.org/10.1016/j.neuroimage.2015.07.020
15. Kelleher, J.D., Mac Namee, B., D'arcy, A.: Fundamentals of Machine Learning for Predictive Data Analytics Algorithms Worked Examples and Case Studies. MIT Press, Cambridge (2015)
16. Kumar, T.: Solution of linear and non linear regression problem by k nearest neighbour approach: by using three sigma rule. In: 2015 IEEE International Conference on Computational Intelligence & Communication Technology. IEEE (2015). https://doi.org/10.1109/cict.2015.110
17. Lal, T., et al.: Support vector channel selection in BCI. IEEE Trans. Biomed. Eng. **51**(6), 1003–1010 (2004). https://doi.org/10.1109/tbme.2004.827827
18. Leistritz, L., Schiecke, K., Astolfi, L., Witte, H.: Time-variant modeling of brain processes. Proc. IEEE **104**(2), 262–281 (2016). https://doi.org/10.1109/jproc.2015.2497144
19. Nakagome, S., Luu, T.P., Brantley, J.A., Contreras-Vidal, J.L.: Prediction of EMG envelopes of multiple terrains over-ground walking from EEG signals using an unscented Kalman filter. In: 2017 IEEE International Conference on Systems, Man, and Cybernetics (SMC). IEEE, October 2017. https://doi.org/10.1109/smc.2017.8123116
20. Pedregosa, F., et al.: Scikit-learn: Machine learning in python. J. Mach. Learn. Res. **12**, 2825–2830 (2011). http://dl.acm.org/citation.cfm?id=1953048.2078195
21. Presacco, A., Goodman, R., Forrester, L., Contreras-Vidal, J.L.: Neural decoding of treadmill walking from noninvasive electroencephalographic signals. J. Neurophysiol. **106**(4), 1875–1887 (2011). https://doi.org/10.1152/jn.00104.2011
22. Raichle, M.E.: The restless brain. Brain Connect. **1**(1), 3–12 (2011). https://doi.org/10.1089/brain.2011.0019
23. Ramos-Murguialday, A., Birbaumer, N.: Brain oscillatory signatures of motor tasks. J. Neurophysiol. **113**(10), 3663–3682 (2015). https://doi.org/10.1152/jn.00467.2013
24. Sakoe, H., Chiba, S.: Dynamic programming algorithm optimization for spoken word recognition, pp. 159–165 (1990). https://doi.org/10.1016/b978-0-08-051584-7.50016-4
25. Vázquez, R.R., Vélez-Pérez, H., Ranta, R., Dorr, V.L., Maquin, D., Maillard, L.: Blind source separation, wavelet denoising and discriminant analysis for EEG artefacts and noise cancelling. Biomed. Signal Process. Control **7**(4), 389–400 (2012). https://doi.org/10.1016/j.bspc.2011.06.005
26. Zhang, Y., Prasad, S., Kilicarslan, A., Contreras-Vidal, J.L.: Multiple kernel based region importance learning for neural classification of gait states from EEG signals. Front. Neurosci. **11**, 170 (2017). https://doi.org/10.3389/fnins.2017.00170
27. Zwillinger, D., Kokoska, S.: CRC Standard Probability and Statistics Tables and Formulae. CRC Press, Boca Raton (1999)

Stewart Robotic Platform for Topographic Measuring System

Carlos Hernández-Santos[1](✉) ⓘD, Donovan S. Labastida[1] ⓘD,
Ernesto Rincón[1] ⓘD, A. Fernández-Ramírez[1] ⓘD, Fermín C. Aragón[2] ⓘD,
and José Valderrama-Chairez[1] ⓘD

[1] Tecnológico Nacional de México/I. T. de Nuevo León,
Av. Eloy Cavazos 2001, Guadalupe, Nuevo Leon, Mexico
carlos.hernandez@itnl.edu.mx
[2] Escuela de ingeniería y ciencias, Tecnológico de Monterrey,
Eugenio Garza Sada 2501, 64849 Monterrey, Mexico

Abstract. In this work, a prototype of an autonomous topographic metrology system that uses a self-leveling Stewart platform system is presented, with the objective of evaluating the angular uncertainty of the azimuth plane adjustment process, which would disperse an associated collimation instrument. The self-leveling process of the prototype is achieved by means of two mutually independent four-bar kinematic chains that regulate the inclination of the platform on the "x" and "y" axes. The control of the prototype is based on the regulation of the motive source, of the kinematic chains, by means of a servomotor coupled to one of the fixed articulations and an accelerometer. The comparison of the angular error of adjustment of the calculated azimuth plane and that measured independently in an array of orthogonal toroid levels shows that the error changes as a function of the initial disturbed position and converges to a fixed value that depends on the accuracy of the source controller motor, the resolution in the range of the sensor and the alignment of the links and articulations of the kinematic chain.

Keywords: Auto levelling · Accelerometer · Topography · Metrology · Stewart system

1 Introduction

The asymptotic condition of a measurement instrument, respect to azimuthal plane is a basic rule in the topographic metrology, [1]. This condition usually must be stablished under static conditions respect to target references. The prototype that is presented is an application to automate this process in a mobile underground mapping robot, that has a Stewart platform tripod, [2], with two control axes (x, y), and two degrees of freedom, a servomotor and an actuator in each chain. The prototype's operation and control process, are programmed on a 16-bit controller, fed back by an analog acceleration sensor, whereby the acceleration components of gravity are acquired, to indirectly calculate the inclination's angle of platform, and determine the appropriate azimuthal horizontality. With the comparison of calculated angles and the sensed inclination in each axis, is determinate a position vector error. This allows evaluates the control's convergence method, considering mechanical induced error. Parallel kinematic structure platforms

© Springer Nature Switzerland AG 2019
L. Martínez-Villaseñor et al. (Eds.): MICAI 2019, LNAI 11835, pp. 633–645, 2019.
https://doi.org/10.1007/978-3-030-33749-0_51

type "Gough-Stewart", for topographic metrology applications, have been studied since 1960, [3] its dynamics was development among others for vehicle simulation, [2], vibration isolation, [4], astrodynamics, [5], vehicle and machinery support, [6], and solar tracing, [7]. As a regulation on topographic technology it was introduced by US Army Corps of Engineers [1]. Then appears control methods focused on inertial stability, [8], adapted geometry, [9], PID for self-balancing platforms over mobile robots, [10], multiple control, [11], and applications as the patent of [12].

2 Mechanical Model

As parallel robot, [13], the platform prototype (Fig. 1) is composed of two kinematic chains, that contains four bars and four joints. See Figs. 1, 2 and 3. Two joins (labeled 1 and 4) are fixed on bench, and others two (labeled 2 and 3) are mobile. Two joins (labeled 3 and 4) are spherical and the others (labeled 1 and 2) are cylindrical. The orthogonal arrangement of the chains, and their two spherical joints minimize the magnitude of mutual affectation, [14].

Fig. 1. Below prototype's mobile plate there are two servo motors MG955, on tops, an accelerometer, and two toroidal levels, referencing each axis (X and Y).

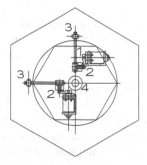

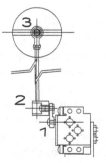

Fig. 2. Plan view of prototype. Orthogonal arrangement of the chains. The join (4), under mobile plate, and join (3) are spherical type.

Fig. 3. The kinematic chain's, side view. The join (1), is between the servomotor shaft and shortest bar. Between longest a shortest bar is the join (2).

The cinematic chain dimensions measured directly on device are: $l_1 = 0.0240$ m, $l_2 = 0.0785$ m, $l_3 = 0.0650$ m y $l_4 = 0.079$ m. The fixed link or bank, and its inclination angle (φ) were determined indirectly with the coordinates of joints 1 and 4, which are: $P_{1x} = 0.0240$, $P_{1x} = 0.0240$, $P_{4x} = 0.0690$ y $P_{4y} = 0.0650$, $\varphi = 0.96525$ rad.

3 Kinematics

The kinematics and dynamics modeling encoded in the c language, focuses on determination error diffusion, considering transference equation. In the four-bar kinematic chains with two fixed joints, the positions of the mobile joints P_2, y P_3, of the angles between the links (θ_1, θ_2, θ_3, θ_4), are show Fig. 4, they are defined by setting one of two parameters: (a) An angle between their links, or (b) The position of one of the mobile joints. Given the restrictions of a closed chain, the first case is as direct kinematics and the second case is the reverse. Since the control variable in the prototype is the angle θ_1, associated with joint 1, on whose axis of rotation the arrow of the actuator is installed, [15, 16].

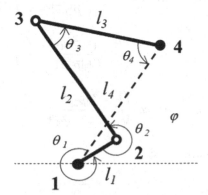

Fig. 4. Kinematic chain's nomenclature, for angles between links. Dark joints are fixed to the bench.

The output variable is the angle (θ_4) of inclination of the platform, this pair of variables are the focus of analysis, and were calculated as follows, the position of the mobile joint (p_2):

$$x_2 = x_1 + \|\hat{l}_1\|cos(\theta_1 + \varphi) = 0.020 + (0.024)cos(\theta_1 + 55.3048°) \tag{1}$$

$$y_2 = y_1 + \|\hat{l}_1\|sen(\theta_1 + \varphi) = 0.024 + (0.024)sen(\theta_1 + 55.3048°) \tag{2}$$

Distance between joints 2 and 4 ($\|\overline{p_2p_4}\|$), Eq. (3) applies from known positions:

$$\|\overline{p_2p_4}\| = \sqrt{(p_2(x) - p_4(x))^2 + (p_2(x) - p_4(y))^2} \tag{3}$$

The angles (θ_2, θ_4), are determined as the sum of the partial attachment angles:

$$\theta_2 = \theta_{2a} + \theta_{2b} \tag{4}$$

$$\theta_4 = \theta_{4a} + \theta_{4b} \tag{5}$$

And by the law of cosines the partial angles, [23], will be determined θ_{2a}, θ_{4a}, θ_{2b} y θ_{4b}:

$$\theta_{2a} = arc\ cos\left(\frac{l_1^2 - (\|\overline{p_2p_4}\|)^2 - l_4^2}{2l_4(\|\overline{p_2p_4}\|)^2}\right) \tag{6}$$

$$\theta_{4a} = arc\ cos\left(\frac{l_4^2 - (\|\overline{p_2p_4}\|)^2 - l_1^2}{2l_1(\|\overline{p_2p_4}\|)^2}\right) \tag{7}$$

$$\theta_{2b} = arc\ cos\left(\frac{l_3^2 - (\|\overline{p_2p_4}\|)^2 - l_4^2}{2l_4(\|\overline{p_2p_4}\|)^2}\right) \tag{8}$$

$$\theta_{4b} = arc\ cos\left(\frac{l_4^2 - (\|\overline{p_2p_4}\|)^2 - l_3^2}{2l_1(\|\overline{p_2p_4}\|)^2}\right) \tag{9}$$

Addition of partial attachments:

$$\theta_2 = arc\ cos\left(\frac{l_4^2 - (\|\overline{p_2p_4}\|)^2 - l_3^2}{2l_3(\|\overline{p_2p_4}\|)^2}\right)$$
$$+ arc\ cos\left(\frac{l_1^2 - (\|\overline{p_2p_4}\|)^2 - l_2^2}{2l_2(\|\overline{p_2p_4}\|)^2}\right) \tag{10}$$

$$\theta_4 = arc\ cos\left(\frac{l_3^2 - (\|\overline{p_2p_4}\|)^2 - l_4^2}{2l_4(\|\overline{p_2p_4}\|)^2}\right)$$
$$+ arc\ cos\left(\frac{l_2^2 - (\|\overline{p_2p_4}\|)^2 - l_1^2}{2l_1(\|\overline{p_2p_4}\|)^2}\right) \tag{11}$$

$$\theta_3 = arc\ cos\left(\frac{(\|\overline{p_2p_4}\|)^2 - l_2^2 - l_3^2}{2l_2l_3}\right) \tag{12}$$

Position of the mobile joint (p_3):

$$x_3 = x_2 + \|\hat{l}_2\|\cos(\theta_2) = x_2 + (0.078492)\cos(\theta_2) \tag{13}$$

$$y_3 = y_2 + \|\hat{l}_2\|sen(\theta_2) \tag{14}$$

$$= y_2 + (0.078492)sen(\theta_2) \tag{15}$$

The other case of interest is when the angle inclination of the platform (θ_4), is known, and must be specially calculated (θ_1) and the rest of angles and joints positions. The process is analogous to the first, when angle θ_4, is defined, the rest of the angles, θ_i and the positions of the mobile joints (2, 3) can be calculated as follows, mobile position joint (p$_3$):

$$\begin{aligned} x_3 &= x_4 + \|\hat{l}_3\|\cos(180° - \theta_4 + \varphi) \\ &= 0.020 + (0.069)\cos(-\theta_4 + 235.3048°) \end{aligned} \tag{16}$$

$$\begin{aligned} y_3 &= y_4 + \|\hat{l}_3\|\sin(180° - \theta_4 + \varphi) \\ &= 0.024 + (0.089)\sin(-\theta_4 + 235.3048°) \end{aligned} \tag{17}$$

Distance between joints 2 and 4 $(\|\overline{p_2 p_4}\|)$, from known positions the equation is applied:

$$\|\overline{p_2 p_4}\| = \sqrt{(p_2(x) - p_4(x))^2 + (p_2(x) - p_4(y))^2} \tag{18}$$

The angles (θ_2, θ_4), they are determined as the sum of the partial attachment angles:

$$\theta_2 = \theta_{2a} + \theta_{2b} \tag{19}$$

$$\theta_4 = \theta_{4a} + \theta_{4b} \tag{20}$$

$$\theta_2 = \theta_{2a} + \theta_{2b} \tag{21}$$

$$\theta_4 = \theta_{4a} + \theta_{4b} \tag{22}$$

And by the law of cosines the partial angles will be determined $\theta_{2a}, \theta_{4a}, \theta_{2b}$ y θ_{4b}:

$$\theta_{2a} = arc\ cos\left(\frac{l_1^2 - (\|\overline{p_2 p_4}\|)^2 - l_4^2}{2l_4(\|\overline{p_2 p_4}\|)^2}\right) \tag{23}$$

$$\theta_{4a} = arc\ cos\left(\frac{l_4^2 - (\|\overline{p_2 p_4}\|)^2 - l_1^2}{2l_1(\|\overline{p_2 p_4}\|)^2}\right) \tag{24}$$

$$\theta_{2b} = arc\ cos\left(\frac{l_3^2 - (\|\overline{p_2p_4}\|)^2 - l_4^2}{2l_4(\|\overline{p_2p_4}\|)^2}\right) \tag{25}$$

$$\theta_{4b} = arc\ cos\left(\frac{l_4^2 - (\|\overline{p_2p_4}\|)^2 - l_3^2}{2l_1(\|\overline{p_2p_4}\|)^2}\right) \tag{26}$$

Addition of partial attachments:

$$\theta_2 = arc\ cos\left(\frac{l_4^2 - (\|\overline{p_2p_4}\|)^2 - l_3^2}{2l_3(\|\overline{p_2p_4}\|)^2}\right) + arc\ cos\left(\frac{l_1^2 - (\|\overline{p_2p_4}\|)^2 - l_2^2}{2l_2(\|\overline{p_2p_4}\|)^2}\right)\theta_4 \tag{27}$$

$$= arc\ cos\left(\frac{l_3^2 - (\|\overline{p_2p_4}\|)^2 - l_4^2}{2l_4(\|\overline{p_2p_4}\|)^2}\right)$$

$$+ arc\ cos\left(\frac{l_2^2 - (\|\overline{p_2p_4}\|)^2 - l_1^2}{2l_1(\|\overline{p_2p_4}\|)^2}\right) \tag{28}$$

$$\theta_3 = arc\ cos\left(\frac{(\|\overline{p_2p_4}\|)^2 - l_2^2 - l_3^2}{2l_2l_3}\right) \tag{29}$$

Defined the position of the movable joint (p_3), and known the lengths of the links (l_1, l_2, l_3, l_4) and the positions of the fixed joints, p_1, p_4. To determine the angles ($\theta_1, \theta_2, \theta_3, \theta_4$), by means of the law of cosines, the all interior angles of the triangles defined between the joints 1, 2, 3 and 1, 3, 4 are determined. From the sum of the partial attachment angles of θ_1 y θ_3, they will be defined:

$$\theta_1 = \theta_{1a} + \theta_{1b} \tag{30}$$

$$\theta_3 = \theta_{3a} + \theta_{3b} \tag{31}$$

In the triangle analysis of joints 1, 4 and 3, to determine the length between joints 1 and 3 ($\|\overline{p_1p_3}\|$), the equation applies to known positions:

$$\|\overline{p_1p_3}\| = \sqrt{(p_1(x) - p_3(x))^2 + (p_1(x) - p_3(y))^2} \tag{32}$$

Then apply the law of cosines:

$$\theta_4 = arc\ cos\left(\frac{(\|\overline{p_1p_3}\|)^2 - l_4^2 - l_3^2}{2l_3l_4}\right) \tag{33}$$

To determine partial angles θ_{1a} y θ_{3a}:

$$\theta_{3a} = arc\ cos\left(\frac{l_4^2 - (\|\overline{p_1p_3}\|)^2 - l_3^2}{2l_3(\|\overline{p_1p_3}\|)^2}\right) \tag{34}$$

$$\theta_{1a} = arc\ cos\left(\frac{l_3^2 - (\|\overline{p_1p_3}\|)^2 - l_4^2}{2l_4(\|\overline{p_1p_3}\|)^2}\right) \tag{35}$$

To determine the angle (θ_2) the law of cosines will be directly applied, considering the joints 1, 3 and 2:

$$\theta_2 = arc\ cos\left(\frac{(\|\overline{p_1p_3}\|)^2 - l_2^2 - l_1^2}{2l_2l_1}\right) \tag{36}$$

To determine partial angles θ_{1b} y θ_{3b}:

$$\theta_{3b} = arc\ cos\left(\frac{l_2^2 - (\|\overline{p_1p_3}\|)^2 - l_1^2}{2l_1(\|\overline{p_1p_3}\|)^2}\right) \tag{37}$$

$$\theta_{1b} = arc\ cos\left(\frac{l_1^2 - (\|\overline{p_1p_3}\|)^2 - l_2^2}{2l_2(\|\overline{p_1p_3}\|)^2}\right) \tag{38}$$

Where angles θ_1 y θ_3, are:

$$\theta_1 = arc\ cos\left(\frac{l_4^2 - (\|\overline{p_1p_3}\|)^2 - l_3^2}{2l_3(\|\overline{p_1p_3}\|)^2}\right) + arc\ cos\left(\frac{l_1^2 - (\|\overline{p_1p_3}\|)^2 - l_2^2}{2l_2(\|\overline{p_1p_3}\|)^2}\right) \tag{39}$$

$$\theta_3 = arc\ cos\left(\frac{l_3^2 - (\|\overline{p_1p_3}\|)^2 - l_4^2}{2l_4(\|\overline{p_1p_3}\|)^2}\right) + arc\ cos\left(\frac{l_2^2 - (\|\overline{p_1p_3}\|)^2 - l_1^2}{2l_1(\|\overline{p_1p_3}\|)^2}\right) \tag{40}$$

4 Dynamics

Considering null inertial influence of collimator mass, [17], the Euler-Langrage approaches revised by [18–22], stablish the Energy Equation as:

$$L = K - U \tag{41}$$

where: K is the kinetic energy, U is the potential energy. Depending on the position, the Lagrangiane is defined as:

$$\frac{d}{dt}\left(\frac{\partial K}{\partial \dot{q}_i}\right) - \frac{\partial K}{\partial q_i} + \frac{\partial U}{\partial q_i} = Q_i \tag{42}$$

where, T is the kinetic energy of the system, Q_i is Generalized forces. Kinetic energy of a rigid solid body is:

$$K = \frac{1}{2}J\dot{q}^2 \tag{43}$$

where J is the moment of inertia of the body, $\dot{q}$ is the angular velocity of the system. Kinetic energy of the platform:

$$K = \frac{1}{2}J\dot{q}^2 + \frac{1}{2}mv^2 \tag{44}$$

where, v is the speed of the system, m is the mass of the system. Angular velocity (45) and velocity (47):

$$\dot{q}_b = \frac{dq}{dt} \tag{45}$$

$$v^2 = \dot{x}^2 + \dot{y}^2 \tag{46}$$

and the position of the centroid of the mass of the system are:

$$x = q \cos \theta \tag{47}$$

$$y = q \, \text{sen}\theta \tag{48}$$

The kinetic energy in the system is:

$$K = \frac{1}{2}(J+m)\dot{q}^2 + \frac{1}{2}mq^2\dot{q}^2 \tag{49}$$

The Potential Energy equation, Ghobakhloo [19], applied in this system is:

$$U = mg \, q \, \sin \theta \tag{50}$$

Substituting the energy components in the Lagrangian:

$$L = \frac{1}{2}(J+m)\dot{q}^2 + \frac{1}{2}\left(mq^2+J\right)\dot{q}^2 - mg \, q \, \sin \theta \tag{51}$$

In terms of the external torque of the system:

$$\tau = \left(mq^2+J\right)\ddot{q}^2 + 2mq\dot{q}\dot{\theta} + mg \, q \, \cos \theta \tag{52}$$

where q it's speed of the center of mass, $\dot{\theta}$ Angular velocity, M it's the mass, J it's the inertia tensor. Lagrangian movement equation:

$$\ddot{r} = \left(-\frac{1}{\frac{J}{R^2} + m} \right) + \left(mg \sin(\theta) - mr\left(\dot{\theta}^2\right) \right) \qquad (53)$$

5 Control

Main electronic components on control circuit are: MPU acceleration sensor, MG995 servomotor, and a 16 bit driver. The connection between the controller card, acceleration sensor, and servomotor are show in the Table 1 (See Fig. 5):

Table 1. MPU's connections

MPU	Controlador
VCC	3V3
GND	GND
SCL	A5
SDA	A4
INT	DIG 2
Servo 1,2	Controlador
V_1, V_2	3V3
G_1 y G_2	GND
C_1	DIG 8
C_2	DIG 9

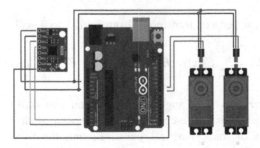

Fig. 5. Connection between the controller circuit configuration.

6 Joint Positioning Error

It was defined as the difference between the real position of the joints, measured in the model and corroborated with the toroidal levels and the determinants in the control algorithm by means of the acceleration sensor and the position equations. The sources of position error are derived from the characteristics and installation of the MG995 servomotor, the MPU6050 accelerometer sensor, the alignment and orthogonality of the articulations and links of both kinematic chains. In reference to the servomotor, it has an angular domain of $0°$ to $180°$, with a PMW (Pulse Width Modulation) range of 1.0 to 2.0 ms, with a resolution of $1°/0.00556$ ms. The 16-bit controller, with ADC (Digital Analog Converter), provides a 10-bit scale, for the PWM, which admits values between 0 and 1023 that for a range of $0°$ to $180°$, has a resolution of $0.17595°$/unit ($0°$ 10' 33.42"/unit). The MPU6050 sensor has a range of 0 to -32768 to 32768 and a domain of 0 to $250°$ which gives a resolution of 3.81469×10^{-3} in each axis (x, y, z). The kinematic chain introduces an error that affects the orthogonality of the system, when the alignment of the joints with respect to their axes of rotation and the links with respect to their design axes has an angular phase shift, this is significant for the x, z of articulation 1 and 2 and in its adjacent orthogonal y, z for joints 1 and 2. The effect on joints that have pins (3 and 4) is considered negligible.

The angular offset also influences the adjustment of the accelerometer sensor mount and the servo motor mount of each chain. The geometric effect of the angular phase shift generates:

1. Difference in the real and theoretical positioning of the joints.
2. Difference in the real and theoretical angle of the inclination of the platform.
3. These differences can avoid the convergence of the control method.

For the parametrization of the angular phase shift, the axes defined for the prototype geometry were compared against the real axes in the manufactured prototype. Its difference can be quantified as an angle in space. Thus, the composition of the position error in each articulation product of the angular phase shift is:

$$E_i(x, y, z) = E_i(\hat{1} \cos \alpha + \hat{j} \cos \beta + \hat{k} \cos \gamma) \tag{54}$$

And the total error per axis transferred from joint 1 to 4 will be:

$$E_x = \sum_{i=1}^{n} E_i(x), \quad E_y = \sum_{i=1}^{n} E_i(y), \quad E_z = \sum_{i=1}^{n} E_i(z) \tag{55}$$

In the parameterization of the angular errors, the angular shift was measured on the prototype, extending the axis references to measure with graduated scale in units of degree, on the axis of the cylindrical joints, finding the following ones (data in degrades), see Table 2.

Table 2. Kinematics chains, error angles.

	Chain 1			Chain 2		
	α	β	γ	α	β	Γ
MPU sit	1.0	1.5	0.0	0.0	1.0	0.0
Servomotor sit	0.5	0.5	0.0	0.0	0.5	0.0
Join 1	1.0	1.5	1.0	1.0	0.5	0.0
Join 2	0.5	1.5	1.5	1.0	0.0	1.0
Join 3	0.0	0.0	1.0	0.0	0.0	1.0
Join 4	0.0	0.0	0.5	0.0	0.0	0.0

The magnitude of the linear error transferred in each joint through the links in each axis are:

$$\varepsilon_{xi} = \|l_i\| \cos \alpha_i, \quad \varepsilon_{yi} = \|l_i\| \cos \beta_i, \quad \varepsilon_{zi} = \|l_i\| \cos \gamma_i \qquad (56)$$

The linear error transfer by axis is in Table 3.

Table 3. Kinematic chains, linear error.

Join	Chain 1				Chain 2			
	Link length	x	y	z	Link length	x	y	z
1	0.0240	0.007	0.006	0.003	0.0240	0.006	0.004	0.001
2	0.0784	0.021	0.018	0.002	0.0784	0.023	0.012	0.001
3	0.0650	0.017	0.015	0.003	0.0650	0.016	0.013	0.002
4	0.0790	0.022	0.018	0.001	0.0790	0.021	0.014	0.002

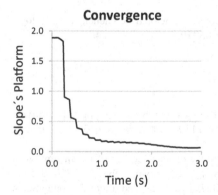

Fig. 6. Transference of the linear position error to the orthogonal kinematic chain.

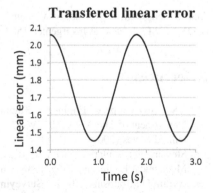

Fig. 7. Slope platform evolution's after disturbance.

7 Conclusions and Future Work

To determine the effects of error dispersion magnitude, caused by the geometric construction defects of robot platform, was quantified and discriminated all the kinematic sources of positioning error, caused by the joint's axes alignment, orthogonality and sensor's orientation, observing if the maximum ranges still allowed the control method applied convergence, to the platform leveling process. In addition, the critical positions of the chains that maximize the position error were found. This was achieved by expressing the discrepancy between the actual and setpoint position during the control process. The error quantification in each mobile joint was formulated as a position vector (Eq. 53), depending on the position of link 1 (see Fig. 4). The behavior of this error with respect to time was associated with a sine curve due to the cyclic nature of the kinematic chains (see Fig. 6). It was found that the change in error value increases as the axes of links l_1 and l_2 in both chains tend to align. The magnitude of error's position on platform and joint l_2 respect to time (Eq. 54), and the adjustment derived from the control gradually attenuates (see Fig. 7) the platform position error. This implies that it is possible to determine which the maximum error caused by the alignment defects of the kinematic chains that can still allow the control method to converge to the desired position of plate. For this calculation, position error parameters are established, quantifying the differences in a complete cycle of the coordinates of components that should not be affected if the links were correctly aligned. These linear error parameters (one for each axial component) are organized in a matrix of factors, for each articulation they allow the platform position error to be calculated based on a reference link with respect to time, as a transfer function. The eligibility for the integration of this prototype is based on its accuracy and the evaluation of its possible miniaturization, the ease of manufacturing and calibration in the field. This is evidenced in the behavior of error, that allows to focus the important parameters that govern during manufacturing. The control of error generated in joint 2, improve notoriously the device general performance.

Acknowledgments. This study was supported by Consejo Nacional de Ciencia y Tecnología (CONACYT), located at Insurgentes 1582, Zip Code 03940.

References

1. US Army Corps of Engineers, Engineering and design, control and topographic survey, Department of The Army, CECW-CE, Manual EM 1110-1-1005, pp. 3-10–3-11, 1 January, United States (2007)
2. Stewart, D.: A platform with six degrees of freedom. In: Proceedings of the Institution of Mechanical Engineers, 1965–1966, United States, vol. 180, no. 15, pp. 371–386 (1965)
3. Avram D., Bratosin I., Ilie D.: Surveying theodolite between past and future. J. Young Sci. **4** (2016). University of Agronomic Sciences and Veterinary Medicine of Bucharest, Romania
4. Hanieh, A.A.: Active isolation and damping of vibrations via stewart platform. Universite Libre de Bruxelles, Faculty of Applied Sciences, Active Structures Laboratory, Department of Mechanical Engineering and Robotics, Belgium (2003)

5. Bai, X., Turner, J., Junkins, J.: Dynamic analysis and control of a stewart platform, using a novel automatic differentiation method. In: AIAA/AAS Astrodynamics Specialist Conference, United States, vol. 1 (2006). https://doi.org/10.2514/6.2006-6286
6. Kazemi, M., Jooshani, M., Tehran, S.: Vehicle suspension inspection by stewart robot. Int. J. Automot. Eng. 2(4), 242–251 (2012)
7. Basim, M., Sharma, R., Vignesh, A., Dinesh, I.: Design of modified stewart platform for solar tracing applications. Int. J. Comput. Appl. 180(38) (2018). 0975–8887
8. Khodadadi, H., Reza, M., Gorji, M.: Robust control and modeling a 2-DOF inertial stabilized platform. In: International Conference on Electrical, Control and Computer Engineering, Malaysia (2011)
9. Borras, J., Thomas, F., Torras, C.: New geometric approaches to the analysis and design of stewart-gough platforms. IEEE/ASME Trans. Mechatron. 19(2), 445–455 (2012)
10. Ali, M.M.: Development of self-balancing platform on mobile robot using pid controller, Faculty of Electrical and Electronic Engineering, Universiti Tun Hussein Onn, Malaysia (2013)
11. Jarrah, A., Salah, M., Banihani, S.: Applications of various control schemes on a four-bar linkage mechanism driven by a geared DC motor. WSEAS Trans. Syst. Control 10, 584–597 (2015)
12. Orlov, M., Shkurko, A.: Support structure with features for precision leveling. United States Patent, 9,163,774 B2, United States (2015)
13. Patel, Y., George, M.: Parallel manipulators applications, a survey. Modern Mechanical Engineering 2, 57–64 (2012)
14. Hua, C., Weishan, C., Junkao, L.: Optimal design of stewart platform safety mechanism. Chin. J. Aeronaut. 20, 370–377 (2006)
15. Incerti, G.: On the dynamic behavior of a four-bar linkage driven by a velocity-controlled dc motor. World Acad. Sci. Eng. Technol. Int. J. Mech. Mechatron Eng. 6(9), 598–604 (2012)
16. Tang, C.P.: Lagrangian dynamic formulation of a Four-Bar mechanism with minimal coordinates. Technical Notes, February, China (2010)
17. Iqbal, S., Bhatti, A., Ahmed, Q.: Dynamic analysis and robust control design for stewart platform with moving payloads. In: Proceedings of the 17th World Congress, The International Federation of Automatic Control, Korea, vol. 41, no. 2, pp. 5324–5329 (2008)
18. Knuplez, A., Chowdhury, A., Svecko R.: Modeling and control design for the ball and plate system. In: IEEE International Conference on Industrial Technology, Slovenia, vol. 2 (2003)
19. Ghobakhloo, A., Eghtesad, M., Azadi, M.: Position control of a stewart-gough platform using inverse dynamics method with full dynamics. In: 9th IEEE International Workshop on Advanced Motion Control, United States (2006)
20. Orman, A., El-Bayoumi, G., Bayoumi, M., Kassem, A.: Genetic algorithm based optimal control for a 6-DOF non redundant stewart manipulator. Int. J. Mech. Ind. Aerosp. Eng. 2, 73–79 (2008)
21. Pedrammehr, S., Mahboubkhah, M., Khani, N.: Improved dynamic equations for the generally configured Stewart platform manipulator. J. Mech. Sci. 26(3), 711–721 (2011)
22. Kassem, A., Haddad, H., Albitar, C.: Comparison between different methods of control of ball and plate system with 6DOF stewart platform. IFAC-PapersOnLine 48(11), 47–52 (2015)
23. Zhang, Y.-X.: Modeling, identification and control of a redundant planar 2-DOF parallel manipulator. Int. J. Control Autom. Syst. 5(5), 559–569 (2007)

A Knowledge and Probabilistic Based Task Planning Architecture for Service Robotics

Elizabeth Santiago$^{(\boxtimes)}$, Sergio A. Serrano , and L. Enrique Sucar

Instituto Nacional de Astrofísica, Óptica y Electrónica,
Luis Enrique Erro No. 1, Sta. María Tonantzintla, 72840 San Andrés Cholula,
Puebla, Mexico
eliza.stgo@gmail.com, {sserrano,esucar}@inaoep.mx

Abstract. Service robots have to face task diversity, large, uncertain and partially observable environments, which are inherent aspects of the domestic domain and increase the task planning problem's complexity. Thus, in an attempt to overcome these challenges, in this work a task planning architecture for service robotics is proposed, which integrates a knowledge base approach with partially observable Markov decision processes (POMDP), and is constituted by three main components: (a) a knowledge base, (b) a POMDP construction module and (c) a task controller. Through a knowledge representation scheme, domain relevant information is exploited to define useful sub-regions in the planning search space. Once the search space is segmented, local POMDP policies are computed for each sub-region, then, a graph-based policy for the main task is built as a collection of these policies, for which the controller will determine the order in which they will be executed. Additionally, our architecture is able to integrate new functionalities as the robot is endowed with them. For evaluation purposes, a mobile robot navigation problem was used as case study to test our architecture, which shows the advantages of using domain specific knowledge in a task planning problem.

Keywords: Task planning · Service robotics · Knowledge base · Partially observable Markov decision processes · State abstraction

1 Introduction

Nowadays, the design of task planning architectures for robotics is an active and challenging field of research, since it involves a wide variety of problems related to robotics and artificial intelligence. In addition, an inherent aspect in decision making in robotic tasks is the uncertainty, mainly due to dynamic environments and to the diversity of scenarios that must be taken into account at the moment of solving a task. Also, being able to execute plans without human intervention results to be critical. In order to address these challenges,

© Springer Nature Switzerland AG 2019
L. Martínez-Villaseñor et al. (Eds.): MICAI 2019, LNAI 11835, pp. 646–657, 2019.
https://doi.org/10.1007/978-3-030-33749-0_52

various approaches have been proposed for the development of task planning architectures, for instance, probabilistic strategies, logic models (construction of rules, relational maps, ontologies) and graph theory. Markov decision processes (MDPs) are one of the most widely used probabilistic models employed to deal with uncertainty and to enable an agent to make decisions based on its states, which are assumed to be fully observable. However, most real-world problems do not have complete observability, in this manner, partially observable Markov decision processes (POMDP) have resulted to be an important tool to model and solve task planning problems in robotics scenarios [9].

Furthermore, the design of architectures for planning is not only focused on single activities, but it rather requires of the organized and coherent integration of various abilities for carrying out a task. This integration involves various problems, such as to represent and manage the knowledge, to capture new knowledge, and to associate a task with different functionalities of a robot (navigation, recognition of objects, people tracking, etc.), which cannot be programmed prior to its operation, because each task requires different abilities. Moreover, through decomposition, robotic tasks can be efficiently solved by fragmenting them into smaller sub-tasks, whose solutions are computed in a given order (sequential or concurrent) so they are eventually integrated into a global solution.

In this work, a task planning architecture based on a knowledge representation and teh POMDP framework for service robotics is presented. Using the proposed knowledge representation schema, which is defined by a set of facts and logic rules, the state space of a domain is segmented into sub-regions that enable the architecture to compute local policies, over these sub-regions, that a controller can invoke in a specific order to solve a particular task. The proposed architecture was evaluated in a mobile robot navigation problem, over a set of different configurations for the size and uncertainty of the environment, showing that by abstracting the state space into sub-regions, more reliable and time-efficient solutions can be achieved in comparison to when no abstraction is performed.

The organization of this work is as follows. Section 2 summarizes some works related with probabilistic and logic strategies for robotics task planning. Section 3 presents the POMDP formulation and some approximate solution methods. Section 4 explains the proposed methodology, the main components, the specification of the POMDP parameters, and the functionality of the planning and execution stages. In Sect. 5, the experimental setting and obtained results for different configurations of the navigation domain are described. Section 6 includes a discussion. Finally, in Sect. 7, the conclusions and future work are presented.

2   Related Work

Planning in partially observable domains is a challenging problem due to the uncertainty present in different environments of real-world problems, as well as the integration of the components required in the execution of a certain task. As aforementioned, probabilistic models have been widely used for searching a policy that maximizes the profit from the formulation of uncertain states and observations. In particular, POMDPs have been employed in many works for task planning [3, 10, 14]. In some real-world scenarios, planning has been simplified by decomposing the task into smaller planning problems. Such decomposition has been used to abstract temporally small solutions, where the conjunction of them solves the main task.

Some recent works have introduced a hierarchical decomposition for the navigation problem using a probabilistic model, which are described as follows. In [10], a hierarchy is built by setting at the bottom level a collection of simpler tasks, represented each by a POMDP. Planning is performed in a bottom-up manner, and the solutions of smaller POMDPs are combined to obtain the solution of the global task. The parameters of each POMDP, no matter at which level they are located, are defined over the same space of states and observations; however, the abstraction is performed in each POMDP using a dynamic belief network in order to compute its policy. Actions are clustered into abstract actions, termed sub-tasks. These sub-tasks are defined manually in the form of a hierarchy task network (HTN), and the states that have the same reward in the execution of a certain task are grouped. Nonetheless, this work does not have warranty in the reduction of states and observations. In [3], the policies are defined as finite-state controllers (FSC) which build exact models for each abstract action, and then use a bottom-up approach to traverse the hierarchical tree. The policy of a sub-problem is represented as an FSC and treated as an abstract action by a POMDP in the immediate upper level of the hierarchy.

In [14] they represent a hierarchical POMDP as a dynamic Bayesian networks (DBN) and show that the DBN can train faster and with fewer samples than a regular hierarchical POMDP or a joint POMDP. In [2] they propose an architecture using POMDPs, named RN-HPOMDP, for the navigation task of an autonomous robot. This architecture efficiently models, at a fine resolution, the state and action space by means of a hierarchical structure. They introduce, for sake of memory efficiency, what they have called *reference POMDPs* to represent the transition and observation matrices for each POMDP in every level. In [15] they define a learning stage for capturing the hierarchical representation of a POMDP, based on maximum likelihood estimation, and use a mixture of DBNs along with a parameter estimation, based on Expectation-Maximization.

On the other hand, knowledge processing methods have also been designed for task planning in robotics [5]. Some knowledge bases (KB) have been structured with logical, PDDL-based, and probabilistic representations, among others. Usually, the initial knowledge is analyzed and translated into logical rules that are employed to reason about how the robot can make decisions. In this part, one important aspect is the association of causal laws that relate actions and their effects. In recent works, such as [17] they propose a logic-based planning which defines a logic state space for the environment of the robot, and designs search strategies to explore it locally. They use logic rules to find out an optimized path from the state space without developing a map of the environment through range sensors. The environment is divided into blocks where the robot can navigate,

and such blocks are treated as states. In this way, the obtained plan is a sequence
of states that leads to a goal state and updates its beliefs, in the form of logical
facts, by adding and removing them from its KB. In [7] they introduce a way for
representing and defining a common vocabulary which describes important elements of the environment and establishes inference procedures that are applied
on this initial knowledge.

In [13] they present an architecture that combines probabilistic graphic models and a logic language to enable a robot to reason about facts observed or
inferred from its environment. This approach inserts structured commonsense
knowledge about objects and relations, and applies two levels of granularity to
describe the domain. In the first level, a coarse-resolution transition diagram is
defined and associated to a set of abstract actions. In the second level, a refined
version of the first level diagram is built, which is used to model a POMDP and
compute a policy to execute an abstract action.

Unlike the reviewed work, besides using POMDP for plan execution, the
proposed architecture uses domain specific knowledge to maintain a factorized
representation of the original state space and to perform abstraction over each
individual state space. By introducing the concept of inter-domain influence
graph, it is possible to determine an order in which actions that belong to different domains shall be executed. Therefore, tasks that require of several abilities
from the robot can be solved without having to perform a cross product of all
the state variables of each domain, which would result in a significantly larger
state space than the factorized one.

3   Partially Observable Markov Decision Processes

Partially observable Markov decision processes (POMDPs) is a framework widely
used for modeling the behavior of agents in order to learn how to act in
their environment. The formal description of the model and its parameters is
described as follows. A discrete time POMDP is formally defined as a 6-tuple
(S, A, P, R, Z, O), where S is a finite set of states termed as belief state, A is a
finite set of actions, P is the transition model, this is, $P^a(s'|s)$ is the probability
of reaching state s' if action a es taken in state s. R is the reward of the model,
$R^a(s)$ is the immediate reward of taking the action a in the state s. Z is a finite
set of observations that the agent can perceive. O is the observation function,
$O^a(z|s')$ is the probability of observation z if the action a is taken from the
state s'. Where the goal is to find an optimal policy that maximizes (minimize)
the reward (costs). The formulation of a POMDP can be solved by updating
the belief state until the optimal solution is obtained by the value function V
expressed in Eq. (1). This recursive formula is derived from Bellman's equation
[11]. Where $\beta = [0, 1)$ is the discount factor, and in this model the belief state b
is expressed by a probability distribution on the state space $b : S \to [0, 1]$, such
that $\sum_{s \in S} b(s) = 1$.

$$V'(b) = \max_{a \in A} \left\{ R_B^a(b) + \beta \sum_{z \in Z} P^a(z|b) V(T(b)) \right\}, \forall b \in B \qquad (1)$$

Existing methods in literature for solving these models were initially the methods [1,6,16]. However, solving problems with a very large set of states results intractable. Later, to deal with this problem, approximate algorithms have been proposed [8]. Recently, some methods have employed the idea based on a fixed point which have shown to be efficient, such as Point based policy iteration [4] and Randomized Point-based Value Iteration (PERSEUS) [12].

4 Proposed Methodology

The proposed methodology for task planning is constituted by two major parts, the architecture's components and the interactions among them that lead to solving a task. The architecture's components encompass a knowledge base (KB), a POMDP construction module (POMDP-CM) and a controller, that altogether, interplay with each other to build a problem-specific POMDP-based planner that is able to solve a requested task, see Fig. 1a. A human expert structures information referent to the robot's skill sets (general knowledge, *i.e.* basic modules' descriptions) and its environment (specific knowledge) into the KB. On the other hand, the architecture's functionality is defined by the way in which the POMDP-CM and controller use information from the KB to decompose a requested task into a set of smaller sub-tasks and build a plan that considers only relevant information for this task, instead of the whole state space. Finally, the controller combines their solutions to solve the original problem. Next, each of the components is described in detail.

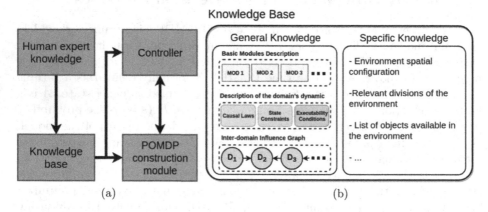

Fig. 1. (a) Architecture general schema for task planning, and (b) knowledge base structure.

4.1   Components' Description

Knowledge Base. Is a collection of facts and rules that comprise the information required to generate a plan whenever the robot is asked to solve a task. The information in the KB is structured under two degrees of specificity: general and specific knowledge. Figure 1b shows the organization of its sub-components. General knowledge comprises a collection of facts and rules that describe the effects the robot's actions have in the world, *e.g.* if a robot moves then its location changes. As for specific knowledge, it contains facts that are only true for the particular environment in which the robot will operate, for instance, a building's furniture arrangement.

General knowledge: Made of three main blocks, as described below.
- **Basic modules description:** A description of the skill sets the robot is equipped with, which in this work is represented by a basic module (BM). A BM is a list of actions the robot can perform with its corresponding skill set, the variables such actions are capable of modifying and the probabilities for the actions' outcomes, in this way a single domain is fully described (*e.g.* navigation domain, object manipulation domain, etc.).
- **Description of domain's dynamic:** A description of the domains' dynamics, based on the robot's BMs, defines how the actions of each BM change the variables they are associated with, that is, under which situations an action can modify a variable, and what are the possible outcomes.
- **Inter-domain influence graph:** Represents the dependency between domains, a directed acyclic graph in which there is a node for each domain described in the KB. In the inter-domain influence graph, if there is an edge going from the node of domains D_i to D_j, it represents that the state of the robot in D_i affects the outcome of actions in D_j, *i.e.* D_j is influenced by D_i. For instance, assuming that for the navigation and object manipulation domains, their states are defined by the robot's location and whether the robot is holding an object or not, respectively. Since the location of the robot influences the result to be obtained after executing a grasping action with its arm, we say that the navigation domain influences the object manipulation domain.

Specific knowledge: Refers to the list of facts that do not change over time, are true for a particular scenario and, along with the domains' description, are employed by the architecture to infer new facts about a particular environment, which are used in the construction of the POMDP-based planners.

POMDP Construction Module. This module is in charge of modeling a task as a POMDP and computing its policy, so that the robot solves the task at hand. When it is invoked, three input parameters are passed: the domain (d), the goal state (s_{goal}) and a sub-region (if any) that encompasses the task's state space. Then, from the description of the BM associated to d, the list of actions A is extracted, along with their general transition and observation probabilities. The sets of states (S) and observations (Z) are elicited from the specific knowledge (also, bounded to the sub-region passed as input parameter), and are used in conjunction with the dynamics description of domain d to build the transition (T) and observation (O) matrices for each action in A. For the reward function (R), the architecture uses a simple heuristic that assigns a large positive value to any transition ending in s_{goal}, while any other transition is assigned a small negative value. Finally, an approximate algorithm computes the policy for the modeled POMDP.

Controller. This component is responsible for conducting the execution of a set of policies that will allow the robot to accomplish its main task. The controller operates at two levels, *inter* and *intra*-domain. At the *inter*-domain level, it decides in which order to solve the sub-tasks of each domain, based on the inter-domain influence graph. Meanwhile, at the *intra*-domain level, the controller uses the sub-regions (if any) defined over the state space to decompose a single domain task into a sequence of sub-tasks. Then, it models each sub-task as a POMDP and executes in sequence the resulting policies.

4.2   Functional Description

With regards to the architecture's functionality, it is organized in two main phases: initialization and operation. In its initialization, the architecture computes and stores policies for each domain, that can be reused in different tasks. Therefore, in operation they are ready and waiting to be invoked. For operation, when the architecture receives a task request at this phase, a POMDP-based planner is built specifically to fit the needs of the task at hand. Both phases are depicted in more detail as follows.

Initialization. At this phase, the architecture revises in each of the domains described in its KB if there are sub-regions defined over their state space, if so, for each sub-region it identifies border states that connect with other sub-regions, and for each neighboring sub-region it uses the POMDP-CM to compute a policy that has as goal states those that border with such sub-region. In this way, the architecture builds some sort of macro actions that can be used later by the controller to traverse between sub-regions.

Operation. As previously mentioned, at the operation phase, the task solving procedure is triggered whenever the user issues a task request (in the form of a vector of goal states, each one assigned to a different domain). Next, according to the domains for which a goal state is defined in the task request, the controller generates the order in which the domain sub-tasks will be solved (based on the inter-domain influence graph). Then, for each domain sub-task, the following steps are performed.

Planning: Using the robot's current state (s_0) the controller computes the shortest path (sub-region-wise) to the sub-region (SR_{goal}) that contains the goal state (s_{goal}) for this domain sub-task. Next, the POMDP-CM computes a policy (P_{final}) for a POMDP modeled over SR_{goal}, and defining s_{goal} as the POMDP's goal state.

Plan execution: The controller sequentially executes the policies that were computed in the initialization phase, which it requires to traverse the shortest path to arrive to SR_{goal}. Once it reaches SR_{goal}, it executes P_{final} to reach s_{goal}. An example of the shortest path is shown and is described in Fig. 2.

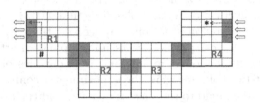

Fig. 2. Example of a navigation domain state space made of 4 sub-regions connected in a ring configuration, since the leftmost sub-region is also connected to the rightmost one, as indicated by the arrows.

5 Experiments and Results

The evaluation of the proposed architecture is applied to the domain of a mobile robot navigation problem, and is performed by simulating its execution within an environment made of several sub-regions configured in the form of a ring. Each sub-region is constituted by a grid of 4×4 resulting in a total of 16 cells, while the connectivity between a pair of them is established by a sub-set of their bordering cells. In example shown in Fig. 2, in order for the agent to reach goal state $*$ from the initial state $\#$, the architecture would invoke the policy to transit from $R1$ to $R4$, and then execute the policy computed for the POMDP modeled over the cells in $R4$ to reach cell $*$.

For these experiments, the BM for navigation is described as follows. The actions ($A = \{move\_up, move\_down, move\_left, move\_right\}$) enable the robot to move to one of its neighbor cells. The transition distribution (T) consists of 2 possible outcomes: stay in the current cell or transit to the target cell (with probabilities of 0.1 and 0.9, respectively). The observation distribution (O) was modeled as a 3×3 Gaussian discrete distribution centered in the action's target cell. The domain's state (S) and observation (Z) spaces are defined by all the cells that constitute the environment. As for the computation of local POMDP (the ones used by our architecture) and full-POMDP (the one defined over the full state space) policies, the PBVI [8] algorithm was used with the following parameters: discount factor ($\gamma = 0.95$), error margin ($\epsilon = 0.1$), horizon ($h = 10$), and amount of initial belief points ($n = 200$).

The two evaluated methods (POMDP and our architecture), were tested in different experimental configurations, which are specified by size of the state-space and the uncertainty of the robot's state. For both methods, when the execution of a policy was terminated while being in a non-goal state or it took an amount of steps greater than $|S|$, that simulation was considered a failure. Additionally, for our architecture, if during execution a policy perceived an observation that was not modeled in its POMDP, then that run is regarded as a failed one. In Fig. 3 is shown the average performance of each method as result of increasing the amount of sub-regions (first row) and standard deviation in the observation function (second row). From the leftmost to the rightmost column, the vertical axes represent the following metrics: Manhattan distance between final state and goal state as a measure of error (E), the executed plan length to optimum plan length ratio (R) and planning time (P). In the rightmost column, the dotted line represents the time required by the proposed architecture to compute the set of local policies at its initial phase. Furthermore, Table 1 summarizes the results for lower, middle and upper values of the independent variables. The first two columns show the experimental configuration, while the last four columns correspond to the success rate (S) and the average of the three evaluation metrics. The values reported in the R metric were averaged with respect the runs in which the agent had a Manhattan error of 2 or smaller, while the other three metrics were computed over 100 runs for each configuration.

From the experiments in which the amount of sub-regions is the control variable, the architecture seems to have a greater impact in maintaining a lower values for E, R and P than the POMDP as the size of the environment increases. By segmenting the state space, the architecture seems to successfully bound the error as it sequentially executes several local policies, while the POMDP has to reach the goal state with a single policy. As for the experiments in which the standard deviation is the control variable, they show that the POMDP obtained higher average values in the E and R metrics than the proposed architecture, while it also does not seem to stabilize its performance, contrary to the archi-

Table 1. Comparative results between a POMDP and the proposed architecture over several navigation scenarios.

# Sub-regions	O-dist. std. dev.	Method	S (%)	R	P	E
3	0.4	POMDP	58	2.39 ± 2.75	1.93 ± 0.26	0.46 ± 0.61
		Ours	63	2.52 ± 1.61	0.72 ± 0.08	0.52 ± 1.01
30	0.4	POMDP	2	7.48 ± 11.1	175.6 ± 39.8	42.88 ± 23.19
		Ours	52	1.45 ± 0.35	1.33 ± 0.11	4.41 ± 12.5
50	0.4	POMDP	3	1.91 ± 0.83	1019.89 ± 136.25	69.06 ± 41.81
		Ours	51	1.52 ± 0.66	3.47 ± 0.21	13.2 ± 27.43
5	0.2	POMDP	13	2.77 ± 2.03	3.34 ± 0.44	3.58 ± 4.69
		Ours	32	1.84 ± 1.05	0.45 ± 0.04	1.4 ± 2
5	0.6	POMDP	54	2.5 ± 1.54	6 ± 0.71	1.94 ± 3.89
		Ours	56	2.32 ± 1.34	0.89 ± 0.07	1.25 ± 2.35
5	1.4	POMDP	42	2.62 ± 1.88	4.83 ± 0.66	1.96 ± 3.58
		Ours	50	2.21 ± 1.36	0.71 ± 0.05	1.03 ± 1.66

tecture. Since the POMDP's state space size is 5 times greater than the one of the policies computed in our architecture, the approximate solving algorithm struggles to consistently find good policies in larger spaces, even though the observation distribution is locally bounded for each state. With regards to the R metric, the use of local policies also appears to reduce the chances of having the agent wandering around as the architecture obtained a lower average value in R than the POMDP. As for the planning time, even though the proposed architecture requires of an initial planning phase, this procedure is executed only once and is considerably lower (dotted trace) than the time required by the POMDP to plan every time a task request is received.

6   Discussion

As the experimental results showed the great benefits performing state abstraction has in comparison to a standard POMDP, the proposed architecture still depends to certain degree on the information the designer encodes as knowledge (in the form of facts and rules using an answer set programming language). That is, although the architecture is able to infer information from the knowledge originally provided, such information will be as good as the initial knowledge. Similarly, the better the provided transition and observation probabilities represent the domain, the greater chances the system will have to solve tasks.

Another important limitation of our work is that, so far, it does not incorporate a mechanism exclusive for the interaction with people, which certainly will be required at some point. Although one could design a basic module that includes speaking actions, a reactive mechanism would fit better human-robot interaction tasks, since announcing to the robot that a conversation is about to start would be very inconvenient. Whereas, a robot that is always alert to

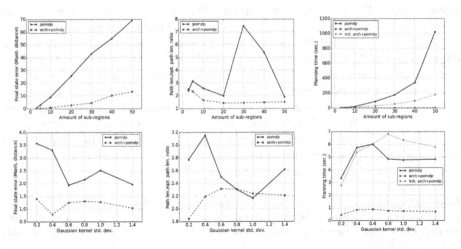

Fig. 3. Performance comparison of the evaluated methods. The solid line corresponds to the POMDP and the dashed line to the proposed architecture.

respond to spoken commands, or questions, would be preferable. To deal with continuous domains, the architecture is able of integrating the necessary parameters to the model; however, it is clear that the architecture will require of a discretization stage of actions or states into the definition of initial knowledge, and the application of the rest of the steps in the methodology will work in the same way.

7 Conclusions and Future Work

In this paper, a task planning architecture for service robotics applications is presented. The methodology integrates a scheme for representing domain specific knowledge, so that it can be employed to define POMDPs over sub-regions of the state space, a module that constructs POMDPs and computes their policy, and a controller that executes POMDP policies in order to solve a given task. The main contributions of the proposed architecture are the concepts of basic module and inter-domain influence graph, that enable to represent the state, observation and action spaces of several domains in a factorized manner, which we hope will help mitigate the computational workload required to solve tasks. With the application of the decomposition of a task into several smaller ones (one for each domain), the use of probabilistic models for planning in uncertain and partially observable environments (such as service robotics scenarios), in terms of time efficiency and robustness, becomes a feasible option.

Furthermore, by enabling the definition of sub-regions in the knowledge base, the system employs state and action abstraction within a domain's state space, which contributes in the decomposition of tasks. According to the obtained results from the navigation domain experiments, it is shown that state abstraction significantly reduces the amount of time required to plan, and increases the system's effectiveness to solve single-domain tasks as the state space of the problem grows. Both, low time response and high reliability, are highly desirable features in task planning and, we believe, are essential for service robotics systems. After showing that the proposed architecture is able to efficiently solve a single-domain task, as future work, we will evaluate how effectively the factorized representation can solve multi-domain tasks, i.e., tasks in which the decomposition requires of the participation of a variety of abilities (manipulation, object recognition, voice, navigation, etc.). Because the planning approach here presented has shown to consistently find near optimal policies, as future work, we will evaluate the proposed architecture in tasks defined by multiple domains, as well as we will explore the idea of modeling the process of bounding regions at several levels of abstraction into a hierarchy.

Acknowledgments. Elizabeth Santiago thanks the postdoctoral fellowship support by CONACYT and also to the robotics laboratory of the National Institute of Astrophysics, Optical and Electronic which were important parts for the realization of this work.

References

1. Cassandra, A.R.: Exact and approximate algorithms for partially observable Markov decision processes. Brown University (1998)
2. Foka, A., Trahanias, P.: Real-time hierarchical pomdps for autonomous robot navigation. Robot. Auton. Syst. **55**(7), 561–571 (2007)
3. Hansen, E.A., Zhou, R.: Synthesis of hierarchical finite-state controllers for POMDPs. In: International Conference on Automated Planning and Scheduling (2003)
4. Ji, S., Parr, R., Li, H., Liao, X., Carin, L.: Point-based policy iteration. In: AAAI, pp. 1243–1249 (2007)
5. Juba, B.: Integrated common sense learning and planning in POMDPs. J. Mach. Learn. Res. **17**(1), 3276–3312 (2016)
6. Kaelbling, L.P., Littman, M.L., Cassandra, A.R.: Planning and acting in partially observable stochastic domains. Artif. Intell. **101**(1–2), 99–134 (1998)
7. Moritz, T., Beetz, M.: Representations for robot knowledge in the KnowRob framework. Artif. Intell. **247**, 151–169 (2017)
8. Pineau, J., Gordon, G., Thrun, S.: Point-based value iteration: an anytime algorithm for POMDPs. In: International Joint Conference on Artificial Intelligence (IJCAI), vol. 3, pp. 1025–1032 (2003)
9. Pineau, J., Gordon, G.J.: POMDP planning for robust robot control. In: Thrun, S., Brooks, R., Durrant-Whyte, H. (eds.) Robotics Research. STAR, vol. 28, pp. 69–82. Springer, Heidelberg (2007). https://doi.org/10.1007/978-3-540-48113-3_7
10. Pineau, J., Thrun, S.: An integrated approach to hierarchy and abstraction for POMDPs (2002)
11. Puterman, M.L.: Markov Decision Processes: Discrete Stochastic Dynamic Programming. Wiley Series in Probability and Statistics. Wiley, Hoboken (1994)
12. Spaan, M.T., Vlassis, N.: Perseus: randomized point-based value iteration for POMDPs. J. Artif. Intell. Res. **24**, 195–220 (2005)
13. Sridharan, M., Gelfond, M., Zhang, S., Wyatt, J.: REBA: a refinement-based architecture for knowledge representation and reasoning in robotics (2018)
14. Theocharous, G., Mahadevan, S.: Hierarchical learning and planning in partially observable Markov decision processes. Ph.D. thesis, Michigan State University. Department of Computer Science & Engineering (2002)
15. Toussaint, M., Charlin, L., Pascal, P.: Hierarchical POMDP controller optimization by likelihood maximization. In: UAI (2008)
16. White, C.C.: A survey of solution techniques for the partially observed Markov decision process. Ann. Oper. Res. **32**(1), 215–230 (1991)
17. Zaman, S., Haq, N.U., Gul, M.I., Habib, A.: Robotic navigation based on logic-based planning. In: 2017 International Conference on Communication, Computing and Digital Systems (C-CODE), pp. 396–401. IEEE (2017)

Best Paper Award, First Place

RGB-D Camera and 2D Laser Integration for Robot Navigation in Dynamic Environments

Orlando Lara-Guzmán[1]([✉])[ID], Sergio A. Serrano[2][ID], David Carrillo-López[2], and L. Enrique Sucar[2]

[1] Instituto Tecnológico y de Estudios Superiores de Monterrey-Campus Guadalajara, Avenida General Ramón Corona 2514 Nuevo México, 45138 Zapopan, Jalisco, Mexico
a01631142@itesm.mx
[2] Departamento de Ciencias Computacionales, Instituto Nacional de Astrofísica, Óptica y Electrónica, Luis Enrique Erro 1, Tonantzintla, 72840 San Andrés Cholula, Puebla, Mexico
{sserrano,dabyte,esucar}@inaoep.mx
https://tec.mx/es/guadalajara, https://ccc.inaoep.mx

Abstract. Navigation, localization, and mapping are challenging tasks that any mobile service robot needs to solve. Given that this type of robots generally navigate in 2D planar environments, a common and highly effective solution is laser-based mapping (SLAM) and navigation. Unfortunately, due to their incapability to detect obstacles outside of a single plane view, these algorithms are affected by irregular obstacles in the environment; even more when there are dynamic obstacles. To address this problem, we propose a method to integrate data from a 2D laser range finder (LRF) and an RGB-D camera. In this paper, our goal is to enrich a 2D grid-based map by extracting and processing a depth image from an RGB-D camera, fusing this with the information from the LRF. To test the algorithm, we set up five different scenarios in which pure laser navigation would be an ambitious task. Comparative results between pure LRF and LRF + RGB-D navigation are presented. In spite of the simplicity of the method, results show a significant improvement in the robot's navigation, making it more robust in complex, dynamic environments.

Keywords: Mobile robot · Navigation · Dynamic environment · Obstacle detection · Collision avoidance

1 Introduction

Usually, service robots are equipped with a mobile platform that enables them to travel to any location of their environment. Moreover, in order to move from one point to another within environments, mapping, localization and navigation techniques have been successfully applied in tandem, which has extended

L. Martínez-Villaseñor et al. (Eds.): MICAI 2019, LNAI 11835, pp. 661–674, 2019.
https://doi.org/10.1007/978-3-030-33749-0_53

the horizon of what mobile robots are able to do in real-world scenarios. These techniques enable a system to build a representation (map) of the environment's spatial configuration that will later be used, in conjunction with its sensors, to estimate its location within its map at any time; then, using its location and a planning algorithm, the robot will build a path that leads to a goal location. Thus, these steps are a common approach for navigation problems in static environments (those that do not change over time), since no feedback is performed to monitor the state of the environment, but only for the robot's location.

For some service robotics applications, assuming that the environment is static seems a reasonable assumption due to how unusual it is to have elements in the map changing their location (e.g. furniture) compared to how greatly it decreases the computational cost of planning for navigation. Nonetheless, service robots might encounter drawbacks as a consequence of human activities that violate the static-assumption. Since the map's construction is performed once at the beginning of its operation, sub-optimal and/or unfeasible plans might be generated. In either case, the robot's performance is decreased as a direct consequence of not updating the map it uses to locate itself and navigate.

What is more, because sensors are required to constantly sample observations from the environment in order to locate the robot within the map, these observations can also be used to modify the original map so it matches the recently observed changes. By doing so, the robot becomes more aware of its surroundings and robust against the presence of unexpected obstacles, e.g. people and opening/closing doors. Additionally, a navigation system can benefit from increasing its sensor data sources, that is, it will enable it to build a richer map that describes the actual environment better, by capturing more intricate features, in comparison to what a single sensor would. Therefore, in the face of these challenges, in this paper we present a method that integrates data from a 2D laser range finder and an RGB-D camera to constantly enrich and adjust a 2D grid-based map in order to avoid dynamic obstacles, as well as those which are not detected by one of the sensors (i.e. laser). The proposed method employs a finite state machine to switch between navigation and collision avoidance, whose transitions are triggered by a hysteresis-based algorithm that uses laser and RGB-D information to determine which pixels in the 2D grid-based map are occupied. Moreover, experimental results show that, in comparison to pure LRF navigation, the proposed method significantly improves the robot's navigation in terms of robustness within complicated and dynamic environments.

2   Related Work

It's common for navigation, localization, and mapping in mobile robotics to employ 2D-based algorithms since they can be quite robust and reliable. Nonetheless, there has been an interest in recent years for the consideration of 3D environments. One idea proposed by [1] was to fuse 3D laser and RGB-D camera data to generate a 3D depth profile of the robot's environment, however, due to a high computational cost, only one third of the information could be processed. Meanwhile, [12] managed to build accurate indoor maps with the proposal of a fusion-ICP method. Although their method was sped up with the help of a 2D laser, processing time was still too large for real-time applications. A 2D laser was also used to reduce the high demanding processing times in [4], by dividing the 3D world environment in discretized 2D planes. This was done by making use of a LRF for 2D SLAM, and by handling with IMU and stereo vision the localization in the vertical axis.

Data fusion is a common approach, fusion of 2D with 3D sensors leads to lower processing time in comparison to pure 3D sensor fusion. The idea of sensor fusion has also been extended to obstacle detection and avoidance. Instead of concatenating the data coming from each sensor to create a 3D map, [6] extract obstacles from a stereo camera and a 2D laser individually to then match and fuse them into a single data set. The pair of sensors are used in such way that their assets are exploited, and their drawbacks are cooperatively compensated. As for [5], a matching algorithm is also used to fuse the two data sets of obstacles, but by using a model based obstacle trajectory algorithm, a 99% accuracy is obtained. In [8], a framework for multi-sensor integration based on the signed distance function is developed. Unlike previous works where point clouds are used to locate obstacles, or recreate a 3D environment, their framework employs the fusion of multi-sensor data to model the 3D or 2D environment with voxels or pixels, by means of occupancy grids.

Both 3D environments and obstacles can be represented by an occupancy grid in which a mobile robot navigates. The creation of such maps has been proposed in [9] by generating two separate 2D occupancy grid maps, one from a 2D laser and another from a stereo camera, and merging them for a later use in obstacle avoidance and path planning. Their approach involves directly using the information from the disparity image provided by the stereo camera for ground plane and obstacle detection, unfortunately, as a result of the noisiness of the camera, the robot cannot navigate without the help of a LRF. On the other hand, regarding these same type of sensors, [7] managed to accomplish this same task with more accuracy by extracting 3D points from a disparity image instead of directly processing the raw data.

RGB-D cameras have been used for sensor fusion and occupancy grid map generation. Following the work done with stereo cameras for navigation, [2] combined the data from various sensors including 2D laser, sonar, and RGB-D to generate a 2D map for navigation. Depth data from the RGB-D sensor was used to project chairs and tables onto the map, while the color image was used to identify rough terrains where the robot could not navigate. In this work, 2D SLAM was performed with 2D laser alone whereas [3], on the other hand, decided to extract virtual scans from the depth image (provided by the RGB-D cameras), and feed them in conjunction with 2D laser data to a navigation algorithm, which can simultaneously handle incoming information from various sensors. Rather than using the virtual scans to fuse them with 2D laser scans, [10] suggested that 2D navigation could be done with RGB-D alone. To do this, the virtual scans were directly passed to a 2D navigation algorithm, reporting results similar to those obtained by pure 2D laser navigation.

With our proposed method, we intend to take into account the 3D space so that a mobile service robot can navigate in dynamic environments without the computational burden of reconstructing the map with 3D sensors as [1,12]. Like all the previously mentioned works, we believe that sensor fusion is a necessity for an accurate reconstruction of the robot's surroundings and robust navigation. However, unlike [7,9] we avoid dealing with the disadvantages of stereo cameras. Our method fuses data from a 2D LRF and an RGB-D camera to generate a 2D occupancy grid. Contrary to [3,10], we don't intend to add the RGB-D information to the SLAM algorithm, but rather embed the information into the generated map to later use it for path planning and navigation in dynamic environments.

3   Sensors' Integration

Since each sensor delivers data in different ways, in this section we describe how the data from different sensors is merged, so that it can be used by the navigation algorithm to travel from one point to another without affecting the SLAM algorithm. For example, data obtained by the LRF is given as ranges in polar coordinates with respect to the laser, while the data obtained by an RGB-D camera is a gray scale depth image. In order to merge these types of data, our approach creates two separate occupancy grid maps and then concatenates them, so that a single merged map is passed to the navigation algorithm.

The first step is to obtain a map M^l from the laser-based mapping algorithm, while simultaneously processing every incoming 640×480 depth image to obtain points in $\mathbb{R}^3$. Consider P_c the set of 3D points obtained from a single depth image I with respect to the camera frame, where P_{cz}, P_{cy}, and P_{cx} are the set of points in each axis defined by Eqs. 1, 2, and 3, with ($k = u + 640v$) representing the k'th element of the set.

$$P_{cz}^k = I_{uv} \tag{1}$$

$$P_{cx}^k = \frac{u - u_c}{f_x} P_{cz}^k \tag{2}$$

$$P_{cy}^k = \frac{v - v_c}{f_y} P_{cz}^k \tag{3}$$

In Eqs. 1, 2, and 3, f_x and f_y are the horizontal and vertical focal lengths (in pixels) in image I, u and v are the pixel positions, I_{uv} is a pixel of I defined by u and v, and u_c and v_c are the pixel coordinates of the center of the image.

Given the pose T_m^c of the camera with respect to the map, we can obtain the set of 3D points P_m in the map's frame of reference with Eq. 4.

$$P_m = T_m^c P_c \tag{4}$$

Just like the set of points P_c, P_m also has subsets of points P_{mx}, P_{my}, and P_{mz} that are used for point-pixel correspondence and filtering. Filtering in the

z axis is done with P_{mz} to eliminate the points conforming part of ground plane and certain obstacles that are too high above the robot to cause a collision, by defining the *min_height* and *max_height* parameters.

The next step is to match the remaining points to a grid cell of the occupancy map. When the algorithm starts, all the cells are marked as *unknown* and they can later be set as *obstacle* or *free*. Let M^c represent the 701×701 grid-based map of elements generated with RGB-D data, while i and j are the row and column number, respectively. For every point in the subsets P_{mx} and P_{my}, there exists a corresponding grid cell that can be calculated with Eqs. 5 and 6.

$$i = \frac{P_{mx}^k - O_x}{\mu} + 0.51 \tag{5}$$

$$j = \frac{P_{my}^k - O_y}{\mu} + 0.51 \tag{6}$$

where, (O_x, O_y) is the center coordinate of the grid map given in meters (-17.525 in our case) and μ is the resolution of each pixel (0.05 m). Note that i and j are truncated to a whole number. In Eqs. 5 and 6, the addition of 0.51 is needed so that a row or column transition won't occur until $P_{mx}^k = \pm 0.05$ given in meters, otherwise it would occur when $P_{mx}^k = \pm 0.03$.

Now that we know to which pixel every point of the set P_m corresponds to, we need a way to determine if that cell will be set as *obstacle* or *free* depending on the observations, which is performed for incoming depth image. To accomplish this, we propose an algorithm based on hysteresis that is individually computed for every grid cell. We set an *observation_threshold* and an *observation_limit* to indicate when a cell needs to be shifted from *free* to *obstacle*, and vice versa. In Algorithm 1, we can see that if an obstacle remains in the same spot until the amount of acquired observations equals the *observation_limit*, then the algorithm will not free up its corresponding pixels as easily as it would for an obstacle that was only present long enough to reach the *observation_threshold*. Lastly, the final merged occupancy grid map M^m, that is used for navigation and path planning in dynamic environments, is obtained by combining information from M^l and M^c. The occupancy of every pixel M_{ij}^m is determined in a hierarchical manner. First, all the pixels are set to *unknown* and for every pixel M_{ij}^l or M_{ij}^c that is set to *obstacle*, the corresponding pixel M_{ij}^m will also be set to *obstacle*. In case neither M_{ij}^l nor M_{ij}^c are set to *obstacle* then if at least one of the pixels in either map are set to *free*, the corresponding pixel M_{ij}^m is set to *free*, otherwise it will remain unchanged as *unknown*.

Our algorithm has two modes of operation to be used under different circumstances: dynamic and static. Both modes operate as described by Algorithm 1, with the difference being that static mode omits lines 10–12 of it. The former mode is for navigating in dynamic environments, while the latter for mapping static obstacles that the laser can't contemplate. Obstacles mapped in static mode are always present in the map while those mapped in dynamic mode are cleared once the robot has reached it's target point. A visual representation of

---

Algorithm 1. Hysteresis-based algorithm for setting pixel occupancy

1: $M_{ij}^c \leftarrow unknown$
2: **if** in field of view **then**
3:     **for** number of points in P_m **do**
4:         **if** P_m^k corresponds to M_{ij}^c **and** Observations of M_{ij}^c $<observation\_limit$
   then
5:             Observations of M_{ij}^c $\leftarrow$ Observations of M_{ij}^c + 1
6:             Exit loop
7:         **end if**
8:     **end for**
9:
10:     **if** no points corresponded to M_{ij}^c **and** Observations of M_{ij}^c > 0 **then**
11:         Observations of M_{ij}^c $\leftarrow$ Observations of M_{ij}^c - 1
12:     **end if**
13: **end if**
14:
15: **if** $M_{ij}^c \neq obstacle$ **and** Observations of $M_{ij}^c \geq observation\_threshold$ **then**
16:     $M_{ij}^c \leftarrow obstacle$
17: **end if**
18:
19: **if** $M_{ij}^c = obstacle$ **and** Observations of $M_{ij}^c = 0$ **then**
20:     $M_{ij}^c \leftarrow free$
21: **end if**

---

the algorithm's output is provided in Fig. 1, where Fig. 1a is M^l given by the SLAM algorithm, Fig. 1b is M^c endowed by camera data and Fig. 1c is M^m the final result.

4 Navigation Algorithm

The navigation algorithm that we are currently using, with some modifications, was designed by the Active Vision Group (AGAS) [11]. In their chapter, they present and explain the use of their software which they call homer gui[1], homer mapping and homer navigation[2] corresponding to the graphical user interface, mapping algorithm and navigation algorithm, respectively. This software uses a particle filter to solve the SLAM problem and an A* algorithm for path planning.

A general overview of the navigation algorithm is shown in Fig. 2. First, the map is used to calculate a safe path to the target point; any obstacles the robot may encounter while it travels it's trajectory are handled apart from the calculated path, by analyzing data from the two sensors independently. Obstacle detection, which is performed at every sensor data callback, checks (within a certain area in front of the robot) for any 3D points that are thought to correspond to an obstacle in the robot's path. If a 3D point is too close, the robot will

---

[1] homer gui: https://gitlab.uni-koblenz.de/robbie/homer_gui.
[2] homer mapping and navigation algorithm: https://gitlab.uni-koblenz.de/robbie/homer_mapnav.

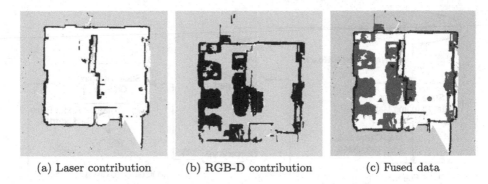

(a) Laser contribution   (b) RGB-D contribution   (c) Fused data

Fig. 1. Static occupancy grid map used for small aperture scenario.

begin to move back until the obstacle is at a distance that the robot considers safe. At this moment, the path is recalculated considering any occupied pixels that weren't present in the previously computed path.

With regards to the information coming from each sensor, data from the LRF has a high value of confidence and accuracy, which is why it is trusted. Therefore, if during navigation the LRF identifies a 3D point (obtained by converting it's readings from polar ranges) at a certain *collision_distance* or less in front of the robot, the algorithm enters the *Avoid Collision* state. On the other hand, RGB-D data isn't as reliable, hence, the algorithm is a little more conservative about marking a reading as an obstacle. Instead, points are placed on the vertices of the pixels marked as obstacles in the RGB-D generated occupancy grid map. Then, using the camera's intrinsic parameters with Eqs. 1, 2, 3, and 4, the 3D points are transformed into the map frame (provided by the RGB-D camera) and treated equally by the algorithm as those generated by the LRF.

As opposed to LRF generated 3D points, that are cleared and computed at every sensor callback, those given by the RGB-D are produced in the previously described manner, due to the drawbacks of the camera. By this, we mean that an obstacle detected at 0.6 m from the robot can suddenly disappear in the next reading according to the camera, yet this can be the result of the obstacle being closer than the camera's minimum range view.

5   Experiments and Results

We are working on a domestic service robot[3] that can help with certain tasks around the house. Our robot is a mobile manipulator RB-1 by Robotnik which has a differential platform and a vertical moving torso. The hardware used for localization, mapping and navigation are a Hokuyo LRF (URG-04LX) and an RGB-D camera (Orbbec Astra). The algorithms presented in this paper all run on an Intel nuc i7 with four cores running at 3.1 GHz and eight gigabytes of RAM.

---

[3] Link to our official web page: www.robotic.inaoep.mx/~markovito.

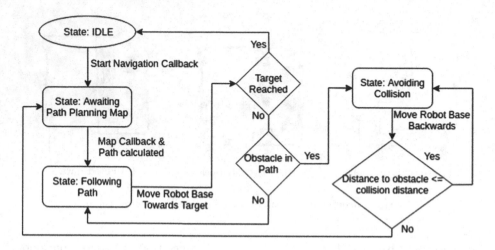

Fig. 2. Flowchart representing the general navigation algorithm.

The robot was submitted to a set of five different scenarios (small scattered obstacles, irregularly shaped obstacles, dynamic human obstacles, walking in front of the mobile robot and passing through a small aperture) to exhaustively test the capabilities of the robot, which include: detecting small obstacles, constantly refreshing the generated map for dynamic obstacles, and of course, evading each one of these. In every scenario the objective was to travel from one point to another with as few collisions as possible, if any. A convenient manner to determine the success of the method was to compare how well the robot navigated with and without the added camera data. The robot was tested in all five scenarios, with ten test runs for each scenario, for a total of 100 test runs. The results obtained in each scenario with both types of navigation approaches are summarized in Table 1 with the duration in seconds and a standard deviation for the sample of the experiment. The total amount of collisions per experiment are also displayed.

5.1   Avoidance of Small Scattered Obstacles

For this test, six small objects were scattered on the floor in an arrangement such that there was no straight path that the robot could take. The robot had previously generated a map with the absence of these obstacles. By small obstacles we are referring to objects that have a height small enough to be undetectable to the LRF; in our case, we used: canned food, wooden blocks, a plastic cup, and a soda can. Prior to executing the test, a map was generated for the static environment; this map is displayed in Fig. 3, while the start and end points are the circle and triangle respectively shown in Fig. 3c. The locations of the obstacles are shown in one of the test runs[4] that include RGB-D data which is available in YouTube™.

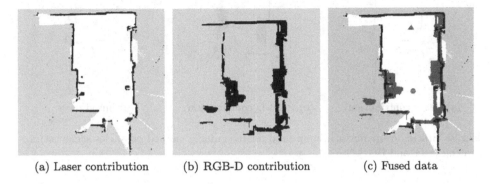

(a) Laser contribution   (b) RGB-D contribution   (c) Fused data

Fig. 3. Static occupancy grid map used for small scattered obstacles scenario integrating laser and RGB-D.

5.2 Avoidance of Irregularly Shaped Obstacles

In this scenario, the ability of the robot to detect and evade irregular obstacles that might be partially or mostly invisible to the LRF was evaluated. Examples of such obstacles would be chairs and tables, which by the way, are what we used. We placed a total of four chairs and one table in the environment. These obstacle weren't moved around during each test run; however, they were considered as dynamic due to the fact that they don't form part of the robot's map so there is a need for rerouting its path once the objects appear. The map used for this scenario is presented in Fig. 4, and a complete test run can be viewed in our YouTube™channel[5]. The beginning and end points of the robot's trajectory can be precisely seen in the mentioned video but are also approximately indicated in Fig. 4c by a circle and triangle respectively.

5.3 Avoidance of Dynamic Human Obstacles

In the previous tests, obstacles were difficult to detect but they weren't moving around, which means that up until this point, we hadn't tested the robots ability to clean its own map, in other words, refresh the data to determine the permanence or absence of the recently projected obstacle. To do this, we blocked the robot's path three to four times with the purpose of making the goal unreachable, given a planned route. If the robot managed to update its map then it

---

[4] The complete test run for small scattered obstacles scenario can be viewed at https://youtu.be/XomosxqqsvM.

[5] Irregular shaped obstacles scenario test run available at https://youtu.be/OkTQYaHHaGM.

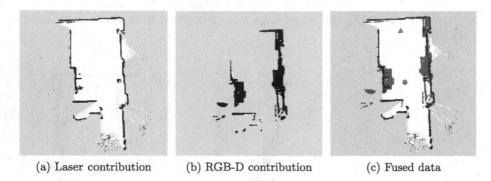

(a) Laser contribution   (b) RGB-D contribution   (c) Fused data

Fig. 4. Static occupancy grid map used for irregularly shaped obstacles scenario integrating laser and RGB-D.

would have no problem finding a route to it's target point, on the other hand, if it couldn't clean it, then the robot would consider the goal unreachable. The same map in Fig. 4 was used for this test, and a video is provided[6].

5.4   Walking in Front of the Mobile Robot

So far, we knew how well the robot evaded obstacles and refreshed the occupancy grid, though false positives could also be an issue. For this test, we walked through the robot's planned path, without stopping, twice and then stood in front of it. Since the minimum view distance of the RGB-D camera is 0.6 m, we decided to perform the two pass by walks approximately 0.8 m in front of its field of view. The experiment was considered a success if the robot did not detect the first two pass by walks as an obstacle but did evade the person that stood in front of it at the end. The generated static map for this scenario was practically the same as the ones in previous scenarios so in Fig. 5a and b we present the bottom right and top left perspective view, respectively, of the real world environment used for these experiments. A demonstration video was also produced for this scenario[7].

5.5   Passing Through a Small Aperture

The previous experiments were designed to test how well the method detected, evaded and cleared obstacles from its map, yet we had to make sure that the algorithm wasn't so conservative that it couldn't compute a path through a door. In this test, we asked the algorithm to navigate from one point to another with the only possible way being to pass through a 0.8 m opening. The largest map

---

[6] Footage of the robot in the dynamic human scenario at https://youtu.be/77IImkjriFw.

[7] Demonstration video of walking in front robot scenario at https://youtu.be/mIdDDreSwyo.

(a) Bottom right perspective view   (b) Top left perspective view

Fig. 5. Real world environment used to perform all the tests with minor adjustments in furniture placement.

created in all the tests was the one made in this scenario with an approximate area of 9.8×9.8 m, this map can be visualized in Fig. 1. We have a video uploaded to YouTube™, in which the robot is navigating through this small entrance[8]. Similarly to previous maps, in Fig. 1c we illustrate the approximate start and end points of the robot's trajectory.

Table 1. Comparative results for all five scenarios between LRF and LRF+RGB-D.

Test	Experiment	Method	Mean duration	Total collisions
1	Small & scattered	LRF	23.968 ± 0.659	20
		LRF+RGB-D	44.359 ± 5.95	1
2	Irregularly shaped	LRF	N/A	N/A
		LRF+RGB-D	46.154 ± 5.556	0
3	Dynamic human	LRF	46.07 ± 5.111	9
		LRF+RGB-D	58.341 ± 4.038	0
4	Walking in front	LRF	30.407 ± 1.171	10
		LRF+RGB-D	34.76 ± 1.168	0
5	Small aperture	LRF	30.423 ± 1.459	0
		LRF+RGB-D	36.468 ± 6.739	0

In Table 1, we can see that with LRF+RGB-D integration, the robot managed to detect and avoid 99% of the obstacles; additionally, this was accomplished without any false positives. The results for the pure LRF trials obtained in every scenario were expected. In Sect. 5.1 none of the obstacles were visible to the LRF, while in Sects. 5.2 and 5.3 the geometry of the objects were not correctly interpreted, rendering the salient parts of the table and the feet of the person undetectable. With regards to Sect. 5.4, the robot didn not report any false positives as predicted, nonetheless, it could not see the dimensions of

---

[8] Video of the robot navigating through a small entrance at https://youtu.be/ qprdONPSrig.

the feet in front of it and collided almost every time. Pure LRF actually had slightly better results than LRF+RGB-D in Sect. 5.5 because the latter is a bit more cautious and has difficulties navigating in tight spaces. Navigation with the fused data approach completely outperformed pure LRF navigation, due to its acquired ability of perceiving 3D information dynamically.

It should be noted that the camera has minimum depth range of view of 0.6 m and a maximum depth range of view of 6.0 m. The camera also has a FOV (field of view) of 53.13°, a value that we empirically obtained, since the brand claims that it is 60°. Given these conditions, there exist certain obstacle position arrangements that could allow the robot to approach an obstacle without the object being detected. This could happen if the obstacle is outside the FOV and once it enters it, the object is closer than the 0.6 minimum distance required for detection. Another situation of possible failure is if the robot is advancing forward at a constant speed and an object enters it's path at 0.75 m or less in front of it. The minimum depth distance is 0.6 m, however, our algorithm needs a certain amount of positive observations to determine a grid cell as containing an obstacle. Both of these conditions were taken into account at the moment of designing the scenarios to test the algorithm and will be addressed in our future work. There is no issue concerning the maximum depth range distance because as long as the camera is detecting the object the amount of positive observations will increase and thus, the corresponding grid cells will be marked as obstacles. This distance is restricted by the physical limitations of the camera but it can be decreased with software. Another concern might be large lighting variations; however, the only lighting that considerably affects both the LRF and the RGB-D camera is direct sunlight. The robot is meant for indoor navigation and this is even possible in dark rooms since each sensor has it's own infrared illuminator. With this in mind, there is actually no need to switch between LRF and LRF+RGB-D navigation.

6   Conclusion and Future Work

We proposed a method to enrich a 2D occupancy grid map, which a 2D laser-based navigation algorithm employs, by integrating information from an RGB-D camera. The purpose of the method was to allow a service robot to navigate in a real 3D world environment without the need of reconstructing a computational burdening 3D map. To accomplish this task, our approach was to leave the SLAM problem strictly to the realm of LRF data, while providing 3D information to the path planning algorithm in real time; in other words, the navigation algorithm could avoid obstacles that the LRF couldn't normally see in a dynamic environment. Since the navigation algorithm is 2D-based, two different occupancy maps were generated independently with each sensor and were dynamically merged. To test the method, the robot was submitted to a total of five scenarios, coming across obstacles in which navigation based solely on LRF input, would be futile. The obtained results demonstrate that a 2D navigation algorithm can be substantially enhanced by projecting 3D information to an occupancy grid map at a computational cost so low that we can be processing the information at more than 17 Hz. The only drawback found were the physical limitations of the camera: small field of view of 53.13° and a minimum range of view of 0.6 m that makes, under certain conditions, obstacles undetectable. In future work we plan to address said drawbacks to obtain a more robust navigator even in conditions in which depth information is not available. The idea is to detect and integrate obstacles, into the map, using the information provided by the RGB image to account for the minimum view range.

References

1. Budzan, S., Kasprzyk, J.: Fusion of 3D laser scanner and depth images for obstacle recognition in mobile applications. Opt. Lasers Eng. (2016). https://doi.org/10.1016/j.optlaseng.2015.09.003
2. Filliat, D., et al.: RGBD object recognition and visual texture classification for indoor semantic mapping. In: 2012 IEEE Conference on Technologies for Practical Robot Applications, TePRA 2012 (2012). https://doi.org/10.1109/TePRA.2012.6215666
3. Gonzalez, J., Ruiz, J.R., Galindo, C.: Improving 2D reactive navigators with kinect. In: Proceedings of the 10th International Conference on Informatics in Control, Automation and Robotics, pp. 393–400. SciTePress - Science and and Technology Publications (2013). https://doi.org/10.5220/0004485503930400, http://www.scitepress.org/DigitalLibrary/Link.aspx?doi=10.5220/0004485503930400
4. Iocchi, L., Pellegrini, S.: Building 3D maps with semantic elements integrating 2D laser, stereo vision and IMU on a mobile robot. In: Proceedings of the 2nd ISPRS International Workshop on 3D-ARCH (2007)
5. Kim, S., Kim, H., Yoo, W., Huh, K.: Sensor fusion algorithm design in detecting vehicles using laser scanner and stereo vision. IEEE Trans. Intell. Transp. Syst. (2016). https://doi.org/10.1109/TITS.2015.2493160
6. Labayrade, R., Royere, C., Gruyer, D., Aubert, D.: Cooperative fusion for multi-obstacles detection with use of stereovision and laser scanner. Auton. Robots **19**(2), 117–140 (2005). https://doi.org/10.1007/s10514-005-0611-7
7. Lin, K.H., Chang, C.H., Dopfer, A., Wang, C.C.: Mapping and localization in 3D environments using a 2D laser scanner and a stereo camera. J. Inf. Sci. Eng. **28**, 131–144 (2012)
8. May, S., et al.: A generalized 2D and 3D multi-sensor data integration approach based on signed distance functions for multi-modal robotic mapping. In: 19th International Workshop on Vision, Modeling and Visualization. VMV 2014 (2014). https://doi.org/10.2312/vmv.20141281
9. Moghadam, P., Wijesoma, W.S., Feng, D.J.: Improving path planning and mapping based on stereo vision and lidar. In: 2008 10th International Conference on Control, Automation, Robotics and Vision, ICARCV 2008 (2008). https://doi.org/10.1109/ICARCV.2008.4795550
10. Nardi, F., Lázaro, M.T., Iocchi, L., Grisetti, G.: Generation of laser-quality 2D navigation maps from RGB-D sensors. In: Holz, D., Genter, K., Saad, M., von Stryk, O. (eds.) RoboCup 2018. LNCS (LNAI), vol. 11374, pp. 238–250. Springer, Cham (2019). https://doi.org/10.1007/978-3-030-27544-0_20

11. Seib, V., Memmesheimer, R., Paulus, D.: A ROS-based system for an autonomous service robot. In: Koubaa, A. (ed.) Robot Operating System (ROS). SCI, vol. 625, pp. 215–252. Springer, Cham (2016). https://doi.org/10.1007/978-3-319-26054-9_9
12. Wen, C., Qin, L., Zhu, Q., Wang, C., Li, J.: Three-dimensional indoor mobile mapping with fusion of two-dimensional laser scanner and RGB-D camera data. IEEE Geosci. Remote Sens. Lett. **11**, 843–847 (2014). https://doi.org/10.1109/LGRS.2013.2279872

Adaptive Controller Based on IF-THEN Rules and Simultaneous Perturbation Stochastic Approximation Tuning for a Robotic System

Ludivina Facundo[(✉)], Chidentree Treesatayapun, and Arturo Baltazar

Robotics and Advanced Manufacturing Program CINVESTAV-Saltillo,
25903 Ramos Arizpe, Mexico
lfacundo04@gmail.com

Abstract. This study presents an adaptive controller based on neuro-fuzzy networks and stochastic approximation techniques. The algorithm assumes that the mathematical model of the plant is unknown. An adaptive Fuzzy Rule Emulated Network (FREN) structure is implemented as the main controller. While, a modified version of the Simultaneous Perturbation Stochastic Approximation (SPSA) technique is added as the adaptation algorithm, which estimates the gradient of the plant with respect to the control effort. The proposed FREN+SPSA performance for position control is compared to conventional FREN and classical PID controllers. Experimental tests were performed on a cartesian robotic system, regulating the frequency of a DC motor to follow a desired trajectory. Experimental results show better performance of the proposed FREN+SPSA controller than the conventional FREN and PID controller.

Keywords: Stochastic approximation · Simultaneous perturbation · Fuzzy neural networks · Position control

1 Introduction

In the development of new technologies, industrial processes are more complex to model by fundamental mathematics or system identification methods. Accurate models are difficult to extract because of nonlinear terms and uncertainties. Fortunately, several control schemes called Data-Driven Controllers (DDC) [6, 12] have been proposed to operate as model-free. A set of input-output data is the only requirement to design the controller. Following this idea, several schemes of model-free adaptive controllers have been reported [5, 13].

In the field of control engineering, the integration of fuzzy logic and neural network, known as Fuzzy Neural Network (FNN) has drawn the attention of many researchers [2, 9, 14]. Combining the learning ability of neural network and human-like reasoning of fuzzy logic renders a flexible and intelligent FNN

© Springer Nature Switzerland AG 2019
L. Martínez-Villaseñor et al. (Eds.): MICAI 2019, LNAI 11835, pp. 675–686, 2019.
https://doi.org/10.1007/978-3-030-33749-0_54

control technique for many applications [7,10]. An adaptive controller inspired by similar principles is called Fuzzy Rules Emulated Network (FREN) and is proposed by Treesatayapun in [20]; its structure is simple and allows the initial settings of network parameters to be intuitively selected. FREN has been implemented in different plants; in [24] a stabilized version of FREN was applied to control a DC motor based on Pulsed-Width Modulation (PWM) techniques. In [23] a Multiple-input FREN (Mi-FREN) controller was applied for grasping force regulation task considering the contact mechanism unknown and the industrial gripper as a nonlinear-discrete time system. In [1] a force feedback controller based on FREN was implemented to control an ultrasound probe based on Hertzian contact, determining instantaneous contact and regulating the contact force. Recently, a robust version of FREN controller, involving sliding mode techniques was presented in [4], for positioning control of a 3DoF robotic system. In mentioned works, FREN's control parameters were tuned based on the steepest descendent technique. Here, we propose a tuning algorithm based on the simultaneous perturbation stochastic approximation methodology.

The Stochastic Approximation (SA) algorithms are based on direct noisy measurements of the gradient vector of a function. However, when only loss function measurements are available, the gradient can be approximated by free-gradient SA methods. One of these, is the Simultaneous Perturbation Stochastic Approximation (SPSA) method, proposed by Spall in [19] as an alternative method to the Kiefer-Wolfowitz procedure in [8], showing a significant advantage especially for large-dimensional problems. SPSA has been implemented in the control area [16,18], and for real-world control problems, such as real-time traffic signal control [17]. In reference [11] a modified version of SPSA is introduced to tune the control parameters for a flexible robotic arm. It includes simultaneous perturbation of all parameters using only one perturbation vector and a limited number of measurements. Recently, in [3] an adaptive weighted gradient version of SPSA was implemented as the learning rule for a NN controller, showing good results over different simulated plants.

In this work, a novel data-driven controller based on FREN as the direct controller and a modified version of SPSA technique as the adaptation algorithm is proposed. The controller assumes that the parameters and structure of the system dynamics are unknown. The tuning of the proposed controller is carried out implementing the modified version presented in [11], using direct output measurements of the plant to optimize the control parameters of FREN controller.

2   Control System Configuration

2.1   Controlled Plant

The controlled plant consists in a robotic system of three degrees (prismatic) of freedom developed and integrated in our laboratory. The robotic system is operated in the frequency-mode control, which means that the controller must generate the frequency command to move each DC motor of the system to follow the desired trajectory. In Fig. 1 the setup of the experimental system is described; the control signal establishes the frequency value to feeds the DC motor of the selected axis; the output of the system is a displacement that acts as the feedback position signal used to determine the control input error. Here, the error is the difference between a desired position and the current measured position, which can be reduced with the proper control algorithm.

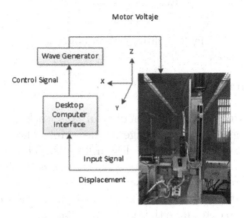

Fig. 1. Setup of the experimental system

2.2 Control Scheme

The control scheme to handle the axis position regulation with unknown mathematical model of the plant is shown in Fig. 2. The controller's inputs are: the error between the desired position and the current measured position $e(k) = x_d(k) - x(k)$ and the delayed error $e(k-1)$, given as a voltage lecture from a linear potentiometer attached to the selected axis of the robotic system. The generated control signal $u(k)$ feeds the plant to generate a new output value $y(k+1)$. In this work, three different control techniques will be implemented in the experimental setup. First, the well known PID with empirical better proportional, derivative and integral gains for this plant, following the rules of [15]. The second algorithm is the conventional adaptive network FREN; and finally, the proposed FREN based on SPSA tuning. FREN and proposed FREN+SPSA version will be introduced in the following sections.

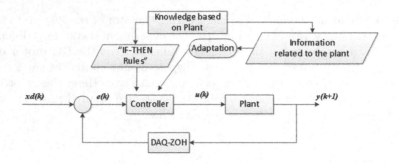

Fig. 2. Control system concept.

3   FREN Controller

The adaptive FREN controller implemented in this work, is based on IF-THEN rules regarding to the human knowledge of the plant. The rules can be directly embedded in the network architecture design [20–22]. They can be seen such as *IF the desired position is far THEN the speed should be high to reach it in short time, or, IF the desired position is close, THEN the speed should be low to arrive in a soft way*; similar to the intuitive control applied when driving. Therefore, IF-THEN rules help to determine the speed of convergence and adaptation of the controller. A general single input-single output fuzzy system could be written as:

$$\text{RULE } i\colon \text{IF } e(k) \text{ is } A_i \text{ THEN } \beta_i = f_i(\mu_i)$$

where, in the i node ($i = 1, 2, ..., N$) if the control input $e(k)$ belongs to the fuzzy set A_i, with the membership function μ_i corresponding to a one linguistic level (e.g. negative, zero, positive), and β_i represents the control parameter to be adjusted. Then, the fuzzy output value $O_i(k)$ is equal to $\beta_i(\mu_i)$ for the time index k.

3.1   FREN Architecture

A brief description of FREN structure is given here, for more details see [20]. FREN architecture shown in Fig. 3 is built by four layers, the first one corresponds to the input of the controller, that is, the error $e(k)$ measured between a reference value and the current output of the system. In the second layer, where the IF-THEN rules are set, the input value is evaluated and assigned to the corresponding membership functions A_i. The third layer, corresponds to the core part of the adaptive control. Where, the adjustable control parameters β_i, also called linear consequence parameters, determine the control system stability. Here, the control performance can be improved by implementing a learning algorithm. Finally, the fourth layer represents the sum of all control parameters resulting in the output of FREN and the control signal to the plant.

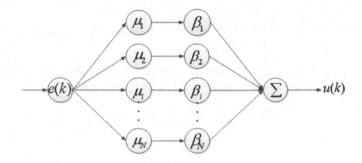

Fig. 3. Network structure of FREN.

3.2   Adaptation Algorithm

A characteristic of FREN is that initial values of the control parameters can be set intuitively as a rough estimation based on the human experience. However, it is necessary a well tuning these values in order to cope with environmental changes. In [24] several FREN adaptation algorithms based on the steepest descendent technique are shown following:

$$\beta_i(k+1) = \beta_i(k) + \eta_i(k)e(k+1)y_p(k)\mu_i(k), \tag{1}$$

where, η_i is the learning rate of the algorithm and y_p is the value of the gradient estimation. The adaptation in FREN, allows the adjustment of control parameters during system operation.

4   Simultaneous Perturbation Stochastic Approximation

A brief review of SPSA approach [17, 19] is given here. This technique is focused in finding the roots θ^* of the gradient equation:

$$g(\theta) \equiv \frac{\partial L(\theta)}{\partial(\theta)} = 0,$$

where the loss function L is observed in the presence of noise. Such that, the scalar-valued differentiable objective function $L(\theta) : R^P \to R^1$ can be minimized with respect to the vector $\theta \in R^P$ of adjustable parameters and assuming that $g(\theta)$ and $L(\theta)$ are not directly available. In SA algorithms, the standard form of $\hat{\theta}$, the estimate value of θ at the kth iteration is:

$$\hat{\theta}_{k+1} = \hat{\theta}_k + a(k)\hat{g}_k(\hat{\theta}_k), \tag{2}$$

where $a(k)$ is defined as the gain sequence that satisfies certain conditions [19], generally given as a small positive value. Letting $J(\cdot)$ denotes a measurement of $L(\cdot)$ for some parameter value represented by $(L(\cdot)+$ noise):

$$J_k^{(+)} = L(\hat{\theta}_k + c(k)\Delta_k) + \varepsilon^{(+)},$$

$$J_k^{(-)} = L(\hat{\theta}_k - c(k)\Delta_k) + \varepsilon^{(-)},$$

where $c(k)$ is a scalar valued related with the perturbation magnitude, and $\varepsilon^{(+)}, \varepsilon^{(-)}$ represent the measurement noise terms that satisfy:

$$E\{\varepsilon^{(+)} - \varepsilon^{(-)} \mid \mathcal{F}_k, \Delta_k\} = 0 a.s. \forall k,$$

$$\mathcal{F}_k \equiv \{\hat{\theta}_0, \hat{\theta}_1, \dots, \hat{\theta}_k\};$$

where $E\{\cdot\}$ is the expected value and $\Delta_k \in R^P$ is a vector of p mutually independent mean-zero random variables $\{\Delta_{k1}, \Delta_{k2}, \dots, \Delta_{kp}\}$ with mutually independent sequence and independent of $\hat{\theta}_0, \hat{\theta}_1, \dots, \hat{\theta}_k$. One form for the estimate of $g(\cdot)$ at kth iteration is:

$$\hat{g}_k(\hat{\theta}_k) = \begin{bmatrix} \frac{J_k^{(+)} - J_k^{(-)}}{2c(k)\Delta_{k1}} \\ \vdots \\ \frac{J_k^{(+)} - J_k^{(-)}}{2c(k)\Delta_{kp}} \end{bmatrix}$$

In general, in SPSA all elements of the control parameters vector $\hat{\theta}_k$ are randomly perturbed together to obtain two output measurements of $y(\cdot)$. However, each component of the estimated gradient $\hat{g}_k(\hat{\theta}_k)$ is formed from a ratio involving the individual components in the perturbation vector and the difference in the two corresponding measurements. The main advantage of SPSA methodology is that it only uses 2 measurements (instead of $2p$ in the usual finite difference approximation) to estimate the gradient.

The SPSA version employed in this work is based on the learning rule given by Maeda in [11], requiring only two values of the error function; the undisturbed $J(\theta(k))$, and $J(\theta(k) + c_k \Delta_k)$ to update the control parameters in the network. Such, the estimated gradient follows:

$$\hat{g}_k(\hat{\theta}_k) = \frac{J_k^{(+)} - J_k}{c(k)} \Delta_k. \tag{3}$$

This rule adopts the simultaneous perturbation with the sign vector Δ_k that is equivalent to the random direction type of optimization methods.

5 FREN Controller Based on SPSA Adaptation Algorithm

The FREN controller structure implemented in this work is defined with five membership functions $\mu_i(k)$, related to the approximated range of $e(k)$ within $[-5, 5]$ cm, as shown in Fig. 4 and a control parameters vector $\beta_i(k)$ of five parameters. The initial adjustable values of $\beta_i(k)$ are set according to the knowledge of the plant, it means, $\beta_1(k)$ is a large negative value, $\beta_3(k)$ is zero and $\beta_5(k)$ is a large positive value.

The control signal without perturbation is given by:

$$u(k) = \beta(k)\mu(e(k)),\tag{4}$$

$u(k)$ is sent to the plant and the error is measured to estimate the cost function $J(k)$ as:

$$J(k) = \frac{1}{2}e(k)^2.\tag{5}$$

At the same kth iteration, a stochastic perturbation Δ_k is added to the control parameter $\beta(k)$:

$$\beta^p(k) = \beta(k) + c(k) * \Delta_k,\tag{6}$$

where the perturbation vector Δ_k contains five random Bernoulli values $(-1, 1)$ and $c(k)$ represents the size of the perturbation, which changes at each iteration as $c(k) = 0.1/(k+1)^{0.101}$, satisfying certain regularity conditions (typically $c(k) \rightarrow 0$ or $c(K) = c, \forall k$ according to the system). The new β^p vector is used to estimate a new perturbed control signal given by:

$$u^p(k) = \beta^p(k)\mu(e(k)),\tag{7}$$

$u^p(k)$ is sent to the plant to estimate $e^p(k)$ and $J^p(k)$. Having both cost function values, the gradient by SPSA is estimated as:

$$\hat{g}(k) = \frac{J^p(k) - J(k)}{c(k)}\Delta_k.\tag{8}$$

The new control parameters are adjusted by

$$\beta_i(k+1) = \beta(k) - a_k * \hat{g}(k),\tag{9}$$

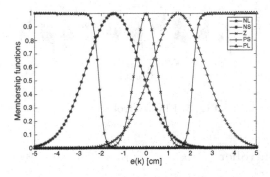

Fig. 4. Membership functions setting; where NL = Negative Large, NS = Negative Small, Z = Zero, PS = Positive Small and PL = Positive Large.

where a_k acts as the learning rate for SPSA. For our plant we found a tuning value of $a(k) = 1700/(k + 1 + A)^{0.602}$ with $A = 1$, which is different from reported by Spall but provides a good performance of the controller.

6   Experimental Results

In order to test the performance of the proposed adaptive controller, three different control techniques were implemented in the x-axis of our 3DOF robotic system shown in Fig. 1. The selected x-axis fluctuates from 20 cm to 15 cm during 5 cycles, as shown in Fig. 5. The position feedback measurement is given by a linear potentiometer attached to the axis as described in Sect. 2.

6.1   PID Controller

The PID gains were selected based on the better empirical results for the plant and following the rules of [15]. PID controller works well on the system for simple tasks, but when compare with FREN its convergence is slower. The equation implemented to estimate the control signal is:

$$u(k) = k_p[e(k)] + k_i[e(k) + e(k - 1)] + k_d[e(k) - e(k - 1)].$$

where $u(k)$ is the control signal to the plant, $e(k)$ is the current error measure and $e(k - 1)$ represents the delay of the error measure. The gains k_p, k_i and k_d for this work were $17000, 150$ and 0.001 respectively. The Fig. 5 shows the performance of the well-tuned PID controller, reaching the desired position in a soft way.

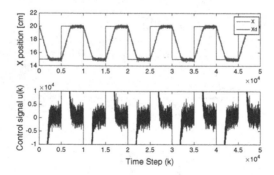

Fig. 5. PID control response.

6.2   FREN Controller

In this work, the gradient value y_p is set as 1 and the learning rate η_i is fixed as 50. The response of FREN controller in the selected task (see Fig. 6), shows faster convergence than PID's response, but a little overshoot when reaching the desired position. The saturation times of control signal $u(k)$ are shorter than PID.

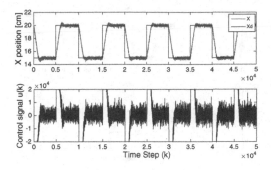

Fig. 6. FREN control response.

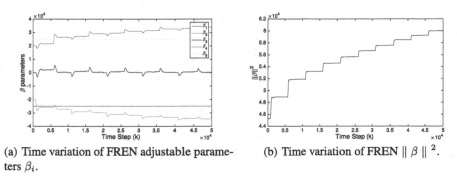

(a) Time variation of FREN adjustable parameters β_i.

(b) Time variation of FREN $\| \beta \|^2$.

Fig. 7. Adaptation results.

The FREN controller allows us to monitor the algorithm's learning process, analyzing the $\beta_i(k)$ performance (see Fig. 7(a)). For a faster evaluation, in Fig. 7(b) the normal value of the $\beta_i(k)$ vector, $\| \beta \|^2$ is presented. It is shown that the process until the last kth iteration, does not reach a stable value.

6.3 FREN Based on SPSA Tuning Algorithm

The FREN+SPSA algorithm, was implemented with the same initial conditions for $\beta_i(k)$ and the same five membership functions $\mu_i(k)$ than conventional FREN. Figure 8 depicts a faster convergence without overshoot. Showing better performance than common FREN and consequently than PID. The time duration of the saturation peaks are shorter in this case than classical FREN and PID.

By analyzing the normal value of the control parameters vector $\| \beta \|^2$ of FREN+SPSA controller (see Fig. 9(b)), it is shown that the learning process reaches a stable value very fast and stays in a quasi-stable state.

However, a deep analysis in real time shows that FREN + SPSA takes twice as much real time to execute the same task as FREN, since it requires a double estimation of the cost function to calculate the gradient within the same iteration (see Fig. 10)

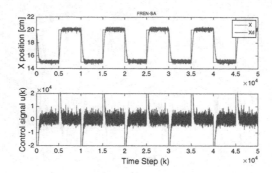

Fig. 8. FREN + SPSA control response.

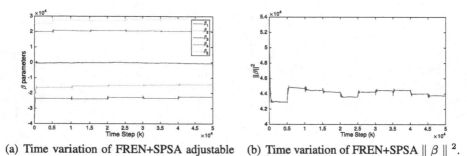

(a) Time variation of FREN+SPSA adjustable parameters β_i.

(b) Time variation of FREN+SPSA $\| \beta \|^2$.

Fig. 9. Adaptation results.

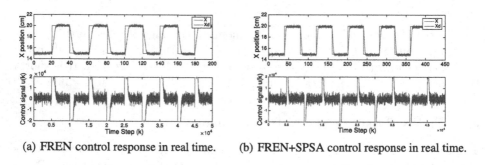

(a) FREN control response in real time.

(b) FREN+SPSA control response in real time.

Fig. 10. Real time comparison.

7   Conclusion

In this paper, an adaptive control methodology based on FREN as the direct controller and a modified version of SPSA as the tuning rule was proposed. The obtained gradient estimation by SPSA is employed in the tuning of the new control parameters value. In order to test the proposed controller, three different control methodologies were compared: the PID, the conventional FREN and the proposed version of FREN tuned by SPSA. The FREN controller based on SPSA technique for gradient estimation and tuning, showed better performance, increasing the convergence speed in time step (k) domain than conventional FREN controller and furthermore, without overshoot. However, in real time domain (s), it was shown that FREN+SPSA takes twice than FREN to complete the task.

Ideally, control methodologies send a control signal per iteration. The SPSA version employed in this work required two measures from the plant per iteration. The next stage of this study is the implementation of one measurement version of SPSA to improve comparison conditions.

Acknowledgments. This document is the result of the 257253 research project funded by CONACyT and the 28875 research project funded by SEP-PRODEP. The first author thanks CONACyT for her Ph.D. scholarship.

References

1. Armendariz, J., Treesatayapun, C., Baltazar, A.: Force feedback controller based on fuzzy-rules emulated networks and Hertzian contact with ultrasound. Mech. Syst. Sig. Process. **27**, 534–550 (2012)
2. Chen, M., Linkens, D.A.: A hybrid neuro-fuzzy PID controller. Fuzzy Sets Syst. **99**(1), 27–36 (1998)
3. Dong, N., Wu, C.H., Gao, Z.K., Chen, Z.Q., Ip, W.H.: Data-driven control based on simultaneous perturbation stochastic approximation with adaptive weighted gradient estimation. IET Control Theory Appl. **10**(2), 201–209 (2016)
4. Facundo, L., Gómez, J., Treesatayapun, C., Morales, A., Baltazar, A.: Adaptive control with sliding mode on a double fuzzy rule emulated network structure. IFAC-PapersOnLine **51**(13), 609–614 (2018)
5. Hahn, B., Oldham, K.R.: A model-free on-off iterative adaptive controller based on stochastic approximation. IEEE Trans. Control Syst. Technol. **20**(1), 196–204 (2011)
6. Hou, Z.S., Wang, Z.: From model-based control to data-driven control: survey, classification and perspective. Inf. Sci. **235**, 3–35 (2013)
7. Jang, J.S.R., Sun, C.T., Mizutani, E.: Neuro-fuzzy and soft computing-a computational approach to learning and machine intelligence [book review]. IEEE Trans. Autom. Control **42**(10), 1482–1484 (1997)
8. Kiefer, J., Wolfowitz, J., et al.: Stochastic estimation of the maximum of a regression function. Ann. Math. Stat. **23**(3), 462–466 (1952)
9. Lee, C.H., Teng, C.C.: Identification and control of dynamic systems using recurrent fuzzy neural networks. IEEE Trans. Fuzzy Syst. **8**(4), 349–366 (2000)
10. Lin, C.T., Lee, C.G., Lin, C.T., Lin, C.: Neural Fuzzy Systems: A Neuro-fuzzy Synergism to Intelligent Systems, vol. 205. Prentice hall PTR, Upper Saddle River (1996)
11. Maeda, Y.: Real-time control and learning using neuro-controller via simultaneous perturbation for flexible arm system. In: Proceedings of the 2002 American Control Conference (IEEE Cat. No. CH37301), vol. 4, pp. 2583–2588. IEEE (2002)
12. Meng, D., Jia, Y., Du, J., Yu, F.: Data-driven control for relative degree systems via iterative learning. IEEE Trans. Neural Netw. **22**(12), 2213–2225 (2011)

13. dos Santos Coelho, L., Pessôa, M.W., Sumar, R.R., Coelho, A.A.R.: Model-free adaptive control design using evolutionary-neural compensator. Expert Syst. Appl. **37**(1), 499–508 (2010)
14. Shi, Y., Mizumoto, M.: An improvement of neuro-fuzzy learning algorithm for tuning fuzzy rules. Fuzzy Sets Syst. **118**(2), 339–350 (2001)
15. Skogestad, S.: Probably the best simple PID tuning rules in the world. J. Process Control 1–28 (2001)
16. Spall, J.C.: Introduction to Stochastic Search and Optimization: Estimation, Simulation, and Control, vol. 65. Wiley, Hoboken (2005)
17. Spall, J.C., Chin, D.C.: Traffic-responsive signal timing for system-wide traffic control. Transp. Res. Part C: Emerg. Technol. **5**(3–4), 153–163 (1997)
18. Spall, J.C., Cristion, J.A.: A neural network controller for systems with unmodeled dynamics with applications to wastewater treatment. In: Proceedings of 1994 9th IEEE International Symposium on Intelligent Control, pp. 273–278. IEEE (1994)
19. Spall, J.C., et al.: Multivariate stochastic approximation using a simultaneous perturbation gradient approximation. IEEE Trans. Automatic Control **37**(3), 332–341 (1992)
20. Treesatayapun, C., Uatrongjit, S.: Adaptive controller with fuzzy rules emulated structure and its applications. Eng. Appl. Artif. Intell. **18**(5), 603–615 (2005)
21. Treesatayapun, C.: A discrete-time stable controller for an omni-directional mobile robot based on an approximated model. Control Eng. Practice **19**(2), 194–203 (2011)
22. Treesatayapun, C.: Discrete-time direct adaptive control for robotic systems based on model-free and if-then rules operation. Int. J. Adv. Manuf. Technol. **68**(1–4), 575–590 (2013)
23. Treesatayapun, C.: Adaptive control based on if-then rules for grasping force regulation with unknown contact mechanism. Robot. Comput.-Integr. Manuf. **30**(1), 11–18 (2014)
24. Treesatayapun, C.: Stabilized adaptive controller based on direct if-then knowledge of electronic systems for PWM drivers. Electr. Eng. **98**(1), 77–85 (2016)

Multi-objective GA for Collision Avoidance on Robot Manipulators Based on Artificial Potential Field

César E. Cea-Montufar[1]([✉]), Emmanuel A. Merchán-Cruz[2],
Javier Ramírez-Gordillo[2], Bárbara M. Gutiérrez-Mejía[1],
Erasto Vergara-Hernández[1], and Adriana Nava-Vega[1]

[1] Unidad Profesional Interdisciplinaria de Ingeniería Campus Hidalgo,
Instituto Politécnico Nacional, 42162 Mexico City, Hidalgo, Mexico
{ccea, bgutierrezm, evergarah, anavav}@ipn.mx
[2] Sección de Estudios de Posgrado e Investigación ESIME Azcapotzalco,
Instituto Politécnico Nacional, 02250 Azcapotzalco, Mexico
{eamerchan, jramirezg}@ipn.mx

Abstract. This paper presents a path planning strategy for robotic manipulators based on genetic algorithms, dual quaternions and artificial potential field, designing a multi-objective function that allow trajectories be planned avoiding collisions in the workspace and singularity-free kinematic restrictions for manipulators as an optimization problem, satisfying position and orientation conditions. Its analysis is based on the problem of generating a trajectory followed by a sequence of coordinated movements capable of moving the manipulator to perform tasks in the workspace, the problem is not only generated these movements, but also implement strategies that define the path with tools that are easy to implement and avoid obstacles autonomously. Robot kinematics solved by dual quaternion can be used to combine translation with orientation on robotic manipulators in a systematic way, simplifying calculation operations compatible with conventional methods. The artificial potential field approach has been extended to collision avoidance for all manipulator links. A genetic algorithm is used to solve the problem, which the fitness of the problem can be measured by a multi-objective function that involves the distance between the initial and desired position/orientation, minimum joint displacement, dual quaternion configuration, the use of attraction potential to the goal and a repulsion potential to the obstacles and its own links. This method has been implemented in MatLab© for an ABB© IRB1600 robot. Collision avoidance demonstrations have been performed by simulating equipment and static objects in the robot's workspace.

Keywords: Artificial potential field · Path planning · Dual quaternion · Multi-objective genetic algorithm · Robot manipulator

1 Introduction

In previous research, robot collision avoidance has been a component of higher levels of control in hierarchical robot control systems. Collision avoidance has been treated as a planning problem, and research in this area has focused on the development of

© Springer Nature Switzerland AG 2019
L. Martínez-Villaseñor et al. (Eds.): MICAI 2019, LNAI 11835, pp. 687–700, 2019.
https://doi.org/10.1007/978-3-030-33749-0_55

collision free path planning algorithms [1]. Path planning of robot manipulator can be classified as an optimization problem, where the route obtained is subject to different criteria such as the length of the route, collision avoidance, etc., at the same time as having to interact with the kinematics and/or dynamics. This makes the problem an ideal candidate for the application of strategies such as genetic algorithms and evolutionary algorithms [2].

The strategy used in multi-objective genetic algorithms can solve complex systems through the constant adjustment of coefficients or weights of each equation in order to obtain a multi-objective fitness function that works properly and in a self-adaptive way [3].

Therefore the manipulator robot can move from an initial configuration to a final point avoiding collisions with obstacles in its path, the problem contemplates the existence of local minimums between certain configurations of the obstacles and the goal, so the search for free collisions in the path involves reaching the global minimum by avoiding obstacles in a series of configurations coordinated by a path planning genetic algorithm capable of escaping from areas where local minimums or singular points are located and to achieve this an optimization approach facilitates the problem and the search for feasible solutions [4].

This strategy considers the goal as an attraction dipole and obstacles as surfaces with a repulsion charge respect to the tip of the manipulator that is attracted by the goal which is a global minimum of the potential function and close to the obstacles. The potential function grows indefinitely causing the manipulator to move away from them, so the idea is to find the shortest path between the manipulator and the goal between collision-free configurations through the descendant gradient as a potential function characterized in the obstacles by a repulsion field [5].

2 Multi-objective Function Design for Path Planning

A rigid body is completely described in space by its position and orientation (*pose*) [6] with respect to a reference frame, the problem statement consists of determining the intermediate *pose* configurations of a rigid body between the initial configuration and a final desired configuration that corresponds when the manipulator reaches a specific goal. For each intermediate position of the *pose* a route is specified and the appropriate values for each articulation will be determined in order to place the *pose* in each specific position of the space. However, this requires a solution to the inverse kinematics along the trajectory. Unfortunately, the analytical solution is a prolonged calculation process due to this requirement to do it at every point along the way.

Therefore, with a genetic algorithm each chromosome represents a set of displacements in angular terms, which can define the appropriate minimum displacements. A constraint-free coordinate system form by three bodies can be used to target rigid body desired position and orientation.

On the other hand, the use of quaternions is very simple and the first applications in robotics were made only for orientation [7]. However, applications with dual quaternions can be used to combined translation with orientation on robotic manipulators in a systematic way, simplifying calculation operations compatible with conventional methods [8]. The equation that governs the kinematics of the system is described by a dual quaternion is given by Eq. (1).

$$q_w = \cos\left(\frac{x}{2}\right)\cos\left(\frac{y}{2}\right)\cos\left(\frac{\theta}{2}\right) - \sin\left(\frac{x}{2}\right)\sin\left(\frac{y}{2}\right)\sin\left(\frac{\theta}{2}\right)$$
$$q_x = \cos\left(\frac{y}{2}\right)\cos\left(\frac{\theta}{2}\right)\sin\left(\frac{x}{2}\right) + \cos\left(\frac{x}{2}\right)\sin\left(\frac{y}{2}\right)\sin\left(\frac{\theta}{2}\right)$$
$$q_y = \cos\left(\frac{x}{2}\right)\cos\left(\frac{\theta}{2}\right)\sin\left(\frac{y}{2}\right) - \cos\left(\frac{y}{2}\right)\sin\left(\frac{x}{2}\right)\sin\left(\frac{\theta}{2}\right)$$
$$q_z = \cos\left(\frac{x}{2}\right)\cos\left(\frac{y}{2}\right)\sin\left(\frac{\theta}{2}\right) + \cos\left(\frac{\theta}{2}\right)\sin\left(\frac{x}{2}\right)\sin\left(\frac{y}{2}\right) \quad (1)$$
$$q_{w\varepsilon} = -\frac{x}{2}q_x - \frac{z}{2}q_z - \frac{y}{2}q_y$$
$$q_{x\varepsilon} = \frac{x}{2}q_z + \frac{x}{2}q_w - \frac{z}{2}q_y$$
$$q_{y\varepsilon} = \frac{z}{2}q_x - \frac{x}{2}q_z + \frac{y}{2}q_w$$
$$q_{z\varepsilon} = \frac{x}{2}q_y - \frac{y}{2}q_x + \frac{z}{2}q_w$$

The process of solution in the generation of paths in a systematic way, starts setting the initial robot configuration, desired position/orientation and minimum joint displacement, the GA parameters, decoding, fitness evaluation, error calculation to pass the next generation or finish the algorithm and the end where the results are given (Fig. 1 shows the flowchart), the design of the fitness function is very important for the complete exploration of the space of solutions and the adequate convergence of the GA.

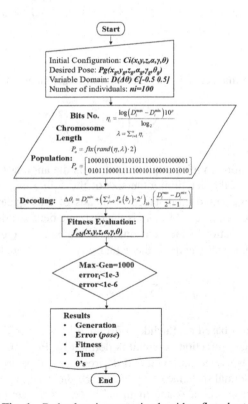

Fig. 1. Path planning genetic algorithm flowchart.

The design of the fitness function is derived from the maximization, however, the objective is to decrease the distance that exists between the initial point of the first configuration and the desired end point. Since the kinematic link equations are given in dual quaternions, two equations can be designed as fitness functions.

Positioning industrial robot's end effector in a specific point of the Cartesian space without resorting to the solution of its inverse kinematics requires the appropriate design of the multi-objective function of the genetic algorithm which depends on the kinematic link equations solved with dual quaternions, the attraction potential function, the repulsion potential and the function of minimum displacement of the links to generate trajectories with safe distances between and the robot and the obstacles present in its workspace.

The Euclidean distance is the objective function, where it is necessary to extract the position coordinates of the dual quaternions referring to it and the fitness function is composed of this minimization of the deviation in the position, combined with a function of minimum displacement, Eq. (2) converts a dual quaternion to a homogenous transformation matrix, where the coordinates of the position vector [x, y, z] T can be taken [9].

$$
T = \begin{bmatrix}
1 - 2\left(q_y^2 + q_z^2\right) & 2\left(q_x q_y - q_z q_w\right) & 2\left(q_x q_z + q_y q_w\right) & 2\left(-q_x q_{w\varepsilon} + q_w q_{x\varepsilon} - q_z q_{y\varepsilon} + q_y q_{z\varepsilon}\right) \\
2\left(q_x q_y + q_z q_w\right) & 1 - 2\left(q_x^2 + q_z^2\right) & 2\left(q_y q_z - q_x q_w\right) & 2\left(-q_y q_{w\varepsilon} + q_z q_{x\varepsilon} + q_w q_{y\varepsilon} - q_x q_{z\varepsilon}\right) \\
2\left(q_x q_z - q_y q_w\right) & 2\left(q_y q_z + q_x q_w\right) & 1 - 2\left(q_x^2 + q_y^2\right) & 2\left(-q_z q_{w\varepsilon} - q_y q_{x\varepsilon} - q_x q_{y\varepsilon} + q_w q_{z\varepsilon}\right) \\
0 & 0 & 0 & 1
\end{bmatrix}
$$

$$(2)$$

Thus, the function that accompanies the minimum displacement is given by Eq. (3).

$$
O_i = \sum_{j=1,k=1}^{j=m,k=n} \left(\theta_k^{j+1} - \theta_k^j\right)^2
$$

$$(3)$$

Where O_i is de minimum joint displacement, θ_k is the angular links solutions, k the number of solutions, i-j the iteration, n the size of the solutions and m the generation.

The fitness function based on distance by means of dual quaternions to represent robot kinematics is shown in Eq. (4), Dq_i is the distance between dual quaternions that tends to zero, i the iteration, j the dual quaternion elements, Qg Goal position and orientation in dual quaternion and Qa the actual *pose* in dual quaternion.

$$
Dq_i = \sqrt{\sum_{j=1}^{j=8} \left(e_i^{Qg} - e_i^{Qa}\right)^2}
$$

$$(4)$$

The fitness function based on Euclidean distance between initial point and desired point and related to the attraction potential is defined by Eq. (5). The problem has to reduces the distance between the initial and desired *pose*, represented by Pa, β is the positive attraction potential scale factor, xg, yg and zg the desired point coordinates, x, y and z the end effector coordinates and finally Δx, Δy, Δz the set of solutions.

$$Pa_i = \beta \sqrt{\left(x_g - (\Delta x + x)_i\right)^2 + \left(y_g - (\Delta y + y)_i\right)^2 + \left(z_g - (\Delta z + z)_i\right)^2} \qquad (5)$$

The fitness function based on Euclidean distance between desired point and obstacles presented in the workspace related to the repulsion potential is defined by Eq. (6). Where Pr is the distance between the desired point and the obstacles in the workspace, ρ is the positive repulsion potential scale factor, $xobs$, $yobs$ and $zobs$ the obstacle point coordinates, x, y and z the desired point coordinates and Δx, Δy, Δz the set of solutions.

$$Pr_i = \rho \sum\nolimits_{k=1}^{l} \sqrt{\left(x_{obs} - (\Delta x + x)_i\right)^2 + \left(y_{obs} - (\Delta y + y)_i\right)^2 + \left(z_{obs} - (\Delta z + z)_i\right)^2} \quad (6)$$

The representative function of the potential generates the difference of forces of attraction and repulsion shown in Eqs. (7) and (8). Pr represents the distance between desired point and obstacles in the workspace, r the imminent contact distance, s the influence zone of the obstacle.

$$Pr < (s + r)\{Pr \qquad (7)$$

$$r \leq Pr \leq (s + r)\{s + r - Pr \qquad (8)$$

Therefore Eq. (9) is the fitness function of the problem, a multi-objective function in order to solve path planning based on genetic algorithms considering to satisfy position/orientation, minimum link movement, kinematics based on dual quaternion and artificial potential field. Where f_i is the multi-objective function, Dqi the distance between two dual quaternions, Pa is the distance between desired and initial configuration, Pr the distance between desired point and obstacles in the workspace, Oi is the minimum joint displacement, i the iteration and C_1 is penalty constant [0, 1].

$$f_i = C_1 e^{-(w1Dqi + w2Pai + w3Pri + w4Oi)} \qquad (9)$$

System penalty changes when restrictions are violated which are presented in Eq. (10), where l_i is the angular movement lower limit and l_s the angular movement upper limit, Eqs. (11) and (12) determine the lower and upper limits by angular changes.

$$C_1 = l_s * l_i \qquad (10)$$

$$l_s = [(\theta_i + \Delta\theta_i) > +\theta] == 0 \qquad (11)$$

$$l_i = [(\theta_i + \Delta\theta_i) < -\theta] == 0 \qquad (12)$$

Since the solution to the problem is to reduce the position and orientation error, it is feasible to have the expression in terms of dual quaternion, because it can do interpolation between displacement and rotation, projecting smooth trajectories satisfying initial conditions, where the translation and rotation of the bodies is seen as a point in common towards the final objective.

The real part of the dual quaternion (DQ) is a quaternion and the dual part is proportional to displacement so when is combined with the exponential function, dual part tends to normalize and remain in the operations range.

3   GA Implementation for a 6DOF Space Manipulator

The problem statement consists of determining intermediate configurations of the links of a space manipulator with six degrees of freedom type ABB © IRB1600, (see Fig. 2) between the initial and ending *pose* configuration, with obstacles in its workspace, generating a free collision path which is planned employing kinematic equations through dual quaternions and is solved by a genetic algorithm.

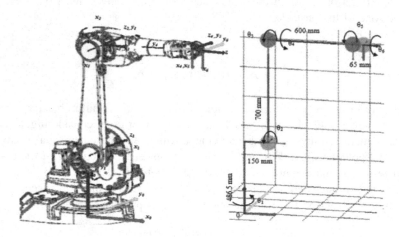

Fig. 2. 6 degrees of freedom robot manipulator ABB © IRB 1600

Table 1 shows arm's D-H parameters that allows the kinematics construction.

Table 1. 6DOF Space manipulator D-H parameters.

i	θ	α	a	d
1	$\theta_1 = 0$	$-\pi/2$	0.15	0.4865
2	$\theta_2 = \pi/2$	0	0.70	0
3	$\theta_3 = \pi$	$\pi/2$	0	0
4	$\theta_4 = 0$	$-\pi/2$	0	0.60
5	$\theta_5 = 0$	$\pi/2$	0	0
6	$\theta_6 = 0$	0	0	0.065

The kinematic link equations are obtained through dual quaternion convention, each joint are shown in Eqs. (13 to 18) respectively, they can be evaluated according to the parameters of Table 1 and by Eq. (19) *pose* can be known from the base to the end effector coordinate frame, Table 2 shows initial position/orientation for each joint.

$$
{}^{0}DQ_1^{DH} = \begin{bmatrix} \frac{\sqrt{2}}{2}\cos\left(\frac{\theta_1}{2}\right), \frac{-\sqrt{2}}{2}\cos\left(\frac{\theta_1}{2}\right)i, \frac{-\sqrt{2}}{2}\sin\left(\frac{\theta_1}{2}\right)j, \frac{\sqrt{2}}{2}\sin\left(\frac{\theta_1}{2}\right)k \\ \left(0.0375\frac{\sqrt{2}}{2}\cos\left(\frac{\theta_1}{2}\right) - 0.1216\frac{\sqrt{2}}{2}\sin\left(\frac{\theta_1}{2}\right)\right)\varepsilon, \left(0.0375\frac{\sqrt{2}}{2}\cos\left(\frac{\theta_1}{2}\right) + 0.1216\frac{\sqrt{2}}{2}\sin\left(\frac{\theta_1}{2}\right)\right)i\varepsilon \\ \left(0.0375\frac{\sqrt{2}}{2}\sin\left(\frac{\theta_1}{2}\right) - 0.1216\frac{\sqrt{2}}{2}\cos\left(\frac{\theta_1}{2}\right)\right)j\varepsilon, \left(0.0375\frac{\sqrt{2}}{2}\sin\left(\frac{\theta_1}{2}\right) + 0.1216\frac{\sqrt{2}}{2}\cos\left(\frac{\theta_1}{2}\right)\right)k\varepsilon \end{bmatrix}
$$
(13)

$$
{}^{1}DQ_2^{DH} = \begin{bmatrix} \cos\left(\frac{\theta_2}{2} - \frac{\pi}{4}\right), \sin\left(\frac{\theta_2}{2} - \frac{\pi}{4}\right)k, 0.350\sin\left(\frac{\theta_2}{2} - \frac{\pi}{4}\right)i\varepsilon, 0.350\cos\left(\frac{\theta_2}{2} - \frac{\pi}{4}\right)j\varepsilon \end{bmatrix}
$$
(14)

$$
{}^{2}DQ_3^{DH} = \begin{bmatrix} \frac{\sqrt{2}}{2}\cos\left(\frac{\theta_3}{2} + \frac{\pi}{2}\right), \frac{\sqrt{2}}{2}\cos\left(\frac{\theta_3}{2} + \frac{\pi}{2}\right)i, \frac{\sqrt{2}}{2}\sin\left(\frac{\theta_3}{2} + \frac{\pi}{2}\right)j, \frac{\sqrt{2}}{2}\sin\left(\frac{\theta_3}{2} + \frac{\pi}{2}\right)k, 0\varepsilon, 0i\varepsilon, 0j\varepsilon, 0k\varepsilon \end{bmatrix}
$$
(15)

$$
{}^{3}DQ_4^{DH} = \begin{bmatrix} \frac{\sqrt{2}}{2}\cos\left(\frac{\theta_4}{2}\right), \frac{-\sqrt{2}}{2}\cos\left(\frac{\theta_4}{2}\right)i, \frac{-\sqrt{2}}{2}\sin\left(\frac{\theta_4}{2}\right)j, \frac{\sqrt{2}}{2}\sin\left(\frac{\theta_4}{2}\right)k\left(0.150\frac{\sqrt{2}}{2}\sin\left(\frac{\theta_4}{2}\right)\right)\varepsilon \\ \left(0.150\frac{\sqrt{2}}{2}\sin\left(\frac{\theta_4}{2}\right)\right)i\varepsilon, \left(0.150\frac{\sqrt{2}}{2}\cos\left(\frac{\theta_4}{2}\right)\right)j\varepsilon, \left(0.150\frac{\sqrt{2}}{2}\cos\left(\frac{\theta_4}{2}\right)\right)k\varepsilon \end{bmatrix}
$$
(16)

$$
{}^{4}DQ_5^{DH} = \begin{bmatrix} \frac{\sqrt{2}}{2}\cos\left(\frac{\theta_5}{2}\right), \frac{\sqrt{2}}{2}\cos\left(\frac{\theta_5}{2}\right)i, \frac{\sqrt{2}}{2}\sin\left(\frac{\theta_5}{2}\right)j, \frac{\sqrt{2}}{2}\sin\left(\frac{\theta_5}{2}\right)k, 0\varepsilon, 0i\varepsilon, 0j\varepsilon, 0k\varepsilon \end{bmatrix}
$$
(17)

$$
{}^{5}DQ_6^{DH} = \begin{bmatrix} \cos\left(\frac{\theta_6}{2}\right), 0i, 0j, \sin\left(\frac{\theta_6}{2}\right)k, 0.0325\sin\left(\frac{\theta_6}{2}\right)\varepsilon, 0i\varepsilon, 0j\varepsilon, 0.0325\cos\left(\frac{\theta_6}{2}\right)k\varepsilon \end{bmatrix}
$$
(18)

Table 2. Initial position and orientation for each joint.

$^{i-1}DQ_i$	w	i	j	k	ε	$i\varepsilon$	$j\varepsilon$	$k\varepsilon$
$^{0}DQ_1$	0.707	-0.707	0	0	0.053	0.053	-0.172	0.172
$^{1}DQ_2$	0.707	0	0	-0.707	0	0.247	-0.247	0
$^{2}DQ_3$	0	0	0.707	-0.707	0	0	0	0
$^{3}DQ_4$	0.707	-0.707	0	0	0	0	0	0.212
$^{4}DQ_5$	0.707	0.707	0	0	0	0	0	0
$^{5}DQ_6$	1	0	0	0	0	0	0	0.032

By Eq. (19) it is possible to know the position and orientation of the end effector from the initial coordinate system of the robot considering the angular configurations of all its joints, Eq. (20) shows end effector's pose.

$$^0DQ_6^{DH} = \Pi_{i=1}^{n}{}^{i-1}DQ_i^{DH} = {}^0DQ_1^{DH1}DQ_2^{DH2}DQ_3^{DH3}DQ_4^{DH4}DQ_5^{DH5}DQ_6^{DH} \tag{19}$$

$$T_f = \begin{bmatrix} 0 & 0 & 1 & 0.815 \\ 0 & 1 & 0 & 0 \\ -1 & 0 & 0 & 1.186 \\ 0 & 0 & 0 & 1 \end{bmatrix} \tag{20}$$

3.1   Study Case 1

The robot manipulator has an initial configuration of (0°, 0°, 0°, 0°, 0°, 180°) and its displaced in (0.2 m, 0.2 m, −0.2 m) of the world coordinate system; on the other hand, the desired *pose* is (0°, 90°, 0°, 1.1 m, 0 m, −0.4 m). Also, the workspace of the robot add a set of obstacles and whose configuration form a body which has to avoid the robot to find the path and plan the movement settings to reach the goal. Therefore, the orientation and position of the end effector of the manipulator is represented by Eq. (21) with respect to the global coordinate system $^wD_6$ and Eq. (22) the desired *pose*.

$$^wDQ_6 = 0.5 + 0.5i + 0.5j + 0.5k - 0.55\varepsilon + 0.057i\varepsilon + 0.042j\varepsilon + 0.45k\varepsilon \tag{21}$$

$$DQ = 0.707 + 0.707j - 0.0707\varepsilon + 0.6717i\varepsilon + 0.0707j\varepsilon + 0.2474k\varepsilon \tag{22}$$

There are constraints on the movement of the links, they have a limit of movement due to the physical configuration of the robotic manipulator, where the links can collide with themselves, so the limits of each joint are described in Table 3.

Table 3. Movement constraints for each joint.

θ's	$+\theta$'s	$-\theta$'s
θ_1	180°	−180°
θ_2	150°	−90°
θ_3	65°	−245°
θ_4	200°	−200°
θ_5	115°	−115°
θ_6	400°	−400°

Movement's solution and the trajectory generation are obtained by the parameters of Table 4, the fitness function for this particular case is based on the multi-objective function Eq. (9), and it has a good performance within the algorithm considering position/orientation and minimum movement of the links. Where θ is the minimum links displacement, ni the number of individuals in the population, p the decimal precision, $Prbcr$ the cross probability, $Prbm$ the mutation probability, Reg the regeneration percentage, fp the disturbance factor and Max-gen the maximum generations allowed.

Table 4. Genetic algorithm parameters.

$f(\Delta\theta's)$	ni	p	P_{rbcr}	P_{rbm}	Reg	fp	$Max\text{-}gen$
$\in[-0.5°,0.5°]$	110	5	0.85	0.11	0.13	0.02	10000

Obstacles represent two surfaces with the vertices in the initial coordinates for O_{b1} (0.75, −0.2, 0.55) and O_{b2} (1.3, −0.2, 0.55), which end in the coordinates O_{b1} (1.3, 0.2, 0.55) and O_{b2} (1.3, 0.2, 0.95) respectively. The trajectory generated by the genetic algorithm (shown in Fig. 3), where each point forming the surface has a radius r = 0.1 and a zone of influence around the obstacle of $rs = 0.05$ without colliding with the obstacles that form the surface and although passes close to the area of influence, depends on the positive scale factor of the repulsion field to approximate or move away the links of the manipulator from obstacles as much as the problem requires.

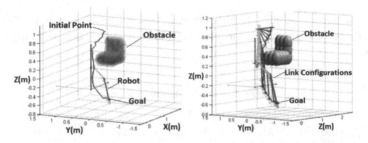

Fig. 3. First image shows the generated trajectory without colliding with the obstacles passing close to the zone of influence, satisfying the *pose* conditions, while the second image shows the link's configurations on some points of the path.

The angular variation for each joint of the robot (see Fig. 4) has a change in the angular position and the time, this positions can determine the variations of speeds, accelerations and torque for each articulation, the movements of the trajectory planned by the algorithm and demonstrates the collision avoidance.

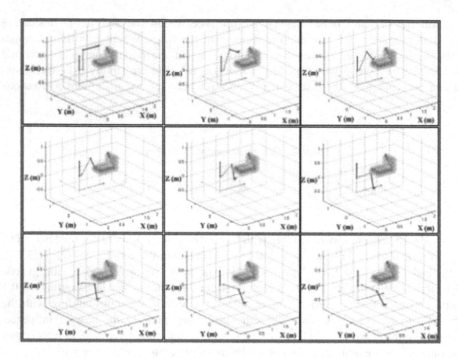

Fig. 4. Robot's configuration profile.

The performance of the algorithm and its results can be seen in Table 5, the decrease of the deviation over the *pose* (see Fig. 5) shows the performance of the algorithm.

Table 5. Genetic algorithm results.

Generations	Segments	Error	Fitness	Average fitness	Time
1000	385	0.103	0.01618	0.02443	5.338

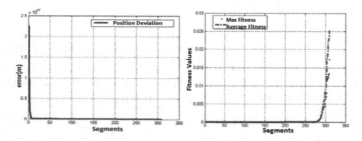

Fig. 5. First image shows the error evolution against the segments through the generations, while the second image shows the fitness vs the segments in the genetic algorithm.

3.2   Study Case 2

The proposed case consist in an industrial robot ABB® IRB1600 has to satisfy conditions of position and orientation without colliding with the obstacles that form two work stations, where the robot has to perform the task without colliding with the first station, plan through of the genetic algorithm and artificial potential field to avoid the second work station in which it has to move from its initial position, besides the robot is in a position known as Gantry, this position is very useful at industrial level since the robot has more free volume workspace since its links and embedment do not interfere in its work. Table 6 indicates the parameters of the genetic algorithm.

Table 6. Genetic algorithm parameters.

$f(\Delta\theta's)$	ni	p	P_{rbcr}	P_{rbm}	Reg	fp	$Max\text{-}gen$
$\in[-0.5°,0.5°]$	50	4	1	0.37	0.2	0.02	10000

The manipulator robot has an initial configuration in $(0°, 0°, 0°, 0°, 0°, 0°)$ and is oriented and displaced in $(180°, 0°, 0°, 0.2\ m, 0.2\ m, 2.2\ m)$ with respect to the world coordinate system; while the desired orientation and position is $(-90°, 0°, 90°, 0.2\ m, 1\ m, 1\ m)$ in addition to adding a set of obstacles whose configuration forms 2 bodies and goal is within one of the objects. Therefore, the orientation and position of the tip of the manipulator is represented by Eq. (23) with respect to the global coordinate system wD6, the desired orientation and position shown in Eq. (24).

$$^wDQ_6 = -0.707i - 0.707k + 0.707\varepsilon - 0.707i\varepsilon + 0.0005j\varepsilon + 0.0707k\varepsilon \qquad (23)$$

$$DQ = 0.5 - 0.5i + 0.5j + 0.5k - 0.45\varepsilon + 0.05i\varepsilon - 0.05j\varepsilon + 0.55k\varepsilon \qquad (24)$$

The obstacles are located in such a way that they represent 2 stations in cubic form, where each point forming the cubes have a radius r = 0.15 and a zone of influence around the obstacle of $rs = 1$, as in study case 1, the limits of movement in each articulation are found in Table 3 are considered to determine the penalty constant in the fitness function by Eq. (10). The resulting path from the algorithm (see Fig. 6) where the goal is reached without colliding with the surfaces present in the path by performing both tasks.

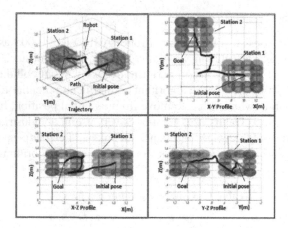

Fig. 6. Path generated by the genetic algorithm.

The angular variation for each joint of the robot (see Fig. 7) has a change in the angular position and the time, this positions can determine the variations of speeds, accelerations and torque for each articulation, the movements of the trajectory planned by the algorithm and demonstrates the collision avoidance.

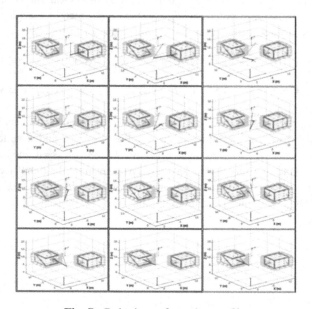

Fig. 7. Robot's configuration profile.

The performance of the algorithm and its results are shown in Table 7, the evolution in the decrease of the error by segments evaluated (see Fig. 8) shows as well as the fitness reached by each segment.

Table 7. Genetic algorithm results.

Generations	Segments	Error	Fitness	Average fitness	Time
761	506	1.0623	0.9119	0.9413	9.4593

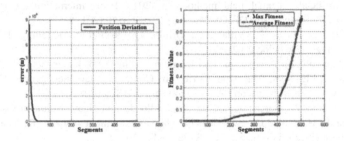

Fig. 8. First image shows the error evolution against the segments through the time, while the second image shows the fitness against the segments in the genetic algorithm.

4 Conclusion

The strategy presented in this work used to generate kinematic link equations using dual quaternions has an advantage compared to homogenous transformation matrices and it is this intuitive relationship between rotation and translation that allows to unify a solution for position/orientation as a function to be solved, the configuration of the dual quaternion is so simple that it allows to have operations in a systematic way even though the product to represent rotations and translations is not commutative, also describes the formulation and implementation of an obstacle avoidance approach based on the artificial potential field. Collision avoidance, generally treated as high level planning, has been demonstrated to be an effective component of low level control.

The Multi-Objective path planning algorithm evolves from a purely genetic approach and the trajectories were obtained based on the performance of the algorithm given by the fitness function, the process of trajectory planning exploits the fact that the manipulators tend to move uniformly in some stages of his career.

Aknowledgements. The authors would like to thank the Instituto Politécnico Nacional (IPN) through the project "Visual servoing on industrial robots for high precision positioning task" *SIP 20196126* for the means and support in the accomplishment of this work.

References

1. Khatib, O.: Real-time obstacle avoidance for manipulators and mobile robots. Int. J. Robot. Res. **5**(1), 90–98 (1986)
2. Merchán-Cruz, E.A., Morris, A.S.: Fuzzy-GA-based trajectory planner for robot manipulators sharing a common workspace. IEEE Trans. Robot. **22**(4), 613–624 (2006). ISSN 1552-3098

3. Fernandez-Figueroa, N.B., et al.: Multi-arm self-collision avoidance: a sparse solution for a big data problem. In: ICRA 2018 (2018)
4. Yuan, Y., Zhang, Y., Cao, H., Yao, R.: New local density definition based on minimum hyper sphere for outlier mining algorithm using in industrial databases. In: The 26th Chinese Control and Decision Conference (2014 CCDC), Changsha, pp. 5182–5186 (2014)
5. Zhang, N., Zhang, Y., Ma, C., Wang, B.: Path planning of six-DOF serial robots based on improved artificial potential field method. In: 2017 IEEE International Conference on Robotics and Biomimetics (ROBIO), Macau, pp. 617–621 (2017)
6. Siciliano, B., Sciavicco, L., Villani, L., Oriolo, G.: Robotics: Modelling, Planning and Control. Springer, Heidelberg (2011)
7. Sahul, S., Biswall, B.: A novel method for representing robot kinematics using quaternion theory. In: IEEE Sponsored Conference on Computational Intelligence, Control and Computer Vision in Robotics and Automation, pp. 75–82 (2008)
8. Ramírez-Gordillo, J., Merchán-Cruz, E.: Desarrollo de una Nueva Solución Compacta a la Cinemática de Manipuladores Robóticos basada en Cuaterniones Duales. Revista iberoamericana de automática e informática Ind. **8**, 334–344 (2011)
9. Dapeng, H., Qing, W., Zexiang, L., Weimeng, S.: Control of oriented mechanical systems: a method based on dual quaternion. In: 17th IFAC

Vertex Codification Applied to 3-D Binary Image Euler Number Computation

Humberto Sossa[1,2(✉)], Elsa Rubío[1], Víctor Ponce[1],
and Hermilo Sánchez[3]

[1] Instituto Politécnico Nacional, CIC, CDMX, Mexico
humbertosossa@gmail.com, {erubio,vponce}@cic.ipn.mx
[2] Tecnológico de Monterrey, Unidad Guadalajara, Zapopan, Jalisco, Mexico
[3] Universidad Autónoma de Aguascalientes, CCB, Aguascalientes, Mexico
hsanchez@correo.uaa.mx

Abstract. A three dimensional (3-D) digital image emerges as a straightforward extension of a two dimensional (2-D) digital image. A 3-D digital image can be obtained by digitizing the 3-D space in which one or more objects of interest can be contained. From each object in the digital image, several features describing their geometry and topology can be computed. One of these features is the Euler number. An alternative method to compute the Euler number of a 3-D digital object (image) in terms of a codification of the vertices of the object voxels is described. The set of formal propositions baseline of the proposal operation are provided, demonstrated and numerically validated with simple objects. Examples with images of different complexity show the applicability of the proposal. The proposed method emerges as an extension of the proposal introduced for the 2-D case in [21] and as alternative of the formulation well described in [22].

Keywords: Three-dimensional image · Three-dimensional object · Object description · Topological descriptor · Topological invariant · Euler number

1 Introduction

A three dimensional (3-D) digital image emerges as a straightforward extension of a two dimensional (2-D) digital image. A 3-D digital image can be obtained by digitizing the 3-D space in which one or more objects of interest can be contained. From each object in the digital image, several features describing their geometry and topology can be computed. The Euler number, or Euler-Poincare characteristic, e is one of these features. Mathematically speaking, the Euler number of a 3-D object or a set of 3-D objects can be expressed in terms of three Betti numbers [1] as follows:

$$e = b_0 - b_1 + b_2. \tag{1}$$

where, b_0 is the number of objects, b_1 is the number of holes or tunnels, and b_2 is the number of bubbles, cavities, voids ([2] and [3]).

© Springer Nature Switzerland AG 2019
L. Martínez-Villaseñor et al. (Eds.): MICAI 2019, LNAI 11835, pp. 701–713, 2019.
https://doi.org/10.1007/978-3-030-33749-0_56

One problem with Eq. (1) is that Betti numbers cannot be obtained by computing local features of the 3-D object such as the number of vertices and edges. In other words, its computation cannot be broken into subtasks. This means that Eq. (1) cannot be used to compute local measures.

An equivalent formula that allows computing the Euler number of a 3-D object follows [4]:

$$e = n_0 - n_1 + n_2 - n_3. \tag{2}$$

where variables n_0, n_1, n_2, n_3 correspond to the number of vertices of 1-voxels[1], edges, faces, and 1-voxels contained in a 3-D object, respectively.

As can be observed, the computation of the Euler number of a 3-D object composed of 1-voxels, requires counting the total number of vertices, edges, faces and its voxels.

Different methods have been reported in literature to compute the Euler feature of a 3-D digital image. The first method to accomplish this was reported in [5] and [6], but it was only applicable for 6-connectivity. Another important and influential work reported can be found in [7]. In this paper, authors report several methods to compute the Euler number of a discrete digital image in both 2-D and 3-D.

Other interesting works in this direction can be found in [8–13]. Five interesting applications of the Euler feature are fully described in [14–20].

With the aim of offering a better method to compute the Euler number of a 3-D digital object (image), our method is designed in terms of a codification of the object vertices that are directly in touch with the background voxel vertexes. Corresponding formal propositions that are basic to the proposal operation are then given and demonstrated. Examples with simple and complex objects are also provided to show the method operation.

It is worth mentioning that the introduced method in this paper to compute the Euler number of a 3-D digital object (image) is an extension of the method well described in [21]. Another similar approach can be found in [22].

The rest of the paper is organized as follows. In Sect. 2, definitions and preliminary results are stated to support the paper reading and to demonstrate the formal propositions that base the functioning of the proposal are given. In Sect. 3, the new proposal to compute the Euler feature of a 3-D digital object or 3-D digital image is explained in detail. The formal propositions and their demonstration, which are basic to the proposal, are also outlined in this section. To test the proposal operation, Sects. 4 and 5 present results with simple and complex objects, respectively. Finally, Sect. 6 points out the conclusions.

---

[1] (a voxel with the value 1).

2 Underlying Definitions

In order for the reader to understand the idea behind the proposal, several concepts are defined and others taken from literature [4, 10]. Such concepts are helpful to derive and prove the formal propositions that govern the operation of our proposed method to compute the Euler number of ,3-D objects.

A 3-D digitized picture is defined as a 3-D array $F = \{f_{xyz}\}$, where x, y and z are integers such that $1 \geq x \geq M$, $1 \geq y \geq N$, and $1 \geq z \geq L$, and f_{xyz} represents a density value at a sample point (or a cube) located at coordinates x, y and z. Each cube is called a *voxel*. A picture is called a *binary picture* if each voxel has a value of either 1 or 0. Voxels of a picture with values 0 and 1 are called 0-voxels and 1-voxels, respectively. The set of all 1-voxels and its complement (0-voxels) are called object and background, respectively. Figure 1 shows an image of dimensions $M \times N \times L$, with three objects composed of six, three and one voxel, respectively.

Definition 1 (neighbourhood). For each voxel $p = (x, y, z)$, three kinds of neighbourhood (Fig. 1(b)), the 6-neighbourhood (6-n) $N_6(p)$, the 18-neighbourhood (18-n) $N_{18}(p)$, and the 26-neighbourhood (26-n) $N_{26}(p)$ are defined as follows:

$$N_6(p) = \{(i, j, k) \,||\, i - x| + |j - y| + |k - z| = 1\} \tag{3}$$

$$N_{18}(p) = \left\{(i, j, k) \,|\, 0 < |i - x|^2 + |j - y|^2 + |k - z|^2 \leq 2\right\} \tag{4}$$

$$N_{26}(p) = \left\{(i, j, k) \,|\, \max(|i - x|, |j - y|, |k - z|) = 1\right\}. \tag{5}$$

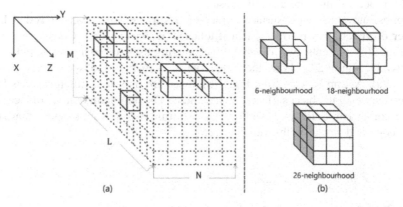

(a)   (b)

Fig. 1. (a) A digitized 3-D binary image of dimensions $M \times N \times L$ voxels with three objects composed of three, six and one voxels, respectively. (b) Three kinds of neighbourhoods in 3-D.

Note, under these kinds of neighbourhood, a voxel p shares at least one face (edge, vertex) with another voxel q. In this way, if a voxel p is in the m-neighbourhood of voxel p, then voxel p is said to be adjacent to voxel q, and vice versa ($m = 6, 18, 26$).

Definition 2 (Connectivity). Two voxels p and q with the same value (1 or 0) are said to be (6-c), (18-c), (26-c) connected, if a sequence of voxels $p_0(=p), p_1, p_2 \ldots, p_n(=q)$ exists, such that each p_l is in the 6-n (18-n, 26-n) neighbourhood of $p_{l-1}(1 \leq l \leq n)$, and all the p_l have the same value (1 or 0) as p and q.

These definitions show that if a set of voxels with the same value (0 or 1) is 6-c, 18-c, 26-c connected then this set defines an *equivalence class*.

Definition 3 (Connected component or 3-D binary object). A binary 3-D object O_n composed of (6-c, 18-c and 26c) n connected voxels (with the same value 0 or 1) is a m-connected component if its n voxels define an equivalence class.

According to this definition, we could have (6-c) connected objects, (18-c) connected objects and (26-c) connected objects. From now on, objects are considered to be composed of 1-voxels, whereas the background is composed of 0-voxels.

Definition 4 (Surface voxel). Let an object O_n with p being one of its 1-voxels, p is a surface voxel if at least one of its faces touches the background.

Example 1. Under 26-connectivity, with the exception of the central voxel of the object Fig. 1(b), all the remaining 26 voxels are surface voxels.

Definition 5 (Surface corner). Let p being a surface voxel, the surface corners of p, are the corners directly touching background voxels.

Example 2. Under 26-connectivity, the upper central voxel possesses 4 exterior corners, while any of the 8 voxels at the corners of the $3 \times 3 \times 3$ cube (Fig. 1(b)) possesses 7 exterior corners.

In this paper, different object classes will be considered including bubbles (voids) and tunnels (holes), and those with no bubbles and tunnels at all. Furthermore, the object surface is built by the bounding surface plus the bounding bubble surfaces and tunnel surfaces, if they are actually present.

Suppose now that each surface corner of a surface voxel can be coded by the number of voxel sides (surfaces) that it touches at that position. Considering such a fact, Fig. 2(a) presents two discrete objects composed of four and seven voxels, respectively. Figure 2(b) shows the coded visible corners of the two objects presented in Fig. 2(a). As can be seen from Fig. 2(b), there are only four different cases for the corners belonging to object surfaces: 3, 4, 5 and 6. The minimum number of faces that a surface corner can touch is 3, while the maximum is 6. Let us suppose that such a corner code is denoted by the variable: vc.

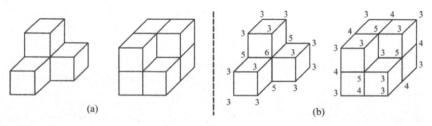

(a)   (b)

Fig. 2. (a) Two objects, one composed of four voxels and the other composed of seven voxels. (b) The objects and the corner codes of their visible surface voxels.

Definition 6. Let O_n^c represent the set of surface voxels of an object O_n. Let $n3$ be the number of vertices of O_n^c for which $vc = 3$, $n5$ be the number of vertices of O_n^c for which $vc = 5$, and $n6$ be the number of vertices of O_n^c for which $vc = 6$.

Thus, for the first object in Fig. 2(b), $n3 = 13$, $n5 = 3$, and $n6 = 1$. Similarly, for the second object in Fig. 2(b), $n3 = 11$, and $n5 = 3$.

3   The Novel Proposal for Computing the Euler Number of a 3-D Binary Object

The Euler number is an intrinsic property of objects, which is used to describe their topology. As mentioned in Sect. 1, the Euler number e as specified by Eq. (2), is defined as: the number of vertexes n_0, less the number of edges n_1, plus the number of faces n_2, less the number of voxels n_3. In the presence of a topological transformation, e is an invariant. As such, it can be used in many applications, such as object detection and object classification.

This section shows how the numbers: $n3$, $n5$, and $n6$ (Sect. 2) can be used to derive two topological features of a binary 3-D object: its number of bubbles and tunnels (combined) and its Euler number.

Proposition 1(a). The number of bubbles and tunnels (taken together) bt of a binary 3-D object O_n is always given as follows:

$$bt = \frac{n3 - n5 - 2n6}{8} - 1. \tag{6}$$

Proof. The proof proceeds by mathematical induction on the number of voxels of O_n. For the base case, O_1 consists of a single voxel. Therefore, we have $bt = 0$, $n3 = 8$, and $n5 = n6 = 0$, values which satisfy Eq. (6).

For the induction step, let us assume that Eq. (6) holds for O_n. Let bt' and $n3', n5'$, and $n6'$ be the number of bubbles-tunnels and the numbers of vertices of O_{n+1}^c (Definition 6) for which $vc' = 3, 5$, and 6, respectively, of object O_{n+1} that is obtained by adding one voxel to O_n.

Let $N3$, $N5$ and $N6$ be the corresponding numbers of this new voxel. We have that:

$$n3' = n3 + N3. \tag{7}$$

$$n5' = n5 + N5. \tag{8}$$

$$n6' = n6 + N6. \tag{9}$$

It must be shown that Eq. (6) holds for O_{n+1}, i.e.

$$bt' = \frac{n3' - n5' - 2n6'}{8} - 1 \tag{10}$$

By substituting Eqs. (7) to (9) into (10) and by regrouping terms, Eq. (19) can be rewritten as follows:

$$bt' = \frac{n3 + N3 - n5 + N5 - 2(n6 + N6)}{8} - 1 = \frac{n3 - n5 - 2n6}{8} - 1 \atop + \frac{N3 - N5 - 2N6}{8}.$$

(11)

By taking into account Eq. (6), Eq. (11) simplifies to:

$$bt' = bt + \frac{N3 - N5 - 2N6}{8}.$$

(12)

Which we know is true.   ∎

It is worth mentioning to talk about the following three cases that can occur at the moment of applying Eq. (11) to an object:

(1) If the object presents no tunnels and no voids, $bt' = 0$.
(2) Each tunnel added to the object **subtracts** one to Eq. (11).
(3) Each void added to the object **adds** one to Eq. (11).

To numerically validate Eq. (11), let us use the two object shown in Figs. 3(a) and (b). For the first object, that does not have holes, neither bubbles, we should obtain $bt = 0$, for the second object with one tunnel, in the other hand, we should obtain $bt = -1$. Let us verify this. For object depicted in Fig. 3(a), $n3 = 10, n5 = 2, n6 = 0$, then $bt = \frac{10 - 2 - 2 \times 0}{8} - 1 = 0$. In the same way, for the object shown in Fig. 3(b), $n3 = 8, n5 = 8, n6 = 0$, and $bt = \frac{8 - 8 - 2 \times 0}{8} - 1 = -1$. In both cases the correct results were obtained.

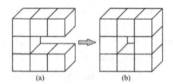

Fig. 3. (a) and (b), objects used to numerically validate Eq. (11).

Proposition 1(b). The number of bubbles and tunnels (taken together) bt of b_0 binary 3-D object O_n is always given as follows:

$$bt = \frac{n3 - n5 - 2n6}{8} - b_0.$$

(13)

Proof. As for Proposition 1(a), we will proceed by mathematical induction on the number of voxels of the b_0 objects. For easy of explanation, let us suppose that each of the b_0 objects has just one voxel. Therefore, we have $bt = 0$, $n3 = 8 \times b_0$, and $n5 = n6 = 0$, values which satisfy Eq. (13).

For the induction step, let us assume that Eq. (13) holds for O_n, where O_n is any of the b_0 objects of the whole set. Let bt' and $n3', n5'$, and $n6'$ be the number of bubbles-tunnels, the numbers of vertices of the set of the surface corners of all the b_0 objects (Definition 5), for which $vc' = 3, 5$, and 6, respectively, of object O_{n+1} that is obtained by adding one voxel to the object O_n.

Let $N3, N5$ and $N6$ be the corresponding numbers of this new voxel. We have that:

$$n3' = n3 + N3. \tag{14}$$

$$n5' = n5 + N5. \tag{15}$$

$$n6' = n6 + N6. \tag{16}$$

It must be shown that Eq. (13) holds for O_{n+1}, i.e.

$$bt' = \frac{n3' - n5' - 2n6'}{8} - b_0. \tag{17}$$

But this equation can be rewritten as follows:

$$bt' = \frac{n3 + N3 - n5 + N5 - 2(n6 + N6)}{8} - b_0 = \frac{n3 - n5 - 2n6}{8} - b_0 \\ + \frac{N3 - N5 - 2N6}{8}. \tag{18}$$

This equation simplifies to:

$$bt' = bt + \frac{N3 - N5 - 2N6}{8}. \tag{19}$$

Which we know is true. ∎

Note that Eq. (19) has exactly the same form that Eq. (13). To numerically validate Eq. (13), let us consider the objects shown in Fig. 3(a) and (b) taken together. We should obtain $bt = -1$. Let us proceed. For the two objects depicted in Fig. 3, taken together, $n3 = 18, n5 = 10, n6 = 0$, then $bt = \frac{18-10-2\times0}{8} - 2 = -1$ as expected.

At this moment the main result concerning the computation of the Euler number e of a 3-D digital object or a collection of 3-D digital objects in an image can be derived. For this, the number of bubbles and tunnels bt are used.

Proposition 2. The Euler number e of b_0 binary 3-D objects is always given as follows:

$$e = \frac{n3 - n5 - 2n6}{8}. \tag{20}$$

Proof. From Eq. (1) by making $bt = -b_1 + b_2$ and by Proposition 1(b):

$$e = b_0 - b_1 + b_2 = b_0 + \left(\frac{n3 - n5 - 2n6}{8} - b_0 \right) = \frac{n3 - n5 - 2n6}{8}. \qquad (21)$$

∎

To validate Eq. (20), let us use the two objects shown in Figs. 3(a) and (b). For the first object: $e = \frac{10-2-2\times0}{8} = 1$, while for the second object: $e = \frac{8-8-2\times0}{8} = 0$. If we apply Eq. (3) to both objects, we obtain the following two results. For the first object: $e = 32 - 60 + 36 - 7 = 1$. For the second object: $e = 32 - 64 + 40 - 8 = 0$. Both results, as expected, coincide with the results obtained with Eq. (20).

To demonstrate the applicability of Eq. (20), next in Sects. 4 and 5 several examples are presented.

4 Examples

To better appreciate the overall operation of the proposed method, this section discusses the computation of the Euler number with some examples. For this, the objects shown in Figs. 4(a), (b), (c), (d), and (e) are used. Second and third columns of Table 1 show the numbers b_1 and b_2 for each of the five objects.

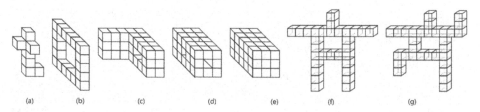

(a)   (b)   (c)   (d)   (e)   (f)   (g)

Fig. 4. (a)–(e). 3-D digital objects used to show the operation of the proposed method. The first object with no voids and tunnels, the second and the third objects with one simple tunnel. The fourth object with a double tunnel; a tunnel with one entrance and two outputs. The fifth object with two voids of one 0-voxel each one. (f)–(g) The Euler number of an object remains unchanged if its topology does not change.

Columns fourth, fifth and sixth show the numbers $n3$, $n5$ and $n6$ as well. Seventh column shows the computed Euler number for each example according to Eq. (1), while eighth column shows the corresponding values obtained by means of Eq. (21). As the reader can see the values for e for each object coincide with the values obtained by means of Eq. (1), showing the validity of Eq. (20).

From this example, notice that numbers: $n3$, $n5$ and $n6$, and the Euler number depend solely on the object's topology. In other words, the object geometry is irrelevant as long as its topology remains unchanged. For instance, consider the example portrayed in Fig. 4(f–g) and Table 2 which show how this fact could be used for shape differentiation. To reinforce the potentiality of the proposal, the next section presents results on several real voxelized objects.

Table 1. The computed features for the objets of Fig. 4.

Object number	b_1	b_2	$n3$	$n5$	$n6$	Euler number by Eq. (1)	Euler number by Eq. (20)
1	0	0	18	6	2	$e = 1 - 0 + 0 = 1$	$e = \frac{18-6-2\times2}{8} = 1$
2	1	0	8	8	0	$e = 1 - 1 + 0 = 0$	$e = \frac{8-8-2\times0}{8} = 0$
3	1	0	10	10	0	$e = 1 - 1 + 0 = 0$	$e = \frac{10-10-2\times0}{8} = 0$
4	2	0	9	17	0	$e = 1 - 2 + 0 = -1$	$e = \frac{9-17-2\times0}{8} = -1$
5	0	2	24	0	0	$e = 1 - 0 + 2 = 3$	$e = \frac{24-0-2\times0}{8} = 3$

Table 2. Euler number of an object in two different postures.

Position	$n1$	$n3$	Euler number
(a)	20	20	0
(b)	20	20	0

5 Examples with Realistic Objects

This section extends the application of the method presented in this paper on a set of four real objects as shown in Fig. 5. With these objects, a series of experiments are presented.

Fig. 5. Set of objects used to test the utility of Eq. (20).

5.1 Euler Number of an Object with Different Number of Cavities and Tunnels

The first object shown in Fig. 5 is altered by adding cavities and tunnels as shown in Fig. 6. For each altered version, Table 3 shows the desired e, the corresponding values for $n3$, $n5$, $n6$, and the obtained e. Note, that in all cases the correct value for e has been obtained by the application of Eq. (20) to the different versions of the sphere.

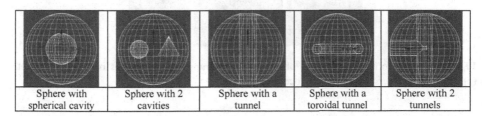

Sphere with spherical cavity	Sphere with 2 cavities	Sphere with a tunnel	Sphere with a toroidal tunnel	Sphere with 2 tunnels

Fig. 6. Sphere and altered versions to test the proposed equation.

Table 3. Euler number of spherical object and several of its altered versions.

Description	Desired value for e	$n3$	$n5$	$n6$	Obtained value for e
Sphere without cavities and tunnels	1	19673	12793	3436	$e = \frac{19673-12793-2\times3436}{8} = 1$
Sphere with a cavity	2	22913	15179	3859	$e = \frac{22913-15179-2\times3859}{8} = 2$
Sphere with two cavities	3	21926	14374	3764	$e = \frac{21926-14374-2\times3764}{8} = 3$
Sphere with a tunnel	0	19529	12657	3436	$e = \frac{19529-12657-2\times3436}{8} = 0$
Sphere with a toroidal tunnel	0	21772	14222	3775	$e = \frac{21772-14222-2\times3775}{8} = 0$
Sphere with a double cylindrical tunnel	−1	19796	12806	3499	$e = \frac{19796-12806-2\times3499}{8} = -1$

5.2 Invariance of Eq. (20) to Image Translations, Rotations and Scale Changes

In this experiment, the three objects of Fig. 5 are translated, rotated and scaled three times. These three versions for each object are shown in Figs. 7(a), (b) and (c).

Table 4 shows the desired value for e, the corresponding values for $n3$, $n5$, $n6$, and the computed value for e. Again, note that in all cases the correct value for e has been calculated by the application of Eq. (20) to the original and transformed versions of the three objects.

It is worth mentioning that sometimes, due to the voxelization, the resulting object can appear disconnected as shown, for example, in Fig. 8(a). As can be seen, 6-connectivity is lost. To eliminate this problem the $2 \times 2 \times 2$ mask shown in Fig. 8(b) is used. It helps to detect pixels not satisfying this connectivity. Now, as depicted in Fig. 8(c) the mask is moved up-down-left-right, trying to find 6-non-connected voxels inside the mask.

Fig. 7. (a) Transformed versions of object bird. (b) Transformed versions of object elephant. (c) Transformed versions of object cheese.

Table 4. Euler number of the three transformed versions of the objects: Bird, elephant, cheese.

Description	Desired value for e	$n3$	$n5$	$n6$	Obtained value for e
First transformed bird	1	3920	1914	999	$e = \frac{3920-1914-2\times999}{8} = 1$
Second transformed bird	1	3132	1516	804	$e = \frac{3132-1516-2\times804}{8} = 1$
Third transformed bird	1	2557	1203	673	$e = \frac{2557-1203-2\times673}{8} = 1$
First transformed elephant	1	3177	1795	687	$e = \frac{3177-1795-2\times687}{8} = 1$
Second transformed elephant	1	6149	4117	1012	$e = \frac{6149-4117-2\times1012}{8} = 1$
Third transformed elephant	1	9970	6226	1868	$e = \frac{9970-6226-2\times1868}{8} = 1$
First transformed cheese	−9	3638	2754	478	$e = \frac{3638-2754-2\times478}{8} = -9$
Second transformed cheese	−9	2136	1672	268	$e = \frac{2136-1672-2\times268}{8} = -9$
Third transformed cheese	−9	6038	3256	1427	$e = \frac{6038-3256-2\times1427}{8} = -9$

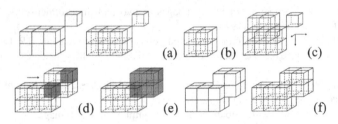

Fig. 8. (a) A 6-non-connected object. (b) $2 \times 2 \times 2$ mask used to correct non-connectivity. (c) Movement of mask. (d) Position where two voxels are non-connected. (e) Voxels are connected. (f) Final result.

As portrayed, the mask is continuously moved until an eventually position is found (Fig. 8(d)). At this moment, all the voxels with value 0 are changed to value 1 (Fig. 8 (e)). The remaining positions are visited and the filling process is repeated. Figure 8(f) shows the final corrected object after the application of the above explained process.

6 Conclusions

This research has shown that it is possible to compute the Euler feature of a 3-D digital object (digital image) in terms of the codes of three of the vertexes of the external voxels of the object (image). The proposal is very simple and can be directly applied to any 3-D digital image.

As a basis for the proposal operation, several formal propositions were provided and demonstrated. To illustrate the method operation, results on several simple and real objects were also given.

Acknowledgements. The authors would like to thank the Instituto Politécnico Nacional for the support to carry out this research. H. Sossa appreciates the economic support received from the SIP-IPN and CONACYT under grants 20190007 and 65 (Frontiers of Science), respectively, to conduct this investigation.

References

1. Lin, X., Xiang, Sh., Gu, Y.: A new approach to compute the Euler number of 3D image. In: Proceedings of the 3rd IEEE Conference on Industrial Electronics and Applications, pp. 1543–1546. IEEE, Singapore (2008)
2. Lee, C.N., Poston, T., Rosenfeld, A.: Winding and Euler numbers for 2D and 3D digital images. CVGIP: Graph. Models Image Process. 53(6), 522–537 (1991)
3. Lee, C.N., Poston, T., Rosenfeld, A.: Holes and Genus of 2D and 3D digital images. CVGIP: Graph. Models Image Process. 55(1), 20–47 (1993)
4. Toriwaki, J., Yonekura, T.: Euler number and connectivity indexes of a three dimensional digital picture. Forma 17, 183–209 (2002)
5. Gray, S.B.: Local properties of binary images in two and three dimensions. IEEE Trans. Comput. C-20(5), 551–561 (1970)
6. Park, C.M., Rosenfeld, A.: Connectivity and genus in three dimension, TR-156. Computer Vision Laboratory, Computer Science Center, University of Maryland, College Park, MD (1971)
7. Kong, T.Y., Rosenfeld, A.: Digital topology: introduction and survey. Comput. Vis. Graph. Image Process. 48, 357–393 (1989)
8. Lee, C.N., Rosenfeld, A.: Computing the Euler number of a 3D image. In: Proceedings of the IEEE First International Conference on Computer Vision, pp. 567–571. IEEE (1987)
9. Xia, F.: BIUP3: boundary topological invariant of 3D objects through front propagation at a constant speed. In: Proceedings of the Geometric Modelling and Processing. IEEE (2004)
10. Bonnassie, A., Peyrin, F., Attaly, D.: Shape description of three-dimensional images based on medial axis. In: Proceedings of the 2001 International Conference on Image Processing, pp. 931–934. IEEE (2001)
11. Schladitz, K., Ohser, J., Nagel, W.: Measuring intrinsic volumes in digital 3D images. In: Kuba, A., Nyúl, L.G., Palágyi, K. (eds.) DGCI 2006. LNCS, vol. 4245, pp. 247–258. Springer, Heidelberg (2006). https://doi.org/10.1007/11907350_21
12. Saha, P.K., Chaudhuri, B.B.: A new approach to computing the Euler characteristic. Pattern Recogn. 28(12), 1955–1963 (1995)
13. Sánchez, H., Sossa, H., Braumann, U.-D., Bribiesca, E.: The Euler-Poincaré formula through contact surfaces of voxelized objects. J. Appl. Res. Technol. 11, 55–78 (2013)
14. Uchiyama, T., Taniazawa, T., Muramatsu, H., Endo, N., Takahashi, H.E., Hara, T.: Three-dimensional microstructural analysis of human trabecular bone in relation to its mechanical properties. Bone 25(4), 487–491 (1999)
15. Vogel, H.J., Roth, K.: Quantitative morphology and network representation of soil pore structure. Adv. Water Resour. 24, 233–242 (2001)
16. Lang, C., Ohser, J., Hilfer, R.: On the analysis of spatial binary images. J. Microsc. 203(3), 303–313 (2001)
17. Lehmann, P., et al.: Impact of geometrical properties on permeability and fluid phase distribution in porous media. Adv. Water Resour. 31, 1188–1204 (2008)

18. Velichko, A., Holzapfel, C., Siefers, A., Schladitz, K., Mücklich, F.: Unambiguous classification of complex microstructures by their three-dimensional parameters applied to graphite in cast iron. Acta Materialia **56**, 1981–1990 (2008)
19. Ohser, J., Mücklich, F.: Statistical Analysis of Microstructures in Materials Science. Wiley, New York (2000)
20. Russ, J.C., Dehoff, R.: Practical Stereology. Kluwer Academic/Plenum, New York (2000)
21. Sossa, H., Santiago, R., Rubio, E., Pérez, M.: Computing the Euler number of a binary image based on a vertex codification. J. Appl. Res. Technol. **11**, 360–370 (2013)
22. Sossa, H., Sánchez, H.: Computing the number of bubbles and tunnels of a 3-D binary object. In: Fred, A., De Marsico, M., Sanniti di Baja, G. (eds.) ICPRAM 2016. LNCS, vol. 10163, pp. 194–211. Springer, Cham (2017). https://doi.org/10.1007/978-3-319-53375-9_11

Comparative Study of P, PI, Fuzzy and Fuzzy PI Controllers in Position Control for Omnidirectional Robots

Leticia Luna-Lobano, Prometeo Cortés-Antonio, Oscar Castillo$^{(\boxtimes)}$, and Patricia Melin

Tijuana Institute of Technology,
Calzada Tecnologico s/n, 22414 Tijuana, Mexico
llunalobano@gmail.com,
prometeo.cortes@tectijuana.edu.mx,
{ocastillo,pmelin}@tectijuana.mx

Abstract. This paper presents the design and analysis of different controller schemes for a three wheeled omnidirectional robot, that is, a robot which can be driven by the control of three independent velocity variables: over x and y linear directions and a rotational direction to perform complex motions. Conventional Proportional, Proportional-Integral, Fuzzy and Fuzzy PI controllers are designed based on the kinematic behavior of the holonomic mobile omnidirectional robot. Velocities of the Robot are estimated by using an odometer module. Also, the implementation performed in Simulink tool of Matlab of the different schemes is presented. The control objective for these designs is to drive the two linear command velocities of the robot and to do it goes from an initial position to a final position without obstacles. Finally, a comparative analysis of the studied controllers in time and distance is performed for determining the performance using a Robotino simulation tool of Festo, which provides an uncertainty environment for the robot control.

Keywords: P control · PI control · Fuzzy control · Omnidirectional robot

1 Introduction

Nowadays, manufacturing companies are working on the implementation of technologies that improve their operations through automation. The use of robots is one of them [1–3]. Robots are programmable devices, they have a wide application in manufacturing industry to perform an individual task or in collaboration with other ones in complex tasks [4, 5].

Many publications have based their study on kinematics of mobile robots, which are controlled by the velocity input [6]. Based on nonlinearities and uncertainty various control systems have been designed [7]. Fuzzy Logic in intelligent computing is strongly applied to robotic solutions to improvement automation processes [8–10]. The feedback information about the robot pose can be estimated from encoder optical sensor [11], and this is used to computed linear and angular command velocities.

© Springer Nature Switzerland AG 2019
L. Martínez-Villaseñor et al. (Eds.): MICAI 2019, LNAI 11835, pp. 714–727, 2019.
https://doi.org/10.1007/978-3-030-33749-0_57

In [12], a simple adaptive fuzzy logic controller is proposed, which utilizes a fuzzy logic system for estimating the unknown robot parameters for tracking control of a wheel mobile robot and it requires only a position measurement. Fuzzy logic theory is a powerful soft computing technique for complex and non-linear control systems based on human expert knowledge [13, 14].

Omnidirectional mobile robots have as a main feature, that they can move simultaneously and independently in rotational and two translational motions on a flat surface [15]. Fuzzy logic is a good alternative for increasing the capabilities of autonomous mobile robots in an unknown dynamics environment by integrating human experience [16]. Fuzzy theory has shown advantage in dealing with uncertainty and nonlinear problems [17]. Fuzzy Logic can be applied in several solutions such as obstacle avoidance [18], Path Navigation in robotic solutions [13], and autonomous Humanoid Robot Control [19]. Other works using Intelligent Control applied in autonomous navigation robots can be found in [20, 21].

In this article the navigation of an omnidirectional robot is addressed using different types of controllers, *P*, *PI*, Fuzzy and Fuzzy-PI controllers. *P* and *PI* controllers are conventional controllers, but the major drawback is the estimation of its parameters in nonlinear systems. Fuzzy control helps to compute command velocities based on fuzzy rules taken from human experience. Last, Fuzzy-PI computes the parameter values for k_p and k_i of a *PI* controller with dynamical parameters.

The paper has the following structure: Sect. 2 introduces the kinematics of the omnidirectional Robot. Section 3 explains the different control schemes, Sect. 4 includes an implementation of control schemes, and Sect. 5 includes results obtained on test execution. Finally, conclusions are about this paper are presented.

2   Kinematics of Omnidirectional Robot

Main characteristic of any omnidirectional robots is that they can move in three directions, that is, they can move on *x*, *y* translational directions, and additionally, they can perform rotational motions. The omnidirectional robot used in this work is the Robotino of Festo [22]. Robotino is a holonomic mobile robot with three omnidirectional drive units, this means that the number of degrees of freedom is equals to the total degree of freedom of the robot [16].

Robot odometer uses data state from the motions of the three actuators to estimate the robot position in time. In the current design problem, we use odometer module (incorporated into Robotino tools) to estimate the mobile robot position relative to the known starting location.

Figure 1 illustrates the kinematics of an omnidirectional robot that contains 3 wheels, each one can be identified by their angular location φ_i and their angular velocity $\dot{\theta}_i$, with $i = 1, 2, 3$. The robot position with respect to reference frame is defined as $x = [x, y, \emptyset]^T$.

According to [13], the kinematics model of Robotino is given by next equation

$$
\begin{bmatrix} \dot{\theta}_1 \\ \dot{\theta}_2 \\ \dot{\theta}_3 \end{bmatrix} = \frac{1}{r} \begin{bmatrix} V_1 \\ V_2 \\ V_3 \end{bmatrix} = \frac{1}{r} \begin{bmatrix} -sin(\emptyset + \varphi_1)\ cos(\emptyset + \varphi_1)R \\ -sin(\emptyset + \varphi_2)\ cos(\emptyset + \varphi_2)R \\ -sin(\emptyset + \varphi_3)\ cos(\emptyset + \varphi_3)R \end{bmatrix} \begin{bmatrix} \dot{x} \\ \dot{y} \\ \dot{\emptyset} \end{bmatrix} \tag{1}
$$

or simpler, in matrix notation

$$
\dot{\theta} = \frac{1}{r}V = \frac{1}{r}P(\emptyset)\dot{x} \tag{2}
$$

with

V_i Linear velocity of the wheel i
R Distance between a wheel and the center of the robot
$\dot{\emptyset}$ Angular velocity of the robot
φ_i Angular location of the wheel i
r Radius of the wheels
$P(\emptyset)$ Transformation matrix between the angular velocities of the wheels and the robot velocity vector $(\dot{x}, \dot{y})^T$

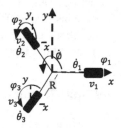

Fig. 1. kinematics of an omnidirectional robot

3 Control Schemes

The main objective of this work is to analyze the behavior of Robotino in reaching a desired position by computing the command velocities v_x and v_y of the robot using different control schemes. In this paper, we study four controllers: (a) proportional, P; (b) proportional-integral, PI; (c) Fuzzy, F and; (d) Fuzzy proportional-integral, FPI. Figure 2 shows the general scheme of the feedback control implemented in this work. Robotino tools provide an odometer module to estimate the pose, x, of the robot. Into the controller block, the different mentioned controllers will be implemented.

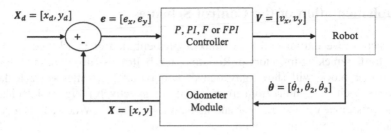

Fig. 2. General feedback control scheme

Table 1 provides the equations to compute the command velocities, v_x and v_y for the P and PI controllers.

Table 1. Equations of the command velocities for P and PI controllers

P	PI
$v_x = k_{px}e_x$	$v_x = k_{py}e_x + k_{ix} \int e_x$
$v_y = k_{py}e_y$	$v_y = k_{py}e_y + k_{iy} \int e_y$

The calculation of v_x and v_y in F and FPI controllers is accomplished through fuzzy logic controllers as it is shown in Fig. 3. The F controller is composed by 2 parallel Mamdani Fuzzy systems with 1-input and 1-output, 5 fuzzy rules and 5 fuzzy sets per variable. The FPI is unlike the F controller as their parallel fuzzy systems have 2 outputs and each output variable has 3 FS, also, it can be noted the output variables are the control parameters k_{px}, k_{py}, k_{ix} and k_{iy} instead of v_x or v_y. For better visualization, Fig. 3 only shows one of two embedded controllers in each scheme.

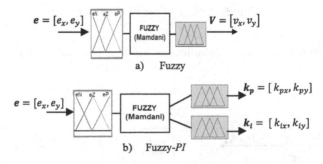

Fig. 3. Schemes of the (a) F and (b) FPI controllers

4   Implementation of the Control Schemes

In this section, we introduce the Simulink implementation of the different controller systems for the tracking trajectory of Robotino. For better visualization, in each system the controller block will show only one of two parallel schemes (to calculate the command velocities v_x and v_y from errors e_x and e_y respectively). Figure 4 depicts the P controller, its input variable is error and its output is velocity. Where, k_p is a constant value and X_d is the desired position.

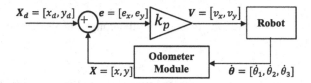

Fig. 4. Scheme of the P controller

Figure 5 depicts the *PI* controller, which its input variable is error and its output is velocity. Where, k_p and k_i are the constants for the proportional and integral terms respectively.

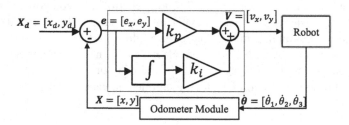

Fig. 5. Scheme of the PI controller

Figure 6 depicts the fuzzy controller, its input is the error and its output is the velocity.

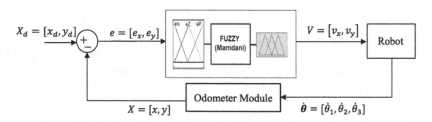

Fig. 6. Scheme of the fuzzy controller

Figure 7 shows the linguistic variables error and velocity, which represent the input and the output the fuzzy model with linguistic values equally spaced along its range. Table 2 lists the linguistic values of the fuzzy variables.

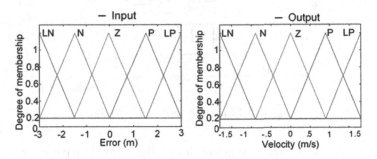

Fig. 7. (a) Input and output variables of the fuzzy controller

Table 2. Linguistic values of fuzzy variables of F controller

Error	Velocity
LN: Negative	LN: Negative
N: Negative	N: Negative
Z: Zero	Z: Zero
P: Positive	P: Positive
LP: Large Positive	LP: Large Positive

The number of Membership Functions (MF) assigned to each input-output variable was chosen empirically. Finally, the rule base created is listed as follows.

$R_1 =$ *if error is Negative Large then Velocity is Negative Large*
$R_2 =$ *if error is Negative then Velocity is Negative*
$R_3 =$ *if error is Zero then Velocity is Zero*
$R_4 =$ *if error is Positive then Velocity is Positive*
$R_5 =$ *if error is Negative Large then Velocity is Negative Large*

Figure 8 depicts the *FPI* controller which each input is the error of the position and outputs are the k_p and k_i variables. Then the *FPI* controller computes the dynamic parameters k_p and k_i to be used by a *PI* scheme to calculate the command velocities v_x and v_y.

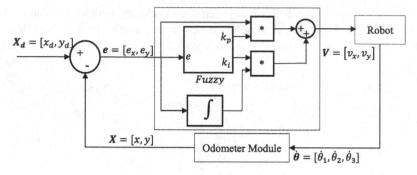

Fig. 8. Schema of the fuzzy-PI controller

Figure 9 depicts the membership functions assigned to the input error, and to the output variables k_p and k_i. Table 3 lists the names of linguistic values of each variable.

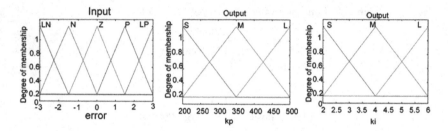

Fig. 9. Error, k_i and k_p variables of the *Fuzzy − PI* controller

Table 3. Linguistic values of fuzzy variables of the *FPI* controller

Error	k_p	k_i
LN: Negative	S: Small	S: Small
N: Negative	M: Medium	M: Medium
Z: Zero	L: Large	L: Large
P: Positive		
LP: Large Positive		

The rule base created for *FPI* controller is listed as follows.

R_1 = *if error is Negative Large then k_i is large and k_p is large*
R_2 = *if error is Negative then k_i is Medium and k_p is Medium*
R_3 = *if error is Zero then k_i is Small and k_p is Small*
R_4 = *if error is Positive then k_i is Medium and k_p is Medium*
R_5 = *if error is Positive Large then k_i is Large and k_p is Large*

5 Results

To compare the different controllers, the Integral Square Error (ISE) is calculated as follows

$$ISE = \int_0^T e^2(t)dt = \int_0^T e_x^2(t)dt + \int_0^T e_y^2(t)dt \tag{3}$$

where e_x and e_y are the errors of each variable. T is the run time. To analyze the different control schemes introduced above, we perform three tests in which, the target position is $x_{d1} = [3, 3]$, $x_{d2} = [5, 4]$ and $x_{d3} = [5, 2]$ respectively. In the first test, run time is 10 s, and the gain parameter values for the P and PI controllers are listed in Table 4.

Table 4. Gains of the P and PI controllers for test 1

Parameters	P	PI
k_{px}, k_{py}	[500, 500]	[300, 500]
k_{ix}, k_{iy}	–	[2, 3]

Table 5 contains the integral square errors and settling time (t_s) obtained from the execution in test 1 of different controllers to go from an initial position [0, 0] to final position [3, 3]. Additionally, it shows if the trajectory had overshoot.

Table 5. Results of the different control schemes for test 1

Results	P	PI	F	FPI
ISE_x, ISE_y	[65.69, 86.34]	[76.90, 41.94]	[14.24, 17.20]	[54.31, 53.57]
ISE	152.03	118.84	31.44	107.88
t_{sx}, t_{sy}	[3.5, 7.14]	[8.36, 4.12]	[1.84, 3.26]	[7.60, 7.00]
Overshoot	No	No	Yes	No

Figure 10 shows the behavior of the Robotino over the x and y positions under the different schemes. It can be noted how the Robotino converges to desired position. Additionally, it is shown the command velocities v_x and v_y applied during execution time for each controller.

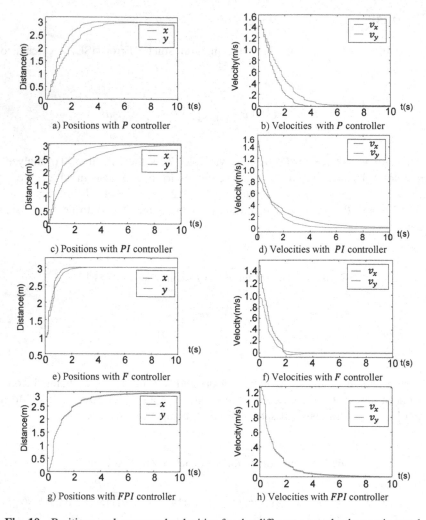

Fig. 10. Positions and command velocities for the different control schemes in test 1

For the second test, the desired position is $x_{d2} = [5, 4]$. The run time is also 10 s, the gain parameter values for P and PI controllers are listed in Table 6.

Table 6. Gains of the P and PI controllers for test 2

Parameters	P	PI
k_{px}, k_{py}	[300, 300]	[300, 500]
k_{ix}, k_{iy}	–	[2, 3]

Table 7 contains the integral square errors and t_s time obtained from the execution of the different controllers to go from an initial position [0, 0] to the final position [5, 4]. Additionally, it shows if the trajectory had an overshoot.

Table 7. Results of the different control schemes for test 2

Results	P	PI	F	FPI
ISE_x, ISE_y	[267.79, 28.57]	[158.01, 161.51]	[252.15, 145.11]	[33.23, 48.90]
ISE	296.36	319.52	397.26	82.13
t_{sx}, t_{sy}	[5.08, 6.44]	[2.38, 5.08]	[9.98, 7.66]	[2.28, 6.00]
Overshoot	Yes	Yes	No	Yes

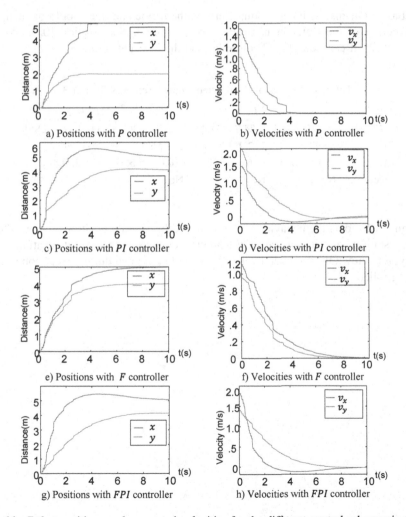

a) Positions with P controller   b) Velocities with P controller

c) Positions with PI controller   d) Velocities with PI controller

e) Positions with F controller   f) Velocities with F controller

g) Positions with FPI controller   h) Velocities with FPI controller

Fig. 11. Robot positions and command velocities for the different control schemes in test 2

Figure 11 shows the behavior of the robot on x and y position under the different schemes. It can be noted how the Robotino converges to desired position. Additionally, it is shown the command velocities v_x and v_y applied during execution time for each controller. Finally, in the third test, $x_{d2} = [5, 2]$. The run time is also 10 s, the gain parameters for P and PI controllers are listed in Table 8.

Table 8. Gains of P and PI controllers for test 3

Parameters	P	PI
k_{px}, k_{py}	[300, 500]	[500, 300]
k_{ix}, k_{iy}	–	[2, 3]

Table 9 contains the integral square errors, the t_s time and overshoot obtained from the execution of the different controllers to go from initial position [0, 0] to final position [5, 2]. It can note that P controller had the best performance.

Table 9. Results of the different control schemes for test 3

Results	P	PI	F	FPI
ISE_x, ISE_y	[52.47, 1.62]	[184.77, 27.43]	[207.07, 26.49]	[144.41, 58.86]
ISE	54.09	212.2	233.56	203.27
t_{sx}, t_{sy}	[4.52, 3.74]	[7.68, 6.55]	[10.00, 5.66]	[3.42, 3.44]
Overshoot	No	No	No	Yes

Figure 12 shows the behavior of the robot on the x and y positions under different schemes studied, and it can see how Robotino converges to desired position. Additionally, it is shown the command velocities v_x and v_y applied during execution time for each controller.

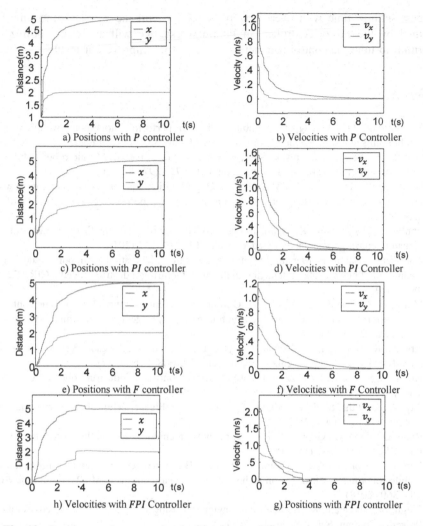

Fig. 12. Positions and command velocities for the different control schemes in test 3

6 Conclusions

In paper, it can be seen that all designed models could arrive to the different desired positions studied. Analyzing the results of the first test, it is identified that the Proportional controller presents the best setting time but it has a small position error. On the other hand, the Fuzzy controller has the worst settling time but it was more accurate. At the second test using same parameters, the Fuzzy controller was the most stable because there was not an overshoot, but settling time was worst, and the fastest was the *FPI*, the rest of the controllers reflected a very large overshoot. At the third test, we try to perform a more extreme scenario, the desired position in x_d and y_d was very different from other ones, The generated results indicate that the *FPI* controller obtains the best settling time with overshoot in its results, and the worst setting time was obtained by the Fuzzy controller. In Future works, we will apply an optimization algorithm to tune the control parameters, which let us improve our results.

References

1. Kermorgant, O.: A magnetic climbing robot to perform autonomous welding in the shipbuilding industry. Robot. Comput.-Integr. Manuf. **53**, 178–186 (2018)
2. Garnier, S., Subrin, K., Arevalo-Siles, P., Caverot, G., Furet, B.: Mobile robot stability for complex tasks in naval industries. Procedia CIRP **72**, 297–302 (2018)
3. Landscheidt, S., Kans, M., Winroth, M.: Opportunities for robotic automation in wood product industries: the supplier and system integrators' perspective. Procedia Manuf. **11**, 233–240 (2017)
4. Phuluwa, H., Mpofu, K.: Human-robot collaboration in a small scale rail industry: demanufacturing operations. Procedia Manuf. **17**, 230–237 (2018)
5. Aaltonen, I., Salmi, T., Marstio, I.: Refining levels of collaboration to support the design and evaluation of human-robot interaction in the manufacturing industry. Procedia CIRP **72**, 93–98 (2018)
6. Martinez, R., Castillo, O., Aguilar, L.: Optimization of interval type-2 fuzzy logic controllers for a perturbed autonomous wheeled mobile robot using genetic algorithms. Inf. Sci. **179** (13), 2158–2174 (2009)
7. Abiyev, R., Günsel, I.S., Akkaya, N., Aytac, E., Çağman, A., Abizada, S.: Fuzzy control of omnidirectional robot. Procedia Comput. Sci. **120**, 608–616 (2017)
8. Krishnaa, S., Vasub, S.: Fuzzy PID based adaptive control on industrial robot system. Mater. Today: Proc. **5**, 13055–13060 (2018)
9. Aly, A., Griffiths, S., Stramandinoli, F.: Towards intelligent social robots: current advances in cognitive robotics (2015)
10. Raun, D., Zhou, C., Gupta, M.: Preface: fuzzy set techniques for intelligent robotic systems. Fuzzy Sets Syst. **134**, 1–4 (2003)
11. Forte, M., Correia, W., Nogueira, F., Torrico, B.: Reference tracking of a nonholonomic mobile robot using sensor fusion techniques and linear control. IFAC-PapersOnLine **51**(4), 364–369 (2018)
12. Singh, N., Thongam, K.: Mobile robot navigation using fuzzy logic in static environments. Procedia Comput. Sci. **125**, 11–17 (2017)
13. Masmoudi, M., Krichen, N., Masmoudi, M., Derbel, N.: Fuzzy logic controllers design for omnidirectional mobile robot navigation. Appl. Soft Comput. **49**, 901–919 (2016)
14. Castillo, O.: Type-2 Fuzzy Logic in Intelligent Control Applications, vol. 272. Springer, Heidelberg (2012). https://doi.org/10.1007/978-3-642-24663-0
15. Sheikhlar, A., Fakharian, A., Adhami-Mirhosseini, A.: Fuzzy adaptive PI control of omnidirectional mobile robot. In: 13th Iranian Conference on Fuzzy Systems (IFSC), pp. 1–4 (2013)
16. Oltean, S., Dulău, M., Puskas, R.: Position control of Robotino mobile robot using fuzzy logic. In: IEEE International Conference on Automation, vol. 1, pp. 1–6 (2010)

17. Huang, H.-C., Wu, T.-F., Yu, C.-H., Hsu, H.-S.: Intelligent fuzzy motion control of three-wheeled omnidirectional mobile robots for trajectory tracking and stabilization. In: 2012 International Conference on Fuzzy Theory and Its Applications (iFUZZY2012), pp. 107–112 (2012)
18. Abiyeva, R., Günsela, I., Akkayaa, N., Aytaca, E., Çağman, A., Abizada, S.: Robot soccer control using behaviour trees and fuzzy logic. Procedia Comput. Sci. **102**, 477–484 (2016)
19. Fujita, M., Kitano, H.: Development of an autonomous quadruped robot for robot entertainment. Auton. Robot. **5**(1), 7–18 (1998)
20. Melin, P., Astudillo, L., Castillo, O., Valdez, F., Garcia, M.: Optimal design of type-2 and type-1 fuzzy tracking controllers for autonomous mobile robots under perturbed torques using a new chemical optimization paradigm. Expert Syst. Appl. **40**(8), 3185–3195 (2013)
21. Montiel, O., Sepulveda, R., Melin, P., Castillo, O., Porta, M., Meza, I.: Performance of a simple tuned fuzzy controller and a PID controller on a DC motor. In: IEEE Symposium on Foundations of Computational Intelligence, pp. 531–537 (2007)
22. Robotino® Festo Didactic. manual.pdf. https://www.festo-didactic.com/int-en/services/robotino. Accessed 14 Aug 2019

Modeling and Control Balance Design for a New Bio-inspired Four-Legged Robot

Hiram Ponce[1]([✉]), Mario Acevedo[2], Elizabeth Morales-Olvera[1],
Lourdes Martínez-Villaseñor[1], Gabriel Díaz-Ramos[1],
and Carlos Mayorga-Acosta[1]

[1] Facultad de Ingeniería, Universidad Panamericana,
Augusto Rodin 498, 03920 Mexico City, Mexico
{hponce,0177650,lmartine,0188401,0188400}@up.edu.mx
[2] Facultad de Ingeniería, Universidad Panamericana,
Álvaro del Portillo 49, 45010 Zapopan, Jalisco, Mexico
macevedo@up.edu.mx

Abstract. Bio-inspired robots have chosen to propose novel developments aiming to inhabit and interact complex and dynamic environments. Bio-inspired four-legged robots, typically inspired on animal locomotion, provide advantages on mobility, obstacle avoidance, energy efficiency and others. Balancing is a major challenge when legged robots require to move over uncertain and sharp terrains. It becomes of particular importance to solve other locomotion tasks such as walking, running or jumping. In this paper, we present a preliminary study on the modeling and control balance design of a bio-inspired four-legged robot for standing on its aligned legs in a straight line. The proposed robot is loosely inspired on the bio-mechanics of the chameleon. Thus, a mathematical modeling, simulation, intelligent control strategy, prototype implementation and preliminary results of control balance in our robot are presented and discussed.

Keywords: Bio-inspired robot · Balancing · Modeling · Rapid prototyping · Four-legged robot · Intelligent control

1 Introduction

Research in mobile robots has been developing rapidly given that they can be used to do tasks dangerous or poisonous for humans [9]. Mobile robot have been proposed for search and rescue when the terrain is unknown or dangerous to access by humans [7]. In particular, legged robots are promising for these tasks because they use biomimetic principles to overcome the difficulties of the terrain.

This research has been funded by Universidad Panamericana through the grant "Fomento a la Investigación UP 2018", under project code UP-CI-2018-ING-MX-02.

L. Martínez-Villaseñor et al. (Eds.): MICAI 2019, LNAI 11835, pp. 728–739, 2019.
https://doi.org/10.1007/978-3-030-33749-0_58

It is important to study legged robot because there is a need of vehicles that can travel in difficult circumstances. Legs provide better mobility in rough terrain than wheels given that isolated footholds optimize support and traction [10]. A legged robot must be able to walk from one point to another without falling. Hence, the control of a legged walking robot must be able to keep the balance even if external forces perturb its walk.

Recently, biologically inspired, or simply bio-inspired, robots have been studied widely. This trend considers the necessity to design robots able to inhabit and interact complex and dynamic environments [3]. In this regard, these types of robots are inspired on animals. Moreover, animal locomotion has been considered important mainly due to the efficiency in motion, shape of body parts and energy used [3]. Hence, bio-inspired robots are typically legged entities.

In particular, four-legged robots are of great importance in the field because they can move in irregular terrains. Advantages of these robots consider: better mobility than wheeled robots, ability to avoid obstacles, presence of active suspension, energy efficiency and velocity management skills [4]. Thus, the analysis, mechanical design, optimization of processes, development of control systems and kinematic simulations, are all important for an efficient and reliable engineering of quadruped robots [4]. Moreover, balancing design of quadruped robots becomes primary relevant [1]. Once this problem is solved all other locomotion tasks can be tackled, in consequence, such as walking, running or jumping.

The balancing task in legged robots has been studied from different points of view: bio-mechanical engineering and control systems. The first approach focuses on the application of interdisciplinary studies of mechanics present in living organisms considered as complex systems [5,12]. The second approach is based on control engineering that allows an electro-mechanical system to regulate interesting variables, such as preserving the robot's angular position in a desired value, i.e. vertical axis [8].

In this paper, we present a preliminary study on the design, modeling and control balance of a bio-inspired four-legged robot for standing on its aligned legs in a straight line. From biological inspiration, this robot is loosely based on the morphology of a chameleon. In this study, we firstly present the mathematical model and the simulation of the robot. Then, we propose a fuzzy proportional-derivative (PD) control system for balancing the robot. After that and using the rapid prototyping approach, we present the first chameleon-like robot prototype, and lastly, we show preliminary results on the balancing control of this prototype using the intelligent controller.

This work corresponds to the first part of an ongoing research for designing a fully robot system inspired on the bio-mechanics of the chameleon for further balancing and walking of the robot over large and stretch working areas, e.g. beams and tubes. The contribution of this paper considers the mathematical modeling, simulation, conceptual design, the rapid prototyping implementation, the intelligent controller, and the resultant robot prototype.

The paper is organized as follows. Section 2 presents the bio-inspired robot, its mathematical modeling and its preview simulation. Section 3 proposes the intelligent control system based on a fuzzy-PD controller for balancing the robot. Section 4 introduces the adoption of rapid prototyping for fast and reliable robot implementation. In Sect. 5, we present preliminary results on the control balance of the robot, and some discussion of the work until now. Lastly, we conclude the paper.

2   Modeling and Simulation of the Bio-inspired Robot

This section introduces our robot system in terms of the mathematical modeling and simulation. Since our robot is committed to move on large and stretch working areas like beams or tubes, this robot is loosely inspired on the bio-mechanics of the chameleon. In that sense, the legs and the body are intended to look like a mechanical chameleon.

2.1   Mechanical Modeling

From the mechanical point of view, the model of the robot is proposing to have a total of nine rigid bodies: the trunk made of a thin plate and four limbs, each one made of a pair of links, as shown in Fig. 1. It has twelve revolute joints, two at each shoulder (points A, B, C and D), and one at each elbow (points I, J, K and L).

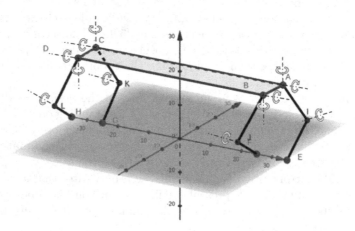

Fig. 1. Simplified model of the chameleon-like robot. Yellow arrows represent the actuated revolute joints. (Color figure online)

This model has different number of degrees of freedom (DoFs) depending on the configuration adopted. The maximum number of DoFs can be reached when the quadruped has no contact with the ground, as "flying". In that case, there are 18 DoFs; but when the paws (points E, F, G and H) are at the ground, it has only 6 DoF. In the latter, the one analyzed here, the system is redundantly actuated as each revolute joint is associated with a motor. Thus it can be actuated with eight torques requiring only six. To constraint the model to have contact at the ground, points E, F, G and H are attached to the surface and they are considered as free spherical joints. To this end, notice that the paws are aligned to a straight line right under the main body of the robot, becoming an unstable state for the system.

The dynamic equations of motion for this robot has been formulated in reference point coordinates: three center of mass displacements in (x, y, z) and three rotations about the three local reference frame axes. Thus the system has a total of 54 dependent coordinates: $\mathbf{q}$, whose first time derivatives form the vector of velocities $\dot{\mathbf{q}}$ are defined as (1), where $\dot{\mathbf{q}}_i^T = [\mathbf{v}_i^T \ \boldsymbol{\omega}_i^T]$, $\mathbf{v}_i^T = [\dot{x}_i, \dot{y}_i, \dot{z}_i]$ and $\boldsymbol{\omega}_i^T = [\omega_x, \omega_y, \omega_z]_i$. In this case $\dot{u}_i \equiv \frac{du_i}{dt}$.

$$\dot{\mathbf{q}}^T = [\dot{\mathbf{q}}_1^T \ \dot{\mathbf{q}}_2^T \ \dot{\mathbf{q}}_3^T \ \dot{\mathbf{q}}_4^T \ \dot{\mathbf{q}}_5^T \ \dot{\mathbf{q}}_6^T \ \dot{\mathbf{q}}_7^T \ \dot{\mathbf{q}}_8^T \ \dot{\mathbf{q}}_9^T] \tag{1}$$

These coordinates are related by a set of 48 constraint equations imposed by the joints: $\boldsymbol{\Phi}(\mathbf{q}) = \mathbf{0}$, whose first and second time derivatives lead to the velocities and accelerations kinematics relations respectively, as expressed in (2) and (3), where $\boldsymbol{\Phi}_{\mathbf{q}}$ is the partial derivative of the kinematic constraints with respect to the dependent coordinates $\mathbf{q}$, also called Jacobian matrix.

$$\boldsymbol{\Phi}_{\mathbf{q}}\dot{\mathbf{q}} = 0; \quad \boldsymbol{\Phi}_{\mathbf{q}} \equiv \frac{\partial \boldsymbol{\Phi}(\mathbf{q})}{\partial \mathbf{q}} \tag{2}$$

$$\boldsymbol{\Phi}_{\mathbf{q}}\ddot{\mathbf{q}} + \dot{\boldsymbol{\Phi}}_{\mathbf{q}}\dot{\mathbf{q}} = 0; \quad \dot{\boldsymbol{\Phi}}_{\mathbf{q}} \equiv \frac{d\boldsymbol{\Phi}_{\mathbf{q}}}{dt} \tag{3}$$

Applying the virtual power method [2], it is possible to express the dynamic equations of motion as in (4):

$$\sum_{i=1}^{9} [\delta\dot{\mathbf{q}}_i^T] \left(\begin{bmatrix} m_i\mathbf{I} & \mathbf{0} \\ \mathbf{0} & \mathbf{J}_i \end{bmatrix} \begin{bmatrix} \mathbf{v}_i \\ \dot{\boldsymbol{\omega}}_i \end{bmatrix} + \begin{bmatrix} \mathbf{0}_1 \\ \tilde{\boldsymbol{\omega}}_i\mathbf{J}_i\boldsymbol{\omega}_i \end{bmatrix} - \begin{bmatrix} \mathbf{f}_i \\ \boldsymbol{\tau}_i \end{bmatrix} \right) = 0, \tag{4}$$

where $\delta\dot{\mathbf{q}}_i^T = [\delta\mathbf{v}_i^T \ \delta\boldsymbol{\omega}_i^T]$ are, $\mathbf{I}$, and $\mathbf{0}$, represent the (3×3) unit and zero matrices, respectively, $\mathbf{0}_1$ represents the null column vector. $\mathbf{J}_i$ and m_i are the tensor of inertia and the mass of body i, respectively, $\tilde{\boldsymbol{\omega}}_i$ is the skew-symmetric matrix of $\boldsymbol{\omega}$, and $\mathbf{f}_i$ and $\boldsymbol{\tau}_i$ are the external applied forces and external applied torques of the body i. These equations can also be written as (5), or in matrix form as in (6).

$$\sum_{i=1}^{9} [\delta\dot{\mathbf{q}}_i^T] (\mathbf{M}_i\ddot{\mathbf{q}}_i + \mathbf{c}_i - \mathbf{g}_i) = 0 \tag{5}$$

$$\delta\dot{\mathbf{q}}^T (\mathbf{M}\ddot{\mathbf{q}} + \mathbf{c} - \mathbf{g}) = 0 \tag{6}$$

The virtual velocities $\delta\dot{\mathbf{q}}_i$ must be kinematically admissible, must satisfy the kinematic constraints, and thus cannot be eliminated from the equation. It is necessary to carry out a reduction of the virtual velocity vector from its actual size to a new vector of independent velocities, $\delta\dot{\mathbf{z}}_i$, whose size is the number of degrees of freedom. Thus the velocities and accelerations of these independent coordinates, the ones associated with the trunk, the joints at the shoulders and the joints at the elbows: $\dot{\mathbf{z}}$ and $\ddot{\mathbf{z}}$, respectively, are related to the dependent velocities by a projection matrix $\mathbf{R}$, where (7) and (8) hold.

$$\dot{\mathbf{q}} = \mathbf{R}\dot{\mathbf{z}}; \quad \boldsymbol{\Phi}_{\mathbf{q}}\mathbf{R} = 0 \tag{7}$$

$$\ddot{\mathbf{q}} = \mathbf{R}\ddot{\mathbf{z}} + \dot{\mathbf{R}}\dot{\mathbf{z}} \tag{8}$$

Thus the reduced final dynamic equations of motion of our model can be expressed as in (9).

$$\mathbf{R}^T\mathbf{M}\mathbf{R}\ddot{\mathbf{z}} = \mathbf{R}^T \left[\mathbf{g} - \mathbf{c} - \mathbf{M}\dot{\mathbf{R}}\dot{\mathbf{z}} \right] \tag{9}$$

The complete procedure for obtaining the dynamic equations of motion in terms of the DoFs can be reviewed in [2].

2.2   Co-simulation

We programmed the model in Matlab's Simscape. This software is able to rapidly create models of physical systems within the Simulink environment [6]. In this paradigm, modeling such as electronics, mechanics and control can be simulated altogether in one environment. In addition to Simulink capabilities, models can be built using 3D CAD designs, variables and expressions from Matlab, and the power of block-diagram schematics of Simulink.

Figure 2 shows the 3D model of our robot created in Simscape. It considers nine rigid parts: the body as the main shape, and eight rigid links forming the four limbs of the robot. The legs are assembled to the body using four universal joints (3-DoF, using only 2-DoFs as shown in Fig. 1). In the elbows, four revolute joints are employed, and four free-spherical joints are located between the paws and the surface (straight line) to model slipping-prevention. As shown later, this co-simulation between Simscape, Simulink and Matlab were employed for testing the torques in the joints for motor design.

3   Fuzzy Control for Robot Balance

As noticed above, the state of the robot is unstable since the four legs are aligned and constrained to be on a straight line under its main body. In that sense, we propose an intelligent control system to balance the robot and keep it in a vertical position.

We developed a Mamdani fuzzy-PD controller which consists of two inputs: the angular position θ and the angular velocity $\dot{\theta}$ of the sagittal plane of the robot (i.e. the plane that divides the body of the robot along the spine). These two inputs are partitioned in three fuzzy sets: *negative* (N), *zero* (Z) and *positive* (P), as shown in Fig. 3. The controller also contains two outputs. One for the motion of the left limbs (u_L) and the other for the motion of the right limbs (u_R). The output membership functions associated to the latter motions correspond to the angular positions of revolute joints at each elbow (I, J, K and L), as shown also in Fig. 3. Three fuzzy partitions were done for the outputs: *counterclockwise* (CCW), *stop* (S) and *clockwise* (CW). To this end, we propose nine fuzzy rules as depicted in Table 1. The fuzzy controller was manually tuned in the prototype robot.

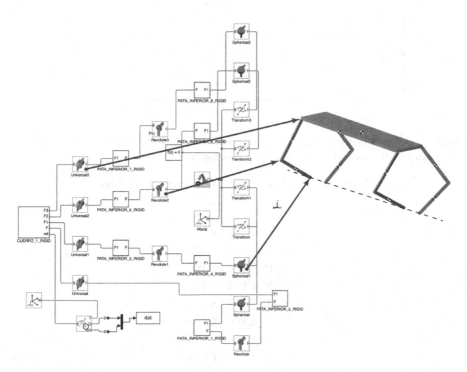

Fig. 2. Schematic of the Simscape modeling. The block diagram programmed in Simulink, at the left, and the assembly model of the robot, at the right. Arrows show the type of joints attached to the assembly.

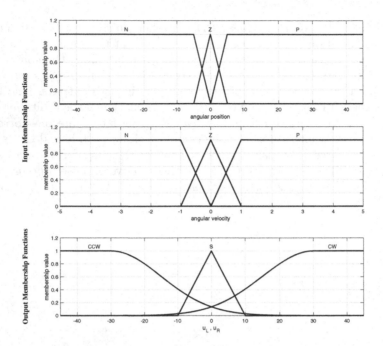

Fig. 3. Input membership functions (top) and output membership functions (bottom) of the Mamdani fuzzy-PD controller for robot balancing.

Table 1. Fuzzy rules for the intelligent controller.

θ	$\dot{\theta}$	u_L	u_R
N	N	CCW	CW
N	Z	CCW	CW
N	P	CCW	CW
Z	N	CCW	CW
Z	Z	S	S
Z	P	CW	CCW
P	N	CW	CCW
P	Z	CW	CCW
P	P	CW	CCW

4   Prototype Implementation

This section describes the implementation of the first version of the robot system. It comprises of three main steps: the CAD design, the fabrication of the prototype, and the instrumentation of the system.

4.1   CAD Design

First, the geometric design of the robot was made, alongside with the manufacturing of each leg and its assembly. The CAD software Solidworks was used to design the different parts needed, including all specifications and measurements. Since we adopted the fast prototyping design, we selected to make this version in a 3D printer. Thus, all pieces were constrained to be modular and in the right dimensions for the printer. Figure 4 shows the assembly robot in CAD. It comprises four limbs attached to the body, and twelve DoFs.

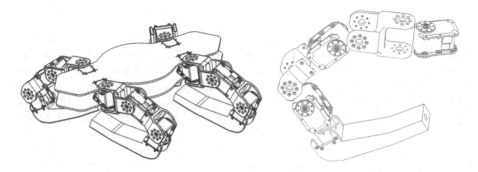

Fig. 4. Isometric view of the assembly robot in CAD. The whole robot comprises a rigid body and four limbs (left). These limbs have 3-DoFs implemented with motors (right).

Each leg can be divided into three subsections separated among them by joints (motors), as shown in Fig. 4(right). Each one of the links of all the limbs (3 per leg) was printed in order to reduce error in manufacturing and to simplify the model by designing a symmetric robot, both in geometry and in materials used. It is important to highlight that the motors represent the three joints in each leg. A total of 12 motors allow the robot the sufficient DoFs to balance itself and, for an ongoing research, to walk over a straight line.

4.2   Construction of the Robot

We built the first robotic prototype (see Fig. 7) using a 3D printer and laser cutting. The material for the body is PMMA (acrylic glass) and consists of a hollow design to reduce total weight and to enable an easy assembly with the limbs; while the links of the legs were printed in ABS plastic.

To determine the technical specifications of the motors, we conducted a testing on the simulation (see Sect. 2.2) to analyze the torques in the revolute joints (elbows). Figure 5 depicted the torques computed by simulation when the robot starts in the initial position (as shown in Fig. 2) and it moves freely. After some milliseconds, the robot falls down and the torques increases in magnitude. At the end of the test, we determined that motors required at least 2 Nm of stall torque.

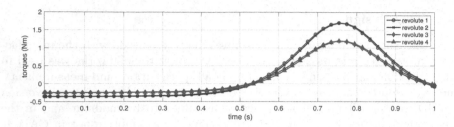

Fig. 5. Graph showing the torques computed in simulation when the robot starts at the initial position and it falls down freely.

From the above, we selected twelve Dynamixel MX-64AT motors from Robotics because of the high angle precision, high torque and a PID control position that they offer [11]. The motors have an easy 3-pin serial communication (VCC-Data-GND) that enables a serial connection to many motors via TTL communication. The main characteristics of these motors are: 10–14 V of input voltage (12 V recommended), 6 Nm of stall torque (12 V and 4.1 A) and absolute (360-degrees) encoder of 12 bits [11].

On the other hand, we installed an inertial measurement unit (IMU) sensor MPU6050 GY-52 that comprises a three-axis accelerometer and a three-axis gyroscope. This device was located on the top of the robot, at the intersection of the sagittal and tranverse planes.

4.3   Automation System

The next step after the manufacturing of the robot was the programming and the synchronization of the twelve motors with a personal computer (PC), as shown in Fig. 6. We use a USBDynamixel [11] device for serial communication between the motors and the PC. All motors are connected in daisy chain and powered with a battery of 12 V and 5 A. In addition, we use an Arduino, connected via USB to the PC, to gather measurement values from the IMU sensor.

To this end, Fig. 7 shows the first robotic prototype built from this methodology.

5   Experimental Results and Discussion

For experimentation, we implemented the Mamdani fuzzy-PD controller in the prototype system. In this work, we only considered to control the balance of the robot in the unstable position without any perturbation.

For the control system, we considered the vertical position ($0°$) as reference. In addition, the angular position θ of the robot is measured from the vertical axis using the IMU sensor. We performed the angular velocity $\dot{\theta}$ using the Arduino and computing the change in angular position. Figure 8 shows the output response using the fuzzy-PD controller and Table 2 summarizes four metrics in well-known in control: IAE (integral absolute error), ITAE (integral time-weighted absolute error), ISE (integral squared error) and ITSE (integral time-weighted squared error).

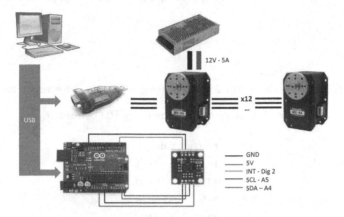

Fig. 6. Schematic of the interface between the PC and the robot.

Fig. 7. Implementation of the robot using the rapid prototype methodology.

As shown from these preliminary results, the chameleon-like robot is able to balance in the unstable state. From Table 2, it is easy to see that the error in steady-state in less than 4° which represents a good achievement. However, improvements in the tuning parameters of the fuzzy control are required to minimize the ITAE and ITSE values which represent the cumulative error over time.

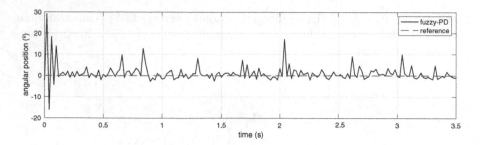

Fig. 8. Output response of the Mamdani fuzzy-PD control for robot balancing.

Table 2. Performance of the fuzzy-PD controller.

metric	value
IAE	3.9884
ITAE	6.0460
ISE	30.5678
ITSE	26.2465

It is remarkable to say that this is the first time a chameleon-like robot is modeled, simulated, implemented and controlled. The basic vertical position of the robot is an unstable state in which the proposed fuzzy-PD controller handles the balancing task well.

Until now, there are several limitations that should be consider in the ongoing research. For instance, a comparative analysis of the controller with others is required. Also, a manual tuning was done in this work, but robustness of the controller have to be tested and validated. In addition, perturbation tests are also pertinent to validate the whole performance of the balancing task in the robot.

To this end, we consider the robot prototype a successful achievement in the sense that we could validate that our bio-inspired modeling can be built and controlled in a balance state position. Thus, our ongoing research can be move further.

6   Conclusions

In this paper, we presented a preliminary study on the design, modeling and control balance of a bio-inspired four-legged robot for standing on its aligned legs in a straight line. From biological inspiration, this robot was loosely based on the morphology of a chameleon. After prototype implementation and experimentation, we concluded that this first iteration of the robot design successfully validated the construction and control of our bio-inspired modeling.

For future work, we are considering to make a deep comparative analysis of the fuzzy-PD control with others, and also to conduct more experiments for testing the robustness to disturbances. Also, we are considering to include an embedding system to replace the remote control processing.

References

1. Agheli, M., Nestinger, S.: Force-based stability margin for multi-legged robots. Robot. Auton. Syst. **83**, 138–149 (2016)
2. de Jalón, J.G., Bayo, E.: Kinematic and Dynamic Simulation of Multibody Systems: The Real-Time Challenge. Mechanical Engineering Series. Springer, Heidelberg (1994). https://doi.org/10.1007/978-1-4612-2600-0
3. Korondi, P., Korcsok, B., Kovacs, S., Niitsuma, M.: Etho-robotics: what kind of behaviour can we learn from the animals? IFAC-PapersOnLine **48**(19), 244–255 (2015)
4. Liang, C., Ceccarelli, M., Carbone, G.: MATLAB for engineers: applications in control, electrical engineering, IT and robotics, chap. In: Design and Simulation of Legged Walking Robots in MATLAB Environment, InTech (2011)
5. Shahbazi, M., Lopes, G., Babuska, R.: Automated transitions between walking and running in legged robots. In: Proceedings of the 19th World Congress of the International Federation of Automatic Control (IFAC), pp. 2171–2176 (2014)
6. Mathworks: Simscape User's Guide (2018). https://www.mathworks.com/help/pdf_doc/physmod/simscape/index.html. Accessed 4 Dec 2018
7. Murphy, R.R., et al.: Search and rescue robotics. In: Siciliano, B., Khatib, O. (eds.) Springer Handbook of Robotics, pp. 1151–1173. Springer, Heidelberg (2008). https://doi.org/10.1007/978-3-540-30301-5_51
8. Najafi, E., Lopes, G., Babuska, R.: Balancing a legged robot using state-dependent Riccati equation control. In: Proceedings of the 19th World Congress of the International Federation of Automatic Control (IFAC), pp. 2177–2182 (2014)
9. Ni, J., Wu, L., Fan, X., Yang, S.X.: Bioinspired intelligent algorithm and its applications for mobile robot control: a survey. Comput. Intell. Neurosci. **2016**, 1 (2016)
10. Raibert, M.H.: Legged Robots that Balance. MIT Press, Cambridge (1986)
11. Robotics: User Manual Dynamixel MX-64AT & AR (2019). http://support.robotis.com/jp/product/dynamixel/mx_series/mx-64at_ar.htm. Accessed 10 Jan 2019
12. Shriyam, S., Agrawal, A., Behera, L., Saxena, A.: Robotic fish design and control based on biomechanics. In: Proceedings of the Third International Conference on Advances in Control and Optimization of Dynamical Systems, pp. 662–669 (2014)

Towards High-Speed Localisation for Autonomous Drone Racing

José Arturo Cocoma-Ortega[1]($\boxtimes$) and José Martínez-Carranza[1,2]

[1] Instituto Nacional de Astrofisica, Optica y Electronica, Puebla, Mexico
{cocoma,carranza}@inaoep.mx
[2] University of Bristol, Bristol, UK

Abstract. The ability to know the pose of a drone in a race track is a challenging task in Autonomous Drone Racing. However, to estimate the pose in real-time and at high-speed could be fundamental to lead an agile flight aiming to beat a human in a drone race. In this work, we present the architecture of a CNN to automatically estimates the drone's pose relative to a gate in a race track. Due to the challenge in ADR, various proposals have been developed to address the problem of autonomous navigation, including those works where a global localisation approach has been used. Despite there are well-known solutions for global localisation such as visual odometry or visual SLAM, these methods may become expensive to be computed onboard. Motivated by the latter, we propose a CNN architecture based on the Posenet network, a work-oriented to perform camera relocalisation in real-time. Our contribution relies on the fact that we have modified and re-trained the Posenet network to adapt it to the context of relative localisation w.r.t. a gate in the track. The ultimate goal is to use our proposed localisation approach to tackle the autonomous navigation problem. We report a maximum speed of up to 100 fps in a low budget computer. Furthermore, seeking to test our approach in realistic scenarios, we have carried out experiments with small gates of 1 m of diameter under different light conditions.

Keywords: Autonomous Drone Racing · High-speed localisation · Convolutional neural network

1 Introduction

One of the most recent challenges that have emerged in the artificial intelligence field is that of drone racing such as the Autonomous Drone Racing (ADR), where the goal is to develop an autonomous drone capable of beating a human in a drone race. In this context, localisation of the drone and control for the navigation are some of the problems to be addressed in this challenge.

To know where the drone is; represents a fundamental task in the planning for autonomous navigation, for this reason, in the last decade several works were

Department of Computer Science at INAOE.

© Springer Nature Switzerland AG 2019
L. Martínez-Villaseñor et al. (Eds.): MICAI 2019, LNAI 11835, pp. 740–751, 2019.
https://doi.org/10.1007/978-3-030-33749-0_59

focused on estimating the pose of a robot employing using a monocular camera and techniques such as visual odometry or visual simultaneous localisation and mapping. Despite the high accuracy in the estimation achieved by these methods, the estimates are usually obtained at low frame rates (20–30 Hz). Pose estimation at high frequency is desirable as it could be exploited in agile flights, such as those expected in a drone race.

More recently and in the context of ADR, the work in [9] have proposed a network to estimate the pose of the drone relative to a gate. However, the estimates are obtained at a frame rate of 10 fps. Motivated by the need for a high-speed drone localisation for autonomous navigation, in this work we propose an algorithm for Autonomous Drone Racing based on Convolutional Neural Networks aiming at estimating the pose of the drone relative to the gate and at a high frequency. Our proposal achieves an estimation speed of 100 fps on average.

In order to present our approach, in Sect. 2 we will discuss the related work, then the methodology used to design and train the network will be described in Sect. 3 in conjunction with the algorithm for autonomous navigation. Section 4 presents the experimental results in where we show that the estimation of the pose is up to 100 fps. Finally, conclusions are discussed in Sect. 5.

2   Related Work

The problem of estimate the position of the camera has been widely studied in recent years. There are two main approaches to Visual Odometry: a geometrical approach and deep learning approach.

Visual Simultaneous Localisation and Mapping (V-SLAM) is one of the most used algorithms to known the robot position in navigation. V-SLAM solves the problem of localisation and mapping the environment by landmarks and features from the frame observed [3]. Hybrid methods reported in the literature, use feature extraction rectification with RANSAC [2]. Some works propose algorithms that employ optical flow [15,17] or a combination of ORB descriptors and optical flow to compute the pose [1]. These works perform geometric approach for visual odometry.

Deep learning-based algorithms have explored different ways to estimate camera pose. In literature are found works that use CNN as the main algorithm and shows the viability of the results instead of geometric ones [7,8], other works resolve localisation via V-SLAM in where estimates VO and also generates a map of the environment [5,22]. In work proposed in [23], a recurrent convolutional neural network is designed to calculate the camera pose from a sequence of input images, the network proposed can process results with high accuracy, but there is no time reported, that indicates that this network is not available to use in real-time problems.

Other algorithms reported in the literature are guided by unsupervised learned [24,25] by the use of stereo images or depth images, the results show good approximations, but not works in real-time, and also there are works not using monocular cameras. Other approaches that such as geometrical ones, employ optical flow for feature extraction and compute visual odometry [4,18,25]. Even these works have shown good accuracy in evaluation over KITTI data-set, they can not perform this in real-time. One relevant work is the reported in [12,13] where they propose a Network they called Posenet. Posenet is based in GoogLeNet [21]. The main contribution of the work is the change of the softmax classifier in the last three layers by a regressor to estimate the pose of the camera. They report high accuracy in their results. Also, it is reported a real-time computation for pose estimation, a time of 5 ms. Some works focus on the estimation of the pose of an object in the image, for instance, those in [6,11,19,20].

In the context of the ADR, seminal works addressed the problem by using visual odometry or visual SLAM algorithms to resolve the drone's localisation [16]. However, more recently, the works in [9,10] present an algorithm where the pose of the drone is estimated relative to the gate using a CNN approach in combination with a filtering scheme. However, this method runs at a frequency of 10 fps. Another approach based on gate detection is presented in [14], in this work they propose a strategy based on colour pixels of the gate for detection (four corners) and subsequently, the problem of perspective n-point (PnP) is solved to estimate the relative position of the drone.

3   Methodology

As previously shown in the works [9,10,14], by the knowledge of the position of the gate is possible to generate planning for drone navigation. In this work, we propose an algorithm to autonomous flight at high-speed based on localisation of the drone relative to the closest gate instead of the complete scene. In our proposal, we do not detect the gate previously; the convolutional neural network designed estimates the drone position relative to the gate without the need for gate detection.

3.1   CNN Architecture

The algorithm proposed, for pose estimation is based on the Posenet [13]. This network allows estimating the 6D camera pose for indoor and outdoor scenes. For drone navigation, we are interested in knowing the position of the drone relative to the gate. To perform the pose estimation, we modify Posenet to predict only the 3D pose of the drone (x, y and z), we eliminate quaternion information from the input and for regressors in dense layers. We also reduce the deep of the network, by the analysis of the results obtained by the regressors, we realise that with only a few layers of the network is enough to estimate the 3D pose. The Fig. 1 shows the modified architecture designed; this architecture has only one regressor as output instead of the three proposed in Posenet. Making this reduction allows the network to speeds up the prediction to 100 fps.

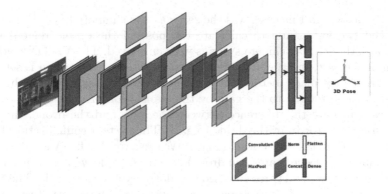

Fig. 1. Reduced Posenet architecture

3.2 Dataset Generation

To train the proposed network, we generate a dataset taking care of the particular needs for the network prediction. The dataset generation was made in two kinds of environments: simulated and real environment.

For the simulated environment, we designed a world using the Gazebo simulator. In this world, two gates were placed and an AR Drone. We develop a script to publish the Gazebo pose of the drone, but the pose is not from the origin of the world, the pose obtained is relative to the closest gate. An example of the images generated for this data set is shown in Fig. 2, in this figure we observe that the floor is not uniform, it has different textures, this is to help the network not to learn specific features of the environment. This dataset for the simulated world contains 2998 images of VGA resolution.

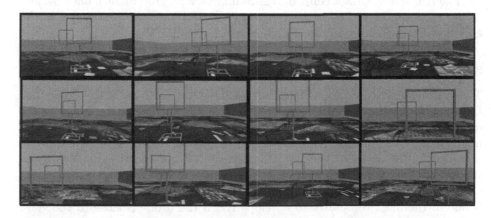

Fig. 2. Example of dataset generated in simulated environment.

The next is the generation of the dataset for the real world. The use of a VICON camera system was necessary to generate images with the ground truth.

The methodology, in this case, was the same as the simulated one. In the scene was placed two gates, and to calculate the pose of the drone, related to the closest gate, the VICON camera systems were employed. The VICON tracks the position of the gate and the drone related to the origin. This origin is set in the configuration in a place in the centre of the scene. The position of the drone is adjusted to be related to the gate by the translation of the coordinates, this means, we calculate the difference between the gate and the drone, the result is the distance vector from the drone to gate. The system configuration for the generation of the dataset is shown in Fig. 3. We use a total of five VICON cameras placed around the scene (gates and drone). The Fig. 3a shows the position of the VICON cameras two and three enclosed in a dotted yellow rectangle. The Fig. 3b shows the drone while dataset generation enclosed in a blue dotted rectangle.

(a) Setup of VICON camera 2 and 3, view from external camera

(b) Setup of VICON and DRONE, view from external camera

Fig. 3. Dataset generation setup (Color figure online)

The real-world dataset consists of 2928 images with groundtruth information. As we can observe in Fig. 4, the light conditions are not the best and also the environment does not generate a high contrast with the gate.

3.3 Autonomous Navigation Algorithm

The Autonomous Navigation Algorithm employs the 6D pose of the drone. For the orientation, the algorithm uses an external IMU to guide the drone facing front the gate in all the time (the Fig. 5 shows the Bebop drone and the IMU used for the experiments); this allows that based on the 3D pose of the drone obtained by the designed network, the algorithm command the drone to fly to the centre of the gate. To perform this, the algorithm first centres the drone in y position related to the gate, and the command to cross the gate. This last task is one of the most complexes to develop. When the drone is close to the gate, a blind point in the view causes the drone to see the next gate before complete the flight through the gate. Our algorithm takes the last measure before entering the blind point and estimates the distance needed to fly to cross the gate, when this distance is reached, the process to centre the drone to the next gate starts again until the drone crosses all the gates.

Fig. 4. Example of dataset generated in the real environment.

Fig. 5. Bebop drone with IMU.

4   Experiments and Results

The experiments were conducted in a real-world indoor scenario. This section describes the results obtained in each experiment. Supplementary video: https://youtu.be/C7goGTZ4F0k.

4.1   Manual Flight with Groundtruth

For the first experiment, we flew the drone with the VICON system to compare 3D pose prediction with the groundtruth pose. We calculate the error en X position and Y position, and the mean error of (x, y) position over a sample of 4380. We obtain $\varepsilon = 0.2162859678$ m with a standard deviation of $\sigma = 0.1357102627$ m, considering the size of the drone and the flyable area of the gate, these results allow the drone to cross the gate properly since the error is smaller than the size of the drone.

Plot in Fig. 6a shows the error in X position, as we can notice the error keep less than 20 cm for a greater time, this is because there is a precision area where the prediction error is minimum, when the drone is flying outside this precision area, the error increases as we can see in the plot. The Fig. 6b shows the plot for Y error, in this plot we can observe that the error on Y is greater than X, and in the same way that in X error, we can notice a precision area where the error is small. Finally, the Fig. 6c shows the error of x and y position (norm), the greater error is caused by Y error.

We measure the time for network prediction; the network allows prediction in an average time of 10 ms, that is, the network estimates the drone pose of a maximum time up to 100 fps.

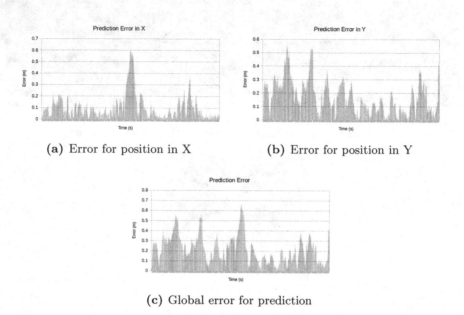

(a) Error for position in X   (b) Error for position in Y

(c) Global error for prediction

Fig. 6. Error in prediction.

4.2   Autonomous Flight

We conducted experiments in a real-world indoor scenario. As we explained in Sect. 3.3, the experiments demonstrate that the algorithm is capable of estimating the drone's pose, which is used by the controller to first, centre the drone w.r.t. the gate and then moving the drone to fly and cross the gate. An exciting aspect of our approach is that it is useful to identify the blind spot when crossing the gate; this is when the drone is inside the window area of the gate. In this case, the main problem is to detect when the drone should stop its forward motion to re-start with the *centering* motion. We detect this by observing the estimated pose as follows: when the drone flies directly to the gate, after centring, the pose estimates will approximate to zero, whilst the next gate will be observed, thus producing a pose estimate that will jump back to a larger distance, given that the estimation is carried w.r.t. the gate. After the jump is detected, the estimate w.r.t. is stored and then compared against the following estimates, as the drone keeps flying forward, the distance to the gate will begin to decrease again, which

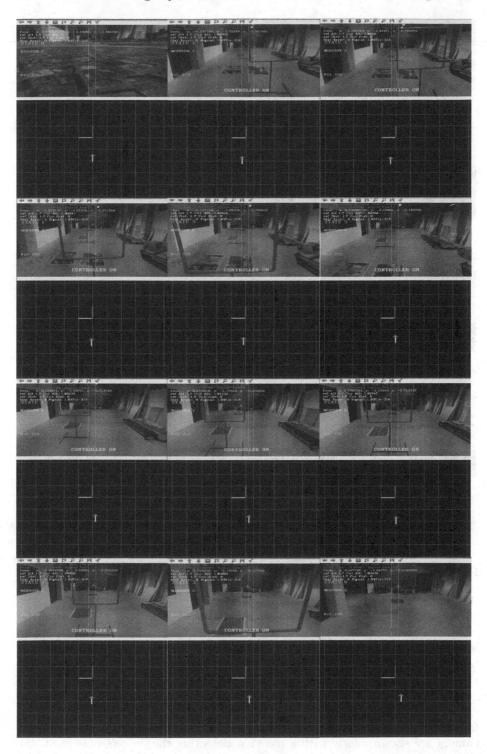

Fig. 7. Drone camera view and RVIZ view of pose prediction.

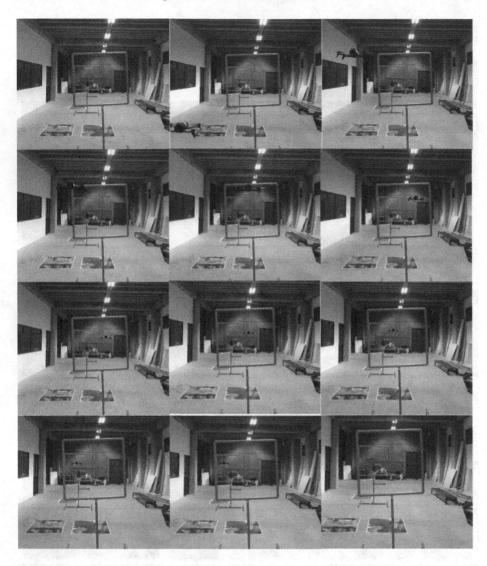

Fig. 8. Back view of autonomous drone flight. The flight sequence is depicted from left to right, top to bottom. The carpets on the floor are used only to provide texture for the optical flow sensor onboard the drone.

is useful to detect when the drone translates 1 m or more from the moment the blind spot was detected. Therefore, after that 1 m of translation is observed, then the controller can switch back to the centring motion.

In total, we performed ten runs where the drone has to take off and cross two gates. From these experiments, eight flights were successful while two of them failed. A representative flight is shown in Fig. 7, where samples of the drone's camera are shown jointly with a top view depicting the drone's pose w.r.t. the gate, estimated with our CNN-base approach, this is represented with a visual marker to see when the drone is close to the gate centre. In the first image, we see the drone before takes off; the controller (algorithm) is off. When the drone takes off, we active the algorithm (green legend "Controller on").

For the same flight, Fig. 8 shows the autonomous drone flight seen from the back. In the beginning, the drone is ready for taking off; the drone takes off, then the algorithm centres the drone to the gate, cross the gate and stop itself to start centre again. Finally, the drone crosses the second gate and then lands. Note that in the images, it can be appreciated when the drone is centred during the centring motion, then it flies in forwarding motion to cross the gate. After crossing the first gate, the algorithm commands the drone to fly to the left and get centred w.r.t. the gate to finally cross the gate and lands.

5 Conclusion and Future Work

Aiming at performing agile fly in the Autonomous Drone Racing challenge, we have presented a CNN approach where the drone's pose is estimated relative to the closest gate in the track. Our approach is based on the Posenet architecture, initially used for camera re-localisation, but modified and adapted here to the ADR problem. We have presented results obtained in simulation and in realistic scenarios to evaluate our localisation approach. In average, we obtain pose estimates at a frequency of 100 fps and with an average error of 20 cm.

Furthermore, we have implemented an autonomous navigation algorithm using our CNN-based localisation approach. For the latter, the main idea is to use the localisation estimates, first to centre the drone w.r.t. the gate, and then it is also used to identify the moment at which the drone crosses the gate.

As future work, we will improve the network to reduce the error. We will also experiment in more massive race tracks. Also, a test with a high-speed camera (>90 Hz) will be performed in order to challenge the network maximum speed prediction.

References

1. Bang, J., Lee, D., Kim, Y., Lee, H.: Camera pose estimation using optical flow and ORB descriptor in SLAM-based mobile AR game. In: 2017 International Conference on Platform Technology and Service (PlatCon), pp. 1–4, February 2017. https://doi.org/10.1109/PlatCon.2017.7883693
2. Camposeco, F., Cohen, A., Pollefeys, M., Sattler, T.: Hybrid camera pose estimation. In: The IEEE Conference on Computer Vision and Pattern Recognition (CVPR), June 2018
3. Casarrubias-Vargas, H., Petrilli-Barcelo, A., Bayro-Corrochano, E.: EKF-SLAM and machine learning techniques for visual robot navigation. In: 2010 20th International Conference on Pattern Recognition, pp. 396–399, August 2010
4. Costante, G., Ciarfuglia, T.A.: LS-VO: learning dense optical subspace for robust visual odometry estimation. IEEE Robot. Autom. Lett. 3(3), 1735–1742 (2018). https://doi.org/10.1109/LRA.2018.2803211

5. DeTone, D., Malisiewicz, T., Rabinovich, A.: Toward geometric deep SLAM. CoRR abs/1707.07410 (2017)
6. Do, T.T., Cai, M., Pham, T., Reid, I.: Deep-6DPose: recovering 6D object pose from a single RGB image (2018)
7. Fanani, N., Stürck, A., Ochs, M., Bradler, H., Mester, R.: Predictive monocular odometry (PMO): what is possible without RANSAC and multiframe bundle adjustment? Image Vis. Comput. **68**, 3–13 (2017)
8. Graves, A., Lim, S., Fagan, T., et al.: Visual odometry using convolutional neural networks. Kennesaw J. Undergrad. Res. **5**(3), 5 (2017)
9. Kaufmann, E., et al.: Beauty and the beast: optimal methods meet learning for drone racing. CoRR abs/1810.06224 (2018)
10. Kaufmann, E., Loquercio, A., Ranftl, R., Dosovitskiy, A., Koltun, V., Scaramuzza, D.: Deep drone racing: learning agile flight in dynamic environments. CoRR abs/1806.08548 (2018)
11. Kehl, W., Manhardt, F., Tombari, F., Ilic, S., Navab, N.: SSD-6D: making RGB-based 3D detection and 6D pose estimation great again. In: The IEEE International Conference on Computer Vision (ICCV), October 2017
12. Kendall, A., Cipolla, R.: Modelling uncertainty in deep learning for camera relocalization. In: 2016 IEEE International Conference on Robotics and Automation (ICRA), pp. 4762–4769, May 2016. https://doi.org/10.1109/ICRA.2016.7487679
13. Kendall, A., Grimes, M., Cipolla, R.: PoseNet: a convolutional network for real-time 6-DOF camera relocalization. In: 2015 IEEE International Conference on Computer Vision (ICCV), pp. 2938–2946, December 2015. https://doi.org/10.1109/ICCV.2015.336
14. Li, S., van der Horst, E., Duernay, P., De Wagter, C., de Croon, G.C.: Visual model-predictive localization for computationally efficient autonomous racing of a 72-gram drone. arXiv preprint arXiv:1905.10110 (2019)
15. Mansur, S., Habib, M., Pratama, G.N.P., Cahyadi, A.I., Ardiyanto, I.: Real time monocular visual odometry using optical flow: study on navigation of quadrotors UAV. In: 2017 3rd International Conference on Science and Technology - Computer (ICST), pp. 122–126, July 2017. https://doi.org/10.1109/ICSTC.2017.8011864
16. Moon, H., et al.: Challenges and implemented technologies used in autonomous drone racing. Intel. Serv. Robot. **12**(2), 137–148 (2019)
17. More, V., Kumar, H., Kaingade, S., Gaidhani, P., Gupta, N.: Visual odometry using optic flow for unmanned aerial vehicles. In: 2015 International Conference on Cognitive Computing and Information Processing (CCIP), pp. 1–6, March 2015
18. Muller, P., Savakis, A.: Flowdometry: an optical flow and deep learning based approach to visual odometry. In: 2017 IEEE Winter Conference on Applications of Computer Vision (WACV), pp. 624–631, March 2017. https://doi.org/10.1109/WACV.2017.75
19. Poirson, P., Ammirato, P., Fu, C.Y., Liu, W., Kosecka, J., Berg, A.C.: Fast single shot detection and pose estimation. In: 2016 Fourth International Conference on 3D Vision (3DV), pp. 676–684. IEEE (2016)
20. Shalnov, E., Konushin, A.: Convolutional neural network for camera pose estimation from object detections. Int. Arch. Photogram. Remote Sens. Spat. Inf. Sci. **42** (2017)
21. Szegedy, C., et al.: Going deeper with convolutions. In: Computer Vision and Pattern Recognition (CVPR) (2015). http://arxiv.org/abs/1409.4842
22. Tateno, K., Tombari, F., Laina, I., Navab, N.: CNN-SLAM: real-time dense monocular slam with learned depth prediction. In: 2017 IEEE Conference on Computer Vision and Pattern Recognition (CVPR), pp. 6565–6574, July 2017

23. Wang, S., Clark, R., Wen, H., Trigoni, N.: DeepVO: towards end-to-end visual odometry with deep recurrent convolutional neural networks. In: 2017 IEEE International Conference on Robotics and Automation (ICRA), pp. 2043–2050, May 2017
24. Wu, Y., Liu, Y., Li, X.: Position estimation of camera based on unsupervised learning. In: Proceedings of the International Conference on Pattern Recognition and Artificial Intelligence, PRAI 2018, pp. 30–35. ACM (2018)
25. Yin, Z., Shi, J.: GeoNet: unsupervised learning of dense depth, optical flow and camera pose. In: The IEEE Conference on Computer Vision and Pattern Recognition (CVPR), June 2018

Author Index